ASP.NET Programmer's Reference

Jason Bell

Mike Clark

Andy Elmhorst

Matt Gibbs

Alex Homer

Bruce Lee

Matt Milner

Jan Narkiewicz

Adil Rehan

John Schenken

Wrox Press Ltd. ®

ASP.NET Programmer's Reference

© 2001 Wrox Press

Published by Wrox Press Ltd,
Arden House, 1102 Warwick Road, Acocks Green,
Birmingham, B27 6BH, UK
Printed in the United States
ISBN 1-861005-30-X

Trademark Acknowledgements

Wrox has endeavored to provide trademark information about all the companies and products mentioned in this book by the appropriate use of capitals. However, Wrox cannot guarantee the accuracy of this information.

Credits

Authors
Jason Bell
Mike Clark
Andy Elmhorst
Matt Gibbs
Alex Homer
Bruce Lee
Matt Milner
Jan Narkiewicz
Adil Rehan
John Schenken

Technical Reviewers
Maxime Bombardier
Paul Churchill
John Godfrey
Vidar Langerget
Wendy Lanning
Don Lee
Sophie McQueen
Gleydson Miguel de Macedo
Christophe Nasarre
Fredrik Normén
Johan Normén
Eric Rajkovic
Juan Ramon Rovirosa
Scott Robertson
Larry Schoeneman
David Schultz
Trevor Scott
Keyur Shah
Andrew Stopford
Ben Taylor
John Timney
Konstantinos Vlassis
Tom Washington

Category Manager
Kirsty Reade
Steve Farncombe

Technical Architect
Chris Goode

Technical Editors
Ewan Buckingham
Matt Cumberlidge
Richard Deeson

Author Agents
Avril Corbin
Laura Jones

Project Administrator
Cathy Succamore
Louise Carr

Production Project Coordinator
Emma Eato

Additional Layout
Natalie O'Donnell

Index
Martin Brooks
Andrew Criddle

Figures
Natalie O'Donnell

Cover
Dawn Chellingworth

About the Authors

Jason Bell

Jason Bell started learning computer programming back in 1981 on his father's TI-99/4A with an incredible 16KB of RAM and a panoramic 10" display supporting resolutions of up to 256x192. After eight years of developing software for the US Air Force, Jason is now an MCSD working as a consultant for Stroudwater NHG, a Microsoft Certified Partner located in Portland, ME. When he's not busy donating out-of-date computer books to the library or reformatting his computer's hard drive to install more beta software, Jason enjoys piloting small aircraft, driving his vintage Porsche, and dreaming about going back to school someday to work toward a PhD in Physics.

Mike Clark

Mike Clark, is senior analyst at Lucin, and is responsible for www.salcentral.com the first web services brokerage. Over the past eight years he has increasingly become more involved in Internet technologies and using his expertise in multi-tier windows development sees the movement into web services as adoption of lessons learned, rather than a completely new environment. Mike now predominantly works in commercial aspects of web services, having developed the web sites www.webservicewatch.com and www.webservicelibrary.com. He is known for his distinctly aggressive style of development and still can't resist a 48 hour working session. Mike Clark can be contacted at mikec@lucin.com.

Andy Elmhorst

Andy Elmhorst is a developer and writer, who spends most of his time architecting and building web applications using Microsoft server technologies. He enjoys delving into the details of every technology he gets his hands on. Andy's currently working for Renaissance Learning, Inc. where he enjoys building cool products with cool people. Every chance he has, he gets away to the Wisconsin Northwoods with his family to enjoy the great outdoors. Andy Elmhorst can be reached at andyelmhorst@hotmail.com.

Matt Gibbs

Matt Gibbs is a software developer at Microsoft where he has been working on Internet technologies since 1997. He is currently working on the Mobile Internet Toolkit. Matt is looking forward to finishing his graduate studies in Computer Science at the University of Washington soon, so that he can spend more time with his wife, son, and daughter.

Alex Homer

Alex Homer is a software developer and technical author living and working in the idyllic rural surroundings of the Derbyshire Dales in England. He started playing with Microsoft's Active Server Pages technology right from the early betas of version 1.0 (remember "Denali"?) – and has watched with awe and excitement as it has evolved into probably the most comprehensive server-side Web programming environment available today. And with the advent of ASP.NET, it gets even better. In fact, he's so excited about the whole new framework and application model that he once nearly referred to it as a "paradigm". In the meantime, he has to be forcibly removed from his computer three times a week for the administration of food and fresh air. You can contact Alex at alex@stonebroom.com.

Bruce Lee

Before he went to Canada, Bruce Lee was a technical support engineer at Microsoft Taiwan. He is also an author and technical writer for a couple of Chinese books, and Windows 2000 Magazine's Traditional Chinese Edition. His focus has always been on Microsoft technologies, especially on operating systems, network management and web development. When not working, you can usually find him with his favorite dog, Jay-Jay, near the St. Lawrence River. You can reach him at yihcheng@hotmail.com.

Bruce wants to give special thanks to Rob Howard for giving him direction and support in his writing.

Matt Milner

Matt Milner works as a Technical Architect for BORN in Minneapolis where he designs and builds Microsoft solutions for clients in a variety of industries. Matt's primary focus has been using Windows DNA architecture, and he is excited about the move to .NET with its powerful new features. When Matt is not working at his computer, he spends his time in his woodshop, reading, or enjoying the many great natural resources of Minnesota.

Jan Narkiewicz

Jan D. Narkiewicz is Chief Technical Officer at Software Pronto, Inc. (jann@softwarepronto.com)

Jan began his career as a Microsoft developer thanks to basketball star, Michael Jordan. In the early 90s Jan noticed that no matter what happened during a game, Michael Jordan's team won. Similarly, no matter what happened in technology Microsoft always won (this strategy is ten years old and may need some revamping). Clearly there was a bandwagon to be jumped upon.

Over the years Jan managed to work on an e-mail system that resided on 17 million desktops, helped automate factories that make the blue jeans you have in your closet (trust me you own this brand!) and developed defence systems. All this was achieved using technology such as COM/DCOM, COM+, C++, VB, C#, ADO, SQL Server, Oracle, DB2, ASP.NET, ADO.NET, Java, Linux, and XML. In his spare time Jan is Academic Coordinator for the Windows curriculum at U.C. Berkeley Extension, he teaches at U.C. Santa Cruz Extension, writes for wwwASPToday.com, and occasionally plays some football (also known as soccer).

Adil Rehan

Adil Rehan works as an independent consultant for a Fortune 500 company. He has been involved with several books, in different roles, and associated with the design and implementation of enterprise Internet-enabled solutions for different clients. He holds a Bachelor of Engineering degree in Electrical Engineering from NED University. When he is not working with computers, he likes watching movies, and traveling to far and distant places to explore the wonders of Nature. He can be reached at adilrehan@yahoo.com.

He would like to thank his parents for bringing him up right and giving him the inspiration to move forward. He'd also like to thank his wife and son for supporting him when he needed it most.

John Schenken

John Schenken is currently Software Test Lead on the Visual Basic Server Enterprise Team for Microsoft. He was previously Test Lead for the Microsoft Script Debugger that shipped with the Windows NT Option Pack, and is still responsible for it in Windows 2000. He has programming experience involving MSMQ, SMTP, NT Event Log, NT Perf Counters, ASP, and ADO – basically that's wide experience writing end-to-end web applications involving business objects.

Table of Contents

Table of Contents

Table of Contents

Table of Contents

Table of Contents

Table of Contents

Table of Contents

Table of Contents

Table of Contents

Table of Contents

xviii

Table of Contents

Table of Contents

Introduction

When Microsoft announced its .NET revolution at PDC 2000, it sent waves through the Microsoft programming community. At its core was this mythical beast called the .NET Framework, which contained many namespaces, each containing classes that could be used to provide a great deal of functionality quite simply. With the introduction of this structured hierarchy came the need to establish the fact that any language that was to be used to create any kind of .NET application, from a Web Form to a Windows Form, would need to follow some strict rules.

VB developers heard that their beloved language was getting a much-needed face-lift with the introduction of proper Object-oriented programming. However, they soon realized that this massive update would require them to effectively re-learn the language from scratch. C++ developers were faced with an interesting path into .NET with the arrival of the new C# language, which looks and feels a lot like Java in its style and structure, but which is designed and built to integrate with the .NET Framework to provide a clean and powerful alternative to the verbosity of VB.NET. In fact, with the leap to VB.NET being so large, many VB developers are considering learning C# instead. However, in among this crowd was a vital part of the community who had been closely involved with the evolution of the Web towards server-side programming – the ASP community.

ASP developers were faced with a difficult upgrade path – VBScript can't be used in ASP.NET applications, and it's been replaced by VB.NET as the default language, although any .NET language can be used to create ASP.NET applications. From the world of interpreted scripting to the world of compiled control-based development is a big change, but it's one that ASP.NET is designed to make as simple as possible.

What is ASP.NET?

ASP.NET is a totally new way of creating web applications. Instead of in-line script in a page, ASP.NET is designed to encapsulate commonly-used code into controls of various kinds, from simple HTML buttons running on the server, through data-bound listboxes and grids, to more complex controls like a calendar that magically appears after placing one single line of code on a page. To have produced something like that with ASP would have taken hours. You have the ability to write your own controls, whether they're simple user controls that just contain a little functionality for one of your site's pages, or pre-compiled controls that you can reuse time and time again, or even sell to other developers.

ASP.NET also embraces the world of Web Services, making it simple to create services that can be accessed using standards like SOAP, WSDL, and UDDI.

ADO.NET is Microsoft's latest data-access technology. It is a central part of the .NET Framework and far more than an update to recent versions of ADO. Many of the concepts and components found in ADO.NET are completely new. It cleanly separates accessing data from manipulating data and is designed for disconnected usage. Accessing various data sources using OLE DB and ODBC is now separated from accessing SQL Server data, which is handled using a managed provider that talks to SQL Server on a lower level. This greatly improves the speed of data access to SQL Server-specific data, and allows developers to make of SQL Server-specific tools. It is likely that many database vendors will soon release high performance .NET providers for their databases.

Support for XML is an important aspect of the .NET Framework. ADO.NET can persist entire data structures to standard XML for transmission over the Internet and communicate with any XML-supporting application.

What Does This Book Cover?

This book is designed as a desktop companion for anyone developing ASP.NET applications. Contained in this book is a reference to all the ASP.NET-specific namespaces, plus some useful namespaces that are needed from time to time while developing with ASP.NET, as well as plenty of example code, and overviews of the technologies that you're likely to encounter as you develop ASP.NET applications.

This book is divided into four sections:

❑ The first section is a straight reference of the main ASP.NET namespaces and the controls that are used in ASP.NET development.

❑ The second section is an overview of some of the other aspects of ASP.NET including configuration, caching, and security. It finishes with an overview of some of the other .NET namespaces that are used regularly in ASP.NET development.

❑ The third section covers Web Services, and includes a discussion of the key concepts, as well as referencing the namespaces.

❑ Finally, there are overviews of both ADO.NET and XML usage within .NET to give you enough information to understand how they fit into the puzzle, along with plenty of sample code to see them in action. The last chapter shows how we can use the concepts learned throughout the book by illustrating them with some broad examples.

Who Is This Book For?

This book is aimed at experienced developers, who have some knowledge of ASP or general development with Microsoft technologies, or experience of programming within the .NET Framework. It is not aimed at beginners and does not cover general programming techniques or the basics of programming languages.

Primarily, it is intended as a reference for .NET developers who are looking to develop ASP.NET applications. For those developers who don't have much programming experience, but who are looking to get started with ASP.NET, we recommend reading *Beginning ASP.NET*, ISBN: 1-861005-04-0 first. For those developers wishing to learn about ASP.NET in detail, who've got more programming experience, possibly of VB application development, or more complex ASP application development, we recommend reading *Professional ASP.NET*, ISBN: 1-861004-88-5. This book is designed to sit alongside either of these titles.

What You Need To Use This Book

To run the samples in this book you need to have the following:

❑ Windows 2000 or Windows XP.

❑ The .NET Framework SDK. *The code in this book will not work with .NET Beta 1.*

The complete source code for the samples is available for download from our web site at http://www.wrox.com/Books/Book_Details.asp?isbn=186100530X.

Conventions

We've used a number of different styles of text and layout in this book to help differentiate between the different kinds of information. Here are examples of the styles we used and an explanation of what they mean.

Code has several fonts. If it's a code word that we're talking about in the text – for example, when discussing a For...Next loop, it's in this font. If it's a block of code that can be typed as a program and run, then it's also in a gray box:

```
<?xml version 1.0?>
```

Sometimes we'll see code in a mixture of styles, like this:

```
<?xml version 1.0?>
<Invoice>
    <part>
        <name>Widget</name>
        <price>$10.00</price>
    </part>
</invoice>
```

In cases like this, the code with a white background is code we are already familiar with; the line highlighted in gray is a new addition to the code since we last looked at it.

Advice, hints, and background information comes in this type of font.

> **Important pieces of information come in boxes like this.**

Bullets appear indented, with each new bullet marked as follows:

❑ **Important Words** are in a bold type font

❑ Words that appear on the screen, or in menus like File or Window, are in a similar font to the one you would see on a Windows desktop

❑ Keys that you press on the keyboard like *Ctrl* and *Enter*, are in italics

Customer Support

We always value hearing from our readers, and we want to know what you think about this book: what you liked, what you didn't like, and what you think we can do better next time. You can send us your comments, either by returning the reply card in the back of the book, or by e-mail to feedback@wrox.com. Please be sure to mention the book title in your message.

How to Download the Sample Code for the Book

When you visit the Wrox site, http://www.wrox.com/, simply locate the title through our Search facility or by using one of the title lists. Click on Download in the Code column, or on Download Code on the book's detail page.

The files that are available for download from our site have been archived using WinZip. When you have saved the attachments to a folder on your hard-drive, you need to extract the files using a decompression program such as WinZip or PKUnzip. When you extract the files, the code is usually extracted into chapter folders. When you start the extraction process, ensure your software (WinZip, PKUnzip, etc.) is set to use folder names.

Errata

We've made every effort to make sure that there are no errors in the text or in the code. However, no one is perfect and mistakes do occur. If you find an error in one of our books, like a spelling mistake or a faulty piece of code, we would be very grateful for feedback. By sending in errata you may save another reader hours of frustration, and of course, you will be helping us provide even higher quality information. Simply e-mail the information to support@wrox.com, your information will be checked and, if correct, posted to the errata page for that title, or used in subsequent editions of the book.

To find errata on the web site, go to http://www.wrox.com/, and simply locate the title through our Advanced Search or title list. Click on the Book Errata link, which is below the cover graphic on the book's detail page.

E-mail Support

If you wish to directly query a problem in the book with an expert who knows the book in detail then e-mail support@wrox.com, with the title of the book and the last four numbers of the ISBN in the subject field of the e-mail. A typical e-mail should include the following things:

- ❑ The **title of the book, last four digits of the ISBN**, and **page number** of the problem in the Subject field.

- ❑ Your **name, contact information**, and the **problem** in the body of the message.

We **won't** send you junk mail. We need the details to save your time and ours. When you send an e-mail message, it will go through the following chain of support:

- ❑ Customer Support – Your message is delivered to our customer support staff, who are the first people to read it. They have files on most frequently asked questions and will answer anything general about the book or the web site immediately.

- ❑ Editorial – Deeper queries are forwarded to the technical editor responsible for that book. They have experience with the programming language or particular product, and are able to answer detailed technical questions on the subject.

❑ The Authors – Finally, in the unlikely event that the editor cannot answer your problem, he or she will forward the request to the author. We do try to protect the author from any distractions to their writing; however, we are quite happy to forward specific requests to them. All Wrox authors help with the support on their books. They will e-mail the customer and the editor with their response, and again all readers should benefit.

The Wrox Support process can only offer support to issues that are directly pertinent to the content of our published title. Support for questions that fall outside the scope of normal book support, is provided via the community lists of our http://p2p.wrox.com/ forum.

p2p.wrox.com

For author and peer discussion join the P2P mailing lists. Our unique system provides **programmer to programmer**™ contact on mailing lists, forums, and newsgroups, all in addition to our one-to-one e-mail support system. If you post a query to P2P, you can be confident that it is being examined by the many Wrox authors and other industry experts who are present on our mailing lists. At p2p.wrox.com you will find a number of different lists that will help you, not only while you read this book, but also as you develop your own applications. Particularly appropriate to this book are the **aspx** and **aspx_professional** lists in the .NET category of the web site.

To subscribe to a mailing list just follow these steps:

1. Go to http://p2p.wrox.com/

2. Choose the appropriate category from the left menu bar

3. Click on the mailing list you wish to join

4. Follow the instructions to subscribe and fill in your e-mail address and password

5. Reply to the confirmation e-mail you receive

6. Use the subscription manager to join more lists and set your e-mail preferences

Why This System Offers the Best Support

You can choose to join the mailing lists or you can receive them as a weekly digest. If you don't have the time, or facilities, to receive the mailing list, then you can search our online archives. Junk and spam mails are deleted, and your own e-mail address is protected by the unique Lyris system. Queries about joining or leaving lists, and any other general queries about lists, should be sent to listsupport@p2p.wrox.com.

1

Introduction to ASP.NET

This chapter introduces ASP.NET – with an emphasis on that ubiquitous suffix, .NET. As a technology, ASP.NET has significant improvements over its predecessor, ASP 3.0. ASP.NET's supporting cast, the Visual Studio.NET troupe, constitutes a similar generational leap from its predecessor, Visual Interdev. Although ASP.NET development can make use of any of a variety of languages, Visual Basic is of particular note because of the improvements that VB.NET (an almost entirely new language suitable for ASP.NET) offers over the legacy VB Script (a language used in ASP). JScript has also been enhanced under ASP.NET. This language in its new incarnation is now called JScript.NET. There's also a brand new language called C#, which is very similar in style to Java, and which is already becoming very popular with the .NET developer community.

Lurking behind the scenes is an intricate infrastructure that makes the magic of ASP.NET possible. In this chapter, we will take an overview of this .NET framework that includes a discussion of how ASP has paved the way for ASP.NET, along with a few high-level points relating to how ASP differs from ASP.NET.

The What

ASP.NET is a server-side technology that, like JSP, PHP, and ASP, allows web content to be created dynamically. Visual Studio.NET is not a requirement of ASP.NET, and many developers will continue to develop web sites without it. As long as the .NET Framework SDK is installed, you're free to develop ASP.NET applications in whatever environment takes your fancy. However, Visual Studio.NET is likely to become the tool of choice in the development of ASP.NET applications. It provides a one-stop shop for the development of ASP.NET solutions and the component infrastructure they require. Visual Studio.NET includes projects that automatically set up appropriate stored procedure calls, shared objects, and Web Services. Visual Studio.NET allows web pages to be put together using a very simple drag-and-drop interface; it greatly facilitates debugging, tracing, project management, and source code control, not to mention Microsoft's 'love-it-or-loath-it' IntelliSense feature.

You may already be aware that as of the time of writing, in addition to the standard ASP.NET that ships withthe .NET Framework SDK, a enhancement pack is available with several extra features, including:

- ❑ Output caching – the caching of frequently requested pages and Web Service results
- ❑ Code access hosting – a form of security that isolates elements of a web site from each other
- ❑ Web farm capability – to take advantage of four or more CPUs on one host

The Premium version also supports the concept of web farm session state. With ASP, state was available at application and session level. With the Premium edition of ASP.NET however, session state can be maintained across multiple computers acting as a single domain – a web farm. The Premium edition is only expected to be available during Beta 2, whereas the release version of ASP.NET will have the custom features allowed for each specific OS it's installed on, so the availability of Premium features will depend on the version of Windows you are running.

ASP.NET requires Windows NT SP6A, Windows 2000, or Windows XP at the server: Windows NT, Windows 9x, and Windows ME are **not** supported server platforms. However, these unsupported Windows versions can run Visual Studio.NET to remotely develop ASP.NET applications for later deployment to a server running a supported platform. Developers who do not have access to Windows 2000 or Window XP can still scrounge a free web site online. Clearly this can encumber the development and debugging process. The Start page of Visual Studio.NET has a Web Hosting menu listing companies that host ASPX applications. Alternatively, sites such as http://www.freewebsiteproviders.com have a large number of sites that provide free hosting, although not all support ASP and ASP.NET.

The Why

In Internet time, ASP is a centuries-old technology. In human time, this translates to a matter of a few years. Before ASP, there was little cohesion when developing web applications, as we required a diverse pot-pourri of tools and technologies. ASP brought a little sanity to this chaos. Web development is still a diverse pot-pourri but ASP provided a core foundation on which to develop. As technologies, ASP and its sidekick Visual InterDev are not without their quirks and shortcomings. Improvements to ASP that many programmers would like to see include simplified debugging, greater flexibility and performance, more complete adoption of standards and support for good software engineering practice, improved setup procedures, and simplified cross-browser support.

Performance

Classic ASP applications are developed in JScript and VBScript. As their names imply, both of these are scripting languages, that is, they are interpreted line-by-line, rather than compiled as a complete program. This generally results in code running significantly slower. ASP does cache such code but it is still interpreted and as such is still subject to scalability and performance limitations. Additionally, because interpreted languages lack the compilation phase that produces executable code, errors that would otherwise be automatically picked up can sometimes be missed.

JScript and VBScript are not type-safe. This means that an integer variable could be used later in the code as an ADO Recordset and then could be used as a string. This infinite flexibility degrades performance and adds a level of potential programmer error to scripting development. A wide range of languages are equally well supported for ASP.NET applications. JScript.NET and VB.NET (replacing VBScript) are still supported development languages, but so are all other managed languages compatible with the .NET framework. All these implementation languages available to ASP.NET are compiled and type-safe, rather than scripted and weakly typed.

ASP's use of interpreted languages does not only affect the speed of ASP applications, however. Because JScript and VBScript do not support strong typing, these languages are forced to use late-bound COM objects. Such COM objects are slower to execute. In C++ it is more difficult to develop such COM objects due to their complexity. Late-bound COM objects expose the IDispatch interface and support a restricted set of types (known as **automation types**). When late-bound COM objects are developed in Visual C++, these types (BSTR, VARIANT, and SAFEARRAY) add a hefty level of complexity to the development process. Concepts such as late binding are the exception rather than the rule in the ASP.NET world where every object is compiled and type-safe. The only place late binding and COM objects are encountered is when ASP.NET accesses legacy COM objects that happen to support late binding only.

Unity

A tremendous amount of ASP code is written in VBScript, a Visual Basic derivative. As a language VB is straightforward to write in, but it is hampered by Dialect Confusion Syndrome (DCS). This just-invented syndrome is associated with languages of the same name but that exhibit subtle variations that cause confusion and frustration in developers moving between dialects. Before .NET there were three flavors of VB: the potentially type-safe, compiled VB language proper; the VBScript language of ASP and the Windows Scripting host; and to top it all off, the VBA language used by developers of Microsoft Office applications. Each incarnation of VB supports subtly different language constructs. Functional support differs, the recommended object models varied between each, and even the online help is stylistically different.

.NET goes a long way to eliminating the headaches caused by Dialect Confusion Syndrome by providing a single flavor of VB: VB.NET, a compiled and type-safe language for use throughout the .NET framework.

Any Language

ASP.NET is a compiled, type-safe environment. This means that development is no longer restricted to scripting languages alone. With .NET at the reins, C++, C#, Perl.Net, Fujitsu COBOL or any .NET-compliant language (managed language) can be used to develop ASP.NET applications. A pleasant side effect is that developers can use whatever language they are most comfortable with. For instance, a C++ team will be able to help out on a project written mostly in another programming language, without getting bogged down trying to figure out simple language variations.

The true elegance in .NET development – and consequently ASP.NET development – is that every managed language can be debugged from the Visual Studio.NET environment. Visual Studio.NET can trace from an ASP.NET application written in VB.NET straight into an object written in C++, and from there step into an object implemented in C#. Gone are the days of developing an ASP application using Visual InterDev, and then having to use the Visual Basic or Visual C++ tools to debug components written in these languages.

A Better Tool

Visual InterDev has been the principal development tool for a large number of ASP developers. The remainder make use of an alternative editor for writing ASP applications, such as Visual C++'s text editor or plain old Windows Notepad. Visual InterDev is analogous to the rotary dial phone. In retrospect, such phones were cumbersome, complicated, and slow, but over the years many a friend and relative has been quite successfully contacted thanks to the rotary phone. Nevertheless, when push button phones (representing the power and convenience of Visual Studio.NET) hit the market, rotary phones didn't take long to disappear.

It is a bit unfair though to judge Visual InterDev against Visual Studio.NET with respect to web development. The latter is the latest and greatest tool from the Microsoft stable. Under Visual Studio.NET, code produced by the designer by dragging and dropping controls is much more reliable than the Visual Interdev equivalent. Visual Studio.NET can manage the development of an entire ASP.NET web site. This includes developing the code infrastructure that sits behind the web site. This infrastructure can include class libraries exposed using .NET assemblies and a variety of database constructs. With Visual Studio.NET the entire development process is encapsulated in a single tool – from the ASP.NET pages themselves, through supporting assemblies, all the way down to the database level. These components could all be written in different languages orchestrated by Visual Studio.NET, providing seamless debugging and compilation, irrespective of the language of any particular component.

Visual Studio.NET also simplifies access to legacy COM objects. This is partially achieved by automatically converting the type libraries of such COM objects into .NET proxy assemblies. These assemblies bridge the gap between legacy COM applications and managed code running under the .NET Framework. Such support makes ASP.NET eminently suitable for upgrading web sites without losing the rich suite of COM components that many companies have built up.

Software Engineering

Old-style ASP mixes code and content, so that ASP pages are littered with a little HTML here, a bit of script there, along with a smidgen more HTML and another scrap of script. This intermingling leads to spaghetti programming that can be very difficult to unravel. In extreme cases, ASP pages that mix code and content with a special ineptness can be classified as "crimes against humanity". Multiple, incompatible, languages are often used on the same page (typically JScript for client-side scripting, HTML and CSS for the representation, XML for data, and VBScript for server-side scripting). Some developers might insert large contiguous chunks of script in a page, while others take a more piecemeal approach. From a software engineer's standpoint, this anarchy makes concepts such as code reuse almost impossible, so jumbled is the cacophony of code and content.

ASP took a sequential approach to code such that script is executed as and when it appears on a page. It is still possible to take this approach in ASP.NET, and intermingle code and content using the `<SCRIPT>` tag and its abbreviated relative, the `<% code here %>` form. Under ASP.NET however, it is not legal to declare global variables and subroutines inside this style of code delimiter. Both variants of code delimiter place server-side script within HTML just as the same mechanisms do in earlier versions of ASP. Under ASP, global variable and subroutine declarations were permitted inside `<%...%>` delimited code for legacy support only. For example, the following is legal under ASP:

```
<%
Dim someVariable
Sub SomeSubroutine
    Response.Write "Mom says to eat your vegetables!"
End Sub
%>
```

Under ASP.NET the previous code would have to be specified between `<script>` delimiters:

```
<script runat="server">
    Dim someVariable As Integer
    Sub SomeFunction()
      Response.Write("Mom says to eat your vegetables!")
    End Sub
</script>
```

The following simple example shows how ASP.NET can execute VB.NET code in legacy ASP fashion (that is, as script embedded within an HTML page):

```
<%@ Page Language="vb"%>
<html>
  <head>
    <title></title>
  </head>
  <body>
    <% Response.Write("Hey, Ungowa! Clipper Power!") %>
  </body>
</html>
```

As in classic ASP, the `Response` object is used here to output messages (such as "Hey, Ungowa! Clipper Power!") to the document. The following screenshot shows the display produced in Internet Explorer by the above code:

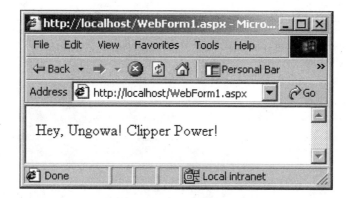

Those who grew up in southern Massachusetts will instantly recognize this as the school cheer of the Norwell High School football team, nicknamed the Clipper Ships. However, the point of this ASP.NET application is not merely to review obscure high school cheers, but to demonstrate that even in the era of ASP.NET, code and content can be mixed up if you wish. This ASP.NET page is clearly trivial, but more complicated pages quickly lead to a quite opaque code/content mix.

To resolve the code/content conundrum, ASP.NET supports a much cleaner, event-driven paradigm where actions (such as page load or page unload) trigger the following event handlers:

❑   `Page_Init` – called when the ASP.NET page framework is initialized

❑   `Page_Load` – called when the code specific to the page is initialized

❑   `Page_Dispose` – called when a page is unloaded (disposed of)

❑   `Page_Error` – called when an unhandled error is encountered

These are the primary events, but there are others such as `Page_DataBind` and `Page_PreRender`. Initialization code given in the `Page_Init` event might open required database connections, retrieve general purpose data, and so on. `Page_Load` could greet the user with "Asalamum Alakum" if it determines that they are in Egypt, or, should it detect that they are in Australia, it could display the message, "G'day".

ASP.NET has another mechanism for the separation of code and content, namely the technique known as **code behind**, which requires that a reference be placed inside a server page linking to a separate source file containing code for the page. An example of this reference follows, where the `Src` attribute refers to a C# source file called `WebForm1.aspx.cs`:

```
<%@ Page language="c#" Description="ASP.NET Component Test"
    Src="WebForm1.aspx.cs" Inherits="WebForm1" %>
```

Next, is an ASP.NET page, `WebForm1.aspx`, which demonstrates how such pages appear when code and content are separated in this way:

```
<%@ Page Language="C#" Description="ASP.NET Component Test"
    Src="WebForm1.aspx.cs" Inherits="WebForm1"%>
<HTML>
```

```
  <body>
    <span id="Message" runat="server"/>
  </body>
</HTML>
```

The external code used by this page is written in C# as indicated by the `Page Language="C#"` attribute, but language is not an issue. Code could just as easily be written in VB.NET, C++, Active Perl, or JScript. The elegance of this approach is that code is not cluttered with HTML tags. A portion of the C# source file, `WebForm1.aspx.cs`, appears below:

```
public class WebForm1 : System.Web.UI.Page
{

    protected System.Web.UI.HtmlControls.HtmlGenericControl Message;

    public WebForm1()
    {
      Page.Init += new System.EventHandler(Page_Init);
    }

    private void Page_Init(object sender, System.EventArgs e)
    {
      Message.InnerHtml = "Go Skippers. Beat Clippers";
    }
}
```

This code clearly can't provide an all-embracing overview of development on the ASP.NET platform, but I hope it sufficiently whets your appetite. We now write text to the `Message` object using the property `InnerHtml` that inserts it into the HTML page at the element `<span id="Message" runat="server" />`. Don't worry too much about other details of this snippet, such as the purpose of the base class, `System.Web.UI.Page`, or the `Page.Init += new System.EventHandler (Page_Init);` statement, as these will be clarified later.

The key to this example lies not in its complexity (or lack of it), but in its components' homogeneity. There is one file, `WebForm1.aspx` that contains the page content. Then there is a second file, `WebForm1.aspx.cs`, that contains all the code associated with the page. This organization helps to keep spaghetti on your dinner plate and off your work-station.

The How – .NET Perks

During the time when ASP ruled the earth there were two types of developers. Some developers (I like to refer to them as Homo Contentus) believed that the world they lived in was ASP alone. Other more wily developers (Homo Senior) understood that ASP was just one part of a larger cosmos, that contained processes, threads, file systems, virtual memory, and so on. The more Homo Senior knew of the world beyond ASP, the more features and optimizations they were able to integrate into their ASP applications.

The .NET era is likely to be dominated by the same two species of developer: Homo Contentus and Homo Senior. The latter will recognize that .NET supports a number of features that can greatly enrich ASP.NET development. They will recognize that ASP.NET sits atop a rich infrastructure that improves the reliability of applications, better facilitates development, improves security, and makes application deployment simpler. ASP.NET developers interested in understanding their environment and subsequently getting the most out of their applications (Homo Senior) should take a look at *Professional .NET Framework*, from Wrox Press, ISBN 1-861005-56-3.

A Unified Language Platform

Whether using C#, C++, JScript, or VB.NET, the underlying objects exposed throughout the .NET Framework are the same. Because each language uses the same .NET Framework objects, it is possible to perform common tasks, such as date/time functions, file I/O, and string manipulation in the same manner across all languages. This substantially reduces the developer's learning curve when jumping between languages. An example of where a unified runtime helps is file I/O. Visual Basic developers use one set of file I/O functions, while VBScript developers use a set of COM objects. This situation is exacerbated by C++: Visual C++ developers can perform file I/O using C runtime functions, C++ runtime objects, MFC objects, or native Win32 function calls.

Under .NET, file I/O is handled by the classes exposed by the `System.IO` namespace. Every managed language can access these classes, greatly simplifying the development process.

Of more significance to ASP.NET development are the data access and XML handling classes that can be shared by ASP.NET applications regardless of language. The shared data access classes can be found in the `System.Data`, `System.Data.Common`, `System.Data.OleDb`, and `System.Data.SqlClient` namespaces. The shared XML classes can be found in namespaces such as `System.Xml`, `System.Xml.Serialization`, `System.Xml.XPath`, and `System.Xml.Xsl`.

Side-by-Side Execution

.NET supports different versions of the .NET environment running on the same machine. It would be possible to develop an ASP.NET application that uses features of .NET version V1.0.2901 while ASP.NET applications could be running on the same machine that require version V1.0.2914. The different ASP.NET applications would run side-by-side using different versions of the .NET Framework without conflict. Gone are the administrative nightmares provoked by different applications requiring different service packs and different versions of the same DLL.

Side-by-side execution is a .NET feature, and can also be used indirectly by ASP.NET applications. Say for example one ASP.NET application requires access to DatabaseX, and this database only runs on .NET version V1.0.2901. ASP.NET applications could be set up to run the most current version of .NET yet still communicate with DatabaseX running on the previous version. It would be up to the installation procedure for DatabaseX to ensure that the required version of the .NET Framework was installed. ASP.NET would simply reap the benefits of this flavor of side-by-side execution.

Managed Code and Type Safety

ASP applications are run inside an ISAPI DLL. This DLL is not actually loaded into the address space of Microsoft's IIS web server. Under Win32, processes have a 4 GB virtual address space and faulty code running in this address space can potentially affect other code in this space. For example, an ASP page might load a COM object written in C++ that uses an invalid pointer that causes the process hosting the ASP application to crash. For this reason ASP applications are run in a separate process of their own. This process, `dllhost.exe`, isolates ASP code and its components from the regular IIS address space. It would be more efficient for IIS to directly load the ISAPI DLL to run ASP applications, but communicating between IIS and an ASP application running in `dllhost.exe`, although slower, is more reliable.

The code under .NET is managed and type-safe. It is not possible for an ASP.NET application built from type-safe assemblies to be brought down by malicious or faulty code accessing data or code that it is not privy to. It is possible to develop code that is not type-safe but ASP.NET applications can be configured to only run in conjunction with type-safe code, and the .NET Framework provides a utility for detecting badly typed code, `PEVerify.exe`.

Managed Heap and Garbage Collection

ASP developers are not renowned for giving thought to dynamic memory allocation, and third-party COM objects (typically written in C++) are notorious for leaking away memory over time, adversely affecting the behavior of the ASP application and potentially that of the web server itself.

ASP.NET developers should be aware of memory management whether they code in VB.NET, C#, JScript.NET, or C++. When objects are created in an ASP.NET application they are placed on the managed heap. This heap is shared between all applications running under .NET regardless of the language originally used for that application. Instances of objects, arrays, and strings used by ASP.NET applications are all placed on this managed heap. The implementation of this heap is quite elegant. Large objects are given their own separate heap space to improve performance for the majority of the objects created, which are relatively small. Per-thread heaps are supported, which reduces contention between threads. Access to the managed heap is quite fast because there is no free space list to traverse as part of object memory allocation.

In the background, the .NET Framework monitors the state of an application's memory. Periodically, or when a threshold is exceeded, garbage collection is initiated. All objects no longer referenced are cleared away, and existing objects are compacted together to maximize memory efficiency. This has the effect that long-term objects come to reside in close proximity, potentially bringing performance benefits. One downside to this approach is that the execution of finalization code is non-deterministic. What this means is that an application does not know precisely when objects will be cleaned up (finalized) and an application will not know when memory cleanup (garbage collection) will take place.

Intermediate Language and JIT

When compiled, the now famous application that displays the message, "Hey, Ungowa! Clipper Power!" generates a DLL, WXCh01SpanDemo01.dll. We already know that ASP.NET applications are compiled, so it should be no surprise that ASP.NET applications generate DLLs. Under Windows DLLs are traditionally compiled to native x86 code, but this is ASP.NET running on the .NET framework. The DLL generated now does not contain machine code but instead contains .NET Intermediate Language (IL) tokens. This language is similar to an object language: lower level than the likes of C# or VB.NET but higher than native machine code.

Why should an ASP.NET developer care what format their compiled code is in? Let's look at the situation of moving an ASP.NET web site from a 32-bit version of Windows to a 64-bit version. There is no porting or recompilation required because the .NET Framework uses Just-in-Time compilation (JIT) to convert from Intermediate Language to native code. When the code in WXCh01SpanDemo01.dll is executed, it is assembled by the JIT engine into x86 machine code. This means that on a 32-bit version of Windows, 32-bit x86 code will always be produced while on a 64-bit version of Windows 64-bit x86 code will be generated. The JIT compilation takes place on a per-method basis. Once compiled to native code, methods are cached so that they can be called more quickly in future.

Even though the .NET Framework ships with an IL assembler, ilasm.exe, there is unlikely to be a rush to develop ASP.NET applications in assembly code. An ASP.NET application that calls computationally intensive utilities for operations such as CRC calculation or data encryption might actually benefit by coding such utilities directly in Intermediate Language. An understanding of IL can also be used in reverse, using the .NET Framework's IL disassembler, ildasm.exe, to study an existing ASP.NET DLL by disassembly.

One particular area of JIT that deserves special note here is the caching of native code. Consider the case of a web site that contains hundreds or thousands of methods exposed as part of shared utility classes. It would certainly make sense to explicitly run JIT to pre-compile these utilities to reduce the load on the server's CPUs when the web site goes live. The .NET Framework provides a utility, `NGen.exe`, which compiles an assembly such as `WXCh01SpanDemo01.dll`, placing the compiled assembly into the native image cache. The native image cache lives up to its name in that it is a cache implemented by the .NET Framework. This cache contains versions of .NET applications that have already been JITed into native code. This style of caching is not the page-level caching available in the premium version of ASP.NET. Caching native code is lower level then page-level caching, but both are capable of leading to better performance.

From Legacy to ASP.NET

Legacy VB to VB.NET

Not all ASP.NET code will be written in VB.NET, just as not all ASP code is written in VBScript. However, a great many developers will be making a move from VBScript to VB.NET, so it is a good idea for us to review the differences between these languages. We shall also look at the differences between VB 6.0 and VB.NET.

VBScript does not support `Option Strict` to force type-safe variables. Under VB.NET, not only is `Option Strict` supported, but it is the default. When `Option Strict` is specified, all variables must have their type specified. Another change from VB to VB.NET is that parameters are passed `ByVal` by default. This is safer than in legacy VB, where `ByRef` is the default. On the subject of parameters, parentheses must be given when making calls to methods. For example, the following code would fail because the parentheses surrounding the string parameter are not present:

```
Response.Write "Hey, Ungowa! Clipper Power!"
```

`Let` and `Set` are no longer required in VB.NET. `Set` is not required because objects can be set using simple assignment. Both `Let` and `Set` are still available keywords under VB.NET, but are now redundant. Another change is that default properties are no longer supported by VB.NET. For example, when retrieving or setting the value of an ADO `Field` or `Parameter`, the `Value` property does not need to be specified in previous versions of VB because it is the default property. Under VB.NET however, this property does have to be explicitly specified. The following line of old-style code shows the value of a `Field` of an ADO `Record` being retrieved (the `EmployeeID` field of the results contained in the `Recordset`):

```
Response.Write "EmployeeID: " & rsEmployees("EmployeeID")
```

Under VB.NET, parentheses are required, and you must explicitly specify the property being retrieved:

```
Response.Write("EmployeeID: " & rsEmployees("EmployeeID").Value)
```

The date format used by older versions of VB is a four-byte `Double`. VB.NET uses the `System.Date` format, represented by an eight-byte integer. The `Integer` type in VB.NET is four bytes wide and `Long` is eight bytes wide. In VB an integer is two bytes and a long four bytes. These type differences are more likely to become an issue when ASP.NET code interacts with legacy COM components.

Error handling under VB uses constructs such as On Error Goto and On Error Resume Next. VB Script used only the latter form for its error handling. Regardless of the legacy VB variant used, the On Error blah blah form is not supported under VB.NET. Error handling under VB.NET is centered on exceptions, and the associated keywords, Try, Catch, and Throw. The Finally keyword is also provided in order to ensure cleanup takes place even when exceptions are raised during execution.

COM Registration

The registration of COM objects is not technically a VB-specific feature and COM object registration represents a legacy issue for all .NET developers. The issue arises because installing a .NET application is simply a matter of copying files without any requirement to register a .NET application in the system registry. COM components on the other hand still require registration (of CLSID, Prog ID, type library, and so on), so .NET applications (including ASP.NET applications) must register any COM objects they utilize. These registered objects are placed in a different directory from that containing the .NET application. Uninstalling a .NET application is simply a matter of deleting the directory that contains the application. Deleting a directory is not the friendliest operation for a COM object. For those lamenting this need to actually tweak the registry when using legacy COM components, recall the words of Michael Corleone, "Just when I think I'm out, they pull me back in".

API Changes ASP to ASP.NET

ASP and ASP.NET both use the same set of Application, Request, Response, Server, and Session objects. These objects have slightly different usage depending on which technology is being used. Recall that the code of a previous ASP.NET sample contained the following line of code germane to the objects exposed by ASP.NET:

```
public class WebForm1 : System.Web.UI.Page
```

The snippet shows that ASP.NET web pages are actually derived from the Page class found in the namespace, System.Web.UI. The fundamental objects used in conjunction with ASP.NET programming (objects Application, Request, Response, Server, and Session) are in fact now implemented as properties of this Page class.

The differences between the ASP and the ASP.NET versions of these objects can be summed up by considering the cases below:

❑ Request(item) – returns an array of strings corresponding to a value found with in a Request object collection. When this variation of Request is called, the variable corresponding to the specified item is retrieved by searching the collections associated with the Request object. The collections are searched in the order QueryString, Form, Cookies, ClientCertificate, and ServerVariables.

❑ Request.QueryString(item) – returns strings corresponding to the query variables of the HTTP response (the variables associated with a GET request).

❑ Request.Form(item) – returns an array of strings corresponding to the form variables of an HTTP response (the variables associated with a POST request).

If the item parameter specified by each of the above methods returns only a single value, then the code for ASP and ASP.NET is the same. When any of these methods return multiple values for one value of item, the ASP and ASP.NET code differs. Although each of the aforementioned methods retrieves an array of strings under ASP, these methods return the collection data type NameValueCollection under ASP.NET. Under VBScript, the first element in a collection is denoted by an index value of one (a one-based collection), but in VB.NET, all collections are zero-based.

ASP.NET Features

Multithreaded Apartments and COM

The threading model associated with ASP.NET is Multithreaded Apartment (MTA), since this threading model offers the best performance. This does mean however that multiple threads can access an ASP.NET object simultaneously and it is up to the developer to provide synchronization of shared data. Legacy COM objects can be accessed from ASP.NET applications using the TlbImp.exe utility or through late binding. The former is a simpler approach. The TlbImp.exe utility can be called either directly from the command line, or indirectly through Visual Studio.NET. Legacy COM objects that only run in a Single Threaded Apartment (STA) must be placed in ASP.NET pages configured using the aspcompat attribute as follows:

```
<%@Page aspcompat=true Language = VB%>
```

Setting the aspcompat attribute to true like this forces the ASP.NET page to run in STA mode. Clearly it benefits a software shop to upgrade such legacy COM objects to run inside MTAs.

ASP and ASP.NET Coexistence

Different extensions (ASP.NET files use the extension .aspx while ASP files use .asp) means that both ASP.NET and ASP can coexist in the same web site. The implication is that a web site does not have to be migrated to .NET all at once. Legacy ASP portions of a site can remain while new portions can be added in ASP.NET. One limitation of this coexistence is that ASP and ASP.NET cannot share state.

When a web page with an .asp extension is accessed, it is loaded as an ASP page using ASP.DLL (the ISAPI DLL that interprets ASP pages). The text of the ASP page is interpreted and run as unmanaged code. The ASP page itself may call managed objects (.NET objects), but the page itself is an unmanaged application.

When an ASP.NET page (.aspx extension) is loaded, the ISAPI DLL, aspnet_isapi.dll, is called to load and run the page's code as a managed application within the .NET Framework. ASP.NET code is run under .NET by using ASP.NET's worker process, aspnet_wp.exe. The specific ISAPI DLL that actually launches ASP.NET code running under this worker process is not documented at present. The DLL, aspnet_isapi.dll, represents an educated guess as to what is the ISAPI DLL. The functions imported and called by this DLL are the same .NET-related functions used to transition from unmanaged code to the managed environment provided by the .NET Framework. If you wish to understand how the hypothesis that aspnet_isapi.dll is the ISAPI DLL that launches ASP.NET pages was arrived at, run VS.NET's dumpbin.exe utility from the command line as follows:

dumpbin /IMPORTS aspnet_isapi.dll

The /IMPORTS option of dumbin displays the functions imported by the specified DLL. Among these functions, you will see some specific to .NET for transitioning code from an unmanaged to a managed environment. These functions include CorBindToRuntimeHost, CorBindToRuntimeEx, and ClrCreateManagedInstance.

This is not a tutorial on dumpbin, .NET run-time hosts, and transitioning from unmanaged to managed code. The point to be made is that the more that is known about an environment, the better equipped a developer is to take advantage of that environment. ASP.NET developers should recognize that they are .NET developers, and that by becoming familiar with the intricacies of this environment, they will have a head start when tackling a new application.

It just so happens that the run-time host can specify the .NET application domain in which an ASP.NET application runs. The application domain either configures an application to run code in a single shared process, or in separate processes if these are to be instantiated. This decision boils down to a tradeoff between reliability and resources (memory). It is just as important for an ASP.NET developer to make sound decisions on reliability versus resource consumption as it is for any developer working with .NET.

Server-Side Controls

ASP.NET supports a variety of server-side controls that include but are not limited to `Label`, `TextBox`, `Button`, `AdRotator`, `Table`, `CheckBox`, and `RadioButton`. These controls are programmable entities that ultimately generate the markup and client script for browsers. Different varieties of browser, such as WAP browsers or those that support an older HTML standard, could have content tailored accordingly.

The following ASP.NET code, found in project `WXCh01Demo01`, demonstrates a basic server-side control (a button) is

```
<%@ Page language="c#" Src="WebForm1.aspx.cs" Inherits="WebForm1" %>
<HTML>
  <body>
    <form id="Form1" method="post" runat="server">
      <asp:button id="ButtonFun" OnClick="btn_ClickToggleButton"
                  runat="server" Text="Scooby"></asp:button>
    </form>
  </body>
</HTML>
```

This ASP.NET code snippet creates a server-side button called `ButtonFun`, with this line:

```
<asp:button id="ButtonFun" runat="server" Text="Scooby"></asp:button>
```

This button toggles between showing the label "**Scooby**" and the label "**Doo**", but the code is contained in the separate file specified by first line of the previous file:

```
<%@ Page language="c#" Src="WebForm1.aspx.cs" Inherits="WebForm1" %>
```

What this ASPX line tells us is that the code associated with the page is written in C# (`Page language="c#"`) and is to be found in the file, `WebForm1.aspx.cs`. Here is an extract from that file:

```
protected void btn_ClickToggleButton(object sender, System.EventArgs e)
{
  if (ButtonFun.Text == "Scooby")
  {
    ButtonFun.Text = "Doo";
  }
  else
  {
    ButtonFun.Text = "Scooby";
  }
}
```

This C# method toggles the button's text between "**Scooby**" and "**Doo**". In this sample, HTML generation is handled by the server-side control and the button text is updated programmatically by a separate C# file. The output displayed is shown in the following screenshots. The browser on the left shows the button as initially displayed (**Scooby**), and the browser window on the right shows the button after it has been clicked once (**Doo**):

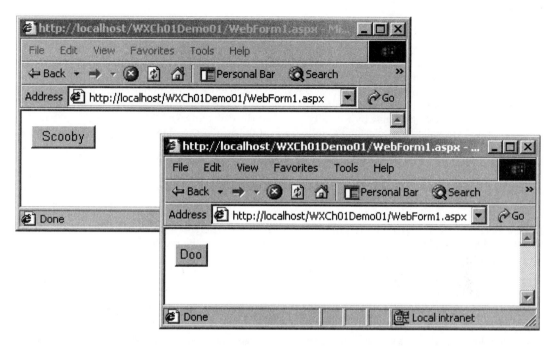

Cross-Browser and Cross-Device Content

ASPX code is executed server-side to produce the markup that the browser ultimately displays. In the Scooby button example, the following HTML code is sent to the browser when the ASPX page is requested:

```
<html>
  <body>
    <form name="Form1" method="post" action="WebForm1.aspx" id="Form1">
      <input type="hidden" name="__VIEWSTATE"
             value="dDwtNTMwNzcxMzI0Ozs +" />
        <input type="submit" name="ButtonFun" value="Scooby"
               id="ButtonFun" />
    </form>
  </body>
</html>
```

The HTML generated by the ASP.NET page is browser-specific. For a browser that supports HTML 4.0, ASP.NET will generate HTML 4.0 content. For a browser that supports only HTML 3.2, ASP.NET will conform to this limitation and generate HTML 3.2-compliant content. ASP on the other hand generates HTML that is not automatically tailored to the browser in which it will run. The task of ensuring the HTML generated matches a user's browser is non-trivial. By fair means or foul, Internet Explorer appears to have pretty much won the browser war, so why is this important? First of all, there are numerous versions of Internet Explorer in use that conform to differing HTML practices. Internet Explorer may rule the PC kingdom, but PDAs, Internet devices, and mobile phones offer specialized browsers. ASP.NET's dynamic generation of content can simplify the development of web pages that display correctly on such diverse devices.

ASP.NET server-side controls generate content according to the browser running client-side, and this content does not necessarily have to be HTML.

Mobile Internet Toolkit

Microsoft ships a separate SDK known as the Mobile Internet Toolkit. This toolkit facilitates the development of device-specific adaptors for mobile applications. Wireless applications can be quickly developed using the Mobile Internet Designer, which is fully integrated into Visual Studio.NET. The toolkit offers useful features oriented towards developers who work in the mobile arena. For instance, specialized mobile controls are made available as part of the toolkit that allow ASP.NET applications to directly generate code consumable by a variety of mobile devices. However, this does not mean that server-side controls will not be migrated to fully support the browser used by a particular mobile device.

Configuration

ASP.NET uses two files for configuration of a given application. The first, `machine.config`, details configuration settings for all ASP.NET applications running on a specific host in an XML format. The second is the `web.config` file, which contains XML specifying compilation options, error handling, tracing, and security for a particular application. An additional perk of such configuration files is that it simplifies deployment by making it no longer necessary to update the registry on the machine on which an ASP.NET application is deployed.

Deployment

.NET applications (including ASP.NET applications) are deployed by simply copying files onto the host that will run the application. The term given to this process is "XCopy Deployment". This style of deployment is possible because each .NET application is self-contained. The required assemblies and configuration files are all included with the installation files. The one exception to this is that legacy COM objects must still be registered when used by .NET applications.

XML Compliance

The standards associated with web development continue to evolve at breakneck pace. ASP.NET is uniquely positioned to evolve in concord with these standards because ASP.NET developers will work primarily with code, rather than HTML. ASP.NET generates HTML 3.2-compliant text. Ultimately it will generate content based on the XHTML specification. This flavor of HTML is in effect HTML 4.01 written in XML-compliant format. Compliance with such standards is not solely dependant on the server. In order to make supporting XHTML a worthwhile option, sufficient browsers that can render it must first be deployed.

Summary

This chapter has presented the benefits of moving from classic ASP development to ASP.NET. Performance, security, reliability, and scalability might not be enough by themselves to coax Homo Contentus to move to ASP.NET, but the ease of use that the Visual Studio.NET environment offers should swing the argument in favor of evolution.

For the benefit of Homo Senior, other .NET concepts have been introduced, such as the Just-in-Time concept, JIT, and the associated possibility of pre-compilation to improve performance. Other .NET benefits such as cross language support, type-safety, and managed heaps have also been described. We have also seen a small subset of .NET related utilities and how they can be exploited by the ASP.NET developer (`ilasm.exe`, `ildasm.exe`, `TlbImp.exe`, `Dumpbin.exe`, and `NGen.exe`).

Both Homo Contentus and Homo Senior should benefit from the fact that ASP and ASP.NET can coexist. Other important features of the new platform include server-side controls, a better IDE, greater XML compliance, simplified deployment, and improved scalability.

2

System.Web

The System.Web namespace contains classes to deal with the base functionality of the web architecture. It includes, among others, objects representing the request and response, as well as objects to access information about the application and file paths. These objects provide useful information about the environment that the application is running in. It also contains some helper functions (utilities) to make working in that environment easier.

In this chapter we'll cover the classes in System.Web that are the most useful, and commonly used, in ASP.NET web applications. These classes make up the bulk of the namespace and provide the majority of its functionality. Before we begin, however, we'll cover some of the basics of creating a page in ASP.NET.

> **Wrox authors Alex Homer and Dave Sussman have an online application, developed for *Professional ASP.NET* (ISBN 1-861004-88-5), that lets you explore the properties of selected Server Controls. It can be found at**
> **http://www.alanddave.com/profaspnet/default.asp**

Creating an ASP.NET Page

In traditional ASP programming, server-side script was embedded into the HTML text of a page. Certainly there were exceptions to this, for example, when a page simply processed code and redirected the user to a display screen, but for the most part, this was the case.

The following simple page mixes ASP code to get the date and time, with HTTP text for the presentation of that information. On the highlighted line we use the <%...%> syntax to indicate to the server that there is code to be processed:

Time.asp

```
<html>
  <head>
    <title></title>
  </head>
  <body>
    <h2>
      The time on the server is:<%=Now%>
    </h2>
  </body>
</html>
```

You can continue to mix code and layout like this in ASP.NET, but the recommended method is to have one file that defines your layout and HTML content, called a **web form**, and another that contains your code. This second file is referred to as a **code behind** file, and is where the server-side processing of your page is defined. This approach has many benefits, not least of which is improved manageability and readability.

We won't cover the differences between ASP and ASP.NET here, but we will show a brief example of the different options for creating a dynamic web page in ASP.NET.

Firstly, here is an example web form where code and layout are mixed. The code is enclosed in `<script>` blocks:

Time.aspx

```
<html>
<head>
  <title>Time Web Form</title>
</head>
<body>
  <script language="C#" runat="server">
    string GetTime()
    {
      return System.DateTime.Now.ToString();
    }
  </script>
  <h2>
    The time at the server is
    <%=GetTime()%>
  </h2>
</body>
</html>
```

The first point to note here is that our page has an ASPX file extension. This tells the web server that it is an ASP.NET web form, and should be handled accordingly. Next, notice that we're using a script block to wrap a function called `GetTime` that returns the system date and time as a string value. The surrounding script block specifies the language and the location to run the script, in this case at the server.

> *You can only use one language in a given web page, as the entire page is compiled to a single instance of a Page class (discussed in Chapter 3). Different languages can be used for different pages.*

Finally, our script returns a value using a function call, though we could just as easily have done it like this:

```
<h2>
  The time at the server is
  <%=System.DateTime.Now.ToString()%>
</h2>
```

The structure we've used so far will be very familiar to ASP developers. Now we're going to compose a similar example, using the suggested ASP.NET architecture, where only the layout elements appear in the ASPX file:

TimeDotNetStyle.aspx

```
<%@ Page Language="vb" Codebehind="TimeDotNetStyle.aspx.vb"
Inherits="TimeDotNetStyle" Src="TimeDotNetStyle.aspx.vb"%>
<html>
  <head>
    <title>Time DotNet Style</title>
```

```
    </head>
    <body>
      <form id="Form1" method="post" runat="server">
        <asp:Label ID="time" Runat="server"></asp:Label>
      </form>
  </body>
  </html>
```

There are a couple of important things to notice here. First, the file now contains an @Page directive at the top of the file, which tells the .NET runtime about the page. Its Language attribute tells the runtime which compiler to use on the file, in this case the Visual Basic.NET compiler. Its CodeBehind attribute specifies the name of the file that contains our server-side code and class rules, and its Inherits attribute indicates that our ASPX page derives from the TimeDotNetStyle class.

Secondly we have used an ASP.NET <asp:Label> and an HTTP <form> element, both with their runat attributes set to "server". This indicates that these items will be available to us as objects in our code behind file. To see how this works, let's examine that file now:

TimeDotNetStyle.aspx.vb

```vb
'This class is representing our page object. It is named
'the same as our page and is inheriting from
'System.Web.UI.Page:

Public Class TimeDotNetStyle
  Inherits System.Web.UI.Page

  'our variable in code behind which represents
  'the label control in our web form and whose
  'name is the same as the ID property of the
  'control.
  Protected WithEvents time As System.Web.UI.WebControls.Label

  Private Sub Page_Init(ByVal sender As System.Object & _
                             ByVal e As System.EventArgs)
                                                            Handles
MyBase.Init

    'we do nothing in the Page Initialization section
  End Sub

  Private Sub Page_Load(ByVal sender As System.Object & _
                             ByVal e As System.EventArgs)
                                                            Handles
MyBase.Load
    'set the text property of our label control to_
    'the current time.
    time.Text = "The time at the DotNet Server is: " &
                                    System.DateTime.Now.ToString()

  End Sub
End Class
```

Here we're defining a class to inherit from System.Web.UI.Page. Within that class we're declaring a variable called time of type System.Web.UI.WebControls.Label that represents our <asp:Label> element from the web form. Then in the Page_Load event handler we're simply setting the Text property of our label to the value that we want to display. It's as simple as that!

The System.Web Namespace

Now we've seen how to make a basic page we'll delve into more detail about the many classes that the ASP.NET `System.Web` namespace makes available to developers. We'll be focusing primarily on classes that deal with communication between the client and the server, including the information sent between the two.

The following classes are covered:

❑ **HttpBrowserCapabilities** – this class encapsulates information about the client browser making requests, and includes information regarding the capabilities of the client, including support for ActiveX controls, Java Applets and JavaScript, cookie support, frames support, and the browser type and version.

❑ **HttpContext** – this class provides information about the current context in which the request is executing including security and error information.

❑ **HttpCookie** – this class allows the creation and manipulation of cookies sent to and from the client.

❑ **HttpCookieCollection** – this class provides access to a collection of cookies. An object of this type is available in both the `HttpRequest` and `HttpResponse` objects to allow access to the cookies sent with a request or to be sent with the response.

❑ **HttpFileCollection** – this class provides a wrapper around a collection of posted files to make managing and working with those files as a group much easier.

❑ **HttpPostedFile** – this class provides an object that represents a file posted to the server via an input tag on the browser and allows easy manipulation and saving of the file.

❑ **HttpRequest** – this class encapsulates information and functionality surrounding the request made to the web server by the client including forms data, query strings, headers, and browser information. Essentially, it encompasses all information sent to the server in an object.

❑ **HttpResponse** – this class encapsulates the outgoing stream from the server and allows for manipulation the information being sent to the client including outgoing cookies, headers, HTML content, and caching information.

❑ **HttpRuntime** – this class provides access to the IIS run-time process and provides information on the host environment including file paths, application IDs and the ability to process a request and to close the runtime.

❑ **HttpServerUtility** – this class encapsulates a great deal of the helper functions for working with web applications including the encoding and decoding of strings, mapping paths, executing other `.aspx` pages, and creating COM objects to be used in the page.

❑ **HttpSessionState** – this class allows for access to the mechanisms for storing information for a given user session. (This class actually belongs to the `System.Web.SessionState` namespace.)

The HttpBrowserCapabilities Class

Knowing the client and the environment in which your pages are being viewed is very helpful in tailoring your pages to them. For example, using different stylesheets and tags in different situations gives a great deal of useful flexibility. You could make a decision about whether to use ActiveX or a Java Applet to perform some functionality based on your knowledge of what the client supports.

It is the means to make these decisions that the `HttpBrowserCapabilities` class provides. It derives from the more general `HttpCapabilitiesBase` class, which provides some base functionality for reading capabilities information from configuration files based on the User-Agent header and Server variables collection for the given request. The `machine.config` file contains the mappings of a User-Agent string (discussed with the `HttpRequest` class) to the capabilities of a browser. Keep in mind that these capabilities only indicate what a client is capable of, not what it will actually support. For example, a user may turn off cookie support in their browser, but because the browser can support cookies in general, the `HttpBrowserCapabilities` class will indicate that the client supports cookies.

HttpBrowserCapabilities Properties

The majority of the properties of the `HttpBrowserCapabilities` class are Boolean values indicating if a particular technology is supported. For that reason, only brief descriptions of the properties are given here. The default values are provided for each property. If a value cannot be determined based on the client requesting a resource, then the default value is used.

- ❑ `ActiveXControls`
- ❑ `AOL`
- ❑ `BackgroundSounds`
- ❑ `Beta`
- ❑ `Browser`
- ❑ `CDF`
- ❑ `ClrVersion`
- ❑ `Cookies`
- ❑ `Crawler`
- ❑ `EcmaScriptVersion`
- ❑ `Frames`
- ❑ `Item` (inherited from `HttpCapabilitiesBase`)
- ❑ `JavaApplets`
- ❑ `JavaScript`
- ❑ `MajorVersion`
- ❑ `MinorVersion`
- ❑ `MSDomVersion`
- ❑ `Platform`
- ❑ `Tables`
- ❑ `Type`
- ❑ `VBScript`
- ❑ `Version`
- ❑ `W3CDomVersion`
- ❑ `Win16`
- ❑ `Win32`

ActiveXControls Property (read-only)

The `ActiveXControls` property indicates if the browser supports ActiveX controls. This value is `false` by default.

```
Boolean = HttpBrowserCapabilities.ActiveXControls
```

AOL Property (read-only)

The `AOL` property indicates whether the browser is an America OnLine browser. This property can be used to determine if the client is using an AOL browser and then target special features of that AOL client, or suppress content that is not appropriate for an AOL browser. The default value for this property is `false`.

```
Boolean = HttpBrowserCapabilities.AOL
```

BackgroundSounds Property (read-only)

The `BackgroundSounds` property indicates whether the browser supports background sounds, embedded links to sound files that play while the page is being displayed, without any user interaction to start them. The default value for this property is `false`.

```
Boolean = HttpBrowserCapabilities.BackgroundSounds
```

Beta Property (read-only)

The `Beta` property indicates whether the browser is a beta version as indicated in the HTTP headers sent to the server. The default value for this property is `false`.

```
Boolean = HttpBrowserCapabilities.Beta
```

Browser Property (read-only)

The `Browser` property indicates the name of the client browser as sent to the server in the user-agent HTTP header. If you want to get a string value representing the browser and the version, use the `Type` property.

```
String = HttpBrowserCapabilities.Browser
```

CDF Property (read-only)

The `CDF` property indicates whether the browser supports the Channel Definition Format (CDF), an implementation of XML that allows for providing software channels such as those found in the Internet Explorer browser. The default value for this property is `false`.

```
Boolean = HttpBrowserCapabilities.CDF
```

ClrVersion Property (read-only)

The `ClrVersion` property indicates the version number of the Common Language Runtime (CLR) on the client machine. Currently, this property will not prove very useful as most clients will not have the CLR installed on their computers. In the future, it will prove useful to target code to the client based on their version of the CLR.

```
Version = HttpBrowserCapabilities.ClrVersion
```

Cookies Property (read-only)

The Cookies property indicates whether the client browser can support cookies. The default value for this property is false.

```
Boolean = HttpBrowserCapabilities.Cookies
```

Crawler Property (read-only)

The Crawler property indicates whether the client requesting the page is a search engine crawler or an Internet browser. A value of true indicates that the client is a search engine crawler. The default value for this property is false.

```
Boolean = HttpBrowserCapabilities.Crawler
```

EcmaScriptVersion Property (read-only)

The EcmaScriptVersion property indicates the version of European Computer Manufacturer's Association (ECMA) script supported by the client. ECMA script is more commonly referred to as JavaScript. This property can be used in conjunction with the JavaScript property which determines if the browser supports JavaScript. For more information about ECMA , see the official web site at http://www.ecma.ch.

```
Version = HttpBrowserCapabilities.EcmaScriptVersion
```

Frames Property (read-only)

The Frames property indicates whether the client browser supports HTML frames. The default value for this property is false.

```
Boolean = HttpBrowserCapabilities.Frames
```

JavaApplets Property (read-only)

The JavaApplets property indicates whether the browser supports Java Applets. The default value for this property is false.

```
Boolean = HttpBrowserCapabilities.JavaApplets
```

JavaScript Property (read-only)

The JavaScript property indicates whether the browser supports JavaScript. The default value for this property is false. This property can be used in conjunction with the EcmaScriptVersion property, which provides the version number of scripting supported.

```
Boolean = HttpBrowserCapabilities.JavaScript
```

MajorVersion Property (read-only)

The MajorVersion property indicates the major version of the browser as sent to the server by the browser. A browser with a version number of 4.7, for instance, has a major version of 4.

```
Int = HttpBrowserCapabilities.MajorVersion
```

MinorVersion Property (read-only)

The `MinorVersion` property indicates the minor version number of the client browser based on information passed from the browser to the server in the request. A browser with a version number of 4.7, for instance, has a minor version of .7.

```
Double = HttpBrowserCapabilities.MinorVersion
```

MSDomVersion Property (read-only)

The `MSDom` property returns the version of the Microsoft XML Document Object Model (DOM) present on the client. Use this property to determine the level of XML functionality supported on the client side.

```
Version = HttpBrowserCapabilities.MsDomVersion
```

Platform Property (read-only)

The `Platform` property indicates the operating system platform that the client is using as sent to the browser in the HTTP request. This comes in handy for managing stylesheets, as the Macintosh, for example, renders pages slightly differently from Windows machines.

```
String = HttpBrowserCapabilities.Platform
```

Tables Property (read-only)

The `Tables` property indicates whether the client's browser supports HTML tables. The default value for this property is `false`.

```
Boolean = HttpBrowserCapabilities.Tables
```

Type Property (read-only)

The `Type` property indicates the version name and number for the client browser. For example, if the client is using Internet Explorer 6, the `Type` property returns `IE6`. This property is different from the `Browser` property, which only gives a representation of the browser and not the version.

```
String = HttpBrowserCapabilities.Type
```

VBScript Property (read-only)

The `VBScript` property indicates whether the client supports VBScript in the browser. The default value for this property is `false`.

```
Boolean = HttpBrowserCapabilities.VBScript
```

Version Property (read-only)

The `Version` property indicates the version of the client browser including the major and minor numbers.

```
String = HttpBrowserCapabilities.Version
```

W3CDomVersion Property (read-only)

The `W3CDomVersion` property indicates the version of the W3C Document Object Model (DOM) that is supported on the client. This property can be useful in determining whether or not to use certain HTML elements.

```
Version = HttpBrowserCapabilities.W3CDomVersion
```

Win16 Property (read-only)

The `Win16` property indicates whether the client is running on a 16-bit Windows platform. The default value for this property is `false`.

```
Boolean = HttpBrowserCapabilities.Win16
```

Win32 Property (read-only)

The `Win32` property indicates whether the client is running on a 32-bit Windows platform. The default value for this property is `false`.

```
Boolean = HttpBrowserCapabilities.Win32
```

HttpContext Class

The `HttpContext` class provides information about the context in which a given web request is executing. This class provides access to methods and properties useful in creating web application such as information about errors, the user, and configuration settings. This class is covered in an abbreviated manner as many of the properties and methods are duplicated on other objects that will be covered here in greater detail. All members have been listed, but only those marked with an * are covered here.

HttpContext Class Static (Shared) Properties

❑   Current*

Current Property (Read-Only)

This static (shared in VB.NET) property provides a reference to the current context object in which the request is executing. This can be useful if you want to access the methods and properties of the context as you can easily get a reference and act on it.

```
HttpContext Context = HttpContext.Current
```

HttpContext Class Static (Shared) Methods

❑   GetAppConfig*

GetAppConfig Method

The `GetAppConfig` method allows the developer to retrieve configuration information from the application's `web.config` file. The object this returns depends on the configuration section accessed. As an example, retrieving a custom `appSettings` element from the configuration file returns a `NameValueCollection` object.

See Chapter 8, Configuration & System.Web.Configuration, *for more information on configuration files and managing configuration information in ASP.NET.*

```
object ConfigSection = HttpContext.GetAppConfig(key)
```

Parameter	Type	Description
key	String	The name of the configuration section you wish to retrieve

HttpContext Class Public Properties

- ❑ AllErrors*
- ❑ Application
- ❑ ApplicationInstance
- ❑ Cache
- ❑ Error*
- ❑ Handler
- ❑ IsCustomErrorEnabled
- ❑ IsDebuggingEnabled
- ❑ Items
- ❑ Request
- ❑ Response
- ❑ Server
- ❑ Session
- ❑ SkipAuthorization*
- ❑ Timestamp
- ❑ Trace
- ❑ User*

AllErrors Property (read-only)

The AllErrors property returns an array of the exceptions that have occurred in the processing of the current request. This property is a convenient way to collect, and act on, all of the errors that occurred during processing, either by logging them, or presenting them to the user.

```
Exception[] Errors = HttpContext.AllErrors
```

Error Property (read-only)

The Error property provides access to the first error encountered during the processing of the request. If you are just looking for the first error, perhaps to indicate the cause of further errors, then this property will give you access to that information.

```
Exception e = HttpContext.Error
```

SkipAuthorization Property

The `SkipAuthorization` property allows the developer to indicate that a given request should skip the authorization process and execute without checking the user's credentials. This property is for use in advanced security schemes where there is a need to allow a user access to a page with anonymous access. The Forms authentication process uses this to allow a user access to a specified login page before being authenticated.

```
HttpContext.SkipAuthorization = Boolean
Boolean Skip = HttpContext.SkipAuthorization
```

User Property

The `User` property indicates the `IPrincipal` object under which the current request is executing. Using this object you can get information about the user making the request. This security identity will be used to attempt to access any resources during the request.

```
HttpContext.User = IPrincipal
IPrincipal WebUser = HttpContext.User
```

HttpContext Class Public Methods

- ❑ `AddError*`
- ❑ `ClearError*`
- ❑ `GetConfig`
- ❑ `RewritePath`

AddError Method

The `AddError` method allows the developer to insert an exception into the errors collection of the context. This can be useful if you want to make your error information available to others. For example, if you create a user control you may want to record exceptions that occur in your control to the error collection of the context so that other objects in the page can be aware of, and get information about, the error.

```
void AddError(error)
```

Parameter	Type	Description
error	Exception	The Exception object contains information about the error you want to add to the collection

ClearError Method

The `ClearError` method clears **all** errors from the `errors` collection of the `context` object. This is especially important when you are providing custom error handling using the `Error` event of the page object (described in Chapter 3, *System.Web.UI*). When you deal with errors that arise in the context of a web request, you must clear this collection if you do not also want the ASP.NET runtime to catch and report those errors.

```
void ClearError()
```

The HttpCookie Class

The Internet, and especially the HTTP protocol, are stateless by nature. A client sends a request to the server and receives a response. Until the client requests another page, the browser is not connected to the server. While this lightens the load on the server because the connection does not need to be maintained, it limits the ability to persist information specific to the client. Each time the client connects to the server to request a page, it could be a different client, or a different user on the same machine.

Cookies, introduced in the early versions of the popular web browsers, allow the web developer to store small pieces of information on the client computer. These "cookies" of information specify an expiration date and a path on the server. The client browser then sends the cookie back to the originating server each time a request is made for a resource in the path specified. When setting a cookie the developer can specify parameters such as expiration date and path on the server where the cookie should be sent. In addition to having cookies that are persisted between visits to the site, in-memory cookies can be created that only last until the browser is closed, which is how session ID has traditionally been maintained.

Using these cookies developers are able to maintain some sense of state or "connectedness" with the client. However, many users do not like the idea of web sites storing information on their computer and tracking their movements on the web, so they may turn cookies off. A good web site needs to be developed with this in mind and come up with alternative methods for maintaining state, such as hidden form fields or passing information in the query string. Use the `HttpBrowserCapabilities` class documented earlier in this chapter to test whether or not cookies are supported on the client and program accordingly.

HttpCookie Properties

- ❏ Domain
- ❏ Expires
- ❏ HasKeys
- ❏ Item
- ❏ Name
- ❏ Path
- ❏ Secure
- ❏ Value
- ❏ Values

Domain Property

The `Domain` property indicates the DNS domain name where the cookie originated and thus where it should be sent when making client requests.

```
String = HttpCookie.Domain
HttpCookie.Domain = String
```

Cookies can only be sent to their originating domain. This practice protects the user because it means that your cookies from the online retailer you shop at do not get transmitted to other sites you visit.

Expires Property

The `Expires` property indicates the expiration date and time of the cookie.

```
DateTime = HttpCookie.Expires
HttpCookie.Expires = DateTime
```

Use this property when setting a new cookie to indicate to the browser when the cookie should no longer be sent with requests. Cookies have a domain and path that indicate **where** they should be sent, and the expiration of the cookie determines **when** the cookie should be sent, or rather, when it should stop being sent.

An application of this property is when a cookie has been set to expire and its life needs to be extended. Or, perhaps you want to know when the user last performed an action that generated a cookie.

HasKeys Property (read-only)

The `HasKeys` property indicates whether the cookie object has sub keys. Unlike a typical name/value pair, a cookie can have multiple values.

```
Boolean = HttpCookie.HasKeys
```

For example, a simple cookie might have a name of "`color`" and a value of "`red`". However, a cookie with sub keys might have a name of "`color`" and values of "`red,blue,yellow`". If we checked the `HasKeys` properties in this second case it would return `true`. We could then use the `Values` property to extract the individual values. If this property returns `false`, then we can use the `Value` property to get the one specific value.

Item Property

The `Item` property indicates a specific value in the cookie. This property would only be used on a cookie that has sub keys, as indicated by the `HasKeys` property. The `Item` property acts as a shortcut to the items in the `Values` collection (as distinct from the `Value` property).

```
String = HttpCookie.Item(key)
```

Parameter	Type	Description
key	String	The name of the item in the cookie to be retrieved

> **This property is deprecated and only available for backward compatibility. Use the `Values` property in ASP.NET.**

Name Property

The `Name` property indicates the name of the cookie to be set, or that has been set.

```
String = HttpCookie.Name
HttpCookie.Name = String
```

Path Property

The `Path` property indicates the path on the server for which the cookie is valid. This property, in conjunction with the domain attribute of the cookie, indicates to the client browser when it should send the cookie along with the request.

```
String = HttpCookie.Path
HttpCookie.Path = string
```

Cookies are intended to maintain state on a given site. Because the information stored in these cookies is specific to a site, and may contain information that should not be shared, client browsers only send cookies to the DNS domain from which they were created. Therefore, a cookie created in the www.wrox.com domain will not get sent when the user visits msdn.microsoft.com.

To further specify when, and where, the cookie should be sent, the path for a cookie can be set to indicate the directory path on the domain that should receive it. So, a cookie from the www.wrox.com domain with a path of /aspprogref would not be accessible for pages requested from http://www.wrox.com/authors, but would be available for pages requested from http://www.wrox.com/aspprogref/examples.

Using a `Path` of "/" indicates that all directory paths on the server should have access to the cookie.

Secure Property

The `Secure` property indicates whether the cookie is only allowed to be sent over a secure (SSL) connection. If so the cookie will only be sent if the protocol of the request is HTTPS.

```
Boolean = HttpCookie.Secure
HttpCookie.Secure = Boolean
```

Use this property when working on a secure site to ensure that the client does not send the cookie over an insecure connection.

Value Property

The `Value` property indicates the value for the cookie. Use this property to either set or get the value of the cookie.

```
String = HttpCookie.Value
HttpCookie.Value = string
```

Values Property (read-only)

The `Values` property returns a `NameValueCollection` of the values for the cookie, or allows for the setting of specific values.

```
HttpCookie.Values[valname] = string
NameValueCollection = HttpCookie.Values
```

The majority of cookies are used as a single name and value. However, a given cookie may have more than one value. This property allows for retrieving all of the values in a cookie with one property. It can be used in conjunction with the `HasKeys` property of the `HttpCookie` object or the `HasKeys` method of the `Values` property itself.

The HttpCookieCollection Class

The `HttpCookieCollection` class encompasses a collection of cookies. The incoming collection can be accessed using the `Cookies` property of the `HttpRequest` object and the outgoing collection can be accessed using the same property of the `HttpResponse` object.

HttpCookieCollection Methods

- ❑ Add
- ❑ Clear
- ❑ CopyTo
- ❑ Getkey
- ❑ Remove
- ❑ Set

Add Method

The `Add` method allows the addition of a single cookie to the collection.

```
HttpCookieCollection.Add(cookie)
```

Parameter	Type	Description
cookie	HttpCookie	The cookie to add to the collection

To add a cookie we simply call the `Add` method passing in a new `HttpCookie` object with a name and a value:

C#
```
Response.Cookies.Add(new HttpCookie("login","username"));
```

VB.NET
```
Response.Cookies.Add(new HttpCookie("login","username"))
```

Clear Method

The `Clear` method allows clearing the collection of all cookies that have been added to it.

```
HttpCookieCollection.Clear()
```

This might be helpful if a collection has been filled with values and then an exception occurs. You'll want the user to get a response stream, but not want to set the cookies, because the page request failed. So you clear the cookies collection on the response object, write a message to the user, and then flush your response:

C#
```
Response.Cookies.Add(new HttpCookie("erased_cook","erased_value"));

try
{
```

```
      //code that may cause an exception
   }
   catch(Exception ex)
   {
      Response.Cookies.Clear();
      Response.Write("Error processing request");
      Response.End();
   }
```

VB.NET

```
   Response.Cookies.Add(New HttpCookie("erased_cook", "erased_value"))
   Try
      'code that may cause an exception
   Catch ex As Exception
      Response.Cookies.Clear()
      Response.Write("Error processing request")
      Response.End()
   End Try
```

CopyTo Method

The CopyTo method allows copying the cookies in the collection to an array.

```
   HttpCookieCollection.CopyTo(destination, index)
```

Parameter	Type	Description
destination	Array	The array to copy the values to
index	Int	The index of the array at which the values should start

Getkey Method

The GetKey method allows for accessing the name of the value specified by the index.

```
   String = HttpCookieCollection.GetKey(index)
```

Parameter	Type	Description
index	Int	The index of the item in the collection

Remove Method

The Remove method allows for taking a single cookie out of the collection. Removing a cookie from the incoming request does not have much impact other than to make it inaccessible to the rest of the code processing the page request. If the cookie has not expired, the client will send it again the next time it requests a resource from the server.

However, a cookie may be removed from the cookies collection on the outgoing response object to keep it from getting written to the client. If the cookie has already been written to the client on a previous visit or request, then removing it from the collection will not remove it from the client browser.

```
   HttpCookieCollection.Remove(name)
```

Parameter	Type	Description
name	String	The name that was given to the cookie as it was added to the collection

Set Method

The Set method allows for updating a cookie that is already present in the collection. This allows you to get a cookie out of the collection, make changes to the properties of that cookie and then use the Set method to update its value in the cookie.

```
HttpCookieColletion.Set(cookie)
```

Parameter	Type	Description
cookie	HttpCookie	The cookie object to be updated

HttpCookieCollection Properties

❑   AllKeys

❑   Item

AllKeys Property (read-only)

The AllKeys property indicates the names of all of the cookies in the collection. A string array is returned with each item containing the name of a cookie.

```
String[] HttpCookieCollection.AllKeys
```

Item Property (read-only)

The Item property indicates a specific cookie in the collection. This method has two overloaded versions to allow for accessing the cookie by name or numeric index.

```
HttpCookie = HttpCookieCollection.Item(index)
```

Parameter	Type	Description
index	Int	The index of the cookie to retrieve

```
HttpCookie = HttpCookieCollection.Item(name)
```

Parameter	Type	Description
name	String	The name of the item in the collection

Working with File Uploads

The ability to upload files to a web server is extremely useful in terms of allowing clients to submit information, or building a content management system. In ASP.NET the `HttpPostedFile` class and the `HttpFilesCollection` class give easy access to the files that are uploaded to the server and enable the developer to manage the file upload process.

The HttpFileCollection Class

The `HttpFileCollection` class provides a container for multiple `HttpPostedFile` objects and is the class used as the data structure to hold files posted to a web server. Knowing how to use this collection means knowing how to work with the posted files collection that is accessible from the `HttpRequest` object via its `Files` property. This collection is accessible once the entire contents of the request have been received by the server.

HttpFileCollection Methods

- ❏ `CopyTo`
- ❏ `GetKey`

CopyTo Method

The `CopyTo` method allows for copying the contents of the collection to an array. This is a common method of collections in the .NET framework that allows moving the objects in one data structure, the collection, to another, the array.

```
HttpFileCollection.CopyTo(destination, index)
```

Parameter	Type	Description
destination	Array	The `Array` that the contents of the collection should be copied into
index	Int	The index of the array where copying will begin

GetKey Method

The `GetKey` method r obtains the name of the item in the collection, that corresponds to the index specified.

```
String = HttpFileCollection.GetKey(index)
```

Parameter	Type	Description
index	Int	The index of the item in the collection to retrieve

HttpFileCollection Properties

- ❏ `AllKeys`
- ❏ `Item`

AllKeys Property (read-only)

The `AllKeys` property returns an array of strings containing all of the keys for the collection.

```
String[] = HttpFileCollection.AllKeys
```

Item Property (read-only)

The `Item` property indicates a specific item in the collection. In C# this property is the indexer, which means that an item can be accessed using a syntax similar to an array.

```
HttpFilePosted=HttpFileCollection.Item[index]
```
or
```
HttpFilePosted=HttpFileCollection.Item[name]
```

The HttpPostedFile class

The `HttpPostedFile` class provides an object to encapsulate a file that has been posted to the server. The binary file content is included in the content body of the incoming request and traditionally required the use of a third-party component or custom code to extract. In ASP.NET we have a built in object to work with that represents an individual file posted to the server.

HttpPostedFile Methods

❑ `SaveAs`

SaveAs Method

The `SaveAs` method allows saving a posted file to a given location on the server with a specific name.

```
HttpPostedFile.SaveAs(fileName)
```

Parameter	Type	Description
fileName	String	The physical path where the file should be saved

The file name must be a physical path to the file. If a simple file name is given without any path information, an attempt will be made to write the file to the Windows System directory (typically `c:\winnt\system32\`), where the IIS executable resides. Since this is probably not the place you want to be collecting posted files, you should provide the file name with a full directory path.

> Writing files to disk requires that your security permissions be such that the account the web request is running under is allowed write access to the server. If you allow users anonymous access to your site, the account under which their requests will be executing is the **IUSER_MahineName** account (where **MachineName** is the name of the server).

HttpPostedFile Properties

- ❑ ContentLength
- ❑ ContentType
- ❑ FileName
- ❑ InputStream

ContentLength Property

The ContentLength property indicates the length, in bytes, of the file that was posted to the server. This information can be important in determining actions to perform on the file. For example, you could have a page that submits files to a BizTalk Server via MSMQ. Because MSMQ has a message size limit of 2MB for Unicode files, a check of the ContentLength property could determine if the file can be sent via MSMQ or whether an alternative transport mechanism will need to be employed.

```
Int = HttpPostedFile.ContentLength
```

ContentType Property

The ContentType property indicates the MIME type of the file posted to the web server such as text/HTML or text/XML.

```
String = HttpPostedFile.ContentType
```

The content type of the file can be extremely important to the security of your site. You may want to ensure that files posted to your web site meet certain criteria in order to be processed, or to process files differently based on their content. For example, you may allow people to post both HTML or text files as well as image files as part of a custom content management system. Incoming images may go to one location while text files get parsed and saved to another location. On the other hand, you probably don't want a user to be able to load an executable application to your server. Therefore, if a file does not meet the requirements you have set you'll want your application to refuse it.

Some common MIME types are shown in the following table along with their file extensions.

Type	Description	FileExtensions
application/msaccess	Microsoft Access	.mdb
application/msword	Microsoft Word	.doc
application/octet-stream	Uninterpreted Binary	.bin
application/pdf	Portable Document Format	.pdf
application/postscript	Postscript file	.ps, .ai, .eps
application/vnd.ms-excel	Microsoft Excel	.xls

Type	Description	FileExtensions
`application/vnd.ms-powerpoint`	Microsoft Powerpoint	`.ppt`
`application/vnd.ms-project`	Microsoft Project	`.mpp`
`application/vnd.visio`	Microsoft Visio	`.vsd`
`application/vnd.wap.wmlc`	Compiled WML	`.wmlc`
`application/vnd.wap.wmlscriptc`	Compiled WML script	`.wmlsc`
`application/zip`	Zip compressed file	`.zip`
`audio/mpeg`	MPEG audio file	`.mpg, .mpeg`
`image/gif`	GIF image	`.gif`
`image/jpeg`	JPEG image	`.jpg, .jpeg, .jpe`
`image/png`	PNG image file	`.png`
`image/tiff`	Tag Image File Format	`.tiff, .tif`
`image/vnd.wap.wbmp`	WAP bitmap	`.wbmp`
`text/css`	Cascading Style Sheets	`.css`
`text/html`	HyperText Markup Language	`.htm, .html`
`text/plain`	Plain text	`.txt`
`text/richtext`	Rich text	`.rtx`
`text/sgml`	Structured Generalized Markup Language	`.sgml`
`text/tab-separated-values`	Tab separated text	`.tsv`
`text/vnd.wap.wml`	Wireless Markup Language	`.wml`

Table continued on following page

Type	Description	FileExtensions
`text/vnd.wap.wmlscript`	Wireless Markup Language Script	`.wmls`
`text/xml`	eXtensible Markup Language	`.xml`
`text/xml-external-parsed-entity`	XML externally parsed entities	`.xml`
`video/mpeg`	MPEG video	`.mpg, .mpeg`
`video/quicktime`	Apple QuickTime video	`.mov`
`video/vnd.vivo`	VIVO movie	`.vivo`

> **For a full list of MIME types visit :**
> **ftp://ftp.isi.edu/in-notes/iana/assignments/media-types/**

FileName Property

The `FileName` property indicates the path of the file on the client's computer. This property matches the text that appears in the file input box on the web page. Don't be confused by this property and think that the path maps to a location on the server. Use the save as method to save a file to a specific location on the server.

```
String = HttpPostedFile.FileName
```

InputStream Property

The `InputStream` property indicates the stream object that the file is on, allowing access to the file as a stream. This object provides an alternative to the simpler `SaveAs` method in that we can act directly on the stream of data provided allowing for more detailed checking of content or specialized processing.

```
Stream = HttpPostedFile.InputStream
```

Below is an example of reading from the input stream and writing that information out to another stream. The `FileStream` object could be replaced with almost any stream to write the data to.

C#

```
System.IO.FileStream OutputFile = new System.IO.FileStream("file" + i.ToString() +
        ".tmp",System.IO.FileMode.OpenOrCreate, System.IO.FileAccess.Write);

//create a buffer for the data
byte[] buffer = new Byte[64];

while(Request.Files[i].InputStream.Read(buffer,0,buffer.Length)>0)
 {
  OutputFile.Write(buffer,0,buffer.Length);
 }
```

VB.NET

```
Dim i As Integer

'loop through the posted files
For i = 0 To Request.Files.Count

'create a file stream to write out the temporary file
Dim OutputFile As New System.IO.FileStream("file" + i.ToString() + ".tmp",_
          System.IO.FileMode.OpenOrCreate, System.IO.FileAccess.Write)

'create a buffer for working with the streams
Dim buffer(64) As Byte

'as long as we are getting data out, we'll write it to the other stream.
While (Request.Files.Item(i).InputStream.Read(buffer, 0, Buffer.Length) > 0)
 OutputFile.Write(buffer, 0, Buffer.Length)
End While
Next
```

Communication Streams: Responses and Requests

In web development, access to a great deal of information comes from the logical and physical request made by the client. Knowing about the client and being able to communicate effectively with the client are essential to building dynamic web sites. The HttpRequest and HttpResponse classes encapsulate the incoming request from the client and the outgoing stream of data being sent back. They afford the developer a powerful framework.

The HttpRequest class

The HttpRequest class represents the incoming request from a client. For example, when a user enters a URL in their browser the browser makes a request to the server identified in the URL for a given resource. This request includes a wide variety of information pertaining to the client and the request. Included in this might be form data, that a user has filled out, or persisted information from cookies.

HttpRequest Methods

❑ BinaryRead

❑ Equals (inherited from Object)

❑ GetHashCode (inherited from Object)

❑ GetType (inherited from Object)

❑ MapImageCoordinates

❑ MapPath

❑ SaveAs

❑ ToString (inherited from Object)

BinaryRead Method

The BinaryRead method reads a specified number of bytes from the request stream into an array. The number of bytes to read will most often be the size of the request in order to get the entire content sent, but can vary depending on the problem you are trying to solve .

45

```
Byte[] Buffer = HttpRequest.BinaryRead(count)
```

Parameter	Type	Description
count	Int	The number of bytes to read. If this value is zero, or greater than the number of bytes available, an `ArgumentException` will be thrown.

When working with posted data on the request object, the bulk of development rests with reading simple text data from the posted information. However, there are cases where the information posted is not plain text. This is where the `BinaryRead` method is useful. This method allows for the reading of binary information, such as an image or file, and working with the bytes returned. In other situations, there may be a need to capture the request in a binary format and transmit it to some other process.

> The `BinaryRead` method is provided for backward compatibility. For new applications use the `InputStream` property of the `HttpRequest` class to read the raw data from the request.

MapImageCoordinates Method

The `MapImageCoordinates` method returns an array of integers representing the map coordinates of a form image input that is submitted to the server. This method works with both HTML input elements, with its type set to `image`, and with the `ImageButton` server control.

```
Int[]Coordinates = HttpRequest.MapImageCoordinates(imageFieldName)
```

Parameter	Type	Description
imageFieldName	String	The field name of the image map as it is defined in the form

MapImageCoordinates Example

In this example we see how to get the x and y coordinates of an image input control that has been clicked.

MapCoords.aspx

```
<%@ Page language="c#" AutoEventWireup="false"
Inherits="AspProgRefChap2.MapCoords" Src = "MapCoords.aspx.cs" %><!DOCTYPE HTML
PUBLIC "-//W3C//DTD HTML 4.0 Transitional//EN" >
<html>
<head>
</head>
<body ms_positioning="FlowLayout">
  <form id="MapCoords" method="post" runat="server">
    <input id="mapimage" type="image" src="" runat="server" width="100"
                                                    height="100">
  </form>
</body>
</html>
```

MapCoords.aspx.cs

```csharp
using System;
using System.Collections;
using System.ComponentModel;
using System.Data;
using System.Drawing;
using System.Web;
using System.Web.SessionState;
using System.Web.UI;
using System.Web.UI.WebControls;
using System.Web.UI.HtmlControls;

    public class MapCoords : System.Web.UI.Page
    {
        //variable for our image input button
        protected System.Web.UI.HtmlControls.HtmlInputImage mapimage;

        public MapCoords()
        {
            Page.Init += new System.EventHandler(Page_Init);
        }

        private void Page_Load(object sender, System.EventArgs e)
        {
            // get the coordinates and write them out to the response
            //if the page has been posted back
            if(IsPostBack)
            {
                int[] Coordinates;
                Coordinates=Request.MapImageCoordinates("mapimage");
                Response.Write("X: " + Coordinates[0] + "<br>Y: " + Coordinates[1]+
                                                            "<br>");
            }
        }

        private void Page_Init(object sender, EventArgs e)
        {
            InitializeComponent();
        }

        private void InitializeComponent()
        {
            this.Load += new System.EventHandler(this.Page_Load);
        }
    }
```

MapCoords.aspx.vb

```vbnet
Public Class MapCoords
  Inherits System.Web.UI.Page
  Protected WithEvents mapimage As System.Web.UI.HtmlControls.HtmlInputImage
    <System.Diagnostics.DebuggerStepThrough()> Private Sub InitializeComponent()
  End Sub

  Private Sub Page_Init(ByVal sender As System.Object,
                                    ByVal e As System.EventArgs) & _
                                                        Handles
MyBase.Init
    InitializeComponent()
  End Sub
```

```
      Private Sub Page_Load(ByVal sender As System.Object,
                                    ByVal e As System.EventArgs)& _
                                                            Handles
     MyBase.Load

        'get the coordinates and write them out to the response
        'if the page has been posted back
        If (IsPostBack) Then
          Dim Coordinates() As Integer
          Coordinates = Request.MapImageCoordinates("mapimage")
          Response.Write("X: " & Coordinates(0) & "<br>Y: " & Coordinates(1) & "<br>")
        End If
      End Sub

    End Class
```

In the web form we add an <input> element with its type set to image. In the code behind, we first check to make sure the page is being posted back to by using the IsPostBack property, and then retrieve the coordinates of the image input. In this example we simply output the coordinates, but we could also determine the location of the click and respond differently depending on where the click occurred.

MapPath Method

The MapPath method maps a given virtual path to the physical path. There are two overloaded forms of this method.

```
String Path = HttpRequest.MapPath(filename)
```

Parameter	Type	Description
filename	String	The name of the file to map

```
String Path = HttpRequest.MapPath(filename, baseVirtualDir, allowCrossAppMapping)
```

Parameter	Type	Description
filename	String	The name of the file to map
baseVirtualDir	String	The base virtual directory from which the file should be mapped
allowCrossAppMapping	Boolean	Determines if the base virtual directory can be outside the current application

In this example we map the path to the directory of another application on the server in order to reference an XML file stored there and output the text of one of the nodes. Notice that in C# we must use the "\" character as an escape character in our strings.

C#

```
//map the path to the file in the other application
string Path;
Path = Request.MapPath("categories.xml", "\\HelperApp", true);
```

```
//open the xml document from the path and output the first category node
XmlDocument Categories = new XmlDocument();
Categories.Load(path);
Response.Write(Categories.SelectNodes("//category").Item(0).InnerText);

//set our variable to null so it can be garbage collected
Categories = null;
```

VB.NET

```
'map the path to the file in the other application
Dim Path As String
Path = Request.MapPath("categories.xml", "\HelperApp", True)

'open the xml document from the path and output the first category node
Dim Categories As New XmlDocument()
Categories.Load(path)
Response.Write(Categories.SelectNodes("//category").Item(0).InnerText)

'set our variable to nothing so it can be garbage collected
Categories = Nothing
```

SaveAs Method

The `SaveAs` method saves the given `HttpRequest` to a text file.

```
HttpRequest.SaveAs(filename, includeHeaders)
```

Parameter	Type	Description
filename	String	The path to the file location for saving this request
includeHeaders	Boolean	Indicates whether the headers from the request should also be saved out to the file

The `SaveAs` method allows the developer to save the client request out to a file. This can be helpful when working with requests that contain data such as XML documents or other messaging systems where the client request as a whole might be saved to a directory to be picked up by another application or if there is a need to keep a history of the requests made to the server, for security or analysis purposes.

HttpRequest Properties

- ❏ AcceptTypes
- ❏ ApplicationPath
- ❏ Browser
- ❏ ClientCertificate
- ❏ ContentEncoding
- ❏ ContentLength
- ❏ ContentType

- ❑   Cookies
- ❑   FilePath
- ❑   Files
- ❑   Filter
- ❑   Form
- ❑   Headers
- ❑   HttpMethod
- ❑   InputStream
- ❑   IsAuthenticated
- ❑   IsSecureConnection
- ❑   Params
- ❑   Path
- ❑   PathInfo
- ❑   PhysicalApplicationPath
- ❑   PhysicalPath
- ❑   QueryString
- ❑   RawUrl
- ❑   RequestType
- ❑   ServerVariables
- ❑   TotalBytes
- ❑   Url
- ❑   UrlReferrer
- ❑   UserAgent
- ❑   UserHostAddress
- ❑   UserHostName
- ❑   UserLanguages

AcceptTypes Property (read-only)

The AcceptTypes property indicates the MIME types of files the requesting client will accept in return. An array of string values each representing a MIME type accepted by the browser is returned.

```
string[] acceptedTypes = HttpRequest.AcceptTypes
```

Most client browsers allow a user to indicate handlers for certain document types. More and more document types are handled by the browser or a helper application. Using this property, the developer can determine if a client supports a specific type. For example, you could have a function on your site that outputs a Microsoft Word file. It might be useful to check that the client will accept the application/msword type. If not, then an alternative format, such as PDF, could be used. See the HttpResponse.ContentType property for a list of popular MIME types.

ApplicationPath Property (read-only)

The `ApplicationPath` property indicates the ASP.Net application's virtual path on the server. This property is useful when you need to determine the root path of the web application in order to determine the location of other files.

```
string appPath = HttpRequest.ApplicationPath
```

For example, we might want to write code to be included in many different web pages. This code could load an XML file that is in a subdirectory of the application. The following code would allow us to find this file, regardless of where in the application hierarchy the code executes:

C#

```
string XmlSettings = Request.ApplicationPath + "/XML/settings.xml";
```

VB.Net

```
dim XmlSettings as String
XmlSettings = Request.ApplicationPath & "/XML/settings.xml"
```

Browser Property

The `Browser` property returns an `HttpBrowserCapabilities` object, which allows access to the abilities and characteristics of the requesting browser. See the `HttpBrowserCapabilities` class earlier in this chapter for more details.

```
HttpBrowserCapabilities BrowseCap= HttpRequest.Browser
```

C#

```
if(Request.Browser.Browser.ToString().Equals("IE"))
{
   //perform an action for the IE browser
}
else
{
   //use code that is supported by all browsers
}
```

VB.NET

```
If Request.Browser.Browser.ToString().Equals("IE")
Then
   'perform an action for the IE browser
else
   'perform an action supported by all browsers
end if
```

ClientCertificate Property (read-only)

The `ClientCertificate` property indicates the certificate sent from the client for secure communications. This object can be used to get access to the information contained in that certificate.

```
HttpClientCertificate ClientCert = HttpRequest.ClientCertificate
```

The client certificate is used in secure communications with the server using SSL technology. Being able to access this certificate allows the developer to ensure the certificate is appropriate and sufficient for the site. In the following example, we check to make sure the client certificate is at least 128 bit encryption. If not, we output a simple message that indicates to the user that they needed a certificate with greater encryption and end the processing of the page immediately using the `End` method of the `HttpResponse` class. The `KeySize` of a certificate indicates the level of encryption. The greater the key size, the greater the encryption.

C#

```
if (Request.ClientCertificate.KeySize<=128)
{
  Response.Write("Your certificate needs to be greater than 128 bit");
  Response.End();
}
```

VB.NET

```
If Request.ClientCertificate.KeySize<=128 then
  Response.Write("Your certificate needs to be greater than 128 bit")
  Response.End()
End if
```

ContentEncoding Property (read-only)

The `ContentEncoding` property indicates the character encoding of the client. This value indicates whether the request is ASCII text, UTF8, etc. For more information on the different encoding values and utility classes to convert from one encoding to another, examine the `Encoding` class in the `System.Text` namespace.

```
Encoding ContentEncode= HttpRequest.ContentEncoding
```

ContentLength Property (read-only)

The `ContentLength` property indicates the length, in bytes, of the request. This information can be used when handling the content using the `BinaryRead` method or the `InputStream` property to read the data from the request.

```
int Length = HttpRequest.ContentLength
```

ContentType Property (read-only)

The `ContentType` property indicates the MIME type of the incoming request such as `text/HTML`.

```
string Type = HttpRequest.ContentType
```

The `ContentType` property can be used to discriminate between the types of files being posted to the server. For example, when the content type is "`multipart/form-data`" files may be included in the posted information.

Cookies Property (read-only)

The `Cookies` property returns all of the cookies sent to the server by the client browser. The `Cookies` collection on the request allows for accessing those cookies being sent to the server. Use the `Cookies` collection of the `HttpResponse` object to send new cookies out to the client, or update existing cookies there. This property returns an `HttpCookieCollection` object, which is referenced later in the chapter.

```
HttpCookieCollection Cookies = HttpRequest.Cookies
```

C#

```
if(Request.Cookies ["user_name"]==null)
{
  Response.Cookies["user_name"] = Request.Form["user_name"];
}
```

VB.NET

```
If Request.Cookies.Item("user_name") Is nothing then
  Response.Cookies.Item("user_name") = Request.Form.Item("user_name")
End if
```

FilePath Property (read-only)

The `FilePath` property indicates the virtual path to the file on the server. In other words, the URL of the file minus any extra path information or server name.

```
String Path = HttpRequest.FilePath
```

For example, given the URL http://www.wrox.com/aspprogref/chapters.aspx the `FilePath` property would return `/aspprogref/chapters.aspx`.

Files Property (read-only)

The `Files` property indicates a collection of files posted to the web server from a client form submission.

```
HttpFilesCollection Files = HttpRequest.Files
```

Uploading files to a web server has come to be an important part of many custom web solutions and content management packages. In the past, the easiest way to manage all of these files was to use a third-party component that did the work of splitting out the files from the uploaded form data. See the `HttpFileCollection` class earlier in this chapter for more information and examples of working with posted files.

> The `Files` collection is only populated when the Content-Type of the form is `"multipart/form-data."`

Filter Property

The `Filter` property indicates a stream object to use as a filter on the incoming request object. The incoming request will be passed through this stream as it is processed, allowing the filtering stream class to read and manipulate the incoming data. This could be used to build a species of incoming proxy by which the data is thoroughly examined before being dealt with in the page.

```
Stream Filter= HttpRequest.Filter
HttpRequest.Filter = Filter
```

Form Property (read-only)

The Form property indicates the contents of an HTML form posted to the server. In order for form data to be accessible, the MIME type of the incoming request must be "application/x-www-form-urlencoded" or "multipart/form-data". The values in the form are returned as a collection, specifically a NameValueCollection class instance.

```
NameValueCollection FormValues = HttpRequest.Form
```

HTML forms are one of the primary ways to allow a user to send information to a web site. The Form property allows the developer to get access to the information that was posted and handle it appropriately, perhaps saving it to a database, or performing actions based on the input.

Form values are accessed from this collection using the names given them in the HTML form at design time, including radio buttons and checkboxes. The following example gives a simple look at accessing items in the collection. For more information on the elements in a form and their properties, see Chapters 4 to 6.

FormProcessing.aspx

```
<%@ Page Language="vb" AutoEventWireup="false" Codebehind="FormProcessing.aspx.vb"
Inherits="AspProgRefChap2VB.FormProcessing"%>
<!DOCTYPE HTML PUBLIC "-//W3C//DTD HTML 4.0 Transitional//EN">
<html>
<head>
  <title>Form Processing Example</title>
</head>
<body>
    <form id="FormProcessing" method="post" action="FormProcessing.aspx">
      <h3>
        Please login:
      </h3>
      Login: <input type="text" size="100" id="login" name="login">
      <br>
      Password: <input type="password" size="75" id="pwd" name="pwd">
      <br>
      <input type="submit" value="Login">
      <br>
      <br>
    </form>
</body>
</html>
```

We have created a simple form with a two textboxes and a submit button. The first box is for plain text and the second for passwords, meaning the actual values typed in will be masked. The following C# and VB.NET code samples show the Page_Load method from the code behind file and how we access the values.

FormProcessing.aspx.cs (Page_Load Method)

```
using System;
using System.Collections;
using System.ComponentModel;
using System.Data;
using System.Drawing;
using System.IO;
using System.Web;
using System.Web.SessionState;
```

```
using System.Web.UI;
using System.Web.UI.WebControls;
using System.Web.UI.HtmlControls;

public class FormProcessing : System.Web.UI.Page
{
  public FormProcessing()
  {
    Page.Init += new System.EventHandler(Page_Init);
  }

  private void Page_Load(object sender, System.EventArgs e)
  {
    // if the form has been posted, then we will act on the
    //values passed in.
    if(Request.Form["login"]!=null)
    {
      //if the password has a value in it then say hi
      if(Request.Form["pwd"]!=null && Request.Form["pwd"] != String.Empty)
      {
        Response.Write("Hello " + Request.Form["login"].ToString());
      }
      //otherwise, ask for the password
      else
      {
        Response.Write("<font color='red'>You did not enter your password
</font>");
      }
    }
  }

  private void Page_Init(object sender, EventArgs e)
  {
    InitializeComponent();
  }

  private void InitializeComponent()
  {
    this.Load += new System.EventHandler(this.Page_Load);
  }
}
```

FormProcessing.aspx.vb (Page_Load Method)

```
Imports System.IO

Public Class FormProcessing
  Inherits System.Web.UI.Page

  Private Sub Page_Load(ByVal sender As System.Object,
                                  ByVal e As System.EventArgs) _ &
                                                        Handles
MyBase.Load
    ' if the form has been posted, then we will act on the
    'values passed in.
    If Not Request.Form.Item("login") Is Nothing Then
      'if the password has a value in it then say hi
      If ((Not Request.Form.Item("pwd") Is Nothing) And
                                (Request.Form.Item("pwd") _ &
                                                  <> String.Empty))
Then
```

```
        Response.Write("Hello " + Request.Form.Item("login").ToString())

        'otherwise, ask for the password
    Else
        Response.Write("<font color='red'>You did not enter a password." & _
                                   " Please try again.</font")
    End If
  End If
 End Sub
End Class
```

Headers Property (read-only)

The `Headers` property indicates the HTML headers sent in the request.

```
NameValueCollection Headers = HttpRequest.Headers
```

When a client makes a request to a server for a resource, a great deal of the information sent to the server is **meta data**: data that describes the request and the client. The headers of a request contain information regarding the client browser, cookies, accepted types, language, and encoding. Much of this information is encapsulated in other properties of the request that may be easier to use. However, the `Headers` property allows the developer to access specialized information from the headers, and, in the `HttpResponse` object, add their own headers. For example, if we wished to view the User-Agent header, we could use the following code.

C#
```
string UserAgent = Request.Headers["User-Agent"];
```

VB.NET
```
dim UserAgent as String = Request.Headers.Item("User-Agent")
```

HttpMethod Property (read-only)

The `HttpMethod` property indicates the method of the HTTP request being made (GET, POST,or HEAD).

```
String Method = HttpRequest.HttpMethod
```

When requesting a resource from a site, there are three different methods that can be used. When typing in a URL to your browser and getting a page back, a GET request is made. When submitting a form, the POST method can be specified, which will include the information in the request itself rather than in the URL. The HEAD request specifies that only the headers that would be sent with a GET request should be returned. It indicates which method was used and can provide insight into where to look for specific data.

InputStream Property (read-only)

The `InputStream` property indicates a stream containing the incoming HTTP request body. This read-only stream object provides access to the body of the incoming request. For example, when we post a form to the server, the values in our form show up in the body of the HTTP request and can, therefore, be seen using this stream.

```
Stream Input = HttpRequest.InputStream
```

As an example, we'll extend the previous form example, and add code to write the contents of the form to a file:

FormProcessing.aspx.cs

```csharp
using System;
using System.Collections;
using System.ComponentModel;
using System.Data;
using System.Drawing;
using System.IO;
using System.Web;
using System.Web.SessionState;
using System.Web.UI;
using System.Web.UI.WebControls;
using System.Web.UI.HtmlControls;

public class FormProcessing : System.Web.UI.Page
{
  public FormProcessing()
  {
    Page.Init += new System.EventHandler(Page_Init);
  }

  private void Page_Load(object sender, System.EventArgs e)
  {
    // if the form has been posted, then we will act on the
    //values passed in.
    if(Request.Form["login"]!=null)
      {
        //if the password has a value in it then say hi
        if(Request.Form["pwd"]!=null && Request.Form["pwd"] != String.Empty)
        {
          Response.Write("Hello " + Request.Form["login"].ToString());
        }
          //otherwise, ask for the password
        else
        {
          Response.Write("<font color='red'>You did not enter your password
</font>");
        }
      }

    //code to show how the InputStream property of the request works

    //open a file
    FileStream Output = new FileStream("c:\\Request.txt",FileMode.OpenOrCreate);

    //create a buffer for the information we are going to read
    Byte[] Buffer = new Byte[Request.InputStream.Length];
    Buffer.Initialize();

    //read the information from the request's input stream
    Request.InputStream.Read(Buffer,0,(int)Request.InputStream.Length);

    //write the information to the file
    Output.Write(Buffer,0,(int)Request.InputStream.Length);
```

```
    //close our variable
    Output.Close();
    Output=null;
  }

  private void Page_Init(object sender, EventArgs e)
  {
   InitializeComponent();
  }


  private void InitializeComponent()
  {
    this.Load += new System.EventHandler(this.Page_Load);
  }
}
```

FormProcessing.aspx.vb

```
Imports System.IO

Public Class FormProcessing
  Inherits System.Web.UI.Page

  Private Sub Page_Load(ByVal sender As System.Object, ByVal e As
System.EventArgs) _
                                                      Handles
MyBase.Load
      ' if the form has been posted, then we will act on the
      'values passed in.
    If Not Request.Form.Item("login") Is Nothing Then
       'if the password has a value in it then say hi
      If ((Not Request.Form.Item("pwd") Is Nothing) And (Request.Form.Item("pwd")_
                                              <> String.Empty))
Then
        Response.Write("Hello " + Request.Form.Item("login").ToString())

         'otherwise, ask for the password
      Else
        Response.Write("<font color='red'>You did not enter a password." & _
                                        " Please try again.</font")
      End If
    End If

      'open a file
      Dim Output As New FileStream("c:\Request.txt", FileMode.OpenOrCreate)

      'create a buffer for the information we are going to read
      Dim Buffer(Request.InputStream.Length) As Byte
      Buffer.Initialize()

      'read the information from the request's input stream
      Request.InputStream.Read(Buffer, 0, CInt(Request.InputStream.Length))

      'write the information to the file
      Output.Write(Buffer, 0, CInt(Request.InputStream.Length))

      'close our variable
      Output.Close()
      Output = Nothing
  End Sub
End Class
```

After opening a `FileStream` object for output, we read the request body into an array of bytes and then write that array out to the file.

IsAuthenticated Property (read-only)

The `IsAuthenticated` property indicates whether the user has been authenticated to the site. There are several methods of authentication available to a developer when building a site in ASP.NET including Windows, Forms-based, and Passport. This property will indicate whether the client making the request has been authenticated by one of these mechanisms. In order for this property to return any thing except `false`, the Authentication element in the `web.config` file must be set to a value other than "none". Similarly, you may have to change the values in the authorization element to allow and deny users.

```
Boolean Authenticated = HttpRequest.IsAuthenticated
```

The example below shows a `web.config` file setup for forms-based authentication and denying initial access to anonymous users. The "?" in the deny element is a wildcard for anonymous. See Example 7 in Chapter 16 for a detailed example of forms-based authentication.

web.config

```xml
<?xml version="1.0" encoding="utf-8" ?>
<configuration>
  <system.web>
  <compilation
      defaultlanguage="c#"
      debug="true"
  />
  <compilation debug="true" />

  <customErrors mode="Off" />
  <!-- AUTHENTICATION
    This section sets the authentication policies of the application. Possible modes
    are "Windows", "Cookie", "Passport" and "None"  -->
  <authentication mode="Forms">
  <forms loginUrl="Home.aspx" name=".northwind_auth" protection="None" />
  </authentication>
  <authorization>
    <deny users="?" />
  </authorization>
  <trace enabled="false" requestLimit="10" pageOutput="false"
      traceMode="SortByTime"
  />
  <sessionState mode="InProc" stateConnectionString="tcpip=127.0.0.1:42424"
      sqlConnectionString="data source=127.0.0.1;user id=sa;password="
      cookieless="false" timeout="20"
  />

  <httpHandlers>
    <add verb="*" path="*.vb" type="System.Web.HttpNotFoundHandler,System.Web"
    />
    <add verb="*" path="*.cs" type="System.Web.HttpNotFoundHandler,System.Web"
    />
    <add verb="*" path="*.vbproj"
type="System.Web.HttpNotFoundHandler,System.Web"
    />
    <add verb="*" path="*.csproj"
type="System.Web.HttpNotFoundHandler,System.Web"
    />
    <add verb="*" path="*.webinfo"
```

```
        type="System.Web.HttpNotFoundHandler,System.Web"
        />
    </httpHandlers>

    <globalization requestEncoding="utf-8" responseEncoding="utf-8" />
  </system.web>
</configuration>
```

IsSecureConnection Property (read-only)

```
Boolean = HttpRequest.IsSecureConnection
```

The IsSecureConnection property indicates whether the user's connection is over a secure HTTPS connection.

When creating secure sites that contain sensitive information or that will be requesting sensitive information from users, a form of data encryption is often employed to protect this information. Today, Secure Sockets Layer (SSL) is the most common security framework used to protect this data.

SSL provides a public/private key framework for ensuring that a client or server is who it says it is and assures the user that they are sending their information only where they want. A hacker cannot get access to the information because they do not have access to the public or private keys existing on the communicating servers.

This security comes at a cost to performance. Encrypting and decrypting data takes time, and the size of the data that needs to be transmitted is larger as well. For this reason, it is important to use SSL only where necessary.

Use this property to determine if the client is requesting pages using SSL encryption. It might be helpful to modify a site to use low resolution images, or different formatting, knowing that the requests to the server will take longer given the increased network traffic related to encrypting and decrypting the data.

Params Property (read-only)

The Params property is a collection combining the Form, QueryString, Cookies, and Server variable values into one collection.

```
NameValueCollection Params= HttpRequest.Params
```

This property allows for accessing a named parameter that might exist in a variety of locations. At times, it might be expected that a parameter will be sent to the page, but it may come in different forms. This property makes it easier to access these values without creating long conditional statements.

Path Property (read-only)

The Path property indicates the path of the current request, including any information trailing the file name. This property differs from the FilePath in that the FilePath property does not include the information following the file itself.

```
String = HttpRequest.Path
```

PathInfo Property (read-only)

The PathInfo property indicates the information in a URL request that follows the file location.

```
String = HttpRequest.PathInfo
```

> The **FilePath**, **Path**, and **PathInfo** properties are all closely related and can be a bit confusing. A sample to show the difference should clarify any confusion. Given the URL: **http://www.wrox.com/aspprogref.aspx/TOC**
>
> The following values would be returned for the three properties:
>
> **FilePath:**   **http://www.wrox.com/aspprogref.aspx**
>
> **Path:**   **http://www.wrox.com/aspprogref.aspx/TOC**
>
> **PathInfo:**   **TOC**

PhysicalApplicationPath Property (read-only)

The `PhysicalApplicationPath` property indicates the disk file path to the application directory.

```
string Path = HttpRequest.PhysicalApplicationPath
```

An example return value for this property would be `"c:\inetpub\wwwroot\asprogrefexamples\"`.

PhysicalPath Property (read-only)

The `PhysicalPath` property indicates the physical disk path to the file requested in the URL. This differs from the above property in that it reflects the path of the actual file requested.

```
String = HttpRequest.PhysicalPath
```

QueryString Property (read-only)

The `QueryString` property indicates a collection of the parameters sent to the server via the URL.

```
NameValueCollection Query = HttpRequest.QueryString
```

For example, given the URL: http://www.wrox.com/aspprogref.aspx?chap=2&section=3:

`HttpRequest.QueryString.Item("chap")` will return the value `"2"`.
`HttpRequest.QueryString.Item("section")` will return the value `"3"`.

RawUrl Property (read-only)

The `RawUrl` property indicates the path to the resource excluding the server and domain information, but including the query string parameters, if present.

```
string URL = HttpRequest.RawUrl
```

For example, the URL http://www.wrox.com/aspprogref/examples/chap2.zip would result in the following return value: `/aspprogref/examples/chap2.zip`

RequestType Property

The `RequestType` property indicates the type of request made by the client (GET or POST).

```
String = HttpRequest.RequestType
```

ServerVariables Property (read-only)

The `ServerVariables` property gets a collection of the properties available from the server.

```
NameValueCollection ServerVars = HttpRequest.ServerVariables
```

Below is a table of the possible server variables in this collection.

Variable	Meaning
ALL_HTTP	All of the HTTP headers with their names in all caps and prefixed with HTTP_
ALL_RAW	All of the HTTP headers in the format they were sent to the server
APPL_MD_PATH	The metabase path of the web application
APPL_PHYSICAL_PATH	The physical path of the web application
AUTH_PASSWORD	The password of the user if using Basic authentication.
AUTH_TYPE	The authentication type used to authenticate the user. Possible values include NTLM and basic
AUTH_USER	The user name of the authorized user
CERT_COOKIE	A cookie providing the ID of the certificate if one is present on the client.
CERT_ISSUER	The name of the company that issued the client certificate; this matches the issuer field on the certificate
CERT_KEYSIZE	The size, in bits, of the encryption key used to encrypt data
CERT_SECRETKEYSIZE	The size, in bits, of the secret or private key on the server
CERT_SERIALNUMBER	The serial number of the client certificate
CERT_SERVER_ISSUER	The issuer field in the server certificate
CERT_SERVER_SUBJECT	The subject field of the server certificate
CERT_SUBJECT	The subject field of the client certificate
CONTENT_LENGTH	The length, in bytes, of the incoming request
CONTENT_TYPE	The MIME type of the request, such as www-url-encoded for a form being posted to the server
GATEWAY_INTERFACE	The Common Gateway Interface (CGI) supported on the server
HTTP_ACCEPT	The MIME types the client can accept

Variable	Meaning
HTTP_ACCEPT_ENCODING	The compression encoding types supported by the client
HTTP_ACCEPT_LANGUAGE	The languages accepted by the client
HTTP_CONNECTION	Indicates whether the connection allows keep-alive functionality
HTTP_COOKIE	The cookies sent with a request
HTTP_HOST	The host name of the server
HTTP_USER_AGENT	Information about the browser used to connect to the server including version and type.
HTTPS	Indicates whether HTTPS was used for the request. Returns "On" if the request came through SSL, or "Off" if not.
HTTPS_KEYSIZE	The number of bits in the encryption used to make the SSL connection
HTTPS_SECRETKEYSIZE	The size, in bits, of the private key on the server
HTTPS_SERVER_ISSUER	The name of the issuing authority for the server certificate as found in the Issuer field of the certificate.
HTTPS_SERVER_SUBJECT	The subject of the server certificate as found in the subject field of the certificate
INSTANCE_ID	The metabase ID of the web server instance
INSTANCE_META_PATH	The metabase path of the web server instance
LOCAL_ADDR	The IP address of the server which is handling the request
LOGON_USER	The NT user name of the user if known
PATH_INFO	The virtual path to the requested resource
PATH_TRANSLATED	The physical path to the requested resource
QUERY_STRING	A string containing any information after the name of the resource requested.
REMOTE_ADDR	The IP address of the client making the request
REMOTE_HOST	The host name of the client making the request, if available
REMOTE_USER	The original NT user name sent by the client before it is modified by any authentication filters on the server
REQUEST_METHOD	The type of the HTTP request made. Possible values are "GET", "POST", and "HEAD"

Table continued on following page

63

Variable	Meaning
SCRIPT_NAME	The virtual path to the script currently executing
SERVER_NAME	The host name of the server
SERVER_PORT	The server port to which the request was made
SERVER_PORT_SECURE	If the port is set to use SSL, this value is 1, otherwise it is 0
SERVER_PROTOCOL	The HTTP protocol and version in use on the server.
SERVER_SOFTWARE	The name and version of the web server software running on the server
URL	The virtual path to the file requested

TotalBytes Property (read-only)

The TotalBytes property indicates the total number of bytes posted to the server in the client's request.

```
Int Count = HttpRequest.TotalBytes
```

Url Property (read-only)

The Url property indicates the Universal Resource Identifier (URI) and its associated information regarding the resource requested. For a client using a web browser, this would be the same information that appears in their browser location.

```
Uri RequestedUrl = HttpRequest.Url
```

UrlReferrer Property (read-only)

The UrlReferrer property indicates the URI of the previously accessed page. The UrlReferrer property can be useful for tracking information about how users arrive at your site or the path that users take when in your site. However, it is not a good idea to use this information for security purposes or any other purpose where you need to be guaranteed that a user is coming from a certain page. This property is only populated when the user is navigating to the page from a link in another web page. Therefore, if the client enters the address directly in their browser, or uses a bookmark, this object will be null.

```
Uri Referrer = HttpRequest.UrlReferrer
```

UserAgent Property (read-only)

The UserAgent property indicates the browser being used by the client as the raw string values posted by the client. This property is the basis for much of the information contained in the HttpBrowserCapabilities object retrieved via the Browser property.

```
string Agent = HttpRequest.UserAgent
```

An example of a string for IE 6.0 might look like this:

```
Mozilla/4.0 (compatible; MSIE 6.0b; Windows NT 5.0; .NET CLR 1.0.2914)
```

UserHostAddress Property (read-only)

The `UserHostAddress` property indicates the network address of the requesting client's machine and is most likely an IP address. This can be useful if you want to determine if someone's connecting from your local network or not. It also has potential for allowing customization based on whether you know of the user's network or not. For example, a company may want to have different content or navigation on their home page for employees browsing to the site from the office, versus the content that users outside the company get.

```
String Address = HttpRequest.UserHostAddress
```

UserHostName Property (read-only)

The `UserHostName` property indicates the host name of the requesting client's machine.

```
string Host = HttpRequest.UserHostName
```

UserLanguages Property (read-only)

The `UserLanguages` property indicates the languages preferred by the user's browser. This property returns an array of languages supported by the client. In Internet Explorer the user can set these values via the **Internet Options** control panel. You can use this array of values to search for a preferred language to present your information in.

```
string[] languages = HttpRequest.UserLanguages
```

The HttpResponse class

The `HttpResponse` class encompasses all of the content getting written out to the client, including headers, cookies, and other non-UI items. Writing to this stream is equivalent to sending data to the client. The `HttpResponse` object is accessible via the intrinsic `Response` object allowing syntax like the following:

```
Response.ContentType="text/XML"
```

HttpResponse Methods

- ❏ AddFileDependencies
- ❏ AddFileDependency
- ❏ AddHeader
- ❏ AppendHeader
- ❏ AppendToLog
- ❏ ApplyAppPathModifier
- ❏ BinaryWrite
- ❏ Clear
- ❏ ClearContent
- ❏ ClearHeaders

- ❏ Close
- ❏ End
- ❏ Equals (inherited from Object)
- ❏ Flush
- ❏ GetHashCode (inherited from Object)
- ❏ GetType (inherited from Object)
- ❏ Pics
- ❏ Redirect
- ❏ ToString (inherited from Object)
- ❏ Write
- ❏ WriteFile

AddFileDependencies Method

The AddFileDependencies method allows addition of multiple files to the list of files the current response is dependent on. These file dependencies are related to the caching mechanisms in ASP.NET. Setting file dependencies indicates that a cached response is dependent on the files and the cache should be refreshed when the file(s) change. See Chapter 7 for more information on caching in ASP.NET.

```
HttpResponse.AddFileDependencies(fileNames)
```

Parameter	Type	Description
fileNames	ArrayList	An array list filled with string values representing the file path of the files to add

AddFileDependency Method

The AddFileDependency method allows addition of a single file as a dependency for the given response object. This is a quicker method to add a single file dependency than using an array of file names as above. Caching is an important part of many high volume sites and having a response that can be cached based on when a file changes is a very powerful mechanism for achieving high throughput on a web site.

```
HttpResponse.AddFileDependency(fileName)
```

Parameter	Type	Description
fileName	String	The path to the file on which this response should be dependent

AddHeader Method

The AddHeader method allows addition of an HTTP header to the outgoing response. See the HttpRequest class's Headers property for more information on common headers.

```
HttpResponse.AddHeader(name, value)
```

Parameter	Type	Description
name	String	The name of the header to add
value	String	The value to be set for the header named in the first parameter

> This method is only provided for backward compatibility with ASP. In ASP.NET the **AppendHeader** method should be used instead.

AppendHeader Method

The AppendHeader method allows addition of a header to the outgoing response stream.

```
HttpResponse.AppendHeader(name, value)
```

For example, maybe we have a server farm and want to indicate to the calling program the actual server that serviced the request. We could append a custom header indicating this value:

```
Response.AppendHeader("SERVICING_SERVER",Request.ServerVariables.Item("LOCAL_ADDR"
));
```

Parameter	Type	Description
name	String	The name of the header to add
value	String	The value to set for the header named in the first parameter

There are standard headers in HTTP communications with a browser, but this method allows for adding your own custom ones, in addition.

AppendToLog Method

The AppendToLog method allows appending information to the IIS web log entry for the request. In this way, specialized information can be included in the log based on the events of the page processing.

```
HttpResponse.AppendToLog(param)
```

Parameter	Type	Description
Param	String	The parameter to be added to the IIS web log entry for this response

Being able to extend the web log can be a powerful mechanism for performing business analysis on a web site. While the standard web logs can be useful for understanding basic traffic patterns, being able to add information to the log can allow you to understanding user's actions by giving more information about what they're doing on any given. The information in the logs can be imported into a database or other source to provide more powerful analysis.

ApplyAppPathModifier Method

The `ApplyAppPathModifier` method allows addition of a virtual path to the response and returns a string representation of the new virtual path. This method can be used if you need to create links to content in sub-directories but do not want your links to be dependent on a statically defined base path.

```
string Path = HttpResponse.ApplyAppPathModifier(virtualPath)
```

Parameter	Type	Description
virtualPath	String	The virtual path to be appended to the path of the outgoing response

BinaryWrite Method

The `BinaryWrite` method allows writing out binary data, such as an image or PDF file, to the response stream.

```
HttpResponse.BinaryWrite(buffer)
```

Parameter	Type	Description
buffer	Byte[]	The byte array containing the binary data to be written

Clear Method

The `Clear` method allows cleaning out the response stream buffer. This might be helpful if information has been written out and the page logic requires the information not to be displayed. For example, if the request begins processing, and the logic dictates that a redirect is necessary, then this method can be used to clear the headers that have already been written to the response before redirecting the client.

```
HttpResponse.Clear()
```

ClearContent Method

The `ClearContent` method allows clearing out just the content portion of the buffer stream but not the header information.

```
HttpResponse.ClearContent()
```

ClearHeaders Method

The `ClearHeaders` method allows clearing any custom or standard headers that have been set for the response. This can be useful if you are designing pages that do not contain any user interface. For example, if you have a page that serves as an interface to another application, you may want to remove the headers for your communication between the two applications.

```
HttpResponse.ClearHeaders()
```

Close Method

The `Close` method allows closing the response object such that no other data can be written to it. In actuality the physical socket connection between the client and the server is closed.

```
HttpResponse.Close()
```

End Method

The `End` method allows stopping execution of the page and flushing the output buffer.

```
HttpResponse.End()
```

In the middle of a page execution, a situation might arise that causes the page execution to end without completing the processing. Calling this method stops the execution at the point of call and returns the output to the client.

Flush Method

The `Flush` method allows for flushing all of the currently buffered content out to the client.

```
HttpResponse.Flush()
```

When buffering the response (see the `BufferContent` property) the `Flush` method can be used to send the buffered content to the browser in chunks. This provides for faster display on the client. The `Flush` method is called intrinsically when the `End` method is called.

Pics Method

The `Pics` method allows addition of a `Pics-label` HTTP header to the outgoing response object. This `Pics-label` identifies a content rating for the material contained in the page. Any value can be set using this method, as the .NET runtime does not set any requirements or do any checking on the value. The only restriction is that the value must be less than 255 characters. This `PICS` header is the indicator of content that is checked when you set content restrictions in Internet Explorer. For more information on PICS, visit the World Wide Web Consortium's web site at http://w3c.org/PICS/.

```
HttpResponse.Pics(value)
```

Parameter	Type	Description
value	String	The value to be set for the `Pics-label` header

Redirect Method

The `Redirect` method allows sending a redirection directive to the client browser. Many browsers support this type of response and will make a new request for the specified resource. This method requires another round trip between the client and server. As such, you should, instead, try to use either the `HttpServerUtil.Transfer` method or the `HttpServerUtil.Execute` method as neither of these requires the client to make a new request.

```
HttpResponse.Redirect(url)
```

or

```
HttpResponse.Redirect(url, endResponse)
```

Parameter	Type	Description
url	String	The URL to send the client to.
endResponse	Boolean	Indicates whether to end the current response, by implicitly calling the End method. The default value for this property, if only specifying the URL, is true.

The endResponse parameter is useful if you want code to continue executing even if the user has been redirected. For example, if you decide at some point in your code to redirect the user, but you have code that follows in your page that still needs to execute in order for the page to successfully process, then you can set this value to false to ensure that the rest of the code in your page executes.

Write Method

The Write method allows writing output to the outgoing stream. There are several overloaded versions of this method to allow for the output of a variety of data types.

```
HttpResponse.Write(char)
```

Parameter	Type	Description
char	Char	The character to write to the output stream

```
HttpResponse.Write(object)
```

Parameter	Type	Description
object	Object	Writes the object to the output stream by calling its ToString method intrinsically

```
HttpResponse.Write(value)
```

Parameter	Type	Description
value	String	The string value to write to the output stream

```
HttpResponse.Write(buffer, index, count)
```

Parameter	Type	Description
buffer	Char[]	The character array to write to the outgoing stream
index	Int	The array index to begin writing from
count	Int	The number of elements to write out to the stream

WriteFile method

The `WriteFile` method allows writing a file out to the output stream. This file could contain HTML and other text elements that would help make up the page content. This method has four overloaded versions:

```
HttpResponse.WriteFile(filename)
```

Parameter	Type	Description
filename	String	The name or path of the file to write out to the stream

```
HttpResponse.WriteFile(fileName, readIntoMemory)
```

Parameter	Type	Description
fileName	String	The name or path of the file to write out to the stream
readIntoMemory	Boolean	Indicates whether the file should be read into a memory block

```
HttpResponse.WriteFile(fileHandle, offset, size)
```

Parameter	Type	Description
fileHandle	IntPtr	The handle to the file that should be written out to the stream
offset	Long	The starting position in the file at which reading should begin
size	Long	The number of bytes to read and then write out to the stream

```
HttpResponse.WriteFile(filename, offset, size)
```

Parameter	Type	Description
fileName	String	The name of the file that should be written out to the stream
offset	Long	The starting position in the file at which reading should begin
size	Long	The number of bytes to read and then write out to the stream

HttpResponse Properties

❑ Buffer

❑ BufferOutput

❑ Cache

❑ CacheControl

❑ Charset

❑ ContentEncoding

❑ ContentType

❑ Cookies

❑ Expires

❑ ExpiresAbsolute

❑ Filter

❑ IsClientConnected

❑ Output

❑ OutputStream

❑ Status

❑ StatusCode

❑ StatusDescription

❑ SuppressContent

Buffer Property

The Buffer property indicates whether or not the output to the response stream will be buffered and therefore cleared before being sent to the client.

```
boolean Buffered = HttpResponse.Buffer
```

> This method has been deprecated and is only available for backward compatibility with ASP. Use the **BufferOutput** property instead in ASP.NET.

BufferOutput Property

The BufferOutput property indicates whether the response output should be buffered until the page has completed processing and then be sent to the client, instead of being sent as the page is processed.

```
boolean Buffered = HttpResponse.BufferOutput
```

The default value for this property is true to allow buffering. Buffering the content before it goes out to the client has several benefits. For example, because the output is buffered, if after processing a portion of the page it is determined that the response should be redirected, then there is no problem. However, if the response had not been buffered, the header would have already been sent to the client. In this case the "302" header cannot be written to the response and an error will be thrown.

Cache Property (read-only)

The Cache property indicates the caching policy in effect for the page by returning a Cache object. This property is the preferred mechanism for setting information about page caching expirations. Caching allows for maintenance of a copy of the page output in memory and servicing requests for the page from memory rather than processing the page again. The policy set through the Cache property indicates such parameters as when the in-memory cached data should expire and where the information can be cached (Server, Client, or Intermediate Server).

```
Cache Policy= HttpResponse.Cache
```

CacheControl Property

The CacheControl property indicates the value to set for the HTTP cache-control header. This value can be "public", "private", or "no-cache". public indicates that the page can be cached at any point between the client and the server, such as on a server designed specifically for caching. private indicates that the content can only be cached on the client. no-cache indicates that the page cannot be cached.

```
HttpResponse.CacheControl=string
```

> The **CacheControl** property has been deprecated. You should use the methods and properties of the **HttpCachePolicy** object exposed through the **Cache** property to set the cacheability of the page.

Charset Property

The Charset property indicates the character set to use for the output stream.

```
HttpResponse.Charset = string
```

The default character set is determined by the settings in the <globalization> section of the web.config file but can be overridden by setting this property. In this section you can set the default values for many of the properties related to globalization. The sample section from a web.config file below shows some of the properties that can be set:

web.config (globalization)

```
<globalization
    fileEncoding="utf-8"
    requestEncoding="utf-8"
    responseEncoding="utf-8"
    culture="en-US"
    uiCulture="de-DE"
/>
```

The settings listed here, with the exception of fileEncoding, can also be set at the page level by placing them in a page directive.

The difference between the CharSet property and the ContentEncoding property is that the CharSet can be set to a null value (Nothing in VB.NET) and the content-type header will be suppressed. The ContentEncoding property cannot be set to null.

ContentEncoding Property

The ContentEncoding property indicates an Encoding object that represents the character set in use on the outgoing stream. This property provides a more robust, object-oriented approach for setting the character set for the outgoing response when compared with the CharSet property. It becomes important when working with international applications, which need to be flexible in the languages they display.

```
Encoding EncodedSetting= HttpResponse.ContentEncoding
HttpResponse.ContentEncoding = Encoding EncodedSetting
```

ContentType Property

The ContentType property indicates the MIME type of the outgoing response stream. The default value for this property is text/html as the majority of content served by web servers is HTML text. This property can be set to reflect the type of the document being sent back. For example, if you were returning XML data directly to the client, then this property would be set to text/xml.

```
string Type = HttpResponse.ContentType
HttpResponse.ContentType = string Type
```

Cookies Property (read-only)

The Cookies property indicates the cookies collection, which allows addition of cookies to the outgoing stream. The HttpCookiesCollection is discussed earlier in the chapter and provides a wrapper for a collection of cookies.

```
HttpCookiesCollection = HttpResponse.Cookies
```

Expires Property

The Expires property indicates the number of minutes that the page should be cached on the client browser.

> The **Expires** property has been deprecated. You should use the methods and properties of the **HttpCachePolicy** object exposed through the **Cache** property to set the expiration for the page in ASP.NET.

ExpiresAbsolute

The ExpiresAbsolute property indicates the specific date and time until which the page should be cached by the client browser.

```
HttpResponse.ExpiresAbsolute = DateTime
```

> The **ExpiresAbsolute** property has been deprecated. You should use the methods and properties of the **HttpCachePolicy** object exposed through the **Cache** property to set the absolute expiration for the page.

Filter Property

The Filter property indicates the stream applied as a filter to the outgoing response. A custom stream class can be set to filter the outgoing content and apply any changes necessary. A simple example would be a stream class that capitalizes all of the HTML tags in the output.

```
HttpResponse.Filter = stream Filter
```

IsClientConnected Property (read-only)

The IsClientConnected property indicates whether the client is still connected to the server. This property can be useful when running a lengthy request. Perhaps you have a long running query, or are waiting for a response from another server. If the client is no longer connected, it does not pay to continue processing the request. In a high volume site, it's important to only process what is necessary.

```
Boolean IsConnected= HttpResponse.IsClientConnected
```

Output Property (read-only)

The Output property indicates a TextWriter object that can be used to directly send output to the HTTP response stream. The Response.Write syntax is much more familiar for traditional ASP developers, but ultimately does the same thing. Writing with the Response.Write or Response.Output.Write methods performs the same operation, and will produce the same results. The Output property simply allows for another mechanism of doing this and provides a TextWriter class as the object.

```
TextWriter Writer= HttpResponse.Output
```

OutputStream Property (read-only)

The OutputStream property indicates a stream object that can be used to write output directly onto the response stream. This is useful if you have content that you are streaming from another source or if you are using a business object, or helper function, that requires a stream to write to. This stream is very similar to the Response object in that it is written to in similar ways, but this property gives you direct access to the stream as an object that derives directly from the abstract stream class.

```
Stream = HttpResponse.OutputStream
```

Status Property

The Status property indicates the HTTP status that is being sent to the client. This is a string value representing both the code and text versions (for example 200 OK).

```
String = HttpResponse.Status
```

StatusCode Property

The StatusCode property indicates the numeric representation of the server's ability to return the requested resource. For example, a successful request is indicated by a 200 status code while a status code of 302 is a redirection. Most users are probably familiar with the 404 status code meaning that a resource was not found. These codes indicate to the web browser the outcome of the request made to the server.

```
Integer Status = HttpResponse.StatusCode
HttpResponse.StatusCode = Integer Status
```

StatusDescription Property

The StatusDescription property indicates the string representation of the server's ability to return the requested resource.

```
String = HttpResponse.StatusDescription
```

SuppressContent

The SuppressContent property indicates whether the content in the page should be sent to the client. A true value indicates that the content should be suppressed and not sent. If this property is set to true, and the response is being buffered, then the response to the client will be blank. If buffering is turned off and this property is set to true, then only that content sent to the output stream before setting this property to true will be sent.

```
HttpResponse.SuppressContent = boolean
```

Utilities and Helpful Information

When working with web applications, it is often useful to get information about the environment in which the application is running. The HttpRuntime, HttpServerUtility, and HttpBrowserCapabilities objects allow the developer to access information about the files and directories involved in the web application environment and the client environment. Knowing the abilities of the client allows the developer to program in such a manner as to ensure the best experience when visiting their site.

The HttpRuntime class

The HttpRuntime class offers methods and properties regarding the run-time environment in which the web application is running as well as information about the runtime itself. This information can be useful for finding path information or locating files needed in processing pages, as well as in more advanced development where the programmer needs to work with the ASP.NET internals.

HttpRuntime Static (Shared) Methods

- ❑ Close
- ❑ ProcessRequest

Close method

The Close method allows shutting down the runtime and clearing the cache.

```
HttpRuntime.Close()
```

ProcessRequest method

The ProcessRequest method is the method that drives all requests made to the web site. This method is the invocation that actually starts a web request.

```
HttpRuntime.ProcessRequest(request)
```

Parameter	Type	Description
request	HttpWorkerRequest	The request that represents the actual request made by the client

HttpRuntime Static (Shared) Properties

- ❑ AppDomainAppId
- ❑ AppDomainAppPath
- ❑ AppDomainAppVirtualPath
- ❑ AppDomainId
- ❑ AspInstallDirectory
- ❑ BinDirectory
- ❑ Cache
- ❑ ClrInstallDirectory
- ❑ CodegenDir
- ❑ IsOnUNCShare
- ❑ MachineConfigurationDirectory

AppDomainAppId Property

The AppDomainAppId property indicates a string value that represents the ID of the application within the AppDomain that the web application is currently executing in. See the AppDomainId property to get the ID for the application domain itself. An application domain is a unit of processing that is used to separate the code executing in different applications. While the runtime generally takes care of creating application domains, they can be created by a developer to execute code in separate spaces.

```
string ID = HttpRuntime.AppDomainAppId
```

AppDomainAppPath Property

The AppDomainAppPath property indicates the file path to the physical directory where the files for the web application reside.

```
string = HttpRuntime.AppDomainAppPath
```

AppDomainAppVirtualPath Property

The AppDomainAppVirtualPath property indicates the virtual path to the directory where the files for the web application exist.

```
string = HttpRuntime.AppDomainAppVirtualPath
```

AppDomainId Property

The AppDomainId property indicates the ID of the AppDomain in which the web application is running.

```
string=HttpRuntime.AppDomainId
```

AspInstallDirectory Property

The AspInstallDirectory property indicates the physical path to the directory where the ASP.NET runtime files exist.

```
string = HttpRuntime.AspInstallDirectory
```

BinDirectory Property

The `BinDirectory` property indicates the `bin` directory for the current web application. This directory is where all assemblies used in the application, other than those in the Global Application Cache, are located.

```
string = HttpRuntime.BinDirectory
```

Cache Property

The `Cache` property indicates a `Cache` object that allows the developer to insert and retrieve items to be cached. This built-in `Cache` object can be extremely useful in caching data or other information that is expensive to retrieve and does not change often.

```
cache = HttpRuntime.Cache
```

See Example 5 in Chapter 16 for an example of using the `Cache` object to cache data from a database. These `Cache` objects can also have dependencies, such as a file dependency. For example, we might load information from an XML document and store it in the `Cache` object. This cache can be dependent on the file we loaded our data from, such that when our file changes, the cache can be updated.

ClrInstallDirectory Property

The `ClrInstallDirectory` property indicates the physical path to the file system directory where the Common Language Runtime binary files are located.

```
string = HttpRuntime.ClrInstallDirectory
```

CodegenDir Property

The `CodegenDir` property indicates the physical path to the directory on the file system that acts as the default location for assemblies generated dynamically.

```
string = HttpRuntime.CodegenDir
```

One of the benefits of ASP.NET over traditional ASP programming is that the code and web pages are compiled as opposed to being interpreted. This compilation allows faster execution of the code. When a page is requested, if it has not been compiled, it is compiled at that time and the compiled files are accessed from that point on. This property provides the path to the directory where these compiled files are created.

IsOnUNCShare Property

The `IsOnUncShare` property indicates whether the application files are located on a UNC share as opposed to being located locally on the web server.

```
Boolean = HttpRuntime.IsOnUNCShare
```

MachineConfigurationDirectory Property

The `MachineConfigurationDirectory` property indicates the physical path to the directory where the machine configuration file is located.

```
String = HttpRuntime.MachineConfigurationDirectory
```

The machine configuration file contains configuration information that covers the entire machine. This information acts as the base configuration information for the machine, which can be overridden by more specific files such as the web.config file. See Chapter 8, *Configuration & System.Web.Configuration*, for more information on using the configuration files in ASP.NET.

The HttpServerUtility Class

The HttpServerUtility class provides helper functions that can be used in your application. These methods and properties are available through the intrinsic Server object of the Page class and can be referenced from within a page as in the following example:

```
Server.HtmlDecode(string);
```

HttpServerUtility Methods

- ❑ ClearError
- ❑ CreateObject
- ❑ CreateObjectFromClsid
- ❑ Execute
- ❑ GetLastError
- ❑ HtmlDecode
- ❑ HtmlEncode
- ❑ MapPath
- ❑ Transfer
- ❑ UrlDecode
- ❑ UrlEncode
- ❑ UrlPathEncode

ClearError Method

The ClearError method allows clearing the last exception. The exception still needs to be caught, but this method clears it from memory so that it does not appear that there have been, or are currently errors with the application.

```
HttpServerUtility.ClearError()
```

CreateObject Method

The CreateObject method allows creation of COM objects using their PROGID or using the type of the object. This method is similar to the Server.CreateObject method in traditional ASP. There are two overloaded versions of this method.

```
HttpServerUtility.CreateObject(progid)
```

Parameter	Type	Description
progid	String	The prog ID of the COM object to be created as it is found in the registry

```
HttpServerUtility.CreateObject(type)
```

Parameter	Type	Description
type	System.Type	The type of the object to create as a COM object

This method creates a COM object on the server and returns an object reference to it allowing the developer to program against the object calling its methods and properties.

One thing to keep in mind when working with COM components is that apartment-threaded components are not creatable by default. In order to be able to use these components, such as the `Scripting.Dictionary` object, the `aspcompat` attribute of the page directive must be set to `true`.

```
<%@ Page aspcompat=true %>
```

This indicates to the runtime that this page should be allowed to run on a single-threaded apartment thread. This offers the benefit of being able to call apartment-threaded components and components in COM+ that need access to the ASP.NET intrinsic objects or object context.

CreateObjectFromClsid Method

The `CreateObjectFromClsid` method allows creation of a COM object from its class ID (`CLSID`) as it appears in the registry.

```
Object = HttpServerUtility.CreateObjectFromClsid(clsid)
```

Parameter	Type	Description
clsid	String	The class ID of the object to be created

This method allows creation of COM objects on the server based on the `CLSID` of these objects. This allows for interoperability between .NET managed code and unmanaged COM code, written in C++ or VB, for example. See the previous discussion on the `CreateObject` method for more information.

Execute method

The `Execute` method allows for execution of an `ASPX` page from within the current page and, optionally, return of the output of that page. This method passes the current `HttpRequest` and `HttpResponse` to the executing page, so it will be able to access the information about the request, and write to the response as if it were requested directly. There are two overloaded versions of this method as outlined below.

```
HttpServerUtility.Execute(path)
```

Parameter	Type	Description
path	String	The URL of the page to execute

```
HttpServerUtility.Execute(path,writer)
```

Parameter	Type	Description
path	String	The URL of the page to execute
writer	TextWriter	The TextWriter onto which the executed page writes its output

It is often the case that a web site using traditional ASP is designed with UI pages and action pages. For example, there might be a page that contains a form and another that processes it. The UI page could still be called and pass execution to the processing page, even returning the UI output to the client. An example of this follows:

```
<html>
<body>
<h2>Thank you for your response.</h2>

<script language="c#" runat="server">

//execute the processing page and return the output to the response object
Server.Execute("processing.aspx", Response.Output);

</script>
</body>
</html>
```

GetLastError Method

The GetLastError method allows the developer to get the last exception that was thrown.

```
Exception = HttpServerUtility.GetLastError()
```

HtmlDecode Method

The HtmlDecode method allows decoding strings that have been encoded in order to be safely sent to a browser. This method has two overloaded versions.

```
string = HttpServerUtility.HtmlDecode (encodedString)
```

Parameter	Type	Description
encodedString	String	The encoded string to be decoded

```
string = HttpServerUtility.HtmlDecode (encodedString, writer)
```

Parameter	Type	Description
encodedString	String	The encoded string to be decoded
writer	TextWriter	The TextWriter object onto which the decoded string will be written

81

HtmlEncode Method

The `HtmlEncode` method allows encoding strings so that they are safe for transmitting to a web browser. There are two overloaded versions of this method.

```
HttpServerUtility.HtmlEncode(inputString)
```

Parameter	Type	Description
inputString	String	The string to be encoded for delivery to the browser

```
HttpServerUtility.HtmlEncode(inputString, writer)
```

Parameter	Type	Description
inputString	String	The string to be encoded for delivery to the browser
writer	TextWriter	The `TextWriter` object that the encoded string will be written to

When working with URL strings it is important to ensure that the browser can interpret them correctly. URL strings are therefore encoded with replacement characters so they will be interpreted correctly by the browser. The `HtmlEncode` and `HtmlDecode` methods provide an easy way to manipulate strings so they are safe to pass to the browser.

For example, the string "Priced < $50", becomes "Priced < $50" after being encoded. Notice that the "<" symbol was replaced as it has special meaning to the HTML rendering engines in web browsers.

MapPath Method

The `MapPath` method allows mapping of the physical path of the file given the file name or relative path.

```
string = HttpServerUtility.MapPath(fileName)
```

Parameter	Type	Description
fileName	String	The relative path of the file to be mapped

Transfer Method

The `Transfer` method allows transfer of page execution from the current page to another page on the server. Unlike its predecessor, the redirect method, this method transfers execution to a new page that returns a result to the browser.

```
HttpServerUtility.Transfer(url)
```

Parameter	Type	Description
url	String	The URL to transfer the execution to. This resource must reside on the same server.

```
HttpServerUtility.Transfer(url, preserve)
```

Parameter	Type	Description
url	String	The URL to transfer the execution to. This resource must reside on the same server.
Preserve	Boolean	Indicates whether the forms and query string collection should be preserved so they may be accessed from the receiving page.

In ASP 2.0, we had access to the `Response.Redirect` method that would send a directive to the client browser with a `302` status code that indicated to the browser that it should request a different resource. In ASP 3.0 and now in ASP.NET, we also have the ability to transfer execution of a page to another page without this round trip to the client. Not only is this faster, but it creates a smoother experience for the user.

UrlDecode Method

The `UrlDecode` method allows decoding of a URL string which has been encoded to allow for special characters in the URL. This method has two overloaded versions

```
string = HttpServerUtility.UrlDecode(url)
```

Parameter	Type	Description
url	String	The URL to be decoded

```
string = HttpServerUtility.UrlDecode(url, writer)
```

Parameter	Type	Description
url	String	The URL to be decoded
writer	TextWriter	The TextWriter object to which the decoded string will be written

UrlEncode Method

The `UrlEncode` method allows encoding a URL string so that is may be understood by the browser. This method has two overloaded versions.

```
string = HttpServerUtility.UrlEncode(url)
```

Parameter	Type	Description
url	String	The URL to be encoded

```
string = HttpServerUtility.UrlEncode(url, writer)
```

Parameter	Type	Description
url	String	The URL to be encoded
writer	TextWriter	The TextWriter object to which the encoded URL will be written

Given the URL http://www.mysite.com/default.aspx?name=my site the UrlEncode method would return: `http%3a%2f%2fwww.mysite.com%2fdefault.aspx%3fname%3dMy+site`.

All spaces and special characters in the string are replaced with character codes so that the string is safe to pass to the browser.

UrlPathEncode Method

The UrlPathEncode method allows encoding the directory path portion of a URL. This method does not encode the resource name itself, the path info, or query string parameters.

```
HttpServerUtility.UrlPathEncode(url)
```

Parameter	Type	Description
url	String	The URL to be encoded

Given the URL http://www.mysite.com/default.aspx?name=my site the UrlPathEncode method would return: `http%3a%2f%2fwww.mysite.com%2fdefault.aspx?name=My site`

Notice that while all spaces and special characters in the URL are replaced with special characters, as in the UrlEncode method, the information following the page name is not encoded.

HttpServerUtility Properties

❑ MachineName

❑ ScriptTimeout

MachineName Property (read-only)

The MachineName property indicates the name of the server that hosts the application.

```
string = HttpServerUtility.MachineName
```

ScriptTimeout Property

The `ScriptTimeout` property indicates the number of seconds that are allowed to elapse before the processing of a page will be terminated and a timeout error sent to the client.

```
Integer = HttpServerUtility.ScriptTimeout
HttpServerUtility.ScriptTimeout = Integer
```

A script running in IIS may encounter issues that keep it from continuing execution, such as waiting for a database query to return. This property indicates how long the script will run before being canceled. If a script needs a long time to run, for example you know the query will take a long time and wish to avoid the timeout, this property can be set higher. Be sure to alert your users that the action they are about to take is going to take some time. Many users will not wait more than a few seconds for a response from a web server.

HttpSessionState Class

While the `HttpSessionState` class is not part of the `System.Web` namespace (it belongs to the `System.Web.SessionState` namespace), maintaining state is an integral part of many web developers' core activities. As such, it makes sense to talk briefly about this class and how to use it. First, it should be noted that Session in ASP.NET has grown considerably from the ASP 3.0 days. In traditional ASP, the session object allowed storage of name-value pairs. These items where stored in memory and were accessible only for a given client and for a specified duration; the client's "session". Two big problems with maintaining state using the session object in traditional ASP were that the storing a value in session tied a user to a given server so load balancing and server farms could not take full advantage of spreading the web hits across multiple servers. Second, storing objects in session could cause nightmarish performance problems when the object was not free-threaded, as it caused a given session not only to be tied to a machine, but to be tied to a specific thread on that machine. So, when the user made a request, if the thread they needed was busy, they would have to wait until it was ready to process their request. The first problem is solved by providing several different storage mechanisms and improvements to the way session information is handled and the second is less of an issue with .NET as components are thread-safe and have the ability to easily serialize themselves to a persistent storage medium.

In ASP.NET we have three options for storing session values. A description of each appears in the table below along with some of the benefits and drawbacks of each.

Mode	Description	Benefits	Drawbacks
InProc	Session data is stored in memory on the web server. This is comparable to the session object in traditional ASP. This is the default setting.	Fastest access to items in session of the three options.	The drawbacks are the same as they always have been for session: a user is tied to a single server so this is not as scalable as other modes.

Table continued on following page

Mode	Description	Benefits	Drawbacks
SqlServer	Session data is stored in a SQL Server database. A SQL script is provided to set up the database.	This provides a scalable solution in that it does not tie a user to a given server for their requests. This method has the ability to provide failure recovery as the database is a persistent and transactional system that can recover the state if necessary.	While this method does not tie a client to a given web server, performance is degraded a bit by the overhead of reading and writing to the database.
StateServer	Session data is stored in memory on a specified server. An NT service runs on a central server and state data is sent to and retrieved from this service, which keeps the data in memory.	This method provides a bit more scalability in that clients are not tied to a given server, but there is some added overhead involved in traversing the network to read and write values.	Like the InProc method, this option does not have any disaster recovery. If the StateServer crashes or hangs for some reason, all session data is lost and the site will not be able to continue to work with session data.

In choosing an option for session state you should consider the needs of your application and what the most important factors are. In general, session state management in ASP.NET is greatly improved. In addition to the options for the storage location, session state is processed on separate threads so that a crash of an application does not mean a loss of state information. And, for those browsers that do not support cookies, there is a cookieless session mechanism that utilizes the query string to pass the session ID back to the server.

In order to set the mode for session, edit the web.config file. The three examples below show typical settings for the three different modes.

InProc

```
<sessionState mode="InProc"
  cookieless="false"
  timeout="20" />
```

SqlServer

```
<sessionState mode="SqlServer"
  sqlConnectionString="data source=127.0.0.1;database=state;user id=sa;password="
  cookieless="false"
  timeout="20" />
```

StateServer

```
<sessionState mode="StateServer" stateConnectionString="tcpip=127.0.0.1:42424"
  cookieless="false"
  timeout="20" />
```

One final note on session: if you are not using session in your application, disable it. Like many of the other features of ASP.NET, session can be very powerful, but if it is not being used, it adds extra overhead to the processing on the server.

As with the `HttpContext` class, we will only be covering a portion of the `HttpSessionState` class including those items that are most commonly used. Items marked with a "*" are covered in detail.

HttpSessionState Properties

- ❑ CodePage
- ❑ Contents*
- ❑ Count
- ❑ IsCookieLess*
- ❑ IsNewSession
- ❑ IsReadOnly
- ❑ IsSynchronized
- ❑ Item*
- ❑ Keys*
- ❑ LCID
- ❑ Mode*
- ❑ SessionID
- ❑ StaticObjects*
- ❑ SynchRoot
- ❑ Timeout*

Contents Property (read-only)

The `Contents` property provides a reference to the given `HttpSessionState` object. This property is provided for backward compatibility with ASP 3.0. Traditionally, this property was implemented as a collection of the `Session` object that allowed access to the contents of `Session` with a collection interface.

```
HttpSessionState State = HttpSessionState.Contents
```

IsCookieLess Property (read-only)

The `IsCookieLess` property returns a Boolean value indicating whether the session mechanism is operating in a cookieless fashion. For those browsers with cookie support disabled, or that do not support cookies, the Session ID is passed to the server as part of the query string. This property can be used to determine if the session is using cookies so a developer can make decisions about interacting with the client.

```
Boolean Cookies = HttpSessoinState.IsCookieLess
```

Item Property

The `Item` property provides access to a given item stored in session in order to retrieve or store the item. This method has two overridden versions that allow the developer to use integer-based indexing or key names to work with the values.

C#

```
object SessionObject = HttpSessionState.[key]
```

VB.NET

```
object SessionObject = HttpSessionState.Item(key)
```

Parameter	Type	Description
key	String	The key name of the item you wish to retrieve

C#

```
object SessionObject = HttpSessionState[index]
```

VB.NET

```
object SessionObject = HttpSessionState.Item(index)
```

Parameter	Type	Description
index	Integer	The index in the collection of the item you wish to retrieve

Keys Property (read-only)

The Keys property indicates a collection of the key names of items stored in the current session. This property is useful if you just want to know what items are in session.

```
NameValueCollection Keys = HttpSessionState.Keys
```

Mode Property (read-only)

The Mode property returns an enumerated value indicating the storage mechanism for the session. These options were discussed in the introduction of this section.

```
SessionStateMode Mode = HttpSessionState.Mode
```

The possible values for the Mode property are indicated below:

Value	Meaning
Off	Session is disabled and therefore not available for storage of values
InProc	Session is being maintained on the local machine in memory
SqlServer	Session is using a SQL Server database to store values
StateServer	Session is being stored using the out-of-process NT service state server

StaticObjects Property (read-only)

The StaticObjects property provides access to items that were declared in the Global.asax file using the <object runat="server"> syntax. This property returns a special collection class that acts as a wrapper around these objects.

```
HttpStaticObjectsCollection Objects = HttpSessionState.StaticObjects
```

Timeout Property

The Timeout property indicates the time, in minutes, that is allowed between requests from a client before the session is destroyed. The default value for this property is 20. This is important because a session is defined as a single user's interaction with your web site. Once that user has stopped interacting with your site, their session is still taking up valuable memory on the server. In a high volume site this can have an impact on performance. On the other hand, if you set this property too low, a user may not have completed working on your site and come back to their computer to find that all of the work they have done is lost and they must start all over again.

You should be sure to consider the ramifications and the needs of your site before changing this value. It can also be set for an application in the web.config file:

C#
```
public int Timeout {get/set};
```

VB.NET
```
Public Property Timeout As Integer
```

HttpSessionState Methods

- ❏ Abandon*
- ❏ Add*
- ❏ Clear*
- ❏ CopyTo
- ❏ GetEnumerator
- ❏ Remove*
- ❏ RemoveAll
- ❏ RemoveAt*

Abandon Method

The Abandon method terminates the session removing all values from it. Essentially, this method notifies the session handlers to drop the session and all of its contents. You can use this method to force a session to be dropped, rather than waiting for a user to close their browser or the timeout to be reached. This can be used to provide "sign out" functionality in which the user indicates they are done working on the site and allows you to cancel their session to recover server resources.

```
void Abandon()
```

Add Method

The `Add` method is used to insert items into session. It takes an object as a parameter for the value, and since all items in .NET are derived from `Object`, you can, potentially, store anything in session. However, you should seriously consider those items that you are storing and the cost of saving and retrieving that information. This will depend both on the object size and the session mode you have chosen for your site. Large items can degrade performance as the user load increases.

```
void Add(name, value)
```

Parameter	Type	Description
name	String	The key name of the item you wish to add to the collection
value	object	The item to store at the named location

Clear Method

The `Clear` method can be used to remove all of the items which are currently stored in session. You can use this method as a shortcut if you need to return the session to a clean state. For example, if you were creating a shopping cart mechanism and wanted to clear out all of the values once an order has been processed. In this way you could prevent a user from accidentally resubmitting their order.

```
void Clear()
```

Remove Method

The `Remove` method allows for removing a named item from session. You can use this feature, along with the `key` used to insert a value, to remove a specific item.

```
void Remove(key)
```

Parameter	Type	Description
key	string	The key name of the item you wish to remove

RemoveAt Method

The `RemoveAt` method is the companion to the remove method, and allows removing an item from session using the index of the item.

```
void RemoveAt(index)
```

Parameter	Type	Description
index	integer	The index in the collection of the item you wish to remove

Summary

The System.Web namespace contains the core classes that support the ASP.NET framework. For developers familiar with traditional ASP, many of the items that have been covered here should be familiar, yet more functional.

In this chapter we looked at:

- ❑ HttpBrowserCapabilities, which offers information on the abilities of the client connecting to our application to allow us to appropriately customize our content

- ❑ HttpCookie and HttpCookieCollection, which provide us with access to cookie information coming in on the request and allow us to easily create cookies on the client

- ❑ HttpPostedFile and HttpFileCollection, which allow us to work with files that a client has posted to the server

- ❑ HttpRequest, which represents a client request for a resource and allows us to gain access to a variety of information about the request

- ❑ HttpResponse and the many options we have for writing content out to a client, including the use of headers, cookies, and globalization information

- ❑ HttpRuntime and the many environment related properties and methods it contains, allowing us to determine the environment in which our application is executing

- ❑ HttpServerUtility, which provides us with several handy tools to use including transferring requests, decoding and encoding strings, and creating objects

In the next chapter we will cover the classes that make up the System.Web.UI namespace and provide the functionality to create a user interface for web applications.

3

System.Web.UI

The System.Web.UI namespace contains the base classes that support the user interface elements of ASP.NET. These classes include elements such as Page, Control, and UserControl, to help you to create the web pages and Web Forms that provide the user interface for your web application.

In ASP.NET, everything reflects the object-oriented model. This means that when you create a web page, an actual Page object representing that page is instantiated. Similarly, the **user controls** your page requires are instantiated as objects. Even literal text and HTML elements that are ignored by the server, are created as **literal controls**. This fully object-oriented approach lends great power and flexibility to those working with web applications. Do not worry if you are wondering what a literal control or a user control is, as we shall cover these next.

Before we dive into specific details of these classes, it's important for us to understand how a Web Form is created and processed and how all the classes fit together. When a client requests a page, the server processes any code contained in the page before it is sent to the client. During this processing, every item on a page, including the page itself, is represented by an object instance. Below is a description of each type of item we might encounter on a page:

❑ **Page object** – this 'top-level' object represents the overall page itself and acts as a container to all of the other items on the page.

❑ **Server Controls** – these are HTML tags that are executed at the server (indicated by having a runat attribute set to server). This means that a developer has programmatic access to these controls as true objects in the code behind a page. Chapters 4 and 5 cover these controls in detail.

❑ **Literal Controls** – a Literal Control is any text or HTML element on a page that is not processed in some way by the server. For instance, each block of text on a page is allocated a Literal Control object at the time that page is processed.

❑ **User Controls** – a User Control object represents a group of related controls and text. The User Control is sometimes called a pagelet because it represents a portion of a page that can be reused as a single unit in any other page. Take a look at Example 3 in Chapter 16 for a quick illustration of User Controls.

Overleaf is a sample web page and a visual depiction of how the items in the page are represented. An easy way to see this for yourself is to enable VS.NET tracing on your pages, and select the Control Tree view. Chapter 11 provides further information on tracing.

Example: Page Heirarchy

```
<%@ Page language="c#" %>
<HTML>
  <HEAD id="head">
    <title id="title">Hierarchy Display</title>
  </HEAD>
  <body id="body">
    <form id="Hierarchy" method="post" runat="server">
      <h2 id="heading2">
        A calendar control
      </h2>
      <asp:Calendar ID="cal" runat="server"/>
      <a href="hierarchy.aspx" runat="server">This is my link</a>
    </form>
  </body>
</HTML>
```

This page has a header containing a title for the page, followed by a body element which comprises an <H2> element, an ASP.NET calendar control, and a link anchor tag that runs at the server. The diagram below shows how these items would be represented as objects.

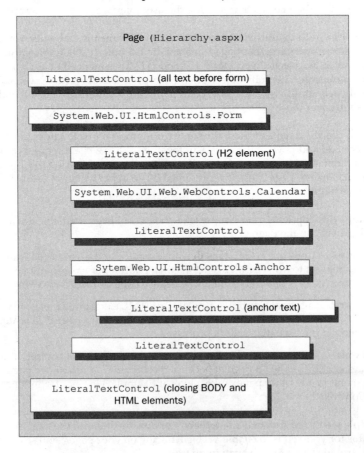

The outer box represents the page object itself. Contained within it are several controls, starting with a literal control that represents all the text which precedes the <FORM> element, including our <HEAD> element, and the opening <BODY> tag. Next, we come to the single form element on the page. Because this form element is set to run at the server, it becomes a server control rather than getting lumped into the opening literal text control.

From our HTML we can see that our form contains three elements: an <H2> element, an ASP.NET calendar control, and an ASP.NET HtmlAnchor. Each of these is represented in the hierarchy above, with a few interesting, and perhaps unexpected side effects. The Anchor control includes a literal text control beneath it which represents the text of the link; the actual wording for the hyperlink. As mentioned above, User Controls can contain text, HTML, and other controls, and this is a perfect example. Note however the literal text controls that follow each of our server controls. These controls represent the line breaks that follow our server controls in the source page. This can be a bit confusing at first. To remove these, we can simply write our server-side elements on a single line. Play around with these items and the formatting of your page, viewing the trace information to get a better understanding of how items in the HTML get mapped to controls.

We have talked about a page *containing* controls, and User Controls *containing* text and other content. In the previous hierarchy diagram, elements are indented to indicate that they exist within each other. For example, the items in the form element are indented to show that they are included inside the Form control. This nested grouping of controls is often referred to as the **control hierarchy**. When working with a control (remember this includes Page objects), we can get access to the controls collection for each item, and add new controls or work with the controls contained in the parent control. See the section later on the Controls property of the Control class for an example.

Knowing the controls and what they represent is helpful, but more important is understanding how they all interrelate. The diagram below shows the relationship between the objects we have been discussing.

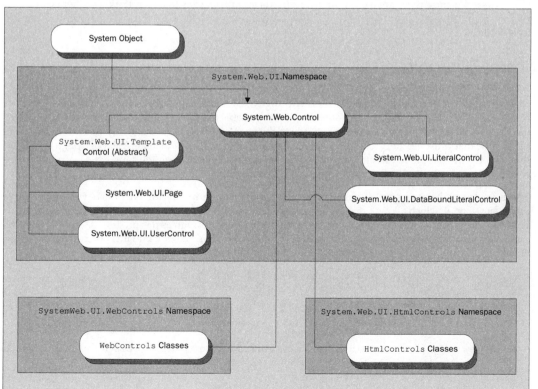

All objects in the .NET framework derive at some level from `System.Object`. This is the base class in the framework and provides the core functionality shared across all objects. `System.Web.Control` is the base class for all controls in the ASP.NET framework. This includes pages, User Controls, Literal Controls, and the framework's server-side controls. Each of these classes inherits the base functionality of the class, so these derived classes can simply use any functions defined by the base `Control` class.

Another important point to note is that the `Page` and `UserControl` classes derive from the Abstract class `TemplateControl`. The `TemplateControl` class defines common functionality useful to both classes encapsulated in a reusable form.

In this chapter we will look at several core classes of the `System.Web.UI` namespace, namely:

❑ `Control` Class – represents the base class for all UI elements in a Web Form. It is the basis for pages, user controls, server controls, HTML controls, and literal text controls.

❑ `TemplateControl` Abstract Class – provides common functionality for the page and user control classes.

❑ `Page` Class – represents a single page, or Web Form, in a web application and houses all objects found on the page. Each page that a developer creates derives from the `Page` class and therefore has all the functionality of this class.

❑ `UserControl` Class – represents small reusable parts of a web page that can be compiled separately and inserted in any page.

Each of these classes is defined in detail in this chapter and examples of using them are provided in many cases. Because there are a great many methods and properties to cover, not all of them can be referenced in full detail, so we have tried to focus on those that will be used most commonly or are the least intuitive.

Control Lifecycle

When a web server receives a request for a simple HTML page, it simply sends the requested file to the client. Traditional ASP pages, however, mix scripting code and HTML text in one file. When an ASP file is requested, Microsoft's Internet Information Server (IIS) passes the file to a DLL, which parses and processes the embedded script to return a pure HTML file to the client. ASP.NET goes one step further. Rather than using code that must be interpreted line-by-line for each request, the code in an ASP.NET page is compiled the first time the page is requested, and only needs to be recompiled when the source file is updated. This results in increased speed and performance as well as providing a very rich object model.

This is not to say that pages are no longer processed; quite the contrary. In ASP.NET we have an event driven processing model, which allows developers to program 'hooks' into the processing of pages and controls. Below is a table that shows the various stages that a control goes through as it is processed. The various stages are shown along with the common activities that occur in that stage. To hook into this process, the developer either handles the event directly, or overrides the method shown in the right-hand column.

Stage	Purpose	Event or Method
Initialize	Initialize the control's state, setting up variables needed for the duration of processing.	`Init` event (`OnInit` method)
Load View State	State information is restored for the control by loading it from the view state or a custom mechanism.	`LoadViewState` method

Stage	Purpose	Event or Method
Process PostBack Data	Incoming form data is processed and control properties are updated accordingly.	`IPostBackDataHandler.LoadPostData`
Load	Perform processing common to all requests. All controls are populated and accessibled at this time.	`Load` event (`OnLoad` method)
Send PostBack Notifications	Controls implementing the `IPostBackDataHandler` interface are notified of changes to their state.	`IPostBackDataHandler.RaisePostDataChanged Event`
Handle PostBack Events	Controls that participate in postback events, such as the button control, handle events associated with the action that initiated the postback.	`IPostBackEventHandler.RaisePostBackEvent`
PreRender	Any final updates are made to the control before it is rendered. This is the very last opportunity to make changes to the state of the control.	`PreRender` event (`OnPreRender` method)
Save State	The control state is saved and persisted to a string, which is sent to the client in a hidden form field.	`SaveViewState` method
Render	The control is written to the output stream to be sent to the client.	`Render` method
Commit/Abort Transaction (page)	For pages run in transactions, any cleanup required after the transaction completes.	`CommitTransaction/AbortTransaction` events
Unload	The control has completed processing and can be removed from memory.	`Unload` Event
Dispose	Final cleanup before the control is released from memory.	`Dispose` method

As controls go through this lifecycle, we can override methods or handle events to run custom code that augments the processing of the control for our purposes.

In the classes detailed below, those items marked as public are accessible from outside the class, while those marked protected are available only from within the class or subclasses. For example, when a Web Form is created, the class generated derives from the `Page` class, so any code you write within that class has access to all of the public and protected members of the Page object, but would only have access to public members of contained objects such as a User Control.

The Control Class

The `Control` class represents the base class for User Interface (UI) elements in ASP.NET pages. As such, it defines a large number of methods, properties, and events that are common to many of the items used to build a web page. Understanding the abilities of the Control class will get you 50% or more of the way towards understanding how to use the other UI controls in ASP.NET.

In this class, as for the others detailed subsequently, remember that public methods and properties are accessible outside the class, while those marked protected are only available within the class or subclasses where they are defined. For example, when a Web Form is created, the class that's generated derives from the `Page` class, so any code you write within that class has access to all of the public and protected members of the `Page` object, but would only have access to public members of any contained objects, such as a User Control.

Control Class Public Methods

- ❑ DataBind
- ❑ Dispose
- ❑ FindControl
- ❑ HasControls
- ❑ RenderControl
- ❑ ResolveUrl
- ❑ SetRenderMethodDelegate

The DataBind Method

The `DataBind` method binds a data source to a server control and any child controls it may have. In a custom control, this method would be overridden to bind data to the control. In ASP.NET we can bind a collection of data to certain controls so that the data is represented in the control. For example, the `DataGrid` control creates an HTML table containing the data in its data source. See Chapter 14 for more information on data binding in ASP.NET.

```
void DataBind()
```

The Dispose Method

The `Dispose` method releases the resources allocated to a control prior to garbage collection. If you are creating your own control, you should override this method to make sure any resources held by your control are correctly released. In addition, you should call `Dispose` on any child controls contained within your control so that the resources held by those controls will also be released. It is also good practice to call this method on any other controls when you are finished working with them.

```
void Dispose()
```

The FindControl Method

The `FindControl` method offers a quick way to select a given child control control of the current naming container. A **naming container** is a sort of namespace for controls. See the `NamingContainer` property and the unique ID property sections later in the chapter for more information. Note that the `FindControl` method has a protected version as well, also discussed in further detail later.

```
Control = FindControl(id)
```

Parameter	Type	Description
id	String	The unique ID for the control you wish to find

The HasControls Method

The `HasControls` method indicates whether the current control has child controls – that is, other controls contained inside it. Use this method to determine if there are such controls available in preference to checking the `Count` property of the `Controls` collection. `HasControls` simply checks that there are controls, and has the better performance when there are none, as the `Controls` collection does not have to be accessed to evaluate the `Count` property.

```
boolean HasControls()
```

The RenderControl Method

The `RenderControl` method causes a control to output its content to an `HtmlTextWriter` and retrieve trace information when tracing is turned on. This public method differs from the protected `Render` method, as the latter cannot retrieve trace information. However, both methods can be overridden to create custom controls for the rendering process. If you create a custom control and override this method, do not forget to call the `RenderControl` method separately for all of your control's children.

```
void RenderControl(writer)
```

Parameter	Type	Description
writer	HtmlTextWriter	The HtmlTextWriter that the output should be written to

The ResolveUrl Method

The `ResolveUrl` method resolves a relative URL to the corresponding absolute URL. This method differs from the more common `MapPath` in that it returns a URL as opposed to a physical path to a file. This method can be helpful when you need to provide the client with a path to a resource that resides on the server but you don't have prior knowledge of the whole path, or you want your code to be flexible enough to run from multiple locations.

```
string = ResolveUrl(relativeURL)
```

Parameter	Type	Description
relativeUrl	String	The relative URL to a file for which you wish to determine the absolute URL

The SetRenderMethodDelegate Method

The `SetRenderMethodDelegate` method lets you specify an alternative method to the `Render` or `RenderControl` method for rendering a control. The `Render` and `RenderControl` methods should suffice in most cases; but this method is available for those situations where you do have to use another method. This method is primarily used by the .NET runtime to set the `Render` method for a control.

```
void SetRenderMethodDelegate(renderMethod)
```

Parameter	Type	Description
renderMethod	Method	The alternative method to handle the Render event. Must have the signature `void(HtmlTextWriter, Control)`.

Control Class Protected Methods

- ❑ AddParsedSubObject
- ❑ BuildProfileTree
- ❑ ClearChildViewState
- ❑ CreateChildControls
- ❑ CreateControlCollection
- ❑ EnsureChildControls
- ❑ FindControl
- ❑ IsLiteralControl
- ❑ LoadViewState
- ❑ MapPathSecure
- ❑ OnBubbleEvent
- ❑ OnDataBinding
- ❑ OnInit
- ❑ OnLoad
- ❑ OnPreRender
- ❑ OnUnload
- ❑ RaiseBubbleEvent
- ❑ Render
- ❑ RenderChildren
- ❑ SaveViewState
- ❑ TrackViewState

The AddParsedSubObject Method

The `AddParsedSubObject` method allows addition of additional parsed content, such as parsed HTML or XML, to the controls collection of the given control.

```
void AddParsedSubObject(subObject)
```

Parameter	Type	Description
subObject	Object	The object to be added to the `ControlCollection` of the current control

This method should be overridden for custom controls for which you wish to inhibit such a feature. For example, if you created a control and did not want users to be able to add their own literal controls to it, then you would override this method with an empty implementation. This is especially important when working with databound templated controls.

The BuildProfileTree Method

The `BuildProfileTree` method is called to build information required for tracing. The information displayed in the control tree display of Visual Studio.NET, showing the hierarchy of controls on the page, is collected by this method. This method is called implicitly when tracing is enabled for a page.

```
void BuildProfileTree(parentID, calcViewState)
```

Parameter	Type	Description
parentID	String	The unique ID for the parent control
calcViewState	Boolean	Indicates whether the view state size of the control should be calculated

The ClearChildViewState Method

The `ClearChildViewState` method clears the view state of all child controls contained in the given control.

```
void ClearChildViewState()
```

View state is turned on by default, so it is important at times to clear the view state of the child controls when working with them in certain situations. For example, if you have a control that allows databinding, then you would use this method to clear the state information of child controls before binding new data to them.

The CreateChildControls Method

The `CreateChildControls` method is called by a control to determine if it should create any child controls that it is to contain. If you develop container controls or templated controls, you must override this method to handle the creation of your child controls.

```
void CreateChildControls()
```

An example of creating child controls follows next. We have a User Control that creates some literal text, an <H3> element, a label object, and an ASP.NET textbox adding each to its collection of controls. This is an example of adding such items dynamically rather than declaratively from the designer tool, but the two forms can be intermingled if desired.

Example: CreateChildControls

This example is available for download from www.Wrox.com and is called `CreateChildren.ascx.cs`

```
namespace AspProgRefChap3
{
  using System;
  using System.Data;
```

```
using System.Drawing;
using System.Web;
using System.Web.UI;
using System.Web.UI.WebControls;
using System.Web.UI.HtmlControls;

public abstract class CreateChildren : System.Web.UI.UserControl
{
  public CreateChildren()
  {
    this.Init += new System.EventHandler(Page_Init);
  }

  protected override void CreateChildControls()
  {
    //create a new literal control and add it
    this.Controls.Add(new LiteralControl("<h3>Dynamically Added Child
     Controls</h3>"));

    //create a label and add it to the controls
    Label TextLabel = new Label();
    TextLabel.Text = "Enter your name: ";
    this.Controls.Add(TextLabel);

    //create a text box and add it to the controls
    TextBox Input = new TextBox();
    Input.Text = "HERE";
    this.Controls.Add(Input);

  }
  private void Page_Load(object sender, System.EventArgs e)
  {
  }

  private void Page_Init(object sender, EventArgs e)
  {
    InitializeComponent();
  }

  private void InitializeComponent()
  {
    this.Load += new System.EventHandler(this.Page_Load);
  }
  }
}
```

We then use this control from within a web page as seen in the following example. Upon rendering, the elements we have added to the controls collection of the UserControl will appear in the document at the point of the UserControl tag. Like all the other samples introduced in this chapter, the following code can be found in the code download available from the Wrox web site. Please note however that the version of UserControlHost.aspx in the download is a combination of the file appearing below, and the other two files of this name referred to later in the chapter.

```
<%@ Page Language="vb" AutoEventWireup="false"
Codebehind="UserControlHost.aspx.vb"
Inherits="AspProgRefChap3vb.UserControlHost"%>
<%@ Register TagPrefix="WROX" TagName="Children" Src="CreateChildren.ascx" %>
<!DOCTYPE html public "-//w3c//dtd html 4.0 transitional//en" >
<html>
```

```
    <head>
    </head>
    <body ms_positioning="FlowLayout">
      <form id="UserControlHost" method="post" runat="server">
        <wrox:children id="ChildControls" runat="server">
        </wrox:children>
      </form>
    </body>
  </html>
```

The CreateControlCollection Method

The `CreateControlCollection` method creates a collection of the child controls contained by the given control. This method is helpful if the `Controls` property of the control is not adequate, or if there is a need to work with a separate control collection.

```
ControlCollection CreateControlCollection()
```

The EnsureChildControls Method

The `EnsureChildControls` method checks the control to make sure it contains child controls. If it does not, then the method creates a child `LiteralControl` based on the literal text contained in the control. Thus, if you need to ensure that your control contains a child control, for instance if you are going to refer to the first control in the collection, call this method first to ensure that there will be at least a dummy control to work with.

```
void EnsureChildControls()
```

The FindControl Method

The `FindControl` method locates the specified control in the current naming container. This protected version of the method allows searching for a control by ID, like the public version. However, the protected version also allows setting how many levels up the control hierarchy to look for the naming container.

```
Control = FindControl(id, levels)
```

Parameter	Type	Description
id	String	The unique ID for the control you wish to find
levels	Int32	The number of levels to go up the hierarchy to find a naming container

The IsLiteralContent Method

The `IsLiteralContent` method tests whether a control is a literal control; that is, the content is literal text only that does not contain any controls to be run on the server. This method can be useful when working with collections of controls to sort those you wish to perform actions on.

```
boolean = IsLiteralControl()
```

The LoadViewState Method

The LoadViewState method allows restoration of the state of a control as previously stored by the SaveViewState method. Generally, this method will not need to be called explicitly, but may be overridden if you require custom routines for maintaining state. For example, if you are building a custom control to act as a container of other controls, you may want to provide an implementation for this method which loads the state of the contained controls, and also sets values for the current control itself.

```
void LoadViewState(state)
```

Parameter	Type	Description
state	Object	Holds the persisted state of the control

The MapPathSecure Method

This method maps the relative file path specified to its absolute path, but only if the control has sufficient security permissions to read the file. Therefore, if you map a file that has security restrictions such that the user would not be able to read it, then this method will fail throwing an HttpException.

```
String = MapPathSecure(relativeUrl)
```

Parameter	Type	Description
relativeUrl	String	The relative URL of the file to map to its absolute path

For example, we could map a path to a configuration file in our application using the following syntax.

C#

```
string Path = MapPathSecure("web.config");
```

VB.NET

```
dim Path as String
Path = MapPathSecure("web.config")
```

The OnBubbleEvent Method

The OnBubbleEvent method is called when a child control event propagates up to this control. In handling the event, the control can indicate that it has handled it, or bubble the event up to its parent control, or both.

There is no defined Bubble event, as this event simply allows for passing other events up the control hierarchy. This is why the source needs to be specified in the method signature. This bubbling mechanism passes events up the control hierarchy so that parent controls have the opportunity to act on events as well. In this way, a parent control, such as a page or user control, can listen for events from all of its child controls and act accordingly.

```
Boolean OnBubbleEvent(source, eArgs)
```

Parameter	Type	Description
source	Object	The object that is the source of the event
eArgs	EventArgs	The arguments that describe the event

As an example, let's create a user control that bubbles its post-back event up to the parent page once it has acted on the event itself.

Example: OnBubble Event User Control

This file is available for download as `Bubbler.ascx`:

```
<%@ Control Language="c#" AutoEventWireup="false" Codebehind="Bubbler.ascx.cs"
Inherits="AspProgRefChap3.Bubbler"%>
<ASP:BUTTON id="Button1" text="Button" runat="server">
</ASP:BUTTON>
<BR>
<ASP:LABEL id="Label1" runat="server">Label</ASP:LABEL>
```

The user control interface consists of a simple button and label, which both run at the server. In the code behind our control, we handle the post-back event of the button and modify the label. This code is provided in both C# and VB.NET:

C#: Bubbler.ascx.cs

```
namespace AspProgRefChap3
{
  using System;
  using System.Data;
  using System.Drawing;
  using System.Web;
  using System.Web.UI.WebControls;
  using System.Web.UI.HtmlControls;

  public abstract class Bubbler : System.Web.UI.UserControl
  {
    protected System.Web.UI.WebControls.Label Label1;
    protected System.Web.UI.WebControls.Button Button1;

    public Bubbler()
    {
      this.Init += new System.EventHandler(Page_Init);
    }

    private void Page_Load(object sender, System.EventArgs e)
    {
    }

    private void Page_Init(object sender, EventArgs e)
    {
      InitializeComponent();
    }

    private void InitializeComponent()
    {
      this.Button1.Click += new System.EventHandler(this.Button1_Click);
      this.Load += new System.EventHandler(this.Page_Load);
```

```
    }
      private void Button1_Click(object sender, System.EventArgs e)
      {
        //handle the event as it pertains to the control
        Label1.Text = "Thanks for clicking!";

        //bubble the event so the parent can also respond
        this.RaiseBubbleEvent(sender,e);
      }
    }
  }
```

VB.NET: Bubbler.ascx.vb

```
  Public MustInherit Class Bubbler
    Inherits System.Web.UI.UserControl
    Protected WithEvents Button1 As System.Web.UI.WebControls.Button
    Protected WithEvents Label1 As System.Web.UI.WebControls.Label

    'This call is required by the Web Form Designer.
    <System.Diagnostics.DebuggerStepThrough()> Private Sub
     InitializeComponent()

    End Sub

    Private Sub Page_Init(ByVal sender As System.Object, ByVal e As
     System.EventArgs) Handles MyBase.Init
      'CODEGEN: This method call is required by the Web Form Designer
      'Do not modify it using the code editor.
      InitializeComponent()
    End Sub

  #End Region

    Private Sub Page_Load(ByVal sender As System.Object, ByVal e As
     System.EventArgs) Handles MyBase.Load
      'Put user code to initialize the page here
    End Sub

    Private Sub Button1_Click(ByVal sender As System.Object, ByVal e As
     System.EventArgs) Handles Button1.Click
      'handle the event as it pertains to the control
      Label1.Text = "Thanks for clicking!"

      'bubble the event so the parent can also respond
      Me.RaiseBubbleEvent(sender, e)
    End Sub
  End Class
```

In this file, the **code behind file**, we create an event handler for the button's click event. In the handler, we deal with the event, in this case changing the label text, and then bubble the event up so the parent control can also react to the event. As you will see below, in the code behind for a page containing the above control, we can then deal with this event when it bubbles up to page level.

This is the ASP.NET page, and is available for download as BubbleParent.aspx:

```
  <%@ Page language="c#" Codebehind="BubbleParent.aspx.cs" AutoEventWireup="false"
  Inherits="AspProgRefChap3.BubbleParent" %>
  <%@ Register TagPrefix="WROX" TagName="Bubbler" src="Bubbler.ascx" %>
```

```
<!DOCTYPE HTML PUBLIC "-//W3C//DTD HTML 4.0 Transitional//EN" >
<HTML>
  <HEAD>
  </HEAD>
  <BODY>
    <FORM id="Form1" method="post" runat="server">
      <asp:Label id="Label1" runat="server">Label</asp:Label>
      <BR>
      <BR>
      <WROX:BUBBLER id="bubbler" runat="server">
      </WROX:BUBBLER>
    </FORM>
  </BODY>
</HTML>
```

This is the Code Behind file for the main ASP.NET page, available as `BubbleParent.aspx.cs`:

```
using System;
using System.Collections;
using System.ComponentModel;
using System.Data;
using System.Drawing;
using System.Web;
using System.Web.SessionState;
using System.Web.UI;
using System.Web.UI.WebControls;
using System.Web.UI.HtmlControls;

namespace AspProgRefChap3
{
  public class BubbleParent : System.Web.UI.Page
  {
    protected System.Web.UI.WebControls.Label Label1;

    public BubbleParent()
    {
      Page.Init += new System.EventHandler(Page_Init);
    }

    protected override bool OnBubbleEvent(object sender,
    System.EventArgs e)
    {
      //handle the event at the page level
      Label1.Text = "Control <b>" + ((Control)sender).ID +
    "</b> was clicked." ;

      //return true indicating that the event has been handled
      return true;

    }
    private void Page_Load(object sender, System.EventArgs e)
    {

    }

    private void Page_Init(object sender, EventArgs e)
    {
      InitializeComponent();
    }
```

```
      private void InitializeComponent()
      {
        this.Load += new System.EventHandler(this.Page_Load);
      }

    }
  }
```

In the parent page, we override the OnBubbleEvent to handle incoming events ourselves. In this case, we simply update another label and then return true to indicate that we have handled the event. Returning false would allow the event to continue bubbling up the control hierarchy.

This event bubbling architecture is extremely powerful in that it lets you pass any kind of event up to parent objects. Using this structure, you can handle aspects of trapped events at more logical locations than when handling events only at their source.

The OnDataBinding Method

The OnDataBinding method fires the DataBinding event and indicates to the control that it should bind the data source to its controls. This method should be overridden if you are developing a custom control that will support data binding to perform the appropriate actions to enumerate the data source and add contents to your control.

```
    void OnDataBinding(eArgs)
```

Parameter	Type	Description
eArgs	EventArgs	The event arguments describing the event

The OnInit Method

The OnInit method fires the Init event to indicate that the control should initialize any values needed for the duration of the request. At this point in the process of creating a control, the child controls and view state are not accessible and therefore actions in this event handler should be limited to the current control.

```
    void OnInit(eArgs)
```

Parameter	Type	Description
eArgs	EventArgs	The event arguments describing the event

The OnLoad Method

The OnLoad method fires the Load event, which indicates that the control should ready itself to be rendered. This is the event containing the bulk of the programming to prepare the control for rendering, such as extracting data from a database and manipulating child controls.

```
    void OnLoad(eArgs)
```

Parameter	Type	Description
eArgs	EventArgs	The event arguments describing the event

The OnPreRender Method

The `OnPreRender` method fires the `PreRender` event, which means that the control should perform any actions required immediately before the view state is saved and the content rendered. At this point in the control lifecycle, the state of the control can be saved. Beyond this point, after the control has been rendered, this ability is lost.

```
void OnPreRender(eArgs)
```

Parameter	Type	Description
eArgs	EventArgs	The event arguments describing the event

The OnUnload Method

The `OnUnload` method fires the `Unload` event, which indicates that the control should perform any clean-up actions resulting from rendering the control. Expensive resources such as database connections or files should be released at this time so that they do not have to wait to be garbage collected.

```
void OnUnload(eArgs)
```

Parameter	Type	Description
eArgs	EventArgs	The event arguments describing the event

The RaiseBubbleEvent Method

The `RaiseBubbleEvent` method passes a given event up to the parent control. Use the `RaiseBubbleEvent` method in another event handler, such as for a button click, to raise an event up to the parent control, where it can be handled by the `OnBubbleEvent` method. See the `OnBubbleEvent` description for a detailed example.

```
void RaiseBubbleEvent(source, eArgs)
```

Parameter	Type	Description
source	Object	The source of the event, usually the control raising the event
eArgs	EventArgs	The event arguments describing the event

The Render Method

The `Render` method outputs content to an `HtmlTextWriter`. Overriding this method allows a control to render its content to the output stream in some other specific manner. If you would like to enable your control to participate in tracing, then the `RenderControl` method must be used instead. As with `RenderControl`, the `Render` method requires that you call `RenderChildren` to render all children (or call the `RenderControl` method for each child control if you need to be more specific about how they are rendered).

```
void Render(writer)
```

Parameter	Type	Description
writer	HtmlTextWriter	The HtmlTextWriter to write the content to

The RenderChildren Method

The RenderChildren method writes the content of the server control's child controls to the output stream. Whenever you override the Render or RenderControl methods, you should include a call to RenderChildren. This method loops through the child controls calling the RenderControl method on each. For greater control over the rendering process, a developer may instead choose to call RenderControl individually for each child control.

```
void RenderChildren(writer)
```

Parameter	Type	Description
writer	HtmlTextWriter	The HtmlTextWriter to write the content to

Example: Rendering

The following example shows a page control that overrides the Render method to handle its own display, available as Rendering.aspx:

```
<%@ Page language="c#" Codebehind="Rendering.aspx.cs" AutoEventWireup="false"
Inherits="AspProgRefChap3.Rendering" %>
<!DOCTYPE HTML PUBLIC "-//W3C//DTD HTML 4.0 Transitional//EN" >
<HTML>
  <HEAD>
    <META name="GENERATOR" content="Microsoft Visual Studio 7.0">
    <META name="CODE_LANGUAGE" content="C#">
    <META name="vs_defaultClientScript" content="JavaScript (ECMAScript)">
    <META name="vs_targetSchema"
content="http://schemas.microsoft.com/intellisense/ie5">
  </HEAD>
  <BODY ms_positioning="GridLayout">
    <FORM id="Rendering" method="post" runat="server">
    </FORM>
  </BODY>
</HTML>
```

C#: Rendering.aspx.cs

```
using System;
using System.Collections;
using System.ComponentModel;
using System.Data;
using System.Drawing;
using System.Web;
using System.Web.SessionState;
using System.Web.UI;
using System.Web.UI.WebControls;
using System.Web.UI.HtmlControls;
```

```csharp
namespace AspProgRefChap3
{
  public class Rendering : System.Web.UI.Page
  {
    public Rendering()
    {
      Page.Init += new System.EventHandler(Page_Init);
    }

    private void Page_Load(object sender, System.EventArgs e)
    {}

    private void Page_Init(object sender, EventArgs e)
    {
      InitializeComponent();
    }

    protected override void Render(HtmlTextWriter writer)
    {
      //do our own custom rendering of the parent control
      writer.Write("<h2>Custom Rendering</h2>");

      //call the render method on all of the child controls
      //commenting out the following line will result in only the
      //above text being displayed by the client
      this.RenderChildren(writer);
    }

    private void InitializeComponent()
    {
      this.Load += new System.EventHandler(this.Page_Load);
    }
  }
}
```

VB: Rendering.aspx.vb

```vbnet
Public Class Rendering
    Inherits System.Web.UI.Page

    'This call is required by the Web Form Designer.
    <System.Diagnostics.DebuggerStepThrough()> Private Sub InitializeComponent()

    End Sub

    Private Sub Page_Init(ByVal sender As System.Object, ByVal e As _
                                                System.EventArgs)
     Handles MyBase.Init
        InitializeComponent()
    End Sub

    Private Sub Page_Load(ByVal sender As System.Object, ByVal e As _
                                                System.EventArgs)
     Handles MyBase.Load
        'Put user code to initialize the page here
    End Sub

    Protected Overrides Sub Render(ByVal writer As HtmlTextWriter)
      'do our own custom rendering of the parent control
      writer.Write("<h2>Custom Rendering</h2>")
```

```
         'call the render method on all of the child controls
         'commenting out the following line will result in only the
         'above text being displayed by the client
        Me.RenderChildren(writer)
     End Sub

  End Class
```

In the `Render` method, we use the `HtmlTextWriter` passed as an argument to write any content that we wish to render on the client. We then call the `RenderChildren` method, passing the same `HtmlTextWriter` used to render the current control. To see what would happen when this method is not called, simply remove (or comment out) the call to `RenderChildren`, which should result in only content that we specifically wrote to the `HtmlTextWriter` appearing on the client page.

The SaveViewState Method

The `SaveViewState` method returns an object representing the view state of the control. This view state allows information to persist between page calls and is passed in hidden form fields inside the HTML.

```
    object SaveViewState()
```

The TrackViewState Method

The `TrackViewState` method initiates tracking of the control's state by the ASP.NET runtime. This method is used when creating templated databound controls to ensure that their state is properly monitored for view state.

Example: Databound Templated Control

This example uses a simple databound control to demonstrate some basic features of the `Control` class. Most importantly, this example shows a custom implementation for saving and loading view state. The control created provides an Item Template and an Alternating Item template which allows the developer to specify different templates according to the position of the element in the data source. In addition, the style for the Item and Alternating Item templates can be specified.

The `UserControlHost.aspx` file listed below shows how this control is used:

```
<%@ Page language="c#" Codebehind="UserControlHost.aspx.cs"
AutoEventWireup="false" Inherits="AspProgRefChap3.UserControlHost" %>
<%@ Register TagPrefix="WROX" Namespace="AspProgRefChap3"
Assembly="AspProgRefChap3"%>
<!DOCTYPE HTML PUBLIC "-//W3C//DTD HTML 4.0 Transitional//EN" >
<HTML>
  <HEAD>
  </HEAD>
  <BODY ms_positioning="FlowLayout">
    <FORM id="UserControlHost" method="post" runat="server">
      <WROX:ViewStateControl id="statecontrol" runat="server">
        <ITEMTEMPLATE>
          Item Color:
          <%# Container.DataItem %>
          <BR>
        </ITEMTEMPLATE>
        <ITEMSTYLE backcolor="gray">
        </ITEMSTYLE>
        <ALTERNATINGITEMTEMPLATE>
          Alternating Item Color:
```

```
            <%# Container.DataItem %>
            <BR>
         </ALTERNATINGITEMTEMPLATE>
         <ALTERNATINGITEMSTYLE backcolor="Yellow">
         </ALTERNATINGITEMSTYLE>
      </WROX:ViewStateControl>
      <ASP:BUTTON id="postbackbutton" runat="server"
      text="post back"></ASP:BUTTON>
    </FORM>
  </BODY>
</HTML>
```

Notice that our `Register` directive at the top of the page has changed to indicate that we are loading a control from an assembly rather than a User Control file (`.ascx`). This allows us to create element tag names with the given prefix that correspond to a control class in our assembly. In this case, `WROX:ViewStateControl` points to the `ViewStateControl` class defined in our code.

In the code file itself, we build a fairly complex control that allows for this templating and styling along with databinding and state management. Note that this is not a code behind file, but rather a stand alone C# code file.

C#: ViewStateControl.cs

```csharp
using System;
using System.Collections;
using System.Web.UI;
using System.Web.UI.WebControls;
using System.ComponentModel;

namespace AspProgRefChap3
{
  /// <summary>
  /// The ViewStateControl class is a very simple, in fact incomplete
  /// example of a DataBound templated control used to show how the
  /// LoadViewState and SaveViewState methods might be used.
  /// </summary>
  [DefaultProperty("Text"),
  ToolboxData("<{0}:ViewStateControl runat=server></{0}:ViewStateControl>")]
  public class ViewStateControl : System.Web.UI.WebControls.WebControl,
                                                    INamingContainer
  {
    //variables for the templates and datasource
    private ITemplate m_ItemTemplate;
    private ITemplate m_AlternatingItemTemplate;
    private IEnumerable m_DataSource;
    private ViewStateContainer m_Container;

    //style variables
    private Style m_ItemStyle;
    private Style m_AlternatingItemStyle;

    //datasource property allowing for a collection
    //to be bound to the control
    public IEnumerable DataSource
    {
      get{return m_DataSource;}
      set{m_DataSource=value;}
    }
```

```
//The ItemTemplate property allowing for an ItemTemplate
//to be specified in the HTML. The continaer for this
//template is indicated as the ViewStateContainer defined below
[TemplateContainer(typeof(ViewStateContainer))]
public ITemplate ItemTemplate
{
  get{return m_ItemTemplate;}
  set{m_ItemTemplate=value;}
}
```

```
//alternating item template property
[TemplateContainer(typeof(ViewStateContainer))]
public ITemplate AlternatingItemTemplate
{
  get{return m_AlternatingItemTemplate;}
  set{m_AlternatingItemTemplate=value;}
}
```

```
public Style ItemStyle
{
  get{return m_ItemStyle;}
  set{m_ItemStyle=value;}
}
```

```
public Style AlternatingItemStyle
{
  get{return m_AlternatingItemStyle;}
  set{m_AlternatingItemStyle=value;}
}
```

```
//overriden databind method which creates instances of the
//container class and instantiates the template in the
//container
public override void DataBind()
{
  base.OnDataBinding(EventArgs.Empty);

  //clear any child controls and their state.
  Controls.Clear();
  ClearChildViewState();

  //make sure we have a datasource and at least one template
  if((m_DataSource!=null) && (m_ItemTemplate!=null))
  {
    IEnumerator Item = m_DataSource.GetEnumerator();
    int Counter =1;
    while(Item.MoveNext())
    {
      //create the container
      m_Container = new ViewStateContainer(this,Item.Current);
      if((Counter%2)!=0)
      {
        m_ItemTemplate.InstantiateIn(m_Container);
        m_Container.ApplyStyle(m_ItemStyle);
      }
      else
      {
        if(m_AlternatingItemTemplate != null)
        {
          m_AlternatingItemTemplate.InstantiateIn(m_Container);
          m_Container.ApplyStyle(m_AlternatingItemStyle);
```

```
        }
        else
        {
          m_ItemTemplate.InstantiateIn(m_Container);
          m_Container.ApplyStyle(m_ItemStyle);
        }
      }

      //make sure the container binds the data and add it to
      //the controls collection
      m_Container.DataBind();
      Controls.Add(m_Container);
      Counter++;
    }
  }

  //indicate that we have created our child controls and that
  //view state should be tracked for our control
  ChildControlsCreated=true;
  TrackViewState();
}
```

```
//override the saveviewstate method to manage
//the saving of our object state
protected override object SaveViewState()
{
  object basestate = base.SaveViewState();
  object ItemStyleState = (m_ItemStyle != null) ?
                  ((IStateManager)m_ItemStyle).SaveViewState() : null;
  object AlternatingItemStyleState = (m_AlternatingItemStyle != null) ?
        ((IStateManager)m_AlternatingItemStyle).SaveViewState() : null;

  object[] thisstate = new object[3];
  thisstate[0] = basestate;
  thisstate[1] = ItemStyleState;
  thisstate[2] = AlternatingItemStyleState;

  return thisstate;

}
```

```
//override the loadviewstate method to control the
//loading of our style information
protected override void LoadViewState(object state)
{
  if(state!= null)
  {
    object[] innerstate = (object[])state;

    if(innerstate[0]!=null)
      base.LoadViewState(innerstate[0]);
    if(innerstate[1]!=null)
      ((IStateManager)m_AlternatingItemStyle).LoadViewState(innerstate[1]);
    if(innerstate[2]!=null)
      ((IStateManager)m_ItemStyle).LoadViewState(innerstate[2]);
  }
}
```

```
}
```

```
/// <summary>
/// The ViewStateContainer class acts as a container to the
```

```
    /// ItemTemplate and AlternatingItemTemplate objects allowing
    /// for the Container.DataItem syntax through its DataItem
    /// property
    /// </summary>
    public class ViewStateContainer: Label, INamingContainer
    {
      ViewStateControl parent;
      object m_DataItem;

      public ViewStateContainer(ViewStateControl parent, object DataItem)
      {
        this.parent = parent;
        m_DataItem = DataItem;
      }

      public object DataItem
      {
        get{return m_DataItem;}
        set{m_DataItem=value;}
      }
    }
  }
}
```

VB: ViewStateControl.vb

```
Imports System.ComponentModel
Imports System.Web.UI

<DefaultProperty("Text"), ToolboxData("<{0}:ViewStateControl
runat=server></{0}:ViewStateControl>")> Public Class ViewStateControl
  Inherits System.Web.UI.WebControls.WebControl
  Implements INamingContainer

  'variables for the templates and datasource
  Private m_ItemTemplate As ITemplate
  Private m_AlternatingItemTemplate As ITemplate
  Private m_DataSource As IEnumerable
  Private m_Container As ViewStateContainer

  'style variables
  Private m_ItemStyle As Style
  Private m_AlternatingItemStyle As Style

  'datasource property allowing for a collection
  'to be bound to the control
  Property DataSource() As IEnumerable

    Get
      Return m_DataSource
    End Get

    Set(ByVal Value As IEnumerable)
      m_DataSource = Value
    End Set

  End Property

    'The ItemTemplate property allowing for an ItemTemplate
    'to be specified in the HTML. The contianer for this
    'template is indicated as the ViewStateContainer defined below
```

```
<TemplateContainer(GetType(ViewStateContainer))> Property ItemTemplate() As ITemplate

  Get
    Return m_ItemTemplate
  End Get

  Set(ByVal Value As ITemplate)
    m_ItemTemplate = Value
  End Set

End Property

'alternating item template property
<TemplateContainer(GetType(ViewStateContainer))> Property &_
                              AlternatingItemTemplate() As ITemplate

  Get

    Return m_AlternatingItemTemplate
  End Get

  Set(ByVal Value As ITemplate)
    m_AlternatingItemTemplate = Value
  End Set

End Property

Property ItemStyle() As Style

  Get
    Return m_ItemStyle
  End Get

  Set(ByVal Value As Style)
    m_ItemStyle = Value
  End Set

End Property

Property AlternatingItemStyle() As Style

  Get
    Return m_AlternatingItemStyle
  End Get

  Set(ByVal Value As Style)
    m_AlternatingItemStyle = Value
  End Set

End Property

'overriden databind method which creates instances of the
'container class and instantiates the template in the
'container
Public Overrides Sub DataBind()

  MyBase.OnDataBinding(EventArgs.Empty)

  'clear any child controls and their state.
  Controls.Clear()
```

```
    ClearChildViewState()

    'make sure we have a datasource and at least one template
    If (Not (m_DataSource Is Nothing) And Not (m_ItemTemplate Is Nothing)) Then

      Dim Item As IEnumerator
      Item = m_DataSource.GetEnumerator()
      Dim Counter As Integer = 1

      While (Item.MoveNext())

        'create the container
        Dim m_Container As New ViewStateContainer(Me, Item.Current)
        If ((Counter Mod 2) <> 0) Then
          m_ItemTemplate.InstantiateIn(m_Container)
          m_Container.ApplyStyle(m_ItemStyle)
        Else
          If (Not m_AlternatingItemTemplate Is Nothing) Then
            m_AlternatingItemTemplate.InstantiateIn(m_Container)
            m_Container.ApplyStyle(m_AlternatingItemStyle)
          Else
            m_ItemTemplate.InstantiateIn(m_Container)
            m_Container.ApplyStyle(m_ItemStyle)
          End If

        End If

        'make sure the container binds the data and add it to
        'the controls collection
        m_Container.DataBind()
        Controls.Add(m_Container)
        Counter = Counter + 1
      End While
    End If

    'indicate that we have created our child controls and that
    'view state should be tracked for our control
    ChildControlsCreated = True
    TrackViewState()
End Sub
```

```
  'override the saveviewstate method to manage
  'the saving of our object state
  Protected Overrides Function SaveViewState() As Object

    Dim basestate As Object = MyBase.SaveViewState()
    Dim ItemStyleState As Object
    If (Not m_ItemStyle Is Nothing) Then
      ItemStyleState = CType(m_ItemStyle, IStateManager).SaveViewState()
    Else
      ItemStyleState = Nothing
    End If

    Dim AlternatingItemStyleState As Object
    If (Not m_AlternatingItemStyle Is Nothing) Then
      AlternatingItemStyleState = CType(m_AlternatingItemStyle,_
                          IStateManager).SaveViewState()
    Else
      AlternatingItemStyleState = Nothing
    End If
```

```vb
      Dim thisstate(3) As Object
      thisstate(0) = basestate
      thisstate(1) = ItemStyleState
      thisstate(2) = AlternatingItemStyleState

      Return thisstate

   End Function


   'override the loadviewstate method to control the
   'loading of our style information
   Protected Overrides Sub LoadViewState(ByVal state As Object)

      If (Not state Is Nothing) Then

        Dim innerstate() As Object = CType(state, Object())

        If (Not innerstate(0) Is Nothing) Then

          MyBase.LoadViewState(innerstate(0))
        End If
        If (Not innerstate(1) Is Nothing) Then
          CType(m_AlternatingItemStyle, IStateManager).LoadViewState(innerstate(1))
        End If

        If (Not innerstate(2) Is Nothing) Then
          CType(m_ItemStyle, IStateManager).LoadViewState(innerstate(2))
        End If
      End If
   End Sub
End Class
```

VB: ViewStateContainer.vb

```vb
'/ <summary>
'/ The ViewStateContainer class acts as a container to the
'/ ItemTemplate and AlternatingItemTemplate objects allowing
'/ for the Container.DataItem syntax through its DataItem
'/ property
'/ </summary>
Public Class ViewStateContainer
  Inherits Label
  Implements INamingContainer

  Private m_parent As ViewStateControl
  Private m_DataItem As Object

  Sub New(ByVal thisparent As ViewStateControl, ByVal DataItem As Object)

    Me.m_parent = thisparent
    m_DataItem = DataItem
  End Sub

  Property DataItem() As Object

    Get
      Return m_DataItem
    End Get

    Set(ByVal Value As Object)
      m_DataItem = Value
```

119

```
      End Set
    End Property

  End Class
```

There is a lot going on in this code, so I will try to pick out a few key areas to aid understanding. First off, we define some private variables and their corresponding property accessors that allow consumers of our control to set templates for items and alternating items as well as their styles. We also have a DataSource property that allows a collection to be set as the source for our information. We override the DataBind method to instantiate our templates, and begin by clearing the child controls and any child view state to ensure that the new data we apply will be the only data in the controls. Next, we create an instance of our simple container class with a single property, and we instantiate our template in this class.

Once our template is loaded into the container, we apply the style indicated and call the DataBind method on the container. Finally, we indicate that we have created the child controls, and ensure that view state is tracked for our control, by the TrackViewState method.

In this example we have overridden the LoadViewState and SaveViewState methods in order to customize the way state is persisted. For the purposes of the sample, we are simply putting the styles for our templates into the view state along with the base class state. We then load this same state and apply it to the styles for the control.

Control Class Public Properties

- ❑ ClientID
- ❑ Controls
- ❑ EnableViewState
- ❑ ID
- ❑ NamingContainer
- ❑ Page
- ❑ Parent
- ❑ Site
- ❑ TemplateSourceDirectory
- ❑ UniqueID
- ❑ Visible

The ClientID Property (read-only)

The ClientID property refers to the ID generated by ASP.NET for the control. Every control on a page is given a unique ID when the page is processed. These IDs appear in the control tree when tracing is enabled.

```
string = ClientID
```

The Controls Property (read-only)

The Controls property returns a ControlCollection consisting of all child controls contained in the given control. The ControlCollection is simply a collection class specifically designed to hold Control objects. You can use this property to add child controls, manipulate child controls, or iterate through performing actions on each control.

```
ControlCollection = Controls
```

The EnableViewState Property

The `EnableViewState` property indicates whether the control maintains state across HTTP requests. This property should be set to `false` if state is not maintained, such as when content is refreshed with data from a database. The default value for this property is `true`.

```
boolean = EnableViewState
EnableViewState = boolean
```

The ID Property

The `ID` property indicates the ID for the control. The value in this property corresponds to the `ID` attribute of the control as it appears in the HTML of a web form. This ID will also match the name of the variable in the code behind file that implements the control.

```
String = ID
ID = String
```

The NamingContainer Property (read-only)

The `NamingContainer` property indicates the control that acts as a container for the given control. Naming containers create a namespace of sorts to ensure that items in the page have a unique ID. Many controls are created with generic names such as `ctrl0` and User Controls could easily have items with an ID identical to an item on the containing page. There are many opportunities for naming collisions, and naming containers provide one mechanism for reducing these collisions. The control returned by this property will be the first control above this one in the hierarchy of the `INamingContainer` interface. This property can be useful for finding other controls being processed, such as other controls on a particular level of a page. You can retrieve the naming container for the control and then use the `FindControl` method on the naming container to find another control in this "namespace".

```
Control = NamingContainer
```

The Page Property (read-only)

The `Page` property gets a reference to the `Page` object hosting the current control. For a `Page` object, this reference will be equal to the `this` or `me` self-reference. For a user control or other contained control, this property can be helpful for accessing the properties and methods of the parent `Page` class.

```
Page = Page
```

The Parent Property (read-only)

The `Parent` property indicates the control immediately containing the current control.

```
Control = Parent
```

The Site Property (read-only)

The `Site` property returns an `ISite` object for communication between a component and its container. The `ISite` object also allows an object to manage controls it contains. This property determines where a control is being hosted, for instance in a designer such as Visual Studio.NET's Web Forms designer.

```
ISite = Site
```

121

The TemplateSourceDirectory Property (read-only)

The `TemplateSourceDirectory` property indicates the virtual directory holding the page or server control that is the parent of the current control. This can be especially useful when designing user controls as it identifies the location of the page file in which a control is housed.

```
String = TemplateSourceDirectory
```

The UniqueID Property (read-only)

The `UniqueID` property indicates the fully qualified unique value for a control. This includes the naming container ID, the client ID, and the control's own ID. With naming containers, the `UniqueID` property of a control is the concatenation of the naming containers in which it resides followed by the control's ID. For example, a server-side label control with an ID of `outputlabel` residing in a `DataList` with an ID of `List` would have a `UniqueID` of `List:ctrl0:outputlabel`, where `ctrl0` is the templated control from the `DataList`. In order to be a naming container, a control must implement the `INamingContainer` interface. This interface does not define any public methods or properties, but serves to indicate that the control acts as a naming container.

```
String = UniqueID
```

The Visible Property

The `Visible` property indicates whether the control is to be visibly displayed on the client. The default value for this property is `true`, so set it to `false` to suppress output for an element and not display it on the page.

```
Boolean = Visible
Visible = Boolean
```

Control Class Protected Properties

- ❑ `ChildControlsCreated`
- ❑ `Context`
- ❑ `Events`
- ❑ `HasChildViewState`
- ❑ `IsTrackingViewState`
- ❑ `ViewState`
- ❑ `ViewStateIgnoreCase`

These properties are not available when working with a control, and are only accessible when creating your own control and deriving from `Control`. These protected properties are most useful when working within a custom control, and would provide little benefit to the consumer of that control.

The ChildControlsCreated Property

The `ChildControlsCreated` property indicates whether the child controls of the control have already been created. If you are writing your own control, be sure to set this to `true` once you have created the child controls. Likewise, unless you particularly wish to add a new set of controls, you should check the value of this property before creating any child controls. Following this guideline will ensure that child controls are only created once.

```
Boolean = ChildControlsCreated
ChildControlsCreated=Boolean
```

The Context Property (read-only)

The `Context` property indicates the `HttpContext` for a control. If it is `null`, or `Nothing`, then the context for the parent control is returned. If that too is `null`, or `Nothing`, then the current `HttpContext` is returned. The `HttpContext` class provides access to a variety of information including error information for the request and application settings such as whether debugging and custom error handling are enabled. In addition, information about the current user, including security context, can be accessed through the `Context` property. See Chapter 2, *System.Web*, for more information about the `HttpContext` class.

```
HttpContext = Context
```

The Events Property (read-only)

The `Events` property lists the event handlers for the control. The retrieved list is an `EventHandlerList` – a rather inefficient structure for searching, so it may be slow if you have a lot of event handlers. This property allows the developer to access the delegates assigned to the events in the control and call them if required. Delegates are essentially object-oriented, type-safe function pointers. They are a primary component underlying the .NET framework event model.

```
EventHandlerList = Events
```

The HasChildViewState Property (read-only)

The `HasChildViewState` property is used to determine whether any of the controls in the current control have view state saved. You can use this property to decide if it's worth a more expensive call to the `ClearChildViewState` method.

```
Boolean = HasChildViewState
```

The IsTrackingViewState Property (read-only)

The `IsTrackingViewState` property indicates whether the control is tracking view state. This property is set to `true` when you call `TrackViewState`.

```
Boolean = IsTrackingViewState
```

The ViewState Property (read-only)

The `ViewState` property represents the `StateBag` object holding the view state of the control allowing it to maintain information between requests. A `StateBag` is essentially a dictionary object that stores name-value pairs. In the context of `ViewState`, this is the primary storage mechanism for storing and retrieving information about the attributes of a control, in order to render the control properly after a post back event. This state information is stored on the client in a hidden form field named "`__VIEWSTATE`", which allows the information to persist for the duration of multiple requests.

```
StateBag = ViewState
```

The ViewStateIgnoreCase Property (read-only)

The `ViewStateIgnoreCase` property indicates whether the `StateBag` object that stores the view state of the control is case-sensitive in its handling of the key values used to identify inserted objects. The default value for this property is `true`, indicating that it is not case-sensitive. If the value is `false`, then the view state is case-sensitive, and more than one value can share the same name as long as their case is different. Note that this does not pertain to the values saved to view state, only the keys. The case of values placed a `StateBag` object will always be maintained.

```
Boolean = ViewStateIgnoreCase
```

For example, if we want to save the state of two items with the same name, but different case, we need to ensure this property is set to `false`.

```
If(ViewStateIgnoreCase == false)
{
  This.ViewState.Add("myvalue", 2);
  This.ViewState.Add("MyValue",3);
}
```

Control Class Events

- ❑ DataBinding
- ❑ Disposed
- ❑ Init
- ❑ Load
- ❑ PreRender
- ❑ Unload

The DataBinding Event

The `DataBinding` event is fired when a control should initiate the databinding process, by a call to the control's `DataBind` method originating from either the external user or the parent control. The event handler for catching this event should manage the binding of items in the control to the data source.

```
EventHandler = DataBinding
```

Example: Databinding

If we want to have a User Control allow databinding, we can give it a data source property and place our databinding code in the `DataBinding` event handler, as in the sample, `Binding.ascx`, below:

C#: Binding.ascx.cs
```
namespace AspProgRefChap3
{
  using System;
  using System.Collections;
  using System.Data;
  using System.Drawing;
  using System.Web;
  using System.Web.UI;
  using System.Web.UI.WebControls;
  using System.Web.UI.HtmlControls;
```

```
public abstract class Binding : System.Web.UI.UserControl
{
   IEnumerable mDataSource; //our internal datasource member

   public Binding()
   {
      this.Init += new System.EventHandler(Page_Init);
   }

   //create property for our control to allow developers
   //to set and get the datasoure of our control
   public IEnumerable DataSource
   {
      get{return mDataSource;}
      set{mDataSource=value;}

   }

   //this method acts as our event handler for the databinding event
   protected void Page_DataBind(object sender, EventArgs e)
   {
      //make sure the datasource has been set before acting on it
      if(mDataSource!=null)
      {
         //clear any child controls and child view state
         ClearChildViewState();
         Controls.Clear();

         //start an unordered list for items
         Controls.Add(new LiteralControl("<ul>"));

         //get an enumerator from our datasource so we can walk
         //the collection
         IEnumerator Enumerator = mDataSource.GetEnumerator();

         //while we still have data, move to the next item
         while(Enumerator.MoveNext())
         {
            //add a literal control which is a list item
            //containing the data item
            Controls.Add(new LiteralControl(
                                 "<li>" + Enumerator.Current.ToString()));
         }

         //add the closing tag for our list
         Controls.Add(new LiteralControl("</ul>"));
      }

   }
   private void Page_Load(object sender, System.EventArgs e)
   {}

   private void Page_Init(object sender, EventArgs e)
   {
      InitializeComponent();
   }

   private void InitializeComponent()
   {
      this.Load += new System.EventHandler(this.Page_Load);
```

```
        //add our Page_DataBind method as an event handler
        //for the DataBinding event
        this.DataBinding += new System.EventHandler(this.Page_DataBind);
    }

  }
}
```

VB: Binding.ascx.vb

```
Public MustInherit Class Binding
    Inherits System.Web.UI.UserControl

  'our internal variable
  Protected mDataSource As IEnumerable

  'create a property to allow for setting the datasource
  Property DataSource() As IEnumerable
    Get
      Return mDataSource
    End Get
    Set(ByVal Value As IEnumerable)
      mDataSource = Value
    End Set
  End Property

  Protected Sub Page_DataBind(ByVal sender As Object, ByVal eArgs As EventArgs)_
                                          Handles MyBase.DataBinding
    'make sure the datasource has been set before acting on it
    If Not mDataSource Is Nothing Then

      'clear any child controls and child view state
      ClearChildViewState()
      Controls.Clear()

      'start an unordered list for items
      Controls.Add(New LiteralControl("<ul>"))

      'get an enumerator from our datasource so we can walk
      'the collection
      Dim Enumerator As IEnumerator = mDataSource.GetEnumerator()

      'while we still have data, move to the next item
      While Enumerator.MoveNext()

        'add a literal control which is a list item containing
        'the data item
        Controls.Add(New LiteralControl("<li>" + Enumerator.Current.ToString()))
      End While

      'add the closing tag for our list as a literal control
      Controls.Add(New LiteralControl("</ul>"))
    End If

  End Sub

  Private Sub Page_Load(ByVal sender As System.Object, ByVal e As
```

```
System.EventArgs) Handles MyBase.Load
  End Sub

  <System.Diagnostics.DebuggerStepThrough()> Private Sub InitializeComponent()
  End Sub

  Private Sub Page_Init(ByVal sender As System.Object, ByVal e As_
                            System.EventArgs) Handles MyBase.Init
    InitializeComponent()
  End Sub
End Class
```

The first thing we do is create a `DataSource` property that allows a user to provide a collection from which we can build our control. We also create an internal variable to hold it. Next, we define our `Page_DataBind` method, which will act as event handler. This method resets the child control values, then walks through the items in the data source creating list items for each, and adding them to the child control collection. To bind data to this control, the consumer would use code such as the following:

C#

```
//create a datasource
ArrayList List = new ArrayList(3);
List.Add("Red");
List.Add("Blue");
List.Add("Orange");

//set the datasource property of our control
//using the findcontrol method here and the id of the control
//as it was set in the HTML
((Binding)this.FindControl("binding")).DataSource=List;

//call DataBind to cause the page and all of it's controls to execute
//their data binding event handlers.
DataBind();
```

VB.NET

```
'create a data source
Dim List As New ArrayList(3)
List.Add("Red")
List.Add("Blue")
List.Add("Orange")

'set the datasource property of our control
'using the findcontrol method and the id of
'the control as it was set in the HTML
CType(FindControl("binding"), Binding).DataSource = List
DataBind()
```

The Disposed Event

The `Disposed` event is fired as the last step in the server control lifecycle. In this event handler, all resources such as database connections or open files should be released so that they do not have to wait until garbage collection before being made available again. In a high traffic site, this step is critical as it releases resources much sooner than the garbage collection process.

```
EventHandler = Disposed
```

The Init Event

The Init event is the first event in the processing of a server control. In this event, a control can be initialized by setting up variables and postback data. However, other controls in the control hierarchy are not guaranteed to be accessible at this time and require use of the Load event to work with them.

```
EventHandler = Init
```

The Load Event

The Load event is fired when a control is loaded onto the page. Other controls are available at this time to manipulate, or use in manipulating the current control. The Load event is where the bulk of control processing occurs. Tasks such as loading data, reading from files, and any other activity required to prepare your control to be rendered or further processed should be located inside this event handler.

```
EventHandler = Load
```

The PreRender Event

When PreRender event is fired, a control must undertake any tasks that need to be accomplished just before being rendered. In the handler for this event, view state should be saved as this is the last opportunity to do so before the control is rendered. For example, if your control has a property, say Size, that can be manipulated by other controls, then that property should be saved to view state at this time.

```
EventHandler = PreRender
```

The Unload Event

The Unload event indicates that a control has been processed and is ready to unload. In this event handler, perform any clean-up tasks for the control such as disposing of resources, closing connections and so on. This event is strongly related to the Disposed event, but the Unload event occurs just before the Disposed event. Either is a good place to put this important clean up code. The Disposed event aligns more closely with the .NET model for cleaning up resources, allowing the consumer of the control to call the Dispose method explicitly to indicate when the control should clean up resources.

```
EventHandler = Unload
```

The Page Class

The Page class represents a single web page. Deriving from the Control class and TemplateClass, it already has a great deal of functionality. On top of these inherited features, the Page class adds a variety of methods and properties that affect everything in the scope of the web page, including items such as the MIME content-type, form fields, script blocks, and transactions.

Page Class Public Properties

- ❑ Application
- ❑ Cache
- ❑ ClientTarget
- ❑ EnableViewState

- ❏ ErrorPage
- ❏ ID
- ❏ IsPostBack
- ❏ IsValid
- ❏ Request
- ❏ Response
- ❏ Server
- ❏ SmartNavigation
- ❏ Trace
- ❏ User
- ❏ Validators
- ❏ Visible

The Application Property (read-only)

The `Application` property is an object of class `HttpApplicationState` that contains state data for the web application in which the `Page` is running. The object returned allows information to be shared among pages in the application. The `Application` object acts as a collection of key-value pairs where any object type can be stored and shared among pages. This object is similar in functionality to the intrinsic `Application` object of traditional ASP.

```
HttpApplicationState = Application
```

Because objects in the application are shared among all its users, the `HttpApplicationState` object supports locking in order to maintain thread synchronization. This mechanism ensures that only one thread at a time can work with the application's state values. Because this locking prevents other threads accessing the object, it is important to release the lock as soon as possible by calling the `Unlock` method. Below is an example that updates values of the `Application` object. Notice that we lock the values first so that another thread cannot update the `SharedValue` member before we get a chance to update our second value.

```
Application.Lock()
Application.Item("SharedValue") = "Value to be shared"
Application.Item("SharedValueCount") =
Application.Item("SharedValue").ToString().Length
Application.Unlock()
```

The Cache Property (read-only)

The `Cache` property represents a `Cache` object, which allows caching data on the web server in order to improve performance. See Chapter 7, *Caching & System.Web.Caching*, for more information on the `Cache` object.

```
Cache = Cache
```

The ClientTarget Property

The `ClientTarget` property indicates the target browser for the page. Use this property to indicate whether the page is targeted at uplevel browsers such as IE 5, which support recent standards such as HTML 4.0, and the MS DOM (Document Object Model). downlevel browsers are assumed to support HTML 3.2. The options available for this property are defined in the `machine.config` file within the `clientTarget` element and provide a value with a corresponding browser type. See Chapter 8, *Configuration & System.Web.Configuration*.

```
String = ClientTarget
```

The `ClientTarget` property can also be set in the `Page` declaration of an `.aspx` file, as here:

```
<%@ Page language="c#" Codebehind="WebForm1.aspx.cs" ClientTarget="downlevel"
Inherits="Chap3_c.WebForm1"%>
```

Use this property to override the default behavior of the page and user controls, for example if you want your page to produce `downlevel` content, even if the client is IE 5+. This provides a common look and feel across browsers at the expense of features that only exist in the richer browsers.

The EnableViewState Property

The `EnableViewState` property indicates whether view state will be saved for the page and its child controls. Disabling view state prevents controls from maintaining state between web page requests. Therefore, if the page is posted back, those controls not responsible for the post back will not maintain their state and corresponding information may have to be re-entered by the user. The default value of this property is `true`.

```
Boolean = EnableViewState
```

The ErrorPage Property

The `ErrorPage` property provides the path to an error page that responses should be redirected to if unhandled exceptions occur while processing the page. Responses will only be directed to this page when the `CustomErrors` element in the `web.config` file has its `mode` attribute set to `On` or `RemoteOnly`. The options for the `CustomErrors` mode attribute include `On`, which allows custom error pages to be shown, `RemoteOnly`, which allows custom errors to be shown only to clients other than the local machine, and `Off`, indicating that custom errors will not be displayed for any user.

```
string = ErrorPage
```

The ID Property

The `ID` property represents a unique ID for the page. This property is an overridden version of the `ID` property found on the `Control` class.

```
string = ID
ID = string
```

The IsPostBack Property (read-only)

The `IsPostBack` property indicates whether the current request for the page is the result of a post-back event. Post back is the mechanism allowing server-side controls to be processed on the server. Certain controls, such as buttons, image buttons, and so on, automatically post back to the server. When they do so, their post-back event, such as a button click, is fired and can be handled. It is important to check this property when loading the page to avoid any processing that only needs to be done on the first request for the page. For example, if you load data into a datagrid, by only doing so when the page is first loaded, you save the cost of connecting to the database and querying it for every subsequent request that uses the same data. To look at it another way, when `IsPostBack` is `false`, the page is being loaded for the first time, and should be processed appropriately. When this property is `true`, then the focus is on processing events from server-side controls, not on loading data and preparing the page.

This property will only be true if the request is a post back, not simply if the request is the result of a form on the page posting to itself. For example, if you create a standard, client-side form in your .aspx file and set its Action property to reference the same .aspx file, this value will remain false.

```
Boolean = IsPostBack
```

The IsValid Property (read-only)

The IsValid property indicates whether the information posted to the page is valid. When using validation controls such as the RegularExpressionValidator, this property is set to true or false according to whether the validation of the content succeeds for each of the validation controls. This property can be used to conditionally act on values passed in. For example, if data is posted to the page to be inserted in a database, you should test the IsValid property before updating the database. To ensure that all validation controls have processed their respective input, you should call the Validate method of the Page object before checking this property, to force the validation controls to perform the checks necessary for the IsValid property.

```
Boolean = IsValid
```

The Request Property (read-only)

The Request property indicates the current HttpRequest that was posted to the server. This object allows access to returned forms, cookie information, browser capabilities, and more. In essence, it wraps up all of the information about the incoming network request from client. See Chapter 2, *System.Web*, for more information on the HttpRequest object.

```
HttpRequest = Request
```

The Response Property (read-only)

The Response property indicates the HttpResponse object that is being sent to the client, and is used for operations such as setting cookies and creating UI elements. The Response object encompasses everything that has to be passed back to the client. See Chapter 2, *System.Web*, for more information.

```
HttpResponse = Response
```

The Server Property

The Server property allows access to an HttpServerUtility object housing utility functions for use in web applications, for instance to create COM components or execute other .aspx pages. See Chapter 2, *System.Web*, for more information on the ServerUtility class.

```
HttpServerUtility = Server
```

The SmartNavigation Property

The SmartNavigation property indicates whether Smart Navigation is enabled. Smart Navigation uses advanced DHTML features to offer a smoother UI experience by using enhanced JavaScript to only post back IFrames and other sections of the page to retrieve only those parts of the page that are to be refreshed. To see how this works, view the SmartNav.js and SmartNavIE5.js files in the asp_client folder. These files can be found under the root directory of your web server. A typical path is:

```
C:\Inetpub\wwwroot\aspnet_client\system_web\build#\
```

where build# is the current build of the .NET framework running on your system.

```
Boolean = SmartNavigation
```

The Trace Property (read-only)

The `Trace` property is a `TraceContext` object representing the tracing context of the current page execution. This object can be used to write information to the trace log, to be displayed when tracing is enabled for the control. Tracing is a new feature of ASP.NET, which eliminates the need for the `Response.Write` approach to web application debugging. Trace information is only processed when tracing is enabled for an application therefore allowing an easy mechanism for turning debug information off and on.

```
TraceContext = Trace
```

The User Property

The `User` property is an `IPrincipal` object providing information about the user accessing the site, such as the security context of the request. This property uses the `User` property of the `HttpContext` object to retrieve the `IPrincipal` object. Through this object, the developer can access the name of the user and the authentication type. In order for this property to be used, the authentication element in the `web.config` file needs to have its `Mode` attribute set to something other than `none`. See Chapter 9, *Security & System.Web.Security*, for details.

```
IPrincipal = User
```

The Validators Property

The `Validators` property denotes the collection of validation controls contained in the page, allowing easy access to update or manipulate them. Validation controls are reusable components that provide a specific form of validation for other controls on a web page. Examples include the `RequiredFieldValidator`, which checks to ensure that a user has entered a value, and the `RegularExpressionValidator`, which validates user input against a specified pattern, such as for a phone number. See Example 4 in Chapter 16, *Examples*, for a sample of how the two controls just mentioned are used.

```
ValidatorCollection = Validators
```

The Visible Property

The `Visible` property indicates whether the page is visible. When the property is set to `false`, controls, either literal or user, are not displayed when the page is rendered on the client. This does not, however, affect items that are written directly to the `HttpResponse` stream. The default value for this property is `true`.

```
Boolean = Visible
Visible = Boolean
```

Page Class Protected Properties

- ❏ `AspCompatMode`
- ❏ `Buffer`
- ❏ `CodePage`
- ❏ `ContentType`
- ❏ `Context`

❑   Culture

❑   EnableViewStateMac

❑   FileDependencies

❑   LCID

❑   ResponseEncoding

❑   TraceEnabled

❑   TraceModeValue

❑   TransactionMode

❑   UICulture

The AspCompatMode Property

The `AspCompatMode` property indicates whether the `.aspx` page runs in a mode compatible with traditional ASP. For this to be possible, the `.aspx` page must be able to run in a Single Threaded Apartment. This compatibility supports many traditional programming practices associated with ASP.

One of the reasons to run in this mode is that it lets you create Single Threaded Apartment (STA) components, such as those made in VB 6.0. If you try to create an STA COM component in an `.aspx` page without setting this property to `true`, an exception will be generated. Setting `AspCompatMode` is one way to get around this. The other is to create a wrapper around the COM component using the `tlbimp` utility or by adding a reference to your project in Visual Studio.NET. When you add a reference to a COM component from VS.NET, the wrapper is created for you automatically.

```
Boolean = AspCompatMode
```

The Buffer Property

The `Buffer` property indicates whether the page is buffered.

```
Boolean = Buffer
```

When ASP.NET pages are requested, the ASP.NET runtime begins processing the page and outputting the resulting HTML to a response stream. By default, this stream is buffered, meaning that nothing is sent to the client until the `flush` or `end` methods of the `Response` object are called. When buffering is turned off, content is streamed to the client immediately.

When page output is not buffered, once the page request begins being processed, it passes beyond a point of no return of sorts because information has begun being sent to the client. Using buffering allows more flexibility in processing the page. Buffering of page output can also improve performance for very large pages because the page can be sent to the client in sections by flushing the stream at regular intervals.

The CodePage Property (write-only)

The `CodePage` property denotes the code page in use on the page. A code page is a numeric identifier for a given encoding, such as ASCII or UTF-8. This property becomes important when dealing with multiple languages and character sets. When the application will run on a computer with a code page different to the one they were developed on, this property needs to be set on the page at development time. This ensures that when the page is run, the system knows which the encoding used for the code to read it correctly.

```
CodePage = int
```

The ContentType Property (write-only)

The ContentType property indicates the MIME type of the page content being sent to the client in the HttpResponse object. MIME types are the industry standard way of indicating content type such as XML, text, HTML, MS-Word, and so on. These types are what web browsers use to determine how to render the content. For text/html, text/xml, or text/text, for example, Internet Explorer will render the item inline. For items such as Word documents, the external application is instantiated. The default value for this property is text/html indicating that the content coming back should be interpreted as HTML text. If the type set for this property is not known on the client, most browsers attempt to deal with this by prompting the user to save the file or attempting to render it as text.

```
ContentType = string
```

The Context Property (read-only)

The Context property indicates the current HttpContext that the page is running under. The Context for the request allows access to configuration information, error collections, and the like. See Chapter 2, *System.Web*, for details of the HttpContext class.

```
HttpContext = Context
```

As an example, we can use the Context object to return a collection of the exceptions that occurred during the request for error tracking or reporting.

C#

```csharp
Exception[] e = Context.AllErrors;
for(int i=0; i< e.Length;i++)
{
    Response.Write(e[i].Message);
}
```

VB.NET

```vbnet
        Dim i As Integer

        Dim ex As Exception() = Context.AllErrors
        For i = 0 To ex.Length -1
            Response.Write(ex(i).Message)
        Next
```

The Culture Property (write-only)

The Culture property indicates the culture group applicable to the page. This affects a variety of items including currency, time, and other formatting issues.

```
Culture = string
```

As an example, the page content below outputs the date and a number formatted as currency:

```
<form id="cultform" method="post" runat="server">
    <%= DateTime.Now.ToString()%>
    <br>
    <% int i = 12345; %>
    <%= i.ToString( "c" )%>
</form>
```

For US users, this displays the following by default:

7/5/2001 10:27:12 PM
$12,345.00

However, if we add the following line to our page before outputting our content, it is rendered according to German formatting conventions:

```
<% Culture="de-DE"; %>
```

05.07.2001 22:30:08
12.345,00 €

The EnableViewStateMac Property

The `EnableViewStateMac` indicates whether the view state of controls and pages will be MAC checked. MAC or Message Authentication Code is a hashing algorithm that generates security checksums for the data in the view state. Based on the default view state framework, state information is passed between the client and the server controls via hidden form fields. Enabling this property allows the server to verify that the viewstate data has not been corrupted or tampered with since being sent to the client. While this provides more security for your site, it does come with a slight performance penalty, as the hashing requires a little processing. The default value for this property is `false`.

```
boolean = EnableViewStateMac
```

The FileDependencies Property (write-only)

The `FileDependencies` property indicates files that the current `HttpResponse` is dependent on. Use this property in conjunction with the caching of the response to make the response dependent on certain files such that if those files are updated, the cached page will be flushed and re-cached. This property internally calls the `AddFileDependencies` method of the `HttpResponse` object described in Chapter 2, *System.Web*. See Chapter 7, *Caching & System.Web.Caching* for more information on file dependencies.

```
FileDependencies=ArrayList
```

The LCID Property (write-only)

The `LCID` property indicates the locale identifier for the executing thread. This property can be used to indicate a specific locale for a page. This information can be used to tailor the output on the client to a specific region.

```
LCID = int
```

The ResponseEncoding Property (write-only)

The `ResponseEncoding` property indicates the character encoding for the outgoing response stream. This property can be used in conjunction with the `AcceptLanguages` property of the incoming `Request` to ensure that content sent to the client is compatible with the browser.

```
ResponseEncoding = string
```

The TraceEnabled Property

The `TraceEnabled` property allows for dynamically turning on tracing at the page level. Having tracing enabled causes information to be dumped to the screen including the control tree, cookies, headers, and other helpful debugging information. Tracing must be enabled in the `web.config` file for tracing to work at the page level.

```
TraceEnabled = Boolean
```

The tracing status of a page can also be set declaratively in the page-level declarations.

```
<%@ Page Trace="true" %>
```

The TraceModeValue (write-only)

The `TraceModeValue` property allows the developer to specify the order in which trace messages should be displayed when tracing is enabled for a page.

```
TraceModeValue = Mode
```

where `Mode` is an enumerated value from the `TraceMode` enumeration with one of the following values:

Value	Description
SortByCategory	Sorts the trace messages alphabetically by the category they are in
SortByTime	Sorts the trace messages by the time they were written to the trace

The TransactionMode Property

The `TransactionMode` property indicates the transactional nature of the page. By setting this value, you can indicate whether the actions taken in the page should be completed in the context of a COM+ transaction. Operations in the page that work with other resources that can be enlisted will be rolled up together into a single transaction. For instance, multiple calls to a SQL server database would be included in the transaction such that if the transaction fails, the actions in the database will be rolled back.

```
TransactionMode = TransactionOption
```

The following are the possible values for the `TransactionOption` enumeration:

Value	Description
Disabled	The page will ignore any transactions in the context in which it is created
NotSupported	The page will be explicitly created in a context without a transaction, even if that means a new context is created
Required	The page requires a transaction so if the context of the current execution is not transacted, the page will be created in a new, transacted context
RequiresNew	The page will be created in its own, new, context with a transaction
Supported	The page will participate in a transaction if one is present, but it does not require one

See the description of the `OnAbortTransaction` method of the `TemplateControl` calss for an example of a transacted web page.

The UICulture Property

The UICulture property indicates the region applicable when loading resources and elements that are culture-specific. It differs from the Culture property in that it directly relates to resources rather than the actual display of information.

```
UICulture = string
```

Page Class Public Methods

- ❑ DesignerInitialize
- ❑ GetPostBackClientEvent
- ❑ GetPostBackClientHyperlink
- ❑ GetPostBackEventReference
- ❑ GetTypeHashCode
- ❑ IsClientScriptBlockRegistered
- ❑ IsStartupScriptRegistered
- ❑ MapPath
- ❑ RegisterArrayDeclaration
- ❑ RegisterClientScriptBlock
- ❑ RegisterHiddenField
- ❑ RegisterOnSubmitStatement
- ❑ RegisterRequiresPostBack
- ❑ RegisterRequiresRaiseEvents
- ❑ RegisterStartupScript
- ❑ RegisterViewStateHandler
- ❑ Validate

The DesignerInitialize Method

The DesignerInitialize method is used by RAD environments to indicate to a control that it should do any initialization required by the development environment.

```
void DesignerInitialize()
```

The GetPostBackClientEvent Method

The GetPostBackClientEvent method retrieves a string that contains the client-side script for the post-back event of a given control with a JScript.NET prefix if the browser making the request is identified as Internet Explorer version 4 or higher.

```
String = GetPostBackClientEvent(control, argument)
```

Parameter	Type	Description
control	Control	The control that should be passed to the post-back method on the client side as the source of the post-back event
argument	String	The argument that will be passed to the post-back method

The GetPostBackClientHyperlink Method

The GetPostBackClientHyperlink method returns a string that represents a hyperlink to the client-side script call which initiates the post-back process.

```
String = GetPostBackClientHyperlink(control, argument)
```

Parameter	Type	Description
control	Control	The control that should be passed to the post-back method on the client side as the source of the post-back event
argument	String	The argument that will be passed to the post-back method

This method allows the developer to create a hyperlink that will cause the page to post back to the server.

```
<a id="link2" href="<%=GetPostBackClientHyperlink(but1,"submit")%>">Link 2</a>
```

In this example, we have created a link to the post-back method associated with the control with the ID but1, and passed in an argument of submit.

The GetPostBackEventReference Method

The GetPostBackEventReference method gets a reference to the client-side function which initiates the post back. When building the web page, it may be helpful to get a reference to the post-back script function in order to programmatically cause the page to post back to the server. The resulting function call causes the page to post back indicating that the specified control caused the post back.

```
String = GetPostBackEventReference(control)
```

Parameter	Type	Description
control	Control	The control that should be passed to the post-back method on the client side as the source of the post-back event

```
String = GetPostBackEventReference(control, argument)
```

Parameter	Type	Description
control	Control	The control that should be passed to the post-back method on the client side as the source of the post-back event
argument	String	The argument that will be passed to the post-back method

The GetTypeHashCode Method

The `GetTypeHashCode` method gets an integer value that represents a hash code for the page. This hash code is generated at run time and indicates a unique ID for the page.

```
Int = GetTypeHashCode()
```

The IsClientScriptBlockRegistered Method

The `IsClientScriptBlockRegistered` method checks to see if a given client script has already been registered. The ASP.NET framework provides for the registration of client-side scripts to avoid sending duplicate script blocks to the browser. See the `RegisterClientScriptBlock` method description for more information.

```
Boolean = IsClientScriptBlockRegistered(key)
```

Parameter	Type	Description
key	String	The key value for the client-side script block that is in question. This same key value would be used to register the block of code.

The IsStartupScriptRegistered Method

The `IsStartupScriptRegistered` method returns a Boolean value indicating whether the startup script for the page has already been registered. A startup script is identified by the developer and registered using the `RegisterStartupScript` method discussed later in this section.

```
Boolean = IsStartupScriptRegistered(key)
```

Parameter	Type	Description
key	String	The key value that uniquely identifies the script block in the page

The MapPath Method

The `MapPath` method returns a physical path for the given virtual path, which can be either relative or absolute.

```
String = MapPath(path)
```

Parameter	Type	Description
path	String	The virtual path to a directory or file for which you want the physical path

The RegisterArrayDeclaration Method

The `RegisterArrayDeclaration` method creates a client-side script block that declares an array. In addition, you can add an element to the array. Subsequent calls to this method using the same array name add further elements to the array declaration. In this way, multiple controls in a page request can add themselves or elements of their content to this array.

```
Void RegisterArrayDeclaration (arrayName, value)
```

Parameter	Type	Description
arrayName	String	The name to give to the client script variable array.
value	String	The value to be added to the array as a value. This can be the name of an object or control on the page.

For example, the following code creates a client-side array named `TextBoxes` with two elements: `TextBox1` and `TextBox2`. These contain the IDs of two different textboxes on our page, so we can loop through the array, and manipulate each in turn.

```
RegisterArrayDeclaration("TextBoxes","TextBox1");
RegisterArrayDeclaration("TextBoxes","TextBox2");
```

The output to the client looks like this:

```
<script language="javascript">
<!--
  var lnkArray = new Array(TextBox1, TextBox2);
  // -->
</script>
```

The RegisterClientScriptBlock Method

The `RegisterClientScriptBlock` method allows creation of a client-side script block with a unique ID. If multiple controls register the same block of script, they are assumed to be the same and the first block registered will take precedence. Using this method to write client-side script to the response ensures that only one copy of a given script will be sent to the client. For example, a page and a user control may both have scripts with the same declaration. If the page has registered its scripts, then the user control will not be able to overwrite them.

```
RegisterClientScriptBlock(key, script)
```

Parameter	Type	Description
key	String	The unique key name for the given script block
script	String	The block of script to be written to the client

The following example shows a registered script block and the resulting client-side code:

C#
```
RegisterClientScriptBlock("uniqueKey","<script><!--\nfunction
    client()\n{alert(\"generated function\");\n}\n--></script>");
```

VB.NET
```
RegisterClientScriptBlock("uniqueKey", _
    "<script><!--" & vbCrLf & "function client()" & vbCrLf & _
    "{alert(""generated function"");" & vbCrLf & "}" & vbCrLf & "--></script>")
```

Client-side code produced:

```
<script><!--
function client()
{alert("generated function");
}
--></script>
```

The RegisterHiddenField Method

The `RegisterHiddenField` method allows a page or control to create a hidden form field on the client. Subsequent calls to this method with the same field name will have no effect and the initial field and value will remain. This ensures that once a hidden field has been registered it cannot be overwritten.

```
Void RegisterHiddenField(key, value)
```

Parameter	Type	Description
key	String	The unique key name for the form field. The form field on the client will use this name.
value	String	The value to provide for the form field.

The RegisterOnSubmitStatement Method

The `RegisterOnSubmitStatement` connects a client-side script function to the `OnSubmit` event of the main form. This causes a block of client-side script to execute when the Submit button of a form is clicked. In this block of code, traditional form validation can take place and the form be submitted or canceled.

```
Void RegisterOnSubmitStatement(key, script)
```

Parameter	Type	Description
key	String	The unique key name for the script block
script	String	The function call for the script block to execute on submission of the form

The RegisterRequiresPostBack Method

The `RegisterRequiresPostBack` method should be called for controls on the page that require post back handling. By default, only a handful of objects require post-back handling, including `Button` and `ImageButton`. This method allows the developer to extend that collection by indicating that a given control should initiate a post back to the server for processing.

```
RegisterRequiresPostBack(control)
```

Parameter	Type	Description
control	Control	The control that requires post-back.

> Note that over-utilization of the post-back mechanism can have a negative impact on the performance of your web application as it can introduce excessive communication between client and server.

The RegisterRequiresRaiseEvents Method

The `RegisterRequiresRaiseEvents` method should be called when a given control is to have events raised when it is processed on the server. This means that, as the control is initialized, loaded, and processed, it will raise events to indicate its current stage of processing.

```
Void RegisterRequiresRaiseEvents(control)
```

Parameter	Type	Description
control	IPostBack Event Handler	The control that should raise events as it is processed

The RegisterStartupScript Method

The `RegisterStartupScript` method registers the script block to execute on page startup. This script block is written inline with the page code and should not include any function blocks. This differs from `RegisterClientScriptBlock` in that the scripts registered with this method are intended to be run when the page is processed by the client application.

```
Void RegisterStartupScript(key, script)
```

Parameter	Type	Description
key	String	The unique name for the client script block
script	String	The actual client-side script to be executed upon loading the page

The RegisterViewStateHandler Method

The `RegisterViewStateHandler` indicates to the page that it should register an object to handle the functions related to view state. Internally, this sets a flag on the page object, which indicates that view state is to be maintained.

```
Void RegisterViewStateHandler()
```

The Validate Method

The `Validate` method causes all of the validation controls on the page to execute their validation logic and set the page's `IsValid` property. Once the `Validate` method has been called, checking the `IsValid` property of the page will indicate whether any of the validation controls found errors in the input. If you check the `IsValid` property before `Validate` has been called, then the result will be invalid because the validation controls will not have been activated.

```
Void validate()
```

The `Validate` method is normally called implicitly as the result of a post back to the server by a control that causes validation by a `CausesValidation` property set to `true`. In addition, the `Validate` method can be called explicitly to force the validation process.

Example: Client-Side Registration

This example pulls together many of the methods of the `Page` class that allow registering client-side code such as scripts and arrays. The ability to register these items to avoid collisions and ensure that all client-side code gets created is important. If a UserControl exists more than one time on a given page, using these methods ensures that a client-side element will only get created one time.

ClientCodeRegistration.aspx

```
<%@ Page language="c#" Codebehind="ClientCodeRegistration.aspx.cs"
AutoEventWireup="false" Inherits="AspProgRefChap3.ClientCodeRegistration" %>
<!DOCTYPE HTML PUBLIC "-//W3C//DTD HTML 4.0 Transitional//EN" >
<HTML>
  <HEAD>
    <TITLE>Client side registration examples</TITLE>
  </HEAD>
  <BODY>
    <FORM id="ClientCodeRegistration" method="post" runat="server">
      <BR>
      <ASP:TEXTBOX textmode="SingleLine" id="text" runat="server"></ASP:TEXTBOX>
      <BR>
      <asp:button id="Button1" runat="server" Text="Button"></asp:button>
      <BR>
      <A href="" id="postbacklink"
       runat="server">Dynamically generated postback</A>
      <BR>
      <BR>
      <A href="javascript:ChangeText()">Change Text Boxes</A>
      <BR>
      <asp:TextBox id="TextBox1" runat="server"></asp:TextBox>
      <BR>
      <asp:TextBox id="TextBox2" runat="server"></asp:TextBox>
      <BR>
    </FORM>
  </BODY>
</HTML>
```

In this page, we have several controls defined to use with our client-side script. The button Button1 serves as the submit button for our form, while the link anchor element will be dynamically set to initiate the post back. The next anchor tag points to a JavaScript function which will be registered on the client by the code behind. The text boxes serve as targets for the `ChangeText` script function.

C#: ClientCodeRegistration.aspx.cs

```
using System;
using System.Collections;
using System.ComponentModel;
using System.Data;
using System.Drawing;
using System.Text;            //needed for string builder
using System.Web;
using System.Web.SessionState;
using System.Web.UI;
using System.Web.UI.WebControls;
using System.Web.UI.HtmlControls;
```

```csharp
namespace AspProgRefChap3
{
  public class ClientCodeRegistration : System.Web.UI.Page
  {
    protected System.Web.UI.WebControls.Button Button1;
    protected System.Web.UI.WebControls.TextBox text;
    protected System.Web.UI.WebControls.TextBox TextBox1;
    protected System.Web.UI.WebControls.TextBox TextBox2;
    protected System.Web.UI.HtmlControls.HtmlAnchor postbacklink;

    public ClientCodeRegistration()
    {
      Page.Init += new System.EventHandler(Page_Init);
    }

    private void Page_Load(object sender, System.EventArgs e)
    {
      //we use a string builder to build our string
      //and provide constants for the opening and closing
      //script tags.
      StringBuilder Builder = new StringBuilder(1024);
      const string ScriptStart = "<script language=\"javascript\">\n<!-- ";
      const string EndScript = "\n-->\n</script>";

      //register an array on the client containing
      //ids of the textbox controls to be used by one
      //of the client side scripts
      RegisterArrayDeclaration("TextBoxes","'TextBox1'");
      RegisterArrayDeclaration("TextBoxes", "'TextBox2'");

      //register new client script block
      //which dynamically fills two text boxes
      //using the array registered earlier
      Builder.Append(ScriptStart);
      Builder.Append("\nfunction ChangeText()\n");
      Builder.Append("{\ndocument.getElementById(TextBoxes[0]).value='dynamic';");
      Builder.Append("\ndocument.getElementById(TextBoxes[1]).value='dynamic';");
      Builder.Append("\n}");
      Builder.Append(EndScript);

      RegisterClientScriptBlock("DynamicScript",Builder.ToString());

      //clear string builder
      Builder.Remove(0,Builder.Length);

      //register startup script which sets the status bar
      //text to a message.
      Builder.Append(ScriptStart);
      Builder.Append("\nwindow.status='Client Side Registrations Example';\n");
      Builder.Append(EndScript);

      RegisterStartupScript("StatusStartup",Builder.ToString());

      //set the click event for the dynamic link to postback
      //this simulates posting back with this control as the
      //source of the event and with the arguments specified
      //which in this case is an empty string.
      postbacklink.HRef=GetPostBackClientHyperlink(postbacklink, "");

      //register a hidden field to be manipulated in the
      //submit script.
      RegisterHiddenField("HiddenFormField","Initialized");
```

```
              //register a submit script which sets the hidden field just registered
              Builder.Remove(0,Builder.Length);
              Builder.Append(ScriptStart);
              Builder.Append("\nfunction SubmitMethod()\n");
              Builder.Append("{\n\tdocument.all.item(\"HiddenFormField\").value=
              \"Set Value\";");
              Builder.Append("\nreturn true;\n}");
              Builder.Append(EndScript);

              RegisterClientScriptBlock("SubmitMethod",Builder.ToString());

              //register the call to the above method when the form submits
              RegisterOnSubmitStatement("SubmitMethod","SubmitMethod()");

              //print out our hidden form field to show that it was
              //changed when we submitted the form.
              if(Request.Form["HiddenFormField"]!=null)
              {
                Response.Write("Hidden Field:" + Request.Form["HiddenFormField"]);
              }
            }
```

```csharp
    private void Page_Init(object sender, EventArgs e)
    {
      InitializeComponent();
    }

    private void InitializeComponent()
    {
      this.Load += new System.EventHandler(this.Page_Load);
    }
  }
}
```

VB: ClientCodeRegistration.aspx.vb

```vb
Imports System
Imports System.Collections
Imports System.ComponentModel
Imports System.Data
Imports System.Drawing
Imports System.Text      'needed for string builder
Imports System.Web
Imports System.Web.SessionState
Imports System.Web.UI
Imports System.Web.UI.WebControls
Imports System.Web.UI.HtmlControls

Public Class ClientCodeRegistration
  Inherits System.Web.UI.Page
  Protected WithEvents Button1 As System.Web.UI.WebControls.Button
  Protected WithEvents TextBox1 As System.Web.UI.WebControls.TextBox
  Protected WithEvents TextBox2 As System.Web.UI.WebControls.TextBox
  Protected WithEvents postbacklink As System.Web.UI.HtmlControls.HtmlAnchor

  <System.Diagnostics.DebuggerStepThrough()> Private Sub InitializeComponent()

  End Sub

  Private Sub Page_Init(ByVal sender As System.Object, ByVal e As
System.EventArgs) Handles MyBase.Init
```

```
    InitializeComponent()
End Sub

Private Sub Page_Load(ByVal sender As System.Object, ByVal e As_
System.EventArgs) Handles MyBase.Load
    'we use a string builder to build our string
    'and provide constants for the opening and closing
    'script tags.
    Dim Builder As New StringBuilder(1024)
    Const ScriptStart As String = "<script language=""javascript"">" & vbCrLf &_
    "<!-- "
    Const EndScript As String = vbCrLf & "-->" & vbCrLf & "</script>"

    'register an array on the client containing
    'ids of the textbox controls to be used by one
    'of the client side scripts
    RegisterArrayDeclaration("TextBoxes", "'TextBox1'")
    RegisterArrayDeclaration("TextBoxes", "'TextBox2'")

    'register new client script block
    'which dynamically fills two text boxes
    'using the array registered earlier
    Builder.Append(ScriptStart)
    Builder.Append(vbCrLf & "function ChangeText()" & vbCrLf)
    Builder.Append(vbCrLf &_
    "{document.getElementById(TextBoxes[0]).value='dynamic'")
    Builder.Append(vbCrLf &_
    "document.getElementById(TextBoxes[1]).value='dynamic'")
    Builder.Append(vbCrLf & "}")
    Builder.Append(EndScript)

    RegisterClientScriptBlock("DynamicScript", Builder.ToString())

    'clear string builder
    Builder.Remove(0, Builder.Length)

    'register startup script which sets the status bar
    'text to a message.
    Builder.Append(ScriptStart)
    Builder.Append(vbCrLf & "window.status='Client Side Registrations Example'" &_
    vbCrLf)
    Builder.Append(EndScript)

    RegisterStartupScript("StatusStartup", Builder.ToString())

    'set the click event for the dynamic link to postback
    'this simulates posting back with this control as the
    'source of the event and with the arguments specified
    'which in this case is an empty string.
    postbacklink.HRef = GetPostBackClientHyperlink(postbacklink, "")

    'register a hidden field to be manipulated in the
    'submit script.
    RegisterHiddenField("HiddenFormField", "Initialized")

    'register a submit script which sets the hidden field just registered
    Builder.Remove(0, Builder.Length)
    Builder.Append(ScriptStart)
    Builder.Append(vbCrLf & "function SubmitMethod()" & vbCrLf)
    Builder.Append(vbCrLf & vbTab &_
    "{document.all.item(""HiddenFormField"").value=""Set Value""")
    Builder.Append(vbCrLf & "return true" & vbCrLf & "}")
```

```
    Builder.Append(EndScript)

    RegisterClientScriptBlock("SubmitMethod", Builder.ToString())

    'register the call to the above method when the form submits
    RegisterOnSubmitStatement("SubmitMethod", "SubmitMethod()")

    'print out our hidden form field to show that it was
    'changed when we submitted the form.
    If Not Request.Form.Item("HiddenFormField") Is Nothing Then
      Response.Write("Hidden Field:" + Request.Form.Item("HiddenFormField"))
    End If
  End Sub
End Class
```

In our code behind, we first create a `StringBuilder` to do our string manipulation. This is the preferred method for string concatenation as the class is designed to optimally manage the memory demands of these operations. We also create constant string values for the opening and closing tags of our script blocks. Next, we register a client-side array that contains the ID values of our two text boxes. While these controls were declared in our page, they could just have easily been dynamically added to the page or a control at run time. Because we declare the array twice, with the same name, we end up with one array of two elements. We then create and register the `ChangeText` function on the client, which will dynamically change the text in the two textboxes by referencing the registered array.

A startup script is an inline script in a page, and therefore runs when the page loads. We have created and registered a startup script, which changes the status bar of the browser to display a message. We then use the `GetPostBackClientHyperlink` method to set the `HREF` property of the HTML anchor element to call the `__doPostback` function, passing in the element itself as the target and empty event arguments. Finally, we register a hidden form field and create a function that changes the field's value. The call to this function is then set as the `OnSubmitStatement` event handler for the page.

While this simple example only really shows the steps needed to register client-side code, hopefully it will also give you some idea of how these methods can be helpful in your own applications.

Page Class Protected Methods

- ❑ AspCompatBeginProcessRequest
- ❑ AspCompatEndProcessRequest
- ❑ CreateHtmlTextWriter
- ❑ DeterminePostBackMode
- ❑ InitOutputCache
- ❑ LoadPageStateFromPersistenceMedium
- ❑ RaisePostBackEvent
- ❑ SavePageStateToPersistenceMedium

The AspCompatBeginProcessRequest Method

The `AspCompatBeginProcessRequest` method processes the current request using legacy ASP objects asynchronously. The current context is passed as well as a `Callback` method to invoke when the request has been processed. This method is provided for compatibility with legacy ASP applications.

```
IAsyncResult AspCompatBeginProcessRequest(context, callback, data)
```

Parameter	Type	Description
context	HttpContext	The HttpContext object representing the current context of the executing request
callback	AsyncCallback	The method to be called when the request is done executing
data	Object	Extra data to be used in processing the request

The AspCompatEndProcessRequest Method

The AspCompatEndProcessRequest method represents the end of the ASP processing of the given request. This method is called in the Callback method invoked by AspCompatBeginProcessRequest at the end of the processing of the request.

```
Void AspCompatEndProcessRequest(result)
```

Parameter	Type	Description
result	IAsyncResult	The result of the AspCompatBeginProcessRequest method

The CreateHtmlTextWriter Method

The CreateHtmlTextWriter method creates an HtmlTextWriter to write HTML content. If the output is targeted at downlevel browsers, then an Html32TextWriter will be created. This method can be overridden in pages should you wish to use a custom writer for output. The CreateHtmlTextWriter method is useful when you want to pass an HtmlTextWriter to a function or business object so it can write to the output stream directly.

```
HtmlTextWriter = CreateHtmlTextWriter(writer)
```

Parameter	Type	Description
writer	TextWriter	An object that derives from TextWriter that represents the output stream to which the content should be written

The DeterminePostBackMode Method

The DeterminePostBackMode method obtains the form values posted, whether they were sent using the POST or the GET method. If the GET method was used, then the values are extracted from the query string, whereas, if the values are sent using the POST method, they are extracted from the Form collection of the request. This method will only work for server-side forms used with the post-back mechanism. The method of the request can also be determined from the Headers property of the HttpRequest class. If the page is being requested for the first time, that is, it is not a post back, then this method will return null (in C#) or Nothing (in Visual Basic).

```
NameValueCollection = DeterminePostBackMode()
```

The InitOutputCache Method

The `InitOutputCache` method sets caching options for the page at run time. The duration of caching, location of caching, and variance of caching based on parameters or controls can be set using this method.

```
Void InitOutputCache(duration, varyByHeader, varyByCustom, location, varyByParam)
```

Parameter	Type	Description
duration	Int	The duration, in seconds, that the page should be cached
varyByHeader	String	The headers for which the page should be cached
varyByCustom	String	A string that gets sent to the "Vary" HTTP header allowing varying the caching based on this header
location	OutputCache Location	An enumerated value indicating the location at which the page content should be cached: the client, server, another server, any of the above, or not at all
varyByParam	String	A string containing the names of the parameters by which the page content should be varied

The `location` parameter can take one of the following enumerated values:

Value	Description
Any	The content can be cached at any location in this list
Client	The content can be cached on the client browser
Downstream	The content can be cached at a server between the client and the web server processing the request
Server	The content can be cached on the web server
None	The content cannot be cached

The output caching of a page can also be set in a page-level declaration as shown below:

```
<%@ OutputCache Duration="60" VaryByParam="*" %>
```

The caching framework in ASP.NET allows storage of copies of pages, controls, data, and other objects so that subsequent requests can be serviced with much less processing required by the server. See Chapter 7 for a detailed explanation of caching in ASP.NET.

The LoadPageStateFromPersistenceMedium Method

The `LoadPageStateFromPersistenceMedium` method loads the page's state. This method is intended to be overridden if the page state needs to be loaded from anything other than a hidden form field.

```
Object LoadPageStateFromPersistenceMedium()
```

The RaisePostBackEvent Method

The `RaisePostBackEvent` method raises the `PostBack` event of a particular control. With the introduction of server controls comes the introduction of the associated server-side events as well. When a button is clicked and posts back to the server, an event handler can be assigned to handle that event. The `RaisePostBackEvent` method allows programmatically calling the post back event of a given control. For example, if a button is clicked and its event method is fired and executing, another control's method can also be executed by calling the `RaisePostBackEvent` method with the other control specified as an argument. This allows us to respond to a single action from the user with multiple events.

```
Void RaisePostBackEvent(handler, arguments)
```

Parameter	Type	Description
handler	IPost BackEvent Handler	A control that implements this interface, and whose event handling method you wish to call
arguments	String	The arguments to send to the event handling method

Example: RaisePostBack

As an example, the web form below has a standard button and a link button. When the standard button is clicked, the event handlers for both are carried out. However, if the link button is clicked then only its event handler is called.

RaisePostBack.aspx

```
<%@ Page language="c#" Codebehind="RaisePostBack.aspx.cs" AutoEventWireup="false"
Inherits="AspProgRefChap3.RaisePostBack" %>
<!DOCTYPE HTML PUBLIC "-//W3C//DTD HTML 4.0 Transitional//EN" >
<HTML>
  <BODY>
    <FORM id="RaisePostBack" method="post" runat="server">
      <asp:Button id="MainButton" runat="server" Text="Main Button"></asp:Button>
      <BR>
      <asp:LinkButton id="TriggeredButton"
                             runat="server">Triggered Button</asp:LinkButton>
      <BR>
      <asp:Label id="Message" runat="server"></asp:Label>
      <BR>
    </FORM>
  </BODY>
</HTML>
```

C#: RaisePostBack.aspx.cs

```
using System;
using System.Collections;
using System.ComponentModel;
using System.Data;
using System.Drawing;
using System.Web;
using System.Web.SessionState;
using System.Web.UI;
using System.Web.UI.WebControls;
using System.Web.UI.HtmlControls;
```

```
namespace AspProgRefChap3
{

  public class RaisePostBack : System.Web.UI.Page
  {
    protected System.Web.UI.WebControls.Button MainButton;
    protected System.Web.UI.WebControls.LinkButton TriggeredButton;
    protected System.Web.UI.WebControls.Label Message;

    public RaisePostBack()
    {
      Page.Init += new System.EventHandler(Page_Init);
    }

    private void Page_Load(object sender, System.EventArgs e)
    {
      // start each request with an empty label.
      Message.Text = String.Empty;
    }

    private void Page_Init(object sender, EventArgs e)
    {
      InitializeComponent();
    }

    private void InitializeComponent()
    {
      //assign event handlers for the buttons
      this.MainButton.Click += new System.EventHandler(this.MainButton_Click);
      this.TriggeredButton.Click += new
                          System.EventHandler(this.TriggeredButton_Click);
      this.Load += new System.EventHandler(this.Page_Load);

    }

    //event handler for the main button
    private void MainButton_Click(object sender, System.EventArgs e)
    {
      //output a message and then raise the event for the other button
      Message.Text = Message.Text + "Main Button Clicked<br>";
      RaisePostBackEvent(TriggeredButton, "");
    }

    //event handler for the triggered button (link button)
    private void TriggeredButton_Click(object sender, System.EventArgs e)
    {
      //output a text message
      Message.Text = Message.Text + "Triggered Button Clicked<br>";
    }
  }
}
```

VB: RaisePostBack.aspx.vb

```
Public Class RaisePostBack
  Inherits System.Web.UI.Page
  Protected WithEvents MainButton As System.Web.UI.WebControls.Button
  Protected WithEvents TriggeredButton As System.Web.UI.WebControls.LinkButton
  Protected WithEvents Message As System.Web.UI.WebControls.Label

  'This call is required by the Web Form Designer.
  <System.Diagnostics.DebuggerStepThrough()> Private Sub InitializeComponent()
```

```
      End Sub

      Private Sub Page_Init(ByVal sender As System.Object, ByVal e As_
                                  System.EventArgs) Handles MyBase.Init
        InitializeComponent()
      End Sub

      Private Sub Page_Load(ByVal sender As System.Object, ByVal e As_
                                  System.EventArgs) Handles MyBase.Load
        'start each request with an empty label
        Message.Text = String.Empty

      End Sub
```

```
      'event hadnler for the main button
      Private Sub MainButton_Click(ByVal sender As System.Object, ByVal e As_
                                    System.EventArgs) Handles MainButton.Click
        'output a message and then raise the event from the other button
        Message.Text = Message.Text & "Main Button Clicked <BR>"
        RaisePostBackEvent(TriggeredButton, "")
      End Sub

      'event handler for the triggered button (link button)
      Private Sub TriggeredButton_Click(ByVal sender As System.Object, ByVal e As_
                                  System.EventArgs) Handles TriggeredButton.Click
        'output a message
        Message.Text = Message.Text & "Triggered Button Clicked"

      End Sub
    End Class
```

As you can see, we have simply added an event handler for each of our two buttons. In the handler for the first we not only handle the event, in this case displaying a message, but we also call the event handler for the link button as well, which simply adds to the message text.

The SavePageStateToPersistenceMedium Method

The `SavePageStateToPersistenceMedium` method saves the state of the page. This method should be overridden for pages where state should be saved somewhere other than a hidden form field.

```
    Void SavePageStateToPersisteneMedium(viewState)
```

Parameter	Type	Description
viewState	Object	The object into which the view state information will be saved

The TemplateControl Class

The `TemplateControl` class represents the base set of functionality for the `UserControl` and `Page` classes. It is presented here for simplicity. The benefits of having a common base class include improved code manageability and modularity. This class is an abstract class, which means that it cannot be created explicitly but must be inherited from in order to gain the functionality it exposes.

TemplateControl Class Public Methods

- ❑ `InstantiateIn`
- ❑ `LoadControl`
- ❑ `LoadTemplate`
- ❑ `ParseControl`

The InstantiateIn Method

The `InstantiateIn` method creates the control tree for a control, and is used to add controls to the control tree (that is, the control hierarchy) of the current control. For example, when creating a templated control, this method can add child controls to the control tree. In effect, this relates the current control to a given parent control. For instance, to add a table row to a table, you would call `InstantiateIn` on the row object, passing the table object as a parameter. If you enable tracing for your web application, then the actual hierarchy of controls will be displayed.

```
Void InstantiateIn(control)
```

Parameter	Type	Description
control	Control	The `Control` object to contain the tree

The LoadControl Method

The `LoadControl` method obtains a reference to a `UserControl` by loading the file that contains the control definition. This means that a user control, defined in a file with the extension `.ascx`, can be loaded dynamically at run time, as opposed to declaratively inserting the control in the HTML of the Web Form. This method allows a specific control to be loaded at run time, providing greater flexibility in your design.

```
UserControl = LoadControl(path)
```

Parameter	Type	Description
path	String	The virtual path to the file that contains the definition for the user control

For example, if we have a navigation control defined in `nav.ascx`, we can load it with the following code:

```
UserControl uc = LoadControl("nav.ascx")
```

We can now add the `nav.ascx` control to the collection of child controls associated with a page or control. In this way, we can load different controls onto the page or user control according to information present at run time. For example, perhaps you have a page on which you want to conditionally load a navigation tree for certain users. You can check the user information and if the user is allowed access, continue to load and display the navigation control.

The LoadTemplate Method

The `LoadTemplate` method loads a template, that is an object implementing the `ITemplate` interface, from a file. Templates allow you to define the layout for the contents of a server control. Only a few of the controls that ship with ASP.NET support templates, including the `Repeater`, `DataList`, and `DataGrid`. For example, the `DataGrid` has both a Header Template and a Footer Template to allow the developer to specify the layout for the header and footer of the grid. The `LoadTemplate` method loads the template definition, comprising HTML and text, from a file at run time rather than specifying it in the page or control at design time.

```
ITemplate = LoadTemplate(path)
```

Parameter	Type	Description
path	String	The virtual path of the file that contains the template

Example: ItemTemplate

For instance, if we wanted to set the `ItemTemplate` of a `Repeater` control, we could load the template from a file at run time as in the example below:

UserControlHost.aspx

```
<%@ Page language="c#" Codebehind="UserControlHost.aspx.cs"
AutoEventWireup="false" Inherits="AspProgRefChap3.UserControlHost" %>
<!DOCTYPE HTML PUBLIC "-//W3C//DTD HTML 4.0 Transitional//EN" >
<HTML>
  <HEAD>
  </HEAD>
  <BODY ms_positioning="FlowLayout">
    <FORM id="UserControlHost" method="post" runat="server">
      <ASP:REPEATER id="repeat" runat="server"></ASP:REPEATER>
      <BR>
    </FORM>
  </BODY>
</HTML>
```

We have a simple form with an ASP Repeater element but no templates defined. We will load the template from the following code behind file, given in both C# and VB.NET:

C#: UserControlHost.aspx.cs

```
using System;
using System.Collections;
using System.ComponentModel;
using System.Data;
using System.Drawing;
using System.Web;
using System.Web.SessionState;
using System.Web.UI;
using System.Web.UI.WebControls;
using System.Web.UI.HtmlControls;

namespace AspProgRefChap3
{
  public class UserControlHost : System.Web.UI.Page
  {
```

```
   //our ASP repeater control
   protected System.Web.UI.WebControls.Repeater repeat;

   public UserControlHost()
   {
     Page.Init += new System.EventHandler(Page_Init);
   }

   private void Page_Load(object sender, System.EventArgs e)
   {
     //create a datasource
     ArrayList List = new ArrayList(3);
     List.Add("Red");
     List.Add("Blue");
     List.Add("Orange");

     //set the datasource of the repeater item to
     //the array list created above
     repeat.DataSource = List;

     //load the item template from a file
     repeat.ItemTemplate = LoadTemplate("Template.ascx");

     //call DataBind to cause the page and all of its controls to execute
     //their data binding event handlers.
     DataBind();

   }

   private void Page_Init(object sender, EventArgs e)
   {
     InitializeComponent();
   }

   private void InitializeComponent()
   {
     this.Load += new System.EventHandler(this.Page_Load);

   }

 }
}
```

VB: UserControlHost.aspx.vb

```
Public Class UserControlHost
    Inherits System.Web.UI.Page
  Protected WithEvents repeat As System.Web.UI.WebControls.Repeater
    <System.Diagnostics.DebuggerStepThrough()> Private Sub InitializeComponent()

  End Sub

  Private Sub Page_Init(ByVal sender As System.Object, ByVal e As_
                        System.EventArgs) Handles MyBase.Init
    InitializeComponent()
  End Sub

    Private Sub Page_Load(ByVal sender As System.Object, ByVal e As_
                          System.EventArgs) Handles MyBase.Load
    'create a collection for our data source
    Dim List As New ArrayList(3)
```

```
    List.Add("Red")
    List.Add("Blue")
    List.Add("Orange")

    'set the datasource property of our control
    'and call databind
    CType(FindControl("binding"), Binding).DataSource = List

    'set the repeater control's datasource to the list
    'created above
    repeat.DataSource = List

    'load the item template from a file
    repeat.ItemTemplate = LoadTemplate("Template.ascx")

    'call databind to cause the page and all of its controls
    'to bind to their data sources
    DataBind()

    End Sub
End Class
```

In the `Page_Load` method, we create a simple data source and set it as the source for our repeater control. Next, we load the item template from a file and then databind all of our controls. The template file itself is a simple text file containing the HTML text to put inside the template elements of the control, with a directive at the top declaring the language used. Below are the two versions of this file for C# and VB.NET. Notice that the only difference comes from casting the container to a `RepeaterItem` class.

C#: Template.ascx

```
<%@ Language="C#" %>
<B>My favorite color:</B>
<%# ((RepeaterItem)Container).DataItem %>
<BR>
```

VB: Template.ascx

```
<%@ Language="VB" %>
<B>My favorite color:</B>
<%# (ctype(Container,RepeaterItem)).DataItem %>
<BR>
```

The ParseControl Method

The `ParseControl` method parses a specified string into a control. This allows creation of control objects dynamically based on the text in the string. A similar process is performed to parse the elements in a web form into control objects in a page.

```
Control = ParseControl(content)
```

Parameter	Type	Description
content	String	The value to parse into a control

For example, if we want to create a label control dynamically at run time, and add it to our controls collection, we could do so with the following line of code:

C#

```
Controls.Add(ParseControl("<asp:label id='mylabel' runat='server'>This is a
label</asp:label>"));
```

VB.NET

```
Controls.Add(ParseControl("<asp:label id='mylabel' runat='server'>This is a
label</asp:label>"))
```

TemplateControl Class Protected Methods

❏ FrameworkInitialize

❏ OnAbortTransaction

❏ OnCommitTransaction

❏ OnError

The FrameworkInitialize Method

The FrameworkInitialize method allows the ASP.NET framework to initialize the control or page. While this method can be overridden, it is best to allow the framework to handle it, and use the Init event to initialize controls.

```
Void FrameWorkInitialize()
```

The OnAbortTransaction Method

The OnAbortTransaction method indicates that a transaction has terminated and should be aborted. This method raises the AbortTransaction event to be captured to clean up the event handler as required when a transaction is aborted. The method is called implicitly by the framework when a transaction is aborted, or it can be used by the developer, perhaps when handling exceptions, to indicate a failure of one or more steps.

```
void OnAbortTransaction(eArgs)
```

Parameter	Type	Description
eArgs	EventArgs	The event arguments to be passed to the event handler

ASP.NET pages can run under a transaction that groups a series of actions that will either all succeed or fail. Transactions in ASP.NET are actually COM+ transactions. For example, say we have a page that makes two different updates to a database and both must succeed or both fail. The standard example for this is the case of a banking transaction where we need to decrement the balance of one account and increment the balance in another account. If the first operation fails, we should not update the second piece of information. Likewise, if the second operation fails, we need to make sure we don't actually reduce the balance in the first account.

This event handling method is called at the end of processing the page only when the transaction property of the page has been set to Requires or Requires New. This allows the developer to respond to the result of the transaction appropriately by notifying the user of the result of their request. Because the page must have completed its processing, these events are fired directly before the Unload and Disposed events, and after all content has been rendered.

Example: Transactions

In the next example, we attempt to send a simple message to a transactional MSMQ message queue. If any step cannot be executed, then all actions will have to be rolled back. We shall put all the code into a single page to make a more compact example. In the real world, you would most likely separate the display code from the action code, as the displaying of the form does not need to be done in a transaction, and the transaction has a processor and memory overhead.

Let's look at a transacted Web page:

Transactions.aspx

```
<%@ Page Transaction="Required" language="c#" Codebehind="Transactions.aspx.cs"
AutoEventWireup="false" Inherits="AspProgRefChap3.Transactions" %>
<!DOCTYPE HTML PUBLIC "-//W3C//DTD HTML 4.0 Transitional//EN" >
<HTML>
  <HEAD>
  </HEAD>
  <BODY>
    <FORM id="Transactions" method="post" runat="server">
      Enter data to be sent to the message queue:
      <BR>
      <ASP:TEXTBOX textmode="MultiLine" id="body" runat="server">
       </ASP:TEXTBOX>
      <BR>
      <ASP:BUTTON id="QueueSubmit" runat="server" text="Send MSMQ message">
       </ASP:BUTTON>
    </FORM>
  </BODY>
</HTML>
```

C#: Transactions.aspx.cs

```
using System;
using System.Collections;
using System.ComponentModel;
using System.Data;
using System.Drawing;
using System.Messaging;
using System.Web;
using System.Web.SessionState;
using System.Web.UI;
using System.Web.UI.WebControls;
using System.Web.UI.HtmlControls;

namespace AspProgRefChap3
{
  /// <summary>
  /// Summary description for Transactions.
  /// </summary>
  public class Transactions : System.Web.UI.Page
  {
    protected System.Web.UI.WebControls.TextBox body;
    protected System.Web.UI.WebControls.Button QueueSubmit;

    public Transactions()
    {
      Page.Init += new System. EventHandler(Page_Init);
    }

    private void Page_Load(object sender, System.EventArgs e)
    {}
```

```csharp
private void Page_Init(object sender, EventArgs e)
{
  InitializeComponent();
}

private void InitializeComponent()
{
  this.QueueSubmit.Click += new System.EventHandler
   (this.QueueSubmit_Click);
  this.Load += new System.EventHandler(this.Page_Load);
  this.CommitTransaction += new System.EventHandler
   (this.Page_Commit);
  this.AbortTransaction += new System.EventHandler(this.Page_Abort);
}

//event handler for the button click
private void QueueSubmit_Click(object sender, System.EventArgs e)
{
  const string MQ_PATH = ".\\private$\\WROX";

  //connect to a private queue on the local machine, making sure
  //it exists first
  if(!MessageQueue.Exists(MQ_PATH))
  {
    //abort the transaction b/c there is no queue
    this.OnAbortTransaction(new System.EventArgs());
    return;
  }

  //open the queue
  MessageQueue q = new MessageQueue(MQ_PATH,false);

  //create a message object containing the text
  //from our text box object
  Message Msg = new Message(body.Text);

  //set the label on the message
  Msg.Label = "Transacted Message";

  //send the message and cleanup
  q.Send(Msg);

  q.Close();
  q = null;

}

private void Page_Commit(object sender, EventArgs eArgs)
{
  if(IsPostBack)
    Response.Write("Message sent successfully!");
}

protected void Page_Abort(object sender, EventArgs eArgs)
{
  if(IsPostBack)
    Response.Write("There were errors with your message. Please try
    again.");
}
}
}
```

VB: Transactions.aspx.vb

```vb
Imports System.Messaging
Imports System.EnterpriseServices

Public Class Transaction
  Inherits System.Web.UI.Page
  Protected WithEvents body As System.Web.UI.WebControls.TextBox
  Protected WithEvents QueueSubmit As System.Web.UI.WebControls.Button

  <System.Diagnostics.DebuggerStepThrough()> Private Sub InitializeComponent()

  End Sub

  Private Sub Page_Init(ByVal sender As System.Object, ByVal e As _
                      System.EventArgs) Handles MyBase.Init
    InitializeComponent()
  End Sub

  Private Sub Page_Load(ByVal sender As System.Object, ByVal e As _
                      System.EventArgs) Handles MyBase.Load

  End Sub

  Private Sub QueueSubmit_Click(ByVal sender As System.Object, ByVal e As _
    System.EventArgs) Handles QueueSubmit.Click
    Const MQ_PATH As String = ".\\private$\\WROX"

    'connect to a private queue on the local machine, making sure
    'it exists first
    If Not MessageQueue.Exists(MQ_PATH) Then

      'abort the transaction b/c there is no queue
      'this static method allows us to abort the transaction
      System.EnterpriseServices.ContextUtil.SetAbort()
      Return
    End If

    'open the queue
    Dim QueWrox As New MessageQueue(MQ_PATH, False)

    'create a message object containing the text
    'from our text box object
    Dim Msg As New Message(body.Text)

    'set the label on the message
    Msg.Label = "Transacted Message"

    'send the message and cleanup
    QueWrox.Send(Msg)

    QueWrox.Close()
    QueWrox = Nothing

  End Sub

  'handler for the CommitTransaction event
  Private Sub Page_Commit(ByVal sender As System.Object, ByVal eArgs As _.
                   System.EventArgs) Handles MyBase.CommitTransaction

    'if this is a post back, then write a response
    'indicating success
    If IsPostBack Then
```

```
        Response.Write("message sent successfully!")
      End If

   End Sub

   'handler for the AbortTransaction event
   Private Sub Page_Abort(ByVal sender As System.Object, ByVal eArgs As _
                 System.EventArgs) Handles MyBase.AbortTransaction
      'if this is a post back, then write a response
      'indicating failure
      If IsPostBack Then
        Response.Write("There were errors with your message. Please tryagain.")
      End If
   End Sub
End Class
```

In the code, we create event handlers for the button's click event and the `AbortTransaction` and `CommitTransaction` events. Within the handler for the button, we attempt to open a message queue and send a message containing the text in the text box. If the send succeeds, the transaction will be committed and our handler will be called, writing a success message. However, if the call fails, the abort transaction handler will be executed, displaying a failure message. Also note that if we find there is no queue with the given name, we manually abort the transaction.

The OnCommitTransaction Method

The `OnCommitTransaction` method indicates that a transaction has completed successfully. This method fires the `CommitTransaction` event to indicate to the calling program that it may continue executing with the assurance that actions in the transaction have completed successfully. You can call this method manually on completion of a transaction, and catch the `CommitTransaction` event to deal with that situation. See the `OnAbortTransaction` method for a detailed explanation of transactions.

```
void OnCommitTransaction(args)
```

Parameter	Type	Description
args	EventArgs	The event arguments describing the event taking place

The OnError Method

The `OnError` method raises the `Error` event to indicate that an error has occurred in processing the control. Use this method in conjunction with the `Error` event to centralize your response to errors. Use exception handling in your methods that catch `Error` events and provide an appropriate response for the UI. In addition to this error handling mechanism, the `ErrorPage` property of the `Page` object can be used for page redirection to provide custom error messages.

```
void OnError(args)
```

Parameter	Type	Description
args	EventArgs	The event arguments that describe the event taking place

> It is important to note that after handling the errors in the **Error** event, you need to empty out the **Error** collection by calling the **ClearError** method of the **HttpContext** class.

TemplateControl Class Protected Properties

❑ SupportAutoEvents

The SupportAutoEvents Property (read-only)

The SupportAutoEvents property indicates whether the control supports **Auto Events**, that is, events that can have handlers automatically set up by the compiler.

```
Boolean = SupportAutoEvents
```

For example, if this property is `true` for a page, then a method with the following signature would be automatically assigned by the compiler as the event handler for the `Load` event:

```
void Page_Load(object sender, EventArgs eArgs)
```

TemplateControl Class Public Events

❑ AbortTransaction

❑ CommitTransaction

❑ Error

The AbortTransaction Event

The AbortTransaction event is fired when a transaction has not completed successfully, and indicates that actions necessary for cleanup should be initiated. See the OnAbortTransaction method in the protected methods of the TemplateControl class for more information on working with transactions.

```
EventHandler = AbortTransaction
```

The CommitTransaction Event

The CommitTransaction event is raised when all steps in a transacted process have completed as planned, and is an indication to continue as the transaction was a success. See the OnAbortTransaction method for more information on transactions.

```
EventHandler = CommitTransaction
```

The Error Event

The Error event is raised when a controlled error has occurred and allows a centralized response to errors during the processing of the page. Page output that occurs before the error in question will still be rendered, but the rest of the page processing will not occur.

```
EventHandler = Error
```

As an example, we can add the following Error event handler to our transacted page so that, when an exception is thrown, the error handler is invoked and returns a message to the user, at the same time aborting the transaction.

Example: Error event

This code should be added to the `Transaction.aspx.cs` or `Transactions.aspx.vb` file as appropriate. The `Transactions.aspx` file example can be found with the transacted web page example provided in the previous section.

C#: Transactions.aspx.cs

```
//add error handling method
protected void Page_Error(object sender, EventArgs eArgs)
{
    //write a message to the UI with information about the error.
    Response.Write("Error occurred: " + Context.Error.Message);

    //clear the error so the framework does not also handle it
    Context.ClearError();

    //abort our transaction
    System.EnterpriseServices.ContextUtil.SetAbort();
}
```

VB: Transactions.aspx.vb

```
'add an error handling method to deal with any unexpected errors
Private Sub Page_Error(ByVal sender As System.Object, ByVal eArgs As_
                            System.EventArgs) Handles MyBase.Error

    'write a message to the UI with some information about the error
    Response.Write("Error occurred:" & context.Error.Message)

    'clear the error so the framework does not also handle it
    context.ClearError()

    'abort our transaction
    System.EnterpriseServices.ContextUtil.SetAbort()

End Sub
```

The UserControl Class

The `UserControl` class is the base class for custom UI components that are reusable in various pages. Similar to include files, which allow text or code from an external file to be inserted into a page at runtime, the User Control is much more powerful as it has all of the functionality of the `Control` class. User Controls are used to form parts of a page, including text, HTML, and other controls, in addition to their own code behind page. Much like the built-in server controls, they can be added to a page using HTML style tags and attributes to set their properties. A User Control can only exist in the scope of a page, that is, a user control cannot be requested directly by the client. By default, the `machine.config` file defines an HTTP handler, of type `System.Web.HttpForbiddenHandler`, to handle requests for user controls so that the runtime does not attempt to process the file outside the scope of a page request.

UserControl Class Public Methods

❑ `DesignerInitialize`

❑ `InitializeAsUserControl`

The DesignerInitialize Method

The `DesignerInitialize` method performs operations necessary to prepare a `UserControl` for manipulation in a RAD environment such as Visual Studio.NET.

```
void DesignerInitialize()
```

The InitializeAsUserControl Method

The `InitializeAsUserControl` method initializes a `UserControl` inside a `Page` object. As mentioned above, the `UserControl` is like a `Page` object except that it cannot be created on its own, so this method can ensure that the control is created properly and instantiated in the control tree of the page object.

```
Void InitializeAsUserControl(page)
```

Parameter	Type	Description
page	Page	The page object in which the user control should be instantiated

UserControl Class Protected Methods

- ❑ LoadViewState
- ❑ SaveViewState

The LoadViewState Method

The `LoadViewState` method causes the `UserControl` to retrieve its view state and apply it appropriately. For example, when this method is called on a control, that control retrieves its view state information and is then able to set text for labels or alter other control states. The method should be overridden when you wish to intervene in the process of loading view state.

```
Void LoadViewState(savedstate)
```

Parameter	Type	Description
savedstate	Object	The object containing the state information

The SaveViewState Method

The `SaveViewState` method causes the `UserControl` to save its current state so that it can be retrieved later during a subsequent request. This method returns an object that contains the state of the user control.

```
object SaveViewState()
```

UserControl Class Public Properties

- ❑ Application
- ❑ Attributes
- ❑ Cache

- ❏ IsPostBack
- ❏ Request
- ❏ Response
- ❏ Server
- ❏ Session
- ❏ Trace

The Application Property (read-only)

The `Application` property indicates the `HttpApplicationState` object that the `UserControl` is running in. The object returned allows information to be shared among pages of the application.

```
HttpApplicationState = Application
```

The Attributes Property (read-only)

The `Attributes` property indicates a collection of name-value pairs that represent the attributes declared on a `UserControl` in the `.aspx` file where it is created.

```
AttributeCollection = Attributes
```

Attributes on a `UserControl` declaration in an `.aspx` file are often directly mapped to special properties or public member variables. However, if there is no corresponding property or field for the attributes, or there is a need to access the entire set of attributes, this method provides access to the entire collection.

The Cache Property (read-only)

The `Cache` property is a `Cache` object for caching data on the web server to improve performance. See Chapter 7, *Caching & System.Web.Caching*, for more information on the `Cache` object.

```
Cache = Cache
```

The IsPostBack Property (read-only)

The `IsPostBack` property indicates whether the current request for the page is the result of a post-back event, returning `true` when the page request is the result of a post-back action from a server control. The post-back process begins when a client-side script runs and submits a form to the server containing view state, the target of the post-back, and any event arguments. However, using other client-side forms and submitting them to the page will not result in this property returning `true`.

```
Boolean = IsPostBack
```

The Request Property (read-only)

The `Request` property indicates the `HttpRequest` object that was posted to the server. This object allows access to returned forms, client cookies, browser capabilities, and more. In sum, it wraps up all the information related to the incoming client request and is analogous to the `Request` object in traditional ASP. See Chapter 2 for more information on the `HttpRequest` object.

```
HttpRequest = Request
```

The Response Property (read-only)

The `Response` property indicates the `HttpResponse` object that is to be sent to the client. This object is used for tasks such as setting cookies and creating UI elements. The `Response` object encompasses everything passed back to the client, serving a similar purpose to the `Response` object in traditional ASP, with added functionality appropriate to .NET. See Chapter 2 for more information.

```
HttpResponse = Response
```

The Server Property

The `Server` property allows access to an `HttpServerUtility` object housing utility functions for use in web applications, for instance to create COM components or execute other `.aspx` pages. See Chapter 2, *System.Web,* for more information on the `ServerUtility` class.

```
HttpServerUtility = Server
```

The Session Property

The `Session` property supplies an `HttpSessionState` object to allow access to the state maintenance mechanisms of ASP.NET. There are several different configurations for session state in ASP.NET, including the traditional in-process as well as database and centralized server in-memory implementations. This object is similar to the `Session` object in previous versions of ASP, in that it stores name-value pairs. However, that is where the similarities end. See Chapter 2, *System.Web,* for a brief introduction to the `HttpSessionState` object.

```
HttpSessionState = Session
```

The Trace Property (read-only)

The `Trace` property is an object representing the tracing context of the current page execution. This object can be used to write information to the trace to be displayed when tracing is enabled for the control.

```
TraceContext = Trace
```

Summary

In this chapter we have covered a great deal of core information for the ASP.NET framework. Pages, User Controls, and Server Controls are an integral part of user interfaces in ASP.NET. The object-oriented nature of the framework, in conjunction with the event-driven programming model, provide the developer with a great deal of flexibility and power.

In this chapter we have covered:

❑   The `Control` class — this class serves as the base class to almost all of the UI elements in ASP.NET and provides a great deal of functionality

❑   The `Page` class — this class serves as the basis for all pages and provides the driving events for processing requests

❑   The `TemplateControl` class — this class provides common functionality to the `Page` and `UserControl` classes

❑   The `UserControl` class — this class allows creation of portions of code that can be reused between pages

In the next few chapters, we will dive into the server controls that derive from `Control` and are used to build increasingly feature-rich pages.

System.Web.UI.HTMLControls

At this point you should have a good idea of how ASP.NET pages work and how to work with the classes in the .NET framework. In this and the following chapter, we will show you some of the classes in the .NET framework that are at the heart of the new techniques in ASP.NET for building interactive Web Forms and web pages. These classes allow us to program in a way that is much closer to the event-driven approach of traditional executable programs, as we can now adopt a programming model based around server-side event handling.

In this chapter we will work on HTML server controls. HTML server controls are very easy to use: if you know some native HTML tags, then you already know most of the syntax for HTML controls. These server controls look like HTML tags, except that HTML server controls have the attribute `runat="server"` at the end of the HTML element. HTML server controls give the web developer the power of the Web Forms page framework while retaining the familiarity and ease of use of HTML tags. For example, HTML server controls not only create an HTML element on a web page, but also create an instance of a server control. The big advantage with HTML server controls over using native HTML tags is that they give us more powerful functionality than native HTML tags. We can, for example, use the cache to increase performance so code can be run much faster after its first request, a feature that is unavailable with native HTML tags. See the following HTML server control example:

```
<input type="button" id="button1" value="Click" runat="server">
```

Without the `runat="server"` attribute, this line of HTML would be parsed into a standard HTML button. With the `runat="server"` attribute, it will be parsed into an HTML server control. After you create a server control, you can access its properties, methods, and events through server-side code, and it can obtain input from as well as provide feedback to the user. This interaction cannot be achieved with simple HTML. This is why HTML controls are so useful for building ASP.NET web applications. Of course, we could also achieve this through the use of server-side scripting and classic ASP, but HTML controls offer a much cleaner and less awkward methodology.

The `System.Web.UI.HtmlControls` namespace provides the functionality required for HTML controls. It includes the following three main classes: `HtmlImage` for image handling, `HtmlInputControl` for server-side controls, and `HtmlContainerControl` for block elements. Before we go into these in depth, however, let's first see the structure of the namespace, `System.Web.UI.HtmlControls`.

> **Wrox authors Alex Homer and Dave Sussman have an online application, developed for Professional ASP.NET, that lets you explore the properties of selected Server Controls. It can be found at http://www.daveandal.com/profaspnet/default.asp.**

System.Web.UI.HtmlControls

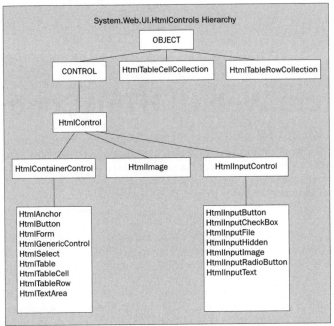

Let's see how these new HTML controls relate to their corresponding plain old native HTML tags:

HtmlControl Name	Native HTML
HtmlAnchor	`<a href="URL">Hyperlink text</a>`
HtmlButton	`<button>text</button>`
HtmlForm	`<form action="URL">...</form>`
HtmlGenericControl	Other tags, for example: `<span>`,`<font>`,`<div>`,`<body>`
HtmlSelect	`<select>...</slsect>`
HtmlTable	`<table>...</table>`
HtmlTableCell	`<td>...</td>`
HtmlTableRow	`<tr>...</tr>`

HtmlControl Name	Native HTML
HtmlTextArea	`<textarea>...</textarea>`
HtmlImage	`<img>`
HtmlInputButton	`<input type="button">` or `<input type="submit">`
HtmlInputCheckBox	`<input type="checkbox">`
HtmlInputFile	`<input type="file">`
HtmlInputHidden	`<input type="hidden">`
HtmlInputImage	`<input type="image">`
HtmlInputRadioButton	`<input type="radio">`
HtmlInputText	`<input type="text">` or `<input type="password">`

HtmlControl Class

The `HtmlControl` class provides basic properties that are inherited from all of the HTML server controls. It inherits from the `Control` class in the `System.Web.UI` namespace, in the same way that any HTML server controls inherit from this `HTMLControl` base class. It doesn't have a corresponding HTML tag because it provides the methods, properties, and events that are inherited by all HTML server control classes in the Web Forms Page namespace. This class has the following properties:

HtmlControl Properties

Attribute

The `Attribute` property gets all attribute name-value pairs expressed on a server control tag within a selected ASP.NET page.

Disabled

The `Disabled` property gets or sets `true` or `false` indicating whether it is included when a server control is rendered.

Style

The `Style` property gets all cascading style sheet (CSS) properties that are applied to a specific HTML server control in a `.aspx` file.

TagName

The `TagName` property displays the name of an HTML tag that contains the `runat="server"` attribute.

Example: HtmlControl Properties

Let's see an example of how some of these properties are used. This code is available for download from www.wrox.com with the filename `HtmlControl.aspx`:

```
<html>
<head>

<script language="VB" runat="server">
  Public Sub button_click1(s As Object, e As EventArgs)
    button1.disabled = true
    div1.innertext = button1.tagname
    div2.innertext = button1.attributes.tostring()
    div3.innertext = button1.style.tostring()
  End sub
</script>

</head>
<body>
  <form id="form1" runat="server">
    <button id="button1" onserverclick="button_click1" runat="Server">Click
1</button>
  </form>
<hr>
<div id=div1 runat="server" />
<div id=div2 runat="server" />
<div id=div3 runat="server" />
</body>
</html>
```

As you can see in this example, we can tell what kind of HTML tag we are dealing with by the `TagName` property. We have to convert `attributes` and `style` to a string value for the purposes of demonstration because they are collections. The following picture shows the result after the button is clicked.

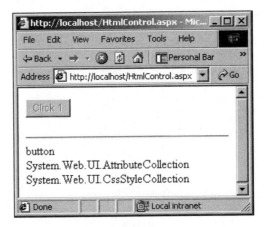

HtmlContainerControl Class

The `HtmlContainerControl` class defines the properties available to all HTML server controls that must have a closing tag. For example: `<span>, <div>`. This class is also inherited by HTML server controls, and has no visible HTML element itself.

HtmlContainerControl Properties

There are two properties in addition to those inherited from classes further up the hierarchy.

InnerHtml

The `InnerHtml` property displays the appearance of the string between the opening and closing tags of the specified HTML server control when in HTML mode.

InnerText

The `InnerText` property displays the appearance of the string between the opening and closing tags of the specified HTML server control when in text mode.

Example: HtmlContainerControl Properties

Let's see these two properties in a quick example. This code is available for download with the filename `Container.aspx`:

```
<html>

<head>
<script language="VB" runat="server">
Public Sub Page_Load(s As Object, e As EventArgs)
   span1.innerHtml = "<font size=+3>InnerHtml</font>"
   span2.innerText = "<font size=+1>InnerText</font>"
End sub
</script>
</head>

<span id="span1" runat="server" />
<hr>
<span id="span2" runat="server" />
</html>
```

The code includes a `PAGE_LOAD` event that displays the results of `InnerHtml` and `InnerText` when the web page is loaded. The result of the above code is shown below:

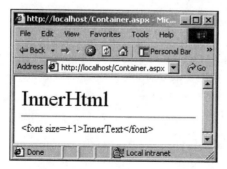

From the above screenshot we can clearly see what the difference is between `InnerHtml` and `InnerText`. The `InnerHtml` property tells our control to take everything between the quotes and interpret it as HTML and parse it as such. The `InnerText` property tells our control to interpret everything between the quotes as text, and to produce HTML code behind the scenes that will output the required content as it is displayed in our code. For example, each instance of a < character is escaped into `&lt;` behind the scenes.

173

HtmlAnchor Class

The HtmlAnchor class allows programmatic access to the HTML <a> tag on the server. The HtmlAnchor class can be used in two ways. Firstly, it can be used as a hyperlink just like the HTML <a> tag, using 'href' properties for navigation; the other way it can be used is for handling a click event of the HtmlAnchor class that is generated by the user, which cannot be done by a simple HTML tag. It has the following syntax:

```
<a id="id_name"
   href="URL"
   name="bookmark"
   target="target_option"
   title="display name"
   onserverclick="function_name"
   runat="server">
Hyperlink_Text
</a>
```

HtmlAnchor Properties

The following are the properties of the HtmlAnchor class, excluding those inherited from upper-level controls.

HRef

The HRef property gets or sets the URL target of the link specified in the HtmlAnchor server control.

Name

The Name property gets or sets the bookmark name defined in the HtmlAnchor server control.

Target

The Target property gets or sets the target window or frame into which to load linked web page content.

Title

The Title property gets or sets the title that the browser displays when identifying linked content.

Example: HtmlAnchor Properties

Let's see these properties in the following example. This code is available for download with the filename Anchor.aspx:

```
<html>
<head>
<script language="VB" runat="server">
Public Sub Page_Load(s As Object, e As EventArgs)
  anchor1.href = "http://www.wrox.com"
  anchor1.name = "NewWindow"
  anchor1.target = "_blank"
  anchor1.title = "To Wrox"
end sub
</script>
```

```
    </head>
    <body>
    <a id="anchor1" runat="server">HtmlAnchor Link</a>
    </body>
    </html>
```

You can easily see what happens by running the above example, as shown below:

The most important thing here is the `Target` property. It can have four values as follows:

Target Property Value	Description
_blank	Renders web page to a new and unframed browser window
_parent	Renders web page in the immediate frameset parent in the same browser window
_self	Renders web page in the current frame in the same browser window
_top	Renders web page in the full and unframed window in the same browser

HtmlAnchor Events

When a user clicks on the text of the `HtmlAnchor` instance on a web page, the browser will navigate to the location that is specified in the `HRef` property of the control. ASP.NET has the ability to react whenever a user clicks this link, by firing the `OnServerClick` event. This event is represented on the control by an attribute, which assigns a name to the event. We can then write an event handler method that intercepts this event and runs some code whenever the event is fired. This is different from the native HTML tag, `<a>`, because these simple tags are static. The ability to react to a user clicking a hyperlink specified by this control means that we can, for example, record how many times a link is clicked.

OnServerClick

The `OnServerClick` event reacts to the action of clicking on the linked text of a hyperlink.

Example: OnServerClick

This code is available for download with the filename `OnServerClick.aspx`:

```
<html>
<head>

  <script language="VB" runat="server">
    Public Sub aclick(s As Object, e As EventArgs)
       span1.innerText = "You clicked the hyperlink"
    end sub
  </script>

</head>
<body>

<form runat="server">
  <a id="anchor1" onserverclick="aclick" runat="server">HtmlAnchor Link</a>
  <hr>
  <span id="span1" runat="server" />
</form>

</body>
</html>
```

This produces the following:

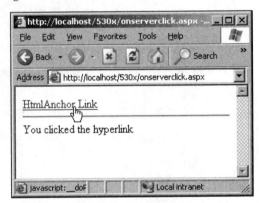

When we run this example, we will see a simple hyperlink, which, when we click it, will cause a message to be shown: "You clicked the hyperlink". This method can also be found within the <form> server control, which will meet later.

The OnServerClick method is common to many HTML server controls, so we won't repeat our discussion of this method in the following server controls.

HtmlButton Class

The HtmlButton class allows programmatic access to an HTML <button> tag on the server. Although the simple HTML <button> is defined in the HTML 4.0 specification, it is only supported by Internet Explorer 4.0 and above; however, with ASP.NET the button server control is accessible by, and displays for, all types of browsers. It has the following syntax:

```
<button id="id_name"
        onserverclick="function_name"
```

```
          runat="server">
Button_name, Button_image, or Button_control
</button>
```

Example: HtmlButton Control

Let's see a quick example. This code is available for download with the filename `HtmlButton.aspx`:

```
<html>
<head>

<script language="VB" runat="server">

  Public Sub button_click1(s As Object, e As EventArgs)
    span1.innerText = "You clicked button 1"
    button1.Visible = false
  End Sub

  Public Sub button_click2(s As Object, e As EventArgs)
    span1.innerText = "You clicked button 2"
    button1.Visible = true
  End Sub

</script>

</head>
<body>

<form id="form1" runat="server">
  <button id="button1" onserverclick="button_click1"
  runat="Server">Click 1</button>
  <button id="button2" onserverclick="button_click2"
  runat="server">Click 2</button>
</form>

<hr>
<span id="span1" runat="server" />
</body>
</html>
```

In the preceding example, we have methods for two 'click' buttons. The first button will display a message and hide itself after it has been clicked by the user. The second button will clear the message created by the first button and the first button will re-appear on the web page. In this example we use the `Visible` property that is inherited from the `Control` class within the `System.Web.UI` namespace. Using the .NET framework classes, we can make a relatively complex button server control quite easily. For example, we can use the `Disabled` property that is inherited from the `HtmlControl` class to disable the button, simply by changing the `Visible` property to `Disabled` in the above example:

```
button1.Disabled = true
```

or

```
button1.Disabled = false
```

HtmlForm Class

The `HtmlForm` class provides programmatic access to the HTML `<form>` tag. Its functionality and usage is very similar to HTML `<form>`. Therefore, you can see how we would use this class in many examples that contain server controls with an `OnServerClick` method. It has the following syntax:

```
<form id = "id_name"
      method= "POST | GET"
      enctype = "Encoding_Type_Name"
      action = "target_page_filename"
      runat = "server">
Other controls, input forms, and so on.
</form>
```

HtmlForm Properties

Action

This is the URL of the page that is to process the form data on a postback. The default setting is the current page.

```
<form action="action_page_name" runat="server">...</form>
```

Enctype

This is the encoding type that browsers use when posting form data to the server. The standard encoding format is `applicaton/x-www-form-urlencoded`, although `multipart/form-data`, `text/plain`, and `image/jpeg` formats are also acceptable.

Method

This is the way in which a browser will post form data to the server. The two most common methods supported by all browsers are `GET` and `POST`. The default value is `POST`.

```
<form method="post | get" runat="server">...</form>
```

Name

This will get the value of the HTML `name` attribute that will be rendered to the browser.

```
<form name="form_name" runat="server">...</form>
```

Target

This will get or set the URI of the frame or window that will be used to render the results of a form's `POST` request. Users can use this property to redirect these results to another browser window or frame.

```
<form target="URI of frame" runat="server">...</form>
```

We won't show an example specifically for HtmlForm because it's in use throughout all of the examples in this chapter. It's worth noting, however, that the HtmlForm class doesn't support the action attribute, but the HTML <form> tag does, so you cannot use this attribute to pass values to other web form pages. So, if action is no longer supported, how should we pass values between web form pages? Generally speaking, you can consider the following three ways. First, using Querystring, which will gather the information you want and append it to a URL, passing this in a GET request to retrieve a specific resource that can be cached or reused. However, when using this method, all of the information we are requesting is visible in the address line of the browser. While this is useful if, for example, we're doing a search on a search engine, where the results can be cached and reused, it's definitely not what we want for passing around things like credit card details, which need to be encapsulated in POST requests. Second, using Session, which will keep all the information you want in memory in the user's current session. Before it expires, you can read the information from session variables from other web form pages. The advantage with this is that all web form pages in a web site can read the session information, and the disadvantage is more session means more memory. Third, use custom page properties and then redirect from the original page to the target page in such a way that you can still read values in the old page.

HtmlGenericControl Class

The HtmlGenericControl class defines the methods, properties, and events for all HTML server controls not represented by a specific .NET Framework class. For example, <span>, <div>, <body>, and so on.

HtmlGenericControl Property

TagName

This property is similar to the TagName property of the HtmlControl class.

HtmlSelect Class

The HtmlSelect class allows programmatic access to an HTML <select> element on the server. It has the following syntax:

```
<select id="select_id"
        datasource = "databindingsource name"
        datatextfield = "field to databind option"
        datavaluefield = "field to databind option"
        multiple
        items = "a collection of options"
        selectindex = "index of current selecteditem"
        size = "number of visible items"
        value = "current item value"
        runat = "server">
   <option> Option1_name </option>
   <option> Option2_name </option>
</select>
```

HtmlSelect Properties

DataSource

The `DataSource` property gets or sets the data source to databind `<option>` values. For example, here's some code to illustrate this – available for download as `DataSource.aspx`:

```
<html>
<head>

<script language="VB" runat="server">
  Sub Page_Load(sender As Object, e As EventArgs)
    Dim values as ArrayList= new ArrayList()

    values.Add ("Illinois")
    values.Add ("Indiana ")
    values.Add ("California ")

    StateSelect.DataSource = values
    StateSelect.DataBind
  end sub
</script>

</head>
<body>Select the following states :
<select id="StateSelect" runat="server" />
</body>
</html>
```

DataTextField

The `DataTextField` property gets or sets the field in the data source that provides the text for an option entry.

DataValueField

The `DataValueField` property gets or sets the field in the data source that provides the option item value.

Items

The `Items` property gets or sets the values of option items.

Example: HtmlSelect

Let's see a quick example, `Select.aspx`, available in the code download:

```
<html>
<head>

<script language="VB" runat="server">
  Public Sub bclick(s As Object, e As EventArgs)
    select1.items.add("text3")
    span1.innertext = select1.items.count
  End Sub
```

```
</script>

</head>

<body>

<form runat="server">
  <select id="Select1" runat="server">
  <option>text1</option>
  <option>text2</option>
  </select>
  <button id="button1" onserverclick="bclick" runat="server">Add</button>
</form>

<hr>Number of Items now is:
<span id="span1" runat="server" />
</body>
</html>
```

As you can see when you run the example, the option of "text3" will be added to the drop-down list when you click the button. With the `Items` property, we can modify the list of option items for the `HtmlSelect` server control:

- ❑   `Add` – adds a new option item
- ❑   `Clear` – clears all option items
- ❑   `Remove` – deletes a selected option item
- ❑   `Count` – lists the total number of option items

Let's see these in a more advanced example, `Selectadv.aspx`:

```
<html>
<head>

<script language="VB" runat="server">

  Sub bclick(sender As Object, e As EventArgs)
    select1.items.add("text3")
  end sub

  Sub bclick2(sender As Object, e As EventArgs)
    select1.items.add(word1.value)
  end sub

  Sub bclick3(sender As Object, e As EventArgs)
    select1.items.remove(word1.value)
  end sub

</script>

</head>
<body>

<form runat="server">
```

```
<input type="text" id="word1" runat="server">
<button id="button2" onserverclick="bclick2" runat="server">Add word</button>
<button id="button3" onserverclick="bclick3" runat="server">Remove word</button>
<select id="select1" runat="server">
<option>text1</option>
<option>text2</option>
</select>
<button id="button1" onserverclick="bclick" runat="server">Add text3</button>
</form>

</body>
</html>
```

Multiple

The Multiple property gets or sets a value indicating whether multiple option items can be selected from the <select> list. The default value is false.

```
<select multiple="true" id="select1" runat="server">
```

If you add the Multiple property to the previous example, you will see how multiple selection can be enabled.

SelectedIndex

The SelectedIndex property gets or sets the ordinal index of the selected option item. If multiple items are selected, SelectedIndex holds the index of the first item selected in the list.

Size

The Size property gets or sets the number of visible option items. A value greater than one will typically cause browsers to display a scrolling list.

Value

The Value property gets or sets the current item selected. It is null when no item is selected.

HtmlTable Class

The HtmlTable class allows programmatic access to the HTML <table> tag on the server. You can bind the <table> server control and add rows and columns to a table by methods within the HtmlTableRowCollection and HtmlTableCellCollection classes. It has the following syntax:

```
<table id="table_id"
       align = "left | center | right"
       bgcolor = "background_color"
       border = "border_width"
       bordercolor = "border_color"
       cellpadding = "spacing_width_within_cell"
       cellspacing = "spacing_width_between_cells"
       height = "table_height"
       rows = "number_of_rows"
       width = "table_width"
       runat="server">
  <tr><td><td></tr>
</table>
```

HtmlTable Properties

Align

The Align property gets or sets the alignment of a table.

```
<table align="left" runat="server">...</table>
```

BgColor

The BgColor property gets or sets the background color of a table.

```
<table bgcolor="#336699" runat="server">...</table>
```

Border

The Border property gets or sets the width of border of a table. The default value is -1 which means no border.

```
<table border="2"  runat="server">...</table>
```

BorderColor

The BorderColor property gets or sets the color of the border of a table.

```
<table border="2"  bordercolor="#336699" runat="server">...</table>
```

You can also use the names of common colors instead. For example, "red", "blue".

CellPadding

The CellPadding property gets or sets the cell padding of a table. Its unit is pixels.

```
<table cellpadding="10"  runat="server"><tr><td>table...</td></tr></table>
```

CellSpacing

The CellSpacing property gets or sets the cell spacing of a table. Its unit is pixels.

```
<table cellspacing="10"  runat="server"><tr><td>table...</td></tr></table>
```

Height

The Height property gets or sets the height of a table.

```
<table height="100"  runat="server">...</table>
```

Rows

The Rows property gets a collection that contains all of the rows in a table. An empty collection is returned if no <tr> elements are contained within the table.

Width

The Width property gets or sets the width of a table.

```
<table width="100" runat="server">...</table>
```

The next two classes that we will see, `HtmlTableRow` and `HtmlTableCell`, will introduce how to create a table dynamically.

HtmlTableRow Class

The `HtmlTableRow` class allows programmatic access on the server to individual HTML `<tr>` tags as well as allowing you to dynamically add, remove, and insert rows to a table, an example of which we'll see later. It has the following syntax:

```
<tr id="id_name"
    align = "horizontal alignment of content in a row"
    bgcolor = "background color of row"
    bordercolor = "border color of row"
    height = "height of table row"
    cells = "collection of table cells"
    valign = "the vertical alignment of row content"
    runat = "server">
  <td>Content of cell</td>
</tr>
```

HtmlTableRow Properties

Align

The `Align` property gets or sets the horizontal alignment of the cells. Possible values are `left`, `center`, `right`, `justify`, and `char`.

```
<tr align="right" runat="server">...</tr>
```

BgColor

The `BgColor` property gets or sets the background color of a table row.

```
<tr bgcolor="red" runat="server">...</tr>
```

BorderColor

The `BorderColor` property gets or sets the border color of a row.

```
<tr bordercolor="yellow" runat="server">...</tr>
```

Cells

The `Cells` property gets or sets the group of table cells contained within a row.

Height

The `Height` property gets or sets the height of a table row. Note that this value will be influenced by the `Height` property of the table. For example, if you set the height of a table to 100 and the height of a table row to 200, then the height of the table row will be limited by the height of the table.

VAlign

The `VAlign` property gets or sets the vertical alignment of cells. Possible values are `top`, `middle`, `bottom`, and `baseline`.

HtmlTableCell Class

The `HtmlTableCell` class allows programmatic access on the server to individual HTML `<td>` and `<th>` tags. You can dynamically add, remove, and insert cells to an `HtmlTableRow` server control, as we saw above. It has the following syntax:

```
<td or th id="id_name"
        align = "horizontal alignment of content in a cell"
        bgcolor = "background color of cell"
        bordercolor = "border color of cell"
        colspan = "the number of columns cell spans"
        height = "height of cell"
        nowrap = "true | false"
        rowspan = "the number of rows cell spans"
        valign = "vertical alignment of cell content"
        width = "the width of cell"
        runat="server">
   Content of cell
</td or /th>
```

HtmlTableCell Properties

Align

The `Align` property gets or sets the horizontal alignment of cell content. Possible values are `left`, `center`, `right`, `justify`, and `char`.

```
<td align="right"  runat="server">...</td>
```

BgColor

The `BgColor` property gets or sets the background color of the cell.

```
<td bgcolor="red"  runat="server">...</td>
```

BorderColor

The `BorderColor` property gets or sets the border color of the cell.

```
<td bordercolor="blue"  runat="server">...</td>
```

Note that in order for this property to be available you have to set a value for `border` in a table. Otherwise you won't see the `BorderColor` of a cell.

ColSpan

The `ColSpan` property gets or sets the number of columns that the cell spans.

```
<td colspan="2"  runat="server">...</td>
```

Height

The `Height` property gets or sets the height of cell. Its unit is pixels.

```
<td height="10"  runat="server">...</td>
```

Note that this value will be influenced by the height of the table.

NoWrap

The `NoWrap` property gets or sets a value indicating whether text within a cell should be wrapped. Possible values are `true` and `false`; `false` is the default value.

RowSpan

The `RowSpan` property gets or sets the number of rows that the cell spans.

```
<td rowspan="2"  runat="server">...</td>
```

VAlign

The `VAlign` property gets or sets the vertical alignment of cell content. Possible values are `top`, `middle`, `bottom`, and `baseline`.

Width

The `Width` property gets or sets the width of a cell. Note that this value will be influenced by the width of the table.

Rows and Cells

The `Rows` property of the `HtmlTable` control is a new property and is a collection of `HtmlTableRow` controls. Similarly, the `Cells` property of the `HtmlTableRow` control is also a new property and is a collection of `HtmlTableCell` controls.

Example: HtmlTableCell

Let's see an example of how to create a dynamic table with the above controls, available for download as `Table.aspx`:

```
<html>
<head>

<script language=VB runat="server">
  sub bt_ck(s as object, e as eventargs)
    dim i,j as integer
    dim row as HtmlTableRow
    dim cell as HtmlTableCell
    for i = 1 to rowt.value
      row = new HtmlTableRow
      for j = 1 to cellt.value
        cell = new HtmlTableCell
        cell.innertext = "cell"
        row.cells.add (cell)
      next
      table1.rows.add (row)
    next
```

```
   end sub
</script>

</head>

<body>

<form runat="Server">
  Rows: <input type="text" id="rowt" runat="server"><br>
  Cells per row: <input type="text" id="cellt" runat="server"><br>
  <button id=button1 onserverclick="bt_ck" runat="server">Create Table</button>
</form>

<table id="table1" border="3" bordercolor="blue"
cellpadding="2" cellspacing="2" runat="server" />
</body>
</html>
```

This little example gives a perfect illustration of how we can operate row and cell collections to create a table dynamically. By entering the value 3 in Rows and 5 in Cells per row, then clicking on Create Table, the result will be:

HtmlTableRowCollection Class

The `HtmlTableRowCollection` contains all of the table rows within an `HtmlTable`. With this class we can dynamically add, remove, and insert rows using the methods provided by `HtmlTableRowCollection`. In fact, in the preceding example, `Table.aspx`, we have already shown how to dynamically add rows to a table using the `Add` method provided by `HtmlTableRowCollection`. This works with `HtmlTable` and `HtmlTableRow`.

HtmlTableRowCollection Properties

Count

The Count property shows the number of items in the HtmlTableRowCollection.

IsReadOnly

The IsReadOnly property gets a Boolean value to indicate whether HtmlTableRowCollection is read-only.

IsSynchronized

The IsSynchronized property gets a Boolean value to indicate whether access to HtmlTableRowCollection is synchronized.

Item

The Item property gets an HtmlTableRow from an HtmlTableRowCollection.

SyncRoot

The SyncRoot property can be used to synchronize access to the HtmlTableRowCollection.

HtmlTableRowCollection Methods

Add

The Add method adds rows to a table.

Clear

The Clear method deletes all rows from an HtmlTableRowCollection.

CopyTo

The CopyTo method copies items in the HtmlTableRowCollection to an array.

GetEnumerator

The GetEnumerator method gets the enumerator that contains all HtmlTableRow objects in the HtmlTableRowCollection.

Insert

The Insert method adds a row at a specified location in the HtmlTableRowCollection.

Remove

The Remove method deletes the specified row from the HtmlTableRowCollection.

RemoveAt

The RemoveAt method deletes the row at a specified index location from HtmlTableRowCollection.

Example: HtmlTableRowCollection

Let's see a quick example. This code is available for download with the filename
`TRCollection.aspx`:

```
<html>
<head>

<script language="VB" runat="server">

  Public Sub Page_Load(s As Object, e As EventArgs)
    dim i,j as integer
    dim row as HtmlTableRow
    dim cell as HtmlTableCell
    for i = 1 to 7
      row = new HtmlTableRow
      for j = 1 to 7
        cell = new HtmlTableCell
        cell.innertext = "R"& i &"C"& j
        row.cells.add (cell)
      next
      table1.rows.add (row)
    next
End sub

  Public Sub btck(sender As Object, e As EventArgs)
    Dim remove As HtmlTableRow
    remove = table1.rows(2)
    table1.Rows.Remove(remove)
  End Sub

</script>

</head>
<body>

<form runat=server>
  <table id="table1" border="3" bordercolor="blue"
  cellpadding="2" cellspacing="2" runat="server" />
  <br>
  <input type=button id=button1 onserverclick=btck value="Remove R3"
                                             runat="server">
</form>

</body>
</html>
```

In this example, we create a table when the page is first loaded, then we use the `Remove` method to
delete the third row in the table. Similarly, we could have used the `Add` or `Insert` methods to
dynamically add or insert rows into the table.

HtmlTableCellCollection Class

The `HtmlTableCellCollection` contains all of the table cells within an `HtmlTable`. With this class we can dynamically add, insert, and remove cells in a table using the methods provided by `HtmlTableCellCollection`. In fact, in the preceding example, `Table.aspx`, we showed how to dynamically add cells to a table using the `Add` method provided by `HtmlTableCellCollection`.

HtmlTableCellCollection Properties

Count

The `Count` property shows the number of items in the `HtmlTableCellCollection`.

IsReadOnly

The `IsReadOnly` property gets a Boolean value to indicate whether `HtmlTableCellCollection` is read-only.

IsSynchronized

The `IsSynchronized` property gets a Boolean value to indicate whether access to `HtmlTableCellCollection` is synchronized.

Item

The `Item` property gets an `HtmlTableCell` from an `HtmlTableCellCollection`.

SyncRoot

An object that can be used to synchronize access to the `HtmlTableCellCollection`.

HtmlTableCellCollection Methods

Add

The `Add` method adds cells to a table.

Clear

The `Clear` method deletes all cells from an `HtmlTableCellCollection`.

CopyTo

The `CopyTo` method copies items in the `HtmlTableCellCollection` to array.

GetEnumerator

The `GetEnumerator` method gets the enumerator that contains all `HtmlTableCell` objects in the `HtmlTableCellCollection`.

Insert

The `Insert` method adds a cell at a specified location in the `HtmlTableCellCollection`.

Remove

The `Remove` method deletes the specified cell from the `HtmlTableCellCollection`.

RemoveAt

The `RemoveAt` method deletes the cell at a specified index location from `HtmlTableCellCollection`.

Example: TableCellCollection

Let's look at another quick example. This code is available for download with the filename `TCCollection.aspx`:

```
<html>
<head>

<script language="VB" runat="server">
  Public Sub Page_Load(s As Object, e As EventArgs)
    dim i,j as integer
    dim row as HtmlTableRow
    dim cell as HtmlTableCell
    for i = 1 to 7
      row = new HtmlTableRow
      for j = 1 to 7
        cell = new HtmlTableCell
        cell.innertext = "R"& i &"C"& j
        row.cells.add (cell)
      next
      table1.rows.add (row)
    next
End sub

Public Sub btck(s As Object, e As EventArgs)
  Dim k As Integer
  For k = 0 To 6
    Dim c As New HtmlTableCell()
    c.innerHtml = "<font color=red>9</font>"
    Table1.Rows(k).Cells.insert(3, c)
  Next k
End Sub

</script>
</head>
<body>

<form runat="server">
  <table id="table1" border="3" bordercolor="blue"
  cellpadding="2" cellspacing="2" runat="server" />
  <br>
  <input type="button" id="button1" onserverclick="btck"
  value="Add Cells at Column 3" runat="server">
</form>

</body>
</html>
```

In this example, we use the `Insert` method to insert cells at the third column in this table dynamically. Similarly, we could use `Add` or `Remove` method to dynamically adjust the cells in a table.

HtmlTextArea Class

The `HtmlTextArea` class allows programmatic access on the server to individual HTML `<textarea>` tags. You can use the `HtmlTextArea` control to gather feedback from users just as with the `HtmlSelect` control. It has the following syntax:

```
<textarea id="id_name"
          cols = "number of columns in textarea"
          name = "name passed to browser"
          rows = "number of rows in textarea"
          runat = "server">
  TextArea Content
</textarea>
```

HtmlTextArea Properties

Cols

The `Cols` property indicates the width in characters of a `textarea`. The default value is not set, or -1.

```
<textarea cols="10" runat="server">...</textarea>
```

Name

The `Name` property indicates the value of the HTML `Name` attribute that will be rendered to the browser.

```
<textarea name="textarea_name" runat="server">...</textarea>
```

Rows

The `Rows` property indicates the display height, in characters, of a `textarea`. The default value is not set, or -1.

```
<textarea rows="10" runat="server">...</textarea>
```

Value

The `Value` property gets or sets the contents of a `textarea`.

```
<textarea value="contents" runat="server">...</textarea>
```

Note that this is equal to `<textarea runat="server">contents</textarea>`.

Here's a quick example, available as `Textarea.aspx`:

```
<html>
<head>

<script language=VB runat=server>
  sub b_click(s as object, e as eventargs)
    span1.innerHtml = "The value in textarea is <b>" + textarea1.value +"</b>"
  end sub
```

```
</script>

</head>
<body>

<form runat=server>
  <textarea id="textarea1" cols=15 rows=5 runat=server />
  <button id="button1" onserverclick="b_click" runat=server>Click</button>
</form>

<hr>
<span id=span1 runat=server />
</body>
</html>
```

HtmlImage Class

The HtmlImage class provides programmatic access on the server to the HTML <img> tag. The HtmlImage control doesn't require a closing tag like the HTML <img>. Most e-commerce web sites have product lists and corresponding product images. Most online users like to see the product image when they click the product. In the past, we used scripts to achieve this. With ASP.NET, this can be done by working with the OnServerClick method of other HTML server controls, like Button or Anchor. This control has the following syntax:

```
<img id="id_name"
     alt = "alternative text"
     align = "alignment of image"
     border = "border width"
     height = "height of image"
     src = "URI of image"
     width = "width of image"
     runat = "server">
```

HtmlImage Properties

Align

The Align property gets or sets the alignment of an image. Valid values are top, middle, bottom, left, and right.

Alt

The Alt property gets or sets a caption that the browser displays if the image is either unavailable or has not been downloaded yet.

Border

The Border property gets or sets the width of border of an image in pixels.

Height

The Height property gets or sets the height of an image in pixels.

193

Src

The `Src` property gets or sets the path and filename of an image that will be displayed in a browser.

Width

The `Width` property gets or sets the width of an image in pixels.

```
<img id="image1" align="middle" alt="test image" border="2"  height="300"
width="300" src="/image/test.gif">
```

Example: HtmlImage Properties

Let's see a simple example for a product list with product images of a typical e-commerce web site. This code is the `default.aspx` page contained in the `ProductPage` folder of the download:

```
<html>
<head>

<script language="VB" runat="server">

  Public Sub bt1(s As Object, e As EventArgs)
    image1.src = "4-1.gif"
    image1.alt = "This is image1"
  End Sub

  Public Sub bt2(s As Object, e As EventArgs)
    image1.src = "4-2.gif"
    image1.alt = "This is image2"
  End Sub

</script>

</head>
<body>

<form runat="server">
  <table height="100%" cellpadding="0" cellspacing="0" width="100%">
    <tr>
      <td width="35%">
        <button id="button1" OnServerClick="bt1" runat="server">Product
A</button><Br>
        <button id="button2" OnServerClick="bt2" runat="server">Product B</button>
      </td>
      <td>
        <img id ="Image1"
           src="4-1.gif"
           Alt = "This is an image"
           runat=server/>
      </td>
    </tr>
  </table>
</form>

</body>
</html>
```

This produces the following:

HtmlInputControl Class

The HtmlInputControl class is the base class for all HTML input controls. It provides properties, methods, and events to all HTML input controls, for example HtmlInputButton, HtmlInputCheckBox, HtmlInputFile, HtmlInputHidden, HtmlInputImage, HtmlInputRadioButton, and HtmlInputText.

HtmlInput Properties

The following properties can be used in all HTML input controls.

Name

The Name property gets or sets a unique identifier name for all HTML input controls. For example:

```
<input name="button1" type="submit" OnServerClick="btfunction" runat="server">
```

Type

The Type property gets the type of an HTML input control. The most common type of course is the 'Submit' input button. The following table shows all of the different types of HTML input controls.

Type	Description
Button	A command button: `<input type="button" runat="server">`
Checkbox	The checkbox type, which can be either true or false: `<input type="checkbox" runat="server">`
File	In ASP.NET, this is a new function for uploading files from client-side to server-side: `<input type="file" runat="server">`

Table continued on following page

Type	Description
Hidden	The field is hidden so that you can persist information between posts to the server without the user knowing: `<input type="hidden" runat="server">`
Image	Acts like an image button: `<input type="image" runat="server">`
Password	A textbox which masks user input: `<input type="password" runat="server">`
Radio	You can only select one of these buttons from its group: `<input type="radio" runat="server">`
Reset	Clears the values in the HTML input controls within a form and act like a button for cleaning up: `<input type="reset" runat="server">`
Submit	A button that submits information to the server: `<input type="submit" runat="server">`
Text	A text box for data entry: `<input type="text" runat="server">`

Value

The `Value` property gets or sets the content value of an HTML input control.

Example: HtmlInputControl

Let's see a quick example, available for download with the filename `Input.aspx`.

```
<html>
<head>

<script language="VB" runat="server">
  Sub btfunction(s As Object, e As EventArgs)
    span1.innerHTML = text1.value
  End Sub
</script>

</head>
<body>

<form runat="server">
  <input id="text1" type="Text" size="10" runat="server">
  <input id="button1" type="Button" OnServerClick="btfunction"
   value="Enter" runat="server">
  <input id="reset1" type="Reset" value="Reset" runat="server">
</form>

<hr>
<span id=span1 runat="server" />
</body>
</html>
```

In this example, we use the HTML input control with types of 'Text', 'Button', and 'Reset'. We also demonstrate how to use the `Value` property.

HtmlInputButton Class

The `HtmlInputButton` class allows programmatic access to the HTML `<input type=button>`, `<input type=submit>`, and `<input type=reset>` tags on the server. Note that `HtmlInputButton` does not require a closing tag. It has the following syntax:

```
<input id="id_name"
       type = "button | submit | reset"
       onserverclick = "onserverclick handler"
       runat = "server">
```

HtmlInputButton Property

CauseValidation

The `CauseValidation` property is new with Beta 2 of the .NET Framework, and it can be set on buttons to cancel their validation behavior. The valid values are `true` and `false`, and the default value is `true`. If `true`, validation will be performed when the button on a web page is clicked. This property will most often be set in the event handler of an `HtmlInputButton`.

HtmlInputButton Method

OnServerClick

The `OnServerClick` method will raise the `ServerClick` event.

HtmlInputButton Event

ServerClick

The `ServerClick` event will occur when an input button is clicked on a web page by a user.

Example: HtmlInputButton

Let's see a quick example, available for download with the filename `InputButton.aspx`:

```
<html>
<head>

<script language=VB runat=server>

  sub sclick(s as object, e as eventargs)
    span1.innerText = text1.value
  end sub

  sub rclick(s as object, e as eventargs)
    text1.value = ""
  end sub
```

```
   sub dclick1(s as object, e as eventargs)
     sub1.disabled = true
     re1.disabled = true
   end sub

   sub dclick2(s as object, e as eventargs)
     sub1.disabled = false
     re1.disabled = false
   end sub

</script>

</head>
<body>

<form runat=server>
  <input type=text id="text1" runat="server"><br>
  <input type=button id="sub1" onserverclick="sclick" value=Show runat=server>
  <input type=button id="re1" onserverclick="rclick" value=Clear runat=server>
</form>

<span id="span1" runat=server /><br>
<input type=button onserverclick="dclick1" value="Disable All" runat=server>
<input type=button onserverclick="dclick2" value="Enable All" runat=server>
</body>
</html>
```

We use buttons to submit a value from the text bar and to clear a value in the text bar. Furthermore, we also use the `Disabled` property that was used in the previous examples to disable or enable the functionalities of the buttons.

HtmlInputCheckBox Class

The `HtmlInputCheckBox` class allows programmatic access to the HTML `<input type=checkbox>` tag on the server. Note that the `HtmlInputCheckBox` class does not require a closing tag. It has the following syntax:

```
<input id="id_name"
       type = "checkbox"
       checked
       runat = "server">
```

HtmlInputCheckBox Property

Checked

The `Checked` property gets or sets a value to determine whether the `HtmlInputCheckBox` is selected or not.

HtmlInputCheckBox Method

OnServerChange

The `OnServerChange` method will raise the `ServerChange` event.

HtmlInputCheckBox Event

ServerChange

The `ServerChange` event will occur when the checkbox changes its state between checked and unchecked.

Example: HtmlInputCheckBox

Let's see this in action in a quick example, available for download with the filename `InputCheckBox.aspx`:

```
<html>
<head>

<script language="VB" runat="server">

  Public Sub bclick(s As Object, e As EventArgs)
    if hidden1.value = check1.checked.tostring() then
      div2.innerhtml = "CheckBox's state is not changed."
    end if
    if check1.checked then
      div1.innertext = "CheckBox is checked"
      hidden1.value = "True"
    else
      div1.innerText = "CheckBox is not checked"
      hidden1.value = "False"
    end if
  End sub

  Public Sub cbc(s As Object, e As EventArgs)
    div2.innerhtml = "CheckBox's state is changed."
  End Sub

</script>

</head>
<body>

<form runat="server">
  <input id="check1" type="checkbox" OnServerChange="cbc" runat="server" checked>
CheckBox1
<input id="button1" type="button" onserverclick="bclick" value="Go"
runat="server">
<input id="hidden1" type="hidden" runat="server">
</form>

<div id=div1 style="color:green" runat="server" />
<div id=div2 style="color:red" runat="server" />
</body>
</html>
```

This produces the following:

As you can see from the example, the checkbox is checked when the page is first loaded because we have included the `Checked` property. We can use the `Checked` property to get the status of a checkbox. This can be useful for a surveying or reporting on a web application.

HtmlInputFile Class

The `HtmlInputFile` class allows programmatic access to the HTML `<input type="file">` tag on the server. In the past, we could not upload files from a client to the server within the functionality of ASP. Instead, we had to write an ActiveX DLL component or use a third-party program and run it on the server to enable us to upload files from a browser to the server. In other words, people who were not familiar with VB programming could not do this by ASP code alone. Thankfully, things have now changed. We can easily reach this functionality with the `HtmlInputFile` class provided by the .NET Framework. This is arguably the most complex and powerful class in the `System.Web.UI.HtmlControl` namespace of the .NET framework. Note that this control does not require a closing tag. It has the following syntax:

```
<input id = "id_name"
       type = "file"
       accept = "MIME encodings"
       maxlength = "Maximum length of path"
       size = "width of file-path textbox"
       postedfile = "uploaded file"
       runat = "server">
```

HtmlInputFile Properties

Accept

The `Accept` property gets or sets a comma-separated list of MIME encodings that can be used to constrain the file types that the browser lets the user select.

MaxLength

The `MaxLength` property gets or sets the maximum length of the path of a file that will be uploaded from a client to the server.

PostedFile

The `PostedFile` property gets access to the file that will be uploaded from a client. To upload files from a client to the server, it needs some additional methods, events, and properties. In order to work on uploading files from a client to the server, we still need to reference some resources in the `HttpPostedFile` class, which is located in the `System.Web` namespace. This class has the following properties:

- ❑ `ContentLength`
- ❑ `ContentType`
- ❑ `FileName`
- ❑ `InputStream`

It has one method:

- ❑ `SaveAs`

We will see how these work in an example.

Size

The `Size` property gets or sets the file-path textbox displaying in a browser.

Example: HtmlInputFile

Let's see a quick example of uploading a file from a client to the server, available for download with the filename `InputFile.aspx`:

```
<html>
<head>

<script language=vb runat=server>
  sub upfile(s as object, e as eventargs)
    dim fname as string
    if file1.PostedFile.ContentLength > 1000 then
      fname = file1.postedfile.filename
      fname = mid(fname, fname.LastIndexOf("\") + 1)
      file1.postedFile.saveas("c:\temp\" & fname)
      span1.innerHtml = "Upload complete ... "
    else
      span1.innerHtml = "Please select a file ..."
    end if
  end sub
</script>

</head>
<body>
<h3>Uploading files example</h3>

<form method="post" enctype="multipart/form-data" runat=server>
  Select a file to upload :
  <input type=file id=file1 runat=server><br>
  <input type=submit value=Go onserverclick=upfile runat=server>
```

```
</form>

<span id=span1 runat=server />
</body>
</html>
```

In the preceding example, we can see some points worth noting about how to create an upload control. The most important thing is the setting of the `<form>` property's `enctype`. You must specify `enctype` as 'multipart/form-data'. The code above will cause the uploaded file to the `temp` directory on the C drive on the server.

```
fname = file1.postedfile.filename
fname = mid(fname, fname.LastIndexOf("\") + 1)
```

In the above code we use the `LastIndexOf` method to get the filename from the `filename` property. In the next example, `InputFile2.aspx`, we will only allow files less than 1,000,000 bytes to be uploaded. It's easy to limit the size of a file to protect server performance or network bandwidth. We can also change our code to accept multiple files simultaneously:

```
<html>
<head>

<script language=vb runat=server>
  sub upfile(s as object, e as eventargs)
    dim fname as string
    dim report as string
    dim allfiles as HttpPostedFile
    dim i as integer
    for i = 0 to request.files.count-1
      allfiles = request.files(i)
      if allfiles.ContentLength > 1000 and allfiles.ContentLength < 1000000 then
        fname = allfiles.filename
        fname = mid(fname, fname.LastIndexOf("\") +2 )
        allfiles.saveas("c:\temp\" & fname)
        report = report & "<font color=green>File " & i+1 & _
                                        " Uploading Complete
...</font><br>"
      else
        report =  report & "<font color=red>File " & i+1 & _
                                " non-selected or fails
uploading...</font><br>"
      end if
    next
    span1.innerHtml = report
  end sub
</script>

</head>
<body>
<h3>Uploading files example</h3>

<form method="post" enctype="multipart/form-data" runat=server>
  Select files to upload :<br>
  File 1 : <input type=file id=file1 runat=server><br>
  File 2 : <input type=file id=file2 runat=server><br>
```

```
        File 3 : <input type=file id=file3 runat=server><br>
        <input type=submit value=Go onserverclick=upfile runat=server>
    </form>

    <span id=span1 runat=server />
    </body>
    </html>
```

This is much more advanced than our first example, as we now have three files uploading at the same time with just one button click. This shows how easy it would now be to code for such a situation as one of the popular Web Hard Disk sites. We use the `HttpPostedFile` class within the `System.Web` namespace in our example.

HtmlInputHidden Class

The `HtmlInputHidden` class allows programmatic access to the HTML `<input type=hidden>` tag on the server. Note that the `HtmlInputHidden` class does not require a closing tag. We often use `<input type="hidden">` to pass an embedded, non-visible piece of information when a user performs a post-back action. It has the following syntax:

```
<input id = "id_name"
       type = "hidden"
       value = "hidden content"
       OnServerChange = "Method name"
       runat = "server">
```

HtmlInputHidden Method

OnServerChange

The `OnServerChange` method raises the `ServerChange` event.

HtmlInputHidden Event

ServerChange

The `ServerChange` event will occur when the value of the `Value` property is changed.

Example: HtmlInputHidden

Let's see an example, available for download with the filename `InputHidden.aspx`:

```
<html>
<head>

<script language=VB runat=server>

  sub hclick(s as object, e as eventargs)
    span1.innerText = hidden1.value
  end sub

</script>
```

```
    </head>
    <body>

    <form runat=server>
      <input id=hidden1 type=hidden value=hiddenvalue runat=server>
      <input id=button2 type=button onserverclick=hclick Value=Hidden runat=server>
    </form>

    <span id=span1 style="color:green" runat=server />
    </body>
    </html>
```

You won't visibly see a 'hidden' object in a browser, so these hidden controls can be used to contain a string of information that you want to trigger by an action. Of course, you can hide information that you don't want to show in a page, and pass it to another page in a normal 'form' action. An `HtmlInputHidden` can also save viewstate information across requests using hidden text fields.

`HtmlInputHidden` has no properties of its own, only inherited ones.

HtmlInputImage Class

The `HtmlInputImage` class allows programmatic access to the HTML `<input type="image">` tag on the server. Note that the `HtmlInputImage` class does not require a closing tag. As this control is the `<input type="image">` element that is run on the server, it offers the same button customization as with the other Input Controls. When it is clicked, the form containing the element is submitted to the server along with the coordinates of the mouse pointer within our image. Note that the `HtmlInputImage` control offers greater support for down-level browsers than the `HtmlButton` control. With the `ServerClick` event, an `HtmlInputImage` can change its alignment dynamically and have the same behavior as a button. It also can use DHTML events, for example `OnMouseOver`, `OnMouseOut`. It has the following syntax:

```
<input id = "id_name"
       type = "image"
       align = "alignment of image"
       alt = "text of alert"
       src = "image path"
       width = "image width"
       onserverclick = "onserverclick handler"
       runat = "server">
```

HtmlInputImage Properties

Align

The `Align` property gets or sets the alignment of the image. Valid values are: `top`, `middle`, `bottom`, `left`, and `right`.

Alt

The `Alt` property gets or sets the alternative text for the specified image that the browser should display if the image cannot be shown.

Border

The `Border` property gets or sets the border width of an image in pixels.

Src

The `Src` property indicates the path and filename of the image file.

HtmlInputImage Method

OnServerClick

The `OnServerClick` method will raise the `ServerClick` event.

HtmlInputImage Event

ServerClick

The `ServerClick` event will occur when the image is clicked.

Example: HtmlInputImage

Let's see an example, available for download with the filename `InputImage.aspx`.

```
<html>
<head>

<script language="VB" runat="server">
  Public Sub image_ck(s As Object, e As ImageClickEventArgs)
    dim x as integer
    dim y as integer
    x = e.x.tostring()
    y = e.y.tostring()
    span1.innertext = "The coordinates you clicked are (" & x &","& y &")."
  End sub
</script>

</head>
<body>

<form runat=server>
  <input id="image1" type="image" width="180" onserverclick="image_ck"
    src="nyc.jpg" runat="server" />
</form>

<hr>
<span id="span1" runat="server" />
</body>
</html>
```

In the preceding example we show the coordinates of an image. The origin, (0,0), is the upper-left corner of the image. We use the `ImageClickEventArgs` class from the `System.Web.UI` namespace to achieve the display of the coordinates.

HtmlInputRadioButton Class

The HtmlInputRadioButton class allows programmatic access to the HTML <input type=radio> tag on the server. Note that the HtmlInputRadioButton class does not require a closing tag. Because HtmlInputRadioButton doesn't have any methods or events it must rely on other controls, for example HtmlInputButton, to make a 'ServerChange'-like event. It has the following syntax:

```
<input id="id_name"
       type = "radio"
       name = "radio group"
       checked
       runat = "server">
```

HtmlInputRadioButton Properties

Checked

The Checked property gets or sets a value to determine whether a radio button is selected or not.

Name

The Name property allows us to group these controls together by specifying a Name that is common to all <input type=radio> elements within the group.

Value

The Value property gets the value of a radio button.

Example: HtmlInputRadioButton

Let's see a quick example, available for download with the filename `InputRadio.aspx`:

```
<html>
<head>

<script language="VB" runat="server">
  Public Sub Button1_Click(s As Object, e As EventArgs)
    If Radio1.Checked Then
      Span1.InnerHtml = radio1.value & " is selected"
    elseif Radio2.Checked Then
      Span1.InnerHtml = radio2.value & " is selected"
    elseif Radio3.Checked Then
      Span1.InnerHtml = radio3.value & " is selected"
    End if
  End Sub
</script>

</head>
<body>

<form runat=server>
  <input type="radio" id="Radio1" name="radio" value="First radio"
                                                runat="server"/>
  The first radio<br>
  <input type="radio" id="Radio2" name="radio" value="Second radio"
                                                runat="server"/>
  The second radio<br>
  <input type="radio" id="Radio3" name="radio" value="Third radio"
                                                runat="server"/>
  The third radio<br>
  <input type="button" id="Button1" value="Enter"
   OnServerClick="Button1_Click" runat="server">
</form>

<hr>
<span id="Span1" runat="server" />
</body>
</html>
```

In this example we have used all of the properties of `HtmlInputRadioButton` to show how they work. We have also added a button control to show a message about the radio selection when the button is clicked.

HtmlInputText Class

The `HtmlInputText` class allows programmatic access to the HTML `<input type=text>` and `<Input type=password>` tags on the server. Note that it does not require a closing tag. In general, it is often used for the input of a username and password in the browser.

Syntax:

```
<input id="id_name
        type = "text | password"
        maxlength = "Maximum length of content"
        size = "width of textbox"
        value = "content of textbox"
        runat = "server">
```

HtmlInputText Properties

MaxLength

The `MaxLength` property gets or sets the maximum number of characters that can be typed into the textbox.

Size

The `Size` property gets or sets the width of a textbox, in characters.

Value

The `Value` property gets or sets the contents of a textbox.

HtmlInputText Method

OnServerChange

The `OnServerChange` method will raise the `ServerChange` event.

HtmlInputText Event

ServerChange

The `ServerChange` event will occur when the value of the `Value` property of `HtmlInputText` is changed.

Example: HtmlInputText

Let's see a quick example, available for download with the filename `InputText.aspx`:

```
<html>
<head>

<script language="vb" runat="server">
  Public Sub check1(s As Object, e As EventArgs)
    if username.value = "Ginny" and password.value = "123456" then
      span1.innerText = "Okay !"
    else
      span1.innerText = "Fail !"
    end if
  End sub
</script>

</head>
<body>

<form runat="server">
  Username : <input type="text" id="username" size="15" runat="server"><br>
  Password : <input type="password" id="password" runat="server"><br>
  <input type="button" id="button1" onserverclick="check1"
   value="Check" runat="server">
</form>

<span id=span1 runat=server />
</body>
</html>
```

Unless we enter Ginny as the username and 123456 as the password authentication will fail. This is a simple way to authenticate with a username and password.

System.Web.UI.WebControls

In this chapter we will look at arguably the most important part of the user interface of ASP.NET: the Web Controls defined within the `System.Web.UI.WebControls` namespace. This namespace contains many control classes that expose complex, extensible functionality and offer a range of capabilities. We can divide the web controls into four groups by their functionalities and features. In the first group are controls that mirror the functions of the HTML controls described in the previous chapter. The main reason that they recur in the `System.Web.UI.Webcontrols` namespace is that web form controls are server-side equivalents of the HTML controls (which generally are run on the client). You will also find the web controls to be more intuitive than their HTML counterparts. For example, we use the HTML controls `<input type="checkbox">` and `<input type="button">` to represent a checkbox and a button respectively. However, in the web controls, we can use their names directly. For example, `<asp:Checkbox>` and `<asp:Button>`. Many developers will find this a much clearer and more intuitive arrangement, and it can simplify the process of creating interactive web pages.

The `System.Web.UI.Webcontrols` namespace can be divided into the following four groups:

- ❑ **Web Form Controls (HTML intrinsic controls)** – the `Button`, `CheckBox`, `Hyperlink`, `Image`, `ImageButton`, `Label`, `LinkButton`, `Literal`, `Panel`, `RadioButton`, `PlaceHolder`, `Table`, `TableCell`, `TableHeadCell`, `TableRow`, `TextBox`, and `XML` server controls.

- ❑ **List Controls** – the `ListItem`, `CheckBoxList`, `DropDownList`, `ListBox`, `RadioButtonList`, `Repeater`, `DataGrid`, and `DataList` server controls. We can also call the last three controls "Data-Bound" list controls.

- ❑ **Rich Controls** – the `AdRotator` and `Calendar` server controls.

- ❑ **Validation Controls** – the `CompareValidator`, `RangeValidator`, `RegularExpressionValidator`, `RequiredFieldValidator`, `ValidationSummary` and `CustomValidator` server controls.

All of the above controls are created simply by adding the `asp:` namespace prefix (upper and lower case are equally acceptable) to indicate that the control belongs to the `System.Web.UI.WebControls` namespace. Like the HTML Controls in the previous chapter, there's no need to import any namespaces into your `.aspx` page to use these controls. Note that, as with any other XML element, all web controls must have well-formed names that don't overlap – controls must have either an ending slash within the tag or a separate closing tag. For example, `<asp:Checkbox runat="server" />` or `<asp:Checkbox runat="server"> ... </asp:Checkbox>`. No doubt you'll find the first format easier and clearer for your ASP.NET code.

The WebControl Class

Before we get into details, let's first examine the base class of the `System.Web.UI.Webcontrols` namespace: the `WebControl` class, which defines properties, methods, and events for all controls within this namespace.

Properties of the WebControl class

The AccessKey Property

The `AccessKey` property gets or sets a keyboard shortcut key to move focus to the web control. This property can be very useful, and makes web form pages resemble a Visual Basic application.

The Attributes Property

This gets a collection of attribute name-value pairs for a web control. It can be used to get or set custom attributes where a control doesn't provide a specific property for a purpose.

The BackColor Property

The `BackColor` property gets or sets the background color of a web control.

The BorderColor Property

This gets or sets the border color of a web control.

The BorderStyle Property

This property gets or sets the border style of a web control.

The BorderWidth Property

Use this property to get or set the border width for a particular web control.

The ControlStyle Property

This property gets the style of a web control, and is primarily used by control developers.

The CssClass Property

This property gets or sets a CSS class rendered by a web control.

The Enabled Property

The `Enabled` property gets or sets a Boolean value indicating whether a web control is enabled. The default value is `True`.

The Font Property

This gets the font information of a web control. For example, it can be used to change the text of a label control to underlined:

```
Label1.Font.Underline = True
```

The sub-properties available are `Bold`, `Italic`, `Name`, `Names`, `Strikeout`, `Underline`, and `Size`.

The ForeColor Property

Use this to get or set the foreground color of a web control.

The Height Property

This property gets or sets the height of a web control.

The Style Property

The `Style` property gets a collection of CSS style properties that apply to a web control.

The TabIndex Property

This gets or sets a tab order of a web control.

The TagKey Property

This property returns the HTML tag for the control.

The TagName Property

This property gets the name of the control's tag, and is primarily used by control developers.

The ToolTip Property

The `ToolTip` property gets or sets the pop-up text displayed by a web control when the mouse cursor hovers over the web control. This property can let a web form page act like a Visual Basic style application.

The Width Property

This property gets or sets the width of a web control.

Web Form Controls (HTML Intrinsic Controls)

Web Form Controls are also commonly known as HTML Intrinsic Controls because they are used in much the same way as you would use the HTML controls explained in the previous chapter. The biggest difference is the prefix, "asp:". This prefix must be added to every web control, and if you don't then the control will not be treated as a web server control. However, Web Form Controls are distinctly different from HTML Controls because of the following benefits they offer:

❑   Web Form Controls provide a standard naming convention for similar controls. One of the problems with HTML server controls has been the lack of a consistent naming convention for similar controls and attributes, a problem shared by the HTML server controls. Web Form Controls eliminate this problem. For example, if we need a button, a checkbox, and a radio button in a page, we can write our code with HTML Server Controls as follows:

```
<input type="button" runat="server">
<input type="checkbox" runat="server">
<input type="radio" runat ="server">
```

All of these controls are input controls, but they all behave in different ways. Web Form Controls can provide an alternative, more intuitive, way to declare different controls.

```
<asp:Button runat="server" />
<asp:Checkbox runat="server" />
<asp:RadioButton runat="server" />
```

❑ Web Form Controls provide common attributes for determining certain characteristics of all controls. For example, `BackColor` means the background color for any Web Form server control. When you want to set the background color for a control, you always use the same attribute irrespective of the control. For example:

```
<asp:Button backcolor="red" runat="server" />
<asp:TextBox backcolor="blue" runat="server" />
```

This feature is available for web controls only, as the HTML server controls are still restricted to old-style attributes.

❑ Web Form Controls provide greater power and flexibility for creating web pages that might be viewed by a variety of browsers and devices.

❑ Web Form Controls provide composite controls with very rich functionality, such as the `Calendar` and `AdRotator` controls.

Generally speaking, if you want a Visual Basic-like programming model, then Web Form Controls are more capable and have a richer object model than the corresponding HTML server controls. If you want all controls running on the server to have good performance, functionality, and capability, then Web Form Controls are a good choice and are in general better than HTML server controls. To sum up then:

Web Control	HTML Control
Provides a VB-style programming model	Provides a HTML-style programming model
Web pages that consist of web controls can be readily viewed by a variety of browsers	When you want to add web forms functionality to an existing HTML site, these controls can be the better choice
Certain richer controls, such as the `Calendar` and `Datagrid`, are only available using web controls	

Let's start with the `Button` server control as the first of the Web Form Controls we shall look at.

The Button Control

A `Button` control renders a clickable button on a Web page. It corresponds to the `<input type="submit">` in HTML controls. The `Button` web control can submit the form to the server and it can raise an event that fires the appropriate event code in our server-side script.

Syntax:

```
<asp: Button id="id_name"
    Text = "button's caption"
    CommandName = "Command name"
    CommandArgument = "Command argument"
    Onclick = "event name" | OnCommand = "event name"
    Runat = "server" />
```

You can create either a Submit button or a Command button on a Web page. When you don't specify a `CommandName` property, the button is by default a Submit button. You can provide an event handler for the `Click` event to programmatically control the actions performed when the submit button is clicked. An example of a simple event handler is given here:

```
Sub event_handler_name( s As Object, e As EventArgs)
```

A button with a command name is called a Command button. You can create Command buttons by specifying the `CommandName` property, which is used to programmatically determine the button that was clicked. You can also provide additional information in the `CommandArgument` property for a button. Furthermore, you can specify an event handler for the `Command` event that programmatically controls the action performed when the Command button is clicked.

A fundamental difference between a Submit button and a Command button is that you can have multiple Command buttons in a web form pages for different purposes. For example, you may have two Command buttons in a web page; one for sorting data by time order and the other for sorting data by alphabetic order, say. In this case, the sort order, as either time or character, would be given by the `CommandArgument` property for each of these two button web controls. On the other hand, there can only be one Submit button in a web page, and when it is clicked, it passes data in the form to the server.

Properties of the Button Control

The CauseValidation Property

This property gets or sets a value that determines whether validation is to occur when the button is clicked. The default value is `True`, which means validation of supplied data is to be performed when the button is clicked. This property works with the `Validation` controls. If you don't want to validate a button control when the validation controls are active, then you should set this property to `false`.

```
<asp:button causevalidation="false" text="button1" runat="server" />
```

The CommandArgument Property

This gets or sets an argument for a button. When you set the `CommandName` property indicating that the button is a Command button, then this property provides the means for passing arguments to a Command event.

The CommandName Property

This gets or sets the command name associated with the `Button` control that is passed to the `Command` event. This command name can be used on the server to determine which control was triggered.

Let's see a quick example that demonstrates the `CommandArgument` and `CommandName` properties in action. Say we want to search a database by keyword; we use the `CommandName` property to specify the search action, and the `CommandArgument` property for the keyword:

```
<asp:Button id="button1"
    Text = "Search"
    CommandName = "search"
    CommandArgument = "keyword"
    OnCommand = "button1_click"
    Runat = "server" />
```

In the event handler for the button, we can declare two variables to get the values of `CommandName` and `CommandArgument` to use as the parameters for searching the database:

In VB.NET:

```
Sub button1_click( s as object, e As CommandEventArgs)
    Dim search_pa as string = button1.CommandName
    Dim kw_pa as string = button1.CommandArgument
    ...
End sub
```

Note that the button in this above example is a Command button, and not a Submit button, which doesn't require these properties to be set.

The Text Property

This property gets or sets the caption text for the button.

```
<asp:Button text="Button1" runat="server" />
```

Methods of the Button Control

The OnClick Method

This method will raise a 'click' event when a Submit button is clicked. A Submit button is one for which no `CommandName` or `CommandArguments` properties have been specified. The code section for the event handler will look like this:

In VB.NET:

```
Sub button1_click( s As Object, e As EventArgs)
...
End sub
```

The OnCommand Method

The `Command` event is raised when a Command button is clicked. A command button must have the `CommandName` and `CommandArguments` properties specified. The code section for the event handler will look like this:

VB.NET

```
Sub button1_click( s as object, e As CommandEventArgs)
    ' Code for handling this command button
    ...
End sub
```

Events of the Button Control

The Click Event

The `Click` event will occur when a button control is clicked and the button is a Submit button, which it is when no `CommandName` and `CommandArgument` properties are specified.

The Command Event

The Command event will occur when a Button control is clicked and the button is a Command button, that is, it specifies its CommandName and CommandArgument properties.

Example: Button Control

Let's see a quick example of a Submit button and a Command button:

```
<html>
<head>
  <script language="VB" runat=server>
    Sub CommandBtn_Click(sender As Object, e As CommandEventArgs)
      label1.Text = "You clicked the command button: Name - " & e.CommandName & _
                               ", Parameter - " & e.CommandArgument &"."
    End Sub 'CommandBtn_Click
    Sub clickBtn_Click(sender As Object, e As EventArgs)
      label2.Text = "You clicked the submit button."
    End Sub 'CommandBtn_Click
  </script>
</head>
<body>
  <form runat="server">
    <h3>Button Example</h3>
    <asp:Button id="Button1"
      Text="Command button"
      CommandName="Name"
      CommandArgument="Parameter"
      OnCommand="CommandBtn_Click"
      runat="server"/><br>
    <asp:Button id="Button2"
      Text="Submit button"
      OnClick="clickBtn_Click"
      runat="server"/><br>
    <asp:label id="label1" runat="server"/><br>
    <asp:label id="label2" runat="server"/>
  </form>
</body>
</html>
```

This code will display the following in a browser:

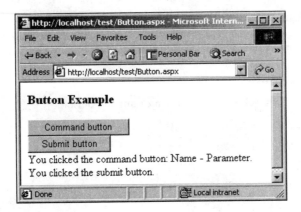

CheckBox

The CheckBox control will display a checkbox on a Web page to let the user select either true or false for a given value. It corresponds to the <input type="checkbox"> element of the HTML Controls.

Syntax:

```
<asp:Checkbox id = "id_name"
    AutoPostBack = "True | False"
    Text = "Label for check box"
    TextAlign = "Right | Left"
    Checked = "True | False"
    OnCheckedChanged = "Method of Checkbox changing state"
    Runat = "server" />
```

Properties of the CheckBox Control

The AutoPostBack Property

This property gets or sets a value to determine whether the state of CheckBox is posted back to the server automatically. The default value is False, so set to True for the state of a CheckBox to be posted back to the server automatically when it changes.

The Checked Property

This gets or sets a value according to whether the CheckBox control is checked. The default value is False meaning that the CheckBox is unchecked by default. Set to True for the CheckBox to appear checked initially. The property reflects the current state of the CheckBox, and changes immediately as the user selects or deselects it.

Let's see the property's usage in the following quick code example.

In VB.NET:

```
Sub Check_Clicked(sender As Object, e As EventArgs)
    If checkbox1.Checked Then
        Label1.Text = "The CheckBox is checked."
    Else
```

```
        Label1.Text = "The CheckBox is not checked."
     End If
  End Sub
```

We now have an event handler for the CheckBox control. When a user changes its state from unchecked to checked or vice versa, the text of the label will change accordingly.

```
<asp:CheckBox id="checkbox1" runat="server"
        AutoPostBack="True"
        Text="Click"
     TextAlign = "Right"
     OnCheckedChanged="Check_Clicked"/>
```

In order for a checkbox to react immediately on a Web page as the user changes its check state, you must assign `True` to the `AutoPostBack` property and assign an event handler for the `OnCheckedChanged` method as discussed later.

The Text Property

The `Text` property gets or sets the text label associated with the `CheckBox` control. The default is an empty string.

The TextAlign Property

The `TextAlign` property is used to get or set the alignment of the text label associated with the `CheckBox` control. The valid values are `Right` and `Left`.

Methods of the CheckBox Control

The OnCheckedChanged Method

The `OnCheckedChanged` method will raise the `CheckedChanged` event when the state of the `CheckBox` control is changed.

Events of the CheckBox Control

The CheckedChanged Event

The `CheckedChanged` event occurs when the `Checked` property is changed.

Example: The CheckBox Control

Let's see this event in action in the following quick example:

```
<html><head>
<script language="VB" runat="server">
Sub checkbox1_check ( s As Object, e As EventArgs )
   if checkbox1.checked then
     label1.text = "It is checked."
   else
     label1.text = "It is not checked."
   end if
```

```
End Sub
</script>
</head>
<body>
<form runat="server">
<asp:checkbox id="checkbox1"
    AutoPostBack="True"
    text="Checkbox"
    textalign = "Right"
    oncheckedchanged = "checkbox1_ch"
    runat="server" /><Br>
<asp:Label id="label1" runat="server" />
</form>
</body></html>
```

This code will have the following output in the browser:

The HyperLink Control

The HyperLink control displays a link on a Web page to let people go to another page or web site. It corresponds to the HTML control `<a runat="server">`.

Syntax:

```
<asp:HyperLink id="id_name"
    NavigateUrl = "Url of target page"
    Text = "Visible Text for the HyperLink"
    ImageUrl = "Url of image"
    Target = "_blank | _parent | _self | _top"
    Runat = "server" />
```

or:

```
<asp:HyperLink id="id_name"
    NavigateUrl = "Url of target page"
    ImageUrl = "Url of image"
    Target = "_blank | _parent | _self | _top"
    Runat = "Server">Visible Text for the Hyperlink</asp:HyperLink>
```

The HyperLink control is quite basic in comparison to other controls in that it only carries a minimal number of properties and has no methods or events.

Properties of the HyperLink Control

The ImageUrl Property

The ImageUrl property gets or sets the path of an image that is displayed on a Web page as the HyperLink control. The default value is empty.

The NavigateUrl Property

The NavigateUrl property gets or sets the URL that is linked to when the HyperLink control is clicked. The default value is empty.

The Target Property

The Target property gets or sets the target window or frame to display the Web page content linked to when the HyperLink control is clicked. The default value is empty. We have already seen the four target parameters in the previous chapter. Here we'll just briefly recap them as follows:

❑ _blank – displays the web page in a new and unframed browser window

❑ _parent – displays the web page in the immediate frameset parent in the same browser

❑ _self – displays the web page in the current frame in the same browser window

❑ _top – displays the web page in a full and unframed window in the same browser

If you don't set any values for the Target property, then by default it will display the content in the current frame in the same browser window. If you set any other values for the Target property, remember that it treats unknown parameters as the _blank parameter.

The Text Property

The Text property gets or sets the text of the HyperLink control.

Let's see a quick example of how these two properties work together:

```
<asp:HyperLink id="hyperlink1"
    ImageUrl="images/wrox.jpg"
    NavigateUrl="http://www.wrox.com"
    Text="Wrox Press"
    Target="_blank"
    runat="server" />
```

This is equivalent to the following:

```
<asp:HyperLink id=" hyperlink2"
    ImageUrl="images/wrox.jpg"
    NavigateUrl="http://www.wrox.com"
    Target="_blank"
    runat="server">Wrox Press</asp:HyperLink>
```

The HyperLink control doesn't have any methods or events. Unlike the majority of the Web Server Controls, the HyperLink control doesn't raise a server-side event when the user clicks it, and simply performs the specified navigation directly.

The Image Control

The Image control displays an image on a Web page and roughly corresponds to the HTML tag <img>.

Syntax:

```
<asp:Image id="id_name"
      ImageUrl = "Url of image"
      AlternateText = "text of alert"
      ImageAlign = "alignment of image"
      Runat = "server" />
```

Properties of the Image Control

The AlternateText Property

The AlternateText property gets or sets the alternative text displayed in the Image control on a Web page when the image is unavailable or is downloading. If a browser supports the ToolTips feature, then the alternative text will also display as a ToolTip when the cursor hovers over the image.

The ImageAlign Property

The ImageAlign property gets or sets the alignment of the image with reference to some other control or element. This property has a range of parameters, described in the following table:

Alignment Parameter	Description
AbsBottom	In the same HTML line, the image will be aligned with the lower edge of the highest element.
AbsMiddle	In the same HTML line, the image will be aligned with the middle of the highest element
Baseline	In the same HTML line, the lower edge of the image will be aligned with the bottom line of the first text in this line
Bottom	In the same HTML line, the lower edge of the image will be aligned with the bottom line of the first text in this line
Left	The image will be aligned with the left side of a web page in the next line rather than original line
Middle	In the same HTML line, the middle point of the image will be aligned with the bottom edge of the first line of text
NotSet	It sets nothing to this property
Right	The image will be aligned with the right side of a web page in the next line rather than original line
TextTop	In the same HTML line, the top side of the image will be aligned with the top edge of the highest text in this line
Top	In the same HTML line, the top side of the image will be aligned with the top edge of the highest element in this line

The ImageUrl Property

The `ImageUrl` property gets or sets the URL of the image that is to be displayed by the control.

Like the `Hyperlink` control, the `Image` control is quite simple in that it doesn't have any methods or events.

The ImageButton Control

The `ImageButton` control enables you to click an image, which will in turn raise an event. It corresponds to the HTML control `<input type="image">`.

Syntax:

```
<asp:ImageButton id = "id_name"
      ImageUrl = "URL of image"
      CommandName = "Command name"
      CommandArgument = "Command argument"
      OnCommand = "Method name" | OnClick = "Method name"
      Runat = "server" />
```

As you can see, the syntax of the `ImageButton` control is very similar to that of the Button control. The `ImageButton` control has Click and Command button functionality. A Command image button will have `CommandName` and `CommandArgument` properties specified for it, whereas a Click image button, like a Submit button, will not. The `OnCommand` method will be invoked by clicking on a Command image button and the `OnClick` method will be invoked by clicking on a Click image button.

Properties of the ImageButton Control

The CauseValidation Property

The `CausesValidation` property gets or sets a Boolean value to determine whether validation should occur when the image button is clicked. The default `True` means validation is performed when an image button is clicked; set to `False` to inhibit such checking.

The CommandArgument Property

The `CommandArgument` property gets or sets an optional argument that is passed to the `Command` event along with the associated `CommandName` property.

The CommandName Property

The `CommandName` property gets or sets the command name associated with the `ImageButton` control, and can be used by the `Command` event to determine which control has been fired.

Methods of the ImageButton Control

The OnClick Method

This method is fired when the `Click` event is raised by the user clicking on a Click image button. This applies when no `CommandName` and `CommandArguments` properties are specified. It is possible to determine the exact coordinates of the cursor on the image inside this method, relative to the top-left corner of the image as (0, 0). The code section for the event handler will look as follows:

```
Sub ImageButton_Click(s as Object, e as ImageClickEventArgs)
    ...
End Sub
```

The OnCommand Method

This method is fired when the Command event is raised by the user clicking on a Command image button, that is, an image control that specifies values for the CommandName and CommandArguments properties. The particular Command button that invoked the call can be determined from within the Command event handler by examining the CommandName property. The code section for the event handler would look something like the following:

```
Sub ImageButton_Command(s as Object, e as CommandEventArgs)
    If (e.CommandName = "Spellcheck") And (e.CommandArgument = "US-English") Then
        ...
End Sub
```

Events of the ImageButton Control

The Click Event

The Click event will be raised when an ImageButton control is clicked and the button is a Click image button, which means it has no CommandName or CommandArgument properties specified.

The Command Event

The Command event is raised when an ImageButton control is clicked and the button is a Command image button, which it is when it has CommandName and CommandArgument properties specified.

The Label Control

The Label control displays static text on a Web page and allows you to manipulate it programmatically. It corresponds to the HTML <span> element.

Syntax:

```
<asp:Label id = "id_name"
    Text = "text of Label"
    runat = "server" />
```

or:

```
<asp:Label id = "id_name"
    runat = "server">Text of Label</asp:Label>
```

Properties of the Label Control

The Text Property

The Text property gets or sets the text content of a Label control.

```
<asp:Label id="label1" text="This is a Label control" runat="server" />
```

The `Label` control doesn't have any methods or events.

The LinkButton Control

The `LinkButton` control has the appearance of a `Hyperlink` but acts like a `Button` control.

Syntax:

```
<asp:LinkButton id = "id_name"
      Text = "Text of LinkButton"
      CommandName = "Command name parameter"
      CommandArgument = "Command argument parameter"
      OnCommand = "Method of LinkButton" | OnClick = "Method of LinkButton"
      Runat = "server" />
```

or:

```
<asp:LinkButton id="id_name"
      Command="Command name parameter"
      CommandArgument="Command argument parameter"
      OnCommand = "Method of LinkButton" | OnClick = "Method of LinkButton"
      Runat = "server" >Text of LinkButton</asp:LinkButton>
```

The `LinkButton` control allows you to create either a Submit link button or a Command link button on a Web page. By default if you do not specify `CommandName` and `CommandArgument` properties, the link button is a Submit link button. You can provide an event handler for the `Click` event to programmatically control the actions performed when such a Submit link button is clicked.

A link button with a command name is a Command link button. You can create Command buttons by specifying the `CommandName` property on a Web page and programmatically determining which link button is clicked. You can also provide additional information by specifying a `CommandArgument` property for the link button. You can also add an event handler for the `Command` event to programmatically control the actions performed when the Command link button is clicked.

Properties of the LinkButton Control

The CauseValidation Property

The `CausesValidation` property gets or sets a Boolean value to indicate whether validation should occur when the link button is clicked. The default value is `True`, which means validation is performed when a link button is clicked; set this to `False` to inhibit such checking.

The CommandArgument Property

The `CommandArgument` property gets or sets an optional argument passed to the `Command` event along with the associated `CommandName` property.

The CommandName Property

The `CommandName` property gets or sets the command name associated with the `LinkButton` control that is passed to the `Command` event.

The Text Property

The Text property gets or sets the text displayed on a link button. For example:

```
<asp:LinkButton id="LinkButton1"
    Text="Click Me"
    Font-Name="Comic Sans MS"
    Forecolor = Green
    runat="server"/>
```

The Forecolor property is inherited from the WebControl class, with the other properties and methods it defines. Because the WebControl class is the base class from which all web controls in the System.Web.UI.Webcontrols namespace are derived, we can use its properties and methods equally on all controls in that namespace.

Methods of the LinkButton Control

The OnClick Method

This method is fired when the Click event is raised by the user clicking a Submit link button. This applies when no CommandName and CommandArgument properties are defined for the link button. The code section for the event handler will look like the following:

In VB.NET:

```
Sub lnkBtn_click ( s As Object, e As EventArgs)
...
End sub
```

The OnCommand Method

This method is fired when the Command event is raised by the user clicking on a Command link button. This applies when CommandName and CommandArgument properties are specified for the link button. The code section for the event handler will look as follows:

In VB.NET:

```
Sub lnkBtn_command( s As Object, e As CommandEventArgs)
...
End sub
```

Events of the LinkButton Control

The Click Event

The Click event is fired when the LinkButton control is clicked and it is a Submit link button, meaning that it has no CommandName or CommandArgument properties.

The Command Event

The Command event will be raised when the LinkButton control is clicked and it is a Command LinkButton, that is, one with CommandName and CommandArgument properties specified.

The Literal Control

The `Literal` control displays static text on a Web page that you can manipulate programmatically.

Syntax:

```
<asp:Literal id = "id_name"
     Text="Text of Literal"
     Runat="server" />
```

or:

```
<asp:Literal id = "id_name"
     runat = "server">Text of Literal</asp:Literal>
```

Unlike the `Label` web control, the `Literal` control does not allow you to apply styles to the text it contains, because text displayed by `Literal` controls only appears on a web page without any HTML code. For example, say you have the following code in a web page:

```
<asp:Literal id="Literal1" text="This is a Literal control" runat="Server" />
```

When you now open this web page with IE, you will find it contains no HTML code, only the text "This is a Literal control" in the HTML source. This is because that `Literal` controls only provide plain, unadorned, text on a web page. This text will however inherit the style and formatting of its parent elements, according to the standard cascading rules of HTML. For instance, `Literal` controls can be used to place content in a table's cells.

Properties of the Literal Control

The Text Property

The `Text` property gets or sets the text content of a `Literal` control.

The Panel Control

The `Panel` control is a control that acts as a container for other controls. It corresponds to the HTML `<div>` element.

Syntax:

```
<asp:Panel id = "id_name"
     BackImageUrl = "Url of background image"
     HorizontalAlign = "Center | Justify | Left | NotSet | Right"
     Wrap = "True | False"
     Runat = "server">
          Other controls
</asp:Panel>
```

If you want to set a group of controls that are displayed or hidden together, then the `Panel` control provides a good way of achieving this. Just like the `<div>` tag, it allows you to manipulate it programmatically.

Properties of the Panel Control

The BackImageUrl Property

The `BackImageUrl` property gets or sets the URL of a background image.

The HorizontalAlign Property

The `HorizontalAlign` property gets or sets the horizontal alignment of the contents of the `Panel` control with respect to its width. It returns one of the following values from the `HorizontalAlign` enumeration:

- ❑ `Left`
- ❑ `Right`
- ❑ `Center`
- ❑ `Justify`
- ❑ `NotSet`

The default value is `NotSet`.

The Wrap Property

The `Wrap` property gets or sets a Boolean value that determines whether the contents of the `Panel` control wraps within its boundaries. The default value is `True`.

The `Panel` control has no methods or events.

Example: The Panel Control

Let's see a quick example of the `Panel` control. Here a `CheckBox` control is used to toggle the visibility of the Panel contents:

```
<html>
<head>
<script language=vb runat="server">
Sub cb1(sender As Object, e As EventArgs)
   if checkbox1.checked then
     panel1.visible = false
   else
     panel1.visible = true
   end if
End Sub
</script>
</head>
<body>
   <h3>Panel Example</h3>
   <form runat=server>
     <asp:Checkbox id=checkbox1 Oncheckedchanged="cb1"
           AutoPostBack="True"
           text="Show/Hide" runat=server />
<br>
   <asp:panel id=panel1 horizontalalign=center
```

```
            backcolor="yellow"
            height=80
            width=300 runat=server>
        <asp:label id=label1 text="This is Label1" runat=server /><br>
        <asp:HyperLink id="hyperlink1"
            NavigateUrl="http://www.wrox.com"
            Text="Wrox Press" runat="server" />
    </asp:Panel>
    </form>
</body>
</html>
```

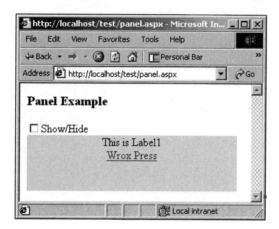

The PlaceHolder Control

The `PlaceHolder` control reserves an area of a Web page in which you may add, insert, and remove items programmatically via the `Control.Controls` collection of a `PlaceHolder` instance.

Syntax:

```
<asp:PlaceHolder id="id_name"
        runat="server"/>
```

Example: The PlaceHolder Control

This sample page demonstrates how to add a new Button control to a `PlaceHolder` control.

```
<html>
<head>
<script runat="server">
Public Sub Page_Load(s As Object, e As EventArgs)

Dim myButton As HtmlButton = New HtmlButton()

myButton.InnerText = "A"
PlaceHolder1.Controls.Add(myButton)
myButton = New HtmlButton()
```

```
myButton.InnerText = "B"
PlaceHolder1.Controls.Add(myButton)
End Sub

Sub button1_click(s As Object, e As EventArgs)
Dim myButton As HtmlButton = New HtmlButton()
myButton = New HtmlButton()
myButton.InnerText = "C"
PlaceHolder1.Controls.Add(myButton)
End Sub
</script>
</head>

<body>
<asp:PlaceHolder id="PlaceHolder1" runat="server"/>

<form runat="server">
<asp:button id="button1" onclick="button1_click" text="Add a button to
Placeholder" runat="Server" />
</form>

</body>
</html>
```

The `PlaceHolder` control has no properties, methods, or events.

The RadioButton Control

The `RadioButton` control represents radio buttons on a Web page, which allow the user to select one of a set of mutually exclusive choices. It corresponds to the HTML `<input type="radio">` tag.

Syntax:

```
<asp:RadioButton id = "id_name"
     AutoPostBack = "True | False"
     Checked = "True | False"
     GroupName = "GroupName"
     Text = "Text of RadioButoon"
     TextAlign = "Right | Left"
     OnCheckedChanged = "Method name"
     Runat = "server" />
```

Properties of the RadioButton Control

The GroupName Property

The `GroupName` property gets or sets a group name for a set of interrelated radio buttons on a Web page. When this property is set, only one radio button can be checked per group of `RadioButton` controls.

`AutoPostBack`, `Checked`, `Text`, `TextAlign`, and `OnCheckedChange` of the `RadioButton` control are inherited from the `CheckBox` control.

Example: The Radio Button Control

Let's see a quick example:

```
<html>
<head>
<script language="VB" runat="server">
sub ch1(s as object, e as eventargs)
  label1.text = "Radio1 changed"
end sub
sub ch2(s as object, e as eventargs)
  label1.text = "Radio2 changed"
end sub
</script>
</head>
<body>
<form runat=server>
    <h3>RadioButton Example:</h3>
    <asp:RadioButton id=Radio1
      Text="1"
      AutoPostBack = true
      Checked="false"
      GroupName="Group1"
      oncheckedchanged = "ch1"
      runat="server" /><br>
    This is RadioButton1
  <p>
    <asp:RadioButton id=Radio2
      AutoPostBack = true
      Checked="true"
      Text="2"
      GroupName="Group1"
      oncheckedchanged = "ch2"
      runat="server"/><br>
    This is RadioButton 2
  <p>
</form>
<br><asp:label id=label1 backcolor=yellow runat=server />
</body>
</html>
```

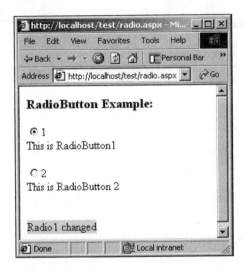

The Table Control

The `Table` control allows you to build a table on a Web page, and corresponds to the HTML `<table>` element. The `Table` control can also be manipulated programmatically.

Syntax:

```
<asp:Table id = "id_name"
     BackImageUrl = "Url of background image"
     CellSpacing = "width of cell spacing"
     CellPadding = "width of cell padding"
     GridLines = "None | Horizontal | Vertical | Both"
     HorizontalAlign = "Center | Justify | Left | NotSet | Right"
     Runat = "server">
  <asp:TableRow>
    <asp:TableCell>
      Text ......
    </asp:TableCell>
  </asp:TableRow>
</asp:Table>
```

We will discuss the `TableRow` and `TableCell` controls later. At design time, you can code static contents for a table. However, the `Table` web control can be constructed programmatically, dynamically assembling content for the table as appropriate. Later in the chapter, there is an example that shows how to build a table using code. Programmatic additions or modifications to a table row or cell will not persist in between posts to the server, so if substantial modifications are expected, use the `DataList` or `DataGrid` controls instead of the `Table` control. The `Datagrid` and `Datalist` controls have powerful features that allow them to maintain their state over successive server round trips. Further information on the `Datagrid` and `Datalist` controls is provided later in the chapter.

Properties of the Table Control

The BackImageUrl Property

The `BackImageUrl` property sets the URL of the background image of the table.

The CellPadding Property

The `CellPadding` property gets or sets the width of the cell padding of a table. Its units are pixels.

The CellSpacing Property

The `CellSpacing` property gets or sets the width of the cell spacing of a table. Its units are pixels.

The GridLines Property

The `GridLines` property gets or sets the grid lines for a `Table` control. The property uses the `GridLine` enumeration and can take one of the values below:

- ❑ `Horizontal`
- ❑ `Vertical`
- ❑ `None`
- ❑ `Both`

The default value is `None`.

The HorizontalAlign Property

The `HorizontalAlign` property gets or sets the horizontal alignment for the `Table` control in the web page in which it appears. This property can take any value from the `HorizontalAlign` enumeration:

- ❑ `Left`
- ❑ `Right`
- ❑ `Center`
- ❑ `Justify`
- ❑ `NotSet`

The default value is `NotSet`.

The Rows Property

The `Rows` property gets the collection of rows in a table. Note that this property is only used when you are building a table programmatically, and it is set by declaring a `TableRow` control at design time.

The `Table` control has no methods or events.

The TableCell Control

The `TableCell` control allows you to declare a table cell in a `Table` control. It corresponds to the HTML `<td>` element, and you are free to manipulate it programmatically. You also can specify a `Table` control in a table cell.

Syntax:

```
<asp:TableCell id = "id_name"
    ColumnSpan = "number of columns"
    RowSpan = "number of rows"
```

```
        HorizontalAlign = "Center | Justify | Left | NotSet | Right"
        Text = "Content text"
        VerticalAlign = "Bottom | Middle | NotSet | Top"
        Wrap = "True | False"
        Runat = "server" />
```

or:

```
<asp:TableCell id = "id_name"
        ColumnSpan = "number of columns"
        RowSpan = "number of rows"
        HorizontalAlign = "Center | Justify | Left | NotSet | Right"
        VerticalAlign = "Bottom | Middle | NotSet | Top"
        Wrap="True | False"
        Runat = "server">Content text</asp:TableCell>
```

Properties of the TableCell Control

The ColumnSpan Property

The ColumnSpan property specifies the number of columns in the Table control that a particular cell spans. The default value is 0.

The HorizontalAlign Property

The HorizontalAlign property gets or sets the horizontal alignment of the content in the cell of a table with respect to the cell width as a value of the HorizontalAlign enumeration, that is, one of the following:

- ❏ Center
- ❏ Justify
- ❏ Left
- ❏ NotSet
- ❏ Right

The default is NotSet.

The RowSpan Property

The RowSpan property specifies the number of rows in the Table control that a particular cell spans. The default value is 0.

The Text Property

The Text property gets or sets the content text of a cell in a table. The default is empty.

The VerticalAlign Property

The VerticalAlign property gets or sets the vertical alignment of the content in the cell of a table. The valid values are Bottom, Middle, NotSet, and Top. The default value is NotSet.

The Wrap Property

The Wrap property gets or sets a value that indicates whether the contents of the cell wrap in the cell. The valid values are True and False. The default value is True.

The TableCell control has no methods or events.

The TableRow Control

The TableRow control represents rows in a table in a form that allows you to manipulate the rows programmatically. It corresponds to the HTML <tr> tag.

Syntax:

```
<asp:TableRow id = "id_name"
     HorizontalAlign = "Center | Justify | Left | NotSet | Right"
     VerticalAlign = "Bottom | Middle | NotSet | Top"
     Runat = "server">

  <asp:TableCell>
     Content Text
  </asp:TableCell>

</asp:TableRow>
```

Properties of the TableRow Control

The Cells Property

Only use this property when you are building a table programmatically to get a collection of the TableCell objects so that you can add, insert, and remove TableCell objects in the collection. An example is provided later in the chapter.

The HorizontalAlign Property

The HorizontalAlign property gets or sets the horizontal alignment of the contents in a row using the HorizontalAlign enumeration, that defines the following values:

❑ Center

❑ Justify

❑ Left

❑ NotSet

❑ Right

The default is NotSet.

The VerticalAlign Property

The VerticalAlign property gets or sets the vertical alignment of the contents in a row using the VerticalAlign enumeration, that defines the following values:

❑ Bottom

❑ Middle

❑ NotSet

❑ Top

The default value is `NotSet`.

The `TableRow` control has no methods or events.

Example: Table Controls

The sample given here demonstrates how to use the `Cell` and `Row` properties to build a table programmatically.

```
<html>
<head>
<script language="VB" runat="server">
Public Sub bt(s As Object, e As EventArgs)
  Dim rows As Integer = row1.value
  Dim cells As Integer = cell1.value
  Dim j As Integer
  For j = 0 To rows - 1
    Dim r As New TableRow()
    Dim i As Integer
    For i = 0 To cells - 1
      Dim c As New TableCell()
      c.Controls.Add(New LiteralControl("Content Text"))
      r.Cells.Add(c)
    Next i
    Table1.Rows.Add(r)
  Next j
End Sub
</script>
</head>
<body>
<form runat="server">
<h3><font face="Verdana">Table Example</font></h3>
    <asp:Table id="Table1"
        Font-Name="Verdana"
        Font-Size="8pt"
        CellPadding="3"
        CellSpacing="3"
        BorderWidth="1"
        Gridlines="Both"
        runat="server" />
<hr>
Row : <input type="text" id="row1" size="10" runat="server"><br>
Cell : <input type="text" id="cell1" size="10" runat="server"><Br>
<Button id=button1 onserverclick="bt" runat=server>Create Table</button>
</form>
</body>
</html>
```

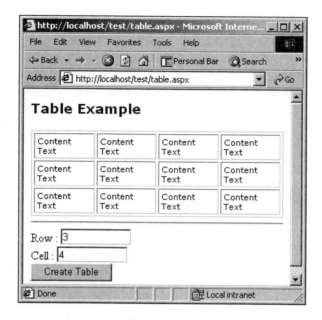

The TextBox Control

The TextBox control displays a textbox on a Web page just like the HTML <input type=text> or <input type=password> elements. Furthermore, the TextBox control acts as a combination of the HTML <input type=text> and <textarea> tags because we can set the TextMode property to determine which type it will be. If we set TextMode to SingleLine, then the textbox control will appear as if produced by an HTML <input type="text"> tag. On the other hand, if we set TextMode to MultiLine, then the textbox control will appear just like an HTML <textarea> element.

Syntax:

```
<asp:TextBox id = "id_name"
     AutoPostBack = "True | False"
     Columns = "number of columns"
     MaxLength = "maximum characters in the textbox"
     Rows = "number of rows"
     Text = "content text"
     TextMode = "Singleline | Multiline | Password"
     Wrap = "True | False"
     OnTextChanged = "OnTextChangedMethod"
     Runat = "server"/>
```

Properties of the TextBox Control

The AutoPostBack Property

The AutoPostBack property gets or sets a value that indicates if an event will automatically be raised when the user changes the text of the TextBox control. The default value is False.

The Columns Property

The Columns property gets or sets the width of the textbox in characters.

The MaxLength Property

The MaxLength property gets or sets the maximum number of characters that the user is allowed to type.

The ReadOnly Property

The ReadOnly property locks the textbox so the users can't input anything.

The Rows Property

The Rows property gets or sets the height in characters of the textbox when you set the TextMode property to Multiline.

The TagKey Property

The TagKey property gets the HTML tag for the TextBox control.

The Text Property

The Text property gets or sets the contents of a textbox.

The TextMode Property

The TextMode property gets or sets the type of a textbox. The valid types are from the TextMode enumeration, and can be one of:

❑   SingleLine

❑   MultiLine

❑   Password

The default type is SingleLine.

The Wrap Property

The Wrap property gets or sets a value indicating whether the text content wraps within the textbox. It only works when the TextMode property is set to Multiline.

Methods of the TextBox Control

The OnTextChanged Method

This method handles the TextChanged event fired when the user changes the contents of the TextBox. The TextChanged event is also raised for parent controls to handle if appropriate.

Events of the TextBox Control

The TextChanged Event

The TextChanged event occurs when the text of the contents of the TextBox control is changed and is thus automatically posted back to the server.

Example: The TextBox Control

The following code provides a simple example of how the `TextBox` control can be used:

```
<html>
<head>
<script language=vb runat=server>
Sub txtMulti_OnChange(s as object, e as eventargs)
   spnMessage.innerHTML = "<font color='red'>Multi line textbox has been
                                          changed.</font>"
End Sub

Sub txtSingle_OnChange(s as object, e as eventargs)
   spnMessage.innerHTML = "<font color='blue'>Single line textbox has been
changed.</font>"
End Sub

</script>
</head>
<body>
<form runat=server ID='Form1'>
  <asp:textbox
    id = 'txtMulti'
    accesskey = 1
    rows = 5
    textmode ='multiline'
    wrap =true
    autopostback ='true'
    MaxLength =10
    ontextchanged ='txtMulti_OnChange'
    runat = 'server' /><Br>
  <asp:textbox
    id = 'txtSingle'
    accesskey = 2
    autopostback = 'true'
    MaxLength = 10
    textmode = 'singleline'
    ontextchanged = 'txtSingle_OnChange'
    runat = 'server' />
</form>
<span id=spnMessage runat=server />
</body>
</html>
```

The Xml Control

The Xml control displays an XML document or the results of an XSL transform on a Web page.

Syntax:

```
<asp:Xml id = "id_name"
     Document = "XML Document"
     DocumentContent = "String of XML"
     DocumentSource = "Path of XML Document"
     Transform = "XslTransform"
     TransformSource = "Path of XSL Transform Document"
     Runat = "server">
```

Properties of the Xml Control

The Document Property

The Document property gets or sets the System.Xml.XmlDocument object to display.

The DocumentContent Property

The DocumentContent property gets or sets a string that contains the XML document to display in the Xml control.

The DocumentSource Property

The DocumentSource property gets or sets the XML filename.

The Transform Property

The Transform property gets or sets the System.Xml.Xsl.XslTransform object that represents the XSLT stylesheet to format the XML document before writing it to the output stream.

The TransformSource Property

The TransformSource property gets or sets the filename of an external XSL stylesheet to use for transforming the XML data.

That completes the round up of the HTML intrinsic controls defined within this namespace. Now let's head over to look at List Controls.

List Controls

In this section, we will examine the List Controls of ASP.NET. We can divide List controls into two categories. The first category is the General List controls, and comprises the `ListItem`, `CheckBoxList`, `DropDownList`, `ListBox`, and `RadioButtonList` controls. The other category is the Special Data-Bound List controls, which includes the `Repeater`, `DataGrid`, and `DataList` controls. It doesn't mean that you can't use General List controls for data binding. In fact, they can all achieve this; it's just that the `Repeater`, `DataGrid`, and `DataList` controls have more powerful capabilities than other List controls. It makes sense therefore to group these three controls into their own category.

The ListControl Class

Before we talk about List web server controls, we must first discuss the abstract base class, the `ListControl` class, which provides properties, methods, and events for the `CheckBoxList`, `DropDownList`, `ListBox`, and `RadioButtonList` controls.

Properties of the ListControl Class

The AutoPostBack Property

This property is a Boolean value. If it is `True` and a user then changes the list selection, then a postback to the server will occur automatically. The default value is `False`.

The DataMember Property

When data source contains more than one table, the `DataMember` property specifies the name of the table within the data source. For example, when your data source is a dataset that contains a couple of datatables, then you should set the `DataMember` property for a list control, so that data within a table can be bound to the control. Refer to Chapter 14 for more information.

The DataSource Property

This property specifies a data source that provides the values to populate. Refer to Chapter 14 for more information.

The DataTextField Property

This gets or sets the name of the field in the data source that provides the text to the list items.

The DataTextFormatString Property

This property gets or sets a formatting string. This string will control how to display the data that is bound to a control.

The DataValueField Property

The `DataValueField` property gets or sets the name of field in the data source that provides the values to the list items.

The Items Property

Use this property to retrieve the collection of the items within the list control, where the collection is within `ListItemCollection` class. The default value is a empty list.

The SelectedIndex Property

This gets or sets an integer index. The integer index presents an item in a list where the item is first selected by a user. The default is -1 that means nothing is selected.

The SelectedItem Property

This property retrieves the item that was first selected by a user from a list. The default is `null`, or `Nothing` in VB.NET.

Methods of the ListControl Class

The OnSelectedIndexChanged Method

This method raises the `SelectedIndexChanged` event when a user changes the selection in the list.

Events of the ListControl Class

The SelectedIndexChanged Event

This event is fired when a selection in the list has been changed and the page is automatically posted back to the server.

The samples given for the following List controls show how these event, method, and properties are used.

The ListItem Class

`ListItem` is not really a control, but rather an object that represents a data item within a list control. In this way, it acts just like the HTML <option> tag and will create the <option> element in a list.

Syntax:

```
<asp:ListItem
    value="value"
    selected = "True | False">
  Text of ListItem
</asp:ListItem>
```

or:

```
<asp:ListItem
    value = "value"
    text = "ListItem text"
    selected = " True | False" />
```

Properties of the ListItem Class

The Attributes Property

This property gets an attribute collection of name-value pairs expressed on the list item. This property is not supported by control's typed property.

The Selected Property

This returns or sets a Boolean value that indicates whether the item in a list is selected. The default is False (meaning not selected).

The Text Property

This property gets or sets a text that is displayed in the list for the item.

The Value Property

The Value property gets or sets a value that belongs to the item in the list.

We will demonstrate the ListItem class in action with some interesting examples in the next section. For now however, let's take a look at some of the different list types.

The CheckBoxList Control

The CheckBoxList control, which is similar to the CheckBox control, creates multiple selections that can be checked by the users, and it can be dynamically generated by using data-binding. The control will create a HTML <table> with the checkboxes in the table cells, or a simple list where the checkboxes are the items in the simple list.

Syntax:

```
<asp:CheckBoxList id = "id_name"
    AutoPostBack = "True | False"
    CellPadding = "Pixels"
    CellSpacing = "Pixels"
    DataSource = "name of data source"
    DataTextField = "DataSourceField"
    DataValueField = "DataSourceField"
    RepeatColumns = "ColumnCount"
    RepeatDirection = "Vertical | Horizontal"
    RepeatLayout = "Flow | Table"
    TextAlign = "Right | Left"
    OnSelectedIndexChanged = "Method for selected index changed"
    Runat = "server">
  <asp:ListItem>
    Content text
  </asp:ListItem>
</asp:CheckBoxList>
```

The AutoPostBack, DataSource, DataTextField, and DataValueField properties are inherited from the ListControl class, which if you remember is the base class for general List Controls. The OnSelectedIndexChanged method is also inherited from the ListControl class.

Properties of the CheckBoxList Control

The CellPadding Property

This property gets or sets the width between the table cell border and the content in the table cell. The default value is -1, meaning not set.

The CellSpacing Property

This property gets or sets the width between the cells in the table. The default value is-1, meaning not set.

The RepeatColumns Property

This property gets or sets the number of columns in the table to display for the CheckBoxList control. The default value is 0 and means not set.

The RepeatDirection Property

This property gets or sets a value that indicates the layout of cells in the CheckBoxList control to display vertically or horizontally. The valid values are from the RepeatDirection enumeration, and may be either vertical or horizontal. The default is vertical.

For example,

Vertical is as follows:

Item 1	Item 3
Item 2	Item 4

Horizontal is as follows:

Item 1	Item 2
Item 3	Item 4

The RepeatLayout Property

This property gets or sets the layout of checkboxes in a CheckBoxList control. The valid values are from the RepeatLayout enumeration, and may be either flow or table. The default value is table, and ensures the checkboxes follow a table structure.

flow Layout is as follows:

- ❑ This is Item 1 ☐ This is Item 2
- ❑ This is a good day ☐ It is good

The flow layout is essentially whatever will fit best with the current format.

table layout is as follows:

□This is Item 1	□This is Item 2
□This is a good day	□It is good

The table layout will put the checkboxes within a table structure.

The TextAlign Property

This property gets or sets the text alignment for the checkboxes. The valid values are given by the TextAlign enumeration, and may be either Left or Right.

A value of Left means that the text of the associated checkbox will be flush with the left-hand side of the control, while Right means that the text of the associated checkbox appears flush with the right-hand side of the control. The default is Right.

Example: CheckBoxList

The code here illustrates the usage of some properties of the CheckBoxList control. We also have the OnSelectedIndexChanged method inherited from the ListControl base class. When we change the selection of the items in the CheckBoxList control, a postback to the server will occur that will list the selected items in the list automatically. Of course, you can hold down the *Ctrl* key for multiple selections.

```
<html>
<head>
<script language="VB" runat="server">
Sub Check_Clicked(s as Object, e as eventargs)
    Dim i As Integer
    label1.text = ""
    For i=0 To checkboxlist1.Items.Count - 1
      If checkboxlist1.Items(i).Selected Then
        label1.Text += checkboxlist1.Items(i).Text + "<br>"
      End If
    Next
End Sub
</script>
</head>
<body>
<form runat="server">
<h3>CheckBoxList Example</h3>

    <asp:CheckBoxList id="checkboxlist1"
        AutoPostBack="True"
        CellPadding="1"
        CellSpacing="1"
        RepeatColumns="1"
        TextAlign="Right"
        OnSelectedIndexChanged="Check_Clicked"
        Runat = "server">

    <asp:ListItem value=Apple text=Apple />
    <asp:ListItem value=Banana text=Banana />
    <asp:ListItem value=Kiwi text=Kiwi />

    </asp:CheckBoxList>
```

```
     <br><br>The fruit you checked is:<br>
     <asp:label id=label1 runat=server />
</form>
</body>
</html>
```

The resulting output is shown here:

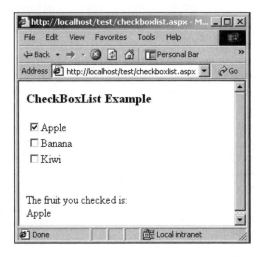

The DropDownList Control

The `DropDownList` control allows you to select items from a drop-down list. It is a single selection control whereas the `CheckBoxList` control is a multiple selection control. The `DropDownList` control is inherited from the `ListControl` base class; therefore you can use the properties of `DataSource`, `DataTextField`, and `DataValueField` for data-binding. Some of the properties that are inherited from the `WebControl` class are not applicable to the `DropDownList` control; such as `BorderColor`, `BorderStyle`, `BorderWidth`, and `ToolTip`.

Syntax:

```
<asp:DropDownList id = "id_name"
     DataSource = "name of data source"
     DataTextField = "Data Source Field"
     DataValueField = "Data Source Field"
     AutoPostBack = "True | False"
     OnSelectedIndexChanged = "Method for selected index changed"
     Runat = "server">
  <asp:ListItem text="content of ListItem" value="value of ListItem" />
</asp:DropDownList>
```

Properties of DropDownList Control

The SelectedIndex Property

This property gets or sets a number that represents the currently selected item of a DropDownList control. The default is 0 meaning the first item in the DropDownList control.

Example: SelectedIndex

Here, we set up an event that will be raised when the selected item in the DropDownList control is changed. This example is similar to the example for CheckBoxList control earlier, the most significant difference between them being the selection mode: the DropDownList control is for single selection, while the CheckBoxList control is for multiple selections. In this sample, the SelectedItem property is inherited from the ListControl class.

```
<html>
<head>
<script language="VB" runat="server">
Sub ddl1(s as Object, e as eventargs)
  Dim i as Integer
  i = dropdownlist1.selectedindex
  Select Case i
   Case 1
    label1.text = "You selected the first fruit, " &
                  dropdownlist1.selecteditem.text
   Case 2
    label1.text = "You selected the second fruit, " &
                  dropdownlist1.selecteditem.text
   Case 3
    label1.text = "You selected the third fruit, " &
                  dropdownlist1.selecteditem.text
   Case Else
    label1.text = "You selected nothing."
  End Select
End Sub
</script>
</head>
<body>
  <form runat="server">
    <h3>DropDownList Example</h3><br>
    <asp:DropDownList id = "DropDownList1"
        autopostback = "True"
        OnSelectedIndexChanged = "ddl1"
        Runat = "server">
      <asp:ListItem text="" value="" />
      <asp:ListItem text=Apple value=Apple />
      <asp:ListItem text="Banana" value="Banana" />
      <asp:ListItem text="Kiwi" value="Kiwi" />
    </asp:DropDownList>
  </form>
    <asp:Label id="Label1" runat="server"/>
</body>
</html>
```

The resulting output is:

Let's change the preceding example a bit to show how we can perform data-binding with the DropDownList control. There's no major change made, except that we change the way of adding items into the DropDownList control. The code provides a simple example of how to use data-binding with the DropDownList control:

```
<html>
<head>
<script language="VB" runat="server">

Function CreateDataSource() As ICollection
Dim myArray() As string = {"","Apple","Banana","Kiwi"}
        Return myarray
End Function

Sub Page_Load(s As Object, e As EventArgs)
If Not IsPostBack Then
            DropDownList1.DataSource = CreateDataSource()
            DropDownList1.DataBind()
End If
End Sub

Sub ddl1(s as Object, e as eventargs)
  dim i as integer
  i = dropdownlist1.selectedindex
  select case i
  case 1
    label1.text = "You selected the first fruit, " &
                  dropdownlist1.selecteditem.text
  case 2
    label1.text = "You selected the second fruit, " &
                  dropdownlist1.selecteditem.text
  case 3
    label1.text = "You selected the third fruit, " &
                  dropdownlist1.selecteditem.text
  case else
    label1.text = "You selected nothing."
  end select
End Sub
</script>
```

```
    </head>

    <body>
      <form runat="server">
        <h3>DropDownList Example</h3><br>
        <asp:DropDownList id = "DropDownList1"
              autopostback = "true"
              OnSelectedIndexChanged = "ddl1"
              Runat = "server" />
      </form>
        <asp:Label id="Label1" runat="server"/>
    </body>
    </html>
```

The ListBox Control

The ListBox control is basically a combination of the CheckBoxList control and the DropDownList control. The ListBox control can either be a single or a multiple selection control, and it allows you to perform data-binding programmatically.

Syntax:

```
<asp:ListBox id = "id_name"
      DataSource = "name of data source"
      DataTextField = "DataSourceField"
      DataValueField = "DataSourceField"
      AutoPostBack = "True | False"
      Rows = "number of row"
      SelectionMode = "Single | Multiple"
      OnSelectedIndexChanged = "Method for selected index changed "
      Runat = "server">
  <asp:ListItem text="text of ListItem" value="value of ListItem" />
</asp:ListBox>
```

Properties of the ListBox Control

Note: the BorderColor, BorderStyle, BorderWidth, and ToolTip properties inherited from the WebControl class are not applicable to the ListBox control.

The Rows Property

This property gets or sets how many rows can be displayed on a web page in the ListBox control. This property allows you to control the height of the ListBox control and determine how many items are displayed on a Web page at any one time. The value of this property must be in the range between 1 and 2000. The default value is 4.

The SelectionMode Property

This property will determine which selection mode the ListBox control will accept. It can take one of the values of the ListSelectionMode enumeration, and may either be Single or Multiple. The default value is Single.

Example: ListBox

In the following code, we set up a multiple selection `ListBox` control that displays five rows on the Web page. The user can press and hold down the *Shift* or *Ctrl* keys to make multiple selections. Notice the sub-property `Items` in the `list_change` event handler. This is inherited from the `ListControl` class.

```
<html>
<head>
<script language="VB" runat="server">
Sub list_change(s As Object, e As EventArgs)
  Dim i As Integer
  label1.text = ""
  For i=0 To listbox1.Items.Count - 1
    If listbox1.Items(i).Selected Then
    label1.Text += listbox1.Items(i).Text + " "
  End If
  Next
End Sub
</script>
</head>
<body>
<form runat="server">
<h3>ListBox Example</h3>

    <asp:listbox id="listbox1"
        AutoPostBack="True"
        rows = "5"
        selectionmode = "multiple"
        OnSelectedIndexChanged="list_change"
        Runat = "server">

      <asp:ListItem value=Apple text=Apple />
      <asp:ListItem value=Banana text=Banana />
      <asp:ListItem value=Kiwi text=Kiwi />
      <asp:ListItem value=Orange text=Orange />
      <asp:ListItem value=Peach text=Peach />
      <asp:ListItem value=Watermelon text=Watermelon />

    </asp:listbox>

</form>
  <br>The fruit you selected is:<br>
  <asp:label id=label1 runat=server />
</body>
</html>
```

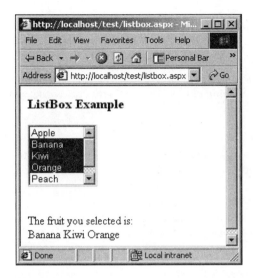

The RadioButtonList Control

The RadioButtonList control allows you to build a single radio selection list and also allows you to automatically generate the list by data-binding. The RadioButtonList control is a single-selection mode control like the DropDownList control, but they take on a different appearance on the web page. The RadioButtonList control creates an HTML <table> or a simple list that implements the radio buttons within the table structure or within the simple list. The properties of the RadioButtonList control are practically the same as the properties of the CheckBoxList control; the most significant different being that the RadioButtonList control only allows the selection of a single item, while the CheckBoxList control permits both single and multiple selections as determined by the SelectionMode property.

Syntax:

```
<asp:RadioButtonList id = "id_name"
    AutoPostBack = "True | False"
    CellPadding = "Pixels"
    CellSpacing = "Pixels"
    DataSource = "name of data source"
    DataTextField = "Data Source Field"
    DataValueField = "Data Source Field"
    RepeatColumns = "Column Count"
    RepeatDirection = "Vertical | Horizontal"
    RepeatLayout = "Flow | Table"
    TextAlign = "Right | Left"
    OnSelectedIndexChanged = "Method of SelectedIndexChanged"
    Runat = "server">
  <asp:ListItem Text="text of ListItem" Value="value of ListItem" />
</asp:RadioButtonList>
```

The RadioButtonList control is inherited from the ListControl class, therefore you can populate it by using data binding.

Properties of the RadioButtonList Control

The CellPadding Property

This property gets or sets the width in pixels between the table cell border and the content in the table cell. Its default value is -1, meaning not set. This property only works when the `RepeatLayout` property is set to `Table`.

The CellSpacing Property

This property gets or sets the width in pixels between the cells in the table. Its default value is -1, meaning not set. This property only works when the `RepeatLayout` property is set to `Table`.

The RepeatColumns Property

This property gets or sets the number of columns in the table to display for the `RadioButtonList` control. The default value is 0, meaning all items in the `RadioButtonList` control will be displayed in a single column.

The RepeatDirection Property

This property gets or sets a value that indicates whether the layout of cells in the `RadioButtonList` control should proceed vertically or horizontally. The valid values are from the `RepeatDirection` enumeration, and may be either `vertical` or `horizontal`. The default is `vertical`.

For example,

`Vertical` is as follows:

```
Item 1      Item 3
Item 2      Item 4
```

`Horizontal` is as follows:

```
Item 1      Item 2
Item 3      Item 4
```

The RepeatLayout Property

This property gets or sets the layout of checkboxes in a `RadioButtonList` control. The valid values are from the `RepeatLayout` enumeration, and may be either `flow` or `table`. The default value is `Table`.

`Flow` Layout is as follows:

```
o This is Item 1      o This is Item 2
o This is a good day  o It is good
```

The flow layout is essentially whatever will best fit the current format.

`table` layout is as follows:

○This is Item 1	○This is Item 2
○This is a good day	○It is good

The table layout will force the radio buttons to follow a table structure.

The TextAlign Property

This property gets or sets the text alignment for the radio buttons. The valid values are given by the `TextAlign` enumeration, and may be either `Left` or `Right`.

A value of `Left` means that the text of the associated radio button will be flush with the left-hand side of the control, while `Right` means that the text of the associated radio button appears flush with the right-hand side of the control. The default is `Right`.

Example: The RadioButtonList Control

Let's see radio buttons at work in a quick example:

```
<html>
<head>
<script language="VB" runat="server">
Sub radiobutton_ch(s as Object, e as eventargs)
  Dim i As Integer
  For i=0 To radiobuttonlist1.Items.Count - 1
    If radiobuttonlist1.Items(i).Selected Then
      label1.Text = radiobuttonlist1.Items(i).Text
    End If
  Next
End Sub
</script>
</head>
<body>
<form runat="server">
<h3>RadioButtonList Example</h3>

    <asp:radiobuttonlist id="radiobuttonlist1"
        AutoPostBack="True"
        RepeatLayout = Table
        OnSelectedIndexChanged="radiobutton_ch"
        Runat = "server">

    <asp:ListItem value=Apple text=Apple />
    <asp:ListItem value=Banana text=Banana />
    <asp:ListItem value=Kiwi text=Kiwi />
    <asp:ListItem value=Orange text=Orange />
    <asp:ListItem value=Peach text=Peach />
    <asp:ListItem value=Watermelon text=Watermelon />

    </asp:radiobuttonlist>

</form>
    <br>The fruit you selected is:<br>
```

```
      <asp:label id=label1 runat=server />
   </body>
   </html>
```

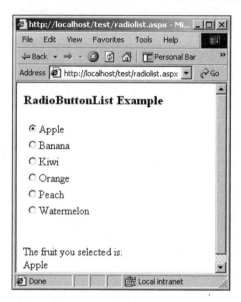

The BaseDataList Class

ASP.NET provides three server controls that get data directly from a `DataSet`. In this section we examine the `DataGrid`, `DataList`, and `Repeater` controls. Before we go into any details of these controls, we should first discuss the `BaseDataList` class. This is the base class for the `DataGrid` and `DataList` controls, and so these both inherit the properties, events, and methods that it defines. These common properties, events, and methods from the `BaseDataList` class are discussed here.

Properties of the BaseDataList Class

The datagrid and datalist controls create an HTML `<table>` on a web page, and it is possible for you to set table-related properties, such as `CellPadding` and `CellSpacing`, for these controls.

The CellPadding Property

This property gets or sets the width in pixels between the border of a cell and the area of the cell where contents will appear. The default value is `-1` meaning not set.

The CellSpacing Property

This gets or sets the width in pixels between the cells in a table. The default value is `0`.

The DataKeyField Property

This property gets or sets the name of the primary key field of the data source.

The DataKeys Property

This gets or sets a collection of key fields from the data source. The collection is from the `DataKeysCollection` class.

254

The DataKeysArray Property

This property returns a list containing the key fields of the data source.

The DataMember Property

If your data source contains more than one table, then the `DataMember` property lets you specify which table in the data source you want to use for binding to a particular control.

The DataSource Property

This property gets or sets the data source for data-binding.

The Gridlines Property

The `Gridlines` property gets or sets the type of the grid line, as a value of the `GridLines` enumeration, and may be one of:

- ❑ `Horizontal` – only horizontal grid lines appear
- ❑ `Vertical` – only vertical grid lines appear
- ❑ `None`
- ❑ `Both`

The default is `Both`.

The HorizontalAlign Property

This property gets or sets the horizontal alignment of a control with respect to its container as a value of the `HorizontalAlign` enumeration, and can be one of the following:

- ❑ `Center`
- ❑ `Justify`
- ❑ `Left`
- ❑ `NotSet`
- ❑ `Right`

The default is `NotSet`.

Methods of the BaseDataList class

The DataBind Method

This method will bind the control and its child controls to the data source specified by the `DataSource` property.

The IsBindableType Method

This method determines whether the data type can be bound to a list control from the `BaseDataList` class. This method will return a Boolean value, either `True` meaning that binding is allowed, or `False` meaning that binding will not work.

The OnSelectedIndexChanged Method

This method raises the `SelectedIndexChanged` event when an item in the list is selected.

Events of BaseDataList class

The SelectedIndexChanged Event

This event occurs when a new item in the list is selected.

The DataGrid Control

The `DataGrid` control is a very complex control, full of features for selecting, editing, deleting, paging, and sorting its contiained data via data-binding. In the past, using ASP 2.0 or ASP 3.0 to get data from a database or other data source, there was no control that unified and simplified the actions involved with selection, editing, deleting, paging, and sorting elements of a displayed list. To achieve such goals then, we had to write a lot of ASP code and associated scripts. Now, ASP.NET comes charging to the rescue, with the excellent `Datagrid` control that lets us easily show, edit, page, and sort our data on a web page.

Syntax:

```
<asp:DataGrid id = "id_name" runat=server
    DataSource='name of data source'
    AllowPaging = "True | False"
    AllowSorting = "True | False"
    AutoGenerateColumns = "True | False"
    BackImageUrl = "URL of background image"
    DataKeyField = "DataSourceKeyField"
    GridLines = "None | Horizontal | Vertical | Both"
    HorizontalAlign = "Center | Justify | Left | NotSet | Right"
    PageSize = "ItemCount"
    ShowFooter = "True | False"
    ShowHeader = "True | False"
    VirtualItemCount = "ItemCount"
    OnCancelCommand = "OnCancelCommandMethod"
    OnDeleteCommand = "OnDeleteCommandMethod"
    OnEditCommand = "OnEditCommandMethod"
    OnItemCommand = "OnItemCommandMethod"
    OnItemCreated = "OnItemCreatedMethod"
    OnPageIndexChanged = "OnPageIndexChangedMethod"
    OnSortCommand = "OnSortCommandMethod"
    OnUpdateCommand = "OnUpdateCommandMethod">

  <AlternatingItemStyle property="value"/>
  <EditItemStyle property="value"/>
  <FooterStyle property="value"/>
  <HeaderStyle property="value"/>
  <ItemStyle property="value"/>
  <PagerStyle property="value"/>
  <SelectedItemStyle property="value"/>

</asp:DataGrid>
```

or:

```
<asp:DataGrid id = "id_name" runat=server
    DataSource = 'name of data source'
    AutoGenerateColumns = "False"
    'Other properties'

    <AlternatingItemStyle property="value"/>
    <EditItemStyle property="value"/>
    <FooterStyle property="value"/>
    <HeaderStyle property="value"/>
    <ItemStyle property="value"/>
    <PagerStyle property="value"/>
    <SelectedItemStyle property="value"/>

<Columns>
 <asp:BoundColumn
      DataField = "DataSourceField"
      DataFormatString = "FormatString"
      FooterText = "FooterText"
      HeaderImageUrl = "url"
      HeaderText = "HeaderText"
      ReadOnly = "True | False"
      SortField = "DataSourceFieldToSortBy"
      Visible = "True | False"
      FooterStyle-property = "value"
      HeaderStyle-property = "value"
      ItemStyle-property = "value"/>

 <asp:ButtonColumn
      ButtonType = "LinkButton | PushButton"
      Command = "BubbleText"
      DataTextField = "DataSourceField"
      DataTextFormatS tring="FormatString"
      FooterText="FooterText"
      HeaderImageUrl="url"
      HeaderText = "HeaderText"
      ReadOnly = "True | False"
      SortField="DataSourceFieldToSortBy"
      Text="ButtonCaption"
      Visible = "True | False"/>

 <asp:EditCommandColumn
      ButtonType = "LinkButton | PushButton"
      CancelText="CancelButtonCaption"
      EditText="EditButtonCaption"
      FooterText="FooterText"
      HeaderImageUrl="url"
      HeaderText="HeaderText"
      ReadOnly="True|False"
      SortField="DataSourceFieldToSortBy"
      UpdateText="UpdateButtonCaption"
      Visible = "True | False"/>

 <asp:HyperLinkColumn
      DataNavigateUrlField="DataSourceField"
```

```
        DataNavigateUrlFormatString="FormatExpression"
        DataTextField="DataSourceField"
        DataTextFormatString="FormatExpression"
        FooterText="FooterText"
        HeaderImageUrl="url"
        HeaderText="HeaderText"
        NavigateUrl="url"
        ReadOnly = "True | False"
        SortField="DataSourceFieldToSortBy"
        Target="window"
        Text="HyperLinkText"
        Visible = "True | False"/>

<asp:TemplateColumn
        FooterText="FooterText"
        HeaderImageUrl="url"
        HeaderText="HeaderText"
        ReadOnly="True|False"
        SortField="DataSourceFieldToSortBy"
        Visible = "True | False">

    <HeaderTemplate>
     Header template HTML
    </HeaderTemplate >
    <ItemTemplate>
     ItemTemplate HTML
    </ItemTemplate>
    <EditItemTemplate>
     EditItem template HTML
    </EditItemTemplate>
    <FooterTemplate>
     Footer template HTML
    </FooterTemplate>

  </asp:TemplateColumn>
 </Columns>

</asp:DataGrid>
```

Because the DataGrid control is a complex control laden with functionality, the best approach is to discuss it with reference to the specific funcationalty offered. To this effect, we shall arrange the components of the DataGrid control into five groups, namely selection, editing, deleting, paging, and sorting. We will discuss how to manipulate the DataGrid control to achieve these five principal tasks.

Let's start with selection, as this is perhaps the easiest task in the list. All we have to do is get data from a data source, and bind it to the DataGrid control.

Example: DataGridExample

We shall start with the following simple example for selection using the DataGrid control.

```
<%@ Import Namespace="System.Data" %>
<html>
<head>
<script language="VB" runat="server">
```

```
Function CreateDataSource() As ICollection

Dim dt As New DataTable()
Dim dr As DataRow
Dim i As Integer
Dim dv As New DataView(dt)

  dt.Columns.Add(New DataColumn("Product Index", GetType(Int32)))
  dt.Columns.Add(New DataColumn("Product Item", GetType(String)))
  dt.Columns.Add(New DataColumn("Product Value", GetType(Double)))

  For i = 0 to 5
          dr = dt.NewRow()
          dr(0) = i
          dr(1) = "Item " + i.ToString()
          dr(2) = 11.17 *(i + 1)
          dt.Rows.Add(dr)
  Next i
  Return dv
End Function

Sub Page_Load(s As Object, e As EventArgs)
If Not IsPostBack Then
     Datagrid1.DataSource = CreateDataSource()
     Datagrid1.DataBind()
End If
End Sub

   </script>
</head>
<body>
<h3>DataGrid Example</h3>
<form runat=server>

Product List:
<asp:DataGrid id="Datagrid1"
             CellSpacing="2"
             CellPadding="2"
             runat="server" />
</form>
</body>
</html>
```

The result is shown below:

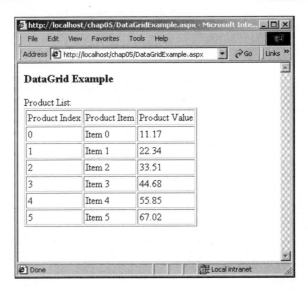

In this example, we import the `System.Data` namespace for a `DataTable`. You can find more information about this in Chapter 14.

Properties of the DataGrid control

The AllowCustomPaging Property

The `AllowCustomPaging` property gets or sets a Boolean value indicating whether custom paging is being used, and it is only relevant when the `AllowPaging` property is set to `True`. The default for `AllowCustomPaging` is `False`. It belongs to the Paging functionality.

The Paging functionality of the `DataGrid` control is aimed at situations where large data files are used, and it allows us to divide the data rows from the data source into sub-sections that are much more manageable for display on a web page. When we move forward or back between sub-sections, the data source will be rebound to the `DataGrid` control as appropriate. It the data source is very large, the binding process will consume more computer resources, and the whole thing becomes increasingly inefficient. The `AlowCustomPaging` property lets us load the sub-section that will be displayed in the `DataGrid` control. For example, if we want to view the eleventh to twentieth items, only the required ten items will be loaded.

The AllowPaging Property

This property gets or sets a Boolean value indicating whether 'Paging' is to be enabled. If you have many data rows in a data source, then you may wish to divide them into groups that will be displayed one group at a time on the web page. This property must be set to `True` if we wish to split data in this way. Because it belongs to the Paging functionality, we will discuss it more and have an example of it in the Paging section.

The AllowSorting Property

This property gets or sets a Boolean value to indicate whether data sorting is enabled. The default value is `False`. Set to `True` to make the heading section of each column within a grid to show as a `LinkButton` control. This property works with the `SortExpression` property and the `SortCommand` event. It belongs to the Sorting section of the `DataGrid` control.

The AlternatingItemStyle Property

This property allows us to set the style properties for every other item from the data source. The valid values are given by the `TableItemStyle` class. The default value is empty meaning no style is defined. We will have an example of this property later after this section on the properties of the `DataGrid` control.

The AutoGenerateColumns Property

This property gets or sets a Boolean value that indicates whether `BoundColumn` objects are automatically created and displayed in the `DataGrid` control for each field in the data source. The default value is `True`. Explicitly declared columns may be used in conjunction with such columns. When using both, explicitly declared columns will be rendered first, followed by the automatically generated ones. Note that automatically generated columns are not added to the `Columns` collection. We shall discuss `BoundColumn` objects in more detail later.

The BackImageUrl Property

This property gets or sets the URL of the background image that will appear in the background of the `DataGrid` control. If the size of the background image is smaller than the `DataGrid` control, then the background image will be stretched to fit.

The Columns Property

Use this property to retrieve the collection of objects that represent the columns in the `DataGrid` control. The valid values are defined in the `DataGridColumn` class, and are the following objects:

- ❑ `BoundColumn`
- ❑ `ButtonColumn`
- ❑ `EditCommandColumn`
- ❑ `HyperlinkColumn`
- ❑ `TemplateColumn`

We will discuss these column objects more detail later.

The CurrentPageIndex Property

This property gets or sets the index number that displays in the `DataGrid` control currently when Paging is active for the `DataGrid` control. For example, say there are 100 data rows in your data source and you have set the `AllowPaging` property to `True`. You will then have ten items displayed in the `DataGrid` control at any one time, and the index number for the first page displayed by the `DataGrid` control will be 0. By setting the `CurrentPageIndex` property to 0, you will force the control to display the first ten items from the data source in the area allocated to it on the web page. An example of this property follows in the Paging section.

The EditItemIndex Property

This property gets or sets the index number in the `DataGrid` control for editing. For example, say you want to edit the tenth item of a `DataGrid`, then this property should be set to 9.

The EditItemStyle Property

This property let us set the style properties for editing items in the `DataGrid` control. The valid values are defined in the `TableItemStyle` class.

The FooterStyle Property

This property lets us set the style properties for the footer section of the `DataGrid` control. The valid values are defined in the `TableItemStyle` class. An example of this property is provided later.

The HeaderStyle Property

This property lets us set style properties for the header section of the `DataGrid` control. The valid values are defined in the `TableItemStyle` class. We will have an example of this property later.

The Items Property

This property returns a collection of the `DataGridItem` objects that represent the individual items in the `DataGrid` control. This property is important for editing and deleting the items in the `DataGrid` control.

The ItemStyle Property

This property lets us set style properties for the items in the `DataGrid` control. The valid values are defined in the `TableItemStyle` class. We will have an example of this property later.

The PageCount Property

This property retrieves the total number of pages spanned by the `DataGrid` control. If we want to use this property, we must ensure that paging for the `DataGrid` control is enabled by setting the `AllowPaging` property to `True`.

The PagerStyle Property

This property lets us set the style properties for the paging section of the `DataGrid` control when paging is enabled. The valid values are defined in the `DataGridPagerStyle` class. The default is empty. An example demonstrating this property can be found in the Paging section later in the chapter.

The PageSize Property

This property lets us set how many items should be displayed per page of the `DataGrid` control. The default value is 10; so set this property to specify how many items you wish the `DataGrid` to display at any one time. This property is only relevant when the `AllowPaging` property is set to `True`.

The SelectedIndex Property

This property lets us get or set an index number for a selected item in the `DataGrid` control. If you want to de-select the item, you need to set this property to -1. This property is important for editing and deleting items in a `DataGrid` control.

The SelectedItem Property

This property returns the `DataGridItem` object that represents the selected item in the `DataGrid` control.

The SelectedItemStyle Property

This property lets us set the style properties for the currently selected item in the `DataGrid` control. The valid values are defined in the `TableItemStyle` class. We will see an example of this property later.

The ShowFooter Property

This property lets us get or set a Boolean value that indicates whether the footer section in the `DataGrid` control is to be displayed. The default is `False`.

The ShowHeader Property

This property lets us get or set a Boolean value that indicates whether the header section in the `DataGrid` control is to be displayed. The default is `True` meaning that a header section is normally displayed.

The VirtualItemCount Property

When we set the `AllowCustomPaging` property to `False`, then all the items in the data source will be bound to the `DataGrid` control at once. If the `AllowCustomPaging` property is set to `True`, then the number of items bound to the `DataGrid` control at any one time is given by the `VirtualItemCount` property. This property is the key to letting us get or set the number of items to show in a `DataGrid` control when we are using custom paging.

Example: DataGridExample2

In this code, we set up a `DataGrid` control to demonstrate some of the properties described above. We are using the same code as in the preceding example, with just the following change to the code of the `DataGrid` control:

```
<asp:DataGrid id="Datagrid1"
              CellSpacing="2"
              CellPadding="2"
              showfooter="true"
              showheader="true"
              runat="server">

    <AlternatingItemStyle BackColor="LightGreen">
    </AlternatingItemStyle>

    <FooterStyle BackColor="LightBlue">
    </FooterStyle>

    <HeaderStyle BackColor="LightYellow">
    </HeaderStyle>

</asp:DataGrid>
```

The result is:

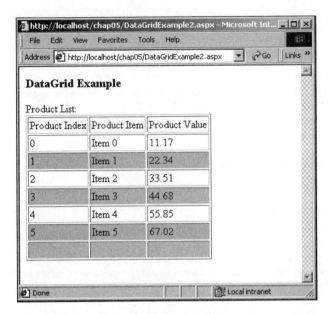

By setting style properties for the header, listed items, and the footer, we can make our DataGrid control quite colorful. Before we move on to cover the other features offered by the DataGrid control, I'd first like to look at the style properties that can be set for headers, list items, and footers.

Style Properties for the DataGrid Control

In the properties of the DataGrid control just listed, you will notice the AlternatingItemStyle, EditItemStyle, FooterStyle, HeaderStyle, ItemStyle, SelectedItemStyle, and PagerStyle properties. The values allowed by the PagerStyle property are defined by the DataGridPagerStyle class, while all the others are from the TableItemStyle class. To begin with, I shall discuss the properties of the TableItemStyle class here, and leave the discussion of the properties of the DataGridPagerStyle class for the section headed *Paging and the PagerStyle Property* later in the chapter.

The TableItemStyle class is inherited from the Style class, so its style properties are also available to the DataGrid control. Here, we shall introduce some of the more useful properties from these classes.

The BackColor Property

We can specify a background color with this property. In the preceding example, we used this style property for FooterStyle, HeaderStyle, and AlternatingStyle.

The ForeColor Property

We can specify a foreground color with this property.

The Height Property

This property specifies the height for rows in the DataGrid control.

The HorizontalAlign Property

This property specifies horizontal alignment of cell content in a `DataGrid` control. The valid values are from the `HorizontalAlign` enumeration, and may be one of:

❑ `Center`

❑ `Justify`

❑ `Left`

❑ `NotSet`

❑ `Right`

The default is `NotSet`.

The VerticalAlign Property

We can specify the vertical alignment for the content of a cell in the `DataGrid` control. The valid values are from the `VerticalAlign` enumeration, and can be one of the following:

❑ `Bottom`

❑ `Middle`

❑ `NotSet`

❑ `Top`

The default is `NotSet`.

Example: DataGridExample3

Now, let's add these style properties to the preceding sample. We only need change the code for the `AlternatingStyle` element:

```
<AlternatingItemStyle backcolor="LightGreen"
                      forecolor="red"
                      height="1cm"
                      horizontalalign="center"
                      verticalalign="top">
</AlternatingItemStyle>
```

The result produced will now look like this:

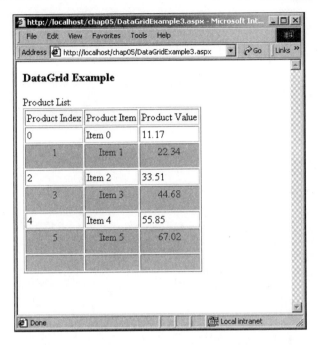

The `DataGrid` control will automatically create any columns needed when the `AutoGenerateColumns` property is set to `True`, the default. If we set it to `False`, then we have to define the columns ourselves. There are five column types that we can specify for the columns of a `DataGrid` control: `BoundColumn`, `ButtonColumn`, `EditCommandColumn`, `HyperlinkColumn`, and `TemplateColumn`.

The BoundColumn Class

This creates columns bound to a field in the data source. A `BoundColumn` will depict each item in the bound field as text, and is the default column type of the `DataGrid` control.

Properties of the BoundColumn Class

The DataField Property

This gets or sets the field name in the data source to bind to the `BoundColumn`.

The DataFormatString Property

This property gets or sets a string specifying the display format for items in the `BoundColumn`.

The display format string consists of two parts, in the form `{A, Bxx}`. The string must be enclosed in curly braces to denote that it is a format string. The first part of the format string (represented by A in this example) specifies the parameter index in a zero-based list of parameters. This can only be set to 0 because there is only one value in each cell. The second part of the format string (represented by Bxx in this example) specifies how numeric values are to be displayed. The following table shows the formatting characters allowed in this part of the format string.

Formatting Character	Description
C	Currency format
D	Decimal format
E	Exponential format
F	Fixed format
G	General format
N	Number format
X	Hexadecimal format

For example, {0:D2} means that the cell will display a number with two decimal places.

The Readonly Property

This returns a Boolean value that indicates whether the items in the BoundColumn can be edited. The default is False.

The ButtonColumn Class

This displays a command button for each item in a ButtonColumn of the DataGrid control.

Properties of ButtonColumn

The ButtonType Property

This property gets or sets the type of button in the ButtonColumn. The types are LinkButton and PushButton

The CommandName Property

This property gets or sets a text that represents the command to perform when the button in the ButtonColumn column is clicked.

The DataTextField Property

This gets or sets the field name in the data source to bind to the ButtonColumn.

The DataTextFormatString Property

This property gets or sets a string that specifies the display format for the caption on the command button. The format string please refers to the property of DataFormatString in the BoundColumn.

The Text Property

Use this property to get or set the text caption for the command button.

The EditCommandColumn Class

This class displays a column with editing capability in the DataGrid control. It is covered in detail in the Editing section.

Properties of EditCommandColumn

The ButtonType Property

This property gets or sets the type of button in the `EditCommandColumn` column. The types are `LinkButton` and `PushButton`.

The CancelText Property

This gets or sets the text displayed on the Cancel button of the `EditCommandColumn` column.

The EditText Property

Use this property to get or set text displayed on the Edit button of the `EditCommandColumn` column.

The UpdateText Property

This property gets or sets a text displayed on the Update button of the `EditCommandColumn` column.

The HyperlinkColumn Class

These types of columns show the contents of contained items as a hyperlinks.

Properties of the HyperlinkCoumn Class

The DataNavigateUrlField Property

This gets or sets the field name in the data source to bind to the URL of the hyperlinks in HyperLinkColumn column.

The DataNavigateUrlFormatString Property

This gets or sets a string that specifies the display format for the URL of the hyperlinks in the `HyperLinkColumn` column. The format string please refers to the property of `DataFormatString` in the `BoundColumn`.

The DataTextField Property

This gets or sets the field name in the data source to bind to the text of the hyperlinks in the HyperLinkColumn column.

The DataTextFormatString Property

This gets or sets a string that specifies the display format for the text of the hyperlinks in the `HyperLinkColumn` column. The format string please refers to the property of `DataFormatString` in the `BoundColumn`.

The NavigateUrl Property

This gets or sets a URL to link when the hyperlink is clicked.

The Target Property

Use this property to get or set the target window or frame to display the Web page content to link to when the hyperlink is clicked. For the valid values it can take, please refer to the `Target` property of the `HyperLink` control.

The Text Property

This property gets or sets a text string to display as the visible label of the hyperlink.

The TemplateColumn Class

Using these types of column, you can display each item in the column according to a specified template. The `TemplateColumn` class allows you to provide custom controls in a column of the `DataGrid` control.

Properties of the TemplateColumn Class

The EditItemTemplate Property

This property gets or sets a template for editing selected items in the column.

The FooterTemplate Property

This property gets or sets a template for the footer section of the `DataGrid` control.

The HeaderTemplate Property

This gets or sets a template for the header section of the `DataGrid` control.

The ItemTemplate Property

The `ItemTemplate` property gets or sets a template for items in a column of the `DataGrid` control.

Paging with the DataGrid Control

For paging items displayed in a `DataGrid`, the `AllowCustomPaging`, `AllowPaging`, `CurrentPageIndex`, `PageCount`, `PagerStyle`, `PageSize`, and `VirtualItemCount` properties, the `OnPageIndexChanged` method, and the `PageIndexChanged` event are all useful. They are described earlier in the chapter.

Example: DataGridPaging

Let's see a simple example of paging with a `DataGrid` control:

```
<%@ Import Namespace="System.Data" %>
<html>
<head>
<script language="VB" runat="server">

Function CreateDataSource() As ICollection
Dim dt As New DataTable()
Dim dr As DataRow
Dim i As Integer
Dim dv As New DataView(dt)

  dt.Columns.Add(New DataColumn("Product Index", GetType(Int32)))
  dt.Columns.Add(New DataColumn("Product Item", GetType(String)))
  dt.Columns.Add(New DataColumn("Product Value", GetType(Double)))

  For i = 1 To 50
```

```
                dr = dt.NewRow()
                dr(0) = i
                dr(1) = "Item " + i.ToString()
                dr(2) = 11.17 *(i + 1)
                dt.Rows.Add(dr)
    Next i
    Return dv
End Function

Sub Page_Load(s As Object, e As EventArgs)

If Not IsPostBack Then
                DataGrid1.DataSource = CreateDataSource()
                DataGrid1.DataBind()
End If

End Sub

Sub Grid_Change(sender As Object, e As DataGridPageChangedEventArgs)
            DataGrid1.CurrentPageIndex = e.NewPageIndex
            DataGrid1.DataSource = CreateDataSource()
            DataGrid1.DataBind()
End Sub
</script>
</head>

<body>
<form runat=server>
<h3>DataGrid Paging Example</h3>

        <asp:DataGrid id="DataGrid1" runat="server"
            BorderColor="black"
            BorderWidth="1"
            CellPadding="3"
            AllowPaging="true"
            OnPageIndexChanged="Grid_Change" />
</form>
</body>
</html>
```

The result from this code will be:

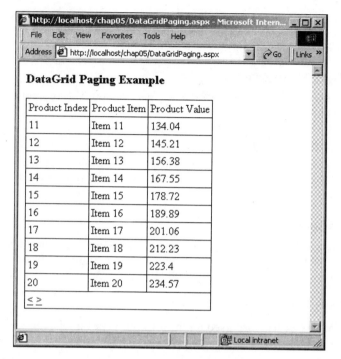

The bottom cell of the DataGrid control is the section for navigating between sub-pages of the control. We will explain it and show how we can make changes to it later.

As you can see in this example, the OnPageIndexChanged method and the PageIndexChanged event are used to allow users to move forward and backward between sub-pages of the DataGrid control. Let's discuss both of these now.

The OnPageIndexChanged Method

This method raises the PageIndexChanged event.

```
Sub DataGrid_Paging ( s As Object, e As DataGridPageChangedEventArgs)
```

The PageIndexChanged Event

This event will be raised when a page element is selected. There is a frequently used parameter for the event, NewPageIndex, as employed in the preceding example. It gets the index number of the page of the DataGrid control selected by the user.

Paging and the PagerStyle Property

In this section, we shall cover the PagerStyle property and how it relates to paging the content of a DataGrid control. The values allowed by the PagerStyle property are defined in the DataGridPagerStyle class, which inherits the TableItemStyle class. So, properties from the TableItemStyle class or Style class, including those discussed earlier in the section *Style Properties for the DataGrid Control*, can also be used here.

The Mode Property

This property gets or sets a value that indicates whether the pager element displays symbol buttons or numeric buttons. The valid values are set by the `PageMode` enumeration, and may be either `NextPrev` or `NumericPages`. The default is `NextPrev` as demonstrated in the preceding example.

The NextPageText Property

This property gets or sets a text displayed for the next page button. This property only works when `PageMode` is set to `NextPrev`.

The PageButtonCount Property

This gets or sets the number of numeric buttons to display concurrently in the page section of the `DataGrid` control. The default is `10`. This property only works when `PageMode` is set to `NumericPages`.

The Position Property

This property gets or sets the position of the next and previous page elements in the `DataGrid` control. The valid values are from the `PagerPosition` enumeration, and can be one of 0, 1, or 2. 0 means 'Bottom', 1 means 'Top', and 2 means 'Top and Bottom'.

The PrevPageText Property

This property gets or sets the text displayed for the previous page button. This property only works when `PageMode` is set to `NextPrev`.

The Visible Property

This property gets or sets a Boolean value to indicate whether the page section is displayed in the `DataGrid` control. The default is `True`.

Example: DataGrid Paging Example2

Now, let's change some code for the page section of the preceding example and manually specify columns in the `DataGrid` control.

```
<%@ Page Language="VB" Debug="true" %>

<%@ Import Namespace="System.Data" %>
<html>
<head>
<script language="VB" runat="server">

Function CreateDataSource() As ICollection
Dim dt As New DataTable()
Dim dr As DataRow
Dim i As Integer
Dim dv As New DataView(dt)

    dt.Columns.Add(New DataColumn("Product Index", GetType(Int32)))
    dt.Columns.Add(New DataColumn("Product Item", GetType(String)))
    dt.Columns.Add(New DataColumn("Product Value", GetType(Double)))
```

```
  For i = 1 To 50
          dr = dt.NewRow()
          dr(0) = i
          dr(1) = "Item " + i.ToString()
          dr(2) = 11.17 *(i + 1)
          dt.Rows.Add(dr)
  Next i
  Return dv
End Function

Sub Page_Load(s As Object, e As EventArgs)

If Not IsPostBack Then
          DataGrid1.DataSource = CreateDataSource()
          DataGrid1.DataBind()
End If
DataGrid1.PagerStyle.Mode = PagerMode.NumericPages
DataGrid1.PagerStyle.Position = "0"
DataGrid1.PagerStyle.PageButtonCount = "3"
End Sub

Sub Grid_Change(sender As Object, e As DataGridPageChangedEventArgs)
        DataGrid1.CurrentPageIndex = e.NewPageIndex
        DataGrid1.DataSource = CreateDataSource()
        DataGrid1.DataBind()
End Sub
</script>
</head>

<body>
<form runat=server>
<h3>DataGrid Paging Example</h3>

      <asp:DataGrid id="DataGrid1" runat="server"
          BorderColor="black"
          BorderWidth="1"
          CellPadding="3"
          AllowPaging="true"
          autogeneratecolumns="false"
          OnPageIndexChanged="Grid_Change">
      <Columns>
        <asp:BoundColumn
            HeaderText="Number"
            DataField="Product Index"/>
        <asp:BoundColumn
            HeaderText="Item"
            DataField="Product Item"/>
        <asp:BoundColumn
            HeaderText="Price"
            DataField="Product Value"
            DataFormatString="{0:c}"></asp:BoundColumn>
      </Columns>
    </asp:DataGrid>
```

```
    </form>
    </body>
    </html>
```

The result will now look like this:

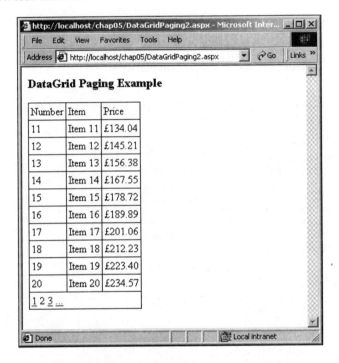

Sorting with the DataGrid Control

Let's now discuss how to perform sorting in a DataGrid control. There are just one method and one event that provide sorting functionality.

The OnSortCommand Method

This method raises the SortCommand event.

```
    Sub Sort_Grid(s As Object, e As DataGridSortCommandEventArgs)
```

The SortCommand Event

This occurs when the text in the header cell of the column is clicked. The most important argument is SortExpression, which contains the text displayed in the header cell in the current column of the DataGrid control. It is demonstrated in the following example.

Example: DataGridSorting

The following is a simple example of sorting with a DataGrid control:

```
<%@ Import Namespace="System.Data" %>
<html>
<head>
<script language="VB" runat="server">
Dim SortExpression As String

Function CreateDataSource() As ICollection

Dim dt As New DataTable()
Dim dr As DataRow
Dim i As Integer
Dim Rand_Num As New Random()
Dim dv As New DataView(dt)

  dt.Columns.Add(New DataColumn("ProductIndex", GetType(Int32)))
  dt.Columns.Add(New DataColumn("ProductItem", GetType(String)))
  dt.Columns.Add(New DataColumn("ProductValue", GetType(Double)))

  For i = 5 To 15
          dr = dt.NewRow()
          dr(0) = i
          dr(1) = "Item " + i.ToString()
          dr(2) = 11.17 * Rand_Num.Next(1, 11)
          dt.Rows.Add(dr)
  Next i
  dv.Sort = SortExpression
  Return dv
End Function

Sub Page_Load(sender As Object, e As EventArgs)

If Not IsPostBack Then

If SortExpression = "" Then
 SortExpression = "ProductIndex"
End If

Datagrid1.DataSource = CreateDataSource()
Datagrid1.DataBind()

End If

End Sub

Sub Sort_Grid(s As Object, e As DataGridSortCommandEventArgs)

SortExpression = e.SortExpression.ToString()
Datagrid1.DataSource = CreateDataSource()
Datagrid1.DataBind()

End Sub
</script>
</head>
<body>

<form runat=server>
```

```
<h3>DataGrid Sorting Example</h3>

<asp:DataGrid id="Datagrid1"
              CellSpacing="2"
              CellPadding="2"
              border="2"
              AllowSorting="true"
              OnSortCommand="Sort_Grid"
              runat="server">

       <AlternatingItemStyle backcolor="LightGreen"
         forecolor="red">
       </AlternatingItemStyle>
</asp:DataGrid>
</form>
</body>
</html>
```

Here is the display that will result from this code:

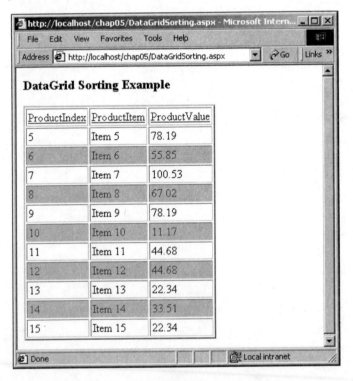

Don't forget to set the `AllowSort` property of the `DataGrid` control to `True`!

Deleting and Editing with the DataGrid Control

Methods for DataGrid Deleting and Editing

The OnDeleteCommand Method

This raises the `DeleteCommand` event when the Delete button is clicked for an item in the `DataGrid` control.

```
Sub MyDataGrid_Delete(sender As Object, e As DataGridCommandEventArgs)
```

The OnCancelCommand Method

This raises the `CancelCommand` event when the Cancel button is clicked for an item in the `DataGrid` control.

```
Sub MyDataGrid_Cancel(sender As Object, e As DataGridCommandEventArgs)
```

The OnUpdateCommand Method

This raises the `UpdateCommand` event when the Update button for an item is clicked.

```
Sub MyDataGrid_Update(sender As Object, e As DataGridCommandEventArgs)
```

The OnEditCommand Method

This raises the `EditCommand` event when the Edit button is clicked for an item in the `DataGrid` control.

```
Sub MyDataGrid_Edit(sender As Object, e As DataGridCommandEventArgs)
```

Events for DataGrid Deleting and Editing

The CancelCommand Event

The `CancelCommand` event occurs when the Cancel button is clicked for an item in the `DataGrid` control. The event handler receives an argument of type `DataGridCommandEventArgs` containing four properties:

Property	Description
`CommandArgument`	The argument of the command
`CommandName`	The name of the command
`CommandSource`	The source of the command
`Item`	The selected item in the `DataGrid` control

The DeleteCommand Event

The `DeleteCommand` event occurs when the Delete button is clicked for an item in the `DataGrid` control. The event handler receives an argument of type `DataGridCommandEventArgs` containing four properties. These properties are the same as the properties of the `CancelCommand` event.

The UpdateCommand Event

The UpdateCommand event occurs when the **Update** button is clicked for an item in the DataGrid control. The event handler receives an argument of type DataGridCommandEventArgs containing four properties. The properties are the same as the properties of the CancelCommand event.

The EditCommand Event

The EditCommand event occurs when the **Edit** button is clicked for an item in the DataGrid control. The event handler receives an argument of type DataGridCommandEventArgs containing four properties. The properties are the same as the properties of the CancelCommand event.

Example: DataGridShoppingCart

The following sample is a simple implementation of a Shopping Cart for an e-commerce site. This example uses ADO.NET features, and is not difficult to understand if you are already pretty conversant with DataTable and DataView.

```VB
<%@ Import Namespace="System.Data" %>
<html>
<head>
<script language="VB" runat="server">
Dim CartTable As New DataTable
Dim CartView As DataView

Sub Page_Load(s As Object, e As EventArgs)
Dim dr As DataRow
If Session("ShoppingCart") Is Nothing Then
            CartTable.Columns.Add(New DataColumn("Quantity", GetType(String)))
            CartTable.Columns.Add(New DataColumn("Item", GetType(String)))
            CartTable.Columns.Add(New DataColumn("Price", GetType(String)))
            Session("ShoppingCart") = CartTable

            Dim i As Integer
            For i = 1 To 11
                dr = CartTable.NewRow()
                If i Mod 3 <> 0 Then
                    dr(0) = "3"
                Else
                    dr(0) = "2"
                End If
                dr(1) = "Item " & i.ToString()
                dr(2) =(11.17 * i).ToString()
                CartTable.Rows.Add(dr)
            Next i
Else
            CartTable= CType(Session("ShoppingCart"), DataTable)
End If
        CartView = New DataView(CartTable)
        CartView.Sort = "Item"

        If Not IsPostBack Then
          DataGrid1.DataSource = CartView
          DataGrid1.DataBind()
        End If
End Sub
```

```
Sub DataGrid_Edit(s As Object, e As DataGridCommandEventArgs)
     DataGrid1.EditItemIndex = e.Item.ItemIndex
     DataGrid1.DataSource = CartView
     DataGrid1.DataBind()
End Sub

Sub DataGrid_Cancel(s As Object, e As DataGridCommandEventArgs)
     DataGrid1.EditItemIndex = - 1
     DataGrid1.DataSource = CartView
     DataGrid1.DataBind()
End Sub

Sub DataGrid_Update(s As Object, e As DataGridCommandEventArgs)

     Dim qtyText As TextBox = CType(e.Item.Cells(1).Controls(0), TextBox)
     Dim priceText As TextBox = CType(e.Item.Cells(2).Controls(0), TextBox)

     Dim item As String = e.Item.Cells(0).Text
     Dim qty As String = qtyText.Text
     Dim price As String = priceText.Text

     Dim dr As DataRow

     CartView.RowFilter = "Item='" & item & "'"
     If CartView.Count > 0 Then
         CartView.Delete(0)
     End If
     CartView.RowFilter = ""

     dr = CartTable.NewRow()
     dr(0) = qty
     dr(1) = item
     dr(2) = price
     CartTable.Rows.Add(dr)

     DataGrid1.EditItemIndex = - 1
     DataGrid1.DataSource = CartView
     DataGrid1.DataBind()
End Sub

Sub DataGrid_Delete(s As Object, e As DataGridCommandEventArgs)
     Dim dr As DataRow
     Dim item As String = e.Item.Cells(2).Text

     CartView.RowFilter = "Item='" & item & "'"
     If CartView.Count > 0 Then
         CartView.Delete(0)
     End If
     CartView.RowFilter = ""

     DataGrid1.DataSource = CartView
     DataGrid1.DataBind()
End Sub
</script>
</head>
```

```
<body>
<form runat="server">
<h3>DataGrid Deleting & Editing Example</h3>
<br>
      <asp:DataGrid id="DataGrid1" runat="server"
            BorderColor="black"
            BorderWidth="1"
            CellPadding="3"
            Font-Name="Verdana"
            Font-Size="8pt"
            OnEditCommand="DataGrid_Edit"
            OnCancelCommand="DataGrid_Cancel"
            OnUpdateCommand="DataGrid_Update"
            OnDeleteCommand="DataGrid_Delete"
            AutoGenerateColumns="false">

            <HeaderStyle BackColor="LightYellow">
            </HeaderStyle>

            <Columns>
                <asp:BoundColumn HeaderText="Item" ReadOnly="true" DataField="Item"/>
                <asp:BoundColumn HeaderText="Quantity" DataField="Quantity"/>
                <asp:BoundColumn HeaderText="Price" DataField="Price"/>
                <asp:EditCommandColumn
                    EditText="Edit"
                    CancelText="Cancel"
                    UpdateText="Update"
                    >
                </asp:EditCommandColumn>
                <asp:ButtonColumn
                    ButtonType="LinkButton"
                    Text="Delete"
                    CommandName="Delete">
                </asp:ButtonColumn>
            </Columns>
      </asp:DataGrid>
</form>
</body>
</html>
```

The result produced is shown below, with the entry for the fourth displayed item being edited:

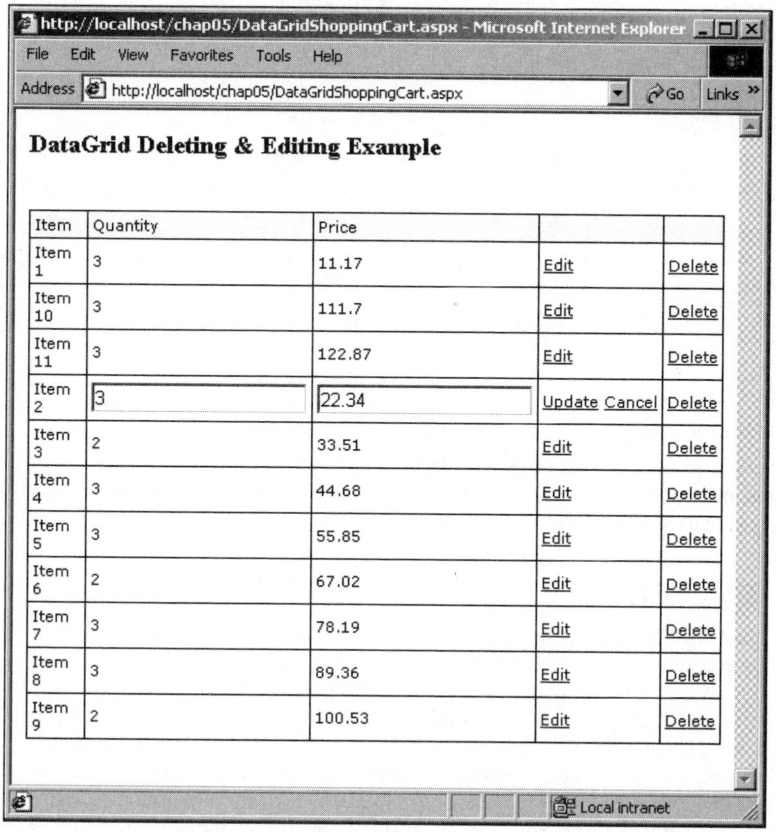

Other Methods and Events of the DataGrid Control

The OnItemCommand Method

The ItemCommand event is raised when any button is clicked in the DataGrid control.

```
Sub MyDataGrid_Item(sender As Object, e As DataGridCommandEventArgs)
```

The OnItemCreated Method

The ItemCreated event is raised when an item in the DataGrid control is created.

```
Sub Item_Created(sender As Object, e As DataGridItemEventArgs)
```

The OnItemDataBound Method

The ItemDataBound event is raised when an item is data bound to the DataGrid control.

```
Sub Item_Bound(sender As Object, e As DataGridItemEventArgs)
```

The ItemCommand Event

The ItemCommand event occurs when any button is clicked in the DataGrid control. The event handler receives an argument of type DataGridCommandEventArgs containing four properties. The properties are the same as the properties in the CancelCommand event.

The ItemCreated Event

The ItemCreated event occurs on the server when an item in the DataGrid control is created. The event handler receives an argument of type DataGridItemEventArgs containing the following single property:

Property	Description
Item	Gets the referenced item in the DataGrid control when the event is raised

The ItemDataBound Event

The ItemDataBound event occurs when an item is data-bound to the DataGrid control. The event handler receives an argument of type DataGridItemEventArgs containing one property. The property is the same as the property in the ItemCreated event.

The DataList Control

The DataList control displays data in a table in a form that can be edited and selected by the user, and you are able to configure how the control should appear. The DataList control provides seven templates for displaying data. However, the DataList control doesn't support paging and sorting as the DataGrid control does. DataGrid provides a complete range of features for displaying and editing data, making it suitable for applications that require complex data processing to generate the output for a web page. Although the DataList control does provide editing functionality, it is much simpler than DataGrid, and data is displayed in a table rather than a grid. DataList focuses primarily on the formatting of data for display, and the seven templates it provides are for this purpose. These seven templates are covered later.

Syntax:

```
<asp:DataList id="id_name"
    DataKeyField = "DataSourceKeyField"
    DataSource = "name of data source"
    ExtractTemplateRows = "True | False"
    GridLines = "None | Horizontal | Vertical | Both"
    RepeatColumns="ColumnCount"
    RepeatDirection = "Vertical | Horizontal"
    RepeatLayout = "Flow | Table"
    ShowFooter = "True | False"
    ShowHeader = "True | False"
    OnCancelCommand = "OnCancelCommandMethod"
    OnDeleteCommand = "OnDeleteCommandMethod"
    OnEditCommand = "OnEditCommandMethod"
    OnItemCommand = "OnItemCommandMethod"
    OnItemCreated = "OnItemCreatedMethod"
    OnUpdateCommand = "OnUpdateCommandMethod"
    Runat = "server">
```

```
<AlternatingItemStyle property="value"/>
<EditItemStyle property="value"/>
<FooterStyle property="value"/>
<HeaderStyle property="value"/>
<ItemStyle property="value"/>
<SelectedItemStyle property="value"/>
<SeparatorStyle property="value"/>

<HeaderTemplate>
  Header template HTML
</HeaderTemplate>
<ItemTemplate>
  Item template HTML
</ItemTemplate>
<AlternatingItemTemplate>
  Alternating item template HTML
</AlternatingItemTemplate>
<EditItemTemplate>
  Edited item template HTML
</EditItemTemplate>
<SelectedItemTemplate>
  Selected item template HTML
</SelectedItemTemplate>
<SeparatorTemplate>
  Separator template HTML
</SeparatorTemplate>
<FooterTemplate>
  Footer template HTML
</FooterTemplate>

</asp:DataList>
```

Properties of the DataList Control

Once you are *au fait* with the `DataGrid` control, you shouldn't have any difficulty understanding how the `DataList` control works. They share many properties for altering their appearance, and for editing and selecting their contents. These properties are listed below:

- ❑ `AlternatingItemStyle`
- ❑ `EditItemIndex`
- ❑ `EditItemStyle`
- ❑ `FooterStyle`
- ❑ `GridLines`
- ❑ `HeaderStyle`
- ❑ `Items`
- ❑ `ItemStyle`
- ❑ `SelectedIndex`
- ❑ `SelectedItem`

- ❑ SelectedItemStyle
- ❑ ShowFooter
- ❑ ShowHeader

All these properties serve the same purpose detailed in the DataGrid section previously, and so are not discussed here.

Methods and Events of the DataList Control

The DataList control also shares the methods of the DataGrid control for editing and deleting items. These methods are listed below:

- ❑ OnCancelCommand
- ❑ OnDeleteCommand
- ❑ OnEditCommand
- ❑ OnItemCommand
- ❑ OnItemCreated
- ❑ OnItemDataBound

The following events are also the same as in the DataGrid control:

- ❑ CancelCommand
- ❑ DeleteCommand
- ❑ EditCommand
- ❑ ItemCommand
- ❑ ItemCreated
- ❑ ItemDataBound
- ❑ UpdateCommand

These six methods and seven events have the same functionalities as in the DataGrid control, except that these methods and events don't support the Paging and Sorting features that are available in the DataGrid control.

Templates of the DataList Control

These seven templates lie at the core of the DataList control's data display mechanism. Each determines certain display characteristics of the control, as described below.

AlternatingItemTemplate

This provides the content and layout to apply to every other item in the DataList control. All other elements are formatted according to the current ItemTemplate. If this template is not defined, then the ItemTemplate is used for all elements in the DataList control.

EditItemTemplate

This provides the content and layout for the items in the DataList control selected for editing. If this template is not defined, then the ItemTemplate will be used to determine content and layout for such items.

FooterTemplate

This provides the content and layout for the footer section in the DataList control. If this template is not defined, then no footer section will be displayed for the DataList control.

HeaderTempate

This provides the content and layout for the header section in the DataList control. If this template is not defined, then no header section will be displayed for the DataList control.

ItemTemplate

This template **must** be defined. It provides the content and layout for all items in the DataList control.

SelecteditemTemplate

This provides the content and layout for the currently selected item in the DataList control. If this template is not defined, then the ItemTemplate will be applied instead.

SeparatorTemplate

This provides the content and layout for the separator between items in the DataList control. If this template is not defined, then no separator section will be displayed for the DataList control.

Example: DataList

The following example illustrates these templates in action. It is an altered version of the previous example for the DataGrid control. We have just changed to use a DataList control and add some tempates for the display of data. It is easy, isn't it?

Where we have columns for altering display of the DataGrid control, the DataList control uses templates.

```
<%@ Import Namespace="System.Data" %>
<html>
<head>
<script language="VB" runat="server">
Function CreateDataSource() As ICollection

Dim dt As New DataTable()
Dim dr As DataRow
Dim i As Integer
Dim Rand_Num As New Random()
Dim dv As New DataView(dt)

   dt.Columns.Add(New DataColumn("Product Index", GetType(Int32)))
   dt.Columns.Add(New DataColumn("Product Item", GetType(String)))
   dt.Columns.Add(New DataColumn("Product Value", GetType(Double)))

   For i = 0 To 8
           dr = dt.NewRow()
           dr(0) = i
           dr(1) = "Item " + i.ToString()
           dr(2) = 11.17 * Rand_Num.Next(1, 11)
           dt.Rows.Add(dr)
   Next i
```

```
    Return dv
End Function

Sub Page_Load(s As Object, e As EventArgs)
If Not IsPostBack Then
      Datalist1.DataSource = CreateDataSource()
      Datalist1.DataBind()
End If
End Sub

   </script>
</head>
<body>
<h3>DataList Example</h3>
<form runat=server>

Product List:
<asp:DataList id="Datalist1"
              showfooter="true"
              showheader="true"
              runat="server">

      <AlternatingItemStyle backcolor="LightGreen"
                            forecolor="red"
                            height="1cm"
                            horizontalalign="center"
                            verticalalign="top">
      </AlternatingItemStyle>

      <FooterStyle BackColor="LightBlue">
      </FooterStyle>

      <HeaderStyle BackColor="LightYellow">
      </HeaderStyle>

       <HeaderTemplate>
       This is the Header
       </HeaderTemplate>

<FooterTemplate>
This is the Footer
</FooterTemplate>

      <ItemTemplate>
      Product Index:<%# DataBinder.Eval(Container.DataItem, "Product Index") %>
      <br>
      Product Item:<%# DataBinder.Eval(Container.DataItem, "Product Item") %>
      <br>
      Product Value:<%# DataBinder.Eval(Container.DataItem, "Product Value") %>
      </ItemTemplate>

<SeparatorTemplate>
<hr color=orange>
 </SeparatorTemplate>
</asp:DataList>
</form>
```

```
    </body>
    </html>
```

This results in the following display:

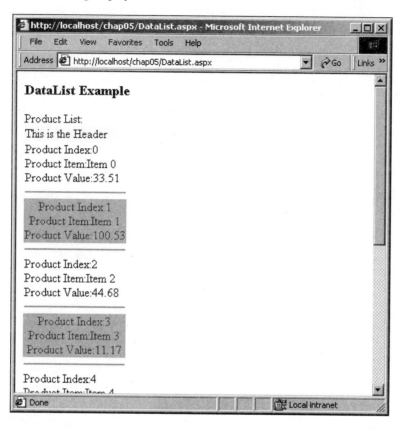

Example: DataListShoppingCart

Let's do a similar thing with the shopping cart example from the DataGrid section, and change the DataGrid control to the DataList control there too. This example is nothing new, apart from the use of the DataList control and associated templates.

```
<%@ Import Namespace="System.Data" %>
<html>
<head>
<script language="VB" runat="server">
Dim CartTable As New DataTable
Dim CartView As DataView

Sub Page_Load(s As Object, e As EventArgs)
Dim dr As DataRow
If Session("ShoppingCart") Is Nothing Then
    CartTable.Columns.Add(New DataColumn("Quantity", GetType(String)))
```

```
    CartTable.Columns.Add(New DataColumn("Item", GetType(String)))
    CartTable.Columns.Add(New DataColumn("Price", GetType(String)))
    Session("ShoppingCart") = CartTable

    Dim i As Integer
    For i = 1 To 11
        dr = CartTable.NewRow()
        If i Mod 3 <> 0 Then
                dr(0) = "3"
        Else
                dr(0) = "2"
        End If
        dr(1) = "Item " & i.ToString()
        dr(2) =(11.17 * i).ToString()
        CartTable.Rows.Add(dr)
    Next i
Else
    CartTable= CType(Session("ShoppingCart"), DataTable)
End If

    CartView = New DataView(CartTable)
    CartView.Sort = "Item"
    If Not IsPostBack Then
            DataList1.DataSource = CartView
            DataList1.DataBind()
    End If
End Sub

Sub EditCommand(s As Object, e As DataListCommandEventArgs)
DataList1.EditItemIndex = e.Item.ItemIndex
DataList1.DataSource = CartView
DataList1.DataBind()
End Sub

Sub CancelCommand(s As Object, e As DataListCommandEventArgs)
DataList1.EditItemIndex = - 1
DataList1.DataSource = CartView
DataList1.DataBind()
End Sub

Sub UpdateCommand(s As Object, e As DataListCommandEventArgs)

Dim item As String = CType(e.Item.FindControl("Label1"), Label).Text
Dim qty As String = CType(e.Item.FindControl("Text1"), TextBox).Text
Dim price As String = CType(e.Item.FindControl("Text2"), TextBox).Text
Dim dr As DataRow

CartView.RowFilter = "Item='" & item & "'"
If CartView.Count > 0 Then
      CartView.Delete(0)
End If
CartView.RowFilter = ""

dr = CartTable.NewRow()
dr(0) = qty
dr(1) = item
```

```
dr(2) = price
CartTable.Rows.Add(dr)

DataList1.EditItemIndex = - 1
DataList1.DataSource = CartView
DataList1.DataBind()
End Sub

Sub DeleteCommand(s As Object, e As DataListCommandEventArgs)

Dim dr As DataRow
Dim item As String = CType(e.Item.FindControl("Label1"), Label).Text

CartView.RowFilter = "Item='" & item & "'"
If CartView.Count > 0 Then
     CartView.Delete(0)
End If
CartView.RowFilter = ""
DataList1.DataSource = CartView
DataList1.DataBind()
End Sub
</script>
</head>
<body>
<form runat="server">
<h3>DataList Deleting & Editing Example</h3>
<br>

    <asp:DataList id="DataList1" runat="server"
        GridLines="Both"
        CellPadding="3"
        CellSpacing="0"
        OnEditCommand="EditCommand"
        OnUpdateCommand="UpdateCommand"
        OnDeleteCommand="DeleteCommand"
        OnCancelCommand="CancelCommand">

      <HeaderStyle BackColor="LightBlue">
      </HeaderStyle>

      <FooterStyle BackColor="LightBlue">
      </FooterStyle>

      <AlternatingItemStyle BackColor="Gainsboro">
      </AlternatingItemStyle>

      <EditItemStyle BackColor="lightgreen">
      </EditItemStyle>

      <HeaderTemplate>
         This is the Header
      </HeaderTemplate>
      <FooterTemplate>
         This is the Footer
      </FooterTemplate>
```

```
        <ItemTemplate>
            <asp:LinkButton id="button1"
                Text="Edit"
                CommandName="edit"
                runat="server"/>
            <%# (CType(Container.DataItem, DataRowView))("Item")  %>
        </ItemTemplate>

        <EditItemTemplate>
            Item:
            <asp:Label id="Label1"
                Text='<%# (CType(Container.DataItem, DataRowView))("Item") %>'
                runat="server"/>
            <br>
            Quantity:
            <asp:TextBox id="Text1" size="6"
                Text='<%# (CType(Container.DataItem, DataRowView))("Quantity") %>'
                runat="server"/>
            <br>
            Price:
            <asp:TextBox id="Text2" size="6"
                Text='<%# DataBinder.Eval(Container.DataItem, "Price") %>'
                runat="server"/>
            <br>
            <asp:LinkButton id="button2"
                Text="Update"
                CommandName="update"
                runat="server"/>
            <asp:LinkButton id="button3"
                Text="Delete"
                CommandName="delete"
                runat="server"/>
            <asp:LinkButton id="button4"
                Text="Cancel"
                CommandName="cancel"
                runat="server"/>
        </EditItemTemplate>
    </asp:DataList>
</form>
</body>
</html>
```

This now results in the following output:

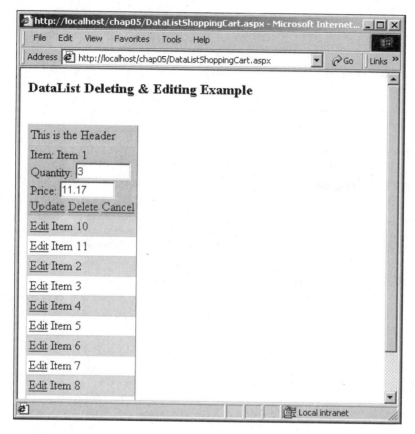

The picture shows the display when the Edit button of the first item is clicked.

The Repeater Control

The Repeater control is much simpler than the DataList control. Basically, a Repeater control displays data only. It doesn't support editing, deleting, paging, or sorting features that the DataGrid offers. It offers a straightforward mechanism for the display of data taken line by line from the data source. The Repeater control has no built-in layout or style, so we must create it within some other HTML structure to provide formatting, such as within a table for instance.

Syntax:

```
<asp:Repeater id = "Repeater1"
    DataSource="name of data source"
    Runat = server>

  <HeaderTemplate>
    Header template HTML
  </HeaderTemplate>
  <ItemTemplate>
```

```
      Item template HTML
   </ItemTemplate>
   <AlternatingItemTemplate>
      Alternating item template HTML
   </AlternatingItemTemplate>
   <SeparatorTemplate>
      Separator template HTML
   </SeparatorTemplate>
   <FooterTemplate>
      Footer template HTML
   </FooterTemplate>

<asp:Repeater>
```

Properties of the Repeater Control

The Repeater control uses two properties from the BaseDataList class, namely DataMember and DataSource, and also the Items property defined by the DataGrid control. Their purposes are as described in the DataGrid control and the DataList control. Apart from these, the only other properties it uses are the template properties that we discuss in their own section below.

Methods and Events of the Repeater Control

The Repeater control is simpler than the DataList control, and as you may expect, it inherits even fewer members from the DataGrid control. While the DataList does not inherit members related to paging or sorting, the Repeater control doesn't inherit members related to paging, sorting, editing, or deleting. This leaves just the following methods:

- ❑ OnItemCommand
- ❑ OnItemCreated
- ❑ OnItemDataBound

and the following events:

- ❑ ItemCommand
- ❑ ItemCreated
- ❑ ItemDataBound

Templates of the Repeater Control

As the Repeater control doesn't support editing of the items displayed, neither EditItemTemplate nor SelectedItemTemplate templates are required. The supported templates are:

- ❑ ItemTemplate
- ❑ AlternatingTemplate
- ❑ SeparatorTemplate
- ❑ HeaderTemplate
- ❑ FooterTemplate

Example: The RepeaterControl

Next, let's see an example to illustrate usage of the Repeater control. The code is based on the DataGrid sample, with changes to use a Repeater control instead of a DataGrid control, and the addition of templates for the Repeater control.

```
<%@ Import Namespace="System.Data" %>
<html>
<head>
<script language="VB" runat="server">
Function CreateDataSource() As ICollection
Dim dt As New DataTable()
Dim dr As DataRow
Dim i As Integer
Dim Rand_Num As New Random()
Dim dv As New DataView(dt)

dt.Columns.Add(New DataColumn("Product Index", GetType(Int32)))
dt.Columns.Add(New DataColumn("Product Item", GetType(String)))
dt.Columns.Add(New DataColumn("Product Value", GetType(Double)))

For i = 1 To 5
    dr = dt.NewRow()
    dr(0) = i
    dr(1) = "Item " + i.ToString()
    dr(2) = 11.17 * Rand_Num.Next(1, 11)
    dt.Rows.Add(dr)
Next i
Return dv
End Function

Sub Page_Load(s As Object, e As EventArgs)
If Not IsPostBack Then
      Repeater1.DataSource = CreateDataSource()
      Repeater1.DataBind()
End If
End Sub
</script>
</head>
<body>

<h3>Repeater Example</h3>

<asp:Repeater id="Repeater1" runat="server">

   <HeaderTemplate>
      <table border=1>
         <tr bgcolor="LightBlue">
             <td>Product Index</td>
               <td>Product Item</td>
               <td>Product Value</td>
         </tr>
   </HeaderTemplate>

   <ItemTemplate>
```

```
        <tr>
                <td> <%# DataBinder.Eval(Container.DataItem, "Product Index") %>
    </td>
                <td> <%# DataBinder.Eval(Container.DataItem, "Product Item") %>
    </td>
                <td> <%# DataBinder.Eval(Container.DataItem, "Product Value") %>
    </td>
        </tr>
   </ItemTemplate>

   <FooterTemplate>
       </table>
   </FooterTemplate>
</asp:Repeater>

</body>
</html>
```

The resulting output is shown below:

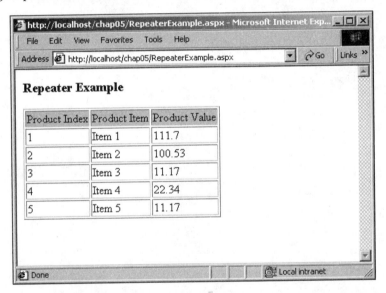

In these pages, we have looked at the three special data-binding list controls, and you have probably noticed how similar to each other they are. Because of the varying sophistication of the functionality they offer, these controls provide a solution for a range of common scenarios. To sum up, the DataGrid control focuses on complex processing in grid format, and allows the user to edit and delete data items. The content of a DataGrid can also be readily split over multiple pages, and sorted dynamically. The DataList control, however, provides templates that allow quite colorful web pages to be built to display data items that the user can edit from their browser. Of course, it no longer offers the powerful paging and sorting capabilities of the DataGrid. Last of all, there is the Repeater control, the simplest of the three. It is purely for the display of data within an external HTML structure on a web page. It doesn't support editing, sorting, paging, or deleting.

Rich Controls

In this section, we discuss rich controls, the third category of controls described in the introduction to this chapter. They are called rich controls because they offer greater functionality and an enriched user interface. For the time being, Microsoft only provides two rich controls: `AdRotator`, and `Calendar`. `AdRotator` is similar to the eponymous control of ASP 3.0. `Calendar`, however, is an excellent new control that all developers will be able to benefit from. To achieve the functionalty of an online diary, you could spend days sweating over reams of JavaScript and bundles of ASP code. In one swoop, the `Calendar` control has obviated the need for such efforts, providing the developer with a very flexible and powerful tool.

The AdRotator Control

The `AdRotator` provides a convenient mechanism for displaying advertisements on a web page in sequence, and makes advertisement management much easier and more practical. In the previous incarnation of ASP, we had to use an ActiveX object to achieve rich features. In ASP.NET, the `AdRotator` control is a dream for developers and administrators alike. The advertisements are detailed in an XML-based file, and thanks to the `PostBack` feature of .NET, when an advertisement is clicked, functions on the server can be executed to perform whatever task is approprate to that advertisement.

Syntax:

```
<asp:AdRotator id = "id_name"
    AdvertisementFile = "XML file of advertisement"
    KeyWordFilter = "KeyWord"
    Target = "Display type"
    OnAdCreated = "Method of AdCreated"
    Runat = "server" />
```

Properties of the AdRotator Control

The AdvertisementFile Property

The `AdvertisementFile` property gets or sets the path of the XML advertisement file. A typical advertisement file is shown below to illustrate the format that is followed:

```
<?xml version="1.0" ?>
<Advertisements>
  <Ad>
    <ImageUrl>1.gif</ImageUrl>
    <NavigateUrl>http://www.wrox.com</NavigatorUrl>
    <AlternateText>This is a gif</AlternateText>
    <Keyword>gif</Keyword>
    <Impressions>20</Impressions>
  </Ad>
  <Ad>
    <ImageUrl>2.gif</ImageUrl>
    <NavigateUrl>http://www.asptoday.com</NavigatorUrl>
    <AlternateText>This is a gif</AlternateText>
    <Keyword>gif</Keyword>
    <Impressions>30</Impressions>
  </Ad>
</Advertisement>
```

Let's summarize the XML elements for a particular advert, as contained within an <Ad> element.

Element	Description
<ImageUrl>	Sets the URL of the image file that is the advertisement banner to show on the page.
<NavigateUrl>	Sets the URL of the page that is displayed when the advertisement image is clicked.
<AlternateText>	If the image is not available, then this text is shown on the page. For Internet Explorer, this attribute is just like the ToolTip property.
<Keyword>	This attribute can be used to organize related advertisements into groups by giving all advertisements of a certain type the same keyword. This keyword can then be used to filter out other advertisement types.
<Impressions>	A weighting indicating how often the image should be displayed on a Web page.

The KeywordFilter Property

This property relates to the keyword of the XML advertisement file. You can set the KeywordFilter property and filter for advertisements with a matching Keyword element. The default is empty.

The Target Property

The Target property gets or sets the name of the browser window or frame to be used to display the contents of the linked web page when the AdRotator control is clicked. The valid values determine the broswer window or frame as follows:

Value	Description
_blank	A new and unframed browser window
_parent	The immediate frameset parent in the same browser
_self	The current frame in the same browser window
_top	The full and unframed window in the same browser

The default value is empty, meaning that the new page will display in the current frame or window.

Methods of the AdRotator Control

The OnAdCreated Method

The OnAdCreated method raises the AdCreated event for the AdRotator control.

Events of the AdRotator Control

The AdCreated Event

The AdCreated event is raised once per round trip to the server after the creation of the control, but before the page is rendered.

```
<script language="VB" runat="server">
      Sub AdCreated_Event(sender As Object, e As AdCreatedEventArgs)
      .......
      End Sub
   </script>
```

The event handler will get some information from `AdCreatedEventArgs`. The following table details the properties of `AdCreatedEventArgs`.

Property	Description
ImageUrl	Sets the URL of the image file to display as the advertisement banner on the Web page.
NavigateUrl	Sets the URL of the page displayed when the advertisement image is clicked.
AlternateText	If the image is not available, then this text appears on the page. For Internet Explorer, this attribute is just like the `ToolTip` property.
AdProperties	Gets an object that contains all the advertisement properties for the currently displayed advertisement. This object represents a collection of key-value pairs.

Example: AdRotator

Let's see a quick example that shows how the `keyword` and `KeywordFilter` properties can be used to select a certain type of advertisement for the `AdRotator` control to display.

```
<html>
<head>
<script language=VB runat=server>
  Sub adcreate( s As Object , e As AdCreatedEventArgs)
    Label1.text = "You will navigate to " & e.NavigateUrl
End sub
</script>
<body>
<h3>AdRotator Example</h3>
<form runat=server />
    <asp:adrotator id=adrotator1
        advertisementfile = advertisement.xml
        keywordfilter = book
        onadcreated = adcreate
        runat = server />
</form><br>
<asp:label id=label1 runat=server />
</body>
</html>
```

The `advertisement.xml` file will be something like the following:

```
<?xml version="1.0" ?>
<Advertisements>
```

```
   <Ad>
      <ImageUrl>wrox.gif</ImageUrl>
      <NavigateUrl>http://www.wrox.com</NavigateUrl>
      <AlternateText>Wrox Press</AlternateText>
      <Impressions>50</Impressions>
      <Keyword>book</Keyword>
   </Ad>
   <Ad>
      <ImageUrl>ms.gif</ImageUrl>
      <NavigateUrl>http://www.microsoft.com</NavigateUrl>
      <AlternateText>MS</AlternateText>
      <Impressions>30</Impressions>
      <Keyword>software</Keyword>
   </Ad>
</Advertisements>
```

When we open up the `adrotator.aspx` file in our browser, it only shows the Wrox Press advertisement because we specified the keyword of `book`:

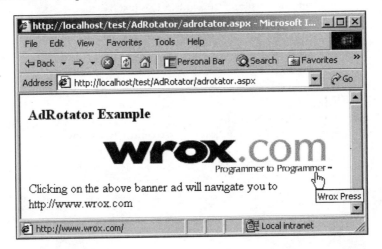

The Calendar Control

The `Calendar` control displays all the dates for a given month on a web page, and allows the user to select dates or move to the next or previous month. It is a more functionally rich control than the `AdRotator` control, and provides many properties, three methods, and three events to make the developer's life easier. The `Calendar` control has the most properties of all the Web controls in the `System.Web.UI.WebControls` namespace.

Syntax:

```
<asp:Calendar id = "id_name"
     CellPadding = "pixels"
     CellSpacing = "pixels"
     DayNameFormat = "The format of day name"
     FirstDayOfWeek = "The first day of a week"
     NextMonthText = "HTML text"
     NextPrevFormat = "The format of Next Previous"
```

```
        PrevMonthText = "HTML text"
        SelectedDate = "date"
        SelectionMode = "None | Day | DayWeek | DayWeekMonth"
        SelectMonthText = "HTML text"
        SelectWeekText = "HTML text"
        ShowDayHeader = "True | False"
        ShowGridLines = "True | False"
        ShowNextPrevMonth = "True | False"
        ShowTitle = "True | False"
        TitleFormat = "Month | MonthYear"
        TodaysDate = "date"
        VisibleDate = "date"
        OnDayRender = "Method of OnDayRender"
        OnSelectionChanged = "Method of OnSelectionChanged"
        OnVisibleMonthChanged = "Method of OnVisibleMonthChanged"
        Runat = "server">

        <TodayDayStyle property = "value" />
        <DayHeaderStyle property = "value" />
        <DayStyle property = "value" />
        <NextPrevStyle property = "value" />
        <OtherMonthDayStyle property = "value" />
        <SelectedDayStyle property = "value" />
        <SelectorStyle property = "value" />
        <TitleStyle property = "value" />
        <TodayDayStyle property = "value" />
        <WeekendDayStyle property = "value" />

    </asp:Calendar>
```

Properties of the Calendar Control

The CellPadding Property

The CellPadding property gets or sets the distance between the contents of a cell and the cell's border. Its unit is pixels and the default value is 2.

The CellSpacing Property

The CellSpacing property gets or sets the space between cells. Its unit is pixels and the default value is 0.

The DayHeaderStyle Property

The DayHeaderStyle property gets the style properties for the section where the weekdays are displayed. The default value is empty. The style properties are the properties of the TableItemStyle class, as with the DataGrid control. Refer to that section for the possible values of this property. This property only applies when the ShowDayHeader property is set to True.

The DayNameFormat Property

The DayNameFormat property gets or sets the name format for the display of days. The valid values are FirstLetter, FirstTwoLetters, Full, and Short. The default value is Short, which means that the first three characters of the name of each day will be displayed. For example, Sunday is Sun, Monday is Mon and so on. The others are self-explanatory.

The DayStyle Property

The `DayStyle` property gets the style properties for the days. The default value is empty. The style properties are the properties of the `TableItemStyle` class in the namespace of `System.Web.UI.WebControls`. You can refer to the `DataGrid` control for `TableItemStyle`. We have discussed the style properties of `TableItemStyle` in the section of the `DataGrid` control.

The FirstDayOfWeek Property

The `FirstDayOfWeek` property gets or sets the day of a week to display in the first day column in the `Calendar` control. The valid values are `Default`, `Monday`, `Tuesday`, `Wednesday`, `Thursday`, `Friday`, `Saturday`, and `Sunday`. The default value is `Default` which means that the value is determined by the system settings.

The NextMonthText Property

The `NextMonthText` property gets or sets the text for the navigational element to select the next month. The text format is HTML, and the default value is `&gt;` which denotes the "greater than" sign.

The NextPrevFormat Property

The `NextPrevFormat` property gets or sets the text format for the navigational elements that select the next and previous months for the `Calendar` control. The valid values are `ShortMonth`, `FullMonth`, and `CustomText`. The default value is `CustomText`, which means that the text specified in the `NextMonthText` and `PrevMonthText` properties is used.

`ShortMonth` will display the first three characters of the month. For example, December is `Dec`.

`FullMonth` will display the whole name of the month.

The NextPrevStyle Property

The `NextPrevStyle` property gets the style properties for the next and previous month navigational text. The style properties are the properties of the `TableItemStyle` class in the `System.Web.UI.WebControls` namespace, and are covered in the section on the `DataGrid` control.

The OtherMonthDayStyle Property

The `OtherMonthDayStyle` property gets the style properties for dates that are not in the displayed month. For example, if a `Calendar` control shows August, then we will see the last few days of July and the first few of September on the calendar as well. The `OtherMonthDayStyle` property contains sub-properties for formatting these dates. The style properties are the properties of the `TableItemStyle` class in the `System.Web.UI.WebControls` namespace, and are covered in the section on the `DataGrid` control.

The PrevMonthText Property

The `PrevMonthText` property gets or sets the text for the navigational element to select the previous month. The text format is HTML, and the default value is `&lt;` which denotes the "less than" sign.

The SelectedDate Property

The `SelectedDate` property gets or sets the day selected by the user. It is in the `DateTime` format, for example `12:12:00 AM, 11/17/2000`. A `System.DateTime` object represents the selected date. The default value is `DateTime.MinValue`. This property is used when the `SelectionMode` property is set to `Day` as discussed later.

When a user selects a date, the `SelectedChanged` event is raised. This event is covered later.

The SelectedDates Property

The `SelectedDates` property gets a collection of `System.DateTime` objects that represent the selected dates. It is a collection of `System.DateTime` objects and the default value is an empty `SelectedDatesCollection`. This property is used when the `SelectionMode` property is set to `DayWeek` or `DayWeekMonth`.

When a user selects a week or a month, the `SelectedChanged` event is raised. The user can not only select a week or a month, but also some special days can be selected in a `Calendar` control. For example, the user could select the range from the 10th to the 19th of a month, or a random selection of days. We can achieve this with the `SelectedDates` collection. We can the `Add`, `Remove`, `Clear`, and `SelectRange` methods to programmatically manipulate the selected dates in the `SelectedDates` collection.

Example: Calendar1

Now, let's see an example for selecting a range programmatically. In this example we use the `VisibleDate` property discussed later. You can also see many properties from the `System.DateTime` object: refer to the `DateTime` structure in the `Sysem` namespace.

```
<html>
<head>
<script language="VB" runat="server">
Sub Page_Load(sender As Object, e As EventArgs)
    If Not Page.IsPostBack Then
       Calendar1.VisibleDate = Calendar1.TodaysDate
    End If
End Sub

Sub Button_Click(sender As Object, e As EventArgs)

    Dim current_month As Integer = Calendar1.VisibleDate.Month
    Dim current_year As Integer = Calendar1.VisibleDate.Year
    Dim a as integer
    Dim b as integer
    a = d1.SelectedItem.Text
    b = d2.selectedItem.Text
    Dim Begin_Date As New DateTime(current_year, current_month, a)
    Dim End_Date As New DateTime(current_year, current_month, b)
    Calendar1.SelectedDates.Clear()
    Calendar1.SelectedDates.SelectRange(Begin_Date, End_Date)
End Sub
</script>
</head>
<body>
<h3>Calendar Example</h3>
<form runat="server">
    <asp:Calendar ID="Calendar1" runat="server"
    SelectionMode="DayWeekMonth"/>
    Start Date :
       <asp:dropdownlist id="d1" runat=server>
       <asp:Listitem text=1 value=1 />
       <asp:Listitem text=2 value=2 />
```

```
        <asp:Listitem text=3 value=3 />
        <asp:Listitem text=4 value=4 />
        </asp:dropdownlist>
        <br>
    End Date :
        <asp:dropdownlist id="d2" runat=server>
        <asp:Listitem text=11 value=11 />
        <asp:Listitem text=12 value=12 />
        <asp:Listitem text=13 value=13 />
        <asp:Listitem text=14 value=14 />
        </asp:dropdownlist>
        <Br>
        <asp:Button id="Button1"
        text="Select range"
        OnClick="Button_Click"
        runat=server /> <br>

    <asp:Label id="Label1" runat=server />
</form>
</body>
</html>
```

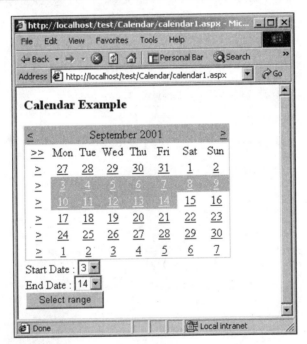

The SelectedDayStyle Property

The `SelectedDayStyle` property gets the style properties for the days selected by a user. The style properties are the properties of the `TableItemStyle` class in the namespace of `System.Web.UI.WebControls`. You can refer to the `DataGrid` control for `TableItemStyle`. We have discussed the style properties of `TableItemStyle` in the section on the `DataGrid` control.

The SelectionMode Property

The `SelectionMode` property gets or sets the selection mode that allows users to select either one day, one week, or one month. The valid values are `None`, `Day`, `DayWeek`, and `DayWeekMonth` and the default value is `Day`.

The SelectMonthText Property

The `SelectMonthText` property gets or sets the text displayed for the month selection element in the selector column. The text format is HTML and the default value is "`&gt;&gt;`" which means two "greater than" signs. The property is only applicable when the `SelectionMode` property is set to `DayWeekMonth`.

The SelectorStyle Property

The `SelectorStyle` property gets the style properties for the week and month selector column. The style properties are the properties of the `TableItemStyle` class in the namespace of `System.Web.UI.WebControls`. The property works only when `SelectionMode` is set to `DayWeek` or `DayWeekMonth`. You can refer to the `DataGrid` control for `TableItemStyle`. We have discussed the style properties of `TableItemStyle` in the section of the `DataGrid` control.

The SelectWeekText Property

The `SelectWeekText` property gets or sets the text displayed for the week selection element in the selector column. The text format is HTML and the default value is "`&gt;`" which means a "greater than" sign. The property is only applicable when `SelectionMode` is set to `DayWeek` or `DayWeekMonth`.

The ShowDayHeader Property

The `ShowDayHeader` property gets or sets a value that indicates whether the name of a day of a week displays in the `Calendar` control. The valid values are `True` and `False` and the default value is `True`.

The ShowGridLines Property

The `ShowGridLines` property gets or sets a value that indicates whether grid lines exist between day cells in the `Calendar` control. The valid values are `True` and `False` and the default value is `False`.

The ShowNextPrevMonth Property

The `ShowNextPrevMonth` property gets or sets a value that indicates whether the text or sign of the next and previous month navigational elements displays in the `Calendar` control. The valid values are `True` and `False` and the default value is `True`.

The ShowTitle Property

The `ShowTitle` property gets or sets a value that indicates whether the title of the `Calendar` control displays. The `Title` section includes next and previous month navigation elements and the name of the current month and year. The valid values are `True` and `False` and the default value is `True`.

The TitleFormat Property

The `TitleFormat` property gets or sets the format of the `Title` section in a `Calendar` control. The valid values are `Month` and `MonthYear` and the default value is `MonthYear`. This property is only applicable when the `ShowTitle` property is set to `True`.

The TitleStyle Property

The TitleStyle property gets the style properties for the Title section in a Calendar control. The style properties are the properties of the TableItemStyle class in the namespace of System.Web.UI.WebControls. The TitleStyle property is only applicable when the ShowTitle property is set to True.

The TodayDayStyle Property

The TodayDayStyle property gets the style properties for today's date in a Calendar control. The style properties are the properties of the TableItemStyle class in the namespace of System.Web.UI.WebControls. The settings of the TodayDayStyle property will override the settings of the DayStyle property.

The TodaysDate Property

The TodaysDate property gets or sets a value for today's date. The default value is the system time on the computer. This property is set using a System.DateTime object.

The VisibleDate Property

The VisibleDate property gets or sets the date that specifies the month to display on the Calendar control. You can programmatically generate a calendar by inputting a year and month. The VisibleDate property is updated before the VisibleMonthChanged event is raised. The VisibleMonthChanged event is discussed shortly.

Example: Calendar2

Let's see this property in a simple example:

```
<html>
<head>
<script language="VB" runat="server">
Sub ButtonClick(sender As Object, e As EventArgs)
  Dim year as Integer
  Dim month as Integer
  year = DropDownList1.SelectedItem.Text
  month = DropDownList2.SelectedItem.Text
  Calendar1.VisibleDate = New DateTime(Year, month, 1)
End Sub
</script>
</head>
<body>
<form runat="server">
   <h3>Calendar Example</h3>
   <asp:Calendar id="Calendar1" runat="server" />
   <hr>
   Year : <Br>
   <asp:DropDownList id="DropDownList1" runat="server">
     <asp:ListItem>1991</asp:ListItem>
     <asp:ListItem>1992</asp:ListItem>
     <asp:ListItem>1993</asp:ListItem>
     <asp:ListItem>1994</asp:ListItem>
     <asp:ListItem>1995</asp:ListItem>
     <asp:ListItem>1996</asp:ListItem>
     <asp:ListItem>1997</asp:ListItem>
```

```
        <asp:ListItem>1998</asp:ListItem>
        <asp:ListItem>1999</asp:ListItem>
        <asp:ListItem>2000</asp:ListItem>
        <asp:ListItem>2001</asp:ListItem>
        <asp:ListItem>2002</asp:ListItem>
    </asp:DropDownList>
    <br>
    Month : <br>
    <asp:DropDownList id="DropDownList2" runat="server">
        <asp:ListItem>1</asp:ListItem>
        <asp:ListItem>2</asp:ListItem>
        <asp:ListItem>3</asp:ListItem>
        <asp:ListItem>4</asp:ListItem>
        <asp:ListItem>5</asp:ListItem>
        <asp:ListItem>6</asp:ListItem>
        <asp:ListItem>7</asp:ListItem>
        <asp:ListItem>8</asp:ListItem>
        <asp:ListItem>9</asp:ListItem>
        <asp:ListItem>10</asp:ListItem>
        <asp:ListItem>11</asp:ListItem>
        <asp:ListItem>12</asp:ListItem>
    </asp:DropDownList>
    <Br>
    <asp:Button id="Button1"
        Text="Create"
        OnClick="ButtonClick"
        runat=server />
</form>
</body>
</html>
```

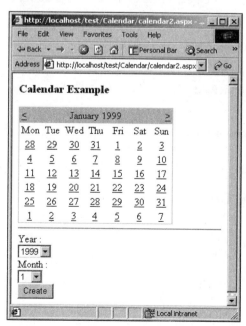

The WeekendDayStyle Property

The WeekendDayStyle property gets the style properties for the days of Saturday and Sunday. The style properties are the properties of the TableItemStyle class in the System.Web.UI.WebControls namespace. When the WeekendDayStyle property is set, it will override the settings of the DayStyle property.

When the TodayDayStyle property is set, it will override the settings of the WeekendDayStyle property if today is Saturday or Sunday.

Methods of the Calendar Control

The OnDayRender Method

The OnDayRender method raises the DayRender event of a Calendar control. The Calendar control does not support data binding, but it is possible for us to change the contents of the date cell in a Calendar control. The DayRender event is raised when the date cells in the Calendar control are created.

You can control the contents and format of the date cells by providing code in the event handler for the DayRender event. The event handler receives a DayRenderEventArgs object that contains two parameters. The two parameters are Cell and Day. The Cell parameter is a TableCell object that contains information about the date cell to render. The Day parameter is a CalendarDay object that contains information about the date to render. These two parameters allow you to create the content and format of the date cell and date programmatically. You can also customize the contents of a cell by dynamically adding controls to the Control.Controls collection of the Cell property.

In the DayRender event, you cannot set any control that will raise an event. Therefore, you can only add static controls in the DayRender event. For example, an Image control, a Literal control and so on.

We will have an example later.

The OnSelectionChanged Method

The OnSelectionChanged method raises the SelectionChanged event when the user clicks a day, a week, or a month.

The OnVisibleMonthChanged Method

The OnVisibleMonthChanged method raises the VisibleMonthChanged event when the user clicks the next or previous month navigational element to move to the next or previous month.

Events of the Calendar Control

The DayRender Event

The DayRender event occurs when the Calendar control is created.

Example: Calendar3

Let's see an example that shows how to customize the content of a day. We define a sample holiday string in the Page_Load event. When the Calendar control is created, the DayRender event is fired. We use DateTime objects to add named holidays into the date cells of the Calendar control.

```
<html>
<head>
<script language="VB" runat="server">
  Dim Holidays(12,31) as string
  Sub Page_Load ( s as object, e as eventargs)
    Holidays(1,1) = "<br<font size=-1>New Year<font>"
    Holidays(7,4) = "<br><font size=-1>Independence Day<font>"
  End Sub
  Sub DayRender( s as object, e as DayRenderEventArgs)
    e.Cell.Controls.Add(New LiteralControl(Holidays(e.Day.Date.Month, _
                                           e.Day.Date.Day)))

  End Sub
</script>
</head>
<body>
<form runat="server">

  <h3>Calendar DayRender Event Example</h3>

  <asp:Calendar id="calendar1"
       OnDayRender="DayRender"
       runat="server">
  </asp:Calendar>
</form>
</body>
</html>
```

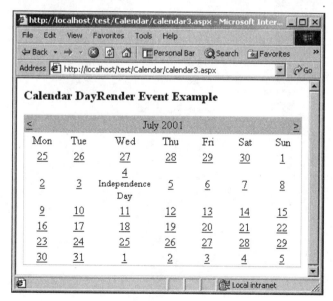

The SelectionChanged Event

The SelectionChanged event occurs when the user clicks a day, a week, or a month in the Calendar control.

Example: Calendar4

Let's have a quick example to demonstrate the SelectionChanged event and the SelectedDayStyle property.

```
<html>
<head>
<script language="VB" runat="server">
Sub Selection_Change(sender As Object, e As EventArgs)
  If Calendar1.SelectedDates.Count = 1 then
    Label1.Text = "You selected :<br>" & Calendar1.SelectedDate
  Else
    label1.Text = "You selected :<br>"
    Dim i as Integer
    For i = 0 to Calendar1.Selecteddates.Count -1
    Label1.text += Calendar1.SelectedDates(i) &"<br>"
    Next
  End if
End Sub
</script>
</head>
<body>

<form runat="server">
 <h3>Calendar SelectionChanged Example</h3>

   Select a date or dates:<br>

   <asp:Calendar ID="Calendar1" runat="server"
      SelectionMode="DayWeekMonth"
      OnSelectionChanged="Selection_Change">

     <SelectedDayStyle BackColor="Yellow"
              ForeColor="Red">
     </SelectedDayStyle>

   </asp:Calendar>
   <hr>
   <asp:Label id="Label1" runat=server />
</form>
</body>
</html>
```

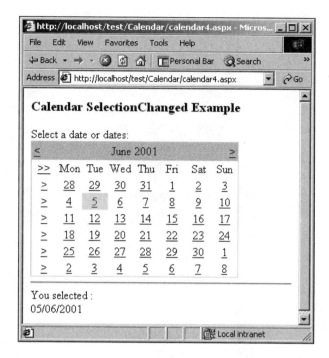

The VisibleMonthChanged Event

The `VisibleMonthChanged` event occurs when the user clicks the navigational element that selects the next or previous month. The event handler receives an argument of type `MonthChangedEventArgs` containing data related to this event. There are two properties contained in the `MonthChangedEventArgs`: `NewDate` and `PreviousDate`. The `NewDate` property represents the month that will be next displayed, and the `PreviousDate` property is the month that the user is coming from.

Example: Calendar5

Let's have another quick example, one that's even simpler than the previous two.

```
<html>
<head>
<script language="VB" runat="server">
Sub MonthChange(source As Object, e As MonthChangedEventArgs)
  If e.NewDate.Month > e.PreviousDate.Month Then
    label1.Text = "You moved forwards one month."
  Else
    label1.Text = "You moved backwards one month."
  End If
End Sub
</script>
</head>
<body>
<form runat="server">
<h3>Calendar VisibleMonthChanged Event Example</h3>
    Click the next or previous month's navigational element.
```

```
    <br><br>

    <asp:Calendar id="calendar1" runat="server"
      OnVisibleMonthChanged="MonthChange">

    </asp:Calendar>
</form>
<hr>
<asp:Label id="label1" runat="server"/>

</body>
</html>
```

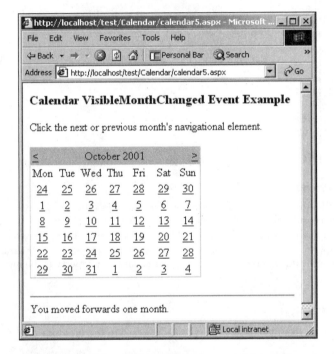

The Calendar control is an extremely sophisticated and powerful tool for web application development. One common example of where a Calendar control can be useful is in an events scheduling Web application. With the Calendar control, it is much easier to write a very good, professional-quality Web Schedule application for your users. Do remember of course that as the Calender control posts back to the server for event processing, users may sometimes have to wait.

Validation Controls

In this section we move on to the fourth category of web controls described in the introduction to this chapter. ASP.NET provides a simple way to validate the information input by users with the following validation controls.

The CompareValidator Control

The CompareValidator control can check values input by the user in a textbox. It will compare the input against some specified value, and throw an exception if it doesn't match the criteria determined by the comparison operator, set by the Operator property.

Syntax:

```
<asp:CompareValidator id = "id_name"
     runat = "server"
     ControlToValidate = "programmatic ID of Server Control to Validate"
     ValueToCompare="104.5"
     Type="Double"
     Operator="LessThan"
     ErrorMessage="Temperature must not exceed 104.5"
     ForeColor = "forecolor"
     BackColor = "background color">
  Text
</asp:CompareValidator>
```

Properties of the CompareValidator Control

The ControlToCompare Property

The ControlToCompare property gets or sets the input control that is to be validated.

The Operator Property

The Operator property gets or sets the comparison operation to perform. The default is '='.

The valid values of the operator are as follows:

Operator	Description
Equal	=
NotEqual	<>
GreaterThan	>
GreaterThanEqual	>=
LessThan	<
LessThanEqual	<=
DataTypeCheck	The data type refers to BaseCompareValidator.Type properties

The ValueToCompare Property

The ValueToCompare property gets or sets a constant value to compare with the value entered by the user into the input control being validated. The default is empty.

Type of validator:

Type	Description
Currency	A currency data type
Date	A date data type
Double	A double data type
Integer	An integer data type
String	A string data type

Example: CompareValidator

Let's see a quick example of this control.

```
<html>
<head>
<script language="VB" runat=server>
Sub compare1(s as object, e as eventargs)
  if (page.isvalid) then
    label1.text = "The number you input is less than 100"
  end if
end sub
</script>
</head>
<body>
<h3>CompareValidator Example</h3>
  <form runat=server>
    Input a number less than 100: <br>
  <asp:textbox id=textbox1 runat=server /><br>
  <asp:comparevalidator id="c1" runat=server
      controltovalidate = "textbox1"
      valueToCompare="100"
      operator = "lessthan"
      Errormessage = "The number is greater than 100"
      type = "Integer" /><Br>
  <asp:button id=button1 text=Compare onclick="compare1" runat=server />
  </form>
<hr>
<asp:label id="label1" runat=server />
</body>
</html>
```

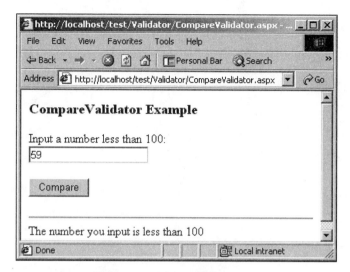

The `CompareValidator` control has no methods or events.

The RangeValidator Control

The `RangeValidator` control checks that a value input by the user falls within in the specified range. You can check ranges for numbers, say 1 to 100, alphabetic characters, like A to F, and dates, such as 2001/5/1 to 2001/6/30.

Syntax:

```
<asp:RangeValidator id ="id_name"
    ControlToValidate = "id name of the control which is validated"
    MinimumValue = "The minimum value of the range"
    MaximumValue = "The maximum value of the range"
    Type = "type of the data"
    ErrorMessage = "Error message"
    Runat = server />
```

Properties of the RangeValidator Control

The range specified for the control is inclusive, so the values provided by the two properties listed here will themselves be permitted input for the control.

The MaximumValue Property

The `MaximumValue` property gets or sets the upper value of the validation range.

The MinimumValue Property

The `MinimumValue` property gets or sets the lower value of the validation range.

Let's see an example for validating dates.

```
<html>
<head>
<script language="VB" runat=server>
```

```
Sub compare1(s As object, e As EventArgs)
  if (page.isvalid) then
    label1.text = "Validation is okay!"
  end if
end sub
</script>
</head>
<body>
<h3>RangeValidator Example</h3>
<form runat=server>
Input a date between May 1st,2001 and June 30th,2001:
<br>
<asp:textbox id=textbox1 runat=server />(Year/Month/Day)<br>
<asp:RangeValidator id="r1" runat=server
    controltovalidate = "textbox1"
    MinimumValue = "2001/5/1"
    MaximumValue = "2001/6/30"
    Errormessage = "The date is not in the range you set."
    type = "Date" />
<br>
<asp:button id=button1 text="Validate" onclick="compare1" runat=server />
</form>
<hr>
<asp:label id="label1" runat=server />
</body>
</html>
```

The resulting output is shown below:

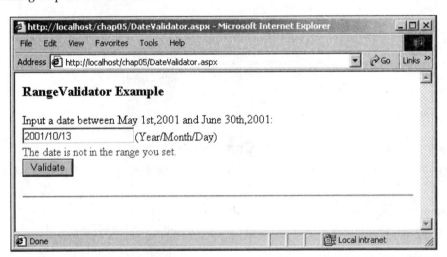

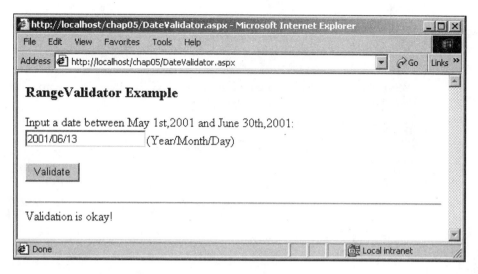

The `RangeValidator` control has no methods or events.

The RegularExpressionValidator Control

The `RegularExpressionValidator` control allows you to check a string input by the user to see if it matches the pattern defined by a regular expression. This type of validation allows you to check for predictable sequences of characters, and can be extremely useful where you need to ensure that the user has entered a correct e-mail address, telephone number, or social security number for instance.

Syntax:

```
<asp:RegularExpressionValidator id="id_name"
    ControlToValidate = "id of control"
    ValidationExpression = "expression"
    ErrorMessage = "Error message"
    Runat = "server" />
```

Properties of the RegularExpressionValidator Control

The ValidationExpression Property

The `ValidationExpression` property gets or sets the regular expression that determines the pattern used to validate a field.

Let's see a few of the regular expression syntax rules.

Symbol	Description
*	Wildcard character representing zero or more unspecified characters. For example, `1*` would match love, lilo, la, l, and so on.
+	Must contain one or more occurrences of the preceding item. For example, `ha+` matches ha and haaaa, but not just h.
.	Matches any character except `\n`.
^	NOT operator. For example, `^a` means that a is not allowed.
?	Zero or one occurrences of the preceding item must be present. For example, `(good)?bye` matches bye or goodbye.
[abdj]	Allowed characters can be given inside square brackets. For example, `[abdj]` means only a, b, d, and j are allowed.
[^abj]	Only a, b, and j are not allowed.
x|y	x or y are allowed.
\w	Matches any word character. Same as `[a-zA-Z_0-9]`.
\s	Matches any whitespace character. Same as `[\f\n\r\t\v]`.
\S	Matches any non-whitespace character. Same as `[^\f\n\r\t\v]`.
\d	Any decimal digit. Same as `[0-9]`.
\D	Any non-digit. Same as `[^0-9]`.

The `RegularExpressionValidator` control has no methods or events.

Example: The RegularExpressionValidator Control

The following example shows how this control can be used to validate an e-mail address.

```
<html>
<head>
<script language="VB" runat="server">
Public Sub Button_Click(s As Object, e As EventArgs)
    If (Page.IsValid) Then
        lbl1.Text = "Email format is right"
    Else
        lbl1.Text = "Email format is wrong"
    End If
End Sub
</script>
</head>
<body>
<h3>RegularExpressionValidator Example</h3>
<p>
<form runat="server">

<asp:TextBox id="textbox1" runat="server" />For example, someone@microsoft.com
<br>
```

```
<asp:Button text="••" OnClick="Button_Click" runat=server />
<hr>
<asp:Label ID="lbl1" runat="server"/>
<asp:RegularExpressionValidator id="RegularExpressionValidator1" runat="server"
        ControlToValidate="textbox1"
        ValidationExpression = " .*@.*\..*"
        ErrorMessage="This is not an email address">

</asp:RegularExpressionValidator>

<asp:RequiredFieldValidator id="Valid1" runat="server"
    ControlToValidate="textbox1"
    ErrorMessage="You must input an email address"
    Display="static"/>
</form>
</body>
</html>
```

The resulting output is:

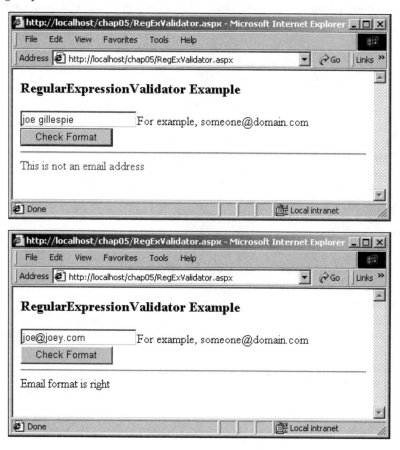

The RequiredFieldValidator Control

You can use the `RequiredFieldValidator` control to check whether the user has provided a value for a particular item.

Syntax:

```
<asp:RequiredFieldValidator id="id_name"
    ControlToValidate = "id of control"
    InitialValue = "Initial value"
    ErrorMessage = "Error message"
    Runat = "server" />
```

Properties of the RequiredFieldValidator Control

The InitialValue Property

The `InitialValue` property gets or sets the initial value of the associated input control. See the e-mail example discussed in the `RegularExpressionValidator` control for an illustration of how this control is used.

The `RequiredFieldValidator` control has no methods or events.

The ValidationSummary Control

The `ValidationSummary` control displays a summary of all validation errors.

Syntax:

```
<asp:ValidationSummary id = "id_name"
    DisplayMode = "BulletList | List | SingleParagraph"
    EnableClientScript = "true | false"
    ShowSummary = "true | false"
    ShowMessageBox = "true | false"
    HeaderText = "TextToDisplayAsSummaryTitle"
    Runat = "server" />
```

Properties of the ValidationSummary Control

The DisplayMode Property

The `DisplayMode` property gets or sets the display mode of the validation summary. The valid values are `BulletList`, `List`, and `SingleParagraph` and the default value is `BulletList`.

The EnableClientScript Property

The `EnableClientScript` property gets or sets a value indicating whether client-side validation is attempted on the browser. The valid values are `True` and `False` and the default value is `True`.

The ForeColor Property

The `ForeColor` property gets or sets the foreground color of the control. The default value is `Red`.

The HeaderText Property

The `HeaderText` property gets or sets the header text that will display at the top of the summary.

The ShowMessageBox Property

The `ShowMessageBox` property gets or sets a Boolean value indicating whether the validation summary should be displayed in a message box. The default is `False`.

The ShowSummary Property

The `ShowSummary` property gets or sets a Boolean value indicating whether the validation summary is displayed inline. The default is `True`.

The `ValidationSummary` control is useful for web pages where many items are input at once.

Example: The ValidationSummary Control

Let's see a small example that validates login textboxes.

```
<html>
<body>

<h3>ValidationSummary Example</h3>
<form runat="server">

Username:
<asp:TextBox id="TextBox1" runat="server" />

<asp:RequiredFieldValidator
     id="RequiredFieldValidator1"
     ControlToValidate="TextBox1"
     ErrorMessage="Username."
     Display="Static"
     runat="server">*
</asp:RequiredFieldValidator>
<br>
password:
<asp:TextBox id="TextBox2" textmode="password" runat="server" />

<asp:RequiredFieldValidator
     id="RequiredFieldValidator2"
     ControlToValidate="TextBox2"
     ErrorMessage="Password."
     Display="Static"
     runat="server">*
</asp:RequiredFieldValidator>

<hr>
<asp:Button id="Button1" text="Validate" runat="server" />

<asp:ValidationSummary
     id="valSum"
     DisplayMode="BulletList"
     runat="server"
     HeaderText="You must enter a value in the following fields:" />
```

```
    </form>
    </body>
    </html>
```

This is the result produced when the button is clicked immediately, without any username or password entered:

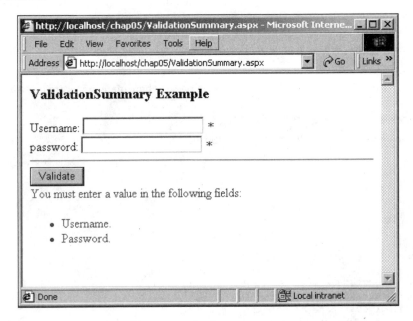

The ValidationSummary control has no methods or events.

The CustomValidator Control

The CustomValidator control allows you to build a validation control with your own specification.

Syntax:

```
<asp:CustomValidator id="id_name"
    ControlToValidate = "id of control"
    ClientValidationFunction = "function for validation"
    OnServerValidate = "ServerValidateID"
    ErrorMessage = "Error message"
    runat="server" />
```

Properties of the CustomValidator Control

The ClientValidationFunction Property

The ClientValidationFunction property gets or sets the name of the custom client script function used for validation. The default is an empty string.

Methods of the CustomValidator Control

The OnServerValidate Method

The OnServerValidate method represents the method that handles the ServerValidate events of a CustomValidator control.

Events of CustomValidator Control

The ServerValidate Event

The ServerValidate event is raised when validation is to be performed by the server.

Example: The CustomValidator Control

Let's see a quick example of the CustomValidator control in action. It is a relatively straightforward task to configure your own validator using this control.

```
<html>
<head>
<script lagnuage=VB runat=server>
sub bt1_ck(s as object, e as eventargs)
  if (page.isvalid) then
    label1.text = "It is an odd number"
  else
    label1.text = "It is not an odd number"
  end if
end sub
sub Runcheck(source As object, e As ServerValidateEventArgs)

  Dim num As Integer = Integer.Parse(e.Value)
  e.IsValid = ((num mod 2) = 1)
 end sub
</script>
</head>
<body>
<h3>CustomValidator Example</h3>
Input an odd number:<Br>
<form runat=server>
Number : <asp:textbox id="number1" runat=server />
<br>
<br>
<asp:button text=Validate id=button1 onclick="bt1_ck" runat=server />
<asp:customvalidator id=cv1
    controltovalidate = "number1"
    onservervalidate ="Runcheck"
    runat=server>
</asp:customvalidator>
</form>
<hr>
<asp:label id=label1 runat=server />
</body>
</html>
```

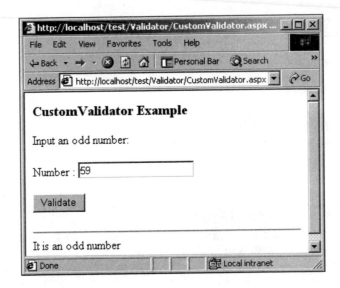

Summary

The `System.Web.UI.WebControls` namespace covered in this chapter provides a selection of flexible and sophisticated tools that the developer can use to rapidly implement powerful, dynamic user interfaces for their applications. The HTML Intrinsic Controls, or Web Form Controls, offer parallel features to the HTML Controls described in the preceding chapter, except that the Web Form Controls execute server-side, allowing the developer to cater for a wider range of browser types consistently.

The List Controls that this namespace contains are a highly customizable set of user interface elements that not only allow the dynamic display of data in tabular form, but also allow that data to be edited by the user through their browser. Used in conjunction with the Validation Controls of this namespace, the List Controls are a potentially essential tool for the development of a range of applications, from e-commerce to online surveys. The Validation Controls are not restricted to List Controls though, and they can be used to automatically check information input in any Web Control against specified criteria.

The inclusion of the Rich Controls, and the possibilities for rapidly developing interactive sites that they offer, makes the `System.Web.UI.WebControls` namespace essential knowledge for any aspiring ASP.NET professional.

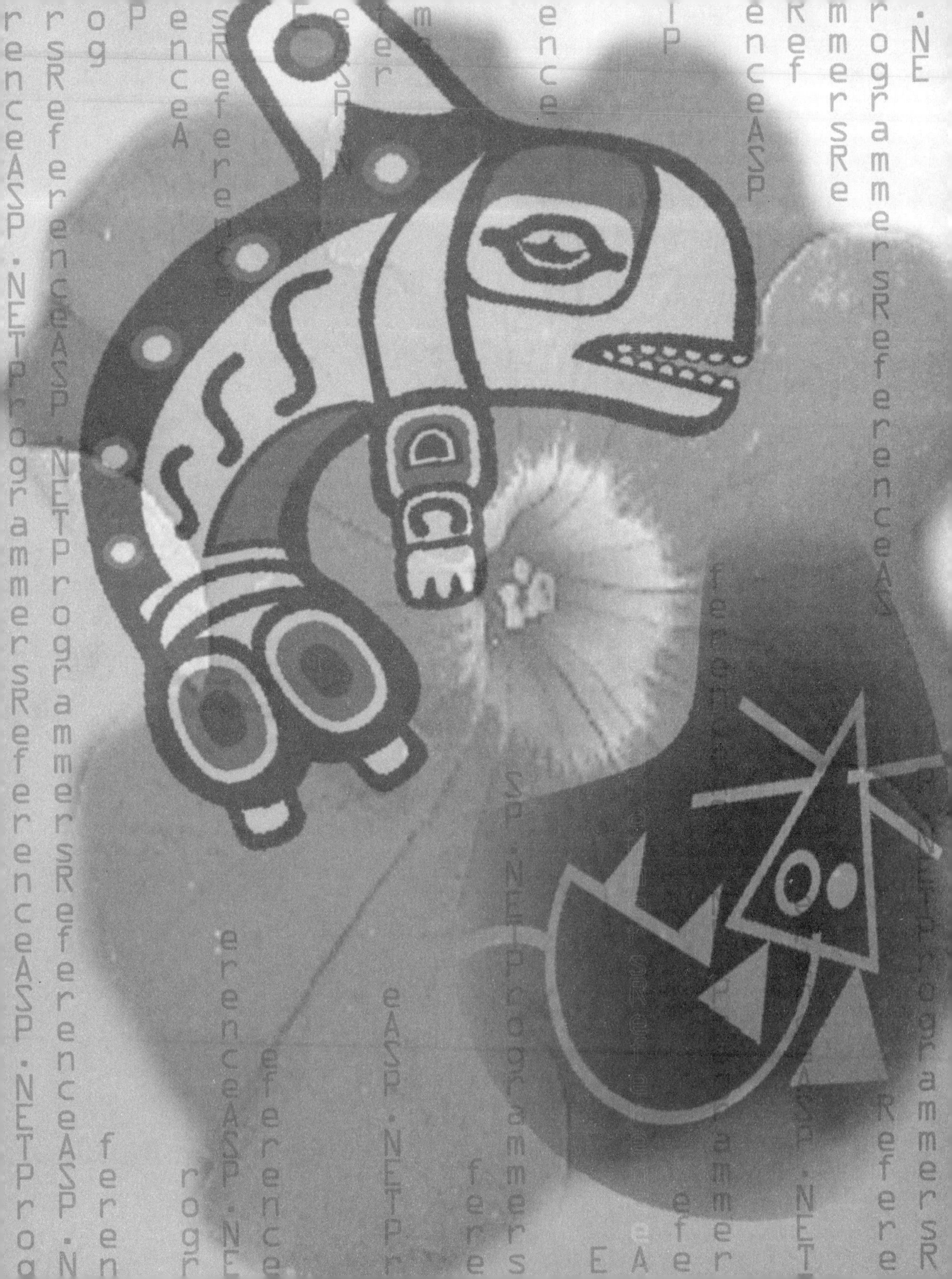

Mobile Internet Toolkit

The Microsoft Mobile Internet Toolkit is an extension to ASP.NET. The mobile controls runtime automatically adapts the content of the mobile controls for various web-enabled cell phones, pagers, and PDAs. The next generation of PDAs and cell phones utilizes several different markup languages. Some devices support the Wireless Markup Language (WML), while others only work with Compact HTML (cHTML). Some only support the Wireless Bitmap Image Format (WBMP), others support JPEG, while others still do not support images at all.

The Mobile Internet Toolkit gives developers the ability to write web applications where output dynamically adapts to the requirements of the requesting device. An ASP.NET page using these mobile controls will automatically tailor its output for a wide variety of mobile browsers, each potentially supporting different markup languages. The controls will render for desktop browsers, as well as the browsers found in mobile devices, although they don't take advantage of all the features found in a desktop client.

The mobile controls, elements, and other sections that make up the Mobile Internet Toolkit together form an extensible framework by extending ASP.NET. You can write a composite control comprising multiple mobile controls, or inherit from a mobile control to specialize it for some specific task. Of course, you can also write your own Mobile control from scratch making use of the base classes of the toolkit. When installed, the toolkit integrates with and expands on the familiar authoring environment of Visual Studio.NET to provide a browser's very rich development environment for Web Services and applications. The developer can select the Mobile Web Application icon when creating a new project. The toolkit can also be used outside of Visual Studio.NET to write Mobile Web Forms pages by hand.

Each Mobile control has a set of device adapters that produce the output appropriate for a specific markup language or device. Microsoft has announced its intention to ship sample source code for a number of device adapters. Developers and independent software vendors will be able to draw on this source code within the extensible framework of the toolkit to support new devices and customize output for particular devices.

In this chapter, we shall discuss the principal features offered by the Microsoft Mobile Internet Toolkit, and provide a reference for the principal controls and elements. Detailed information about the classes available is included with the toolkit download, which can be found under the Software Development Kits heading at http://msdn.microsoft.com/downloads.

To get started, let's establish the minimal mobile page in order to illuminate the use of the mobile controls. A mobile page must contain the following at the beginning of the page with any other directives that may be used:

```
<%@ Register TagPrefix="Mobile" Namespace="System.Web.UI.MobileControls"
                                  Assembly="System.Web.Mobile" %>
<%@Page Inherits="System.Web.UI.MobileControls.MobilePage" Language="C#" %>
```

The first line sets up a relationship between the Mobile Internet Toolkit namespace and page elements prefixed with `Mobile:`. For example, `<Mobile:Label runat="server">` in a mobile page is mapped to the `System.Web.Mobile.dll` assembly. The second line is a page directive, which establishes that the page extends `MobileControls.MobilePage` rather than the default ASP.NET `Page`.

Of course, the language declared can be any language supported by the Common Language Runtime of the .NET platform.

Additionally, every Mobile Page must contain at least one `<Mobile:Form>` element, such as `<Mobile:Form runat="server"/>`. The `runat` attribute is required for the mobile `Form` control and must have the value `server`. So, the canonical "Hello World" application looks like this:

Example: HelloWorld.aspx

```
<%@Register TagPrefix="Mobile" Namespace="System.Web.UI.MobileControls"
Assembly="System.Web.Mobile" %>
<%@Page Inherits="System.Web.UI.MobileControls.MobilePage" Language="C#"%>
<Mobile:Form runat="server">
  Hello World
</Mobile:Form>
```

When this is viewed in the Nokia 7110 Emulator the output looks like this:

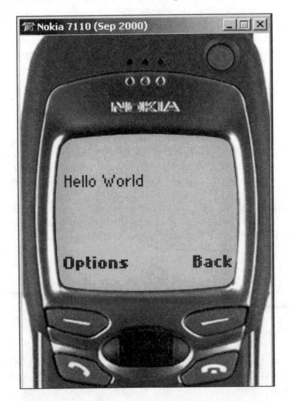

The lifecycle of a mobile page differs slightly from that of the Web Forms page that it extends. When the request is first received, the headers of the device are examined to determine the capabilities of the requesting device, as defined in the `machine.config` file, so that the appropriate set of device adapters for the page output is used. The `machine.config` file is found, as of this writing, in `\WINNT\Microsoft.Net\Framework\version\CONFIG`. For example, the output produced for a `Form` element is very different using WML from in HTML, but the page developer need not be concerned about which device adapter is selected by the server. After the page has been parsed and compiled by ASP.NET when it is requested, it is then executed. By this point, every control on the page has been matched to a corresponding device adapter to tailor the control to output as required. For instance, to render a `Form` control for an HTML-capable device, the `HtmlFormAdapter` class will be used. If the device utilizes WML, `WmlFormAdapter` will be invoked instead.

The run-time pairing of each control to the appropriate adapter means that the toolkit can be readily extended to accommodate new devices with varying capabilities and evolving markup languages. If a new device comes to market, the `machine.config` file can be updated to reflect the capabilities of the device and map the device adapters it requires. When updates to existing devices are made that alter their capabilities, the `machine.config` file can be updated, and the output will straightaway reflect these changes. If a new markup language emerges, or an existing markup language changes significantly, new device adapters can be added. The pages of your applications will not need any modification to keep up with the evolving wireless world.

The MobileControl Base Class

All mobile controls inherit from the base `MobileControl` class, either directly, or indirectly, by extending a class that itself inherits from this base class. In turn, the base class extends the `System.Web.UI.Control` class. Therefore, all controls described here share the properties and methods that are defined by the base class. Rather than list these repeatedly for each control, we'll discuss them first of all, and only indicate where a particular control overrides them. The class is abstract, so it cannot be instantiated directly, but every control that is based on it will share common methods, properties, and events. Controls that inherit directly from the `MobileControl` class are:

- ❏ AdRotator
- ❏ Calendar
- ❏ Image
- ❏ Panel
- ❏ SelectionList
- ❏ StyleSheet
- ❏ TextView
- ❏ ValidationSummary

Public Properties of MobileControl

Adapter Property (read-only)

This property references an object that implements the `IControlAdapter` interface. The methods of that interface are used to render the output for the control for the current request. When a Mobile Web Forms page is requested, the capabilities of the device are matched against the adapters configured on the machine and a set of adapters is chosen. For example, if a device that accepts only WML requests a page, the WML adapters are chosen. Then, when it is time for a control to emit its output, the adapter that will render WML is used, rather than one that produces cHTML. The `Adapter` property gives the developer access to the selected adapter at run-time. This property is not usually used outside of efforts to extend and specialize the toolkit.

```
System.Web.UI.IControlAdapter = Adapter
```

Alignment Property (read/write)

This property specifies the alignment layout desired for the output. It is of type `System.Web.UI.MobileControls.Alignment` and can take any of the following values:

❑   Left

❑   Center

❑   Right

❑   NotSet

If the requesting device does not support alignment, the default adapter may not render markup for this property. The control itself still renders, but without the alignment information that the device would not display properly.

```
System.Web.UI.MobileControls.Alignment = Alignment
Alignment = System.Web.UI.MobileControls.Alignment
```

BackColor Property (read/write)

This property specifies the desired rendering background color. It is of type `System.Drawing.Color`.

```
System.Drawing.Color = BackColor
BackColor = System.Drawing.Color
```

BreakAfter Property (read/write)

This is a Boolean value indicating whether a logical break should appear after the control rendering. Depending on the markup language, a break may correspond to the end of a table, a paragraph, a div, or an explicit break tag. The default value is `true`.

```
Boolean = BreakAfter
BreakAfter = Boolean
```

CustomAttributes Property (read-only)

This property retrieves the `System.Web.UI.StateBag` object that details any custom attributes that have been defined for the control.

```
System.Web.UI.StateBag = CustomAttributes
```

DeviceSpecific Property (read/write)

If the control is not part of a device-specific construct, the property will be null. Otherwise, it will be the `System.Web.UI.MobileControls.DeviceSpecific` that is associated with the control.

```
System.Web.UI.MobileControls.DeviceSpecific = DeviceSpecific
DeviceSpecific = System.Web.UI.MobileControls.DeviceSpecific
```

FirstPage Property (read/write)

This property indicates the first rendered page of the form on which output of this control appears. When a form paginates, it splits up the children across multiple pages to better fit the capabilities of the requesting device. The `FirstPage` property tells us which is the first page, of those that will be rendered, upon which output from this control or its children will appear.

```
Integer = FirstPage
FirstPage = Integer
```

Font Property (read-only)

This property retrieves a `System.Web.UI.MobileControls.FontInfo` object. This object gives more detailed information about the font settings for the control. If the requesting device does not support certain font elements, they will not be rendered for the device. For example, a grayscale display will not be able to take advantage of the `ForeColor` property of the `FontInfo` class, so that particular attribute will not be rendered for that device.

```
System.Web.UI.MobileControls.FontInfo = Font
```

FontFace Property (read/write)

This property specifies the string name of the font to be used in formatting the output for the control. It can be set declaratively, or programmatically, as the `FontFace` property of the `FontInfo` object. It is an empty string by default, which results in the client using its default font or inheriting the `Style` of a parent control if set. The string specified is rendered for devices that support setting the font, but no server checks are made to validate that the font is available on the device.

```
String = Font.FontFace
Font.FontFace = String
```

FontSize Property (read/write)

The `FontSize` property specifies the size of the text rendered by the control. This property can be set declaratively, or programmatically as the `FontSize` property of the `FontInfo` object.

It is of type `System.Web.UI.MobileControls.FontSize`, and its possible values are:

❑ `NotSet`

❑ `Small`

❑ `Normal`

❑ `Large`

```
System.Web.UI.MobileControls.FontSize = Font.FontSize
Font.FontSize = System.Web.UI.MobileControls.FontSize
```

Example: Setting FontSize Declaratively – HelloSmallWorld1.aspx

```
<Mobile:Label runat="server" Font-Size="Small">
  Hello Small World
</Mobile:Label>
```

Example: Setting FontSize Programmatically – HelloSmallWorld2.aspx

```
<script runat="server" language="C#">
public void Page_Load(object sender, EventArgs e)
{
  label1.Font.Size = System.Web.UI.MobileControls.FontSize.Small;
}
</script>
<Mobile:Form runat="server">
<Mobile:Label runat="server" id="label1">
  Hello Small World
</Mobile:Label>
</Mobile:Form>
```

ForeColor Property (read/write)

This property specifies the color used for the foreground where appropriate, typically corresponding to the text color for rendering a control. It is of type `System.Drawing.Color`.

```
System.Drawing.Color = ForeColor
ForeColor = System.Drawing.Color
```

Form Property (read-only)

This property retrieves the `System.Web.UI.MobileControls.Form` object containing the control.

```
System.Web.UI.MobileControls.Form = Form
```

InnerText Property (read/write)

This property specifies the text contained by the control. It may return text coalesced from contained child controls, for example, if the control contains children that are `DataBound` or contain `LiteralText` controls.

```
String = InnerText
InnerText = String
```

IsTemplated Property (read-only)

This property retrieves a Boolean indicating whether the control is part of a template construct where there is a `<DeviceSpecific>` element containing a `<Choice>` filter that is satisfied by the request. Refer to the section later in the chapter on *Device-Specific Rendering* for an explanation of templating.

```
Boolean = IsTemplated
```

LastPage Property (read/write)

This property indicates the last rendered page of the form on which output of this control appears.

```
Integer = LastPage
LastPage = Integer
```

MobilePage Property (read-only)

This property retrieves the `MobilePage` object containing the control. It is of type `System.Web.UI.MobileControls.MobilePage`.

```
System.Web.UI.MobileControls.MobilePage = MobilePage
```

PaginateChildren Property (read-only)

This property retrieves a Boolean indicating whether contained controls can be paginated. Pagination is the separation of controls onto multiple pages. This is done in order to make better use of the limited screen size of devices and transmit smaller amounts of data where the download size of the device is limited.

```
Boolean = PaginateChildren
```

StyleReference Property (read/write)

This string property specifies the ID of the `Style` object associated with this control. This typically serves in the reuse of a set of style settings grouped together in an external stylesheet.

```
String = StyleReference
StyleReference = String
```

VisibleWeight Property (read-only)

This property corresponds to an integer value associated with the control used for calculating pagination. If the return value is -1, it indicates that the default weighting should be used. Refer to the `machine.config` file at `\WINNT\Microsoft.NET\Framework\version\CONFIG` for a listing of the default weights. When a control is undergoing pagination, the `VisibleWeight` of the children is totaled and compared to the `optimumPageWeight` established for the device in the configuration. This determines how many pages the children should be rendered on and where the page breaks should occur.

```
Integer = VisibleWeight
```

Wrapping Property (read/write)

This property specifies the wrapping format for the output. As with the `Alignment` property, there may be no corresponding rendering if a device does not allow control over wrapping functionality.

```
System.Web.UI.MobileControls.Wrapping = Wrapping
Wrapping = System.Web.UI.MobileControls.Wrapping
```

Public Methods of MobileControl

AddLinkedForms Method

This method adds a set of forms that the control should consider itself linked to. There is no return value. It is used internally and by developers extending the toolkit.

Parameter	Type	Description
linkedForms	System.Collections.IList	The set of forms that are linked to the control

```
void AddLinkedForms(linkedForms)
```

CreateDefaultTemplatedUI Method

This method is called to instantiate child templates. There is no return value.

```
void CreateDefaultTemplatedUI(doDataBind)
```

Parameter	Type	Description
doDataBind	Boolean	Indicates whether the templates should perform data binding operations

If the doDataBind parameter is false, it indicates that the template data should use the default values, or data extracted from viewstate. The device adapter will use this method and will typically databind on the first request, while restoring data from viewstate on postbacks.

EnsureTemplatedUI Method

This method can force the template elements of the control to be created, so that they can be accessed programmatically. It is not necessary to call this method during default page processing unless access to the template elements is required. It has a void return value. EnsureTemplatedUI takes no parameters.

```
void EnsureTemplatedUI()
```

GetTemplate Method

This method returns an instance of the object contained by the control with a name matching the parameter. If the control is not templated or no match is found, null is returned.

```
System.Web.UI.ITemplate GetTemplate(templateName)
```

Parameter	Type	Description
templateName	String	The name of the template to retrieve

IsVisibleOnPage Method

This method returns a Boolean indicating whether or not this control produces any output on the specified output page.

```
Boolean IsVisibleOnPage(pageNumber)
```

Parameter	Type	Description
pageNumber	Int32	The page to check for visible output

PaginateRecursive Method

Mobile controls can be split across multiple pages of output, and this method paginates the control and all of its children. No return value.

```
void PaginateRecursive(pager)
```

Parameter	Type	Description
pager	ControlPager	The ControlPager tracks state information about the current pagination

RenderChildren Method

This method is called to cause the rendering of all contained controls to be performed. No return value.

```
void RenderChildren(writer)
```

Parameter	Type	Description
writer	HtmlTextWriter	The TextWriter used to receive output for the rendering

ResolveFormReference

Given a string, this method walks up the control tree to find the Form control with the corresponding name. Used with links of the type #formName. Returns the Form object if found, otherwise returns null.

```
System.Web.UI.MobileControls.Form ResolveFormReference(formID)
```

Parameter	Type	Description
formID	String	The name of the form to resolve

ResolveUrl Method

Takes a relative URL and resolves it to an absolute URL associated with the control.

```
String ResolveUrl(relativeUrl)
```

Parameter	Type	Description
relativeUrl	String	The URL to be resolved into an absolute URL

The TextControl Class

Some of the Mobile Controls inherit directly from the MobileControl base class. Others inherit from the TextControl class, which extends MobileControl by adding a Text property. The class is abstract. The properties, methods, and events common to all mobile controls are explained in the previous section. The text of the control can be set declaratively:

Example: Setting the Text of a Control Declaratively – HelloWorldText1.aspx

```
<Mobile:Label runat=server Text="Hello Text-based World" />
```

The Text property can be used programmatically to achieve the same effect:

Example: Setting the Text of a Control Programmatically – HelloWorldText2.aspx

```
<script runat=server>
public void Page_Load(Object o, EventArgs e)
{
  label1.Text = "Hello Textbased World";
}
</script>
<Mobile:Form runat=server>
  <Mobile:Label runat=server id="label1"/>
</Mobile:Form>
```

These two examples both have the following output:

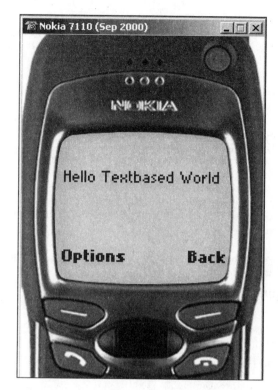

Controls that inherit directly from the TextControl class are:

- PhoneCall
- Command
- Label
- Link
- TextBox
- TextView

Paginated Content

The Mobile Internet Toolkit is able to break up content for display across multiple pages. Since different devices have varying display sizes, this is ideal for adapting the page output to the requesting device. If the Paginate property is set to true for a Panel, it can have its contents split across multiple pages if needed. Since the Form class extends the Panel class, Form contents can also be paginated. By default, the Paginate property is false. When set to true for the form, any Panels contained within the form will still be rendered together on a single page where possible, unless their Paginate property is also set to true.

If the requirement is to mark a group of controls on the page for pagination, set the ControlToPaginate property of the form to the ID of the pagination target. Any children of that control are then able to be broken across multiple pages. This is often used to split the contents of a single panel on a form.

Some controls can render parts of their output across multiple pages. For example, `LiteralText` can be broken up according to the capabilities of the device. Controls that support this internal pagination are:

- ❏ `LiteralText`
- ❏ `List`
- ❏ `ObjectList`

Custom Pagination

These controls also support more fine-grained control over how pagination is to be handled; particularly useful when retrieving individual items of a control incurs an expensive overhead. To utilize custom pagination, set the `ItemCount` property to the total number of items to be displayed. The `LoadItems` event handler must have a delegate registered that the Mobile Internet Toolkit can raise to handle the event, passing the items needed so that the handler can then carry out the work necessary to retrieve the data and populate the items.

In the next code sample, we set the number of items in the list to 100, and show how the event is called to retrieve a subset of the total set of items.

Example: Custom Paging – PagedList.aspx

```csharp
<script runat="server" language="C#">
protected void MyList_OnLoadItems(object sender, LoadItemsEventArgs args)
{
  //clear the current contents of the list
  MyList.Items.Clear();
  //populate the list with the items requested
  for(int i = 0; i < args.ItemCount; i++)
  {
    MyList.Items.Add(new MobileListItem("item # " + i.ToString()));
  }
}
</script>
<mobile:Form runat="server" Paginate="true">
  <mobile:List runat="server"
              id="MyList"
              ItemCount="100"
              OnLoadItems="MyList_OnLoadItems" />
</mobile:Form>
```

The output from the above code can be seen in the following screenshot:

The BaseValidator Class

The TextControl class is further specialized by implementing the IValidator interface in the BaseValidator class. BaseValidator is another abstract class, and so cannot be instantiated directly. It simply defines the validation behavior of controls that inherit from it. The properties, methods and events common to all mobile controls are explained earlier in the chapter.

Controls that extend the BaseValidator class are:

- ❏ CompareValidator
- ❏ CustomValidator
- ❏ RangeValidator
- ❏ RegularExpressionValidator
- ❏ RequiredFieldValidator

Public BaseValidator Properties

The Validation controls extend the BaseValidator class. The validators are used to perform checks on user input. The validators all share some common properties. Validators that inherit from BaseValidator are:

- ❑ CompareValidator
- ❑ CustomValidator
- ❑ RangeValidator
- ❑ RegularExpressionValidator
- ❑ RequiredFieldValidator

ControlToValidate Property (read/write)

This property corresponds to the control whose values will be checked. It is a string type that matches the ID of the target control.

```
String = ControlToValidate
ControlToValidate = String
```

Display Property (read/write)

This property corresponds to the ValidatorDisplay property of the validator.

```
System.Web.UI.WebControls.ValidatorDisplay = Display
Display = System.Web.UI.WebControls.ValidatorDisplay
```

ErrorMessage Property (read/write)

The ErrorMessage property is a string that is displayed when the validation criteria are not met.

```
String = ErrorMessage
ErrorMessage = String
```

IsValid Property (read/write)

A Boolean indicating whether or not the last validation check performed was successful.

```
Boolean = IsValid
IsValid = Boolean
```

Public BaseValidator Methods

Validate Method

This method performs the validation check. This method has no return value, as it sets the IsValid property to indicate the result of the validation.

```
void Validate()
```

The AdRotator Control

The AdRotator control extends the abstract MobileControl class to control the display of a collection of advertisements. An XML file controls the relative frequency each ad is displayed as well as the other pertinent information concerning the advert. The AdRotator of the mobile toolkit extends the functionality of the System.Web.UI.WebControl.AdRotator class by allowing device-specific templates to set properties appropriate for the capabilities of the requesting device.

Public Properties of the AdRotator Control

AdvertisementFile Property (read/write)

This property gets and set the path to the XML advertisement file. Each <Ad> element allows several URLs and image types to be specified to support a range of requesting devices. The `AdvertisementFile` property is used to rotate through a set of ads to display them, in turn, to visitors to the site. Here is a pair of typical <Ad> elements from the XML file:

```
<Ad>
    <ImageUrl>Wrox.gif</ImageUrl>
    <NavigateUrl>http://www.wrox.com</NavigateUrl>
    <AlternateText>Wrox: Programmer to Programmer</AlternateText>
    <Keyword>publisher</Keyword>
    <Impressions>80</Impressions>
    <BmpImageUrl>AspToday.bmp</BmpImageUrl>
    <WbmpImageUrl>AspTopday.wbmp</WbmpImageUrl>
    <WmlUrl>../mobile.aspx</WmlUrl>
</Ad>
<Ad>
    <ImageUrl>AspToday.gif</ImageUrl>
    <NavigateUrl>http://www.asptoday.com</NavigateUrl>
    <AlternateText>ASP Today</AlternateText>
    <Keyword>online</Keyword>
    <Impressions>40</Impressions>
    <BmpImageUrl>.bmp</BmpImageUrl>
    <WbmpImageUrl>AspToday.wbmp</WbmpImageUrl>
    <WmlUrl>../device.aspx</WmlUrl>
</Ad>
```

```
String = AdvertisementFile
AdvertisementFile = String
```

ImageKey Property (read/write)

This property corresponds to the `image` element from the advertisement file that will be rendered. The default behavior is given by the <ImageUrl> element, and this property takes this value by default. It can be altered programmatically, or declaratively by a <choice> element within the <deviceSpecific> section:

```
<deviceSpecific>
  <choice filter="isWml">
    <mobile:adRotator runat=server imageKey="WbmpImageUrl"/>
  </choice>
  <choice>
    <mobile:adRotator runat=server/>
  </choice>
</deviceSpecific>
```

```
String = ImageKey
ImageKey = String
```

KeywordFilter Property (read/write)

A string used to narrow the set of choices. It checks the `Keyword` element of the `Ad` entries in the `AdvertisementFile` to find possible matches. By default, no filter is used, so the choice of which image advertisement to display remains a function of its relative frequency. For example, in the previous sample file, the `impressions` element has a value of `80` for `Wrox` and `40` for `AspToday`. With no `KeywordFilter` specified, the `Wrox` ad will be selected twice as often as the `AspToday` one. If the `KeywordFilter` is set to `"online"`, which is the keyword for the `AspToday` entry, then the `Wrox` entry will be filtered out since it's keyword is `"publisher"`, and is not a match.

```
String = KeywordFilter
KeywordFilter = String
```

NavigateUrlKey Property (read/write)

This property represents the hyperlink for the rendered image. The default string is `NavigateUrl`, indicating the URL given inside the element of the same name in the advertisement file. Change it if you wish an alternative element's URL to be used instead.

```
String = NavigateUrl
NavigateUrl = String
```

Public Events of the AdRotator Control

AdCreatedEventHandler Event

The `OnAdCreated` method is called by this event handler once an advertisement has been selected from the XML file. The developer can react to this event to track information about the ads being displayed. For example, the event could be used to log the frequency with which the various ads are being displayed. It is not necessary for the developer to react to this event in order to have the ad displayed.

The Calendar Control

The `Calendar` control for selecting dates extends the abstract `MobileControl` class, and effectively ports the `System.Web.UI.Calendar` control onto mobile devices. The `Calendar` contains a `WebControls` calendar that can access information not exposed directly as properties of the Mobile Calendar, such as more complex style information that may be rendered only for more capable PC browsers.

Public Properties of the Calendar Control

CalendarEntryText Property (read/write)

This read/write string property can be set and retrieved and is preserved through server roundtrips. On a device where a complete calendar cannot be displayed, the user may be taken through a series of steps to select a date. This text is used for the link to begin the steps for date selection.

```
String = CalendarEntryText
CalendarEntryText = String
```

FirstDayOfWeek Property (read/write)

This property corresponds to the day of the week to display in the first column. The default is derived from the server's locale setting. So, a server with a locale where Saturday is the first day of the week will choose Saturday if the `FirstDayOfWeek` property is left as `Default`. Any of the following values may be used:

❑   Default

❑   Monday

❑   Tuesday

❑   Wednesday

❑   Thursday

❑   Friday

❑   Saturday

❑   Sunday

```
System.Web.UI.WebControls.FirstDayOfWeek = FirstDayOfWeek
FirstDayOfWeek = System.Web.UI.WebControls.FirstDayOfWeek
```

SelectedDate Property (read/write)

The `System.DateTime` property defaults to the current date on the server.

```
DateTime = SelectedDate
SelectedDate = DateTime
```

SelectedDates Property (read-only)

A collection of `System.DateTime` objects. By default, the collection contains just one item: the current server date.

```
System.Web.UI.WebControls.SelectedDatesCollection = SelectedDates
```

SelectionMode Property (read/write)

The calendar selection mode property indicates the way dates are selected, and is of type `System.Web.UI.WebControls.CalendarSelectionMode`. By default, selections are made by day, but can be set to one of:

❑   Day

❑   DayWeek

❑   DayWeekMonth

❑   None

Setting the property to `None` results in disabling selection for the `Calendar` control.

```
System.Web.UI.WebControls.SelectionMode = SelectionMode
SelectionMode = System.Web.UI.WebControls.SelectionMode
```

ShowDayHeader Property (read/write)

The default for this Boolean property is `true`, and means that the days of the week names are shown on the client-side calendar display.

```
Boolean = ShowDayHeader
ShowDayHeader = Boolean
```

VisibleDate Property (read/write)

This `DateTime` property controls the range of dates displayed by the calendar control.

```
DateTime = VisibleDate
VisibleDate = DateTime
```

WebCalendar Property (read-only)

This property retrieves the contained `System.Web.UI.WebControls.Calendar` control.

```
System.Web.UI.WebControls.Calendar = WebCalendar
```

Public Methods of the Calendar Control

RaiseSelectionChangedEvent Method

This method allows adapter authors to raise the `SelectionChanged` event once that condition has been detected. It can be caught by handling the `SelectionChanged` event.

```
void RaiseSelectionChangedEvent()
```

Public Events of the Calendar Control

SelectionChanged Event

The `SelectionChanged` event is raised whenever the choice of the calendar date is modified.

The Command Control

The `Command` control extends the abstract `MobileControl` class by extending the `TextControl` class to provide a UI (User Interface) element for invoking server-side event handlers. Values entered into form elements are posted and therefore available to the event handler. In HTML, the `Command` control is rendered as an input button by default.

Public Properties of the Command Control

CausesValidation Property (read/write)

By default, this property is `true`, and selection of the control causes the page to be validated. Set it to `false` if you wish to inhibit validation of the page for any reason.

```
Boolean = CausesValidation
CausesValidation = Boolean
```

CommandArgument Property (read/write)

This property is used to pass an argument string to the CommandEventHandler when the Command is selected.

```
String = CommandArgument
CommandArgument = String
```

CommandName Property (read/write)

The CommandEventHandler identifies the control that triggered the event to be invoked by the CommandName property. This string property has a default value of null. The CommandName is usually set when a single handler will be used for the same event and the developer wants to identify the control source.

```
String = CommandName
CommandName = String
```

Format Property (read/write)

The Format property is of type CommandFormat, and it defines how the Command control should be rendered. By default, it appears as a button. It has possible values of:

❑   CommandFormat.Button

❑   CommandFormat.Link

```
System.Web.UI.MobileControls.CommandFormat = Format
Format = System.Web.UI.MobileControls.CommandFormat
```

ImageUrl Property (read/write)

When this property is set with a valid URL for an image, and the requesting device supports it, the button uses that image for its face.

```
String = ImageUrl
ImageUrl = String
```

SoftkeyLabel Property (read/write)

Some devices have a key or button that can be associated with selecting elements on the page. By default, this string property is null and the word Go is used as the label for this button, which is referred to as the softkey.

```
String = SoftkeyLabel
SoftkeyLabel = String
```

Public Events of the Command Control

Click Event

The Click event is raised when the Command element is activated. The event is not bubbled up.

ItemCommand Event

The ItemCommand event is raised when the Command element is activated. The event is then cascaded to its parent, unlike the Click event.

The CompareValidator Control

The CompareValidator control extends the abstract BaseValidator class and shares the properties, methods and events of the MobileControl of the BaseValidator base class as detailed earlier in this chapter. This control compares the contents of one mobile control to another, verifying that the user-specified comparison operation is satisfied.

Public Properties of the CompareValidator Control

ControlToCompare Property (read/write)

This string identifies the control against which validation will be performed – ControlToValidate (see the BaseValidator class description) is verified against the control given by this ControlToCompare property. It defaults to null, indicating that the string value of the ValueToCompare property is to be used instead.

```
String = ControlToCompare
ControlToCompare = String
```

Operator Property (read/write)

This property defines how ControlToValidate and ControlToCompare are to be contrasted during the validation process. The Operator property is of type System.Web.UI.WebControls.Validation CompareOperator, and may take any of the following values:

- ❑ Equal – verifies if the controls are equal to each other
- ❑ NotEqual – verifies if the controls are not equal to each other
- ❑ GreaterThan – verifies if one control has a higher value than another
- ❑ GreaterThanEqual – verifies if one control has a higher or equal value to that of another
- ❑ LessThan – verifies if one control has a lesser value than another
- ❑ LessThanEqual – verifies if one control has a lesser or equal value to that of another
- ❑ DataTypeCheck – verifies that the two controls are of a legal data type

The default is Equal.

```
System.Web.UI.WebControls.ValidationCompareOperator = Operator
Operator = System.Web.UI.WebControls.ValidationCompareOperator
```

Type Property (read/write)

The Type is a System.Web.UI.WebControls.ValidationDataType, and it defines the type of the compared controls. It can be one of the following:

- ❑ String
- ❑ Integer

- ❑ Double
- ❑ Date
- ❑ Currency

If not specified, the property defaults to `String` type.

```
System.Web.UI.WebControls.ValidationDataType = Type
Type = System.Web.UI.WebControls.ValidationDataType
```

ValueToCompare Property (read/write)

If `ControlToCompare` is null, then the string value of `ValueToCompare` is used for the validation. It defaults to `null` which can be used for comparison. The string is coerced into the appropriate type for validation.

```
String = ValueToCompare
ValueToCompare = String
```

The CustomValidator Control

The `CustomValidator` class also extends `BaseValidator`, and provides a control for executing custom validation. The control raises an event for use in checking `ControlToValidate`.

Public Events of the CustomValidator Control

ServerValidate Event

When `ControlToValidate` is to be checked by the custom validator, the `ServerValidate` event is raised. By default, the `OnServerValidate` method is called. The event takes an argument of type `System.Web.UI.WebControls.ServerValidateEventArgs`. If the validation is deemed successful, the `IsValid` property of that argument is set to `true`.

The Form Control

The `Form` control extends `System.Web.UI.MobileControls.Panel`, and one must be present in every mobile page. All other controls are contained inside a `Form`. The types of controls that can be placed inside a form in a mobile ASP.NET application are limited to mobile controls and custom controls that inherit from the `MobileUserControl` class. A mobile page may contain multiple forms, but only one will be active during any given request.

Public Properties of the Form Control

Action Property (read/write)

The `Action` property is a string specifying the destination URL that the form should be submitted to. When not specified, the current form is assumed to be the postback destination.

```
String = Action
Action = String
```

ControlToPaginate Property (read/write)

Panels support the `Paginate` element attribute. In order for the contents of a panel contained in a form to be paginated, it is necessary for the form to be set to paginate. However, this property provides an alternative means to specify a target control that can be paginated. By programmatically specifying the ID of a control in the form, that control can be paginated while the form contents in general are not.

```
System.Web.UI.Control = ControlToPaginate
ControlToPaginate = System.Web.UI.Control
```

CurrentPage Property (read/write)

This integer property specifies the number of the page currently being displayed. The first page is given by the value 1, so this property should always be set within the range from 1 to `PageCount`.

```
Integer = CurrentPage
CurrentPage = Integer
```

Footer Property (read-only)

Like the `Header` property, the `Footer` property returns an object of type `System.Web.UI.MobileControls.Panel` when the form is templated. The contents of the panel, after filtering for the requesting device, are rendered at the bottom of each page. Templating is discussed in detail later on in this chapter.

```
System.Web.UI.MobileControls.Panel = Footer
```

Header Property (read-only)

When the contents of a form are templated for device-specific rendering based on filters, a header can be defined to appear at the top of each page. This property is of type `System.Web.UI.MobileControls.Panel` and will contain the controls that match the device-specific selection criteria. Templating is discussed in detail later on in this chapter.

```
System.Web.UI.MobileControls.Panel = Header
```

Method Property (read/write)

Forms are submitted using HTTP POST by default. Although the quantity of data that can be passed using HTTP GET is fairly limited, the form will do so when the `Method` property specifies it. The property can take the following `FormMethod` values:

❑ Post

❑ Get

```
System.Web.UI.MobileControls = Method
Method = System.Web.UI.MobileControls
```

PageCount Property (read-only)

This property returns an integer indicating the number of pages for the form. Without pagination, the form contents will be rendered on a single page.

```
Integer = PageCount
```

PagerStyle Property (read-only)

This property is of type `PagerStyle`, which derives from
`System.Web.UI.MobileControls.Style`. When the contents of a form are split across multiple pages, the pager is generated to allow navigation between the elements. The property can be accessed programmatically, or it can be specified by placing a `<PagerStyle>` element in the form.

```
System.Web.UI.MobileControls.PagerStyle = PagerStyle
```

Script Property (read-only)

The `Script` property is also of type `System.Web.UI.MobileControls.Panel`. It accesses an optional element of the device-specific template for sending content at a particular point of the rendering process. `ScriptTemplate` support was not included for WML in beta 2, but it will be included for RTM. For WML devices, the contents of the script panel are sent immediately after the `<card>` element (representing a single display page on such devices). For HTML, the script is sent as part of the HTML `<head>` element. Either way, the contents of the script template are naturally not formatted for rendering.

```
System.Web.UI.MobileControls.Panel = Script
```

Example: Script Template – clientscript.aspx

WML doesn't support client-side JavaScript, and WMLScript is handled via callbacks, so the `scriptTemplate` is more useful for adding something like a WML timer event. The example below demonstrates a client-side redirect when the timer event hits.

```
<%@Register TagPrefix="Mobile" Namespace="System.Web.UI.MobileControls"
Assembly="System.Web.Mobile" %>
<%@Page Inherits="System.Web.UI.MobileControls.MobilePage" Language="C#"%>
<Mobile:Form runat=server>
<deviceSpecific>
<Choice Filter="IsHtml">
  <ScriptTemplate>
    <script language='Javascript'>
    <!--
      function ShowGreeting()
      {
        sample.innerText = "client-side hello";
        Alert("client-side hello");
      }
    // -->
    </script>
  </ScriptTemplate>
  <HeaderTemplate>
    is html
    <h2 id="sample" onMouseOver="ShowGreeting();">mouse over me</h2>
  </HeaderTemplate>
  <ItemTemplate>
  </ItemTemplate>
  <FooterTemplate>
  </FooterTemplate>
</Choice>
<Choice Filter="IsWml" Argument="">
  <ScriptTemplate>
    <onevent type="ontimer">
      <go href="http://mobile.msn.com" />
    </onevent>
```

```
      <timer value="40" />
   </ScriptTemplate>
   <HeaderTemplate>
     <Mobile:Label runat=server>is wml</Mobile:Label>
     <Mobile:Label runat=server>timer event to client redirect </Mobile:Label>
   </HeaderTemplate>
 </Choice>
 </deviceSpecific>
 </Mobile:Form>
```

Title Property (read/write)

This property is empty by default. When set to a string value, it determines the title to use for the currently viewed page, when supported by the requesting device.

```
String = Title
Title = String
```

Public Methods of the Form Control

CreateDefaultTemplatedUI Method

When a control is templated, the adapter can invoke this method to cause the creation of the templated structure. This is primarily used when writing new controls or adapters.

```
void CreateDefaultTemplatedUI()
```

GetLinkedForms Method

This method returns an `IList` collection of the forms linked to by the current form. A form is considered to be linked if there is a direct route for the user to invoke that form. If the current form has a `Deactivate` handler or the target form has an `Activate` handler, it is not considered to be linked. The linked forms are those that can be accessed without requiring server-side code execution.

```
IList = GetLinkedForms()
```

HasActivateHandler Method

This method returns a Boolean value indicating whether a handler has been added for the `Activate` event.

```
Boolean HasActivateHandler()
```

HasDeactivateHandler Method

This method returns a Boolean value indicating whether a handler has been added for the `Deactivate` event.

```
Boolean HasDeactivateHandler()
```

Public Events of the Form Control

Activate Event

When a page is first requested, the default form is made current and its `Activate` event is called. When another form on the page is made active, the previous form is deactivated, and the `Activate` event of the new form is invoked. A form is made active by the first request for it, by a postback, or by setting the `ActiveForm` property.

Deactivate Event

The `Deactivate` event is called when a new form is made active. Because the deactivate event is only raised when a new form is activated, the deactivate event for a form may never be invoked. Even if the developer has not explicitly provided an `Activate` handler, the `Deactivate` event for the previous form is raised.

Paginated Event

When a form undergoes pagination, the `Paginated` event is raised. This will occur during the `PreRender` stage, but can also happen whenever the `ControlToPaginate` property is set, or the `PaginateRecursive` method is called.

The Image Control

The `Image` control extends the abstract `MobileControl` base class to display an image where the requesting device supports them. Such images can be used for user navigation. They can also be applied to Softkeys where this feature is provided by a device.

Public Properties of the Image Control

AlternateText Property (read /write)

The `AlternateText` is displayed when the image cannot be displayed or is not set. It is a `String` type.

```
String = AlternateText
AlternateText = String
```

ImageUrl Property (read/write)

The `ImageUrl` corresponds to the image to be displayed on the client device. The `<deviceSpecific>` element can be used to set this property to an image appropriate for the requesting device. See the section on *Templates* for more detailed information.

```
String = ImageUrl
ImageUrl = String
```

NavigateUrl Property (read/write)

If this property is set, the `NavigateUrl` represents a hyperlink associated with the image.

```
String = NavigateUrl
NavigateUrl = String
```

SoftkeyLabel Property (read/write)

Some devices provide keys, known as Softkeys, devoted to interacting with web pages. They can be bound to a certain action by your applications, often have a separate label associated with them, and this string property provides the means to set this label.

```
String = SoftkeyLabel
SoftkeyLabel = String
```

The Label Control

The Label control extends the abstract TextControl base class, so it also exposes the properties, methods, and events of the TextControl class and therefore the MobileControl base class as covered earlier in the chapter. The Label control is used for formatting and displaying text. The text can be supplied as inner child text of the element, or by using the Text attribute.

Example: Declaratively Setting Label Text – HelloLabeledWorld1.aspx

```
<%@Register TagPrefix="Mobile" Namespace="System.Web.UI.MobileControls"
Assembly="System.Web.Mobile" %>
<%@Page Inherits="System.Web.UI.MobileControls.MobilePage" Language="C#"%>
<Mobile:Form runat=server>
  <Mobile:Label runat=server>
    Hello World from some child text
  </Mobile:Label>
  <Mobile:Label runat=server Text="Hello World from a text attribute"/>
</Mobile:Form>
```

Label text can be set programmatically as well, as in this next example.

Example: Programmatically Setting Label Text – HelloLabeledWorld2.aspx

```
<%@Register TagPrefix="Mobile" Namespace="System.Web.UI.MobileControls"
Assembly="System.Web.Mobile" %>
<%@Page Inherits="System.Web.UI.MobileControls.MobilePage" Language="C#"%>
<script runat=server>
protected void Page_Load(object o, EventArgs e)
{
  MyLabel.Text = "Hello Programmatically Labeled World";
}
</script>
<Mobile:Form runat=server>
  <Mobile:Label runat=server id="MyLabel"/>
</Mobile:Form>
```

The Link Control

The Link control extends the abstract TextControl base class, so it also exposes the properties, methods, and events of the TextControl class and therefore the MobileControl base class as covered earlier in the chapter. The Link control is used to present a navigation option to the user. If the Text property is null, the NavigateUrl property of the Link is used as the label for the hyperlink.

Public Properties of the Link Control

NavigateUrl Property (read/write)

This string property can be set to either a relative or fully-qualified file path, and is `null` by default. A form of the indicated page can be specified to link to by appending the ID of that form to the URL, separated by the pound character (#). If `NavigateUrl` starts with this character, it is assumed that the link indicates a form identifier on the current page.

```
String = NavigateUrl
NavigateUrl = String
```

SoftkeyLabel Property (read/write)

On devices that support Softkey actions for selecting a hyperlink, this string property is rendered as a label for the softkey. If `null`, the default value is Go.

```
String = SoftkeyLabel
SoftkeyLabel = String
```

The List Control

The `List` control extends the abstract `PageControl` base class not only to provide a means for displaying a set of `MobileListItems`, but also to encapsulate event handling so that the server may react when the user makes selections from this set. The list can, of course, be used to simply display a collection of items. The `List` supports internal pagination, which means that it is able to automatically render its content across multiple pages without additional code from the developer.

Public Properties of the List Control

DataMember Property (read/write)

This string property is used in conjunction with data binding when the `DataSource` is of type `IListSource`. It indicates which field of the `DataSource` should be extracted to generate the items of the list.

```
String = DataMember
DataMember = String
```

DataSource Property (read/write)

The `List` control supports data binding for the list items. The property can be either of type `IEnumerable` or `IListSource`. When using data binding, the `DataBind` method of the list must be called to populate the list. If the `DataSource` is of type `IEnumerable`, the enumerated member specified in the `DataTextField` and `DataValueField` is used for the list item. If it is of type `IListSource`, the `DataMember` property must be set to indicate which member should be used.

```
Object = DataSource
DataSource = Object
```

DataTextField Property (read/write)

This string property specifies which databound field should be used for the display text of the listed items.

```
String = DataTextField
DataTextField = String
```

DataValueField Property (read/write)

This string property indicates the value to use for databound list items.

```
String = DataValueField
DataValueField = String
```

Decoration Property (read/write)

The Decoration property determines how list elements should be presented. It is of type System.Web.UI.MobileControls.ListDecoration. The possible values are:

❑ None

❑ Bulleted

❑ Numbered

The default Decoration is ListDecoration.None. Bulleted lists use the browser default for placing highlighted list items. Numbered lists render the items preceded by sequential numbers.

```
System.Web.UI.MobileControls.ListDecoration = Decoration
Decoration = System.Web.UI.MobileControls.ListDecoration
```

HasItemCommandHandler Property (read-only)

This property returns a Boolean value indicating whether the List control has an associated ItemCommand handler registered. If true, the ItemCommand handler is invoked when the user selects an item from the list.

```
Boolean = HasItemCommandHandler
```

Items Property (read-only)

The Items property retrieves a System.Web.UI.MobileListItemCollection containing the items of the list.

```
System.Web.UI.MobileListItemCollection = Items
```

ItemsAsLinks Property (read/write)

By default, this Boolean property is false. When set to true, the items of the list are rendered as hyperlinks. The text of the MobileListItem is displayed as the visible label of the hyperlink, while the value of the MobileListItem is taken to be the URL for navigation.

```
Boolean = ItemsAsLinks
ItemsAsLinks = Boolean
```

Public Methods of the List Control

DataBind Method

The `DataBind` method can be called once the `DataSource` has been populated. The `MobileListItem` collection is then populated using the text and values specified in the `DataTextField` and `DataValueField` properties. It has a `void` return value.

```
void DataBind()
```

Public Events of the List Control

ItemCommand Event

If a `ListCommandEventHandler` is registered for the `List` control, then it will be invoked when the `ItemCommand` event is caught. This event is raised when the user selects an item from the list. The `ListCommandEventHandler` takes two arguments, an `Object` corresponding to the event originator, and further parameters inside a `ListCommandEventArgs` collection. The handler can be declared using the name of the event delegate:

```
<script language="C#" runat=server>
public void MyItemCommandHandler(Object o, ListCommandEventArgs e)
{
  //react to event here
}
</script>
<Mobile:Form runat="server">
  <Mobile:List runat="server" OnItemCommand="MyItemCommandHandler" />
</Mobile:Form>
```

ItemDataBind Event

The `ItemDataBind` event is raised during data binding so that the properties of the `MobileListItem` being created can be set programmatically. As arguments, the event delegate takes a sender object, which will be another control on the page, and a `ListDataBindEventArgs`. The handler can be declared using the `OnItemDataBind` property:

```
<script language="C#" runat=server>
public void MyItemDataBindHandler(Object o, ListCommandEventArgs e)
{
  //react to event here
}
</script>
<Mobile:Form runat="server">
  <Mobile:List runat="server" OnItemDataBind="MyItemDataBindHandler" />
</Mobile:Form>
```

The ObjectList Control

The `ObjectList` control extends the abstract `PagedControl` class that provides more flexibility than the `List` control but is restricted to data binding. When an item from the list is selected, a view can be produced that provides an even greater level of detail about the selected item. The `List` control provides just a single item for each list and only allows it to react to a single default command when it is selected. The `ObjectList` can automatically provide a detailed view of the data when the user selects an item. See the `ObjectList.aspx` example further on.

Public Properties of the ObjectList Control

AllFields Property (read-only)

This property is read-only so cannot be altered. It will retrieve an `IObjectListFieldCollection` corresponding to the fields to be used for the data binding. It is only set after data binding has occurred and cannot be modified thereafter.

```
System.Web.UI.MobileControls.IObjectListFieldCollection = AllFields
```

AutoGenerateFields Property (read/write)

The default behavior of the `ObjectList` is to automatically generate the fields to be displayed from the `DataSource`. If this Boolean property is set to `false`, it indicates that rendering should instead correspond to the `Fields` collection.

```
Boolean = AutoGenerateFields
AutoGenerateFields = Boolean
```

BackCommandText Property (read/write)

To return from the details view of an `ObjectListItem` to the main list view, a command is invoked by selecting a UI element labeled with the `BackCommandText` string. By default, it will be a localized version of "Back".

```
String = BackCommandText
BackCommandText = String
```

Commands Property (read-only)

The `Commands` property returns a modifiable `ObjectListCommands` collection that corresponds to the delegates defined for execution when an item from the list is selected. The delegates are invoked when the `ItemCommand` event is raised.

```
System.Web.UI.MobileControls.ObjectListCommandCollection = Commands
```

DataMember Property (read/write)

When `DataSource` is set to an `IListSource` type, the `DataMember` string property determines the member to use when creating `ObjectListItems`.

```
String = DataMember
DataMember = String
```

DataSource Property (read/write)

The `DataSource` property is an object that should be set to an `IEnumerable` or `IListSource` type. If the `AutoGenerateFields` property is set to `true`, the members of the `IEnumerable` collection are created as fields for each `ObjectListItem`. If the `DataSource` implements `IListSource`, the data binding operation looks to the types of the `DataSource` when generating `ObjectListItems`. Otherwise, the first item of the enumeration is used to determine the types of the `ObjectListItem` fields (using the field specified in the `DataMember` field of the `ObjectList`), so all elements of the `DataSource` enumeration must be of the same type.

```
Object = DataSource
DataSource = Object
```

DefaultCommand Property (read/write)

The DefaultCommand has a default value of an empty string. If the property is set, however, the rendering of the ObjectList will provide, where possible, a method for invoking the command given by this property.

```
String = DefaultCommand
DefaultCommand = String
```

Details Property (read-only)

When templating the contents of the ObjectList, the Details property will return a Panel object corresponding to the template that applies to the requesting device.

```
System.Web.UI.MobileControls.Panel = Details
```

DetailsCommandText Property (read/write)

When the ObjectList is displayed on devices that require a text message to link to the detailed view of a selected item, the text of the DetailsCommandText property is used. By default, this property is the string "Details", or a localized version of this message.

```
String = DetailsCommandText
DetailsCommandText = String
```

Fields Property (read-only)

The Fields property provides access to an ObjectListFieldCollection that corresponds to the fields that have been defined for the ObjectList. The members of the Fields collection can be modified.

```
System.Web.UI.MobileControls.ObjectListFieldCollection = Fields
```

HasItemCommandHandler Property (read-only)

This Boolean property returns true when the ObjectList has a handler registered for the ItemCommand event.

```
Boolean = HasItemCommandHandler
```

Items Property (read-only)

The Items property returns an ObjectListItemCollection, allowing access to the items that have been bound for the ObjectList. This collection cannot be modified by the Items property.

```
System.Web.UI.MobileControls.ObjectListItemCollection = Items
```

LabelField Property (read/write)

The LabelField property defaults to an empty string. When it is left empty, the first field of the DataSource is used as a label. When the ObjectList is rendered as a table, the LabelField is not used, as a more explicit delineation determined by the names of the individual fields of the ObjectListItemCollection is displayed. The LabelField will be overridden by the <LabelTemplate> element if present.

```
String = LabelField
LabelField = String
```

LabelFieldIndex Property (read-only)

This property indicates the index of the Fields collection to use as the label. The default is 0, that is, the first member. When LabelField is set, this property is updated accordingly.

```
Integer = LabelFieldIndex
```

SelectedIndex Property (read/write)

This integer field defaults to -1, which indicates that no item is selected. The ObjectList can only have a single item selected, and the SelectedIndex will be updated accordingly.

```
Integer = SelectedIndex
SelectedIndex = Integer
```

Selection Property (read-only)

When an item from the ObjectList is selected, the Selection property will return the selected ObjectListItem. If no item is selected, this property will return null.

```
System.Web.UI.MobileControls.ObjectListItem = Selection
```

TableFields Property (read/write)

The TableFields string is a set of comma-separated field names. When the ObjectList is rendered as a table, the DataFields specified in the TableFields property will be used as the columns for the table.

```
String = TableFields
TableFields = String
```

TableFieldIndices Property (read-only)

By default, the TableFieldIndices property returns null. When the TableFields property has been set, the TableFieldIndices property returns an array of integers. This array corresponds to the indices of the AllFields collection to use when displaying the ObjectList as a table.

```
Integer[] = TableFieldIndices
```

ViewMode Property (read/write)

This property sets and retrieves a type from the ObjectListViewMode enumeration. It corresponds to the way that the ObjectList is to be displayed for this request, and can take on the following values:

❑   List

❑   Commands

❑   Details

```
System.Web.UI.MobileControls.ObjectListViewMode = ViewMode
ViewMode = System.Web.UI.MobileControls.ObjectListViewMode
```

Public Methods of the ObjectList Control

CreateTemplatedItemDetails Method

When the details of a list item are to be displayed using templates, the control adapter calls `CreateTemplatedItemDetails`, passing a Boolean value to indicate the need for data binding. The detail view of the currently selected list item is constructed according to the templates that match the requesting device.

```
void CreateTemplatedItemDetails(doDataBind)
```

Parameter	Type	Description
doDataBind	Boolean	Specifies whether a data binding operation is required to create the detail view for the current item

CreateTemplatedItemsList Method

The `CreateTemplatedItemsList` is invoked by adapters to build the `ObjectList` when the `ObjectList` is templated. It has no return value. The Boolean parameter indicates whether data binding should be performed when building the list.

```
void CreateTemplatedItemsList(doDataBind)
```

Parameter	Type	Description
doDataBind	Boolean	Specifies whether a data binding operation is required to create the list

DataBind Method

The `DataBind` method must be called once the `DataSource` has been populated. The `ObjectListItem` collection is then populated according to the values of `ObjectListField` and appropriate collections.

```
void DataBind()
```

PreShowItemCommands Method

This method is called by control adapters prior to displaying a particular item to call the events that may be triggered by `ShowItemCommands`. The `itemIndex` argument indicates which member of the `ObjectListItems` is being prepared.

```
void PreShowItemCommands(itemIndex)
```

Parameter	Type	Description
itemIndex	Integer	An index into the `ObjectListItems` specifying the item for which the default event should be raised

RaiseDefaultItemEvent Method

When an item is selected, the default event will be raised. Control adapters can invoke this method specifying which item should have the default command handler invoked.

```
void RaiseDefaultItemEvent(itemIndex)
```

Parameter	Type	Description
itemIndex	Integer	An index into the `ObjectListItems` specifying the item for which the default event should be raised

Public Events of the ObjectList Control

ItemCommand Event

By default, the list view of the `ObjectList` renders each item as a hyperlink. When the link is selected, the `ItemCommand` event is raised, and bubbled up to the parent of the templated item. The events can be set by modifying the `ObjectListCommand` collection returned by the `Commands` property. Its handler can also be established declaratively by setting `OnItemCommand`.

ItemDataBind Event

The `ItemDataBind` event is called for each `ObjectListItem` when the data bind operation occurs. The `ObjectList` can only be populated via data binding, so this event is called for every item of every `ObjectList`.

ShowItemCommands Event

Individual `ObjectListItems` have associated commands. When these are rendered for the details view of a list item, the `ShowItemCommands` event is raised. The delegate to invoke when this event is raised can be set declaratively by the `OnShowItemCommands` attribute.

Example: Using the ObjectList Control – Developers.aspx

In this example, we create an `ArrayList` of custom developer objects to display in the `ObjectList`. The `ArrayList` is then data bound, and the information about the developers is rendered as a list with detail views for each developer.

```
<%@ Page Inherits="System.Web.UI.MobileControls.MobilePage" Language="cs" %>
<%@ Register TagPrefix="Mobile" Namespace="System.Web.UI.MobileControls"
Assembly="System.Web.Mobile" %>
<script runat=server>
private class Developer {
  private string devName;
  private string preferredLanguage;
  private int phoneExtension;

  public Developer(String devName, String preferredLanguage, int phoneExtension)
  {
    this.devName = devName;
    this.preferredLanguage = preferredLanguage;
    this.phoneExtension = phoneExtension;
  }

  public String Name { get { return devName; } }
  public String Language { get { return preferredLanguage; } }
  public int Extension { get { return phoneExtension; } }
}

protected void Page_Load(object sender, EventArgs e)
{
  if(!(IsPostBack))
  {
    //create an ArrayList of Developer objects
    ArrayList developers = new ArrayList();
    developers.Add(new Developer("Chris",   "VB.NET",  130));
    developers.Add(new Developer("Allen",   "C++",     815));
    developers.Add(new Developer("Glenda",  "Fortran", 699));
    developers.Add(new Developer("Mike",    "JScript", 180));
    developers.Add(new Developer("Matt",    "C#",      549));

    //set DataSource and DataBind
    developerList.DataSource = developers;
    developerList.DataBind();
  }

}
</script>
<Mobile:Form runat=server>
  <Mobile:ObjectList runat=server id="developerList" />
</Mobile:Form>
```

The Panel Control

The `Panel` control extends the abstract `MobileControl` base class and is primarily used to group a set of contained controls. All of the controls contained within a panel inherit the style attributes set on the panel unless overridden. A `Panel` control can be selectively paginated using the `Paginate` property. For an explanation of paginated content, see the corresponding section earlier in this chapter.

The visibility of the panel affects the visibility of the entire group of child controls it contains. Because a panel has no visible elements itself, a handy technique is to place an empty panel on a form, and then add controls to it programmatically. The controls will only be visible if the Panel is visible. However, even if the Panel is visible, an individual control will not be rendered if its Visible property is set to false.

Public Properties of the Panel Control

Content Property (read-only)

The Panel object supports device-specific templating of its contained controls. This property retrieves the Panel corresponding to the contained choice.

```
System.Web.UI.MobileControls.Panel = Content
```

Paginate Property (read/write)

The Mobile Internet Toolkit makes it quite easy to automatically split the content of controls across multiple display pages. By default, the Paginate property is false, so set it to true if you wish the panel contents to be split up when required. Not only does this allow large documents to be rendered in a user-friendly way on the variable screen sizes of mobile devices, but as each logical page is sent by the ASP.NET server separately, it can be very important for devices that can only handle relatively small amounts of data at a time.

```
Boolean = Paginate
Paginate = Boolean
```

Public Methods of the Panel Control

CreateDefaultTemplatedUI Method

This method is called to instantiate child templates. It has no return value.

Parameter	Type	Description
doDataBind	Boolean	Indicates whether the templates should perform data-binding operations

The PhoneCall Control

The PhoneCall control (referred to as the Call control in the beta version of the Toolkit) extends the abstract TextControl class for displaying telephone numbers. On devices with dynamic dial-out support, it is possible to call the number by selecting the link. The PhoneCall control can optionally render a hyperlink for the displayed number for devices that do not support this feature.

Public Properties of the PhoneCall Control

The PhoneCall control is used for displaying phone numbers, and adds just a few properties to the TextControl class. When the device supports it, the device can automatically call the telephone number when selected by the user.

AlternateFormat Property (read/write)

This string property is used to format the output for devices that do not support placing calls. By default it has a value of "{0} {1}" where the {0} will be replaced by the Text property and the {1} will be replaced by the PhoneNumber.

```
String = AlternateFormat
AlternateFormat = String
```

AlternateUrl Property (read/write)

If this string property is set to a non-null value and the AlternateText is rendered indicating the current device does not support dynamic dial-out, this property provides a hyperlink alternative, using AlternateText as the label.

```
String = AlternateUrl
AlternateUrl = String
```

PhoneNumber Property (read/write)

This string property corresponds to the phone number. It can contain digits as well as any of the following:

- +
- #
- (
-)
- -
- .

```
String = PhoneNumber
PhoneNumber = String
```

SoftkeyLabel Property (read/write)

This property is the string to use as the label for the built-in function key (if available on the device) for placing the phone call or linking to the AlternateUrl. The default label is Go.

```
String = SoftkeyLabel
SoftkeyLabel = String
```

Text Property (read/write)

This string is displayed on devices that do not support dialing the number.

```
String = Text
Text = String
```

The RangeValidator Control

The `RangeValidator` extends the abstract `BaseValidator` class to check that the value of `ControlToValidate` falls within a specified range.

Public Properties of the RangeValidator Control

MaximumValue Property (read/write)

The `ControlToValidate` must be less than or equal to the numeric value of the `MaximumValue` string, which is `null` by default.

```
String = MaximumValue
MaximumValue = String
```

MinimumValue Property (read/write)

This string property is `null` by default. The `ControlToValidate` must be greater than or equal to the numeric value of `MinimumValue`.

```
String = MinimumValue
MinimumValue = String
```

Type Property (read/write)

The validation uses the `System.Web.UI.WebControls.ValidationDataType` type specified by this property. It can take any of the following values:

❑   `String`

❑   `Integer`

❑   `Double`

❑   `Date`

❑   `Currency`

If not specified, the default is `String`.

```
System.Web.UI.WebControls.ValidationDataType = Type
Type = System.Web.UI.WebControls.ValidationDataType
```

The RegularExpressionValidator Control

The `RegularExpressionValidator` control extends the abstract `BaseValidator` class to validate the value of `ControlToValidate` according to the constraints of a particular Regular Expression.

Public Properties of the RegularExpressionValidator Control

ValidationExpression Property (read/write)

This string property is used to set the `RegularExpression` that will be applied to validate the `ControlToValidate`'s value.

```
String = ValidationExpression
ValidationExpression = String
```

The RequiredFieldValidator Control

The `RequiredFieldValidator` ensures that the `ControlToValidate` has a value. It does not perform any validation on the control's value, merely verifying that a value has been provided.

The SelectionList Control

The `SelectionList` control extends the abstract `MobileControl` base class to allow for the selection of items from a list. It supports allowing multiple items in a list to be selected simultaneously. The `SelectionList` does not support pagination. Selecting an item in the list does not automatically result in firing off corresponding server events, but there are events for changes in the selected items when the form is posted. The `SelectionList` can render in a variety of ways depending upon the value of the `SelectType` property.

Public Properties of the SelectionList Control

DataMember Property (read/write)

If `DataSource` is set to an object of type `IListSource`, the `DataMember` property selects the member to extract from the `DataSource` object for data binding.

```
String = DataMember
DataMember = String
```

DataSource Property (read/write)

The default value for this property is `null`. It can be set to a type of `IEnumerable` or `IListSource`. The `DataSource` corresponds to the object to use when applying data binding to a `SelectionList`. The `DataBind` method must be called for data binding to occur, but not until after the `DataSource` property is set.

```
Object = DataSource
DataSource = Object
```

DataTextField Property (read/write)

The `Text` field of the list corresponds to the item identified by this string property during the data binding process.

```
String = DataTextField
DataTextField = String
```

DataValueField Property (read/write)

The `Value` field of the list corresponds to the item identified by this string during the data-binding process.

```
String = DataValueField
DataValueField = String
```

IsMultiSelect Property (read-only)

When `true`, this Boolean read-only property indicates that multiple selections are permitted when the `SelectType` is one of the following:

❑   `CheckBox`

❑   `MultiSelectListBox`

Note however, that the `SelectionList` will only permit single selections when `SelectType` is one of the following:

❑   `DropDown`

❑   `ListBox`

❑   `Radio`

❑   `CheckBox`

```
Boolean = IsMultiSelect
```

Items Property (read-only)

This property returns the `MobileListItemCollection` containing all the chosen items of the `SelectionList`.

```
System.Web.UI.MobileControls.MobileListItemCollection = Items
```

Rows Property (read/write)

This integer corresponds to the visible row count when the `SelectType` is a `ListBox`. This rendering is dependent on the ability of the device to render a logically grouped set of options. If the device does not support dynamically displaying more of the available options, they may all be displayed at once.

```
Integer = Rows
Rows = Integer
```

SelectedIndex Property (read/write)

This integer property has a value of –1 if no item from the `SelectionList` has been selected. After form submission, the selected value will default to 0, which corresponds to the first item in the zero-based counting scheme of .NET. The first selected value will be returned when the `SelectionList` is multi-select, even if other items have also been selected. Use the `Items` property to retrieve the complete list of selected items. The `Selected` property of a specific item will determine if that item has been selected.

```
Integer = SelectedIndex
SelectedIndex = Integer
```

`SelectedIndex` may only be set programmatically, as in the following code sample.

Example: Setting SelectedIndex – SelectedIndex.aspx

```
<script runat=server>
protected void Page_Load(object o, EventArgs e)
{
  foreach(MobileListItem item in selectionList1.Items)
  {
    if (item.Value == "2001")
      selectionList1.SelectedIndex = 2;
  }
}
</script>

<Mobile:Form runat=server>
<Mobile:SelectionList runat=server id="selectionList1" >
    <Item Text="1999" Value="1999"/>
    <Item Text="2000" Value="2000"/>
    <Item Text="2001" Value="2001"/>
    <Item Text="2002" Value="2002"/>
    <Item Text="2003" Value="2003"/>
</Mobile:SelectionList>
<Mobile:Command runat=server Text="submit"/>
</Mobile:Form>
```

When we test this and select an index we get the following output:

Selection Property (read-only)

The `Selection` property is used to retrieve the `MobileListItem` that has been selected. Like the `SelectedIndex` property, when the control is a multi-select list, the property returns the first item selected. Use the `Items` property to retrieve the complete list of selected items. If no item has been selected, this accessor property returns `null`.

```
System.Web.UI.MobileControls.MobileListItem = Selection
```

SelectType Property (read/write)

The `SelectType` property can be set to one of the `ListSelectType` values:

- ❑ `DropDown`
- ❑ `Listbox`
- ❑ `Radio`
- ❑ `MultiSelectListBox`
- ❑ `CheckBox`

The control supports multiple selections to be made by the user when the `SelectType` is `CheckBox` or `MultiSelectListBox`. In general, to determine if an individual item has been selected, use its `Selected` property.

```
System.Web.UI.MobileControls.ListSelectType = SelectType
SelectType = System.Web.UI.MobileControls.ListSelectType
```

Public Events of the SelectionList Control

ItemDataBind Event

When using data binding to populate the `SelectionList`, the `ItemDataBind` event is called for each `MobileListItem` to be added to the list.

SelectedIndexChanged Event

This event is raised when the selection is changed by the user.

The TextBox Control

The `TextBox` control extends the abstract `TextControl` class to provide for a mechanism allowing a single line of input to be entered by the user. When the form is submitted, the string entered by the user can be retrieved using the `Text` property.

Public Properties of the TextBox Control

MaxLength Property (read/write)

The `MaxLength` integer defaults to 0, which indicates that there is no limit to the size of the entry, otherwise user input is restricted to no more than `MaxLength` characters.

```
Integer = MaxLength
MaxLength = Integer
```

Numeric Property (read/write)

This property is an indication that the user input should be restricted to numbers. It is `false` by default and not typically supported in HTML. It is advantageous on devices (like cell phones) where a single key is used to enter several characters and the device can automatically skip cycling through the non-numeric characters.

```
Boolean = Numeric
Numeric = Boolean
```

Password Property (read/write)

The default value of this Boolean property is `false`. When set to `true`, it indicates that the user input should be hidden when this feature is available. On some devices, this results in the characters entered appearing on the screen as asterisks. For others, there may be a slight delay before the masking is applied.

```
Boolean = Password
Password = Boolean
```

Size Property (read/write)

This integer property indicates the length for the textbox on the user's screen. Not all devices support this, since the textbox is simply a blank link for input. The input is not restricted to the size and may scroll. The default value is 0, which will result in using the client default.

```
Integer = Size
Size = Integer
```

Public Events of the TextBox Control

TextChanged Event

This event occurs on form submission when the `Text` property has changed from the value it was set to during the previous request. The default behavior of the `TextChanged` event is to fire the `OnTextChanged` method.

The TextView Control

The `TextView` control extends the abstract `TextControl` class. It is akin to the `Label` control, except that its contents are parsed to create `Link` controls (where appropriate) and `LiteralText`. The `Text` property can be set during page execution, and child controls will be created as appropriate for rendering.

Public Properties of the TextView Control

Elements Property (read-only)

The `Elements` property is read-only, and returns an `Arraylist` containing the controls parsed from the `Text`. At run-time, the `Text` property is parsed into child controls that can be either of type `LiteralText` or `Link`. The `Elements` property is an array of the controls after they have been parsed.

```
ArrayList = Elements
```

Text Property (read/write)

This property is a string that can be set and retrieved dynamically, but will actually be translated to indicate the relevant child controls for rendering. It can be data-bound with text that contains `LiteralText` as well as `Links`.

```
String = Text
Text = String
```

Public Methods of the TextView Control

PaginateRecursive Method

This method can be called to explicitly paginate the control's contents. It is used internally to perform default pagination if the `Paginate` property is set to `true`, but the developer may use it directly for custom pagination.

```
void PaginateRecursive(pager)
```

Parameter	Type	Description
pager	ControlPager	The ControlPager to use in paginating the contents of the TextView

The ValidationSummary Control

The `ValidationSummary` control extends the abstract `MobileControl` base class to display the errors encountered in processing the validation controls of a form. This is useful for providing a group of errors for the user to fix instead of confronting them with one error message at a time.

Public Properties of the ValidationSummary Control

BackLabel Property (read/write)

The `BackLabel` is displayed as a link to return the user to the page where the error was encountered. This string property has a default value of Back.

```
String = BackLabel
BackLabel = String
```

FormToValidate Property (read/write)

The `FormToValidate` property is `null` by default but must be set in order for the `ValidationSummary` to produce any output. Its value corresponds to the ID of the form that is to be validated. Error messages produced by any validation controls of that form that encountered errors are displayed by the `ValidationSummary` control.

```
String = FormToValidate
FormToValidate = String
```

HeaderText Property (read/write)

The `HeaderText` is a string with a `null` default. It is displayed at the top of the summary of errors.

```
String = HeaderText
HeaderText = String
```

StyleReference Property (read/write)

The `StyleReference` is a string that refers to the `Style` object that will be used when rendering the `ValidationSummary` control. The default is the `Error` style provided with the Mobile Internet Toolkit.

```
String = StyleReference
StyleReference = String
```

Public Methods of the ValidationSummary Control

GetErrorMessages Method

This method returns an array of strings representing the error messages produced by the validator controls that detected validation problems.

```
String[] GetErrorMessages()
```

Device-Specific Rendering

The ability to render content based on the specific capabilities of the requesting device is the central theme underlying the Mobile Internet Toolkit. The flexibility provided by device-specific constructs allows an application to develop rich content while still using a single page to target a variety of devices with varying capabilities.

A set of qualifying filters is first defined using the ASP.NET configuration files, as can be seen in the extract from `web.config` below. These filters are checked during execution using the `MobileCapabilities` object of the page when a `<deviceSpecific>` element is encountered. The `MobileCapabilities` object is covered in detail in the next section. When a `<Choice>` child element of `<deviceSpecific>` is found that matches a filter in the `web.config`, the content of that element is used for the rendering, and other choices of that `<deviceSpecific>` element are skipped.

For example, in the next example, we will define filters to determine whether the requesting device is using HTML or WML and alter the graphic displayed accordingly.

First, the device filters section of the `web.config` file must be altered to declare the required filters:

```
<system.web>
  <deviceFilters>
    <filter name="CheckHtml" compare="PreferredRenderingType" argument="html32"/>
    <filter name="CheckWml" compare="PreferredRenderingType" argument="wml11"/>
  </deviceFilters>
</system.web>
```

The filters both check the `PreferredRenderingType` defined in the `MobileCapabilities` class using the argument specified by the `compare` attribute for comparison. For instance, when the requesting device is configured to use HTML 3.2, the `CheckHtml` filter will return `true` and the `CheckWml` filter will be `false`. It is not necessary to specify a filter for every possible device, as a default image can be provided by the mobile page as described next.

The `compare` attribute must correspond to a mobile capability found in the configuration and the argument needs to be valid for that capability.

Next, the `<deviceSpecific>` element must be inserted on our mobile page to indicate which `<Choice>` element applies for each possible filter result. In this example, the `<ImageUrl>` element is given, to provide the default when no filter is matched. The `<Choice>` elements are evaluated in order, and the first qualifying choice is selected. If no `filter` attribute is provided, and the choice is evaluated, it will always match. This provides a method for providing a default choice when no appropriate filter is found. The `<Choice>` element that is selected will override the `ImageURL` property of the containing `Image` control.

Example: Device-Specific Rendering – DeviceSpecificImage.aspx

```
<Mobile:Image runat=server>
  <deviceSpecific>
    <Choice filter="CheckHtml" ImageUrl="pda.gif" />
    <Choice filter="CheckWml" ImageUrl="phone.wbmp" />
    <Choice ImageUrl="gizmo.gif" />
  </deviceSpecific>
</Mobile:Image>
```

Templates

The Mobile Internet Toolkit allows the template constructs of ASP.NET to be utilized within a `<deviceSpecific>` section. The templating is performed according to the matching of the `<Choice>` element filters.

Template	Template Purpose
HeaderTemplate	Rendered at the top of the control's output. When control is internally paginated, it is duplicated on each page.
FooterTemplate	Rendered at the bottom of the control's output. When control is internally paginated, it is duplicated on each page.
ContentTemplate	Replaces panel contents.
ItemTemplate	When rendering an `Items` collection, this template is applied to each item.
AlternatingItemTemplate	When rendering an `Items` collection, this template is alternated with the `ItemTemplate` for each item.
SeparatorTemplate	When rendering an `Items` collection, this template is rendered between each item.
ItemDetailsTemplate	Applied to the details view for an item of the `ObjectList`.
LabelTemplate	Rendered as the label for each item in the list view of an `ObjectList`.

Here we extend the `Developers.aspx` example from the `ObjectList` section to demonstrate using template elements within a `<deviceSpecific>` section. The contents of the `HeaderTemplate` and `FooterTemplate` are repeated on each page. Notice that the `<Choice>` element has no filter, which means no check against `MobileCapabilities` is required.

Example: Using Template Elements – ObjectList.aspx

```
// Uses Developer class and Page_Load code from Developers.aspx
<Mobile:Form runat=server>
  <Mobile:ObjectList runat=server id="developerList">
    <deviceSpecific>
      <Choice>
        <HeaderTemplate>
          <Mobile:Label runat=server Font-Bold=true Font-Size=Large>
            The Developers
          </Mobile:Label>
        </HeaderTemplate>
        <ItemTemplate>
          <%#((Developer)((MobileListItem)Container).DataItem).Name %>
          <Mobile:Label runat=server/>
        </ItemTemplate>
        <FooterTemplate>
          <Mobile:Label runat=server Font-Size=Small>
            Brought to You by Wrox
          </Mobile:Label>
        </FooterTemplate>
      </Choice>
    </deviceSpecific>
  </Mobile:ObjectList>
</Mobile:Form>
```

The Item Element

The `List` control supports declarative construction of the list using the `Item` element.

Attribute	Descriptions
Text	A string corresponding to the text that is displayed for the `MobileListItem`
Value	A string corresponding to the value used for the `MobileListItem` if submitted
Selected	Boolean indicating that the item should be constructed and rendered as a selected item
DataItem	Sets or returns the data bound item for the `MobileListItem`

Below is an example of populating a list using the `Item` element.

Example: Using the Item Element – SelectionList.aspx

```
<Mobile:SelectionList SelectType=Checkbox runat=server>
  <Item Text="Heather"  />
  <Item Text="Matthew" />
  <Item Text="Joshua" Selected=true />
  <Item Text="Kelley" />
</Mobile:SelectionList>
```

MobileCapabilities

The capabilities of the requesting device can be used programmatically as well. This allows the developer to make decisions at run-time without the use of the `<deviceSpecific>` element. To populate the `MobileCapabilities` object, simply cast the `Request.Browser` object as `MobileCapabilites`:

```
using System.Web.Mobile;
MobileCapabilities theCapabilities = (MobileCapabilities)Request.Browser;
Bool IsColor = theCapabilites.IsColor;
```

Following are some of the properties of the `MobileCapabilities` class that can be used for customizing output:

MobileCapability Type	Property Name
String	MobileDeviceManufacturer
String	MobileDeviceModel
String	PreferredRenderingType
String	PreferredRenderingMime
String	PreferredImageMime
Int	ScreenCharactersHeight
Int	ScreenPixelsWidth
Int	ScreenPixelsHeight
Int	ScreenBitDepth
Bool	IsColor
String	InputType
Int	NumberOfSoftkeys
Int	MaximumSoftkeyLabelLength
Bool	CanInitiateVoiceCall
Bool	CanSendMail
Bool	HasBackButton
Bool	SupportsCss
Bool	IsMobileDevice
Bool	SupportsImageSubmit
Bool	SupportsSelectMultiple
Bool	SupportsAccesskeyAttribute

The deviceFilters Section

The `<deviceFilters>` element should be placed within a `<system.web>` section of the web.config or machine.config file. The machine.config is appropriate for global settings, whereas the web.config is local to a specific application. It can contain multiple child `<filter>` elements that define filters for use in `<deviceSpecific>` elements of mobile pages.

The Filter Element

The `<filter>` element is placed within a `<deviceFilters>` section of either the web.config or the machine.config file. The `<filter>` element has three attributes for declaratively establishing a filter. The first is name, which is used to identify the filter from within the `<deviceSpecific>` element of the mobile page. The second is compare, which identifies which device capability to check. The third is argument and is compared to the device capability specified by the compare attribute.

The DeviceSpecific Control

This control corresponds to the `<deviceSpecific>` element, which declaratively establishes the set of available choices based on the `<deviceFilters>` element, which must be placed within a mobile control or Style element on the page.

Properties of the DeviceSpecific Control

Choices Property (read-only)

This property returns the child `<Choice>` elements of the corresponding `<deviceSpecific>` element. It is a DeviceSpecificChoiceCollection. The Choices property cannot be set, and the DeviceSpecificChoiceCollection it returns cannot be modified.

```
System.Web.UI.MobileControls.DeviceSpecificChoiceCollection = Choices
```

HasTemplates Property (read-only)

This property returns a Boolean indicating if there are `<Choice>` elements defined within the corresponding `<deviceSpecific>` element.

```
Boolean = HasTemplates
```

MobilePage Property (read-only)

This property returns the MobilePage object that contains the DeviceSpecific element. It cannot be modified.

```
System.Web.UI.MobileControls.MobilePage = MobilePage
```

Owner Property (read-only)

The Owner property returns an object derived from the parent element of the `<deviceSpecific>` element that corresponds to this DeviceSpecific instance. It can be either a Style or a Mobile control.

```
Object = Owner
```

SelectedChoice Property (read-only)

The `SelectedChoice` property returns the contained `<Choice>` element selected by the associated filters.

It is of type `System.Web.UI.MobileControls.DeviceSpecificChoice` and cannot be modified.

```
System.Web.UI.MobileControls.DeviceSpecificChoice = SelectedChoice
```

The DeviceSpecificChoice Class

In a .NET mobile page, each `<Choice>` element in a `<deviceSpecific>` element defines one of the possible choices for customized rendering based on a device filter specified in the application configuration files named `web.config` or `machine.config`. The `DeviceSpecificChoice` class directly reflects a single such `<Choice>` element.

Properties of the DeviceSpecificChoice Class

Contents Property (read-only)

The `Contents` property is of type `IListDictionary`. It will be populated with the properties that are overridden by selection of this choice.

```
IDictionary = Contents
```

Filter Property (read/write)

This property identifies the value of the `filter` attribute of the `<Choice>` element, which in turn indicates the `<filter>` element defined in the system configuration files applicable to this choice. Note that the match between the `filter` attribute and the `<filter>` element name attribute is case-sensitive. If this property is an empty string, evaluation of this choice will always succeed.

```
String = Filter
Filter = String
```

HasTemplates Property (read-only)

This Boolean property returns `true` if templates have been defined for this `Choice` element.

```
Boolean = HasTemplates
```

Templates Property (read-only)

This property returns an `IDictionary` corresponding to the templates defined for this choice.

```
IDictionary = Templates
```

Style Information

The Mobile Internet Toolkit provides several ways for designating the stylistic qualities to apply when rendering a control on devices that support such settings. Contained controls inherit the styles set higher in the control hierarchy, in the same way that styles cascade down through the layers of an HTML page. For example, if the `Bold` property is set to `true` on a `Form`, all elements in that form that support rendering as bold will do so. A set of styles can be grouped together in a `<StyleSheet>` element to be shared throughout various elements of a page. Those styles can then be applied to any control by simply setting their `StyleReference` to the ID of the `<StyleSheet>`. The Microsoft Mobile Internet Toolkit establishes two pre-defined styles: the `Title` style renders an emphasized element, while the `Error` style sets the rendering apart from the default styles.

Style Properties

The following style properties are available to be set on the `Style` element, and can be set on other mobile controls as well:

- ❑ `Alignment`
- ❑ `BackColor`
- ❑ `Font-Name`
- ❑ `Font-Size`
- ❑ `Wrapping`

The StyleSheet

The `<StyleSheet>` element provides a way to group styles for reuse, control inheritance, and the programmatic control of settings. `<StyleSheet>` can be declared inside the mobile page, or it can be created in a separate file and referenced by setting the `ReferencePath` attribute of a `<StyleSheet>` element in the page. Next is an example of using the `StyleSheet` with `Style` element declared inline:

Example: Using a StyleSheet – Style.aspx

```
<%@Register TagPrefix="Mobile" Namespace="System.Web.UI.MobileControls"
                                Assembly="System.Web.Mobile" %>
<%@Page Inherits="System.Web.UI.MobileControls.MobilePage" Language="C#"%>
<Mobile:StyleSheet runat="server">
  <Style name="LargeRed" ForeColor="red" Font-Size="Large" />
  <Style name="SmallBlue" ForeColor="blue" Font-Size="Small" />
</Mobile:StyleSheet>
<Mobile:Form runat="server">
<Mobile:Label runat="server" StyleReference="LargeRed">
  large red text
</Mobile:Label>
<Mobile:Label runat="server" StyleReference="SmallBlue">
  small blue text
</Mobile:Form>
```

Style elements can inherit another style and add to the information already specified:

```
<Style name="LargeRed" ForeColor="red" Font-Size="Large" />
<Style name="LargeRedBold" StyleReference="LargeRed" Font-Bold=True />
```

375

When the `ReferencePath` for a `<StyleSheet>` element is set to a non-empty string, the `Style` properties of the `<StyleSheet>` element contained in the designated file are used as the stylesheet for that page. This makes it possible to reuse a single stylesheet across multiple files.

```
<Mobile:StyleSheet runat="server" Referencepath="./SharedStyles.ascx"/>
```

PagerStyle

`PagerStyle` extends the `Style` element for use with paginated content. When the contents of a control are paginated, a UI element is displayed for navigating forward and backward through the pages. In addition to the properties and methods of the `Style` object, `PagerStyle` provides a means for overriding the defaults of the pager.

Properties of PagerStyle

NextPageText Property (read/write)

By default, to move forward through paginated content, a localized equivalent of the word Next is rendered. This is a string property.

```
String = NextPageText
NextPageText = String
```

PageLabel Property (read/write)

This property sets or returns a label for the current page that is rendered between the `PreviousPage` and `NextPage` navigation elements. By default, it is an empty string. It supports the `{0}` and `{1}` substitution specifiers, where `{0}` is replaced by the number of the current page, and `{1}` is replaced by the total number of pages.

```
String = PageLabel
PageLabel = String
```

PreviousPageText Property (read/write)

To move backward through paginated content, a localized equivalent of the word Previous is rendered. This is a string property.

```
String = PreviousPageText
PreviousPageText = String
```

Summary

This chapter has taken an in-depth look at the Microsoft Mobile Internet Toolkit, a very powerful extension to ASP.NET. Using the toolkit, it is possible to write web applications where content is automatically adapted to display on a wide array of browsers running on many different devices.

The capabilities of the requesting device are ascertained when a request is received, and a predefined set of device adapters can then be selected to render content for the controls on the page.

The Mobile Internet Toolkit can be extended quite painlessly to accommodate new devices simply by adding to the `machine.config` file so that the best set of existing device adapters is used for requests from the new device. If new or customized markup is needed, new device adapters can be added to the framework to extend the capabilities of existing web applications to deal with devices configured for those adapters in `machine.config`.

The Mobile Internet Toolkit integrates seamlessly with the authoring environment of Visual Studio.NET, providing developers with an accessible way to create web applications that can extend beyond the desktop to cell phones, pagers, PDAs, and the PocketPC.

Caching & System.Web.Caching

Caching is really a very simple concept. When a request is made that requires work to be done, caching allows the result of that work to be saved in memory. When subsequent requests are made, the cached result can be delivered without needing to redo the work. In the context of a web application, this means retaining pages or data in memory across HTTP requests so they can be used without the expense of recreating them. The actual amount of performance gained by using caching varies greatly depending on the type of application. However, in the right circumstances, caching can provide one of the biggest boosts in performance for your ASP.NET application and, in many cases, this increase for your entire application can be as much as two- or three-fold.

One example of where caching can have a significant impact is the scenario of a typical e-commerce application. While an e-commerce site may offer many services, a process similar to the browsing of a product catalog is usually by far the most common user operation. There are a variety of reasons why information related to products should be (or has to be) stored in a database. This means that a page that displays products from the catalog will be dynamically generated for each request and could entail significant overhead by having to access the database, possibly travel over the network, and so on, every time the user request a page. However, if we think about it, the type of information generated for such a catalog page is really static over a specific period of time. This span of time could be hours, or maybe even days. So, as this chapter will show, we can use the caching features in ASP.NET to retrieve this product information only once and use an in-memory copy of the data until it is no longer valid. Our overhead then becomes only a handful of in-process calls to check if an item has been cached, versus the possible several thousand calls (and network latency) to retrieve the data from a remote data source.

This idea of storing something in memory for use later on is not, however, a new concept for ASP developers. Using the `Application` and `Session` objects in classic ASP allowed us to store a piece of data in memory across multiple requests on a per-application or per-user basis respectively. However, this was a very manual process when it came to providing caching-style functionality. An item was programmatically added to one of these objects and remained there until explicitly removed (or until the application/session came to an end). Another problem with using these objects was that as the number of users increased, you could very easily consume the available memory on your server. As we will see in this chapter, the caching functionality provided in ASP.NET solves this and many other issues that developers were presented with when trying to reap the benefits of caching in classic ASP applications.

ASP.NET provides for two distinct methods of caching. The first method is referred to as output caching and simply involves using a directive to mark a page, partial page, or web service method as "cacheable"; the system will then handle all of the work for you. This type of caching will be covered in the first part of this chapter. The second type of caching available in ASP.NET is more akin to using the `Session` object and is commonly referred to as "traditional application (or programmatic) caching". This form of programmatic caching is a big improvement over using the `Session` object since it was specifically designed for the task. We will discuss this type of caching in the second part of this chapter.

> At the time this chapter was written, .NET was in beta 2 and required the installation of "ASP.NET Premium Edition" for the caching features described in this chapter to function. This product is available for free download from **msdn.microsoft.com**. However, this should no longer be necessary in future releases as the availability of "premium" features will depend on the version of Windows and not on the runtime itself.

Output Caching

As was discussed in the introduction, output caching provides a way to store the responses generated by a request for a dynamic page or user control. What is actually stored in the cache is exactly that – the response. In other words, what is actually sent back to the browser when the specific HTTP request is sent for that page. For example, if a page includes images, the images themselves are retrieved using separate HTTP requests and are therefore not stored in the cache with the page. Keep in mind that, in this case, images are often cached client-side by the browser itself.

It's been said several times that output caching can be used for complete pages, partial pages, and Web Service methods. It will be these three types of output caching that we will examine next:

❏ Page output caching

❏ Partial page caching (or Fragment Caching)

❏ Web Service caching

Each of these output caching types only requires that we mark the item as "cacheable" and let the system handle the management of our cached items. However, what is actually going on behind-the-scenes is that the system is using members of the `HttpCachePolicy` class, which is exposed for an individual response through the `Page.Response.Cache` property. This is in fact exactly what we will be looking at and working with when we cover programmatic caching in the latter part of this chapter.

Page Output Caching

The first type of output caching that we will examine is page output caching. This allows the response of an entire dynamic page to be stored in the cache for future requests. To demonstrate the different options available for page output caching, we will be using a classic example used to demonstrate that caching is actually taking place, which is a page that outputs the current time. Without caching enabled, the code for the page in this case looks like this (see `PageOutput.aspx` in the code download available from **www.wrox.com**):

VB.NET:

```
<SCRIPT runat="server">
  Public Sub Page_Load()
    span1.InnerHtml = DateTime.Now
  End Sub
</SCRIPT>

<SPAN id="span1" runat="server" />
```

As you might expect, this page simply outputs the date and time and re-executes each time you make a request for the page. Each time you refresh the browser, you should see a new value displayed for the time (you will of course see the same value if it's still the same second as the first view of the page). This page could just as easily be one that goes off and runs a query on a database, returns a set of data, and fills a grid with the results but we'll keep things simple so as not to get distracted.

To let the system know that we would like the results of this page to be cached, we just need to add a directive to the top of the page similar to the following:

```
<%@ OutputCache [List of Attributes] %>
```

We will cover each of the possible attributes in detail in the following sections, but a summary is provided below:

Attribute	Required	Value(s)
Duration	Yes	Number of seconds an item is considered valid and will remain in the cache
Location	No	Specifies which cache-capable network applications involved in delivering the response can be used to cache the item
VaryByCustom	No	Determines whether different versions of an item will be cached depending on either the browser type or a custom string you specify
VaryByHeader	No	A determination is made on whether to cache an item based on the HTTP headers, either by the value of a single header or by multiple header values
VaryByParam	Yes	Makes a determination on whether to cache an item based on parameters passed to the request (typically as a form or on the query string)

As noted in the table above, `Duration` and `VaryByParam` are the two required attributes for page output caching. Keep in mind that ASP.NET does provide much more in the way of functionality and flexibility when it comes to caching than the options available through the use of the `OutputCache` directive. However, in order to take advantage of this, we would need to use programmatic caching which is examined in the latter part of this chapter.

Duration Attribute

The Duration attribute is required for the OutputCache directive and specifies the amount of time in seconds that a page will remain in the cache. The first time a request is made for the page, the page is executed and the output is stored in the cache. When subsequent requests are received, the cache engine will check to see if a copy of the page output is in the cache. Independent of the number of requests that are received while the page is cached, once the specified duration of time has passed, the cache engine will automatically evict that item from the cache. Therefore, the next request received after the duration has expired will cause the page to be re-executed and the new result placed back in the cache for a new period of the specified duration.

Building on our previous example page that displayed the current time, we will now add a line to enable page output caching with a Duration of ten seconds:

```
<%@ OutputCache Duration="10" VaryByParam="None" %>
<SCRIPT runat="server">
  Public Sub Page_Load()
    span1.InnerHtml = DateTime.Now
  End Sub
</SCRIPT>

<SPAN id="span1" runat="server" />
```

When you view this page in a browser, you should still see the current data and time. However, now you can refresh the browser window as many times as you wish within ten seconds and the time should remain constant. Once ten seconds have elapsed since the page was first executed, the next refresh should cause the page to re-execute and a current value to display. Notice that we did have to include the VaryByParam attribute, which we will discuss in the next section.

There are two factors that can have an effect on how long an item remains in the cache regardless of the Duration value you specify.

The first factor is system memory. When the web server that is hosting a particular ASP.NET application begins to run low on system memory, the cache engine will automatically begin selectively purging items from the cache to avoid it having an adverse effect on application performance. Items in the cache are assigned a priority that will affect the order in which items are removed. This will be covered in more detail during the section of the chapter on programmatic caching.

The second factor that can override the Duration attribute you specify in the OutputCache directive is something called **sliding expiration**. The cache in ASP.NET is designed to store frequently used items and therefore includes this mechanism to avoid the cache growing too large with items that are accessed infrequently. This slidingExpiration property is set to five minutes by default and will cause an item to be evicted from the cache if it is not accessed within that period. Once again, this is regardless of the duration period you specify. However, unlike the Duration, this sliding expiration clock is reset each time the item in the cache is accessed. Also, it is possible to override this sliding expiration property and we will discuss this in the section on programmatic caching.

The amount of overhead necessary to support these steps required by the caching process is very small but should be taken into consideration. Because every situation is different, the only truly accurate way to determine the effectiveness of caching for a particular page or the most appropriate duration value to use is through testing and performance monitoring.

VaryByParam Attribute

In addition to `Duration`, `VaryByParam` is the other required attribute for the `OutputCache` directive. Often in an ASP.NET application, you will use the HTTP GET (query string) and POST (form) methods (or HEAD) to send information to a page. This can generate different responses from the page as a result. The `VaryByParam` attribute allows you to control when these different views of a page are cached.

These are the possible values for `VaryByParam`:

Value	Description
None	Only GET requests with no query string values are cached. Any requests that include a GET or POST parameter will not result in a new item being added to the cache.
*	An item is created in the cache for each page requested with a different value in either the query string or the POST collection.
[Custom]	Allows you to list which GET or POST parameters will result in the output being cached. Multiple parameters are separated by semicolons.

To illustrate this attribute, we will expand on the page we developed earlier that outputs the current date and time. However, now we will decide whether or not to display the time based on a value supplied as part of the query string.

```
<%@ OutputCache Duration="10" VaryByParam="None" %>
<SCRIPT runat="server">
  Public Sub Page_Load()
    If Request.QueryString("ShowDate") = "No" Then
      span1.InnerHtml = DateTime.Now.ToShortTimeString
    Else
      span1.InnerHtml = DateTime.Now
    End If
  End Sub
</SCRIPT>

<SPAN id="span1" runat="server" />
```

If you bring this page up in your browser, you will see the same output as before. If you refresh the page several times, you should see the same value for the time until after the ten seconds have expired, at which time you should get an updated value. However, there is a problem here. Keep refreshing the page until you get an updated value and then change the URL to include the ShowDate parameter. The URL should look something like the following (your directory and page name may be different):

http://localhost/CacheExamples/PageOutput2.aspx?ShowDate=No

Request this page and then refresh it immediately. What has happened? Perhaps more appropriately, what has not happened? If you completed these steps within ten seconds, you should still see a page that displays the date. Now, if you continue to refresh the page, you will eventually see an updated value for the time and the date should also be removed. This behavior can also be seen in the opposite direction if you now delete the query string parameter and refresh the page.

What is happening is that the cache engine is caching our page but is ignoring our query string parameter. This is because of the `VaryByParam="None"` attribute that we included with our `OutputCache` directive. This basically tells the cache engine to cache only cache one version of our page and to serve that version from the cache regardless of any query string or form values that are supplied. This is acceptable when the page doesn't expect to receive any values in this way. However, in this case, this behavior is undesirable because the look of our page changes depending on the value of `ShowDate`.

To solve this problem, we can use one of the other possible values for `VaryByParam`. In this case, go ahead and change the `OutputCache` directive to read as follows:

```
<%@ OutputCache Duration="10" VaryByParam="ShowDate" %>
```

If we now repeat our previous experiment, we should see the results that we would expect in this case. The cache engine will now add a new instance of our page to the cache each time a different value is used for `ShowDate`.

If we were instead to use a line like the following:

```
<%@ OutputCache Duration="10" VaryByParam="*" %>
```

then the cache engine would now cache a different version of the page whenever a request arrives for the page that has a different array of query string or form parameters from the one that already existed in the cache. This approach may be advantageous for a page you expect to be requested very frequently and that presents many different possible views. Again, one example of this may be a page that displays products for a web storefront. The page may take a parameter that identifies the category and then retrieves items from a database to display to the user. If this one page takes a lot of hits, you can be serving up these individual category pages from memory rather than hitting your database every time. Even though the cache engine will monitor memory usage and evict items from the cache before degrading application performance, it's a good rule of thumb not to use this approach unless you expect each of these category pages to be accessed much more frequently than the default five-minute sliding expiration.

It is also possible to base caching decisions on more than one parameter without using the "*", all, wildcard. This simply involves listing out multiple parameter names separated by a semicolon. For example, we could add yet another parameter to our time page that would allow us to use the short or long form of the time. We could call this parameter `TimeFormat` and accept values of `Long` or `Short`. Our `OutputCache` directive would then look like the one shown below:

```
<%@ OutputCache Duration="10" VaryByParam="ShowDate;TimeFormat" %>
```

Parameters that are listed for `VaryByParam` are not case-sensitive.

VaryByHeader Attribute

The attribute `VaryByHeader` operates in much the same way as the `VaryByParam` attribute. The only difference is that this attribute makes a determination of whether to add a separate item to the cache based on the HTTP header values instead of the query string and form values. One example of where this capability can be useful is for web applications that provide a single page in more than one language. How to implement such a page is beyond the scope of this chapter. However, the browser will send an HTTP header that is named `Accept-Language`. This value will be a code that identifies the preferred language for the browser. For example, `en-us` for English-US or `fr` for French. We can then modify our `OutputCache` directive to cache the different language versions of our page:

```
<%@ OutputCache Duration="10" VaryByParam="None" VaryByHeader="Accept-
    Language" %>
```

VaryByCustom Attribute

The VaryByCustom attribute is the last that we can use to control what variations of a specific page are cached. This attribute allows you to cache different views of a page depending on the browser version of the request and to optionally extend the functionality of output caching by allowing you to specify your own custom string to use in controlling the behavior of the OutputCache directive.

To vary by browser type, you specify VaryByCustom="browser". The cache engine will then use the value of Request.Browser.Type to determine whether a new item should be created in the cache. Only the browser's name and major version is used for this evaluation. Therefore, a different item will exist in the cache for IE 4 and IE 5 requests but not for IE 5 and IE 5.5 requests. This will happen automatically without writing any specific browser detection code in your ASP.NET pages. However, the real benefit of this capability is if you do write a page that will produce different output depending on the browser version. Then the cache engine will automatically cache this different output and deliver it to any future request made by a browser with the same name and major version. Otherwise, the same output will be cached twice with no added benefit.

To use your own custom string in the VaryByCustom attribute, you must override the HttpApplication.GetVaryByCustomString method in your application's Global.asax file. The code in this method will be used by the cache engine to determine whether a new item is added to the cache.

As an example, VaryByCustom would be useful for a site that provides different versions of a page depending on whether the browser supports frames or client-side JavaScript. You could accomplish this using the VaryByCustom attribute within your OutputCache directive:

```
<%@ OutputCache Duration="600" VaryByParam="*" VaryByCustom="Frames;JavaScript" %>
```

You would then need to add your own custom logic to set the value for each of these name-value pairs to allow the cache engine to determine which versions of the output to cache and which to retrieve and return for future requests. The following is an example of what the code in your Global.asax file may look like:

VB.NET:

```
Public Overrides Function GetVaryByCustomString(context As HttpContext, _
                                      arg As String) As String
  Select Case arg
    Case "Frames"
      Return "Frames=" & context.Request.Browser.Frames
    Case "JavaScript"
      Return "JavaScript=" & context.Request.Browser.JavaScript
    Case Else
      Return ""
  End Select
End Function
```

The Case Else clause that returns an empty string in this case simply represents the fact that no other strings are used in resolving the VaryByCustom attribute. This does not affect any other caching that may occur due to VaryByParam or VaryByHeader attributes.

Partial Page Caching

Often, caching an entire page as described in the previous section isn't feasible. It is very often the case that while the main content of the page is static, some other features are dynamic to support things like personalization or advertisements. In these cases, it is desirable to cache the static portions of the page while not caching the more dynamic portions. This can be accomplished through the use of partial page caching (also known as Fragment Caching).

The ability to separate relatively static content (that could be cached) from dynamic content in ASP.NET is provided through the use of User Controls. Although we will be using a User Control in an enhanced version of the page that we developed earlier that outputs the current time; you may want to refer back to Chapter 3 for more details on the development and use of User Controls.

So, our first step in creating an example that will use Partial Page Caching is to create a User Control that will represent our dynamic (or possibly personalized) content. Our User Control in this case will simply be another version of our time example, but which will display in red and be a little bigger:

VB.NET:

```
<SCRIPT runat="server">
    Public Sub Page_Load()
        span1.InnerHtml = DateTime.Now
    End Sub
</SCRIPT>
```

```
<H2><FONT color="red">
<SPAN id="span1" runat="server" />
</FONT></H2>
```

We will now save this file with the default name of `WebUserControl1.ascx`. Notice that this file uses the extension `.ascx` instead of `.aspx` since this is a control and not a page.

The next step is to insert this User Control into our parent page. You can do this in design mode in VS.NET simply by dragging the User Control from the Solution Explorer and dropping it onto the page. If you leave all of the default names, you should have a parent page that looks something like the following (you should remove or comment out all of the caching-related code for now):

VB.NET:

```
<%@ Register TagPrefix="uc1" TagName="WebUserControl1" Src="WebUserControl1.ascx"
%>
<SCRIPT runat="server">
  Public Sub Page_Load()
    span1.InnerHtml = DateTime.Now
  End Sub
</SCRIPT>
```

```
<SPAN id="span1" runat="server" />
<UC1:WEBUSERCONTROL1 id="WebUserControl1" runat="server" />
```

Once again, you can refer back to Chapter 3 for more on User Controls. If you bring this page up in your browser, the output should resemble that shown opposite:

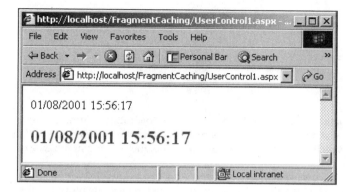

Since we have included no `OutputCache` directives, you can refresh this page and you should see updated values for the time for each instance.

We already saw how the contents of the `.aspx` page can be cached. Now we can use the same technique to have the parent page be executed with every request but the content of the user control be cached. All that is required is to add an `OutputCache` directive to the User Control itself like the following:

```
<%@ OutputCache Duration="10" VaryByParam="None" %>
```

If we now bring up the parent page in a browser, we see that one part of the page (smaller text) refreshes with the current time every second while another part of the page (larger red text) only refreshes with a new value every ten seconds.

As you can see, caching in ASP.NET combined with User Controls can obviously provide a very flexible way of maximizing reuse of relatively static content while still allowing areas of a page to be dynamically generated with every request.

> **There is one very important caveat to caching a User Control. Because the cached item represents the end result of the execution of the User Control, you cannot write server-side code to manipulate the User Control anywhere except in the control itself (such as in the control's Load and PreRender events). An error will occur if you try to do so elsewhere such as in the parent page.**

VaryByControl

One attribute that becomes available when using an `OutputCache` directive in a User Control is `VaryByControl`. This is in addition to the other attributes that we discussed as being available for the directive.

What this allows you to do is to define a property in the User Control that you can then reference in the `VaryByControl` attribute to control what versions of the User Control are cached. For example, you could include code in a User Control similar to the following:

VB.NET:

```
<%@ OutputCache Duration="10" VaryByControl="CategoryID" %>
<SCRIPT runat="server">
  Public Property CategoryID() As String
    Get
```

```
        Return cmbCategoryID.Value
    End Get
    Set
        cmbCategoryID.Value = CategoryID
    End Set
  End Property
</SCRIPT>
```

In this case, the property just represents the value of a ComboBox control on the User Control. This User Control could then just be dropped onto a parent page and the cache engine will use this property in much the same way as it uses parameters passed on the query string in the case of VaryByParam.

For example, if you have a user control that renders a drop-down list for choosing the category of books to display, you could use the value of the drop-down list to vary the output cache.

Web Service Caching

Everything we have discussed up until now has involved storing the result of an executed ASP.NET page or User Control. Another powerful feature of caching in ASP.NET is the ability to provide output caching for the result of a Web Service method.

This can be done simply by adding an additional attribute to the definition of your publicly available web service method. This is possible since the output of a web service method that uses the default SOAP encoding always has its results serialized into XML. It is this resulting XML that is stored in the cache.

Shown below is the "code behind" file for a simple web service that exposes a single method that returns the current time.

VB.NET:

```
Imports System
Imports System.Web
Imports System.Web.Services

Public Class Service1
  Inherits System.Web.Services.WebService

// Web Services Designer Generated Code

    <WebMethod(CacheDuration:=10)> _
    Public Function GetTime() As String
      GetTime = DateTime.Now.ToString
    End Function

End Class
```

If you bring up the system-provided test page and invoke this method, you should see something like the following display in your browser (your time will of course be different):

```
<?xml version="1.0" encoding="utf-8" ?>
<string xmlns="http://tempuri.org/">08/02/2001 12:16:24 AM</string>
```

Just as with the examples using ASP.NET pages and User Controls, the value displayed for the time will not change no matter how many times you refresh the browser until the ten second duration we specified has expired.

With Web Service Caching, the **VaryBy** attributes listed for Page Output and Partial Page Caching do not apply. Web Service Caching behaves in a manner similar to **VaryByParam="*"**. This makes sense since you can always attach additional parameters to a URL even if none are expected, but web service methods on the other hand always explicitly specify what parameters are expected.

Programmatic Caching

Up until this point in the chapter, we have been discussing different ways to use Output Caching in an ASP.NET application. What Output Caching provides is a very easy way to use caching in the search for better performance. However, often, it may become necessary to search out ways to have more control over caching in our web applications. ASP.NET provides a way for us to achieve this control by allowing us to access the members of the System.Web.Caching namespace directly. These are the same classes, methods, and properties that are used behind the scenes by Output Caching. You can think of the OutputCache directive as a high-level cache API and what we will cover here as the low-level cache API.

Rather then caching entire pages or even partial pages, programmatic caching allows us to retain specific objects in memory across HTTP requests. To make the best use of caching, these objects should be expensive to generate, frequently accessed, and static over a specific period of time. However, there are exceptions to the need to be static over time. We will look at ways in which we can set up dependencies that will cause an item to be automatically evicted from the cache when another cached item or file changes.

There are only two classes and one delegate contained within the System.Web.Caching namespace. These three items are listed in the table below and we continue by looking at each of these in turn.

Item	Type	Description
Cache	Class	Implements the cache for a web application
CacheDependency	Class	Tracks cache dependencies, which can be files, directories, or keys to other objects in the cache
CacheItemRemoved Callback	Delegate	Allows us to define a callback method that will be used to notify our application when an item is removed from the cache.

Cache Class

This class implements all of the methods you will need for adding, accessing, and removing cache items. It's important to remember that items in the cache are really just key-value pairs much like application or session variables. The key is a string used to identify the item and the value can be anything that derives from Object (which is of course everything in .NET). An instance of this class is automatically created for you as an application-level variable in your ASP.NET application and is appropriately named "Cache". The properties and methods that are not inherited from Object are listed in the table overleaf:

Item	Type	Description
Add	Method	Adds the specified item to the cache. You can also specify dependency, expiration and priority policies, and a delegate you can use to notify your application when an item is removed from the cache.
Count	Property	Returns the total number of items currently in the cache.
Get	Method	Returns the specified item from the cache.
GetEnumerator	Method	Returns a dictionary enumerator that allows for iterating through the key-values pairs that are in the cache.
Insert	Method	Inserts an item into the cache and returns the object added.
Item	Property	Gets or sets the item at the specified key.
Remove	Method	Removes the specified item from the cache.

Add Method

The Add method allows you to add a specified item to the cache with dependencies, expiration and priority policies, and a delegate that you can use to notify your application when the inserted item is removed from the cache. The following table shows the parameters that are required for this method listed in the order that they are required:

Parameter	Type	Description
key	String	The same as using the Item property, this is the string (or cache key) used to identify the item in the cache.
value	Object	This is the actual item that you would like to be added to the cache.
dependencies	Cache Dependency	The file or cache key dependencies for this item. When any dependency changes, the item is removed from the cache.
absoluteExpiration	DateTime	This is where you can provide a specific time when the item will be removed from the cache.
slidingExpiration	TimeSpan	This allows you to control when an item that is not being accessed is to be removed from the cache (five minutes by default).

Parameter	Type	Description
priority	CacheItem Priority	This is used by the cache engine to determine in what order to remove items in the cache when it needs to free system memory.
priorityDecay	CacheItem Priority Decay	The rate at which an object in the cache decays in importance. Objects that decay quickly are more likely to be removed.
onRemoveCallback	CacheItem Removed Callback	Allows you to specify a method in your application that will be called when the item is removed from the cache.

> The **Add** and **Insert** methods are essentially the same. However, the **Add** method requires all of the parameters listed above and returns an **Object** representing the item just added to the cache. The **Insert** method on the other hand comes in four varieties that each take a subset of these parameters and do not return the object. Please see the section later in this chapter that deals specifically with the **Insert** method for more details.

The statement shown below will add an item to the cache where "d" represents an absolute expiration value and "t" represents a sliding expiration value. It also specifies a priority of "high", a decay of "never", and does not specify a callback method.

VB.NET:

```
Cache.Add("MyItem", MyItemValue, Nothing, d, t, CacheItemPriority.High, _
    CacheItemPriorityDecay.Never, Nothing)
```

We have already discussed the first two parameters of this method – Key and Value. The third parameter of type CacheDependency will be covered in the section on the CacheDependency class itself later in this chapter. The next two parameters involve absolute and sliding expiration and are described in the previous table. The next parameter we will look at in more detail is the one that defines the cached item's priority.

CacheItemPriority

Every item added to the cache carries with it an associated priority value. It is this value that the cache engine will use when the memory used by the cache reaches a high level and may begin to adversely affect overall system performance. That is the only time this value will be used. The possible values are listed below in order from items that will be least likely to be removed from the cache to those that are first to be removed.

❑ NotRemovable – an item with this value will never be evicted from the cache to free system resources.

❑ High – this item would be least likely to be removed from the cache when memory is low

❑ AboveNormal– this priority value is set relatively between Normal and High

❑ Normal – this is the default value for items in the cache

❑ BelowNormal– this priority value is set relatively between Normal and Low

❑ Low – this item would be the first to be removed from the cache when memory is low

CacheItemPriorityDecay

The next parameter required for the Add method involves how the priority of an item will decay over time. This parameter is of type CacheItemPriorityDecay and the system will use this value to downgrade the priority value for an item in the cache that is not being accessed frequently. The possible values for this parameter are listed below in order of decreasing speed:

❑ Fast – when accessed infrequently, an item with this value is the most likely to be removed from the cache when memory is low

❑ Medium – this is the default value for items added to the cache

❑ Slow – an item with this decay value will be least likely to be removed from the cache when accessed infrequently

❑ Never – an item with this value will never have its priority decreased by the cache engine

Count Property

The Count property of the Cache class very simply returns the number of items currently in the cache. Lines similar to the following will store this value in a variable for later use:

```
Dim x As Integer
x = Cache.Count
```

Get Method

The Get method provides an alternative way to retrieve items from the cache, which is in addition to using the Item property that will be described shortly.

```
Public Function Get(ByVal key As String) As Object
```

Once again, the return type of this method is Object. So, the example below shows how you might retrieve a DataView item that was previously added to the cache.

```
Dim Source as DataView
Source = CType(Cache("MyData1"), DataView)
If Not (Source Is Nothing) Then
  MyDataGrid.DataSource = Source
  MyDataGrid.DataBind()
End If
```

It's worth noting that the call to CType is used here to convert the cached item, which is of type Object, to the DataView type that we are expecting.

Insert Method

The Insert method is overloaded to provide four different versions of the method. This allows us to add items to the cache without having to specify all of the parameters that are needed when using the Add method. The four different versions of this method are listed below:

```
Insert(key As String, value As Object)

Insert(key As String, value As Object, dependencies As CacheDependency)
```

```
Insert(key As String, value As Object, dependencies As _
    CacheDependency, absoluteExpiration As DateTime, _
    slidingExpiration As TimeSpan)

Insert(key As String, value As Object, dependencies As _
    CacheDependency, absoluteExpiration As DateTime, _
    slidingExpiration As TimeSpan, priority As _
    CacheItemPriority, priorityDecay As _
    CacheItemPriorityDecay, onRemoveCallback As _
    CacheItemRemovedCallback)
```

The simplest form of this method would simply insert an item into the cache and assign all of the default values for all of the other parameters.

```
Cache.Insert("MyItemKey", MyItemValue)
```

On the other hand the most complex form of this method would look nearly identical to the Add method described earlier in this section.

Item Property

The Item property is the default property of the Cache class that can be used to retrieve items by specifying the item's key. This allows you to use the Cache object that is exposed to your application in much the same way as using the Application object in classic ASP. In other words, we can just reference our application's Cache instance followed by a key value to both retrieve and insert items into the cache as upcoming examples will show.

```
Public Default Property Item(ByVal key As String) As Object
```

Notice that when retrieving items from the cache, this property returns a type of Object. So, for example, when retrieving a String item, you would want to call the ToString method to use the item.

```
Dim MyString As String
myString = Cache("MyItem").ToString
```

The following code shows an example of inserting the value of a textbox into the cache:

```
Cache("UserName") = txtName.Text
```

Remove Method

Items are automatically removed from the cache according to the information you provide regarding duration and dependencies. However, it is sometimes desirable to remove an item from the cache explicitly. This is done by using the Remove method of the Cache class. The Remove method takes only one parameter, which is the key of the item you wish to remove.

```
Public Function Remove(ByVal key As String) As Object
```

For example:

```
Cache.Remove("MyData1")
```

CacheDependency Class

The CacheDependency class is used to track dependencies between an item in the cache and files, directories, or keys to other items in the cache. An instance of the class is taken as a parameter of the Add and Insert methods of the Cache class.

In all cases, whatever is identified as a dependency for a cached item will be monitored by the system. When a change is made to this file, directory, or other cached item, the system will automatically remove the dependent item from the cache.

There are three different constructors for this class:

❑ Public Sub New(filename As String) creates a dependency with the file or directory specified.

❑ Public Sub New(filenames() As String) creates a dependency between the item and an array of files or directories.

❑ Public Sub New(filenames() As String, cachekeys As String) creates a dependency between the item and an array of files or directories and/or an array of cache keys

The following example inserts a new item into the cache identified by the key "CustomerData" and which contains an object identified by the variable MyCustomerObject. In this case, we set this item's existence in the cache to be dependent on an XML file named "cust.xml". Now, whenever a change is made to this XML file, our "CustomerData" item would automatically be evicted from the cache by ASP.NET.

```
Cache.Insert("CustomerData", MyCustomerObject, New _
            CacheDependency(Server.MapPath("cust.xml")))
```

CacheItemRemovedCallback Delegate

This delegate defines a callback method for notifying your application when an item is removed from the cache.

```
Public Delegate Sub CacheItemRemovedCallback(ByVal key As String, _
    ByVal value As Object, ByVal reason As CacheItemRemovedReason)
```

To allow your application to be notified whenever an item is removed from the cache, you must create an event handler that has the same parameters as this delegate declaration. An example of such a method is shown below:

VB.NET:

```
Public Sub RemovedCallback(k As String, v As Object, r As CacheItemRemovedReason)
    'Code to be executed when item is removed
End Sub
```

This callback function can now be declared and used with code similar to the following:

VB.NET:

```
Private Shared onRemove As CacheItemRemovedCallback = Nothing

Public Sub Page_Load(sender As Object, e As EventArgs)
```

```
Dim MyObject As Object
Dim d As New DateTime()
d.AddMinutes(30)
Dim t As New TimeSpan()

onRemove = New CacheItemRemovedCallback(AddressOf Me.RemovedCallback)

'Inserts the item into the cache
Cache.Insert("MyItemKey", MyObject, Nothing, d, t, CacheItemPriority.High, _
        CacheItemPriorityDecay.Never, onRemove)

'Removes item from the cache which causes the callback to execute
Cache.Remove("MyItemKey")
End Sub
```

In this case, we added and removed an item from the cache explicitly in the page's Load event. However, we could do this anywhere in a page and could also just let the item expire instead of calling Remove. The callback method would still get called when the item is removed either explicitly or implicitly by the system for any of the reasons that we have discussed. These reasons are also summarized in the definition of the CacheItemRemovedReason enumeration defined in the next section.

CacheItemRemovedReason Enumeration

This enumeration allows your method that is notified when items are removed from the cache to easily determine the reason why the item was removed.

❑   DependencyChanged – the item was removed because a file or key dependency changed

❑   Expired – the item was removed because it expired

❑   Removed – the item was explicitly removed using either the Remove or Insert method; The Insert method will cause an item to be removed if the key specified already exists in the cache

❑   Underused – the item was removed because the sliding expiration was exceeded or the system needed to remove the item to free system memory

System.Web.Configuration

The System.Web.Configuration namespace provides users with support for easily adding configurable properties to their applications. In the past, most developers will have had some experience with the use of .ini files, or possibly using registry keys, for persisting settings and options for an application. Exactly which of these two storage methods were used usually depended on individual developer's preferences. Regardless of the method used, the point was to allow applications to store and retrieve values and settings without having to recompile the application. It would be a maintenance and deployment nightmare if an application needed to be recompiled each time it needed to connect to a different database server. Instead of storing the database server name hardcoded into the application, developers stored that information separately. The application could then query either the registry or the .ini file and retrieve whatever information was needed.

Now, with ASP.NET, we have a new and more powerful approach to maintaining application settings and preferences – System.Web.Configuration. This approach uses .config files to store the information, and a Configuration object, provided by ASP.NET, to retrieve it.

Configuration File Types

In ASP.NET there are two types of configuration files, each used to specify configuration for a specific scope on the machine. The first type is the machine.config file, of which there can only be one on an ASP.NET server. This file is used to specify settings that apply to all ASP.NET applications on the server. All of the settings stored within the machine.config file are inherited by all of the ASP.NET applications.

The second type of file is the web.config file. Each ASP.NET web application can have its own web.config file, which can be used to override and/or extend the properties specified in machine.config.

To make sure this very important distinction is clear, if the machine.config file contained a setting specifying that session state is to be maintained, then that setting would apply to **all** ASP.NET applications on the server. However, if there were one application that was designed to be run without any session state being maintained, then that application could specify in its web.config file that no session state is to be kept. This information would then **only** be applied to that application.

The machine.config file would have a line of code similar to that overleaf. The file is stored in the .NET framework installation directory, in the Config folder.

```
<sessionState
    mode="InProc"
    cookieless="false"
    timeout="20" />
```

And, in order to disable session state for our ASP.NET application, we would create a web.config file containing this code in the application's root directory:

```
<sessionState
    mode="Off"/>
```

In Visual Studio.NET (and the .NET frameworks) there is also an application configuration file for non-ASP.NET applications.

Win32 applications created with the .NET frameworks can also take advantage of the configuration functionality of .NET. However, as this book is focused on ASP.NET, we will not be covering these topics in any greater detail.

To illustrate this point, let's look at an ASP.NET application that has some reporting, management, and simple browsing capabilities. In all cases, the application will want to access the same database server, but not necessarily the same database, or with the same login credentials. In a case like this, it would be best to include all the settings in the machine.config file and then only override the necessary settings in each application. This diagram shows the specifics:

machine.config

```
<appSettings>
        <add key=DatabaseServer value="MainSql">
        <add key=DatabaseDataSource
        value="Northwind"/>
        <add key=Login value=appUser/>
        <add key=PassWd value=appUser/>
</appSettings>
```

\wwwroot\Reports\web.config

```
<appSettings>
        <add key=DatabaseDataSource
        value="Reporting"/>
        <add key=Login value=reportUser/>
        <add key=PassWd value=reportUser/>
</appSettings>
```

\wwwroot\management\web.config

```
<appSettings>
        <add key=DtatabaseDataSource
        value="Personnel"/>
        <add key=Login value=adminUser/>
        <add key=PassWd value=adminUser/>
</appSettings>
```

In this case all applications, other than those in the Reports and Management directories, will access the Northwind database with the login information provided in the machine.config file. However, the Management ASP.NET application will access the Personnel database using different login credentials. Also, the Reports ASP.NET application will access the Reporting database using another set of login credentials. It is important to note that the child applications need not define a setting for the DatabaseServer property, as they will inherit this from machine.config.

Why use Configurable Properties?

Configurable properties are useful for the following reasons:

- ❑ Low-cost maintenance
- ❑ Flexibility of design
- ❑ Changes can be made without recompiling
- ❑ You can share a setting between multiple sections of code

We're going to illustrate these points with an example. Imagine a situation where an application is running, consisting of a database backend and an ASP.NET user interface, and is also making use of a number of Web Services.

The low cost of maintenance of the system is provided through the ability to quickly reconfigure the system. Instead of storing the database server information in the compiled code, that information can be a configurable property of the application. Once that is done, the administrator can easily configure the application for another server just by changing the values in the web.config file that is in the application's directory. This simple change also demonstrates how the use of configurable properties makes the application flexible. This application could easily be tailored for a variety of rollouts, and could be customized to a customer's needs by simply changing the properties file. Both of these benefits come about because of being able to make changes without having to recompile the code. If it were necessary to recompile the application each time a new database had to be used, then the application would lose its flexibility and low-cost maintenance.

The last benefit we note is the sharing of a setting between multiple sections of code. This benefit is not exclusively due to using configurable properties, but it is important. Understanding that the application may have multiple ASP.NET pages that involve database connections, we can see how each of those pages using the same properties would be important. You could reconfigure in the properties file for a change of database, and that change would then automatically be picked up by the different sections of code.

Configurable Properties versus .INI files

As we mentioned in the above section, the Classic ASP method of persisting a user's settings and preferences is either by storing the data in .ini files or in the system Registry. For this chapter, we will be focusing on the use of .ini files, as that is most similar to the use of configurable properties files.

One of the extremely important advantages of using .NET configuration files is that changes to the configuration are immediately and automatically effected on the application. As soon as the configurable property is changed, that value will be returned the next time the Configuration object is used in a query. With an .ini file, the application must either watch the file for changes, or be restarted in order for changes to be propagated. With configuration files, a change to the configuration file will cause any of the dependent web resources (database connections, and so on), to be updated to the new settings when the resources are next utilized.

As a quick refresher, we will take a look at the basic syntax and layout of an .ini file. Here is an example of what the .ini file might look like for an application:

```
[Login]
UserNameMask=########
PassWordMask=####
```

```
[Database]
DBServerName=db1
UserName=dbUser
Password=PaSsWoRd
Database=Northwind

[WebServices]
WSServerName=ws1
```

From this file, the application would be able to retrieve the settings that determine the username mask and password mask for when users login to the system. The application would also retrieve the information necessary for determining the database server and authentication information. The last bit of the .ini file provides the application with the name of the server providing the web services for this application.

One of the first, and most obvious, differences between an .ini file and an ASP.NET configuration file is that the configuration files are composed using XML, whereas .ini files are composed in plain text. Here is what the above .ini file would look like as a configuration file:

```
<configuration>
  <configSections>
    <section name="appSettings"
        type="System.Web.Configuration.NameValueSectionHandler" />
  </configSections>

  <appSettings>
    <add key="UserNameMask" value="########">
    <add key="PassWordMask" value="####">
    <add key="DBServerName" value="db1">
    <add key="UserName" value="dbUser">
    <add key="Password" value="PaSsWoRd">
    <add key="Database" value="Northwind">
    <add key="WSServerName" value="ws1">
  </appSettings>
</configuration>
```

The first thing that stands out in the XML version is the `<configSections>` tags. We'll discuss these in detail in the next section on *Configuration File Format*, for now we'll just say that this section declares the names and types of the different sections that will be defined within this configuration file.

After the `<configSection>` tags come a pair of `<appSettings>` tags (see their entry under *Configuration File Sections* for more detailed information), containing a number of elements containing key-value pairs. Here the line of:

```
<add Key="UserNameMask" value="########" />
```

is functionally similar to the following .ini file code:

```
UserNameMask="########"
```

Both of these lines create a new setting name and assign a value to that name. The configuration file approach is much more explicit in describing the actions that are occurring. It is clear from the XML file that a new key-value pair must be created for each of the application settings that are being configured. Each of these key-value pairs will 'declare' a new application setting (by the Key) and the value which is assigned to that setting (the value).

Another difference in the configuration files is that these files must be located within the same directory as the ASP.NET application (excepting `machine.config`). If the application is rooted at `c:\inetpub\wwwroot\SampleApp`, then the application's configuration file (`web.config`) would also have to exist at that location. This `web.config` file would then specify the configuration for files in the current directory as well as any child directories. Although it is possible for a `.ini` file to exist in the application's directory, that 'rule' is not enforced and `.ini` files can be placed anywhere on the machine.

There's an important note to make about security at this point, as it would appear at first glance that your configuration files would be obvious targets for people trying to gain unauthorized access to your applications. To prevent this ASP.NET will not serve requests for configuration files over HTTP. While you could configure your system to do this with `.ini` files, it is set up automatically for `.config` files.

Another difference between `.ini` and configuration files is that the configuration files are extensible. An `.ini` file is only extensible in that more key-value pairs may be added to the file, while a configuration file is extensible in any way that a developer desires. For example, you could create a new section handler that will process the XML tags within a section and return the appropriate collection.

Key Differences between Configuration and .INI files

.ini File	Configuration File
Changes not reflected without an application restart	Changes are seen next time property value is queried
Plain text format	XML format
Can be located anywhere that is accessible to the applications (even on network shares)	Must be located within the application's directory
Requires work to be done to prevent web server from processing request for the file	ASP.NET inherently will not serve any requests for `.config` file
Extensible via name-value pairs	Extensible via SectionHandlers however the developer sees fit

Configuration File Format

A configuration file must be created using well-formed XML (that is XML with a full complement of matching beginning and end tags correctly nested).

Bear in mind that XML is case-sensitive.

The root tags for a configuration file are the `<configuration>` tags. All of the application's configuration settings are contained within these tags. The file contains two areas: the `configSections` handler declarations, and the `configSections` definitions (settings). The `configSections` handler area is used to declare which `configSections` will be defined within the file, as well as the full path of the class that will be processing that section. From our above sample of a configuration file, here is a handler declaration:

```
<!-- Declare the section handler for the appSettings section -->
  <configSections>
    <section name="appSettings"
       type="System.Web.Configuration.NameValueSectionHandler" />
  </configSections>
```

This XML specifies that a section called `appSettings` will be defined in the file, and that the `NameValueSectionHandler` (from the `System.Web.Configuration` namespace) will be the class to process the information in that section. Also, you will note that the first line has a comment. Comments can be placed into an XML file just as they would be in an HTML file. They should be prefixed with a "`<!--`" and ending with a "`-->`".

All of the `configSections` handlers must be declared within the `configSections` tags. The `configSections` settings however, are not contained within an XML tag. All XML after the `configSections` tags is considered to be settings information. It is possible, and very likely, that a configuration file will contain more than one configuration section. There are a number of section handlers that are included in the .NET frameworks, and developers can also create their own. Here is a list of the section handles included with ASP.NET:

Handler	Purpose
DictionarySectionHandler	Process key-value pairs from the configuration file into a `Dictionary` object
NameValueSectionHandler	Process name-value pairs from the configuration file
SingleTagSectionHandler	Process and provide access to all key-value pairs from a configuration section
SessionStateSectionHandler	Process web session settings from a configuration section
DiagnosticsConfigurationHandler	Process settings from the <Diagnostics> section.

Two of the provided handlers, `DiagnosticsConfigurationHandler` and `SessionStateSectionHandler`, are used to interact directly with ASP.NET intrinsic objects and settings. The `SessionStateHandler` reads from the configuration file and sets the session state values and properties based on the tags within the `<SessionState>` section of the file. The `DiagnosticsConfigurationHandler` will be applied to all properties within the `<Diagnostics>` section of the file. A typical use of the `Diagnostics` section would be to enable debugging or tracing for the application.

Furthermore, as we noted, it is also possible to create your own configuration section handlers. We mentioned earlier that it is possible that a web application would serve HDML, HTML, and WML clients. It is also very likely that the application would want to set different timeout values for each of these clients. An easy way to expose the different timeout values to the application would be to use the configuration file.

The first step is to create a new section handler. This is done by implementing the `IConfigurationSectionHandler` interface in your class. The only method of this interface is a `Create` method. The definition of the `Create` method is:

```
Object Create( object parent, object configContext, XmlNode section);
```

Parameter	Description
Parent	Contains the configuration settings from the parent configuration in `machine.config` (if such a section exists).

Parameter	Description
configContext	Virtual path for determining config values. Typically is null and not used.
XmlNode	An XmlNode object containing the XML for the section.

Within the Create method, the code would need to iterate through the XML tags within the section and handle them appropriately. If we were writing our own key-value pair handlers for specifying different timeouts based on the client type, then the code would be similar to this:

```
public static object create( object parent, object configContext, XmlNode section)
{
  String sClientName;
  String sTimeout;
  HashtablehashTable = new Hashtable();

  // Ensure that the nodes have values
  if (section.HasChildNodes)
  {
    for (int i=0; i < section.ChildNodes.Count;i++)
    {
      // Then retrieve each name/value pair from node's attributes
      sClientName = section.ChildNodes.Item(i).Attributes.Item(0).Value;
      sTimeout = section.ChildNodes.Item(i).Attributes.Item(1).Value;
      // And add them to the hastable.
      hashTable.Add(sClientName, sTimeout);
    }
  }
  // When completed, return the hashtable
  return hashTable;
}
```

The class would then implement the code to process the XML within a specific section of the configuration file and return a Configuration object. The definition of that Configuration object is up to the developer, as it can be any data structure.

Here is how the settings would appear:

```
<timeoutSettings>
  <add Client="HDML" Timeout="300"/>
  <add Client="WML" Timeout="300"/>
  <add Client="HTML" Timeout="1800"/>
</timeoutSettings>
```

You would create a new configuration section handler that would process the XML tags and add each Client type as a key, and the Timeout value as the value in a Dictionary object. This would allow your application to easily retrieve the timeout value from the configuration object with code similar to this:

```
iTimeOut = myConfig("HTML");
```

Although the included section handlers provide some powerful functionality, the system is designed so that developers can extend the configuration file as needed for their applications. Handlers can be created in VB.NET, C#, or C++. So each developer is able to choose their preference.

Now that we have covered the basics of configuration files, and compared them to .ini files, we will dig even deeper into the multitude of sections that are supported within a standard .NET installation.

Configuration File Sections

Now that we have looked into how a configuration file is processed and used, the next step is to look into the actual contents of the file in greater depth. Within a configuration file, there are a number of sections that have section handlers provided by ASP.NET. We will list them here, and then look at them, individually, in more detail:

- ❑ appSettings
- ❑ browserCaps
- ❑ compilation
- ❑ globalization
- ❑ httpHandlers
- ❑ httpModules
- ❑ identity
- ❑ pages
- ❑ processModel
- ❑ securityPolicy
- ❑ sessionState
- ❑ trace
- ❑ webServices

The appSettings Section

The appSettings section contains application-specific settings. Database connection information would typically be placed here. The section is composed of <add> tags, which add configuration settings as key-value pairs:

```
<appSettings>
  ...
  <add key="<KeyName>" value="<KeyValue>">
  ...
</appSettings>
```

These configuration settings can then be retrieved at run time using the Configuration object and querying for the value of the desired key. For example, if we were storing database connection information in our appSettings section, the configuration file would look like this:

```
<appSettings>
  <add key="DBServerName" value="db1">
  <add key="UserName" value="dbUser">
  <add key="Password" value="PaSsWoRd">
  <add key="Database" value="Northwind">
</appSettings>
```

Then, in the application code, we would be able to build the connection string using these properties:

```
public string getConnectionString()
{
  String sConnString;

  sConnString = "user id=" + ConfigurationSettings.AppSettings("UserName");
  sConnString += ";password=" + ConfigurationSettings.AppSettings ("Password");
  sConnString += ";initial catalog=" + ConfigurationSettings.AppSettings
                                                        ("Database");
  sConnString += ";server=" + ConfigurationSettings.AppSettings ("DBServerName");

  return (sConnString);
}
```

As you can see from this code, all of the properties specified in the `appSettings` section are accessible using the `ConfigurationSettings.AppSettings` property. This returns a name-value collection which makes it possible to query for setting's values based on the setting's name.

The browserCaps Section

The `browserCaps` section is used to specify the default browser capabilities. This is useful in the event that the ASP.NET browser capabilities component is unable to determine any of the browser's capabilities. In those cases, the default value will be returned by the `HttpBrowserCapabilities` class. For those familiar with the classic ASP `Browscap.ini`, you will see that it has basically been converted from an INI file into an XML file and made available through the `System.Web.Configuration` objects.

Here is an example of a `browserCaps` section:

```
<browserCaps>
  <result type="System.Web.HttpBrowserCapabilities" />
  <use var="HTTP_USER_AGENT" />

  browser="Unknown"
  version=0.0
  majorver=0
  minorver=0
  frames=false
  tables=false

  <filter>
    <case match="Windows 95 | Win95">
    platform=Win95
    </case>
    <case match="Windows NT | WinNT">
      platform=WinNT
    </case>
  </filter>
</browserCaps>
```

In the event that the browser capabilities cannot be determined by the `HttpBrowserCapabilites` object, these default values will be used instead. Although it will not happen often, it can do if a new browser is used, or if a request is made to the server from a browser that is not recognized, or not supported. In ASP.NET applications, the browser capabilities are exposed via the `Browser` property of the `Request` object. For a welcome page that redirects browsers to either a frame-based site or a non-frames site, the page could have this code:

```
HttpBrowserCapabilities bc = Request.Browser;
If (!bc.Frames)
   Response.Redirect("NoFrame.aspx");
Else
   Response.Redirect("FrameSet.aspx");
```

In the event that the browser could not be determined by the application, the value of the `bc.Frames` property would be determined by what was set in the configuration file.

The compilation Section

The compilation section is used to specify the compile options for ASP.NET applications. These options include specifying which compiler to use for specific file extensions, which assemblies to reference during compilation, and which namespaces to include at compilation time. An example of this section is:

```
<compilation defaultLanguage="C#"
             debug="false"
             numRecompilesBeforeAppRestart="15"
             explicit="true"
             strict="true"
             batch="false" >

   <compilers>
     <compiler language="VB;VBScript"
               extension=".cls"
               type="Microsoft.VB.VBCodeProvider,System" />
     <compiler language="C#;Csharp"
               extension=".cs"
               type="Microsoft.CSharp.CSharpCodeProvider,System" />
   </compilers>

   <assemblies>
     <add assembly="*" />
   </assemblies>

   <namespaces>
     <add namespace="System.Web" />
     <add namespace="System.Web.UI" />
     <add namespace="System.Web.UI.WebControls" />
     <add namespace="System.Web.UI.HtmlControls" />
   </namespaces>

</compilation>
```

The first tag in this section is the `<compilation>` tag. This has seven properties that can be specified as follows; a second table is included below to show the default values:

Property	Purpose
debug	Specifies whether to compile retail (finished product) binaries or debug binaries.
defaultLanguage	Provides a semicolon-separated list of language names to use in dynamic compilation files. For example, "C#; PERL".

Property	Purpose
explicit	Indicates the setting of the VB explicit option.
batch	Indicates whether batching is supported.
batchTimeout	Indicates the time-out period for batch compilation. If compilation cannot be completed within the time-out period, the compiler reverts to single compilation mode.
numRecompilesBeforeAppRestart	Indicates the number of dynamic recompiles of resources that can occur before the application restarts. This attribute is supported at the global and application level but not at the directory level.
strict	Indicates the setting of the VB strict option.

Here is a listing of the possible values that can be specified for the properties:

debug	
debug=true	Debug binaries are generated by the compiler
debug=false	Retail/Ship binaries are generated by the compiler
defaultLanguage	
defaultLanguage=C#	Use C# as the default language for compiling
defaultLanguage=VB	Use VB.NET as the default language for compiling
explicit	
explicit=true	(VB Only) Force all variables to be declared
explicit=false	(VB Only) Allow use of undeclared variables
batch	
batch=true	Batching is supported
batch=false	Batching is not supported
batchTimeout	

Table continued on following page

debug	
`batchTimeout=n`	Set timeout to *n* seconds for batch compiling

numRecompilesBeforeAppRestart	
`numRecompilesBeforeAppRestart=n`	Dynamically recompile the resources *n* times before restarting the application.

strict	
`strict=true`	(VB Only) For VB to enforce semantics
`strict=false`	(VB Only) For VB not to enforce semantics

The next tag, within the `<compilation>` section, is the `<compilers>` section. This section is used to specify which compilers will handle the different file types. The section is composed of one or more `<compilers>` tags. Each compiler tag specifies which compiler will be used on which files, and also which compile settings will be used. There are five properties that are specified for each `<compilers>` tag:

Property	Purpose
`Language`	Specifies the language type the compiler will handle
`Extension`	Specifies the file extension that the compiler will handle (".cs")
`Type`	Specifies the .NET framework class used to compile the file
`warningLevel`	Specifies the warning level for the compiler
`compilerOptions`	Specifies any compiler-specific options to be used during compilation

The last two tags in the `<compilation>` section are used to indicate which assemblies and namespaces should be included at compile time. The `<assemblies>` tag contains zero or more `<add assembly>` tags, each specifying the name of an assembly to be included. The `<namespace>` tag, similarly, contains zero or more `<add namespace>` tags that each specify a namespace to include.

The globalization Section

The `<globalization>` section is used to specify any globalization options for the ASP.NET application. These options include the encoding options as well as any cultural information. This section is composed entirely of a single XML tag with multiple attributes that can be specified:

```
<globalization
    requestEncoding=<EncodingMethod>
    responseEncoding=<EncodingMethod>
```

```
    fileEncoding=<EncodingMethod>
    culture= <Culture>
    uiCulture= <Culture> />
```

The `requestEncoding`, `responseEncoding`, and `fileEncoding` properties are used to specify the encoding method for requests, responses, and files handled by the ASP.NET application. These settings can be used to override a server's Regional Options settings for the `Encoding` method. The `requestEncoding` property specifies which encoding method is to be used for processing requests, while the `responseEncoding` property specifies the method to be used for processing/generating responses from the server.

In many cases, it is not necessary to specify all of these properties, and it is completely possible not to declare any of them. The properties are given defaults in the `machine.config` file. Any property that is not specified in the configuration file will result in ASP.NET using the default properties specified in the server's Regional Settings. Typically, the `requestEncoding` and `responseEncoding` properties are most often used, though, for the most part, they will not have to be set.

The `Culture` value is used to specify the `CultureInfo` object from which to retrieve culture-specific information. This information typically defines the proper formatting of dates and numbers, default languages, and country or region information. The `Culture` property is used to specify the culture used when handling requests to the web server. The `uiCulture` property is used to specify the culture used when executing locale-dependent resource searches.

The full list of cultures is extensive, and can be found in the .NET framework documentation, though here are some of the most commonly used:

CultureString	Country & Language
en-US	US– English
en-GB	Great Britain – English
de	German
de-DE	Germany – German
fr-CA	Canada – French
it	Italian
ru-RU	Russia – Russian
es-MX	Mexico – Spanish
zh-CHS	China – Chinese (Simplified)

Here is an example of a `<globalization>` section in which we specify encoding methods to be "US ASCII" and the culture to be "US English".

```
<globalization
  requestEncoding="us-ascii"
  responseEncoding="ISO-8859-1"
```

```
        culture="en-US"
        uiCulture="en-US" />
```

The only property from the globalization section that has an easily identified impact on the resulting web pages is the `responseEncoding` property. We can see the effect of this property's setting when examining the headers of an ASP.NET page in the browser's View Source command. In the headers is a line specifying the `content-type` and `charset`. For many pages, the line appears like this:

```
<META HTTP-EQUIV="content-type" CONTENT="text/html; charset=ISO-8859-1">
```

It has a marked impact as it determines the character set to use in displaying the page.

The httpHandlers Section

Using IIS 5, administrators and developers used the MMC Console to configure IIS so that incoming requests were processed by the correct handlers. This caused some issues when products were rolled out and the web server was not correctly configured. Sometimes a web server would completely stop functioning and return either an HTTP 500 (Internal Server Error) or HTTP 404 (File not Found) response to the client machines. In some cases, determining the cause of the issue was very difficult, and it was not at all clear that the problem was caused by a misconfigured server. Now, with ASP.NET, it is possible to configure request handlers via the XML-based configuration files instead of the MMC console. This greatly simplifies the task of rolling out an ASP.NET application from a development web server to a production web server.

Any settings in the configuration files will override those from the Internet Services MMC, but will **only** apply to ASP.NET applications. So now, in order to rollout a product to a web server, it is only necessary to copy the needed web file and the configuration files. Once the configuration files are placed on the machine, it will then have the web configuration that the developer requires for ASP.NET. This makes life much easier, as all settings can now be set simply by copying a file, rather than having to manually set options in the MMC.

The `<httpHandlers>` section is used to specify the classes that will process specific HTTP requests that come into the server. For example, IIS currently uses application mappings to allow for extending a web server's functionality. The IDQ files are a good example of this, as they are query files that interact with Windows 2000's Indexing Service. If you were to look at the Application Configuration settings for the web server, you would see something similar to this:

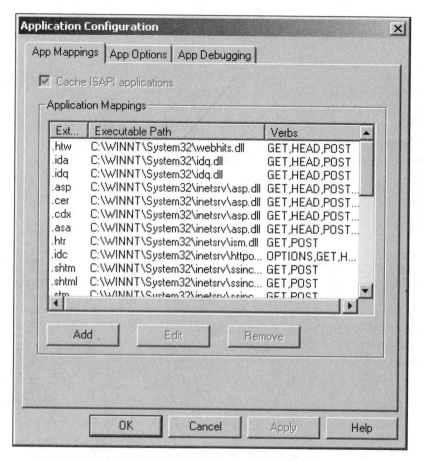

Here you can see that the web server has a mapping such that all files with an .idq extension are processed through the idq.dll. You can also see that this mapping applies to GET, HEAD, and POST requests to the server.

Now, with ASP.NET, this same mapping could be configured using this XML:

```
<httpHandlers>
  <add verb="GET, HEAD, POST"
       path="*.idq"
       type="idq,idq.dll" />
</httpHandlers>
```

In addition to adding httpHandlers, this section can also be used to remove handlers that were inherited from either the system.config or the parent directory. If we wanted to remove the idq handler, the section would appear like this:

```
<httpHandlers>
  <remove verb="GET, HEAD, POST"
          path="*.idq"  />
</httpHandlers>
```

And, as another option in the `httpHandlers` section, it is possible to remove all application `httpHandlers` mappings by using the `<clear>` tag:

```
<httpHandlers>
  <clear />
</httpHandlers>
```

Any of the settings in the `httpHandlers` section will apply not only to the existing directory, but to any directory below it as well. The subdirectories can also define their own `web.config` file and override the inherited settings. For example, if a web application was written such that it wanted not to allow IDQ files to be requested, then it would have this in its `web.config` file:

```
<httpHandlers>
  <remove verb="GET,HEAD, POST"
  path="*.idq" >
</httpHanlders>
```

The httpModules Section

The `httpModules` section is used to determine which `httpModules` will be loaded with the ASP.NET application. `httpModules` are objects that are involved in each request to the server. These modules all expose events, which a developer can catch and process in the web application's `global.asax`. The `httpModules` included with ASP.NET are listed here, along with their function:

Module	Function
DefaultAuthenticationModule	Provides an `Authentication` object that can be used within the application
FileAuthorizationModule	Ensures that a user has the correct permissions to access the requested file
FormsAuthenticationModule	Provides the application with the ability to use `FormsAuthentication`
PassportAuthenticationModule	Provides wrapper functions for integrating `PassportAuthentication` into .NET applications
SessionStateModule	Provides the basic IIS session state object
UrlAuthorizationModule	Provides for authenticating access to a file or server resource via a URL
WindowsAuthenticationModule	Provides the application with the ability to use `WindowsAuthentication`

Once a module is loaded with the application, the ASP.NET code can then make use of it. Since those familiar with Classic ASP will be familiar with `Sessions`, we will look at the `SessionStateModule`. This module provides the application with the `Session` object. In order to be able to use `Session` objects, we must include the `SessionStateModule` in the application's configuration file. The syntax for this would be:

```
<httpModules>
  <add type="System.Web.State.SessionStateModule" name="Session">
</httpModules>
```

But, since session state is widely used in ASP.NET applications, the `machine.config` file already includes this module, so there is no need to declare it in `web.config`.

The inclusion of this module allows the .NET application to handle events for the `Session` object:

```
<Script language="c#" runat="server">
  void Session_OnStart()
{
  Utils.LogSessionStart(sUserID);
}
void Session_OnEnd()
{
  Utils.LogSessionEnd(sUserID);
}
</Script>
```

This code could be used for a data-warehouse application where it is necessary to track user's time spent on the server. In this case, it is assumed that the `sUserID` has either been retrieved from the user's Cookie or from a database lookup.

The identity Section

The `<identity>` section of the configuration file can be used to specify a user account under which the web application is run. This can be used when you wish to have the web processes run with the same permissions as the user accessing the site (using NTFS Authentication) or to always force the web processes to run under a certain account. See Chapter 9 for more information about web security.

The format of the identity section is:

```
<identity
  impersonate="True | False"
  username="<username>"
  password="<password>"
/>
```

The `impersonate` attribute determines whether client impersonation is used. If `impersonate` is set to `False`, then the web application executes with the permissions of the username and password values supplied. If a web application should allow resource access based on the requesting user's own permissions, then the identity section would be:

```
<identity
  impersonate="True"
/>
```

Furthermore, any processes or resource requests executed by the web application would be run under the user account of the user that is requesting the page.

Alternatively, to give all users the same access, then the `<identity>` section should look like this:

```
<identity
  impersonate="False"
  username="WebUser"
  password="WebPass"
/>
```

The pages Section

The `<pages>` section from the configuration files is used to specify any page-specific settings for an ASP.NET application. There are six different page attributes that can be specified in this section. The format is:

```
<pages
  buffer="true | false"
  enableSessionState="true | false | ReadOnly"
  enableViewState="true | false"
  autoEventWireup="true | false"
  pageBaseType="typename, assembly"
  userControlBaseType="typename"/>
```

The attributes for the `<pages>` section are:

Attribute	Function
buffer	Specify whether response buffering is used for requested pages (True=Yes, False=No)
enableSessionState	Specify whether session state variables are available to the page (True=Yes, False=No, ReadOnly=can only be read, not written)
enableViewState	Specify whether View State tracking is enabled or disabled
autoEventWireup	Specify whether page events are automatically executed
pageBaseType	Specify the base class from which .aspx pages inherit
userControlBaseType	Specify the base class from which user controls inherit

For an ASP.NET application that is designed to have buffered pages, use session state, and disable View State tracking, the web.config would have this section :

```
<pages
  buffer=true
  enableSessionState=true
  enableViewState = false />
```

The processModel Section

The `<processModel>` section of the configuration file is used to determine the ASP.NET process model settings for an IIS web server. This section can be used to enable or disable the process model, specify the maximum number of requests that are to be queued before throwing a `"Server Too Busy"` error, and many other settings. The ASP.NET Process Model can be used to improve the scalability of an application, enable multiple processes for an application, and spread those processes across the CPUs in the web server. The format of the section is:

```
<processmodel
  enable="true | false"
  timeout="# minutes"
  idleTimeout"# minutes"
  shutdownTimeout="HH:MM:SS"
  requestLimit="#"
  requestQueueLimit="#"
  memoryLimit="%"
  cpuMask="#"
  webGarden="true | false"
  username="username"
  password="password"
/>
```

The properties are:

Property	Function
enable	True – enable process model False – disable process model
timeout	Number of minutes until IIS replaces a current process with a new one
idleTimeout	Number of minutes until IIS shuts down an idle process
shutdownTimeout	Number of minutes that the process has to shut itself down; after this time, IIS will shut down the process
requestLimit	Number of requests after which IIS will launch a new process and replace the existing one
requestQueueLimit	Number of requests required in the queue before IIS will throw an Error 503, Server Too Busy
memoryLimit	Maximum percentage of system memory that a process can use before IIS will launch a new process
cpuMask	Determines which processors (on a multi-processor system) can be used for ASP.NET processes
webGarden	True – Windows determines which CPU to use False – the cpuMask attribute is used to determine which CPU to use

Table continued on following page

Property	Function
username	The username of an account under which the process will run
password	The password for the username

The securityPolicy Section

The `securityPolicy` section is used to associate named security levels with specific policy files. These policy files contain sets of restrictions and rules that are used when determining what access ASP.NET code will have to other code as well as to the system's resources. The format of this section is:

```
<securityPolicy>
    <trustLevel name="Level" policyFile="FileName" />
    ...
</securityPolicy>
```

The `trustLevel` tag has attributes that specify the name used in reference to the policy file, as well as the full path to the policy file. This section allows administrators to easily configure multiple servers with the same security settings. Once the administrator or developer has created `Low_Security.config`, `High_Security.config`, and `No_Security.config` files for the web servers, each `web.config` file would have this section in it:

```
<securityPolicy>
    <trustLevel name="High" policyFile="High_Security.config" />
    <trustLevel name="Low"  policyFile="Low_Security.config" />
    <trustLevel name="None" policyFile="No_Security.config" />
</securityPolicy>
```

The sessionState Section

Earlier, in the section on `httpModules`, we mentioned the `SessionState` module. Most developers with ASP experience have had experience with the `Session` object. Now, with ASP.NET applications, the `sessionState` HTTP module is configured using the values from the `<sessionState>` section in `web.config`. The format of this tag is:

```
<sessionState
    mode="Off | Inproc | StateServer | SqlServer"
    cookieless="True | False"
    timeout="# Minutes"
    connectionString="Server:Port"
    sqlConnectionString="sql connection string"
/>
```

The `mode` attribute determines where and how the session state is maintained. The `Off` mode means that no session state is maintained. `Inproc` means that the session state is maintained by the local machine. The `StateServer` mode uses a different server to maintain session state, while `SqlServer` mode also uses a different server, but maintains the session state in a SQL database.

Both of these last two options are useful when using a web farm and wishing to maintain user's sessions across multiple servers. With a remote state server, it is not necessary for a user to remain on one server. That user's session will be maintained as their requests are farmed out to the multiple servers, since each of the servers will be configured to use the same, remote server for maintaining the session state.

By default, as specified in the `machine.config` shipped with ASP.NET, session state is set to `InProc` mode, `cookieless` equals `false`, and a `timeout` of 20 minutes is set:

```
<sessionState
  mode="InProc"
  cookieless="false"
  timeout="20" />
```

For this tag, the `connectionString` and `sqlConnectionString` attributes are mutually exclusive. The `connectionString` attribute is only applicable if the session mode is set to `StateServer`. Likewise, the `sqlConnectionString` is only applicable when the session mode is set to `SqlServer`. If the mode is set to `InProc`, then neither the `connectionString` nor the `sqlConnectionString` attributes are used.

Here is how you would configure a web site to maintain session state on the machine, enable the use of cookies, and set a 30 minute timeout for the session:

```
<sessionState
  mode="Inproc"
  cookieless="False"
  timeout="30"
/>
```

And, for a web farm environment, the session state would be configured to use a SQL server for maintaining state:

```
<sessionState
  mode="SqlServer"
  cookieless="False"
  sqlConnectionString="data source=StateServer;user
id=userstate;password=userstate"
  timeout="30"
/>
```

The trace Section

The `<trace>` section of the configuration file is used to enable tracing for the web site, as well as to configure the output from the trace service. The format of the section is:

```
<trace
  enabled="True | False"
  requestLimit="# Requests"
  pageOutput="True | False"
  traceMode="SortByTime | SortByCategory"
  localOnly="True | False"
/>
```

The `enabled` attribute determines whether tracing is enabled (`true`) or disabled (`false`) for the web application. The `requestLimit` attribute specifies the number of requests that are stored. Once the server has processed that number of trace requests, the oldest requests will be over-written on the server. The `pageOutput` attribute determines whether the trace output is appended to the ASP.NET pages (`true`) or if the output is only available via the .NET `Trace` utility (`false`). The `traceMode` attribute is used to sort the trace results, either by Time, or by user-defined Categories. Lastly, the `localOnly` attribute determines if the trace viewer is only available on the local server.

To configure an ASP.NET application to append trace information to ASP.NET pages, the `web.config` would have a trace section like this:

```
<trace
  Enabled="True"
  requestLimit="20"
  pageOutput="True"
  traceMode="SortByTime"
  localOnly="True"
/>
```

The webServices Section

Later in this book we will cover the new ASP.NET feature of Web Services. The configuration and operation of these services is specified within the `<webServices>` section of the configuration file. It is in this section that Web Services on the machine are configured. The section can contain a number of types for the following properties:

`Protocol`	Define which protocols will be used for the Web Service
`returnWriter`	The class that will be used for formatting and writing the return from the Web Service
`parameterReader`	The classes that can be used for reading parameters in Web Service calls
`mimeReflector`	The classes that can be used for determining information on MIME objects
`protocolReflector`	The classes that can be used for determining information on the protocol used
`protocolImporter`	The classes that can be used for importing information on the protocol
`mimeImporter`	The classes that can be used for importing information on MIME objects
`protocolInfo`	The classes used to retrieve information on the protocol
`mimeInfo`	The classes used to retrieve information on the MIME object
`soapExtension`	Allows the developer to specify custom extensions for handling SOAP request/response
`soapExtensionReflector`	The reflector/info class for the custom extensions specified in `soapExtension`
`soapExtensionImporter`	The importer class for the custom extensions specified in `soapExtension`

Since these settings will be covered in detail in Chapter 12 on Web Services, we will not go into great detail on this here, but will simply give a brief example of what a section of `<webServices>` looks like in the `machine.config` file:

```
<webServices>
  <protocolTypes>
    <add type="System.Web.Services.Protocols.SoapServerProtocol" />
    <add type="System.Web.Services.Protocols.HttpServerProtocol" />
    <add type="System.Web.Services.Protocols.DiscoveryServerProtocol" />
  </protocolTypes>
  <returnWriterTypes>
    <add type="System.Web.Services.Protocols.XmlReturnWriter" />
  </returnWriterTypes>
  <parameterReaderTypes>
    <add type="System.Web.Services.Protocols.HtmlFormParameterReader" />
    <add type="System.Web.Services.Protocols.UrlParameterReader" />
  </parameterReaderTypes>
  <protocolReflectorTypes>
    <add type="System.Web.Services.Description.SoapProtocolInfoReflector" />
    <add type="System.Web.Services.Description.HttpPostProtocolInfoReflector" />
    <add type="System.Web.Services.Description.HttpGetProtocolInfoReflector" />
  </protocolReflectorTypes>
  <mimeReflectorTypes>
    <add type="System.Web.Services.Description.XmlMimeInfoReflector" />
    <add type="System.Web.Services.Description.FormInfoReflector" />
  </mimeReflectorTypes>
</webServices>

...
```

It is unlikely that developers will need to make many changes to this section of the configuration files, though those wanting to extend SOAP will need to add extensions to their `web.config` files to utilize their amendments.

The Location Tag

Although it is not a separate section, the `<location>` tag is an important tag for configuration files. This tag allows specification of different configurations within the same configuration file. For example, assume a web application has three subdirectories: HTML, WML, and HDML. In this case, it would be much easier to have a single `web.config` file that specified the properties for all of the directories. The `<location>` tag is what allows this to happen. In order to specify the configuration properties for multiple directories, it is necessary to contain the properties within `<location>` tags.

To specify different session and timeout details for these directories you could create a `web.config` file like this:

```
<configuration>
  <system.web>
    <sessionState cookieless="false"/>
  </system.web>

  <location path="HDML">
    <system.web>
      <sessionState timeout="5"/>
      <httpHandlers>
        <add verb="*" path="*.hdml" type="web.Hdml"/>
      </httpHandlers>
    </system.web>
  </location>

  <location path="WML">
    <system.web>
      <sessionState timeout="2"/>
```

```
    <httpHandlers>
        <add verb="*" path="*.wml" type="web.Wml"/>
    </httpHandlers>
  </system.web>
</location>

<location path="HTML">
  <system.web>
    <sessionState timeout="30"/>
  </system.web>
</location>

</configuration>
```

In this example, both the HDML and WML directories will have an httpHandler included so that the directories can correctly process HDML and WML files respectively. As a result of this configuration file, each of the directories has a different session timeout value as well that so the server can adapt to the different conditions.

Using Configurable Properties

Hopefully by this point you can see what useful, flexible, and powerful structures configuration files are. We're now going to finish the chapter with a brief look at how information can be stored in a configuration file, and then accessed from your code.

The web.config file below specifies a variety of settings that might be of use to a fictional company wanting to access company phone book information both from web browsers (HTML) and wireless devices (HDML).

It stores a connection string to a database, as key-value pairs, in the <appSettings> section, dictates the type of session state to be maintained, specifies the type of encoding to be used, and sets compilation to debug.

```
<configuration>
  <system.web>
  <appSettings>
    <add key="DBServerName" value="PhoneSrv">
    <add key="UserName" value="WebUser">
    <add key="Password" value="WebPass">
    <add key="Database" value="ContactList">
  </appSettings>
  <compilation
    debug="True"
  />
  <globalization
    requestEncoding="UTF-8"
    responseEncoding="UTF-8"
  />
  <sessionState
    mode="Inproc"
    cookieless="True"
    timeout="5"
  />
  </system.web>
</configuration>
```

Using Configurable Properties in code

As we've seen earlier the majority of this information is automatically applied – any compiled code will now be generated as debug code because of the settings we've included in `web.config`. Likewise, session state is now set to be "in process", with no need for us to do anything in our code.

The exception to this is the database connection information, which needs to be actively collected from the configuration file by our code. The function we've outlined below is used to do this.

```
public string getDBConnectionString()
{
  String sConnString;

  // Build the SQL connect string based on settings in the web.config file
  sConnString = "user id=" + ConfigurationSettings.AppSettings("UserName");
  sConnString += ";password=" + ConfigurationSettings.AppSettings("Password");
  sConnString += ";initial catalog=" +
                            ConfigurationSettings.AppSettings("Database");
  sConnString += ";server=" + ConfigurationSettings.AppSettings("DBServerName");

  return (sConnString);
}
```

Here, the connection information is being collected from the `AppSettings` property of the `ConfigurationSettings` class. Once this information has been harvested from the configuration file and placed into a string it can then be used freely within the rest of the application. This technique can be used to collect any information you choose to store as a key-value pair in the configuration files, all you need do is change the key name to that of your custom pair.

Writing Configurable Properties?

As a final note, it is worth pointing out that, unfortunately, the .NET configurable properties do not support writing values at run time. Configurable properties can only be read from `.config` files and they cannot be written to these files from the application. This is important to note because one immediate application for configurable properties could be for persisting user preferences. If it is desirable for the application to persist user preferences, then the application should make use of cookies (or the `viewState` capabilities of ASP.NET).

The one exception to writing to configuration files is the VS.NET development environment. Once an object's property is set to be a configurable property, then changes made to that property in the User Interface will be reflected in the `web.config` file for that application.

Security & System.Web.Security

For many web applications the ability to securely and accurately identify users is paramount. The classes in the `System.Web.Security` namespace enable you to easily implement user authentication in your web applications. User authentication is the process of confirming the identity of a user based on credentials that they provide.

Credentials are pieces of information that allow applications to verify that the user is who they claim to be. The most common credentials offered are a username and password pair. Once the user has been authenticated, ASP.NET's authentication providers maintain the user's identity through out the lifetime of their session. You can interact with this user authentication process at several levels to modify its operation, for example, by creating your own custom objects to hold the users' identities.

In previous versions, ASP did not provide support for any type of authentication, though you could kludge a workaround that enabled Windows authentication. This was because if you enabled authentication in IIS the username of the currently authenticated user would become available in the Server variables collection. This could be accessed with the ASP code, below:

```
Dim aUserName
aUserName = Request.ServerVariables("LOGON_USER")
```

ASP.NET provides built-in support for user authentication through three authentication providers: Forms, Passport, and Windows. In this chapter, we are going to begin with a short primer on the basic concepts behind user authentication. After that, we will move into discussing the three authentication providers in detail. Then, following these overview sections, we'll dig into the actual APIs of the classes involved in authentication from the `System.Security.Principal` and `System.Web.Security` namespaces in .NET.

ASP.NET Security Overview

To understand how security works in ASP.NET, you need to understand its three key aspects: **impersonation**, **authorization**, and **authentication**. Before we start examining user authentication in ASP.NET, let's go over some background information on what impersonation is, and how it works. After that, we'll look at authorization and the part it plays in the authentication process.

Impersonation in ASP.NET

Any web request that runs in IIS is running under the security context of a Windows user account. This process is known as impersonation. In the context of this discussion, this means that a piece of running code is executing under the identity of a specific Windows user account.

For public web sites that do not require users to log in to Windows, IIS provides a guest account under which requests can be impersonated, commonly called the **Anonymous User**. When IIS is installed, it creates this account, with the name IUSR_*machinename* where *machinename* is the name of the computer at the time of installation.

In previous versions, ASP always impersonated the user account that IIS was using to serve the request. In ASP.NET, however, this is no longer the default behavior, because impersonation is disabled by default. This means that all requests in ASP.NET run under the identity of the **System** account. This is a special Windows account with virtually unlimited access to the resources on the local machine. This may be a security concern for some implementations, especially for an Internet Service Provider (ISP) that allows users to upload ASP.NET code to the server. In addition, the System account does not have access to network resources, such as file shares or printers on remote servers.

For situations when impersonation in required in ASP.NET, it can be enabled with the following code:

```
<system.web>
    <identity impersonate="true | false " userName="user" password="Password"/>
</system.web>
```

If the `impersonate` attribute is set to `"true"`, all requests will run under the identity that IIS is using to serve the request, in the manner of the classic ASP model. If enable is set to `"false"`, you can specify a specific Windows account that ASP.NET should impersonate when running requests by specifying a user name and password.

Impersonation can also be imposed at run time. You can switch the current account that code is running under by calling the `WindowsIdentity.Impersonate` method. See the `WindowsIdentity` class under the `System.Security.Principal` section of this chapter for more details.

Authorization in ASP.NET

Authorization is the process of determining if the current user is permitted access to the resources they have requested. If they have not yet logged on, and the resource requires authentication, they will be directed to a login prompt. Once they have logged in, authorization takes place for every request that they make to ensure they're allowed to see the information that they're requesting. This authorization process allows different users to have different levels of permissions. You can ensure that all, or part, of your web site is protected by a login by designing it to fail authorization for requests from users that have not logged in. This can be done in one of two ways:

❑ If you're using the Windows authentication provider you can restrict access to the specific physical files and directories using ACL (Access Control List) Authorization. The main caveat of this approach is that it requires physical configuration changes to the server, which can be tricky to manage.

❑ You can restrict access based on the URL requested by the user. This can be specified in changes to the web.config file. This method allows easier deployment of a web application. Because the web.config is installed with the application, no further server configuration is required.

Let's look at these two methods of restricting access in a little more detail:

ACL Authorization

ACL (Access Control List) authorization is built into the Windows server file system, commonly known as NTFS. Access can be explicitly granted to specific Windows users or groups using the standard Windows server file access control dialogue through the Security sheet of the file, or directory, Property dialog presented by Windows Explorer. ACL authorization will fail for the anonymous user account if one of the following conditions is true:

❑ The anonymous account does not have read access to the file requested in the URL

❑ The anonymous account does not have rights to some other system resource needed to complete the current request

❑ Anonymous authentication is disabled for the current directory or virtual directory in IIS

If ACL authorization fails, IIS issues a challenge to the browser, which results in a login dialog being displayed to the user. The user must then log in with an appropriate Windows Account that has sufficient access rights to complete the current request. For this reason, ACL Authorization is best used in conjunction with Windows Authentication. Windows Authentication will be discussed in more detail later in this chapter.

URL Authorization

URL authorization is a much more flexible method for controlling access in a web application than ACL authorization. Authorization of users for specific URLs is controlled by settings in the web.config file. If URL authorization fails, the user's authentication is challenged by forcing them to log in.

This method of authorization allows applications to use authentication methods such as Forms Authentication and Passport Authentication without creating Windows accounts for each user. Using this system authorization can be configured by roles, as well as by users.

Modifying web.config and adding a <location> element that specifies a directory or file can restrict access to certain areas. An example of this is shown below; the path attribute of the <location> element should refer to a file or directory:

```
<configuration>
    <system.web>
        <!- Configuration for the root application directory -->
        <!- No <authorization> element needed here -->
    </system.web>

    <!- Configuration for the "restricted" subdirectory -->
    <location path="restricted">
        <system.web>
            <authorization>
            <!-- This will force all users to log in
                to the restricted directory. We are denying access to the
                anonymous user -->
            <deny users="?" />
            </authorization>
        </location>
    </system.web>
</configuration>
```

In the example above, anonymous users are denied access to the "restricted" directory. You may add <allow> or <deny> elements within the authorization element to allow or deny users and roles access to the specified resource. Two special characters that are useful here are:

❑   ? means the anonymous account in Windows

❑   * is a wildcard character and means everyone

ASP.NET goes through each of the `<allow>` and `<deny>` tags until it finds the first one that matches the current authenticated user. It will then allow or deny access to the URL, based upon that tag. Here is an example:

```
<configuration>
    <system.web>
        <!-- Configuration for the root application directory -->
        <authorization>
            <!-- Only allow people from the following groups or the Administrator -->
            <allow roles="Sales,Marketing" users="Administrator" />
            <!-- Deny all others -->
            <deny users="*" />
        </authorization>
    </system.web>
</configuration>
```

See Chapter 8 for more details on server configuration.

ASP.NET Authentication Providers

The ASP.NET runtime can be configured to authenticate a user using one of the following authentication providers:

❑   Forms Authentication

❑   Passport Authentication

❑   Windows Authentication

Forms Authentication

Forms authentication is one of the exciting new features of ASP.NET. It is called forms authentication because the user will typically be redirected to an HTML form to log in to the application. Many web site applications today are already built using custom authentication mechanisms that do a lot of work behind the scenes to authenticate a user and maintain the notion of the user's identity throughout the lifetime of the user's session. Forms authentication handles a lot of the underlying work and promises to make many peoples lives much easier.

As an ASP.NET developer, you no longer need to be concerned about how you are going to maintain the identity of users between requests. In addition, you don't need to hold on to the URL that the user attempted to access before they were redirected to your login form. The `FormsAuthenticationModule` handles all of this for you, yet, at the same time gives you complete control over how your user is authenticated.

You provide the login page, and your application's logic handles the work of verifying the user's credentials while the Forms Authentication provider handles the underlying details of authentication management. When a new web request comes into the application, the Forms Authentication provider checks the request for a valid authentication cookie. If the cookie is not present, or is not valid, the user is redirected to your application's login page that is defined in `web.config`. Once the user's identity has been verified by your application, the Forms Authentication provider then handles creating the authentication cookie to identify the user for subsequent requests to the application.

> Note that using Forms Authentication requires that the user have cookies enabled in their browser. Unlike the Session object, it cannot be configured to work without cookies by giving the user a unique URL.

Implementing Forms Authentication

In order to implement Forms Authentication, the `<authentication>` section in `web.config` should be configured like this:

```
<authentication mode="Forms">
  <forms loginUrl="login.aspx"
         name="authCookie" />
</authentication>
```

For a good example of implementing Forms Authentication, see Chapter 16, Example 7.

Passport Authentication

The Passport authentication service confirms the user's identity by validating them using the Microsoft Passport service. Passport is a user authentication Web Service that allows a user to store their profile information in the central Passport database, and then log in to any partner web site using a single sign-in that implements Passport authentication.

The benefits for the web user are numerous:

- ❏ The user can use a single sign-in at all participating web sites. They will not have to remember multiple login usernames and passwords.

- ❏ If the user logs in to one site, they do not have to log in again at the next participating Passport web site. The user's profile information can be retrieved automatically by participating web sites. All of this profile information is shared at the user's discretion.

- ❏ The user can also securely store additional personal information in a Passport wallet. This can then be retrieved by other participating Passport sites that implement the Passport Express service to make purchasing easier.

All Passport web sites share some common GUI characteristics, including the login page, which is controlled centrally by the Passport service. An example passport login screen is shown overleaf:

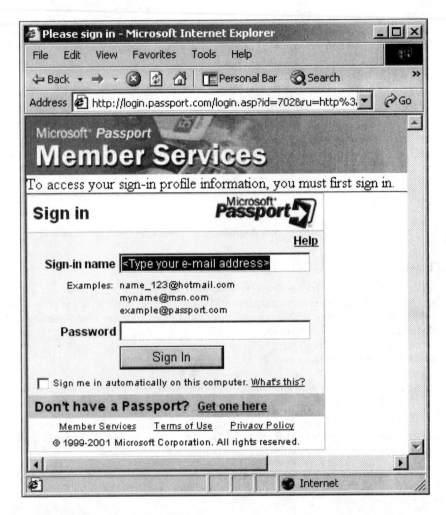

Windows support for Passport

Starting with Windows XP, Windows will have built-in support for Passport authentication. Once a user has logged into the Windows domain on Win XP, they will be able to automatically log in to web sites implementing Passport authentication if they are using Internet Explorer 6.0, or greater.

Implementing Passport Authentication

Implementing Passport authentication requires signing up for the Passport Authentication service, which requires a small fee. See http://www.passport.com/ for details. At the time of writing, implementing Passport on your web site is a free service from Microsoft. However, future licensing models may change that.

Once the Passport service has been installed on the server and configured, you can configure ASP.NET to use it for user authentication. To implement Passport authentication, the <authentication> element of web.config must be configured, as follows:

```
<authentication mode="Passport">
  <passport redirectUrl="internal"/>
</authentication>
```

Windows Authentication

When using Windows Authentication, the user's identity is confirmed by validating them against a Windows domain controller. Users are maintained by managing the accounts in the central Windows domain. Windows Authentication works well in intranet and extranet environments where users of the system are typically already managed users in a Windows domain. It does not work well in most Internet scenarios, especially with large numbers of users.

Overview

IIS is involved in the authentication process in Windows Authentication. When IIS receives a request that needs to be authenticated, it issues a challenge to the browser for authentication information. A login dialog is then presented to the user. Depending on how IIS is configured (see the section below) and the authentication capabilities of the client, the dialog might be a Basic, Digest, or Integrated Windows Authentication dialog.

> Note that Internet Explorer can automatically log a user into an intranet site using Integrated Windows Authentication if the user and the server are on the same domain.

Once the user's identity has been confirmed by the Windows Domain, the `WindowsAuthenticationModule` provider constructs `WindowsIdentity` and `WindowsPrincipal` classes, and attaches them to the current request. These objects will be discussed later in this chapter.

IIS Authentication Methods

IIS supports a number of different methods for authenticating a user. It must be configured appropriately to allow Windows Authentication to take place in your application. Here is what the IIS configuration screen for Directory Security looks like:

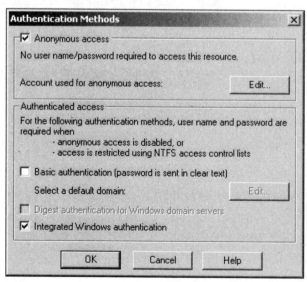

We'll look at these authentication methods more closely in the following sections:

Anonymous Authentication

Anonymous Authentication is a method that, by default, allows IIS to map all incoming web requests to the identity of a single Windows domain account. As previously mentioned, when IIS is installed, it creates a new windows account called IUSR_*machinename*. This account is the one that IIS uses to gain access to the requested web resources. This allows all requests to be handled without requiring the user to log on to the web server. Anonymous Authentication is used for web sites, or portions of web sites, that do not require user authentication.

Be aware that if Anonymous Authentication is still enabled in IIS for the directory in which your application is based, IIS will attempt to authenticate the user using Anonymous Authentication first. If that fails, IIS will send a challenge response to the browser that will result in the user having to log in.

> If you are implementing a site that always requires a login and uses Windows Authentication, you should deny access to anonymous users in the `web.config` file, as shown below:

```
<authorization>
    <deny users="?"/>
</authorization>
```

By using the "?" wildcard in the deny field this element is blocking all users from being authorized, meaning they will all be challenged to login. Of course, you can also remove access to the anonymous user through the IIS manager, but setting it in the `web.config` file makes a lot of sense, because it is much easier to deploy to a new server and copy to other servers.

There may be cases, however, when you allow access to portions of your web application to unauthenticated users. In this case, you will need to enable authorization of the anonymous user for those areas and force authentication for other areas. This is most easily done by placing the secure parts of the site in separate directories from the rest of the site. To force authentication for specific portions of your web site, you may use one of the following methods:

- ❑ Add a `<location>` element to the main `web.config` and modify the `<authorization>` element there. This is the preferred method of setting up authorization on your site because it can be configured at development time without having to make changes to IIS at the time of installation.

- ❑ Create a `web.config` file for a subdirectory, then modify the `<authorization>` element in this file to restrict access to that subfolder from unauthenticated users.

- ❑ Restrict access to those areas using NTFS file permissions – remove "Read" permissions on the files from the anonymous user account. This method is more difficult to manage and requires Windows Authentication to satisfy the authorization requirement.

- ❑ If the restricted sections of your web site are all under specific directories, you can also disable Anonymous Authentication for those directories using IIS.

Basic Authentication

Basic Authentication is part of the HTTP 1.0 specification and most browsers have support for it. To log in to a web site running IIS using Basic Authentication, a user needs to supply their username and password. Here is a sample of the logon form used by a typical browser to handle Basic Authentication:

One weakness of Basic Authentication is that the username and password are sent over the network as plain text and can be easily harvested by hackers. If Basic Authentication is used together with HTTPS, however, the username and password are securely encrypted. Using HTTPS is truly the only secure way to use Basic Authentication.

Digest Authentication

Digest Authentication is a new standard that was proposed as part of the HTTP 1.1 specification. Digest Authentication is similar to, and has been proposed as a replacement for, Basic Authentication. In Digest Authentication, the username and password are passed through a hashing algorithm so that they are not sent as plain text over the network. The original username and password cannot be deciphered from the resulting hash.

Digest Authentication is only available to IIS if the web server is a domain controller. Currently, few browsers support Digest Authentication, but as it becomes more available, it will be a very viable option for authenticating users.

Integrated Windows Authentication

Integrated Windows Authentication has also been known as NTLM Authentication or Windows NT Challenge/Response. If a user has already logged into the same Windows domain as the web server, or one trusted by the web server, a hash of their login credentials can be automatically communicated to the server using a secure communication protocol. If not, a login dialog is displayed to the user as shown overleaf:

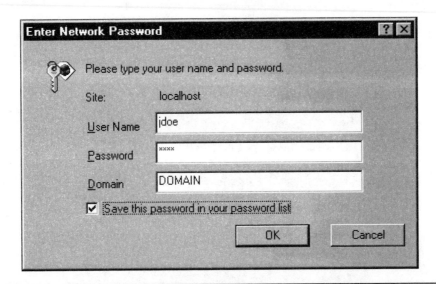

Internet Explorer is the only browser to support Integrated Windows Authentication. In addition, it will not work through most proxy servers, and some firewalls. This method of authentication is best used in intranet environments.

Implementing Windows Authentication

Implementing Windows Authentication is a two-step process. The first step is to make a modification to the web.config file:

```
<configuration>
  <system.web>
    <authentication mode="Windows" />
      <identity impersonate="true | false" />
    <authorization>
      <!-- This will force all users to log in -->
      <deny users="?" />
    </authorization>
  </system.web>
</configuration>
```

The second step is to make the necessary configuration changes to IIS. To enable Windows Authentication, IIS must be configured to allow Basic, Digest, or Integrated Windows authentication, or any combination of them as appropriate.

IIS can also be configured to authenticate users using certificates. Using Active Directory, certificates can be created that map to specific user accounts. If IIS is configured to authenticate users with certificates, the user's certificate takes the place of a login dialog.

System.Security.Principal Namespace

This namespace contains classes that are important to the authentication framework in ASP.NET. Two of the classes (IPrincipal and IIdentity) are interfaces used by all three of the authentication providers. The third, WindowsIdentity, is used by Windows authentication.

Once a user has been authenticated, the `HttpContext` object, which was discussed in Chapter 2, holds information about the current user in the form of a `Principal` object. In .NET, `Principal` represents the security context for the current user. Each `Principal` object implements the `IPrincipal` interface. This interface allows access to the user's identity, and to any groups to which the user belongs. The `Principal` object for the current user can be retrieved from `HttpContext` as shown below:

C#

```
IPrincipal aPrincipal = Page.Context.User;
```

VB.NET

```
Dim aPrincipal as IPrincipal = Page.Context.User;
```

The IIdentity Interface

The `IIdentity` interface is returned by the `Context.User.Identity` property. It contains basic information about the user. Each of the three authentication providers in ASP.NET has an `Identity` object that implements this interface. It contains the following properties.

AuthenticationType Property

The `AuthenticationType` property returns a string that specifically describes how the user was authenticated (more information is given under the individual types in this section). This property is read-only, and can be implemented as follows.

C#

```
string aType = Context.User.Identity.AuthenticationType;
```

VB.NET

```
Dim aType as String = Context.User.Identity.AuthenticationType
```

IsAuthenticated Property

The `IsAuthenticated` property returns a Boolean value that indicates whether the current user has been authenticated yet. It is read-only and implemented as follows:

C#

```
If( Context.User.Identity.IsAuthenticated ) {
   // Do something only authenticated users can do
}
```

VB.NET

```
If Context.User.Identity.IsAuthenticated Then
   'Do something only authenticated users can do
End If
```

Name Property

If the current request has an authenticated user, the `Name` property returns a string containing the username for the currently authenticated user. This should be a string that uniquely identifies the user from all other users. This property is read-only.

C#
```
string aName = Context.User.Identity.Name;
```

VB.NET
```
Dim aName as String = Context.User.Identity.Name
```

Here is a comparison of what the `Name` property will return for all three of the authentication providers:

Parameter	Description
Windows	Returns the domain-qualified username of the currently authenticated user in the form `Domain\UserName`.
Forms	Returns the username that was submitted to the application when the user logged in.
Passport	Returns a Passport PUID. This is a 64-bit Hex string that will be unique across all Passport users.

For more information, consult the documentation for the specific authentication provider you are interested in.

The IPrincipal Interface

The `IPrincipal` interface is implemented by all ASP.NET authentication providers. It defines the basic set of properties and methods that a provider must implement to plugin to the authentication framework. The `IPrincipal` interface is a lightweight interface that is easy to implement using your own classes to maintain the identity of the user.

Identity Property

The `Identity` property returns an object that implements the `IIdentity` interface. We will look at the `IIdentity` interface in the next section. But, briefly, it allows access to the user's name and some information about their authentication status. The `Identity` property is read-only.

C#
```
IIdentity aIdentity = Page.Context.User.Identity;
```

VB.NET
```
Dim aIdentity as IIdentity = Page.Context.User.Identity;
```

IsInRole Method

The `IsInRole` method allows the application to check to see if the user is a member of a particular role:

Parameter	Type	Description
Role	String	The name of the role that should be checked to see if the current user is a member of it

If Windows Authentication is being used, the user's roles are directly mapped to the groups that they belong to in the Windows domain. For example, the following code checks to see if the user belongs to the "Sales" role. The other two built-in providers do not provide the notion of roles, and will therefore return `false`.

C#

```
bool aIsAdministrator = Context.User.IsInRole( "Sales" );
```

VB.NET

```
Dim aIsAdministrator as bool = Context.User.IsInRole( "Sales" )
```

WindowsIdentity Class

The `WindowsIdentity` class represents the `identity` of a user. It is the Windows authentication provider's implementation of the `IIdentity` interface, and contains the following properties and methods.

AuthenticationType Property

This property is inherited from the `IIdentity` interface. It returns a string that indicates the type of authentication that was used to confirm the identity of the current user.

C#

```
string aType = Context.User.Identity.AuthenticationType
```

VB.NET

```
Dim aType as String = Context.User.Identity.AuthenticationType
```

This property will return one of the following values:

- ❑ `" "` – for Anonymous Authentication (the user has not had to log in to the application)
- ❑ `"Basic"` – for Basic Authentication
- ❑ `"Digest"` – for Digest Authentication
- ❑ `"NTLM"` – for NTLM Authentication (Integrated Windows Authentication)
- ❑ `"Kerberos"` – for Kerberos Authentication

IsAnonymous Property

This property returns `true` if the `WindowsIdentity` object represents the identity of an anonymous user. This property is read-only.

IsAuthenticated Property

This property returns `true` once the user has been authenticated by Windows. This property is read-only.

C#

```
bool aIsAuthenticated = Context.User.Identity.IsAuthenticated;
```

VB.NET

```
dim aIsAuthenticated as Boolean = Context.User.Identity.IsAuthenticated
```

IsGuest Property

This property returns true if the WindowsIdentity object represents a guest account in Windows. This property is read-only.

C#
```
bool aIsGuest = ((WindowsIdentity)Context.User.Identity).IsGuest;
```

VB.NET
```
dim aIsGuest as Boolean = CType(Context.User.Identity, WindowsIdentity).IsGuest
```

IsSystem Property

This property returns true if the WindowsIdentity object represents the system account under Windows. This property is read-only.

C#
```
bool aIsSystem = ((WindowsIdentity)Context.User.Identity).IsSystem;
```

VB.NET
```
dim aIsSystem as Boolean = CType(Context.User.Identity, WindowsIdentity).IsSystem
```

Name Property

This property returns the username of the currently logged on user. For a user that is part of a Windows Domain, this string contains the domain-qualified name of the user in the format [Domain Name]\[User Name]. This property is read-only.

C#
```
string aUserName = Context.User.Identity.Name;
```

VB.NET
```
dim aUserName as String = Context.User.Identity.Name
```

Token Property

This property returns an IntPtr representing a pointer to the Windows account token for the user represented by the WindowsIdentity object. This property is for facilitating interoperability with unmanaged code. This property is read-only.

C#
```
IntPtr a = ((WindowsIdentity)Context.User.Identity).Token;
```

VB.NET
```
Dim a as IntPtr = Ctype(Context.User.Identity,WindowsIdentity).Token
```

GetAnonymous Method

The GetAnonymous method is a static ("shared" in VB.NET) method of the WindowsIdentity object. It returns an Identity object that represents the anonymous user account on the system.

C#

```
WindowsIdentity aIdentity = WindowsIdentity.GetAnonymous();
```

VB.NET

```
Dim aIdentity as WindowsIdentity = WindowsIdentity.GetAnonymous()
```

GetCurrent Method

This static method will return a `WindowsIdentity` object representing the current user. This is a shortcut for getting access to the current user object from classes that do not have direct access to the `Context` object.

C#

```
public static WindowsIdentity GetCurrent();
```

VB.NET

```
Public Shared Function GetCurrent() As WindowsIdentity
```

Impersonate Method

By default, impersonation is turned off in ASP.NET. This means that even though a user is logged in using Windows Authentication, the current thread is not running under their security context in Windows. The default account that the ASP.NET framework runs under is the local system account. If the current user needs access to network resources, such as a Web Service that is protected by Windows Authentication, you can allow the current thread to start running under the `Identity` of the current user. The `Impersonate` method of the `WindowsIdentity` object allows the currently running code to run under the security context of the user it represents.

C#

```
WindowsImpersonationContext aImpersonationCtx =
    ((WindowsIdentity)Context.User.Identity).Impersonate();
//Access the restricted resources here
...
//revert back to the default security context
aImpersonationCtx.Undo();
```

VB.NET

```
Dim aImpersonationCtx As WindowsImpersonationContext = _
    CType(Context.User.Identity, WindowsIdentity).Impersonate()
'Access the restricted resources here
...
'revert back to the default security context
aImpersonationCtx.Undo()
```

After you are done using the protected resource, you can return to the previous security context by calling `Undo` on the `WindowsImpersonationContext` object that you are given when you call `Impersonate`.

> Note that the anonymous account cannot be impersonated. Attempting to do so will cause an exception to be thrown.

The `WindowsIdentity` class has a static (shared) version of this method as well that takes, as a parameter, a pointer to the Windows account token for the user:

Parameter	Type	Description
userToken	System.IntPtr	A pointer to the Windows account token for the user

WindowsPrincipal Class

The `WindowsPrincipal` class is used in Windows Authentication to implement the `IPrincipal` interface. This object does not define any behavior beyond that interface.

Identity Property

This `Identity` property is part of the implementation of the `IPrincipal` interface. This property returns a `WindowsIdentity` object representing the identity of the current user. This property is read-only.

C#
```
IIdentity aIdentity = Context.User.Identity;
```

VB.NET
```
Dim aIdentity as IIdentity = Context.User.Identity
```

IsInRole Method

The `WindowsPrincipal` object automatically uses groups from the Windows domain to build a list of roles for the user. As a result, this method can be used to check if the current user is part of a specific Windows group. This method returns `true` if the member is indeed part of the group. For example, the following code checks to see if the user is a member of the Administrators' group.

C#
```
bool aIsAdministrator = Context.User.IsInRole( "Administrators" );
```

VB.NET
```
Dim aIsAdministrator as bool = Context.User.IsInRole( "Administrators" )
```

System.Web.Security Namespace

The `System.Web.Security` namespace contains a collection of classes that ease the implementation of user authentication. In this section we will examine the properties, methods, and events that this namespace makes available to us through the authentication providers.

Forms Authentication Classes

The ASP.NET forms authentication framework provides functionality to easily implement forms authentication in your web application. In the sections below, we'll dig into the specifics of using the APIs provided by these classes.

Important Implementation Details

Let's deviate for a moment and look at a couple of issues that you should be aware of when using forms authentication.

Create a Unique Name for the Authentication Cookie

If you do not specify a name for the authentication cookie in the `web.config`, ASP.NET will use one with the default name of `".ASPXAUTH"`. Here is an example of how you would change the default cookie name by modifying `web.config`:

```
<authentication mode="Forms">
  <forms loginUrl="login.aspx"
         path="/mywebapplication"
         name="CookieName" />
</authentication>
```

You should be aware that if you are running forms authentication on a web host that is also running other web applications that you do not have control over, those applications could overwrite your cookie if they are using the same name, causing your user's authentication ticket to be invalidated. This type of situation is not common, but bears taking into account when determining the name for your cookie, in order to ensure it is as close to being unique as possible.

Issues with the Use of CookiePath

We've already mentioned how dependent forms authentication is upon the use of cookies. A further issue is that cookies can have their paths set. If this occurs a browser will only return the cookie if it is stored at the exact location specified in the path. This `CookiePath` property can be set in `web.config`, as was shown in the previous example. If you are planning on using the path property to dictate where your cookies are stored, you should be aware that it can be prone to problems unless you are aware of the issues.

The cookie path property of an HTTP cookie is **case-sensitive**. This is part of the HTTP specification for cookies. If the case of the request path for a subsequent web request does not exactly match, the cookie will not be returned to your application. This could result from one of the following scenarios:

❑   The user clicks on a hyperlink in your application that invokes a page in your application. You have incorrectly specified the URL in the hyperlink, causing part of the URL path to differ in case from what you specified in your cookie path.

❑   The user comes into your application following a link from another web site or an e-mail that has an incorrect case specified in the URL.

❑   The user manually re-types part of the URL, causing the case of the page URL path to change.

The `CookiePath` property is provided simply for the sake of completeness because it is part of the HTTP specification for a cookie. In most cases, it is best to forget about it when working with cookies, unless you are prepared to deal with the problems.

If you do not specify the `CookiePath` attribute, the default path of `"/"` is used, which means that the cookie will be sent on every request to any URL on the host. The actual cookie will be sent to any application running under the same host name on the server. If you are sharing your web host with other web applications, cookies created with the default path will be sent to any request to any application on the server. An additional limitation on cookies is that a maximum of 20 cookies can be specified for any one host. Therefore, in a shared hosting environment, this is just one more thing that could cause forms authentication to go awry.

For more information on using cookies, please see Chapter 2.

Spanning Multiple Servers

On a side note, remember that if you implement forms authentication across a web garden of servers, or you plan on passing encrypted forms authentication tickets (see the `FormsAuthenticationTicket` class for more details) between servers, the `<machinekey>` element in `web.config` must be configured properly so that all servers are using the same encryption key.

When Forms Authentication creates the cookie that stores the `FormsAuthenticationTicket`, it encrypts the data. The `<machinekey>` setting in web.config is merely a way to ensure that all of the servers that need to be able to decrypt this cookie are using the same encryption key. See Chapter 8 for details on this.

FormsAuthentication Class

The `FormsAuthentication` class consists entirely of static (shared) helper methods for dealing with forms authentication in your application. We will examine the properties and methods of this object in the sections that follow.

FormsCookieName Property

This property returns the name of the cookie that forms authentication is using to store the user's authentication ticket representing their identity. This property is read-only. This setting is configurable in the `web.config` file as was shown in the example above.

C#

```
string aName = FormsAuthentication.FormsCookieName;
```

VB.NET

```
Dim aName as String = FormsAuthentication.FormsCookieName
```

FormsCookiePath Property

This property returns the path assigned to the current cookie used to maintain the user's identity. The forms cookie path can be set in `web.config` as was shown in the previous example. This property is read-only.

C#

```
String aPath = FormsAuthentication.FormsCookiePath;
```

VB.NET

```
Dim aPath as String = FormsAuthentication.FormsCookiePath
```

Authenticate Method

In forms authentication you have an option to store the usernames and passwords of users in the `web.config` file. This option may be an easy solution for small web sites that need an easy way to manage a small user base. However, it may not be a very manageable solution for web sites that intend to have a large user base, as each user will have to be added manually.

```
<authentication mode="Forms ">
   <forms name="AuthCookieName" loginUrl="login.aspx">
      <!-- Usernames and passwords stored here -->
      <credentials passwordFormat="Clear">
         <user name="john" password="password" />
         <user name="kathy" password="password" />
      </credentials>
   </forms>
</authentication>
```

If you do implement this method of storing user's credentials, the `FormsAuthentication` class will do all of the work of verifying the user for you. You pass the username and password, as entered by the user, to the `Authenticate` method and it will return `true` if the username and password match a user that has been configured in the `web.config`.

C#

```
If(FormsAuthentication.Authenticate(lblUserName.Text,lblPassword.Text))
{
    // send the user on their way back to the resource they requested
    FormsAuthentication.RedirectFromLoginPage( lblUserName.Text, false );
}
```

VB.NET

```
If FormsAuthentication.Authenticate( lblUserName.Text, lblPassword.Text ) Then
    'send the user on their way back to the resource they requested
    FormsAuthentication.RedirectFromLoginPage( lblUserName.Text, false )
End If
```

Parameter	Type	Description
name	string	The username of the user who is being authenticated
password	string	The password of the user who is being authenticated

Decrypt Method

This method takes an encrypted string as a parameter. This is known as the user's authentication ticket and returns a `FormsAuthenticationTicket` object. The string is what is actually stored in the cookie used to maintain the user's identity between requests.

Normally you will never need to use this method, as the `FormsAuthenticationModule` does this work for you. It is useful, however, to use the decrypt and encrypt methods if you need to pass the identity of the user securely to another server, such as another web server or a server at another tier in the application.

C#

```
FormsAuthenticationTicket formsAuthTicket;
formsAuthTicket = FormsAuthentication.Decrypt( aEncryptedTicket );
```

VB.NET

```
Dim formsAuthTicket as FormsAuthenticationTicket
formsAuthTicket = FormsAuthentication.Decrypt( aEncryptedTicket )
```

This method is used by the `FormsAuthenticationModule` to build an instance of a `FormsAuthenticationTicket`, which can then be used to create a `FormsIdentity` object.

Parameter	Type	Description
strEncrypted	string	A string representing the user's encrypted authentication ticket

Encrypt Method

This method does the opposite of the decrypt method above. It takes the user's `FormsAuthenticationTicket` and builds an encrypted string representing that ticket.

C#

```
String aEncryptedTicket = FormsAuthentication.Encrypt( formsAuthTicket );
```

VB.NET

```
dim aEncryptedTicket as String
aEncryptedTicket = FormsAuthentication.Encrypt( formsAuthTicket )
```

Parameter	Type	Description
ticket	FormsAuthenticationTicket	The user's authentication ticket.

GetAuthCookie Method

Normally, once you authenticate a user, you will call the `RedirectFromLoginPage` method. The `GetAuthCookie` method is only useful if you need to set some further properties on the cookie that forms authentication could use to maintain the identity of the user that you have just authenticated.

If you need more control over the cookie properties of the authentication ticket, this method can be used to get the cookie, modify it, and then send it to the user yourself.

C#

```
// The user is authenticated, set a cookie that will only work
// if the user is connecting securely
HttpCookie aCookie = FormsAuthentication.GetAuthCookie( lblUserName.Text, false );
aCookie.Secure = true;
Response.Cookies.Add( aCookie );
Response.Redirect("/signedon.aspx");
```

VB.NET

```
' The user is authenticated, set a cookie that will only work
' if the user is connecting securely
Dim aCookie as HttpCookie = FormsAuthentication.GetAuthCookie( _
    lblUserName.Text, False )
aCookie.Secure = True
Response.Cookies.Add( aCookie )
Response.Redirect("/signedon.aspx")
```

This method has an overloaded version, as well, that takes a cookie path as an additional parameter.

GetRedirectUrl Method

The way forms authentication works is that if a user attempts to access a resource that requires authentication and the user is not yet authenticated, they are redirected to the login page specified in `web.config`. Once the user has been authenticated, they need to be sent to the original resource that they requested. Normally you would just use the `RedirectFromLoginPage` method to send the user on their way.

If, however, you wish to control the process yourself for some reason, you can get the URL using `GetRedirectUrl`. This method returns a string that represents the URL that the user requested when they were instead redirected to the login page. This method is only valid if it is called from the login page specified in `web.config`.

C#

```
public static string GetRedirectUrl(
    string userName,
    bool createPersistentCookie
);
```

VB.NET

```
Public Shared Function GetRedirectUrl( _
    ByVal userName As String, _
    ByVal createPersistentCookie As Boolean _
) As String
```

Parameter	Type	Description
username	string	The name of the user
createPersistent Cookie	bool	If set to true, sets the cookie so that it will not expire when the user's session ends

At the time of writing, I don't know why the username and createPersistentCookie parameters are passed to this method call because ASP.NET does not create a cookie or set it when you call the method.

HashPasswordForStoringInConfigFile Method

If you choose to store username and password information in the web.config file, it is a good idea to store the passwords in an encrypted format. This method will allow you to create an encrypted version of the password to store in web.config.

Normally you would use this method in some utility application, or an administrative page. You would then take the encrypted result and manually store it in web.config.

C#

```
string aHashedPassword = FormsAuthentication.HashPasswordForStoringInConfigFile(
        "password", "MD5" );
```

VB.NET

```
Dim aHashedPassword as String =
FormsAuthentication.HashPasswordForStoringInConfigFile(
        "password", "MD5" );
```

Parameter	Type	Description
password	string	The user's password
passwordFormat	string	The encryption type to use when creating the encryption: "SHA1" or "MD5"

RedirectFromLoginPage Method

If a user has been successfully authenticated by your application's custom code, you can call this method to redirect the user to the resource they initially requested, when they were prompted to log on. When you call this method, the FormsAuthentication provider creates a FormsAuthenticationTicket object and stores it in a cookie. Subsequently, when a user hits any page in the application, the Forms Authentication provider can verify that the user is indeed logged in.

After you have authenticated the user, you are responsible for providing the unique username that will be stored in the `Context.User.Identity.Name` property. This username should be unique across all users of the application and has a limit of 32 characters.

C#

```csharp
private void cmdLogin_Click(object sender, System.EventArgs e)
{
    if( BusinessLogicLayer.AuthenticateUser(
        txtUserName.Text, txtPassword.Text ) )
    {
        FormsAuthentication.RedirectFromLoginPage(
            txtUserName.Text, false);
    }
}
```

VB.NET

```vbnet
Private Sub cmdLogin_Click( _
        ByVal sender As System.Object, _
        ByVal e As System.EventArgs) _
        Handles cmdLogin.Click
    If BusinessLogicLayer.AuthenticateUser( _
        txtUserName.Text, _
        txtPassword.Text) Then
            FormsAuthentication.RedirectFromLoginPage( _
                txtUserName.Text, False)
    End If
End Sub
```

As well as the example usage shown above, this method also has an overloaded version that takes a string representing a cookie path for the authentication cookie. If not specified here, or in `web.config`, that path defaults to "/", which means that the cookie will be sent to any path on the current host.

Here is a description of the parameters for the `RedirectFromLoginPage` method:

Parameter	Type	Description
username	string	The name of the user. This string should uniquely identify the user from all other users of the application. It should also be less than 32 characters.
createPersistent Cookie	bool	If set to `true`, sets the cookie so that it will not expire when the user's session ends.
strCookiePath	string	Sets the path property of the cookie to the desired path.

RenewTicketIfOld Method

This method takes a `FormsAuthenticationTicket` and renews its expiration date so that it remains valid. Normally, you do not have to call this method yourself. It is handled by forms authentication automatically as needed. The default behavior is that the user's ticket will be renewed when it is about halfway to its expiration. The default expiration, if not overridden in the `web.config`, is 30 minutes. You would normally only call this method if you want to override the forms authentication default behavior for renewing authentication tickets.

C#

```
public static FormsAuthenticationTicket RenewTicketIfOld(
   FormsAuthenticationTicket tOld );
```

VB.NET

```
Public Shared Function RenewTicketIfOld( _
   ByVal tOld As FormsAuthenticationTicket _
) As FormsAuthenticationTicket
```

SetAuthCookie Method

The `SetAuthCookie` method effectively authenticates the current user but does not redirect them to another page. The `FormsAuthentication` object creates the appropriate cookie to uniquely identify the user and sets it in the `Response.Cookies` collection. The parameters of this method and their usage are exactly the same as for the `RedirectFromLoginPage` method.

Normally, once you authenticate a user, you will call the `RedirectFromLoginPage` method to send the user on their way. If you need more control over the chain of events that happens when a user is authenticated, such as sending them to a specific web page instead of the one they requested, the `SetAuthCookie` method can be used to authenticate the user and then manage the workflow yourself.

An example of this would be if you always wanted a user to go to a specific home page, rather than allowing them to go to any page they want when they first log in, you would use `SetAuthCookie` to log them in and then redirect them to your specific home page. Here is an example of authenticating the user and then sending them to a specific page instead of the page they came from. The parameters for this method are the same as the `RedirectFromLoginPage` method.

C#

```
//The user is authenticated, set the cookie and then
//direct them to the home page for the application
FormsAuthentication.SetAuthCookie( lblUserName.Text, false );
Response.Redirect("/signedon.aspx");
```

VB.NET

```
'The user is authenticated, set the cookie and then
'direct them to the home page for the application
FormsAuthentication.SetAuthCookie( lblUserName.Text, false)
Response.Redirect("/signedon.aspx")
```

SignOut Method

If you provide the option for a user to logout from within your application, you should call the `SignOut` method when the user chooses to sign out. This method clears the forms authentication cookie and sets it to expire immediately. Once this method is called, the user will have to log in again if they attempt to access any resource for which authorization is required.

C#

```
// The user has clicked the sign out link
private void SignOut_Click(object sender, System.EventArgs e)
{
   FormsAuthentication.SignOut();
   // Redirect them to the home page
   Response.Redirect("/",true);
}
```

VB.NET

```
' The user has clicked the sign out link
Private Sub SignOut_Click(ByVal sender As System.Object, _
        ByVal e As System.EventArgs) Handles SignOut.Click
    FormsAuthentication.SignOut()
    ' Redirect them to the home page
    Response.Redirect("/", True)
End Sub
```

FormsAuthenticationModule Class

The `FormsAuthenticationModule` is an `HttpModule` that is called and invoked during each request when `FormsAuthentication` is enabled. This object exposes a single event that can be useful if you plan to write a custom object to store the user's identity.

The Authenticate Event

The `Authenticate` event is called each time the `FormsAuthenticationModule` authenticates the current request. Very early on in the request (long before the actual page object is even created), the `FormsAuthenticationModule` checks for a valid authentication cookie in the current request. If found, it creates a `FormsIdentity` object from the cookie, then fires the `Authenticate` event.

> **Note that once a user is logged in to your web application, this event fires once for each subsequent request.**

The easiest way to hook into this event is to create a method called `FormsAuthentication_OnAuthenticate` in the `global.asax` file with the same method signature as the `FormsAuthenticationEventHandler` delegate. An example of this is shown below.

C#

```
// in the global.asax file
public void FormsAuthentication_OnAuthenticate( object Source,
                                                FormsAuthenticationEventArgs e
)
{
    // Do something here
}
```

VB.NET

```
' in the global.asax file
Public Sub FormsAuthentication_OnAuthenticate( _
                        Source As Object, _
                        e As FormsAuthenticationEventArgs)
    ' Do something here
End Sub
```

The `FormsAuthenticationEventArgs` object passed to this event handler holds the following properties:

Parameter	Type	Description
Context	HttpContext	The `Context` object of the current `HttpRequest`.
User	Iprincipal	Gives access to the newly authenticated user. This property returns an object that implements `IPrincipal`.

For a more advanced example of using an authentication event to handle creating your own custom user principal object, refer back to the `WindowsAuthenticationModule Authenticate` event earlier in this chapter.

FormsAuthenticationTicket Class

The `FormsAuthenticationTicket` is a read-only class that holds all of the data that is stored in the authentication cookie for the current user. The `FormsAuthentication Decrypt` and `Encrypt` methods are typically used by ASP.NET to save a `FormsAuthenticationTicket` to a cookie and recreate the ticket at the beginning of the next request.

CookiePath Property

The `CookiePath` property returns the path currently being used for the cookie that is to hold the `FormsAuthenticationTicket`. This property is read-only.

C#

```
FormsAuthenticationTicket formsAuthTicket =
                       ((FormsIdentity)Context.User.Identity).Ticket;
string aPath  = formsAuthTicket.CookiePath;
```

VB.NET

```
Dim formsAuthTicket As FormsAuthenticationTicket = _
                       CType(Context.User.Identity, FormsIdentity).Ticket
Dim aPath As String = formsAuthTicket.CookiePath
```

Expiration Property

The `Expiration` property is the time that the user's authentication ticket will expire. `Expiration` can be reset by calling `FormsAuthentication.RenewTicketIfOld`. This property is read-only.

C#

```
Datetime aExp = formsAuthTicket.Expiration;
```

VB.NET

```
Dim aExp as Datetime = formsAuthTicket.Expiration
```

Expired Property

The `Expired` property will return `true` if the current user's authentication ticked has expired, otherwise `false`. This property is read-only.

C#

```
bool aExpired = formsAuthTicket.Expired;
```

VB.NET

```
Dim aExpired as Boolean = formsAuthTicket.Expired
```

IsPersistent Property

This property will return `true` if the cookie being used to authenticate the user is a permanent cookie. The user is then automatically logged into the application each time they open their browser and come to the site. This property is read-only.

C#

```
if (formsAuthTicket.IsPersistent)
{
   lblInfo.Text = "You are permanently logged in.";
}
else
{
    lblInfo.Text = "Your login will expire when you close your browser";
}
```

VB.NET

```
If = formsAuthTicket.IsPersistent Then
    lblInfo.Text = "You are permanently logged in."
Else
    lblInfo.Text = "Your login will expire when you close your browser"
End If
```

IssueDate Property

Returns the exact `DateTime` that the authentication ticket for the user was first issued. This property is read-only.

C#

```
DateTime aDate = formsAuthTicket.IssueDate;
```

VB.NET

```
Dim aDate as DateTime = formsAuthTicket.IssueDate
```

Name Property

Returns the username of the currently logged on user. The result is the same as querying the `Name` property of the current `Identity` object. This property is read-only.

> **Note that in Forms Authentication, the user name must be 32 characters or less.**

C#

```
string aName = Context.User.Identity.Name;
```

VB.NET

```
Dim aName as String = Context.User.Identity.Name
```

UserData Property

Returns a string that may have been set when the ticket was created. This property is read-only.

C#

```
string aUserData = formsAuthTicket.UserData;
```

VB.NET

```
Dim aUserData as String = formsAuthTicket.UserData
```

Version Property

Returns an integer that identifies the version of the `FormsAuthenticationTicket`. This is unimportant currently, but may be important as new releases of the ASP.NET framework are released. This property is read-only.

C#

```
public int Version {get};
```

VB.NET

```
Public ReadOnly Property Version As Integer
```

FormsIdentity Class

The `FormsIdentity` class provides the implementation of the `IIdentity` interface that is used when `FormsAuthentication` is enabled. It also has a `Ticket` property that is used to gain access to the information stored in the authentication cookie for the currently logged on user.

AuthenticationType Property

This property returns "`Forms`" for `FormsAuthentication`. It is read-only.

C#

```
// Check to see if Forms authentication has been enabled in the
// current deployment of this application.
If (Context.User.Identity.AuthenticationType == "Forms")
{
    FormsAuthenticationTicket formsAuthTicket =
        ((FormsIdentity)Context.User.Identity).Ticket;
}
```

VB.NET

```
' Check to see if Forms authentication has been enabled in the
' current deployment of this application.
If Context.User.Identity.AuthenticationType = "Forms" Then
    Dim formsAuthTicket As FormsAuthenticationTicket = _
        CType(Context.User.Identity, FormsIdentity).Ticket
End If
```

IsAuthenticated Property

This property is from the `IIdentity` interface. It returns `true` if the current user is authenticated. This property is read-only.

C#

```
bool aIsAuthenticated = Context.User.Identity.IsAuthenticated;
```

VB.NET

```
dim aIsAuthenticated as Boolean = Context.User.Identity.IsAuthenticated
```

Name Property

If `IsAuthenticated` returns `true`, this property will return the username of the authenticated user. Otherwise it will return an empty string (""). This property is read-only.

C#

```
string aName = Contex;
```

VB.NET

```
overridable Public ReadOnly Property Name As String
```

Ticket Property

Returns the `FormsAuthenticationTicket` used to hold authentication data in the cookie for the current user. This property is read-only.

C#

```
public FormsAuthenticationTicket Ticket {get;}
```

VB.NET

```
public ReadOnly Property Ticket As FormsAuthenticationTicket
```

Passport Authentication Classes

The ASP.NET framework provides classes that do the work of providing Passport authentication for your web site. The following sections will go through the methods and properties of the framework classes that implement integration with the Passport Service.

Please note that the following section is not meant to be a thorough discussion of implementing Passport authentication. For more information on Passport implementation, sign up for the Passport authentication service at http://www.passport.com/ and then use the documentation provided with the Passport SDK.

PassportAuthenticationModule Class

Authenticate Event

This event is fired after the user has been authenticated by the Passport authentication provider and at the beginning of each request, thereafter. It can be captured in the `global.asax` file by creating a method with the same method signature as the `PassportAuthenticationEventHandler` delegate. An example is shown here.

C#

```
// in the global.asax file
public void PassportAuthentication_OnAuthenticate( object Source,
            PassportAuthenticationEventArgs e )
{
  // Do something here
}
```

VB.NET

```
' in the global.asax file
Public Sub PassportAuthentication_OnAuthenticate( _
                            Source As Object, _
            e As PassportAuthenticationEventArgs)
  ' Do something here
End Sub
```

The `PassportAuthenticationEventArgs` object passed to this event handler has the following properties.

Parameter	Type	Description
Context	HttpContext	The `Context` object of the current `HttpRequest`.
Identity	PassportIdentity	The currently authenticated `PassportIdentity` object.
User	IPrincipal	Gives access to the newly authenticated user. This property returns an object that implements `IPrincipal`.

PassportIdentity Class

The `PassportIdentity` class contains a lot of behavior that is necessary to implement Passport authentication on your web site. For those of you who are familiar with the classic ASP Passport APIs, the `PassportIdentity` object implements most of the behavior of the COM `PassportManager` object.

AuthenticationType Property

This property is part of `PassportIdentity`'s implementation of the `IIdentity` interface. When Passport authentication has been enabled, this property will return "`Passport`".

C#

```
// Check to see if Passport authentication has been enabled in the
// current deployment of this application.
If (Context.User.Identity.AuthenticationType == "Passport") &&
    (Context.User.Identity.IsAuthenticated)
{
  PassportIdentity aPassportIdentity = (PassportIdentity)Context.User.Identity;
}
```

VB.NET

```
' Check to see if Passport authentication has been enabled in the
' current deployment of this application.
If Context.User.Identity.AuthenticationType = "Passport" And _
        Context.User.IsAuthenticated Then
  Dim aPassportIdentity As PassportIdentity = CType(Context.User.Identity, _

End If
```

Error Property

If an error has occurred in Passport authentication, the `Error` property returns an integer code that identifies the error. Possible values for the error code include the following:

Error Code	Description
1	The Passport provider received an incomplete request
2	The Passport database is offline
3	The request to the Passport database timed out
4	The user's account has been locked out or the user has not signed in
5	The requested extended profile type is not available for the user
6	Some of the Passport network servers are down or queries to them have timed out.
7	The `Ticket` or `Profile` cookie cannot be decrypted
8	The Passport service is having a problem parsing the configuration file for the Passport participant service
9	This signifies an unknown exception
10	This error occurs if the site has attempted to use Kids Passport Features from the Passport network, but the site is not configured to use Kids Passport

GetFromNetworkServer Property

When a user logs in to a Passport server, they are redirected back to the web application. The `GetFromNetworkServer` property returns `true` if the user has just been redirected from logging in at a Passport network server.

HasSavedPassword Property

When a user signs into the Passport service, they have a checkbox on their login screen that asks them whether Passport should remember their username and password between logins. If the user checks this box, they will be automatically logged in, the next time Passport attempts to authenticate them. If the user has chosen this option, the `HasSavedPassword` property will return `True`.

HasTicket Property

The `HasTicket` property returns `true` if the user has a Passport ticket.

C#

```
PassportIdentity aPassportIdentity = (PassportIdentity)Context.User.Identity;
If (aPassPortIdentity.HasTicket)
  Label1.Text = "Your Ticket is " + aPassportIdentity.TicketAge.ToString() +
                                                    " seconds old."
```

VB.NET

```
Dim aPassportIdentity as PassportIdentity = Ctype(Context.User.Identity, _
                                        PassportIdentity)

If aPassPortIdentity.HasTicket Then _
   Label1.Text = "Your Ticket is " & _
      aPassportIdentity.TicketAge & _
            " seconds old."
```

IsAuthenticated Property

The `IsAuthenticated` property is part of the `PassportIdentity`'s implementation of the `IIdentity` interface. This property will return `true` if the user has logged in to Passport.

Item Property

The `Item` indexer property for the `PassportIdentity` class is the primary method for retrieving pieces of profile information that a user has stored in their Passport profile.

C#

```
string aPostalCode = passportIdentity["PostalCode"]
```

VB.NET

```
Dim aPostalCode as String = passportIdentity("PostalCode")
```

Name Property

In Passport Authentication, the `Name` property of the `Identity` object will return a Passport PUID. The Passport PUID is a Hex string representing a 64-bit number. This property is guaranteed to be unique across all Passport users and can be used as a Primary key for the user in your internal user database.

C#

```
string key as String = Context.User.Identity.Name;
```

VB.NET

```
dim key as String = Context.User.Identity.Name
```

TicketAge Property

This property returns the amount of time, in seconds, that have elapsed since the user's authentication ticket has been issued or refreshed. You will need to study the Passport SDK to fully understand the aging of Passport authentication tickets.

C#

```
int a = passportIdentity.TicketAge;
```

VB.NET

```
Dim a As Integer = passportIdentity.TicketAge
```

TimeSinceSignIn Property

This property returns the amount of time, in seconds, since the user logged in to the Passport network.

C#

```
int a = passportIdentity.TimeSinceSignIn;
```

VB.NET

```
Dim a As Integer = passportIdentity.TimeSinceSignIn
```

AuthUrl2 Method

This method returns a URL that can be displayed as a hyperlink on a web page for a user who has not yet signed on, or whose authentication ticket has expired. Please note that this method should not be used to redirect the user directly by using `Response.Redirect`. The `LoginUser` method handles this more efficiently.

C#

```
string URL = ((PassportIdentity)Context.User.Identity).AuthUrl2();
```

VB.NET

```
Dim URL as String=Ctype(Context.User.Identity, PassportIdentity).AuthUrl2()
```

This method has several overloads. The usage of this method is similar to the `LogoTag2` and `LoginUser` methods.

Parameter	Type	Description
strReturnURL	string	A string representing the URL of the page that the user should be redirected to once they have logged in to Passport.
iTimeWindow	integer	The maximum time-span, in seconds, allowed since the user was last signed in to Passport. This value must be between 100 and 1,000,000.
fForceLogin	boolean	If `true`, the user must have logged into the system within the time-span specified in `iTimeWindow`. If `false`, the user must only have a valid ticket.
strCoBrandedArgs	string	See the Passport SDK for more information on using `CoBranding`.
iLangID		The LCID of the language to display on the login page. Defaults to `1033` (US English).
strNamespace	string	The default namespace for the user if they sign on with a new account. Normally this parameter is left blank.
iKPP	integer	**Do not use**. Set this to its default value of `-1`. This parameter is used for Kids Passport Authentication only.
bUseSecureAuth	boolean	Set to `true` if you want Passport to use secure authentication.

> Note that at the time of writing, secure authentication is not supported and the **bUseSecureAuth** parameter is ignored.

Compress Method

The `Compress` method is only used in certain cases for Kids Passport implementations. It reduces the number of characters needed to send a URL string. It only supports low ASCII strings. The `Decompress` method must be used on the string to decode it.

C#

```
string aData = passportIdentity.Compress("string to compress");
```

VB.NET

```
dim aData as String = passportIdentity.Compress("string to compress")
```

CryptIsValid Method

This method is a static (shared) function that can be called after you have set the host name or site in Passport using the `CryptPutHost` or `CryptPutSite` methods. If Passport is configured correctly on the system, it will have a valid encryption key and this property will then return `true`. If it is not, this method will return `false`.

CryptPutHost Method

This method is a static (shared) function that is used in Passport implementations running on machines with more than one host name running on them. For example, a single server could be hosting two separate DNS host names, such as **www.foo.com** and **www.foobar.com**. This method tells Passport to use the encryption key specified by the host name you pass to the method.

C#

```
PassportIdentity.CryptPutHost("www.foo.com");
```

VB.NET

```
PassportIdentity.CryptPutHost("www.foo.com")
```

Normally, the Passport framework automatically selects the appropriate authentication key, based on the host name it gets from the Request *object. Overriding this behavior should only be done in if you have a specific reason to do so.*

CryptPutSite Method

This method is a static (shared) function that is sometimes used in conjunction with the `CryptPutHost` method to change the encryption key used by the Passport framework. Normally this is not necessary.

C#

```
PassportIdentity.CryptPutSite (sitename);
```

VB.NET

```
PassportIdentity.CryptPutSite(sitename)
```

Decompress Method

This method is a static (shared) function that decompresses data compressed using the `Compress` method.

C#

```
string aData = PassportIdentity.Decompress(aCompressedString);
```

VB.NET

```
dim aData as String = PassportIdentity.Decompress(aCompressedString)
```

Decrypt Method

This method is a static (shared) function that decrypts a string that was previously encrypted using the `Encrypt` method.

C#
```
string aData = PassportIdentity.Decrypt(aEncryptedString);
```

VB.NET
```
Dim aData as String = PassportIdentity.Decrypt(aEncryptedString)
```

Encrypt Method

This method is a static (shared) function that securely encrypts a string. The string can then be unencrypted using the `Decrypt` method. One use for this method would be to encrypt data that you wish to store in a user's cookie or pass on the query string to a page, but would like to keep safe from prying eyes.

C#
```
string aData = PassportIdentity.Encrypt("secret data");
```

VB.NET
```
dim aData as String = PassportIdentity.Encrypt("secret data")
```

GetDomainAttribute Method

`GetDomainAttribute` retrieves information for the current Passport domain. Some of the properties that are available are URLs to the Passport registration, profile editing, and privacy policy pages for the current Passport implementation. These properties are useful if you want to build links in your site to allow users to edit their Passport profile.

The `GetDomainAttribute` method defines the following parameters:

Parameter	Type	Description
strAttribute	string	The name of the attribute value to retrieve
int iLCID	integer	An integer identifying the language code
strDomain	string	Indicates the domain for which you are requesting an attribute

Here is an example of retrieving the URL to the page the will allow the user to edit their profile.

C#
```
PassportIdentity aPI = (PassportIdentity)Context.User.Identity;
string aURL = aPI.GetDomainAttribute( "EDITPROFILE", 1033, "Default" );
```

VB.NET
```
Dim aPI as PassportIdentity = Ctype(Context.User.Identity, PassportIdentity)
Dim aURL as String = aPI.GetDomainAttribute( "EDITPROFILE", 1033, "Default" )
```

See the Passport SDK for more details.

GetDomainFromMemberName Method

This method returns the name of the Passport domain, given the user's member name.

C#

```
string aDomain = aPI.GetDomainFromMemberName(Context.User.Identity.Name);
```

VB.NET

```
Dim aDomain as String = aPI.GetDomainFromMemberName( Context.User.Identity.Name )
```

GetIsAuthenticated Method

This method returns `true` if the user currently has a valid Passport authentication ticket. This method returns `false` if the user's login ticket has expired.

GetProfileObject Method

This method is functionally equivalent to the `Item` indexer property. The only real difference is that this method returns an object instead of a string.

C#

```
string city = ((PassportIdentity)Context.User.Identity).GetProfileObject(
              "City" ).ToString();
```

VB.NET

```
dim city As String = CType(Context.User.Identity, _
                          PassportIdentity).GetProfileObject("City")
```

HasFlag Method

The `HasFlag` returns `true` if the given flag is in the user's profile. See the Passport SDK for full documentation on currently available flags.

C#

```
bool aEmailValid = passportIdentity.HasFlag( 1 );
```

VB.NET

```
dim aEmailValid as bool = passportIdentity.HasFlag( 1 )
```

The only parameter on the `HasFlag` method is an integer that determines which flag you are checking the user for. At the time of this writing, the only flag that is documented for use by developers is `1`, which is shown above. If this flag is set, the method, as shown above, will return `true`, which means that the user's e-mail address, from their core profile, has been verified as valid.

HasProfile Method

The `HasProfile` method returns `true` if the Passport account contains profile information. Please note that a user could have a valid Passport Identity, but not have a profile stored in the Passport system. If you call the overloaded version of this method, that takes no parameters, the method checks for the user's core profile.

C#

```
string aPreferredEmail;
PassportIdentity aPassportIdentity = (PassportIdentity)Context.User.Identity;
If(aPassportIdentity.HasProfile())
  aPreferredEmail = aPassportIdentity["PreferredEmail"];
```

VB.NET

```
Dim aPreferredEmail as string
Dim aPassportIdentity as PassportIdentity = Ctype(Context.User.Identity, _
                                                  PassportIdentity)
If aPassportIdentity.HasProfile() Then _
                aPreferredEmail = aPassportIdentity("PreferredEmail")
```

You can also call this method by passing it the name of an extended profile type. The following code checks to see if the user has the Passport Wallet profile.

C#

```
bool aHasWallet;
PassportIdentity aPassportIdentity = (PassportIdentity)Context.User.Identity;
// If the user has a PassportWallet, the aHasWallet variable will have the
// value of TRUE
aHasWallet = aPassportIdentity.HasProfile("Wallet");
```

VB.NET

```
bool aHasWallet;
Dim aPassportIdentity as PassportIdentity = Ctype(Context.User.Identity, _
                                                  PassportIdentity)
' If the user has a PassportWallet, the aHasWallet variable will have the
' value of TRUE
aHasWallet = aPassportIdentity.HasProfile("Wallet")
```

HaveConsent Method

The HaveConsent method is used in implementations of the Kids Passport service. It will return true if the user has their parent's full consent to use the current web site. This property can be used to turn on additional content once the parent's full consent is provided.

LoginUser Method

Logs the user on to Passport. Usually the result of this method is an HTTP status code of 302 being sent to the browser to cause it to redirect to the Passport logon page.

C#

```
//Log the user into passport
passportIdentity.LoginUser();
```

VB.NET

```
'Log the user into passport
passportIdentity.LoginUser()
```

This method also has two overloaded versions. The descriptions of the possible parameters for these methods are shown opposite.

Parameter	Type	Description
strReturnURL	string	A string representing the URL of the page that the user should be redirected to, once they have logged in to Passport.
iTimeWindow	integer	The maximum time-span, in seconds, allowed since the user was last signed in to Passport. This value must be between 100 and 1,000,000.
fForceLogin	boolean	If true, the user must have logged into the system within the time-span specified in iTimeWindow. If false, the user must only have a valid ticket.
strCoBrandedArgs	string	See the Passport SDK for more information on CoBranding.
iLangID		The LCID of the language to display on the login page. Defaults to 1033 (US English).
strNamespace	string	The default namespace for the user if they sign on with a new account. Normally this parameter is left blank.
iKPP	integer	**Do not use.** Leave as blank. This parameter is used for Kids Passport Authentication only.
bUseSecureAuth	boolean	Set to True if you want Passport to use secure authentication.
ExtraParams	string	Extra name-value pair information that can be sent to the login client. See the Passport SDK for more details.

> Note that at time of writing, secure authentication is not supported and the **bUserSecureAuth** parameter is ignored.

Here are the method signatures of the overloaded versions of LoginUser:

C#

```
public int LoginUser( string szRetURL,  int iTimeWindow,
    bool fForceLogin, string szCOBrandArgs, int iLangID,
    string strNameSpace, int iKPP, bool fUseSecureAuth,
    object oExtraParams );
```

VB.NET

```
Overloads Public Function LoginUser( ByVal szRetURL As String, _
    ByVal iTimeWindow As Integer, ByVal fForceLogin As Boolean, _
    ByVal szCOBrandArgs As String, ByVal iLangID As Integer, _
    ByVal strNameSpace As String, ByVal iKPP As Integer, _
    ByVal bUseSecureAuth As Boolean, ByVal oExtraParams As Object _
    ) As Integer
```

Here is the signature of the second overload of the `LoginUser` method:

C#

```
public int LoginUser( string szRetURL,  int iTimeWindow,
    int fForceLogin,   string szCOBrandArgs,  int iLangID,
    string strNameSpace,  int iKPP,  int iUseSecureAuth,
    object oExtraParams );
```

VB.NET

```
Overloads Public Function LoginUser( ByVal szRetURL As String, _
    ByVal iTimeWindow As Integer, ByVal fForceLogin As Integer, _
    ByVal szCOBrandArgs As String, ByVal iLangID As Integer, _
    ByVal strNameSpace As String, ByVal iKPP As Integer, _
    ByVal iUseSecureAuth As Integer, ByVal oExtraParams As Object _
    ) As Integer
```

LogoTag2 Method

Returns a pure HTML string that includes an image tag. The image will appropriately display "Sign In", if the user is not currently signed in, or "Sign Out" if the user is signed in. If the user clicks on the image, the appropriate hyperlink that is embedded into the HTML causes the user to go to the Passport login, or sign-out, screen. The image itself actually resides on a server controlled by the Passport system.

The image might look something like this:

Or this:

C#

```
// Write the HTML directly to the HtmlTextWriter
writer.Write( passportIdentity.LogoTag2() );
```

VB.NET

```
'Write the HTML directly to the HtmlTextWriter
writer.Write( passportIdentity.LogoTag2() )
```

This method also has two more overloads with parameters. Here is a list of the parameters and their usage.

Parameter	Type	Description
strReturnURL	string	A string representing the URL of the page that the user should be redirected to once they have logged in to Passport.
iTimeWindow	integer	The maximum time-span, in seconds, allowed since the user was last signed in to Passport. This value must be between 100 and 1,000,000.

Parameter	Type	Description
fForceLogin	boolean	If true, the user must have logged into the system within the time-span specified in iTimeWindow. If false, the user must only have a valid ticket.
strCoBranded Args	string	See the Passport SDK for more information on CoBranding.
iLangID		The LCID of the language to display on the login page. Defaults to 1033 (US English).
fSecure	boolean	Should be true if the current request is running under HTTPS. Otherwise, false.
strNamespace	string	The default namespace for the user if they sign on with a new account. Normally this parameter is left blank.
iKPP	integer	This parameter is used for Kids Passport Authentication only.
bUseSecure Auth	boolean	true if you want Passport to user secure authentication.

> Note that at the time of writing, secure authentication is not supported and the **bUserSecureAuth** parameter is ignored.

Here are the method signatures of the first overloaded version of the LogoTag2 method:

C#

```
public string LogoTag2( string strReturnUrl, int iTimeWindow,
    bool fForceLogin, string strCoBrandedArgs,
    int iLangID, bool fSecure, string strNameSpace,
    int iKPP, bool bUseSecureAuth );
```

VB.NET

```
Overloads Public Function LogoTag2( ByVal strReturnUrl As String, _
    ByVal iTimeWindow As Integer, ByVal fForceLogin As Boolean, _
    ByVal strCoBrandedArgs As String, ByVal iLangID As Integer, _
    ByVal fSecure As Boolean, ByVal strNameSpace As String, _
    ByVal iKPP As Integer, ByVal bUseSecureAuth As Boolean ) As String
```

And here is the signature of the other overloaded version:

C#

```
public string LogoTag2(string strReturnUrl,int iTimeWindow,
    int iForceLogin, string strCoBrandedArgs, int iLangID,
    int iSecure,string strNameSpace, int iKPP, int iUseSecureAuth );
```

VB.NET

```
Overloads Public Function LogoTag2( ByVal strReturnUrl As String, _
    ByVal iTimeWindow As Integer, ByVal iForceLogin As Integer, _
```

```
         ByVal strCoBrandedArgs As String, ByVal iLangID As Integer, _
         ByVal iSecure As Integer, ByVal strNameSpace As String, _
         ByVal iKPP As Integer, ByVal iUseSecureAuth As Integer) As String
```

SignOut Method

The `SignOut` method is a static (shared) method that signs the user out of all Passport network sites, completely, and removes all Passport authentication cookies:

C#

```
PassportIdentity.SignOut(mSignOutGifURL);
```

VB.NET

```
PassportIdentity.SignOut(mSignOutGifURL)
```

Parameter	Type	Description
strSignOut DotGifFileName	string	A string representing the URL to a GIF file (typically representing a checkmark) that will be displayed on the sign out screen when the user has successfully signed out of your domain.

Windows Authentication Classes

To begin with, let's look at the classes that make up the Windows Authentication provider. Some of these classes are actually part of the `System.Security.Principal` namespace. This is because Windows Authentication is also used quite heavily to enforce code security in .NET. We are including documentation for them here to round out our coverage of the security authentication providers.

WindowsAuthenticationModule Class

HttpModules are classes built to be part of the pipeline for each HTTP request. The `WindowsAuthenticationModule` is an HttpModule that handles determining the identity of the current user and populating the `User` property of the `HttpContext`. If Windows authentication has been enabled in the `web.config`, the `WindowsAuthenticationModule` populates the `Context.User` property with a `WindowsPrincipal` object that represents the current user. This happens for each request that comes into the application.

The Authenticate Event

The `Authenticate` event is raised by the `WindowsAuthenticationModule` each time it authenticates the current request. You can create your own handlers for this event to implement custom behavior during the authentication process.

The easiest way to hook into this event is to create a method called `WindowsAuthentication_OnAuthenticate` in the `global.asax` file with the same method signature as the `WindowsAuthenticationEventHandler` delegate.

The `WindowsAuthenticationEventArgs` object passed to this event handler holds the following properties:

Parameter	Type	Description
context	HttpContext	The `Context` object of the current `HttpRequest`.
identity	WindowsIdentity	The currently authenticated Windows identity.

462

Parameter	Type	Description
user	IPrincipal	Gives access to the newly authenticated user. This property returns an object that implements IPrincipal.

Here is an example of how to do this:

C#
Custom class:

```
public class Customer : IPrincipal
{
  public Customer(IIdentity existingIdentity)
  { mPrincipal = existingPrincipal;}
  // Implement the IPrincipal interface
  // add custom behavior
}
```

In the global.asax file:

```
protected void WindowsAuthentication_OnAuthenticate(
  Object Source, WindowsAuthenticationEventArgs e )
{
  e.User = new Customer(e.Identity);
}
```

In one of the pages in the application:

```
Customer aCustomer = Context.User as Customer;
```

VB.NET
Custom class:

```
Public Class Customer : Inherits IPrincipal
  Public Sub New(ByRef existingIdentity As IIdentity)
    mPrincipal = existingPrincipal
  End Sub
  'Implement the IPrincipal interface
  'Add custom methods
End Class
```

In the global.asax file:

```
Public Sub WindowsAuthentication_OnAuthenticate( _
  Source As Object, _
  e As WindowsAuthenticationEventArgs)
  e.User = New Customer(e.Identity)
End Sub
```

In one of the pages in the application:

```
Dim aCustomer As Customer = CType(Context.User, Customer)
```

This code fragment illustrates a powerful concept. ASP.NET allows the objects created by the authentication providers to be replaced by your own implementation. Instead of using the WindowsPrincipal object provided by the WindowsAuthentication provider, we have created our own class that provides the implementation of the IPrincipal interface. We allow WindowsAuthentication to do the work of authenticating the user in Windows, and then provide our own Principal object with more functionality. This custom Principal implementation is now accessible from any web page, web control, or web service through the Context.User property.

Useful .NET Namespaces

The Microsoft .NET Framework comes complete with a huge number of predefined classes for you to use in your own applications. These classes are found in various different assemblies in your system directory. The intent behind this is partly that one day all the functionality available through the Win32 APIs will be available through the .NET class library, as well as additional features appropriate to .NET applications that the APIs don't offer. Currently this class library addresses a vast number of areas, including networking, memory management, threading, data access, file operations, and more. The library also provides a large number of utility classes ready for use, thus avoiding the need to spend valuable time building such generic classes from scratch. For example, it provides a set of classes that helps us build collections of objects, and another set that allows us to work with streams and serialization, as well as a variety of encoding schemas.

Each of the classes in the .NET framework is located in an appropriate namespace, such as the `System.Text.RegularExpressions` namespace that contains the set of classes for working with regular expressions. Similarly, the `System.IO` namespace contains the classes that handle streams and file-system objects.

Although there is a veritable plethora of classes and namespaces in the Microsoft .NET Framework, we will limit the scope of this chapter to consider only the most important and widely used namespaces and classes not covered elsewhere in the book.

Below is the list of namespaces covered in this chapter:

- ❑ **System.Collections** – classes that implement different types of collections
- ❑ **System.IO** – the set of classes to operate on streams and file system objects
- ❑ **System.Text** – the classes that provide different encoding functionality
- ❑ **System.Text.RegularExpressions** – the set of classes to work with regular expressions

System.Collections Namespace

The ArrayList Class

The `ArrayList` class is a type of collection which implements the `IList` interface to provide the functionality to maintain and manipulate a list of objects in a collection. Internally, it uses an array to maintain all the elements of the collection. The collection can hold any type of object, and the capacity of the collection increases dynamically as you add objects to the collection. The `ArrayList` class can be used as a basic collection object when we don't want to go to the trouble of implementing the `IList` or some other similar interface ourselves to build a collection.

Constructors

The constructors below are available for creating a new instance of the `ArrayList` object:

```
public ArrayList();
public ArrayList( ICollection c );
public ArrayList( int capacity );
```

Here the second constructor takes an object implementing the `ICollection` interface as an argument, for example an `Array` object. The third constructor takes an integer as an argument, which contains the initial size of the `ArrayList` object. The initial size of `ArrayList` is by default 16

Properties of the ArrayList Class

Capacity Property

This property sets or retrieves the current size of an `ArrayList` object.

```
public virtual int Capacity {get; set;}
```

The returned integer indicates how many objects can be added to the `ArrayList` without allocating more resources to the collection. If the collection reaches capacity and further items are added to the collection, its capacity is automatically doubled, grabbing more resources from the system. You can also shrink the collection by setting a smaller number for the `Capacity` property. If this number is less than the total number of items contained in the collection, an `ArgumentOutOfRangeException` is thrown. The default value of this property is `16`. The objects in the collection are unaffected when the capacity of the collection is altered.

Count Property

This read-only property returns the number of objects held in the `ArrayList` object.

```
public virtual int Count {get;}
```

Note that `Count` returns the total number of objects currently stored in the collection, and not the maximum number of objects that the collection can hold.

IsFixedSize, IsReadOnly, and IsSynchronized Properties

The `IsFixedSize` property returns `true` if the `ArrayList` instance is of fixed size. `IsReadOnly` indicates if `ArrayList` is modifiable or read-only. `IsSynchronized` returns `true` if `ArrayList` is thread-safe and can be accessed by different threads without having to worry about thread synchronization.

```
public virtual bool IsFixedSize {get;}
public virtual bool IsReadOnly {get;}
```

```
public virtual bool IsSynchronized {get;}
```

You can get a fixed size version of an `ArrayList` by calling the `FixedSize` method, while you can make an `ArrayList` read-only by the `ReadOnly` static property of the class.

To get a synchronized version of an `ArrayList`, you need to call the `Synchronized` method of the `ArrayList` class.

Item Property

Used to get or set an element at a particular offset in the collection using a zero-based index.

```
public virtual object this[ int index ] {get; set;}
```

For example the following code snippet loops through all of the elements of an `ArrayList` and writes the elements to a `Response` object.

```
ArrayList al = new ArrayList();
// add some elements to the collection here
...
// write the objects contained in the collection to the Response object.
for( int i=0; al.Count-1; i++ )
{
    Response.Write( al[i].ToString() );
}
```

SyncRoot Property

Returns the synchronized object representing the `ArrayList`, providing synchronized access.

```
public virtual object SyncRoot {get;}
```

Methods of the ArrayList Class

Add, Remove, and Clear Methods

These three methods do just what it says on the tin: the `Add` method inserts an object into the `ArrayList`; the `Remove` method deletes an object from the `ArrayList`; and the `Clear` method removes all objects from the `ArrayList` collection.

```
public virtual int Add( object value );
public virtual void Remove( object obj );
public virtual void Clear();
```

The following example illustrates the use of these methods:

```
ArrayList al = new ArrayList();      // Creates an instance of ArrayList
al.Add("Adil");                      // Adds a string to the collection
al.Add(10);                          // Adds an integer to the same collection
al.Add( myClass );                   // Adds a custom class to the collection
al.Remove(10);                       // removes integer previously added
al.Clear();                          // clears all items from the collection
```

The Add method increases the Count property by one, while the Remove method decreases the Count property by one. The Clear method sets the value of Count to zero but the value of the Capacity property remains the same.

AddRange

This method adds all elements from a collection to the end of the ArrayList.

```
public virtual void AddRange( ICollection c );
```

BinarySearch Method

This method searches through the entire ArrayList or through a specified range of elements in an ArrayList for a given object. An integer is returned indicating the location of the object in the ArrayList. If the return value is negative, the object was not found.

```
public virtual int BinarySearch( object value );
public virtual int BinarySearch( object value, IComparer comparer );
public virtual int BinarySearch( int index, int count, object value,
                                                  IComparer comparer );
```

You can also specify an object containing a comparing algorithm. This comparer argument must implement the IComparer interface.

Clone Method

This method creates a new ArrayList, containing references to the elements in this ArrayList. This newly-created ArrayList only contains **references** to the elements in the ArrayList from which it was created, not actual copies.

```
public virtual object Clone();
```

Contains Method

This method is used to check if the object passed as the argument is present in the collection or not. It returns true if it is found, otherwise false.

```
public virtual bool Contains( object item );
```

Being a virtual method, it allows the deriving class to override it.

CopyTo Method

This method copies all the elements or a range of elements from the ArrayList to an array. You can also provide a starting location in the destination array.

```
public virtual void CopyTo( Array array );
public virtual void CopyTo( Array array, int arrayIndex );
public virtual void CopyTo( int index, Array array, int arrayIndex, int count );
```

For example, the following method call copies the five elements starting from the eighth location in the ArrayList called al to an array named arr. It starts coping elements into the destination array from the third location.

```
al.CopyTo( 7, arr, 2, 5 );
```

The next call however copies all elements from the fifth location to the end, inclusive, of the `ArrayList` named a1 to the destination array `arr`:

```
a1.CopyTo( arr, 5 );
```

GetEnumerator Method

This returns an enumerator object that can be used to loop through each item in the collection.

```
public virtual IEnumerator GetEnumerator();
public virtual IEnumerator GetEnumerator( int index, int count );
```

The method can return an enumerator object for looping through every item of the collection, or just a subset of it. If you want to iterate over a selection, you also need to provide the index of the starting element and the number of items that are to be accessed with the enumerator object.

As these methods are virtual, they can be overridden by the deriving class to provide custom enumeration. The following code iterates through the last five items in a collection:

```
IEnumerator e = a1.GetEnumerator( a1.Count-6, 5 );
while( e.MoveNext() )
{
  Response.Write( e.Current );
}
```

GetRange Method

This method returns a subset of elements from an `ArrayList` as a new `ArrayList`.

```
public virtual ArrayList GetRange( int index, int count );
```

IndexOf Method

This method returns the index of a specified object. You can search the entire `ArrayList`, or from one particular location in the `ArrayList` to the end, or within a specified range of the `ArrayList`. To specify a range, you provide the starting location and the number of elements beyond that point to be searched for the `object` argument.

```
public virtual int IndexOf( object value );
public virtual int IndexOf( object value, int startIndex );
public virtual int IndexOf( object value, int startIndex, int count );
```

Insert and InsertRange Methods

These methods insert an object or a collection of objects into an `ArrayList` at a specified offset in the `ArrayList`.

```
public virtual void Insert( int index, object value );
public virtual void InsertRange( int index, ICollection c );
```

The `index` parameter provides the location at which the object or collection is to be inserted. All of the elements after that location are shifted forward.

LastIndexOf Method

Returns the index of the last occurrence of the specified object in an `ArrayList`. You can search for the last occurrence of an object in the entire `ArrayList`, in a subset starting at a given point through to the end, or in a subset starting at a given point through a specified number of consecutive elements of the `ArrayList`.

```
public virtual int LastIndexOf( object value );
public virtual int LastIndexOf( object value, int startIndex );
public virtual int LastIndexOf( object value, int startIndex, int count );
```

ReadOnly, FixedSize, and Adapter Methods

These are static methods and can be called without creating an instance of an `ArrayList` object.

```
public static ArrayList ReadOnly( ArrayList list );
public static IList ReadOnly( IList list );

public static ArrayList FixedSize( ArrayList list );
public static IList FixedSize( IList list );

public static ArrayList Adapter( IList list );
```

The `ReadOnly` method takes either an instance of an `ArrayList` object or an `IList` object and returns the corresponding read-only wrapper object. You cannot insert, remove, or clear this returned object. However, if something is changed in the underlying `ArrayList` or `IList` object, the contents of the read-only wrapper will also change. This is due to the fact that the wrapper object returned by the static `ReadOnly` method does not contain a duplicate of the `ArrayList` or `IList` object, but a reference to the original object passed as the argument. For example, consider the following C# code, which creates an `ArrayList` named `al`, and populates it with two string elements. Next, we use the `ReadOnly` method to create `ro`, a read-only reference to our original `ArrayList` `al`, and print out the items it contains. When another element is added to `al`, the list of objects contained in `ro` is printed a second time, and we can see that this read-only mirror of the original `al` `ArrayList` instantly reflects changes made to the original.

Example: ReadOnlyArrayList

The following file is available in the code download as `ReadOnlyArrayList.aspx`:

```
void Page_Load(Object sender, EventArgs EvArgs) {

  ArrayList al = new ArrayList();
  al.Add("Toronto");
  al.Add("Montreal");

  ArrayList ro = ArrayList.ReadOnly(al);

  string msg += "*******************<BR>";
  foreach( string s in ro )
    msg += s + "<BR>";

  al.Add("Detroit");

  msg += "*******************<BR>";
  foreach( string s in ro )
    msg += s + "<BR>";

  Message.InnerHtml = msg;
}
```

The output from this code is as shown below:

```
********************
Toronto
Montreal
********************
Toronto
Montreal
Detroit
```

Similarly, the `FixedSize` method returns a wrapper object that has a fixed size. You cannot use the `Capacity` property to change its size, and nor may contained elements be removed or new members added. However, the existing elements can be altered.

Use the `IsReadOnly` and `IsFixedSize` properties to determine whether an `ArrayList` is read-only or of fixed size.

The `Adapter` method takes an `IList` object and returns an `ArrayList` object that wraps the provided `IList` object.

Example: WrappedArrayList

The following excerpt from the `WrappedArrayList.aspx` file of the code download illustrates these methods:

```
ArrayList al = new ArrayList();
al.Add("Adil");
al.Add("Saima");
al.Add("Jibran");

ArrayList roal = ArrayList.ReadOnly( al );
ArrayList fsal = ArrayList.FixedSize( al );

Response.Write( roal.IsReadOnly );
Response.Write( fsal.IsFixedSize );

string msg = "********************<BR>";
msg += "Original Read Status: " + al.IsReadOnly;
msg += "<BR>ReadOnly Wrapper Read Status: " + roal.IsReadOnly;
msg += "<BR>********************<BR>";
msg += "Original Fixed Size Status: " + al.IsFixedSize;
msg += "<BR>FixedSize Wrapper Size Status: " + fsal.IsFixedSize;
msg += "<BR>********************";
```

RemoveAt and RemoveRange Methods

These methods remove one object or a range of objects from an `ArrayList` starting from a specific location.

```
public virtual void RemoveAt( int index );
public virtual void RemoveRange( int index, int count );
```

`index` indicates the starting location of the object to be deleted, and when provided, `count` indicates the number of objects after that point that are to be deleted. All the elements in the `ArrayList` after the deleted objects are shifted up to fill the space previously occupied by the deleted object or objects.

Repeat Method

This is a static method that copies the specified object a given number of times and returns the copies as an `ArrayList`.

```
public static ArrayList Repeat( object value, int count );
```

For example, the following code creates an instance of `ArrayList` by dulicating the string `"Wrox"` five times. In other words, the newly created `ArrayList` has 5 elements, each of them being the string `"Wrox"`.

```
ArrayList al = ArrayList.Repeat( "Wrox", 5 );
foreach( string s in al )
  Response.Write( s );
```

Reverse Method

This method reverses the order of all the elements in a collection or a portion of it.

```
public virtual void Reverse();
public virtual void Reverse( int index, int count );
```

In the second overloaded `Reverse` method, you pass the offset of the starting element in the collection and the number of elements after it that are to be set in reverse order. For example, the following code reverses the order of the first five items in the collection.

```
al.Reverse( 0, 5 );
```

SetRange Method

This method copies all of the elements from a collection onto the existing elements of an `ArrayList` starting at the location given by the `index` argument.

```
public virtual void SetRange( int index, ICollection c );
```

Sort Method

This method sorts the elements in an `ArrayList`. You can set a range in the collection that has to be sorted and you can also supply an `IComparer` object to do your custom sorting.

```
public virtual void Sort();
public virtual void Sort( IComparer comparer );
public virtual void Sort( int index, int count, IComparer comparer );
```

The second overloaded `Sort` method allows you to sort the `ArrayList` based on an object that implements the `IComparer` interface, so a `Comparer` or a `CaseInsensitiveComparer` object can be passed in as the argument. The third overloaded method is similar to the second, but allows you to sort a specified subset of the `ArrayList` using an `IComparer` object, so you also need to supply the index of the starting element and the number of elements following it that are to be sorted. For example, the following code creates an instance of an `ArrayList` and a `CaseInsensitiveComparer`, and it adds six strings to the collection. Then it uses the `CaseInsensitiveComparer` object to sort four elements of the collection starting from the second one. Later on all of the elements are output to the page.

Example: SortArrayList

The following file is available in the code download as `SortArrayList.aspx`:

```
<%@ Page Language="C#" Description="Test Collection" %>
<%@ Import Namespace="System.Collections" %>

<html>
<script language="C#" runat=server>

void Page_Load(Object sender, EventArgs EvArgs) {
  string msg = "";
  ArrayList myList = new ArrayList();
  CaseInsensitiveComparer ic = new CaseInsensitiveComparer();

  myList.Add("zzzz");
  myList.Add("adil");
  myList.Add("Saima");
  myList.Add("saima");
  myList.Add("Adil");
  myList.Add("Rehan");

  myList.Sort(1,4,ic);

  foreach( string s in myList )
    msg += s + "<BR>";

  Message.InnerHtml = msg;
}

</script>
<body>
   <span id="Message" runat=server/>
</body>
</html>
```

Here is the output produced by the above code:

zzzz
Adil
adil
saima
Saima
Rehan

Synchronized Method

This method returns a thread-safe wrapper object for the `IList` or `ArrayList` object passed as the argument.

```
public static ArrayList Synchronized( ArrayList list );
public static IList Synchronized( IList list );
```

The thread-safe object returned allows more than one thread to operate on the object without need to be concerned about synchronization between the threads.

ToArray Method

This method copies all of the objects from an `ArrayList` to an array of the object. You can also specify the type of the newly created array, so that when each item is copied from `ArrayList` to an array, it will be cast to this type. This method will fail if the casting cannot be performed for even a single element.

```
public virtual object[] ToArray();
public virtual Array ToArray( Type type );
```

TrimToSize Method

This method sets the capacity of the collection to exactly fit the items present in the collection.

```
public virtual void TrimToSize();
```

If the collection is of a fixed size or if it is read-only, calling this method throws a
NotSupportedException.

As this method is a virtual method, a deriving class can override the functionality it provides.

The BitArray Class

The BitArray class is list of bits that are either 1 or 0 in value. In BitArray, these values can also be referred to as true (meaning 1) or false (meaning 0). BitArray implements the ICollection, IEnumerable, and ICloneable interfaces, so it can be enumerated and cloned.

```
public sealed class BitArray : ICollection, IEnumerable, ICloneable
```

You can use this class to perform all of the most common bitwise operations, such as and, or, xor, and not.

BitArray is not thread safe.

Constructor

This creates a new instance of a BitArray, and can be invoked with the following arguments:

```
public BitArray( BitArray bits );
public BitArray( bool[] values );
public BitArray( byte[] bytes );
public BitArray( int length );
public BitArray( int[] values );
public BitArray( int length, bool defaultValue );
```

The following table describes the different arguments that may be passed to the BitArray constructor.

Argument	Description
bits	bits is another instance of BitArray that will be used to initialize the current bit array
values bool[]	Contains an array of Boolean values that will be used to initialize the BitArray
length	Length (in bits) of the new BitArray
values int[]	Contains a an array of integer values that will be used to initialize the BitArray
defaultValue	A Boolean value that will be used to initialize the new BitArray

Properties of the BitArray Class

Count Property

This property returns the number of elements present in a BitArray.

```
public int Count {get;}
```

This is a read-only property. The value contained in the `Length` property is always the same as this property, the only difference between the two being that the value of the `Length` property can be changed.

IsReadOnly Property

The `IsReadOnly` property contains a Boolean `true` value if the `BitArray` is read-only. It is itself a read-only property.

```
public bool IsReadOnly {get;}
```

IsSynchronized Property

A `true` value for the `IsSynchronized` property indicates that the `BitArray` is thread-safe – that is, more than one thread can operate on the same `BitArray` simultaneously with no threat to integrity.

```
public bool IsSynchronized {get;}
```

It is also a read-only property.

Item Property

This property sets or gets a bit at a specified location in the `BitArray`.

```
public bool this[ int index ] {get; set;}
```

In C#, this property is an indexer for the `BitArray` class.

Example: BitArrayItem

The following code, found in the download as `BitArrayItem.aspx`, sets the eighth bit of a `BitArray`:

```csharp
<%@ Page Language="C#" %>

<SCRIPT runat="server">

protected void Page_Load(object Source, EventArgs e){
  string msg = "";

  BitArray ba = new BitArray( 8 );
  ba[7] = true;
  Response.Write( GetNumber(ba) );
}

private int GetNumber( BitArray bitarray )
{
  int factor = 1;
  int count = 0;

  IEnumerator enu = bitarray.GetEnumerator();
  while( enu.MoveNext() )
  {
    if( (bool) enu.Current )
      count += factor;

    factor *= 2;
  }
```

```
    return count;
}

</SCRIPT>
```

The code outputs the decimal number represented by the binary value of the bit array, which in this case is:

128

Length Property

The Length property contains the actual number of elements present in a BitArray.

```
public int Length {get; set;}
```

You can change the value of the Length property, but if the new value is less than the value of the Count property, the BitArray is truncated. Setting it to a value greater than Count will result in addition of extra bits to the end of the array.

SyncRoot Property

This property returns an object that can be used to synchronize simultaneous operations on BitArray originating from more than one thread.

```
public object SyncRoot {get;}
```

Methods of the BitArray Class

And Method

This method performs an And operation between the bits of the current BitArray and a specified BitArray. The results of the operation are returned as a new BitArray, and placed into the current BitArray as well.

```
public BitArray And( BitArray value );
```

For reference, the following table shows the result of the bitwise AND operation between two bits, a and b. The result is true only if both a and b are true.

a	b	a AND b
0	0	0
0	1	0
1	0	0
1	1	1

Example: AndBitArray

The following sample code, found in the download as AndBitArray.aspx, displays the result of the And method for two BitArrays.

```
<%@ Page Language="C#" %>

<html>
<script language="C#" runat=server>

void Page_Load(Object sender, EventArgs EvArgs) {
  string msg = "";

  BitArray myBitArray1 = new BitArray(8);
  BitArray myBitArray2 = new BitArray(8);

  myBitArray1[2] = true;
  myBitArray1[5] = true;
  myBitArray1[7] = true;

  myBitArray2[4] = true;
  myBitArray2[1] = true;
  myBitArray2[7] = true;

  msg += GetBitPattern(myBitArray1) + "  - BitArray1<BR>";
  msg += GetBitPattern(myBitArray2) + "  - BitArray2<BR>";
  BitArray result = myBitArray1.And( myBitArray2 );
  msg += GetBitPattern(myBitArray1) + "  - BitArray1 AND BitArray2<BR>";

  Message.InnerHtml = msg;
}

private string GetBitPattern( BitArray ba )
{
  string s = "";

  foreach( bool b in ba )
    if( b )
      s = "1" + s;
    else
      s = "0" + s;

  return s;
}

</script>

<body>
<span id="Message" runat=server/>
</body>
</html>
```

The output is shown below:

10100100 BitArray1
10010010 BitArray2
10000000 BitArray1 And BitArray2

Clone Method

This method returns a cloned object of the current BitArray. This cloned object is an exact copy of all the elements in the current BitArray.

```
public object Clone();
```

Changes made to the `BitArray` after cloning are **not** refected in the cloned object. Similarly, if you change something in the cloned `BitArray`, these changes will not be duplicated in the original `BitArray`.

Example: ClonedBitArray

The following sample code, called `ClonedBitArray.aspx` in the download, creates and displays a `BitArray`, and then clones it. After making some changes to both the original `BitArray` and the cloned `BitArray`, the new contents of both are displayed:

```
<%@ Page Language="C#" %>

<html>
<script language="C#" runat=server>

void Page_Load(Object sender, EventArgs EvArgs) {
  string msg = "";

  BitArray myBitArray1 = new BitArray(8);

  myBitArray1[2] = true;
  myBitArray1[5] = true;
  myBitArray1[7] = true;

  BitArray cloned = (BitArray) myBitArray1.Clone();

  msg += "<B>Before Changes</B><BR>";
  msg += GetBitPattern(myBitArray1) + " - BitArray1<BR>";
  msg += GetBitPattern(cloned) + " - clone<BR>";

  myBitArray1.SetAll( true );
  cloned.SetAll( false );

  msg += "<B>After Changes</B><BR>";
  msg += GetBitPattern(myBitArray1) + " - BitArray1<BR>";
  msg += GetBitPattern(cloned) + " - clone<BR>";

  Message.InnerHtml = msg;
}

private string GetBitPattern( BitArray ba )
{
  string s = "";

  foreach( bool b in ba )
    if( b )
      s = "1" + s;
    else
      s = "0" + s;

  return s;
}

</script>

<body>
<span id="Message" runat=server/>
</body>
</html>
```

The output of this code is shown below:

Before Changes
10100100 BitArray1
10100100 cloned
After Changes
11111111 BitArray1
00000000 cloned

CopyTo Method

This method copies the contents of the current elements to an array. The `index` argument specifies the location in the **target** array indicating the offset where the contents are to be copied to.

```
public void CopyTo( Array array, int index );
```

Get Method

This method retrieves the value of a bit at a specified location in the `BitArray`. It is equivalent to accessing the bit using the `Item` property.

```
public bool Get( int index );
```

The following snippet retrieves the value from the fifth location of `myBitArray`.

```
bool value = myBitArray.Get( 4 );
```

GetEnumerator Method

Returns an `IEnumerator` object that may be used to iterate over the elements in the `BitArray`.

```
public IEnumerator GetEnumerator();
```

To loop through each element of the `BitArray`, you can use code like that below.

```
BitArray myBitArray = new BitArray(8);
string BitPattern = "";
myBitArray[7] = true;
IEnumerator enu = myBitArray.GetEnumerator();
while( enu.MoveNext() )
{
  if( (bool) enu.Current )
    BitPattern = "1" + BitPattern;
  else
    BitPattern = "0" + BitPattern;
}
Response.Write(BitPattern);
```

Not Method

This method returns a new `BitArray` containing the inverse of the current `BitArray`. That is, all `true` values are replaced with `false`, and vice versa. Note that it also inverts the values of the current `BitArray`.

```
public BitArray Not();
```

The code below creates a `BitArray` and then inverts all the elements in it by calling the `Not` method. The contents of the `BitArray` are displayed before and after the operation.

479

Example: NotBitArray

The following sample code, found in the download as `NotBitArray.aspx`, displays the result of the `Not` method of a `BitArray`:

```
<%@ Page Language="C#" %>
<%@ Import Namespace="System.IO" %>

<SCRIPT runat="server">

protected void Page_Load(object Source, EventArgs e){
  BitArray ba1 = new BitArray(16);
  ba1[2] = true;
  ba1[9] = true;
  ba1[13] = true;
  Response.Write( GetBitPattern(ba1) + " - <b>Original BitArray</b><BR>" );
  BitArray ba2 = ba1.Not();
  Response.Write( GetBitPattern(ba1) + " - <b>NOT BitArray</b><BR>" );
}

private string GetBitPattern( BitArray ba )
{
  string bitpattern = "";
  IEnumerator enu = ba.GetEnumerator();
  while( enu.MoveNext() )
  {
    if( (bool) enu.Current )
      bitpattern = "1" + bitpattern;
    else
      bitpattern = "0" + bitpattern;
  }
  return bitpattern;
}
</SCRIPT>
```

Output of this code should be as follows:

0010001000000100 - Original BitArray
1101110111111011 - NOT BitArray

Or Method

This method performs a bitwise OR operation between the current `BitArray` and the `BitArray` passed as the argument. The current `BitArray` is populated with the result of this operation, and a new `BitArray` is also returned containing the results.

```
public BitArray Or( BitArray value );
```

The bitwise OR operation between two bits results in `true` if either of the bits are `true`, as indicated by the following table.

a	b	a OR b
0	0	0
0	1	1
1	0	1
1	1	1

Set Method

This method sets a specific element in the `BitArray` to a specified value. The `index` argument denotes the location of the element in the `BitArray` and `value` provides the value to be assigned to that bit.

```
public void Set( int index, bool value );
```

The following code sets the third element of the `BitArray` to `true` (1).

```
myBitArray.Set( 2, true );
```

SetAll Method

This method sets all of the elements in the `BitArray` to the value specified in the `value` argument.

```
public void SetAll( bool value );
```

So, to set all the elements of a `BitArray` to `0`, use the following:

```
myBitArray.SetAll( false );
```

Xor Method

Performs a bitwise XOR operation on the current `BitArray` using a second `BitArray` supplied as an argument. It not only stores the results in the current `BitArray` but returns a new `BitArray` containing the results.

```
public BitArray Xor( BitArray value );
```

The XOR operation, known as the "exclusive OR" operation, is a bitwise operator, meaning that each bit of the operand is compared to the corresponding bit in the other operand. The following table describes the logic of the XOR operation, which returns `true` only when the bits are different.

a	b	a XOR b
0	0	0
0	1	1
1	0	1
1	1	0

Example: XorBitArray

The following sample code, found in the download as `XorBitArray.aspx`, demonstrates the `Xor` method, by creating two `BitArrays` which are then XORed together:

```
<%@ Page Language="C#" %>

<html>
```

```
<script language="C#" runat=server>

void Page_Load(Object sender, EventArgs EvArgs) {
  string msg = "";

  BitArray myBitArray1 = new BitArray(8);
  BitArray myBitArray2 = new BitArray(8);

  myBitArray1[2] = true;
  myBitArray1[5] = true;
  myBitArray1[7] = true;

  myBitArray2[4] = true;
  myBitArray2[1] = true;
  myBitArray2[7] = true;

  msg += GetBitPattern(myBitArray1) + " - <b>BitArray1</b><BR>";
  msg += GetBitPattern(myBitArray2) + " - <b>BitArray2</b><BR>";
  BitArray result = myBitArray1.Xor( myBitArray2 );
  msg += GetBitPattern(myBitArray1) + " - <b>BitArray1 XOR BitArray2</b><BR>";

  Message.InnerHtml = msg;
}

private string GetBitPattern( BitArray ba )
{
  string s = "";

  foreach( bool b in ba )
    if( b )
      s = "1" + s;
    else
      s = "0" + s;

  return s;
}

</script>

<body>
<span id="Message" runat=server/>
</body>
</html>
```

Here is the output of this code:

10100100 - **BitArray1**
10010010 - **BitArray2**
00110110 - **BitArray1 XOR BitArray2**

The CollectionBase Class

The CollectionBase class is an abstract class that can be used as a base class for deriving a strongly typed collection. Writing a collection from scratch for your object can be a painful process as you have to implement certain interfaces to make the whole thing work. To avoid these hassles, you can use the CollectionBase class as the base class when deriving your collection. As this is not an interface, there is no need to implement all of the methods and properties that it offers, and you only need override those methods and properties that you need. The CollectionBase class uses an ArrayList internally to maintain the objects of the collection.

Example: MyCollection

In the following sample, available in the download under the name `MyCollection.aspx`, the `CollectionBase` class is used to derive a class named `MyCollection`. In the derived class we define the single `Add` method only, which accepts a string as an argument and adds this string to the underlying base class's `ArrayList` object. Although this internal `ArrayList` can hold any object, because our `Add` method only accepts a string object, we can only add strings to it. This `ArrayList` object is the instance used by the `CollectionBase` class to contain its members. In the `Page_Load` event, we add three strings to our collection and loop through the collection using an enumerator object.

```
<%@ Page Language="C#" Description="Test Collection" %>
<%@ Import Namespace="System.Collections" %>

<html>
<script language="C#" runat=server>

// Create the MyCollection class derived from CollectionBase class
class MyCollection : CollectionBase
{
  // Implement an Add method to add a string to the base class
  public void Add( string str )
  {
    base.List.Add( str );
  }
}

// Page Load Event
void Page_Load(Object sender, EventArgs EvArgs) {
  MyCollection coll = new MyCollection();

  // Add three strings to the collection
  coll.Add("Jilani");
  coll.Add("Adil");
  coll.Add("Jibran");

  // Loop through each element in the collection and output it
  IEnumerator enu = coll.GetEnumerator();
  string s = "<b>Contents of MyCollection</b><br>";
  while( enu.MoveNext() )
    s += enu.Current + "<BR>";

  // display the string in Message span on HTML page
  Message.InnerHtml = s;
}
</script>

<body>
  <span id="Message" runat=server/>
</body>
</html>
```

Let's now take a look at some of the important properties and methods of the `CollectionBase` class.

Properties of the CollectionBase Class

Count Property

This read-only property returns the number of objects in the derived collection.

```
public int Count {get;}
```

The following code displays the total number of members of the collection coll, which is an instance of the CollectionBase class.

```
Message.InnerHtml = coll.Count.ToString();
```

InnerList Property

This property returns an ArrayList containing all the elements present in the CollectionBase object.

```
protected ArrayList InnerList {get;}
```

List Property

This property gets the list of member objects contained in the collection. It returns an object of type IList.

```
protected IList List {get;}
```

Because the access level of the property is protected, you can access it only from classes derived from the CollectionBase class. It returns an object that implements the IList interface, so you can use all the methods available in that interface to manipulate the object.

Methods of the CollectionBase Class

Clear Method

This method removes all elements from the collection.

```
public void Clear();
```

It sets the Count property to zero and cleans up the inner ArrayList object of the CollectionBase instance.

GetEnumerator Method

This method returns an IEnumerator object that can be used to iterate through the collection.

```
public IEnumerator GetEnumerator();
```

As the returned object implements the IEnumerator interface, you can use any method defined for the interface to manipulate the items in a collection.

The following code gets an IEnumerator object for the collection coll, an instance of the CollectionBase class, and iterates over this collection using that IEnumerator object.

```
IEnumerator e = coll.GetEnumerator();
While( e.Movenext() )
{
  Response.Write( e.Current.ToSting() );
}
```

OnClear and OnClearComplete Methods

These virtual protected methods are respectively called before and after all collection items are removed from the internal ArrayList with the Clear method.

```
protected virtual void OnClear();
protected virtual void OnClearComplete();
```

These allow the CollectionBase class implementation to perform custom tasks when items are removed.

OnInsert and OnInsertComplete Methods

The OnInsert and OnInsertComplete methods can be respectively used to perform actions before and after an element is added to the collection.

```
protected virtual void OnInsert( int index, object value );
protected virtual void OnInsertComplete( int index, object value );
```

These methods are intended to be overridden by the deriving class, so that it can perform some action before and after an element is added to the collection. You can enforce custom rules in these events. The index argument contains the offset of the element being added and value contains the object that is being added.

OnRemove and OnRemoveComplete Methods

The OnRemove and OnRemoveComplete methods provide the derived class with an opportunity to perform tasks before and after an element is removed from the collection.

```
protected virtual void OnRemove( int index, object value );
protected virtual void OnRemoveComplete( int index, object value );
```

If any object is removed from the ArrayList of the CollectionBase class, the CollectionBase class calls the OnRemove method of the deriving class before removing the object from the ArrayList, and calls the OnRemoveComplete method of the deriving class after the element has been removed from the ArrayList.

OnSet and OnSetComplete Methods

The OnSet and OnSetComplete methods allow the deriving class to perform tasks before and after an element in a collection derived from CollectionBase is altered.

```
protected virtual void OnSet(int index, object oldValue, object newValue);
protected virtual void OnSetComplete(int index, object oldValue, object newValue);
```

The argument index indicates which object in the collection is being changed, while oldValue is the previous value of that object that is to be replaced by newValue.

OnValidate Method

The OnValidate method gives the deriving class an opportunity to perform specific validation tasks on an object.

```
protected virtual void OnValidate( object value );
```

The argument of this function is the object to be validated.

RemoveAt Method

This method removes a particular item from the collection at a specified location in the collection.

```
public void RemoveAt( int index );
```

The method takes one input argument, which should be a valid collection offset indicating the element you wish to have removed. As collections in .NET are zero based, the following code will remove the third element from the collection called `coll`.

```
coll.RemoveAt( 2 );
```

When an element is removed with this method, all the following elements move up to occupy the vacated spot.

The DictionaryBase Class

The `DictionaryBase` class provides the base class for creating collections in which each element has a key and an associated value. It provides a foundation for creating a strongly typed custom collection.

```
public abstract class DictionaryBase : IDictionary, ICollection, IEnumerable
```

As this class implements `IDictionary`, `ICollection`, and `IEnumerable`, it can be enumerated to loop through each element contained in it. The `DictionaryBase` class uses a `Hashtable` object internally to store the list of key-value pairs.

Constructor

As this is an abstract class, its constructor is protected and cannot be called explicitly.

```
protected DictionaryBase();
```

To create an instance of `DictionaryBase` class, you must implement a class that derives from it. For example, the following line of code derives `DictionaryBase` class to implement `myDictionary` class.

```
public class myDictionary : DictionaryBase {
   // All code goes here
}
```

Properties of the DictionaryBase Class

Count Property

This property returns the number of elements currently contained in the object.

```
public int Count {get;}
```

Dictionary Property

This property gets a list containing all the elements stored in the `DictionaryBase` object. The retrieved object is of `IDictionary` type.

```
protected IDictionary Dictionary {get;}
```

As this property is protected, it can only be accessed within a deriving class. The following code iterates over all of the elements and builds a string to show how you can use this property in this way.

```
          string s = "";
          IDictionary d = base.Dictionary;

          foreach( DictionaryEntry de in d )
            s += "KEY: " + de.Key + "   { Value: " + de.Value + "}<BR>";
```

InnerHashtable Property

This is a read-only property that returns the internal `Hashtable` object used to maintain the collection of key-value pairs. It is also a protected method, so may only be accessed from a deriving class.

```
          protected Hashtable InnerHashtable {get;}
```

To add an element to the the internal `Hashtable` from a deriving class, you can use code similar to this:

```
          base.InnerHasttable.Add( someKey, someValue );
```

This inner `Hashtable` is not strongly typed, and accepts any object in the key and value arguments. To make the `DictionaryBase` object a strongly typed collection, you will have to perform data-type checking before adding any element to the `innerHashtable` object.

Methods of the DictionaryBase Class

Clear Method

This method removes all elements (keys and values) from a `DictionaryBase` object.

```
          public void Clear();
```

Calling this method sets the `Count` property to zero.

CopyTo Method

This method copies all the elements contained in the `DictionaryBase` instance to an `Array`. The `index` argument specifies the location in the destination array to which you wish the elements to be copied.

```
          public void CopyTo( Array array, int index );
```

GetEnumerator Method

This method gets an enumerator object that can be used to iterate over the elements in the `DictionaryBase` object.

```
          public IDictionaryEnumerator GetEnumerator();
```

The returned enumerator object implements `IDictionaryEnumerator`, useful when we have a key and value pair for every element in the collection. The traditional `IEnumerator` object only fits the situation where only one entity exists in an element. For example, the following code iterates over all the elements of `myDict` object, an instance of `DictionaryBase`:

```
          IDictionaryEnumerator e = base.GetEnumerator();
          while( e.MoveNext() )
            Response.Write( "KEY: " + e.Key + "   { Value: " + e.Value + "}" );
```

OnClear and OnClearComplete Methods

These methods, when implemented by a deriving class, are respectively called before and after the elements in a collection are cleared by the `Clear` method. This gives the deriving class an opportunity to perform custom checking before clearing the collection.

```
protected virtual void OnClear();
protected virtual void OnClearComplete();
```

These methods are intended to be overridden by the deriving class.

OnGet Method

`OnGet` is called whenever an element is retrieved from the `DictionaryBase` instance.

```
protected virtual object OnGet( object key, object currentValue );
```

The `key` object contains the key of the object that is being retrieved, and `value` contains the value associated with that object. This is a protected virtual method that must be overridden by the deriving class in order to be usable.

OnInsert and OnInsertComplete Methods

The `OnInsert` method is called before an element is insert into the internal collection. This allows you perform a custom task before the element is inserted into the collection. `OnInsertComplete` is executed after the element is inserted.

```
protected virtual void OnInsert( object key, object value );
protected virtual void OnInsertComplete( object key, object value );
```

These methods must be overridden by the deriving class in order to be usable.

OnRemove and OnRemoveComplete Methods

The `OnRemove` and `OnRemoveComplete` methods are respectively called before and after an item is removed from the collection.

```
protected virtual void OnRemove( object key, object value );
protected virtual void OnRemoveComplete( object key, object value );
```

`key` specifies the key of the object to be removed, and `value` is the value of the object associated with that key.

These methods are virtual and must be overridden by the deriving class in order to be usable. These methods are like events in nature, and are called asynchronously by the `DictionaryBase` class.

OnSet and OnSetComplete Methods

The `OnSet` and `OnSetComplete` methods are invoked before and after a value associated with a specific key is changed.

```
protected virtual void OnSet(object key, object oldValue, object newValue);
protected virtual void OnSetComplete(object key, object oldValue, object
newValue);
```

The `key` argument is the key of the object whose value is changing. `oldValue` indicates the value before the alteration has been effected, and `newValue` indicates the value after the `Set` process is complete. These methods are invoked asynchronously, and are like events in nature. As these method are virtual, they must be overridden by the deriving class for that class to be able to use them.

OnValidate Method

This method allows the deriving class to perform custom processing when validation of an element in the base collection is performed.

```
protected virtual void OnValidate( object key, object value );
```

The `OnValidate` method is virtual and is therefore intended to be overridden by the deriving class.

The Hashtable Class

The `Hashtable` class maintains a list of key and value pairs based on the hash code of the key object. This provides a simple and easy mechanism to store objects that are accessed by key and not by index. Using a `Hashtable` you can easily search for a value if you know its key. This object is very helpful when your application uses codes to indicate a given description, for example a country code associated with a particular country name. In most cases like this, you have to go back to the database to find the name of the country represented by a particular code. By using a `Hashtable` you can create a list of codes and their corresponding description on the client, so that you don't have to make repeated trips to the database when expanding such codes. It is worth noting that the order of the objects in the collection is not based on the order in which we inserted the object, but on the hash code of the key object. Hash codes are used to speed up the search on the key contained in the `Hashtable` object.

Constructors

Creates an instance of a `Hashtable` object.

```
public Hashtable();
public Hashtable( IDictionary d );
public Hashtable( int capacity );
public Hashtable( IDictionary d, float loadFactor );
public Hashtable( IHashCodeProvider hcp, IComparer comparer );
public Hashtable( int capacity, float loadFactor );
public Hashtable( IDictionary d, IHashCodeProvider hcp,
   IComparer comparer );
public Hashtable( int capacity, IHashCodeProvider hcp,
   IComparer comparer );
public Hashtable( IDictionary d, float loadFactor,
   IHashCodeProvider hcp, IComparer comparer );
public Hashtable( int capacity, float loadFactor,
   IHashCodeProvider hcp, IComparer comparer );
```

Here is the description of the arguments used in the different overloaded constructors:

Argument	Description
d	Represents a dictionary object, which contains a list of key-value pairs of objects
capacity	Represents the initial capacity of the `Hashtable` object

Table continued on following page

Argument	Description
loadFactor	Specifies the growth behavior of the capacity of a Hashtable once the Count reaches the capacity limit
hcp	Represents an object that implements the IHashCodeProvider interface and is used to generate your custom hash codes for your key objects
comparer	Represents an object that implements the IComparer interface and is used to compare keys during a search

Properties of the Hashtable Class

Comparer Property

This property sets or retrieves the IComparer object that is used for all comparisons internally in the Hashtable.

```
protected IComparer comparer {get; set;}
```

As this property is protected, it is only available for the deriving class. You can set a Comparer or CaseInsensitiveComparer class to this property or you can set your own class that implements the IComparer interface.

Count Property

This property returns the total number of key-value pairs contained in a Hashtable object.

```
public virtual int Count {get;}
```

IsFixedSize and IsReadOnly Properties

The IsFixedSize property returns true when the Hashtable is of fixed size. IsReadOnly similarly indicates when the Hashtable is read-only.

```
public virtual bool IsFixedSize {get;}
public virtual bool IsReadOnly {get;}
```

IsSynchronized and SyncRoot Properties

IsSynchronized returns true if ArrayList is thread-safe, meaning that it can be simultaneously accessed by multiple threads without worrying about thread synchronization.

```
public virtual bool IsSynchronized {get;}
```

To get a synchronized copy of an ArayList, call the Synchronized method of Hashtable. The SyncRoot property returns an object that can be used for synchronized access from multiple threads.

```
public virtual object SyncRoot {get;}
```

Item Property

This property sets or retrieves a value for a specified key. It requires the key to be in square brackets to get or set the key's value.

```
public virtual object this[ object key ] {get; set;}
```

To access a value from the `Hashtable` "ht" whose key is "AKBE", we can use the following code:

```
Response.Write( ht["AKBE"] );
```

When amending the `Hashtable`, if the key is already present, its value is replaced with the new one. But if the key is not found in the `Hashtable`, both the key and its values are stored in the `Hashtable`

Keys and Values Properties

The `Keys` property returns a collection containing all the keys in the `Hashtable`, while the `Values` property returns a collection of all the values contained in the `Hashtable`.

```
public virtual ICollection Keys {get;}
public virtual ICollection Values {get;}
```

Methods of the Hashtable Class

Add, Remove, and Clear Methods

The `Add` method adds a key-value pair to the `Hashtable` object. It takes a key and an object (the value) as its arguments.

The `Remove` method removes a value object from the `Hashtable`, it also eliminates the corresponding key from the `Hashtable` object. It only takes the key object as its argument. No exception is thrown if the key is not found in the `Hashtable`.

The `Clear` method removes all key-value pairs from the `Hashtable`.

```
public virtual void Add( object key, object value );
public virtual void Remove( object key );
public virtual void Clear();
```

Example: AddHashtable

The following code, called `AddHashtable.aspx` in the download, demonstrates the above methods:

```
<%@ Page Language="C#" Description="Test Collection" %>
<%@ Import Namespace="System.Collections" %>

<html>
<script language="C#" runat=server>

void Page_Load(Object sender, EventArgs EvArgs) {
  string msg = "";
  Hashtable Students = new Hashtable();

  // Add five key/value pairs in the Hashtable
  Students.Add( 03, "Syed Altaf");
  Students.Add( 10, "Adil Rehan");
  Students.Add( 22, "Rizwan Jamal");
  Students.Add( 25, "Afzal Khan");
  Students.Add( 33, "Iftikhar Ahmed");
  // Sets a new value for the item in the collection with key equals 3
```

```
        Students[03] = "Batkha";
        // Removes item from the collection with key equals 25
        Students.Remove( 25 );  // display each element of Hashtable
        foreach( DictionaryEntry de in Students )
          msg += "<b>Key</b>: " + de.Key + ", <b>Value</b>: " + de.Value + "<BR>";

        Message.InnerHtml = msg;

        // Clear the Hashtable
        Students.Clear();
    }
    </script>

    <body>
        <span id="Message" runat=server/>
    </body>
    </html>
```

Here is the output of the above code:

Key: 10, **Value**: Adil Rehan
Key: 33, **Value**: Iftikhar Ahmed
Key: 3, **Value**: Batkha
Key: 22, **Value**: Rizwan Jamal

Clone and CopyTo Methods

The `Clone` method clones all the elements of the `Hashtable`, and returns them as a new object. The returned object is a generic object, and may be cast to a `Hashtable` object. This is a virtual method and can be overriden by the deriving class.

```
    public virtual object Clone();
```

The `CopyTo` method copies the elements from current `Hashtable` to an array specified as an argument. You can also specify an offset in the destination array as a starting point for appending the `Hashtable`.

```
    public virtual void CopyTo( Array array, int arrayIndex );
```

The `CopyTo` method is also virtual, and so can be overriden by the deriving class.

Contains Method

This method checks the `Hashtable` to determine if the specified key exists in the collection. If it exists, it returns `true`, otherwise it returns `false`.

```
    public virtual bool Contains( object key );
```

Functionally, this method is equivalent to the `ContainsKey` method.

Example: HashtableContains

The following code, called `HashtableContains.aspx` in the download file, demonstrates the use of the `Contains` method. It creates a `Hashtable` and inserts some elements in it, then it checks for a specific key using `Contains`, displaying an appropriate message if the key is found.

```
<%@ Page Language="C#" %>
<%@ Import Namespace="System.IO" %>

<HTML>
<HEAD>

<SCRIPT runat="server">

protected void Page_Load(object Source, EventArgs e){

  Hashtable ht = new Hashtable();
  ht.Add( "KHI", "Karachi");
  ht.Add( "YYZ", "Toronto");
  ht.Add( "YUL", "Montreal");
  ht.Add( "DTW", "Detroit");

  if( ht.Contains("YUL") )
     lblMessage.InnerHtml = "YUL is present in Hashtable";
  else
     lblMessage.InnerHtml = "YUL is not present in Hashtable";
}

</SCRIPT>

</HEAD>
<BODY>
  <span id=lblMessage runat=server />
</BODY>
</HTML>
```

Here is the output of the code:

YUL is present in Hashtable

ContainsKey and ContainsValue Methods

The ContainsKey method returns true if the key is presents in the Hashtable object, otherwise it returns false. Similarly ContainsValue returns true if the value is present in the Hashtable, otherwise it returns false.

```
public virtual bool ContainsKey( object key );
public virtual bool ContainsValue( object value );
```

GetEnumerator Method

This method returns an IDictionaryEnumerator object that can be used to iterate through the key-value pairs in the Hashtable.

```
public virtual IDictionaryEnumerator GetEnumerator();
```

IDictionaryEnumerator is derived from the IEnumerator interface and is used to deal with cases like Hashtable where we have a collection made up of multiple pairs of objects (key-value pairs). You can use the DictionaryEntry object to access both the key and the value of a single element in the Hashtable. For example, the following code illustrates the use of a foreach structure to access each element in a Hashtable. Note that foreach uses IDictionaryEnumerator internally to loop through each element of a collection:

```
Hashtable Students = new Hashtable();
// Add some elements here
foreach ( DictionaryEntry d in Students )
  Response.Write( d.Value + "<BR>" );
```

Or you can explicitly use an `IDictionaryEnumerator` object to loop through the `Hashtable` object:

```
Hashtable Students = new Hashtable();
// Add some key/value pairs in the Hashtable
IDictionaryEnumerator de = Students.GetEnumerator();
while( de.MoveNext() )
  Response.Write( de.Key + ":" + de.Value  + "<BR>" );
```

GetHash Method

This method returns the hash code for the specified key.

```
protected virtual int GetHash( object key );
```

It is a protected method and is therefore available from deriving classes only.

GetObjectData Method

This method implements the `ISerializable` interface, which returns to the calling function the data needed to serialize the `Hashtable` data.

```
public virtual void GetObjectData( SerializationInfo info, StreamingContext context );
```

Here `info` is an object that provides the information needed to serialize the data in the `Hashtable`, and `context` provides information about the source and destination of the serialized `Hashtable` stream.

This is a virtual method and should be implemented in derived classes if it is to be used.

```
Serialization refers to the process of converting any object to a stream of bytes
that can be readily transferred from one machine to another. Normally objects are
serialized in XML format. Once the object arrives at the destination machine, it
is deserialized and reconstructed to form the originally transmitted object.
```

KeyEquals

This method returns `true` if the specified object equals the key value from the Hashtable, otherwise it returns `false`.

```
protected virtual bool KeyEquals( object item, object key );
```

It is a protected method and is therefore available from deriving classes only.

OnDeserialization Method

This method is called implicitly immediately prior to deserialization and must implement the `ISerialization` interface.

```
public virtual void OnDeserialization( object sender );
```

Here `sender` identifies the source of the deserialization event. This is also a virtual method and should be implemented in derived classes if it is to be used.

Queue Class

As opposed to the `Stack` class, which we'll come to later, the `Queue` class is based on a first-in first-out (FIFO) scheme. This means that when you retrieve an object from a `Queue`, the object that has been in the queue the longest will be the next object to be retrieved.

When you put an object in a `Queue`, you "enqueue" that object and when you retrieve an object from a `Queue`, you dequeue it.

The `Queue` class is also an implementation of the `ICollection`, `IEnumerable`, and `ICloneable` interfaces.

```
public class Queue : ICollection, IEnumerable, ICloneable
```

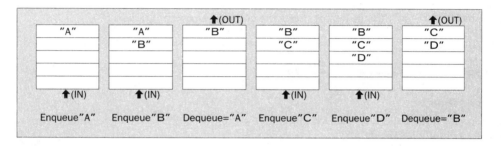

Queue Constructors

These create an instance of a `Queue` object. The constructor for the `Queue` class is overloaded:

```
public Queue();
public Queue( ICollection col );
public Queue( int capacity );
public Queue( int capacity, float growFactor );
```

Here are the descriptions of the different arguments:

Argument	Description
col	Represents a collection, to be used in the constructor. All of the members of the collection are put in the queue in the order they are in the collection object.
capacity	Represents the initial capacity of the `Queue` object; default is 32.
growFactor	Specifies the growth behavior of the queue capacity once `Count` reaches the capacity limit. Default is 2.0, meaning that the `Queue`'s capacity will be doubled when the item count exceeds the current capacity.

Queue Properties

Count Property

This property indicates the number of elements present in the `Queue` object.

```
public virtual int Count {get;}
```

Note the Count property does not contain the maximum capacity of the Queue object, but just the number of objects currently in the Queue object. The queue's capacity is automatically increased when objects are queued past its maximum, so that capacity will always be greater than the Count property's value.

IsReadOnly and IsSynchronized Properties

The IsReadOnly property returns true if the Queue object is read-only, otherwise it returns false. Similarly the IsSynchronized property returns true if the Queue object is thread-safe, otherwise this property returns false.

```
public virtual bool IsReadOnly {get;}
public virtual bool IsSynchronized {get;}
```

For example the following code demonstrates the use of these two properties:

```
Queue que = new Queue();
Response.Write( que.IsReadOnly );
Response.Write( que.IsSynchronized );
```

SyncRoot Property

This property returns the synchronized object for the Queue, which permits safe simultaneous access to a Queue by multiple threads.

```
public virtual object SyncRoot {get;}
```

Queue Methods

Clear Method

This method removes all objects from the queue and sets the Count property to zero.

```
public virtual void Clear();
```

The following code demonstrates the usage to remove all objects from the collection called que:

```
que.Clear();
```

Clone Method

This method creates a new Queue object, which contains references to the elements in the Queue provided as the argument. This newly created Queue only contains references to the elements in the Queue from which it was created. It does not contain a copy of it, so changes to one are reflected immediately in the other.

```
public virtual object Clone();
```

Contains Method

This method returns true if the specified object is present in the queue.

```
public virtual bool Contains( object obj );
```

The following code checks to see if the string object `"adil"` is present in the queue:

```
if( que.Contains("adil") )
    Response.Write("Yes, you are in the queue!!!");
```

CopyTo Method

This method copies all the elements from the `Queue` to a one dimensional array. You can also provide a starting location in the destination array.

```
public virtual void CopyTo( Array array, int index );
```

For example the following code copies all of the elements from the `Queue` named `que` to an array named `arr`. It starts copying elements into the destination array at the third location.

```
que.CopyTo( arr, 2 );
```

Dequeue Method

This method returns and removes the object at the start of the queue.

```
public virtual object Dequeue();
```

The returned object is the earliest queued object in the `Queue` object. It returns an `InvalidOperationException` if the queue is empty, so it is always a good idea to check the `Count` property before attempting to use this method. Consider the following code, which uses a `try...catch` construct with the `Dequeue` method.

```
try
{
    string s;
    if( q.Count > 0 )
        s = (string) q.Dequeue();
}
catch( InvalidOperationException e )
{
    Response.Write( e.Message + "<BR>" );
}
```

As the `Dequeue` method returns a generic object, you may need to cast it to a data type that you require, as in the above code where the object is cast to a string.

Enqueue Method

This method places an object at the end of the queue.

```
public virtual void Enqueue( object obj );
```

The newly queued object will be the **last** one returned when we dequeue the objects from the queue. This is because, as we said before, `Queue` is based on a First-In-First-Out (FIFO) mechanism. You can add any object type to the queue; for example the following code queues a variety of different types of objects:

```
q.Enqueue(1024);
q.Enqueue(3.724543);
q.Enqueue("Adil Rehan");
q.Enqueue( new Queue() );
```

This is a virtual method and can be overridden by the deriving class.

GetEnumerator Method

This method returns an object that implements the `IEnumerator` interface.

```
public virtual IEnumerator GetEnumerator();
```

This enumerator object allows you to iterate through the snapshot of the objects in the queue. If something is changed in the queue after the `IEnumerator` object is returned, the enumerator goes out of sync and throws an exception.

Example: QueueException

The following code, found in the file `QueueException.aspx` of the book download, modifies data in a `Queue` after getting an `IEnumerator` object, and catches an exception when it then tries to execute the `MoveNext` method on it.

```
Queue q = new Queue();

q.Enqueue(1024);
q.Enqueue(3.724543);
q.Enqueue("Adil Rehan");
q.Enqueue( new Queue() );

IEnumerator e = q.GetEnumerator();

object o = q.Dequeue();

try
{
  while(e.MoveNext() )
    Response.Write( e.ToString() + "<BR>" );
}
catch( InvalidOperationException ee )
{
  Response.Write( ee.Message );
}
```

Here is the output produced:

Collection was modified; enumeration operation might not execute.

Peek Method

This method returns the object from the beginning of the queue.

```
public virtual object Peek();
```

Unlike `Dequeue`, this method does not remove the object from the queue, but simply returns it. Keep in mind this will always return the least recently queued object in the queue. In other words, calling this method more than once on a queue whose state has not changed since the last call will return the same object. The following line of code demonstrates the usage of this method:

```
object o = que.Peek();
```

The `Peek` method returns a duplicate of the object at the head of the `Queue`, so altering the returned object will **not** change the content of the queued object. As this method is virtual, the deriving class can override it.

Synchronized Method

This method returns a thread-safe wrapper for the `Queue` object.

```
public static Queue Synchronized( Queue queue );
```

The `Synchronized` method should be used to get a thread-safe version of the `Queue` obejct so that more than one thread can simultaneously operate on it without having to worry about synchronization between the threads.

ToArray Method

This method returns an array of objects that contains copies of all the objects in the queue.

```
public virtual object[] ToArray();
```

The order of objects in the list is the same as that of the queue. The state of the queue remains the same even after calling the method, as this method only returns copies of the objects. You can use this method as in the following code:

```
object[] oa = que.ToArray();
```

The SortedList Class

The `SortedList` is a collection based on key-value pairs, which maintains all of its keys in a specific sorted order. The `SortedList` class maintains two collections internally: one for keys and one for values. So, in terms of memory requirement it is expensive, as it has to maintain two collections internally. All of the elements (key-value pairs) of the `SortedList` are sorted by key when they are inserted in a `SortedList`, thus making operations on a `SortedList` more expensive than a similar operation on a `Hashtable`, which we will cover later. `SortedList` lets you get a value using a key or the index of the item. You can also use a custom sorting algorithm using the `IComparer` object.

Constructors

The constructor for the `SortedList` class is overloaded:

```
public SortedList();
public SortedList( IComparer comparer );
public SortedList( IDictionary d );
public SortedList( int initialCapacity );
public SortedList( IComparer comparer, int capacity );
public SortedList( IDictionary d, IComparer comparer );
```

The following table describes the arguments used in the overloaded constructors:

Argument	Description
comparer	Represents an object that implements the `IComparer` interface and is used to sort the elements in the `SortedList`.
d	Represents an object that implements the `IDictionary` interface. This object contains a list of key-value pairs that are set as elements in the `SortedList`. It is used to populate the sorted list at the time of creating the instance of the `SortedList` object.

Table continued on following page

Argument	Description
`initialCapacity/` `capacity`	Specifies the initial size or the capacity of the `SortedList` object. It just allocates space for a number of key-value pairs, it doesn't necessarily use all of the available capacity. You can reset the capacity of `SortedList` too, after creating the instance. Once the number of elements in a `SortedList` reaches its capacity, it is automatically increased.

Properties of the SortedList Class

Capacity Property

This property returns the size of a `SortedList`. You can also set the value of this property to increase or decrease the size of the collection.

```
public virtual int Capacity {get; set;}
```

As new items are added to the collection, the value of `Capacity` increases automatically. All existing elements of `SortedList` are unaffected when the capacity is increased. Note however that if you remove objects from the collection, the collection size will not decrease unless you explicitly reduce the value of `Capacity`. If the new value for `Capacity` is smaller than the number of items in the collection an `Exception` is thrown.

Count Property

This property returns the number of elements present in a `SortedList`.

```
public virtual int Count {get;}
```

Note that, as indicated by the absence of the `set;` keyword in the definition, this property is read-only.

IsFixedSize and IsReadOnly Properties

The `IsFixedSize` property returns `true` if the `SortedList` is of fixed size. You cannot add or remove objects from a fixed size `SortedList`. However you can change the objects that it contains. It is a virtual property and can be overridden by a deriving class.

```
public virtual bool IsFixedSize {get;}
```

The `IsReadOnly` property returns `true` if the `SortedList` is read-only. It is also a virtual property that can therefore be overridden by a deriving class.

```
public virtual bool IsReadOnly {get;}
```

IsSynchronized Property

The `IsSynchronized` property indicates if the `SortedList` is thread-safe. A synchronized `SortedList` allows multiple threads to operate on it without a need to consider thread synchronization issues.

```
public virtual bool IsSynchronized {get;}
```

You can get a reference to a synchronized version of a `SortedList` object by calling the `Synchronized` method.

Item Property

This property allows you to access any specific key in the collection, using its index.

```
public virtual object this[ object key ] {get; set;}
```

It is important to note that this property can only get or set a key not the value. To iterate through all of the keys in the collection you can use a `for` loop and the `Count` property:

```
for( int i=; i<sl.Count; i++ )
{
   Response.Write( sl[i] );
}
```

Keys Property

Returns an `ICollection` object containing all of the keys contained in the `SortedList`. This collection is a sorted collection and does not return the values in the order in which they were added.

```
public virtual ICollection Keys {get;}
```

Example: SortedListKeys

You can use the following code, taken from the file `SortedListKeys.aspx`, to iterate through the list of keys.

```
string s = "";

SortedList sl = new SortedList();

sl.Add( 2, "Rehan");
sl.Add( 4, "Adil");
sl.Add( 1, "Saima");
sl.Add( 5, "Jibran");

foreach( int i in sl.Keys )
   s += i.ToString() + "<BR>";

Response.Write( s );
```

As this collection is a `SortedList` and all of its elements are sorted at the time of insertion into the collection, the output will not follow the order in which the objects were added. Here is the output:

1
2
4
5

SyncRoot Property

Returns the synchronized object for the `SortedList` instance. This object provides access to the thread-safe object of the `SortedList`, when it is to be used by different threads concurrently.

```
public virtual object SyncRoot {get;}
```

Values Property

Returns an `ICollection` object that contains the list of all values in the collection, sorted by key.

```
public virtual ICollection Values { get; }
```

This method is somewhat similar to the `GetValueList` method except that `GetValueList` returns an `IList` object and this property returns an `ICollection` object.

Example: SortedListValues

The file listed below, `SortedListValues.aspx`, illustrates the `Values` property.

```
<%@ Page Language="C#" Description="Test Collection" %>
<%@ Import Namespace="System.Collections" %>

<html>
<script language="C#" runat=server>

void Page_Load(Object sender, EventArgs EvArgs) {
   string msg = "<b>Contents of SortedList sl</b>=================<br><br>";
   SortedList sl = new SortedList();

   sl.Add( 2, "Naveed");
   sl.Add( 4, "Sadat");
   sl.Add( 1, "Kamran");
   sl.Add( 5, "Bina");
   sl.Add( 6, "Azra");

   foreach( string val in sl.Values )
     msg += val.ToString() + "<BR>";

   Message.InnerHtml = msg;
} </script>

<body>
   <span id="Message" runat=server/>
</body>
</html>
```

The output will be the values of the sorted list as shown below:

Contents of SortedList sl
=====================
Kamran
Naveed
Sadat
Bina
Azra

Methods of the SortedList Class

Add, Remove and Clear Methods

The `Add` method adds a key-value pair to the `SortedList` object. The position of key-value pairs in the `SortedList` depends on the value of the key.

The `Remove` method removes a key-value pair for a specified key.

The `Clear` method removes all of the key-value pairs from the `SortedList`.

```
public virtual void Add( object key, object value );
public virtual void Remove( object key );
public virtual void Clear();
```

For example:

```
mySortedList.Add( "BE", new Student() );
mySortedList.Add( 4, "Kami");
mySortedList.Remove( 4 );
mySortedList.Clear();
```

Clone Method

This method returns a new `SortedList` object that contains a copy of all the objects in the original `SortedList`.

```
public virtual object Clone();
```

After cloning, changes made to the cloned `SortedList` will not be reflected in the original `SortedList` from which the clone was created. Similarly, changes made to the original `SortedList` will not affect the cloned `SortedList`.

Example: ClonedSortedList

The following code, found in the download as `ClonedSortedList.aspx`, creates a `SortedList` and adds some items to it. Then it creates a clone of the object, modifying both the clone and the original object, and displays the objects in both `SortedList`s before and after the modifications.

```
<%@ Page Language="C#" %>
<%@ Import Namespace="System.Collections" %>
<HTML>
<HEAD>

<SCRIPT runat="server">

protected void Page_Load(object Source, EventArgs e){
  string msg = "";

  SortedList sl = new SortedList();

  sl.Add("KHI", "Karachi");
  sl.Add("YYZ", "Toronto");
  sl.Add("YUL", "Montreal");
  sl.Add("DTW", "Detroit");

  SortedList csl = (SortedList) sl.Clone();

  // display both SortedList
  msg += "<B>Objects in original SortedList before changes</B><BR>";
  foreach( DictionaryEntry d in sl )
    msg += d.Key + ": " + d.Value  + "<BR>";
```

```
    msg += "<BR><B>Objects in cloned SortedList before changes</B><BR>";
    foreach( DictionaryEntry d in csl )
        msg += d.Key + ": " + d.Value + "<BR>";

    // make some changes in the original and cloned SortedList
    sl.Add("YQG", "Windsor");
    sl.SetByIndex( 0, "Metro Detroit");
    csl.Add("LHR", "Heathrow");
    csl.SetByIndex(2, "Dorval" );

    // display both SortedList
    msg += "<BR><B>Objects in original SortedList after changes</B><BR>";
    foreach( DictionaryEntry d in sl )
        msg += d.Key + ": " + d.Value + "<BR>";

    msg += "<BR><B>Objects in cloned SortedList after changes</B><BR>";
    foreach( DictionaryEntry d in csl )
        msg += d.Key + ": " + d.Value + "<BR>";

    lblMessage.InnerHtml = msg;
}

</SCRIPT>

</HEAD>
<BODY>
    <span id=lblMessage runat=server />
</BODY>
</HTML>
```

Here is the output produced by the code:

Objects in original SortedList before changes
DTW: Detroit
KHI: Karachi
YUL: Montreal
YYZ: Toronto

Objects in cloned SortedList before changes
DTW: Detroit
KHI: Karachi
YUL: Montreal
YYZ: Toronto

Objects in original SortedList after changes
DTW: Metro Detroit
KHI: Karachi
YQG: Windsor
YUL: Montreal
YYZ: Toronto

Objects in cloned SortedList after changes
DTW: Detroit
KHI: Karachi
LHR: Dorval
YUL: Montreal
YYZ: Toronto

As you can see from the output, changes made to either `SortedList` do not reflect in their counterpart `SortedList`.

Contains Method

This method returns `true` if the key is present in the `SortedList`, otherwise it returns `false`.

```
public virtual bool Contains( object key );
```

For example:

```
if( mySL.Contains("10") )
  Response.Write("Key 10 is present");
```

ContainsKey and ContainsValue Methods

The `ContainsKey` method returns `true` if the specified key exists in the `SortedList`, otherwise it returns `false`. `ContainsValue` checks for the supplied object in the `SortedList`, and returns `true` if one exists, otherwise it returns `false`.

```
public virtual bool ContainsKey( object key );
public virtual bool ContainsValue( object value );
```

The `ContainsKey` method uses a binary search algorithm to search the list, as the list is sorted in key order. It has the same behavior as that the of `Contains` method. `ContainsValue` must use a linear search algorithm.

Example: SortedListContains

The following code, taken from the file `SortedListContains.aspx`, demonstrates these methods:

```
SortedList sl = new SortedList();

sl.Add("KHI", "Karachi");
sl.Add("YYZ", "Toronto");
sl.Add("YUL", "Montreal");
sl.Add("DTW", "Detroit");

if( sl.ContainsKey("YUL") )
  Response.Write("YUL is present");

if( sl.ContainsValue("Windsor") )
  Response.Write("Windsor is present");
```

CopyTo Method

The `CopyTo` method copies the contents of a `SortedList` into an array. You can also specify the offset in the target array to indicate where the `SortedList` is to be copied.

```
public virtual void CopyTo( Array array, int arrayIndex );
```

GetByIndex Method

The `GetByIndex` method returns the object from a specified location in the `SortedList`. As sorted list objects are sorted in order of the key, you will not necessarily access the first inserted element in a `SortedList` using a zero index, as it will be placed in the list according to the value of its key.

```
public virtual object GetByIndex( int index );
```

In the following code, although `"Karachi"` was inserted first in the `SortedList`, the first object in the final `SortedList` is `"Detroit"` because its key, of `"DTW"`, comes before the `"KHI"` key of the `Karachi` element when sorted.

```
SortedList sl = new SortedList();

sl.Add("KHI", "Karachi");
sl.Add("YYZ", "Toronto");
sl.Add("YUL", "Montreal");
sl.Add("DTW", "Detroit");

Response.Write( sl.GetByIndex(0) );
```

The result of the above code snippet is `"Detroit"`.

GetEnumerator Method

This method returns an enumerator object for the `SortedList` that can be used to iterate over the elements in the `SortedList`.

```
public virtual IDictionaryEnumerator GetEnumerator();
```

As each element in a `SortedList` consists of a key-value pair, this enumerated object implements `IDdictionaryEnumerator`.

The following code demonstrates use of this method:

```
SortedList sl = new SortedList();

sl.Add("KHI", "Karachi");
sl.Add("YYZ", "Toronto");
sl.Add("YUL", "Montreal");
sl.Add("DTW", "Detroit");

IDictionaryEnumerator enu = sl.GetEnumerator();
while( enu.MoveNext() )
  Response.Write( enu.Key + ": " + enu.Value + "<BR>" );
```

The code will display all of the elements in the `SortedList`.

GetKey Method

This method returns the key of the element located at the specified index of the `SortedList`.

```
public virtual object GetKey( int index );
```

For example, the following line of code will find the key of the ninth element in the `SortedList`:

```
object myKey = sl.GetKey( 8 );
```

GetKeyList Method

Returns an `IList` object containing a list of the keys in the `SortedList`.

```
public virtual IList GetKeyList();
```

GetValueList Method

Returns an `IList` object containing a list of the values in the `SortedList`.

```
public virtual IList GetValueList();
```

The returned `IList` object is a read-only reference to the values contained in the `SortedList` and changes made to the underlying `SortedList` are immediately reflected in the `IList` object.

Here is a code snippet that gets a list of all the values in the `SortedList`, and writes them to the `Response` object.

```
Stack mySortedList = new SortedList();
...
IList l = mySortedList.GetValueList();

foreach( object o in I )
  Response.Write( o );
```

IndexOfKey and IndexOfValue Methods

The `IndexOfKey` method returns the index of the specified key in a `SortedList`. It uses a binary search algorithm to locate a key in the list. `IndexOfValue` returns the index of the first occurrence of the specified object in the list. It uses a linear search to find the specified element in the list.

```
public virtual int IndexOfKey( object key );
public virtual int IndexOfValue( object value );
```

RemoveAt Method

This method removes the element at the specified location in a `SortedList`.

```
public virtual void RemoveAt( int index );
```

All elements after the deleted element are shifted up to fill the space it occupied.

SetByIndex Method

This method replaces the `value` object at the location specified by `index` in the `SortedList`. The key for that location remains unchanged.

```
public virtual void SetByIndex( int index, object value );
```

Example: SortedListNewValues

The following code taken from `SortedListNewValues.aspx` creates a `SortedList` and adds some elements to it, then changes the value of the first element in the list. As this is a `SortedList`, when elements are inserted, they are sorted according to their key. For this reason, when the value of "`Detroit`" is replaced by the new value "`Lahore`", because the key is unchanged, this element still appears first in the `SortedList`.

```
SortedList sl = new SortedList();

sl.Add("KHI", "Karachi");
sl.Add("YYZ", "Toronto");
sl.Add("YUL", "Montreal");
sl.Add("DTW", "Detroit");
```

```
sl.SetByIndex( 0, "Lahore");

IDictionaryEnumerator enu = sl.GetEnumerator();
while( enu.MoveNext() )
  Response.Write( enu.Key + ": " + enu.Value + "<BR>" );
```

The output should look like this:

DTW: Lahore
KHI: Karachi
YUL: Montreal
YYZ: Toronto

Synchronized Method

This method returns a thread-safe version of the SortedList so that more than one thread can operate on the same object simultaneously without thread synchronization becoming an issue.

```
public static SortedList Synchronized( SortedList list );
```

TrimToSize Method

This method sets the maximum capacity of the SortedList to match the space required by the elements currently in it.

```
public virtual void TrimToSize();
```

The capacity of the SortedList is doubled by default whenever the number of objects contained in it reaches the capacity currently allocated to it. This can adversely affect system resources available for other activities, and this method provides a good way to free up unused memory.

The Stack Class

The Stack class is an implementation of the ICollection, IEnumerable, and ICloneable interfaces.

```
public class Stack : ICollection, IEnumerable, ICloneable
```

Like other collection classes, this implementation also supports generic objects, and you can insert a variety of different types of object into a Stack object.

Stack represents a special kind of collection based on Last-In-First-Out (LIFO) principle. This means that when you retrieve object from the stack, the object most recently put into the stack is the first one that will be retrieved. The next newest object will be the next to be retrieved from the stack and so on.

Putting an object into the Stack is generally referred to as a **push**, while retrieving an object from it is known as a **pop**.

This implementation of a collection keeps a position counter internally, which points to the last inserted object, so when you try to retrieve an object it returns the last inserted object. You cannot retrieve an object randomly in this implementation. Each time you pop an object, the object at the current position is returned to the caller and the position counter is decremented to point to the next last inserted object.

↓(IN)	↓(IN)	↑(OUT)	↓(IN)	↓(IN)	↑(OUT)
				"D"	
	"B"		"C"	"C"	"C"
"A"	"A"	"A"	"A"	"A"	"A"
PUSH"A"	PUSH"B"	POP="B"	PUSH"C"	PUSH"D"	POP="D"

You can set an initial size for the Stack buffer, but the buffer is automatically increased if the number of objects reaches the initial capacity.

As this class also implements the IEnumerable interface, we can use a foreach looping structure to loop through the Stack. The implementation of the ICloneable interface allows it to be cloned.

There is one thing to be noted here, the Stack object is not thread-safe. So when you try to access the same Stack from more than one thread, you might get inconsistent results. To avoid this you can use a Synchronized method of the Stack class. This Synchronized method is a static method, which means that you can invoke this method without explicitly creating an instance of the Stack object. Later in this chapter, we will provide more information on how to use the Synchronized method.

Constructors

The constructors are used to create a new instance of the Stack object. The constructor for the Stack class is overloaded. Here is the list of constructors:

```
public Stack();
public Stack( int initialCapacity );
public Stack( ICollection collection );
```

The first constructor creates an instance of the Stack object and sets its initial size to a default value of 10, meaning that ten objects can be pushed onto this stack. The second constructor lets you set the initial size for the stack. The third constructor takes a collection and populates the stack with the objects from the collection. The size of the stack is set to the size of the collection supplied. The objects are copied onto the stack in the same order as the order they occur in that collection.

After setting the initial size of the stack, you can push objects onto the stack. Once the size limit is reached, the capacity of the stack gets doubled. Unlike the Queue object, you cannot specify the growth factor for a particular Stack object.

Properties of the Stack Class

Count Property

This is a read-only property that tells you the number of objects contained in the Stack.

```
public virtual int Count {get;}
```

Keep in mind that this property does not tell you the size of the stack. It tells you how many objects are currently present in the Stack. The following code sets the size of the stack to 15 when the stack object is created. Then two string objects are pushed onto the stack. When we read the value of the Count property, it will be 2, even though the size of the stack is 15:

```
Stack stack = new Stack(15);
stack.Push("Test1");
stack.Push("Test2");
Console.WriteLine("Count = {0}", stack.Count.ToString());
```

Output:

Count = 2

IsReadOnly Property

This is also a read-only property and returns a Boolean. A `true` value means the stack is read-only.

```
public virtual bool IsReadOnly {get;}
```

Here is a typical use of this property:

```
Stack stack = new Stack();
Console.WriteLine( "IsReadOnly: {0}", stack.IsReadOnly.ToString() );
```

Output:

IsReadOnly: False

IsSynchronized Property

This is also a read-only property. It returns a Boolean indicating if the object is a synchronized object or not. The `Stack` object is not a thread-safe collection. So if you have more than one thread operating on the same `Stack` object, you may end up with an inconsistent result.

```
public virtual bool IsSynchronized {get;}
```

Let's consider the following code where we are creating a `Stack` object and then wrapping it up with a thread-safe, synchronized `Stack` object. Now the value of the `IsSynchronized` property of this new stack object will be `true` because it is thread-safe.

```
Stack myStack = new Stack();
Stack syncStack = Stack.Synchronized ( myStack );
Console.WriteLine( "IsSynchronized: {0}", myStack.IsSynchronized.ToString() );
Console.WriteLine( "IsSynchronized: {0}", syncStack.IsSynchronized.ToString() );
```

Output:

IsSynchronized: False
IsSynchronized: True

As you can see from the above brief example, you can get a `Synchronized` version of a `Stack` object by calling the `Synchronized` method. More information on the `Synchronized` method is given later in this chapter.

Methods of the Stack Class

Clone Method

This method creates a new Stack object containing references to the elements in Stack object. This newly created Stack only contains references to the elements in the Stack from which it was created. It does not contain a copy of it, so changes to one are reflected immediately in the other.

```
public virtual object Clone();
```

Contains Method

This method takes an object as a parameter and returns true if the object is present in the stack. This method uses the Object.Equals method internally to determine if the objects are equal.

```
public virtual bool Contains( object obj );
```

```
if( myStack.Contains("myObject") )
    Console.WriteLine("Result: Found");
else
    Console.WriteLine("Result: Not Found");
```

Clear Method

The Clear method removes all the objects from the Stack and sets the Count property to zero.

```
public virtual void Clear();
```

Example:

```
myStack.Clear();
```

CopyTo Method

This method copies all elements from a Stack object into an array. The index argument provides the starting location in the destination array.

```
public virtual void CopyTo( Array array, int index );
```

For example, the following code copies all the elements in the Stack called myStack to an array named arr. It starts copying elements at the seventh position of the array arr.

```
myStack.CopyTo( arr, 6 );
```

GetEnumerator Method

This method returns an IEnumerator class for the stack.

```
public virtual IEnumerator GetEnumerator();
```

This IEnumerator object provides a read-only cursor on the snapshot of elements in the stack. The following code shows how to get the IEnumerator object and how to loop through the elements in the stack:

```
Stack myStack = new Stack();
...
IEnumerator e = myStack.GetEnumerator();

while( e.MoveNext() )
{
  Response.Write( e );
}
```

Peek Method

This method returns an object from the top of the `Stack` without removing it.

```
public virtual object Peek();
```

This method is exactly the same as the `Pop` method except that it does not remove the object from the stack.

Pop Method

This method removes and returns an object from the top of the `Stack`.

```
public virtual object Pop();
```

This method returns an `InvalidOperationException` when you call this method on an empty stack. The following code snippet shows the use of this method:

```
string s = (string) myStack.Pop();
```

The above code pops an object from `myStack`, which is cast from the generic object type to string before being assigned to `s`.

Push Method

This method places an object onto the stack. As this method takes a generic object as a parameter, you can insert any type of object, including you own defined classes and `null`s, into a stack. If the internal buffer size limit is reached, the stack will automatically expand itself by a factor of two, that is, its size is doubled.

```
public virtual void Push( object obj );
```

Example: StackPush

The following code excerpt from the download file `StackPush.aspx` shows how to use the `Push` method:

```
Stack myStack = new Stack();

myStack.Push("Test");
myStack.Push(1);
myStack.Push(2.731);
myStack.Push(null);
// Any object can be pushed:
myStack.Push(new myClass());

foreach( object o in myStack )
```

```
if( o != null )
  Response.Write("Type: " + o.GetType() + "<BR>");
else
  Response.Write ("Type: Null Object<BR>");
```

When different data types are pushed onto a `Stack`, the `Stack` uses the technique of **boxing** to store them in memory, which in effect means that value of the data type is copied to the stack's memory. Boxing is covered in more detail in Wrox's *Professional C#*, ISBN 1-861004-99-0.

Synchronized Method

The `Synchronized` method returns the thread-safe wrapper of a `Stack` object. The `Stack` object itself is not thread-safe and can create problems when one than one thread tries to perform operations on the same `Stack` object. To avoid this situation and to synchronize the operations between the threads on a stack object, you can get a reference to a thread-safe wrapper object using the `Synchronized` method – a static method that takes a `Stack` object as an argument, and returns a thread-safe wrapper around the `Stack` object.

```
public static Stack Synchronized( Stack stack );
```

As you can see from the definition of this method, it is a static method, meaning you can invoke this method without first creating an instance of the `Stack` object, as shown below:

```
Stack mySyncStack = Stack.Synchronized( new Stack() );
```

This method throws `ArgumentNullException` if we pass a null `Stack` object as its parameter.

```
Stack SomeNullStack = null;
try
{
  Stack mySyncStack = Stack.Synchronized( SomeNullStack );
}
Catch( ArgumentNullException e )
{
  Response.Write( "Invalid value of {0}", e.ParamName );
}
```

ToArray Method

This method copies all the objects in a `Stack` to an array of generic objects.

```
public virtual object[] ToArray();
```

The order of the objects in the array is determined by the order in which they would be popped from the `Stack`, but of course this method does not remove any objects from the `Stack`.

Example: StackToArray

The following code, found in the download as `StackToArray.aspx`, demonstrates this method. It creates a stack, pushes some strings onto it, and then copies the elements to an `object` array, before displaying the contents of both the `Array` and `Stack`.

```
<%@ Page Language="C#" %>
<%@ Import Namespace="System.Collections" %>
<HTML>
<HEAD>
```

```
<SCRIPT runat="server">
protected void Page_Load(object Source, EventArgs e){
  Stack myStack = new Stack();

  myStack.Push("Birmingham");
  myStack.Push("London");
  myStack.Push("Leeds");

  object[] arr = myStack.ToArray();

  // display the elements of stack
  string msg = "<BR><B>Objects in Stack</B><BR>";
  while( myStack.Count > 0 )
    msg += ((string) myStack.Pop()) + "<BR>";

  // display the elements of array
  msg += "<B>Objects in new Array</B><BR>";
  foreach( object o in arr )
    msg += ( (string) o ) + "<BR>";

  lblMessage.InnerHtml = msg;
}

</SCRIPT>

</HEAD>
<BODY>
  <span id=lblMessage runat=server />
</BODY>
```

Here is the output from this code:

Objects in new Array
Leeds
London
Birmingham

Objects in Stack
Leeds
London
Birmingham

System.Text.RegularExpressions Namespace

This namespace contains a set of classes and enumerations that lets you operate on regular expressions. To use any of the classes contained in this namespace, you must include a reference to this namespace in your class or your .aspx page.

For example, you have to include the following line in your class:

```
using System.Text.RegularExpressions;
```

Similarly, if you are using these classes in your .aspx pages, you must include the following line in the top portion of the page:

```
<%@ Import Namespace="System.Text.RegularExpressions" %>
```

This namespace is contained in the System.dll assembly.

Regular Expressions

Regular Expressions are a commonly used notation for complex pattern matching in string-based data. The primary role of a regular expression engine is to quickly search for patterns of strings within other strings, a technique generally referred to as **Pattern Matching**. Most regular expression engines (.NET included) have facilities to allow string manipulation via very fast lookup and replace functionality, replacing matched sub-strings with another string of data. Regular Expressions in .NET are based on the Perl5 rules; as such they come with a high degree of flexibility in identifying the type of string data to match upon, be it numeric, textual, e-mail addresses, URLs, or a whole host of other patterns.

Suppose we have the string "This article is from Wrox!". If we wanted to replace all occurrences of "article" with "book", we would require a fairly simple search-and-replace mechanism. The process would need to loop through each character in the string and check whether the next seven characters are "article". If so, then delete those characters and insert "book" at that location. Now, let's take a look at the following string:

"Technical support phone number is (911) 911-9110 and sales support phone number is (411) 411-4110".

Now, if we had to extract all of the phone numbers from the above string, it would not be a simple character match. As there is no simple set of characters that has to be matched, we have to search for a pattern in the string instead. We know that all US phone numbers have the common pattern *(nnn) nnn-nnnn*, where *n* is a digit. This is exactly the sort of place where Regular Expressions come into action. Using the rules, we can define a pattern string for phone numbers (this pattern string is known as a Regular Expression) and use that pattern to search through the given string for all matching patterns. The regular expression for phone numbers in our case will be:

\([0-9]{3}\) [0-9]{3}-[0-9]{4}

> **NOTE: Different Regular Expressions can indicate the same pattern, for example:** "((\(\d{3}\) ?)|(\d{3}-))?\d{3}-\d{4}" **also represents the same matching pattern.**

Using this pattern, if we search through our string we can easily find all of the occurrences of phone numbers.

A Regular Expression is nothing more than a sequence of characters that defines a pattern. Some of the characters in the sequence have special meaning. For example a Regular Expression [1] will match all occurrences of 1 in the input string. Similarly, [0-9] is the Regular Expression that will match any number between 0 and 9. If you have to find three digits in a string where each of the three digits can be between 5 and 8, you can use the regular expression [5-8]{3}. Regular Expressions provide a very wide range of special characters and escape sequences. You can find more information on Regular expressions at http://msdn.microsoft.com/library/default.asp?url=/library/en-us/cpguidnf/html/cpconcomregularexpressions.asp

The namespace System.Text.RegularExpressions contains a set of classes to handle Regular Expressions. In the next sections, we will be going through some of the more important classes and their methods and properties.

The Capture Class

The `Capture` class represents a substring for a successful capture in the provided string.

```
public class Capture
```

One or more than one `Capture` instances are contained in a `Group`. One or more than one `Group` forms a `Match`. For more information on `Group` and `Match`, see the `Group` class and the `Match` class.

Properties of the Capture Class

Index Property

This property returns the offset in the string being searched where the captured substring has been found.

```
public int Index {get;}
```

Length Property

This property returns the length of the substring captured from the provided string.

```
public int Length {get;}
```

Value Property

This property returns the actual substring that is being captured.

```
public string Value {get;}
```

Example: RegExPhone

The following file, `RegExPhone.cs`, is a console application that demonstrates these properties by searching for a phone number pattern in a string:

```csharp
using System;
using System.Text.RegularExpressions;

public class reg
{
  public static void Main()
  {
    Regex re = new Regex("(?<AreaCode>\\([0-9]{3}\\)) (?<Phone>[0-9]{3}-[0-
9]{4})");
    MatchCollection mc = re.Matches("Work: (313) 123-1234 Home: (519) 245-1235");

    foreach( Match m in mc )
    {
      Console.WriteLine( "Match: "  + m.Value  );
      foreach( Group g in m.Groups )
      {
        Console.WriteLine( "Group: " + g );
        foreach( Capture c in g.Captures )
        {
          Console.WriteLine( "Capture: " + c.Value + "[Index=" + c.Index +
                                "; Length=" + c.Length + "]" );
        }
      }
    }
  }
}
```

Here is the output of this code:

```
Match: (313) 123-1234
Group: (313) 123-1234
Capture: (313) 123-1234[Index=6; Length=14]
Group: (313)
Capture: (313)[Index=6; Length=5]
Group: 123-1234
Capture: 123-1234[Index=12; Length=8]
Match: (519) 245-1235
Group: (519) 245-1235
Capture: (519) 245-1235[Index=27; Length=14]
Group: (519)
Capture: (519)[Index=27; Length=5]
Group: 245-1235
Capture: 245-1235[Index=33; Length=8]
```

As you can see, there are two matches in the string and each match has three groups. Each of these groups has one capture. It also displays the captured substring, its index on the string, and the length of the substring.

Methods of the Capture Class

ToString Method

This method returns the captured substring from the input string.

```
public override string ToString();
```

The returned substring is equivalent to the `Value` property.

The CaptureCollection Class

The `CaptureCollection` is a strongly typed collection of `Capture` objects.

```
public class CaptureCollection : ICollection, IEnumerable
```

This class supports enumeration, that is, you can iterate over its elements using an enumerator object.

Properties of the CaptureCollection Class

Count Property

This property returns the number of `Capture` objects present in the collection.

```
public int Count {get;}
```

IsReadOnly and IsSynchronized Properties

These properties can be used to determine if this `CaptureCollection` instance is read-only and synchronized, respectively. A synchronized instance permits simultaneous access by multiple threads, avoiding the need to pay particular attention to thread synchronization issues.

```
public bool IsReadOnly {get;}
public bool IsSynchronized {get;}
```

Item Property

The Item property returns a Capture object from a specified location in the collection. In C#, this property is an indexer property for the CaptureCollection class.

```
public Capture this[ int i ] {get;}
```

For example, to access the second Capture object in the CaptureCol capture collection you can use the following line of code:

```
Capture c = CaptureCol[1];
```

SyncRoot Property

This property returns a synchronizing object that may be used to synchronize simultaneous operations on CaptureCollection from more than one thread.

```
public object SyncRoot {get;}
```

Methods of the CaptureCollection Class

CopyTo Method

This method copies all the Capture objects contained in the collection to an array. The arrayIndex argument specifies the location in the destination array where the Capture object is to be copied.

```
public void CopyTo( Array array, int arrayIndex );
```

GetEnumerator Method

This method returns an IEnumerator object that can be used to iterate over all the elements in a CaptureCollection instance.

```
public IEnumerator GetEnumerator();
```

For example, you can use this method as shown below:

```
CaptureCollection cc = myGroup.Captures;
IEnumerator e = cc.GetEnumerator();
while( e.MoveNext() )
{
  Response.Write( e.Current );
}
```

The Group Class

The Group class is derived from the Capture class. It represents a group of captured substring in an input string. One or more than one Group makes a Match.

```
public class Group : Capture
```

Properties of the Group Class

Captures Property

This property contains a collection of `Capture` objects.

```
public CaptureCollection Captures {get;}
```

These `Capture` objects represent captured substrings which form a `Group`.

Success Property

This property returns `true` if the match is successful for the `Group`.

```
public bool Success {get;}
```

Methods of the Group Class

Synchronized Method

This method returns a synchronized thread-safe wrapper for the `Group` object, which can be used by more than one thread simultaneously, without having to worry about synchronization between threads.

```
public static Group Synchronized( Group inner );
```

This is a static method, so it may be called without first creating an instance of the `Group` object.

The GroupCollection Class

The `GroupCollection` class is a strongly typed collection of `Group` instances.

```
public class GroupCollection : ICollection, IEnumerable
```

The group collection implements the `IEnumerable` interface so you can iterate over its elements using an `IEnumerator` object.

Properties of the GroupCollection Class

Count Property

This property contains the number of `Group` objects currently contained in this `GroupCollection` object.

```
public int Count {get;}
```

IsReadOnly and IsSynchronized Properties

The `IsReadOnly` property indicates whether the `GroupCollection` object is read-only or not. The `IsSynchronized` property contains a `true` value if the `GroupCollection` is thread-safe. A synchronized instance permits simultaneous access to the `GroupCollection` by multiple threads, avoiding the need to pay particular attention to thread synchronization issues.

```
public bool IsReadOnly {get;}
public bool IsSynchronized {get;}
```

Both of these properties are themselves read-only.

Item Property

The Item property lets you access a specific Group object in GroupCollection using the name of the Group object or its offset in the collection. In C#, the Item property is the indexer for the GroupCollection class.

```
public Group this[ int groupnum ] {get;}
public Group this[ string groupname ] {get;}
```

As you can see from the above definition, which only mentions the get; keyword, this is a read-only property.

SyncRoot Property

This property returns a synchronizing object that can be used to synchronize simultaneous access to a Group object by multiple threads.

```
public object SyncRoot {get;}
```

Methods of the GroupCollection Class

CopyTo Method

This method copies all the Group objects in the GroupCollection to an array. You can also specify the array location where you want the elements to be copied.

```
public void CopyTo( Array array, int arrayIndex );
```

GetEnumerator Method

This method returns an enumerator object that can be used to iterate over the elements in the GroupCollection.

```
public IEnumerator GetEnumerator();
```

The Match Class

The Match object represents a match of the pattern in the input string.

Properties of the Match Class

Empty Property

The Empty property is a static property and is used to get an empty Match object.

```
public static Match Empty {get;}
```

For example:

```
Match m = Match.Empty;
```

Groups Property

The Groups property is an object of type GroupCollection. It is a collection of Group objects. Each match in the input string consists of one or more captured substring. These captured substrings are arranged in Groups.

```
public virtual GroupCollection Groups {get;}
```

Methods of the Match Class

NextMatch Method

This method returns the next Match object from the input string starting from the last position in the string where the match was found.

```
public Match NextMatch();
```

Example: RegExNextMatch

The code download file RegExNextMatch.aspx shows this method in action, by searching for all occurrences of a phone number in the string "Work: (313) 123-1234 Home: (519) 245-1235", with the following code:

```
Regex re = new Regex("\\([0-9]{3}\\) [0-9]{3}-[0-9]{4}");
Match m = re.Match("Work: (313) 123-1234 Home: (519) 245-1235");

while( m.Success )
{
  Response.Write( m.Value + "<BR>" );
  m = m.NextMatch();
}
```

Here is the output of this code:

(313) 123-1234
(519) 245-1235

Result Method

The Result method is used to format the substrings in different groups using a replacement pattern passed to the method as the argument. It returns the newly created formatted version of the string.

```
public virtual string Result( string replacement )
```

Example: RegExParsePhone

The following code, taken from the download file RegExParsePhone.cs, represents a console application that finds two matches in the input string. Each match has three groups. The Result method uses a pattern to format results of the second and third group's substrings.

```
using System;
using System.Text.RegularExpressions;

public class reg
{
  public static void Main()
  {
```

```
      Regex re = new Regex(
                    "(?<AreaCode>\\([0-9]{3}\\)) (?<Phone>[0-9]{3}-[0-9]{4})");
      MatchCollection mc = re.Matches("Work: (313) 123-1234 Home: (519) 245-1235");

      foreach( Match m in mc )
      {
        Console.WriteLine( m.Result("Area Code is $1 and Phone Number is $2") );
      }
    }
  }
```

Here is the output produced by the code:

Area Code is (313) and Phone Number is 123-1234
Area Code is (519) and Phone Number is 245-1235

Synchronized Method

The Synchronized method is a static method that returns a thread-safe wrapper of the Match object.

```
    public static new Match Synchronized( Match inner );
```

The MatchCollection Class

MatchCollection is strongly typed collection of Match objects. If you expect to get more than one match in an input string, you can use MatchCollection to hold all the Match objects in your input string using the Matches method of the Regex object. For example, the following code populates a MatchCollection by calling the Matches method:

```
      Regex re = new Regex(
                    "(?<AreaCode>\\([0-9]{3}\\)) (?<Phone>[0-9]{3}-[0-9]{4})");
      MatchCollection mc = re.Matches("Work: (313) 123-1234 Home: (519) 245-1235");
```

Properties of the MatchCollection Class

Count Property

This property returns the number of Match objects in the MatchCollection.

```
    public int Count {get;}
```

IsReadOnly and IsSynchronized Properties

These properties indicate if the MatchCollection object is read-only and thread-safe respectively. A synchronized instance permits simultaneous access to the MatchCollection by multiple threads, avoiding the need to pay special attention to thread synchronization issues.

```
    public bool IsReadOnly {get;}
    public bool IsSynchronized {get;}
```

They return a Boolean value.

Item Property

The Item property returns or sets a Match object in the MatchCollection object using an index argument i.

```
    public Match this [ int i ] { virtual get;}
```

Example: MatchCollectionItem

The file below, `MatchCollectionItem.aspx`, demonstrates `MatchCollection` and its `Item` property:

```
<%@ Page Language="C#" %>

<HTML>
<HEAD>

<SCRIPT runat="server">

protected void Page_Load(object Source, EventArgs e){
  string msg = "";

  Regex re = new Regex("(?<AreaCode>\\([0-9]{3}\\)) (?<Phone>[0-9]{3}-[0-9]{4})");
  MatchCollection mc = re.Matches("Work: (313) 123-1234 Home: (519) 245-1235");

  for( int i=0; i< mc.Count; i++ )
  {
    msg += mc[i].Value + "<BR>";
  }
  lblMessage.InnerHtml = msg;
}

</SCRIPT>
</HEAD>
<BODY>
  <span id=lblMessage runat=server />
</BODY>
</HTML>
```

Here is the output of the code:

(313) 123-1234
(519) 245-1235

SyncRoot Property

This property returns a synchronizing object that may be used to synchronize simultaneous access to `MatchCollection` by different threads.

```
public object SyncRoot {get;}
```

Methods of the MatchCollection Class

CopyTo Method

This method copies the contents of a `MatchCollection` instance into an array at the specified index.

```
public void CopyTo( Array array, int arrayIndex );
```

GetEnumerator Method

This method returns an `IEnumerator` object that may be used to iterate over the elements of the `MatchCollection`.

```
public IEnumerator GetEnumerator();
```

The Regex Class

In the Microsoft .NET framework, one of the core classes for Regular Expression handling is the `Regex` class. This class is used to compile a regular expression and then search for it in any string and replace it if desired. This compilation process involves converting the pattern string to binary form and storing it in memory in order to enhance performance when searching for the pattern in the input string. Each object of this class represents an unchangeable regular expression. This means that you can define a single pattern only for a `Regex` object that cannot later be changed without reinstantiating the object. However, you can use object of this class as many times as you like on different strings.

This class has some static methods, for example `CompileToAssembly`, `Escape`, `IsMatch`, `Match`, `Matches`, `Replace`, `Split`, and `Unescape`. Static methods can be called without instantiating their parent class, in this case, the `Regex` class.

Constructors

The `Regex` class has overloaded constructors to initialize a new instance of the object.

```
protected Regex();
public Regex( string pattern );
public Regex( string pattern, RegexOptions options );
```

Here the `pattern` argument is of string type and contains the regular expression pattern to match. Also note that the first constructor above may only be used by a deriving class because it is protected.

The RegexOptions Argument

This class has the following arguments:

❑ **Compiled** – this option forces the compiler to include the compiled regular expression in the assembly. This accelerates the execution of code that uses it, as regular expressions do not need be compiled at run-time, but it does have a negative impact on the loading time of the assembly.

❑ **ECMAScript** – indicates to the regular expression compiler that the expression is in ECMA format.

❑ **ExplicitCapture** – instructs the RE (Regular Expression) compiler to search only named RE patterns.

❑ **IgnoreCase** – this option instructs the RE compiler to perform a case-insensitive match.

❑ **IgnorePatternWhitespaces** – ignores unescaped white spaces.

❑ **Multiline** – this option changes the meaning of ^ and $. By setting this flag, the RE compiler treats each line as a separate pattern.

❑ **None** – no option is set.

❑ **RightToLeft** – instructs the RE compiler to search the string from right to left. This option is good for those languages whose script flows right to left.

❑ **Singleline** – tells the RE compiler that the given RE pattern consists of a single line.

In case of failure, the Constructors all throw an `ArgumentException`.

The following code creates an instance of the `Regex` object with the `IgnoreCase` flag. It also provides a pattern for searching for an e-mail address in the constructor. The regular expression builds up a pattern for matching a general e-mail address like this: any word (denoted by [\\w-]), plus @, followed by another word, a period ('.'), and finally another word, thus correctly matching simple e-mail addresses such as `barney@bear.net`.

```
Regex re = new Regex("[\\w-]+@([\\w-]+\\.)+[\\w-]+",
  RegexOptions.IgnoreCase );
```

Properties of the Regex Class

Options Property

This is a read-only property and returns the option that was set while creating the object in the constructor.

```
public RegexOption Options {get;}
```

For a list of possible values of `RegexOptions`, see the previous section.

RightToLeft Property

This is a read-only property and returns `true` if the Regular Expression compiler was set to search the string from right to left while creating the `Regex` object.

```
public bool RightToLeft {get;}
```

Example use:

```
Response.Write( "Option : " + re.RightToLeft );
```

Methods of the Regex Class

IsMatch Method

This method indicates if the pattern has at least one occurrence in the input string. Returns `true` if the pattern is present in the string, otherwise returns `false`.

The `IsMatch` method also has instance and static versions of the overloaded methods:

```
public bool IsMatch( string input );
public bool IsMatch( string input, int startat );

public static bool IsMatch( string input, string pattern );
public static bool IsMatch( string input, string pattern, RegexOptions options );
```

Here `startat` indicates the position in the input string from where the search for the pattern will begin.

Match Method

The `Match` method searches the input string for the first occurrence of the defined pattern and returns a `Match` object.

There are two sets of overloaded `Match` methods. One set is of the instance type, as below:

```
public Match Match( string input );
public Match Match( string input, int startat );
public Match Match( string input, int beginning, int length );
```

The `Match` method returns a `Match` object. We will see the `Match` object in more detail in the next section. All of the overloaded methods take an input string. The `Match` method searches for the defined pattern in this string. You can also search a portion of the input string if you provide a `startat` in the second overload or if you provide `beginning` and `length` in the third overload.

The other set is of static methods, which can be used in creating an instance of the `Regex` object:

```
public static Match Match( string input, string pattern );
public static Match Match( string input, string pattern, RegexOptions options );
```

As these methods are called without creating an instance of the `Regex` object, you also have to provide the pattern and/or `RegexOptions` as the argument.

The following code creates a `Regex` object and calls its `Match` method to get a `Match` object. Then it checks the `Success` property of the `Match` object to make sure that a match was successful, before it writes the found string to the `Response` object. This code finds a telephone number of the format *(XXX) XXX-XXXX* format from the string "My home phone number is (519) 245-1234.":

```
Regex re = new Regex("\\([0-9]{3}\\) [0-9]{3}-[0-9]{4}");
Match m = re.Match("My home phone number is (519) 245-1235.");

if( m.Success )
  Response.Write( m.Value );
```

The same thing can also be done using a static method:

```
Match m = Regex.Match("My home phone number is (519) 245-1235.",
        "\\([0-9]{3}\\) [0-9]{3}-[0-9]{4}");
if( m.Success )
  Response.Write( m.Value );
```

Here is the output that the above code would produce:

(519) 245-1235

We will learn more about the `Match` object in the next section.

Matches Method

The `Matches` method searches for all of the occurrences of the pattern in the input string and returns a `MatchCollection` object. The `MatchCollection` object is a collection of `Match` objects and each item in the collection represents a match on the pattern in the input string.

Just like the `Match` method, the `Matches` method also has two sets of overloaded methods: instance `Matches` methods:

```
public MatchCollection Matches( string input );
public MatchCollection Matches( string input, int startat );
```

and static `Matches` methods:

```
public static MatchCollection Matches( string input, string pattern );
public static MatchCollection Matches( string input, string pattern,
                        RegexOptions options );
```

Let's consider an input string "Home: (519) 123-1234 Work: (313) 987-9876", where we have to find all of the phone numbers from the string. We will use the `Matches` method to search for a telephone number pattern in the string mentioned above to get a collection of `Match` objects:

```
MatchCollection mc = Regex.Matches(
   "Home: (519) 245-1235 Work: (313) 234-2345","\\([0-9]{3}\\) [0-9]{3}-[0-9]{4}");
foreach( Match m in mc )
   Response.Write( m.Value );
```

Replace Method

Like the classic ASP `Replace` function, the `Replace` method of the `Regex` object can be used to replace any matched pattern in a string with an alternative string. The `Replace` method returns a new string containing the replaced entities.

```
public string Replace( string input, MatchEvaluator evaluator );
public string Replace( string input, string replacement );
public string Replace( string input, MatchEvaluator evaluator, int count );
public string Replace( string input, string replacement, int count );
public string Replace( string input, MatchEvaluator evaluator, int count,
               int startat );
public string Replace( string input, string replacement, int count, int startat );


public static string Replace( string input, string pattern,
            MatchEvaluator evaluator );
public static string Replace( string input, string pattern,
            string replacement );
public static string Replace( string input, string pattern,
            MatchEvaluator evaluator, RegexOptions options );
public static string Replace( string input, string pattern,
            string replacement, RegexOptions options );
```

System.IO Namespace

The `System.IO` namespace contains classes that help us to interact with both the file-system object and streams. Contained within it is a set of classes that are used to write to and read from a stream using different encoding schemes.

- ❑ **File-System-Related Classes** – this includes the `File`, `Directory`, `Path`, `FileInfo`, `DirectoryInfo`, and `FileSystemWatcher` classes

- ❑ **Stream-Related Classes** – these include the `FileStream`, `MemoryStream`, and `BufferedStream` classes

- ❑ **Stream Reader and Writer Classes** – these include the `StreamReader/Writer`, `StringReader/Writer`, and `BinaryReader/Writer` classes

The Directory Class

The `Directory` class lets you perform different operations on file system directories. All of the methods for this class are static, so you don't need to create an instance of this class. However, just like the `File` class that we'll see later, it also performs security checking on every call that it makes to the operating system. The `Directory` class has its counterpart instance class, the `DirectoryInfo` class. You have to explicitly create an instance of the class to call any of its methods.

Methods of the Directory Class

CreateDirectory Method

This method creates a directory on the `FileSystem` as specified in the `path` argument.

```
public static DirectoryInfo CreateDirectory( string path );
```

This method returns an instance of the `DirectoryInfo` class, which gives you information about the directory just created. It takes the path name for the directory to be created, limited to a maximum 248 characters. By default, all users have full read and write access to the newly created directory. An exception is thrown if you attempt to create a subdirectory in a directory for which you don't have access rights.

If you pass a path that includes parent directories that do not actually exist at the current time, this method will create them automatically. For example, the following code creates a directory named `Jilani` on the C drive, and under that directory it creates a subdirectory named `Adil`, and then under this subdirectory it creates another one called `Jibran`.

```
Directory.CreateDirectory("C:\\Jilani\\Adil\\Jibran");
```

Don't forget to use the C# escape sequence, \\, if using a backslash character in the path!

Delete Method

The `Delete` method removes the directory specified by the `path` argument. If the directory contains any file or subdirectory in it, an `IOException` will be thrown unless the `recursive` argument is set to `true`.

```
public static void Delete( string path );
public static void Delete( string path, bool recursive );
```

Exists Method

This method returns `true` if the directory name specified in the argument exists, otherwise it returns `false`.

```
public static bool Exists( string path );
```

GetCreationTime, GetLastAccessTime, and GetLastWriteTime Methods

These methods return the creation time, the time when the directory was last accessed, and the time when it was last written to for a directory name specified in the argument, respectively.

```
public static DateTime GetCreationTime( string path );
public static DateTime GetLastAccessTime( string path );
public static DateTime GetLastWriteTime( string path );
```

All of these methods take the path of the directory and return a `DateTime` object.

SetCreationTime, SetLastAccessTime, and SetLastWriteTime Methods

These methods set the time when the directory was created, last accessed, and last written to. These methods take the path of the directory and a `DateTime` object.

```
public static void SetCreationTime( string path, DateTime creationTime );
public static void SetLastAccessTime( string path, DateTime lastAccessTime );
public static void SetLastWriteTime( string path, DateTime lastWriteTime );
```

GetCurrentDirectory and SetCurrentDirectory Methods

The GetCurrentDirectory method returns the current working directory, while the SetCurrentDirectory method sets the directory specified in the argument as the current working directory.

```
public static string GetCurrentDirectory();
public static void SetCurrentDirectory( string path );
```

For example, the following code sets the current working directory to C:\Temp and then gets the current working directory:

```
Directory.SetCurrentDirectory("C:\\Temp");
  Response.Write( Directory.GetCurrentDirectory() );
```

GetDirectories Method

This method returns string array containing all of the subdirectories in the directory specified in the path argument.

```
public static string[] GetDirectories( string path );
public static string[] GetDirectories( string path, string searchPattern );
```

You can also specify a search pattern for the subdirectories' name in one of its overloaded methods. This search pattern follows the rule of DOS-type wild cards. For example, the following code lists all of the subdirectories whose name starts with a letter 's' and are present in the C:\ (root) directory.

```
string[] dirlist = Directory.GetDirectories("C:\\", "s*");
foreach( string s in dirlist )
  msg += s + "<BR>";
Response.Write( msg );
```

The search criteria are case-insensitive.

GetDirectoryRoot and GetParent Methods

The GetDirectoryRoot method returns the root of the directory specified in the input argument.

```
public static string GetDirectoryRoot( string path );
```

The GetParent method returns a DirectoryInfo object for the parent directory.

```
public static DirectoryInfo GetParent( string path );
```

GetFiles Method

This method returns a list of strings containing the complete name of the files in the specified path. You can also provide search criteria for the file names.

```
public static string[] GetFiles( string path );
public static string[] GetFiles( string path, string searchPattern );
```

Here `path` is the directory where the object has to look for the list of files and `searchPattern` indicates the criteria for the files to be searched. For example, the following code will search for all `.exe` files in the `C:\WINNT` directory:

```
string msg = "";
string[] files = Directory.GetFiles("C:\\WINNT", "*.exe");

foreach( string file in files )
  msg += file + "<BR>";

Response.Write( msg );
```

GetFileSystemEntries Method

This method returns a string array containing the names of both directories and files in a specified path.

```
public static string[] GetFileSystemEntries( string path );
public static string[] GetFileSystemEntries( string path, string searchPattern );
```

You can also provide matching criteria in one of its overloaded methods.

Example: RecursiveListFiles

The following code snippet, from `RecursiveListFiles.aspx`, lists all file-system objects in a specified path, and then this path is passed through a `Request` object's `path` entry. Initially the path is set to `C:\`. In this code, the string returned from `GetFileSystemEntries` is checked to see if it contains a directory or a file using the `Directory.Exists` method. If the string contains the name of a directory, the entry in the list is enclosed in a hyperlink and the `HREF` attribute is set to that directory name. This means that clicking on the hyperlink will list all of the entries under that subdirectory. If the string does not contain a directory it is assumed that the string is a filename.

```
string msg = "";
string path = "C:\\";

if( Request["path"] != null )
  path = Request["path"];

string[] list = Directory.GetFileSystemEntries( path );

foreach( string fso in list )
  if( Directory.Exists( fso ) )
    msg += "<A HREF='?path="+ fso + "\\'>" + fso + "</A><BR>";
  else
    msg += fso + "<BR>";

Response.Write( msg );
```

GetLogicalDrives Method

This returns a string array containing all of the logical drives on the machine.

```
public static string[] GetLogicalDrives();
```

The following code, for example, lists all of the logical drives on the machine:

```
string s = "";
string[] sa = Directory.GetLogicalDrives();

foreach( string ss in sa )
  s += ss + "<BR>";

Response.Write( s );
```

Move Method

This method moves a directory along with its contents to a new location.

```
public static void Move( string sourceDirName, string destDirName );
```

Here `sourceDirName` is the name of the directory whose content has to be moved and `destDirName` is the name of the new directory where the contents of the source directory will be moved. The source and destination directories must be different, but both have to be on the same disk volume.

The File Class

The `File` class provides a set of static methods to perform different file operations. Using these methods, you can create a file, delete a file, or append data to a file. You can also obtain information about the file such as its creation time, attributes, etc. Furthermore, you can make changes to file-specific information using methods contained in this class. As all of the members of this class are static, you do not have to explicitly create an instance of the `File` class to call any of its methods. Methods contained in this class perform all of the security checking for the file at the file-system level. So every time you call a method in this class on a specific file, all of the security permissions are checked.

The `System.IO` namespace also provides another class, the `FileInfo` class, which has a subset of the functionality of `File` class. As opposed to the `File` class, however, all of the methods contained in the `FileInfo` class are of the instance type. This means that you have to explicitly create an object of the `FileInfo` class to access its methods. The `FileInfo` class checks the permissions of a file only when the object is created. This makes the `FileInfo` class more useful when you have to perform several tasks at the same time on a particular file, as it will not check its file permissions on every call.

The `File` class does not contain any properties.

Methods of the File Class

AppendText Method

This method opens the file in Append mode and returns a `StreamWriter` object. It also moves to the end of the stream so that everything you write to the stream will go at the end of the file. A new file is created if the file specified does not already exist.

```
public static StreamWriter AppendText( string path );
```

For example, the following code appends a line at the end of a file.

```
StreamWriter sw = File.AppendText("myFile.txt");
Sw.WriteLine("Add this line at the end of file");
```

Copy, Move, Delete, and Exists Methods

You have probably already guessed that these methods can be respectively used to copy, move, or delete a file, as well as checking if a certain file actually exists or not.

```
public static void Copy( string sourceFileName, string destFileName );
public static void Copy( string sourceFileName, string destFileName, bool
                                                            overwrite );
public static void Move( string sourceFileName, string destFileName );
public static void Delete( string path );
public static bool Exists( string path );
```

Here, sourceFileName indicates the file to be copied or moved, and desFileName indicates its new filename. overwrite indicates if a file already exists with the name given in destFileName, it should be overwritten when the source file is copied. The path parameter of the Delete and Exists methods specifies the fully qualified filename of the file to be deleted or checked for existence.

Create and CreateText Methods

The Create method creates a new file at the specified path and returns a FileStream object. This object is a stream for the physical file on the hard disk; if you write anything to this stream this will automatically be written to the physical hard disk. You can also specify the size of the buffer for the FileStream object by specifying bufferSize.

```
public static FileStream Create( string path );
public static FileStream Create( string path, int bufferSize );
public static StreamWriter CreateText( string path );
```

The CreateText method creates a file and returns a StreamWriter object. This object is a wrapper around the FileStream object and uses a specific encoding to write text to the file.

GetAttributes and SetAttributes Methods

These retrieve or set the attributes of a specified file.

```
public static FileAttributes GetAttributes( string path );
public static void SetAttributes( string path, FileAttributes fileAttributes );
```

These methods take a filename as an argument. This filename can either be a relative or an absolute filename. You can also use the Universal Naming Convention (UNC). The GetAttributes method returns a value from the FileAttributes enumeration, while on the other hand, the SetAttributes method takes the same kind of data type in its arguments.

Here is the list of values from the FileAttributes enumeration:

- ❑ ReadOnly – you can only read this file. Write is denied.
- ❑ System – file is a system file (it's a part of the operating system).
- ❑ Hidden – the file is hidden file.
- ❑ Normal – regular file.
- ❑ Compressed – the file is compressed.
- ❑ Encrypted – indicates that the file is encrypted.

- ❑ `Temporary` – indicates that the file is temporary and should be deleted.

- ❑ `Directory` – indicates that the provided filename is a directory.

- ❑ `Offline` – contents of the file folder is not available currently.

- ❑ `NotContentIndexed` – the operating system file indexer will not index the file. In Windows 2000, all of the files marked by this flag are indexed by the operating system to optimize file searching procedures.

- ❑ `ReparsePoint` – the file contains associated user-defined data. On NTFS, applications can attach user-defined data to a file. When the file is opened, this data is used with the file system filter supplied by the application. One example of these files is the NTFS link file.

- ❑ `SparseFile` – indicates that the file is large and a large portion of the file consists of zeros. When this attribute is set for a file, the operating system does not allocate space for every single byte, thus saving disk space for files that are largely empty.

The following code makes the file hidden and read-only:

```
File.SetAttributes("C:\\VS.NET\\File.cs",
  FileAttributes.Hidden | FileAttributes.ReadOnly);
```

GetCreationTime and SetCreationTime Methods

These methods retrieve and set, respectively, the date and time the file was first created.

```
public static DateTime GetCreationTime( string path );
public static void SetCreationTime( string path, DateTime creationTime );
```

These methods take a complete filename as an argument. You can also use UNC to provide the filename in the "path" argument.

GetCreationTime returns a DateTime object indicating the creation time of the file. On the other hand, SetCreationTime uses creationTime as its second argument, which contains the new date and time to set as the creation time of the file.

The following code retrieves the creation time of file1.cs and sets the file creation time of file2.cs to the current date and time.

```
Response.Write( "GetCreationTime : {0}",
  File.GetCreationTime("\\\\SERVER1\\SHARE1\\file1.cs") );
File.SetCreationTime("C:\\file2.cs", DateTime.Now );
```

Failing to provide a valid filename in the arguments will result in an ArgumentException. If the creationTime supplied in the argument of SetCreationTime is invalid, an ArgumentOutOfRangeException will be thrown.

GetLastAccessTime and SetLastAccessTime Methods

These methods retrieve or set, respectively, the date and time the specified file was last accessed.

```
public static DateTime GetLastAccessTime( string path );
public static void SetLastAccessTime( string path, DateTime lastAccessTime );
```

The `GetLastAccessTime` method takes a complete filename as its argument. The `SetLastAccessTime` method takes a filename as well as a date and time. Just like the `Get/SetCreationTime` methods, `ArgumentException` and `ArgumentOutOfRangeException` are thrown when the filename is invalid or when the date and time are invalid respectively.

GetLastWriteTime and SetLastWriteTime Methods

These two methods either retrieve or set the last date and time when something was written to the specified file.

```
public static DateTime GetLastWriteTime( string path );
public static void SetLastWriteTime( string path, DateTime lastAccessTime );
```

Open, OpenRead, OpenWrite and OpenText Methods

The `Open` method opens a specified file in a specified mode and access and returns a `FileStream` object that could be used to write to the file.

The `OpenRead` and `OpenWrite` methods open the specified file in read or write mode and return a `FileStream` object

The `OpenText` method returns a `StreamWriter` object for a specified file.

```
public static FileStream Open( string path, FileMode mode );
public static FileStream Open( string path, FileMode mode, FileAccess access );
public static FileStream Open( string path, FileMode mode,
                            FileAccess access, FileShare share );
public static FileStream OpenRead( string path );
public static FileStream OpenWrite( string path );
public static StreamReader OpenText( string path );
```

FileInfo Class

The `FileInfo` class provides more or less the same functionality as the `File` class. The only difference between these classes is that all of the methods in the `File` class are static, and you do not have to create an instance of the `File` object to work with it. In the `FileInfo` class you have to create an instance of the object to access its methods and properties. Furthermore, the `File` class checks the file permission on every call to the file system. The FileInfo class on the other hand does it only once when the object is created. The `FileInfo` class is derived from the `FileSystemInfo` class.

Properties of the FileInfo Class

Directory Property

This property contains the instance of the `DirectoryInfo` class for the parent directory of the file.

```
public DirectoryInfo Directory {get;}
```

This `DirectoryInfo` object can be used to manipulate different properties of the directory.

Exists Property

This property returns `true` if the file exists. Note that if the file does not exist, or if it is a directory, this property returns `false`.

```
public override bool Exists {get;}
```

You must check if the file exists or not before performing any operations on it, otherwise you may get an exception.

Length Property

This property returns the size of the current file in bytes.

```
public long Length {get;}
```

Calling this property may result in `IOException` or `FileNotFoundException` if an IO error occurred or if the file was not found.

Name and DirectoryName Properties

The `Name` property returns the name of the file.

```
public override string Name {get;}
```

The `DirectoryName` gets the name of the directory where the file is located.

```
public string DirectoryName {get;}
```

For example, the following code gets the directory name of the file:

```
FileInfo fi = new FileInfo("File.cs");
Message.InnerHtml = fi.DirectoryName;
```

If the file is not found, the `DirectoryName` property will contain the default directory of the ASP.NET engine which is `c:\WINNT\system32`.

Methods of the FileInfo Class

AppendText Method

Returns a `StreamWriter` object, and moves the position of the pointer to the end of the file so that everything written to the `StreamWriter` is written to the end of the file.

```
public static StreamWriter AppendText( );
```

The code below shows use of this method:

```
FileInfo file = FileInfo("abc.txt");
StreamWriter sw = file.AppendText();
sw.WriteLine("Some Text");
```

CopyTo, MoveTo, and Delete Methods

These methods copy, move, and delete the current file respectively.

```
public FileInfo CopyTo( string destFileName );
public FileInfo CopyTo( string destFileName, bool overwrite );
public void MoveTo( string destFileName );
public override void Delete();
```

Argument	Description
destFileName	Name of the destination file.
Overwrite	Indicates if it should overwrite the destination file if it is already present. A true value will force it to overwrite if the file already exists.

Calling the CopyTo method copies the current file to a new file as specified by destFileName, returning a new FileInfo object for the copy.

The MoveTo method moves the current file to a new destination, while the Delete method removes the specified file from the file system.

These methods are analogous to their counterpart methods in the File class, except that in the File class, file permission is checked on every call while for FileInfo class it is only checked at the time of creating the instance of the object.

Create and CreateText Method

The Create method creates a file and returns a FileStream. This stream could be used to write to or read from the file. The filename should be provided in the constructor of the FileInfo class.

The CreateText method creates a file and returns a StreamWriter object. This StreamWriter is in fact a wrapper around an underlying FileStream object, and makes it easy to write different .NET data types to the file without worrying about different encoding schemes.

```
public FileStream Create();
public StreamWriter CreateText();
```

These methods create a new file and if the file is already there they overwrite it. So before using these methods, make sure you do not need any data in the existing file.

Open Method

The Open method opens a file with a specified mode, access and sharing attribute. It returns a FileStream object that can read or write data from the file. A new file is created if the file does not already exist.

```
public FileStream Open( FileMode mode );
public FileStream Open( FileMode mode, FileAccess access );
public FileStream Open( FileMode mode, FileAccess access, FileShare share );
```

Here, the mode argument is an enumeration of type FileMode. It can have one of the following values:

❑ **Append** – opens the file and sets the position of the file pointer to the end.

❑ **Create** – creates a new file. Overwrites any file that already exists.

❑ **CreateNew** – creates a new file. If the file already exists, an exception is thrown.

❑ **OpenOrCreate** – creates a file if it does not already exist, or opens it if it does already exist.

❑ **Open** – opens a file.

❑ **Truncate** – opens a file and truncates it to zero length.

The access argument can be any value from the FileAccess enumeration, as listed below:

- ❑ Read – file is opened for read only
- ❑ Write – file is opened for write only.
- ❑ ReadWrite – file is opened for read and write operation

The share argument indicates whether more than one process can work with the file at the same time. It can have any of the following values:

- ❑ None – If one process opens a file, other processes will not be able to open it until after the first process has closed it
- ❑ Read – If one process opens a file, all subsequent processes can open it in read mode only
- ❑ ReadWrite –Processes can read and write to a file even if it is already open by a process
- ❑ Write – Subsequent processes can open the file in write mode

OpenText Method

The OpenText method opens a file to read data from. It returns a StreamWriter object, which is a wrapper around an underlying FileStream object. Every character written to the file is encoded by the UTF8 scheme. For information on UTF8 encoding, refer to the Encoding class later in the chapter.

```
public StreamReader OpenText();
```

It throws an exception if the file does not exist, or you don't have the required permission to access the file. The following code opens a file, reads the first line, and displays it:

```
FileInfo fi = new FileInfo("myFile");
StreamReader sr = fi.OpenRead();
Response.Write( sr.ReadLine() );
sr.Close();
```

OpenRead and OpenWrite Methods

The OpenRead method opens an existing file and returns a read-only FileStream instance. This file can only be used to read data from the file. If the file does not exist, a FileNotFoundException will be thrown. OpenWrite opens a file and returns a write-only FileStream object. It creates the file if does not already exist. You can use the FileStream object only for writing data to the file.

```
public FileStream OpenRead();
public FileStream OpenWrite();
```

Example: OpenCloseRead

The OpenCloseRead.aspx file shown below creates a file using the OpenWrite method, writes some data to it and closes it. Then, it reopens the file using the OpenRead method, and displays the contents of the file as just written.

```
<%@ Page Language="C#" %>
<%@ Import Namespace="System.IO" %>
```

```
<SCRIPT runat="server">

protected void Page_Load(object Source, EventArgs e){
  string msg = "";
  FileStream fs;

  byte[] ba_source = {87, 82, 79, 88};
  byte[] ba_destin = new byte[4];

  FileInfo fi = new FileInfo("C:\\myFile.txt");

  fs = fi.OpenWrite();
  fs.Write( ba_source , 0, 4 );
  fs.Close();

  fs = fi.OpenRead();
  fs.Read( ba_destin, 0, 4 );
  fs.Close();

  foreach( byte b in ba_destin )
    Response.Write( (char) b );
}

</SCRIPT>
```

Here is the output from this code:

WROX

ToString Method

This method returns a string containing the fully qualified path of the file.

```
public override string ToString();
```

The FileStream Class

The `FileStream` class provides a stream for a file, that represents the serialization of the file's contents. This stream may be used to read and write to a file synchronously or asynchronously. Such file streams also supports random access seeking – that is, you can move both forward and backward to search for a specific item in the stream.

The `FileStream` class is derived from the `Stream` class.

Constructors

These create an instance of the `FileStream` object. The constructor for this class is overloaded as below:

```
public FileStream( IntPtr handle, FileAccess access );
public FileStream( string path, FileMode mode );
public FileStream( IntPtr handle, FileAccess access, bool ownsHandle );
public FileStream( string path, FileMode mode, FileAccess access );
public FileStream( IntPtr handle, FileAccess access, bool ownsHandle,
          int bufferSize );
public FileStream( string path, FileMode mode, FileAccess access, FileShare share );
public FileStream( IntPtr handle, FileAccess access, bool ownsHandle,
```

```
                          int bufferSize, bool isAsync );
      public FileStream( string path, FileMode mode, FileAccess access,
              FileShare share, int bufferSize );
```

The following table describes the different arguments that can be used for the constructor:

Argument	Description
IntPtr	Operating system handle for the file.
Path	Filename along with the path that has to be encapsulated in a stream.
access	Access mode for the underlying file. This could be set to one of the values of the FileAccess enumeration.
Mode	The mode in which the underlying file should be opened. This could be set to a value of the FileMode enumeration.
ownsHandle	true if the operating system file handle should be owned by the FileStream object.
bufferSize	The size of the buffer in bytes.
Share	Can be set to one of the values of the FileShare enum. Indicates how the file has to be shared across different processes.
isAsync	true if the file should be open for asynchronous operation.

Here are the possible values for the FileAccess enumeration:

❑   Read – file is opened for read only

❑   Write – file is opened for write only

❑   ReadWrite – file is opened for read and write operation

The following is the list of possible values for the FileMode enumeration:

❑   Append – opens the file and sets the current position of the pointer to the end of the file.

❑   Create – creates a new file. Overwrites if the file is already there.

❑   CreateNew – creates a new file and if the file already exists it throws an exception.

❑   OpenOrCreate – creates a file if it does not already exist and opens it if it does already exist.

❑   Open – opens a file.

❑   Truncate – opens a file and truncates its contents.

Properties of the FileStream Class

CanRead, CanWrite, and CanSeek Properties

The CanRead property indicates if the FileStream object can retrieve data from the source of the stream (from a file in other words). A return type of true in this property means you can read data from the stream.

539

The `CanWrite` property indicates if writing to the stream is permitted or not. A `true` value means you can write to the stream.

The `CanSeek` property returns `true` if the stream supports moving back and forth in the stream.

```
public bool CanRead { override get; }
public bool CanWrite { override get; }
public bool CanSeek { override get; }
```

Some of the stream types coming from the operating system, such as `stdin` and `stdout`, can only accessed for reading or writing, depending on their specific nature. In those cases, you can figure out the operations supported on the streams by using these properties. The following code shows the use of these properties for the `FileStream` object:

```
FileStream fs = new FileStream("abc.txt", FileMode.OpenOrCreate );
Response.Write( fs.CanRead + "<BR>");
Response.Write( fs.CanWrite + "<BR>");
Response.Write( fs.CanSeek + "<BR>");
```

If the `CanSeek` property for a stream is `false`, a call to the `Length`, `Position`, or `SetLength` methods/properties will result in an exception.

Handle Property

This property returns the operating-system's handle for the underlying file.

```
public virtual IntPtr Handle {get;}
```

Using this handle you can make operating system function calls on the file.

IsAsync Property

This property contains a Boolean value indicating if the underlying file was opened asynchronously or synchronously. It returns `true` value if it was opened asynchronously.

```
public virtual bool IsAsync {get;}
```

Length Property

Returns the length of the stream in bytes.

```
public long Length { override get; }
```

For example, the following code opens a stream against a file and then calls the `Length` property to get the length of the file in bytes.

```
FileStream fs = new FileStream("C:\\VS.NET\\abc.txt", FileMode.OpenOrCreate );
Response.Write( fs.Length + "<BR>");
fs.Close();
```

Name Property

The `Name` property gets the fully qualified name of the file used as the source of this `FileStream`.

```
public string Name {get;}
```

Position Property

The `Position` property gets or sets the current position in the stream.

```
public long Position { override get; override set; }
```

This returns the current position in the stream where data will be written to or will be read from. For example the following code sets the position to the end of the stream so that anything written to the stream is written at the end.

```
FileStream fs = new FileStream("C:\\VS.NET\\abc.txt", FileMode.OpenOrCreate );
fs.Position = fs.Length;
// Write some data to the stream
fs.Close()
```

Methods of the FileStream Class

BeginRead Method

This method initiates an asynchronous read from the `FileStream`. Data is read from the stream and put into an array provided as the argument. The `offset` argument specifies the location of the array where the first data item is to be inserted, and `numBytes` indicates the number of bytes to read from the file stream. Once the all of the data has been read from the stream, a call is made to the `userCallback` function specified in the argument list.

```
public override IAsyncResult BeginRead( byte[] array, int offset,
            int numBytes, AsyncCallback userCallback, object stateObject );
```

If more than one asynchronous call is to be made at any one time, you can distinguish between callbacks by specifying a different `stateObject` for each new asynchronous call. This returns an object that implements the `IAsyncResult` interface.

It is not generally advisable to read asynchronously from a file less than 64 kilobytes in length, because of the overheads associated with initiating an asynchronous call.

BeginWrite Method

This method commences an asynchronous write operation to a `FileStream`.

```
public override IAsyncResult BeginWrite( byte[] array, int offset,
        int numBytes, AsyncCallback userCallback, object stateObject );
```

The `array` parameter denotes an array of bytes containing the data to be written to the `FileStream`. The `offset` argument specifies the location in the array of the first data item to be written. `numBytes` indicates the number of bytes that are to be written to the stream. You also need to specify a call-back function with the `userCallback` parameter to be called upon completion of the write task. You can also specify a synchronizing `stateObject`, if you are making more than one asynchronous call, and need to differentiate between calls to the call-back method.

It is not generally advisable to perform asynchronous write operations for files under 64 kilobytes in size, because of the overheads incurred by initiating an asynchronous operation.

Close Method

This method closes the stream and releases all resources associated with the file.

```
public override void Close();
```

Calling this method also closes the underlying file. After executing this method, you may not perform any further operations on the stream and an `ObjectDisposedException` will result if you attempt to do so. The code below shows use of this method:

```
fs.Close();
```

Dispose Method

The `Dispose` method releases managed resources. It can also release unmanaged resources if you provide a `true` value for the `disposing` argument.

```
protected override void Dispose( bool disposing );
```

Managed resources are resources managed by the .NET framework runtime, and all resources not maintained by the .NET framework runtime are referred to as **unmanaged resources**. All code in ASP.NET applications runs under the .NET framework, but `FileStream` also uses resources from the unmanaged heap.

EndRead Method

Calling `EndRead` method waits until any pending asynchronous read operations are completed.

```
public override int EndRead( IAsyncResult asyncResult );
```

It requires the `IAsyncResult` object generated from the `BeginRead` method, and returns the number of bytes read from the stream.

EndWrite Method

This method waits until any pending asynchronous write operations are completed.

```
public override void EndWrite( IAsyncResult asyncResult );
```

It requires the `ISyncResult` object generated by the `BeginWrite` method.

Flush Method

This method clears the internal buffer of a file stream and forces it to write (flush) the contained data to the underlying file.

```
public override void Flush();
```

This method is available for both read-write and write-only streams.

Lock Method

This method locks a file or part of a file so that no other process can access data in that range.

```
public virtual void Lock( long position, long length );
```

The `position` argument provides the starting file offset of the locked area, and `length` indicates the number of bytes from that location that are to be locked to other processes. For example, the following code locks the first 100 bytes of data in the file.

```
FileStream fs = new FileStream("f.txt", FileMode.OpenOrCreate,
FileAccess.ReadWrite );
fs.Lock(0, 100);
```

Read Method

This method reads a specified number of bytes from the current location of the stream to a specified location in an array of bytes. Returns the number of bytes read from the stream.

```
public override int Read( out byte[] buffer, int offset, int count );
```

Here, `buffer` is the array of bytes that will hold the read data and `offset` indicates to the `Read` method the starting location in the buffer, while `count` indicates the maximum number of bytes to be read. For example:

```
int ByteRead fs.Read( myBuffer, 10, 100 );
```

The above code reads 100 bytes from the current position of the stream and writes it to `myBuffer` (an array of bytes) starting from the eleventh byte. `ByteRead` is set to the actual number of bytes read from the stream.

ReadByte Method

This method reads a byte from the current position of the stream. It returns a byte cast to an integer.

```
public override int ReadByte();
```

Seek Method

This sets the current position of the stream to a new specified location and returns the new position.

```
public override long Seek( long offset, SeekOrigin loc );
```

Here `offset` is the number of bytes the current position has to be moved relative to `SeekOrigin`. The `SeekOrigin` enumeration can have one of the following values:

- ❑   `Current` – from the current position of the stream
- ❑   `Begin` – from the beginning of the stream
- ❑   `End` – from the end of the stream

For example the following code sets the current position of the `FileStream` to 10 bytes before the end of the stream.

```
fs.Seek( 10, SeekOrigin.End );
```

SetLength Method

This method sets the length of the stream to the value specified as the argument.

```
public override void SetLength( long value );
```

If the length of the file stream is greater than the number supplied, the file stream will shrink accordingly. Increasing the length of the file stream similarly increases the size of the underlying file. In the code below, a file stream is opened by creating a file and the length of the stream is set to 2048 bytes. The stream is then closed. Although nothing is written to the stream, the size of the file created is 2 kilobytes.

```
    FileStream fs = new FileStream("TestFile.txt", FileMode.OpenOrCreate,
FileAccess.ReadWrite );
    fs.SetLength(2048);
    fs.Close();
```

UnLock Method

This method releases the lock set on a file or a range of a file so that other process may access that portion of the file.

```
public virtual void Unlock( long position, long length );
```

The position argument denotes the file offset of the first data item to be unlocked, and length indicates the number of bytes from that point that are to be unlockcd.

Write Method

This method writes a certain number of bytes to the current location of the stream from a specified location in a byte array.

```
public override void Write( byte[] buffer, int offset, int count );
```

Here buffer contains the data that has to be written to the stream, offset indicates the starting location in buffer and count is the maximum number of bytes to be written to the stream.

```
    fs.Write( myBuffer, 0, myBuffer.Length );
```

The above code writes the entire contents of myBuffer into a file stream.

WriteByte Method

Writes a byte of data into the current position of the stream.

```
public override void WriteByte( byte value );
```

The FileSystemWatcher Class

The FileSystemWatcher class can be used to monitor changes in the file system. This object allows you to perform specific tasks when something is triggered by the file system. For instance, you can monitor any file or directory on your local machine, or on a remote machine. If monitoring a remote machine, it should be running either Windows 2000 or Note that you cannot remotely monitor a file or directory on a machine, and nor can a FileSystemWatcher object monitor events on CDs or DVDs as they are read-only, so their timestamps and properties do not change at all. FileSystemWatcher can also monitor hidden files.

Constructor

```
public FileSystemWatcher();
public FileSystemWatcher( string path );
public FileSystemWatcher( string strPath, string filter );
```

Argument	Description
`Path`	Path to be monitored for any changes in a file or directory. For example, to monitor the files in `C:\TestDir`, you can set this string to `"C:\\TestDir"`. This argument corresponds to the `Path` property of this class. So, if you did not provide this string at the time of construction the `FileSystemWatcher` object, you can still set it, using the `Path` property of the object.
`filter`	Filename or filename pattern to be monitored for change. This property can be set to either a filename or a mask like `"*.*"` or `"*.txt"`. If you did not provided `'filter'` when creating the object, you can still use the `Filter` property of the `FileSystemWatcher` object to set a value.

Properties of the FileSystemWatcher Class

NotifyFilter Property

The `NotifyFilter` property indicates the type of file system activity to be monitored, for example create, delete, permission change, and so on.

```
public NotifyFilters NotifyFilter { get; set;}
```

The `NotifyFilters` enumeration can have any one of the following values:

❑   `Attributes` – only changes to the attribute of the file or directory in the specified path will be monitored.

❑   `LastAccess` – monitors access to the file or directory in the specified path

❑   `LastWrite` – monitors write activity on the file or directory specified

❑   `Security` – monitors changes in security properties of files and directories in the specified path

❑   `Size` – monitors changes to the size of the file in the specified path

The following code sets the `FileSystemWatcher` to monitor any changes to the file's attributes, when it is accessed, and when it is written to.

```
FileSystemWatcher fsw = new FileSystemWatcher();
fsw.NotifyFilter = NotifyFilters.Attributes |
                   NotifyFilters.LastAccess |
                   NotifyFilters.LastWrite;
```

EnableRaisingEvents Property

Setting this property to `true` starts the monitoring of the files.

```
public bool EnableRaisingEvents {get; set;}
```

Filter Property

This property gets or sets a string that contains a filter to restrict the class to monitor only those files that match the filter.

```
public string Filter {get; set;}
```

This filter is based on the standard DOS-type wildcard characters. For example, the following code examines files or directories that start with the letter 'a'.

```
FileSystemWatcher fsw = new FileSystemWatcher();
fsw.Filter = "a*";
```

IncludeSubdirectories Property

This indicates if all subdirectories within the monitored directory are to be monitored.

```
public bool IncludeSubdirectories {get; set;}
```

InternalBufferSize Property

This property gets or sets the size of the internal buffer used by the `FileSystemWatcher` object.

```
public int InternalBufferSize {get; set;}
```

All changes to file system objects being monitored are placed in this buffer to be passed to the appropriate event handlers. The buffer is needed because file system objects may change faster than the assigned event handler can handle them. The default size of the buffer is 8 kilobytes; however this value can be changed according to your specific requirements. Increasing the size of the buffer, is however, expensive, as the buffer memory comes from non-paged memory and cannot be swapped out to disk. But if the internal buffer is too small, you risk buffer overflow occurring when too many changes to the file system take place at the same time. It is recommended to increase the size of the buffer by 4 Kilobyte increments for Intel-based machines.

Path Property

This contains the path to be monitored.

```
public string Path {get; set;}
```

SynchronizingObject Property

This property contains an object that marshals event handler calls triggered by changes detected to the file-system object being monitored.

```
public ISynchronizeInvoke SynchronizingObject {get; set;}
```

The object assigned to this property must implement the `ISynchronizeInvoke` interface. If you do not set any object in this property, events are handled by a thread from the system thread pool. If you do assign an object to this property, the events are handled by the object's thread. For example, a Windows Form application might want to handle the event by a button, or on a form. To do so, assign the `Button` object or `WinForm` object to this property to link the event into the button or form.

Methods of the FileSystemWatcher Class

BeginInit and EndInit Methods

The `BeginInit` method initializes the `FileSystemWatcher` object, ready to be used by a Form or some other component. `EndInit` terminates the initialization of the `FileSystemWatcher` object. This initialization and termination is carried out at run-time.

```
public void BeginInit();
public void EndInit();
```

These methods are also used by the Visual Studio.NET design time environment to begin and end initialization of the `FileSystemWatcher` object.

OnChanged, OnCreated, OnDeleted, OnRenamed, and OnError Methods

These are protected methods and can be used in a deriving class to handle the events when a change occurs in the monitored directory.

`OnChanged` is called whenever a file or directory is changed, such as when any of its attributes are changed, or its file size changes. A `FileSystemEventArgs` object is also passed as an argument containing the information about the changes that have occured.

The `OnCreated` method is triggered when a new file or directory is created. Its argument also contains a `FileSystemEventArgs` object detailing information about the newly created file or directory.

The `OnDelete` method is called when a file or directory is deleted in the monitored path. Information about the file or directory being deleted is contained in the `FileSystemEventArgs` argument.

The `OnError` method is fired when a buffer overflow or other file system error occurs. Information relating to the error is passed in an `ErrorEventArgs` object.

The `OnRenamed` method is called when a file or a directory in the monitored path is renamed. Information about the renamed file or directory is passed in an `RenamedEventArgs` object.

```
protected void OnChanged( FileSystemEventArgs e );
protected void OnCreated( FileSystemEventArgs e );
protected void OnDeleted( FileSystemEventArgs e );
protected void OnError( ErrorEventArgs e );
protected void OnRenamed( RenamedEventArgs e );
```

Whenever these method are used in a deriving class, one should always call the corresponding method on the base class. For example, if we want to handle the `OnChanged` event handler methods in a deriving class, it is necessary for us to call the `OnChanged` method on the base class as shown below.

```
base.OnChanged( e )
```

where e is an object of type `FileSystemEventArgs`.

WaitForChanged Method

Calling this method waits for the file-system change specified in the `changeType` argument. It will either wait indefinitely, or for the time in milliseconds specified by the `timeout` argument.

```
public WaitForChangedResult WaitForChanged( WatcherChangeTypes changeType );
public WaitForChangedResult WaitForChanged( WatcherChangeTypes changeType,
                                            int timeout );
```

This method waits for the first occurance of the specified change in the file system, unless the `timeout` period, when specified, elapses first.

`WatcherChangeTypes` is a enumeration that can take one of the following values:

❑ `All` – monitors the target path for all events (the `Changed`, `Deleted`, `Created`, and `Renamed` events)

- ❑ `Changed` – forces the method to monitor only changes to files or directories in the specified path.

- ❑ `Created` – monitors only creation of files or directories in the specified path

- ❑ `Deleted` – monitors deletion of files or directories in the specified path

- ❑ `Renamed` – monitors any filename or directory name chages in the specified path

The method returns a `WaitForChangedResult` structure. Here are the important members of this structure:

- ❑ `ChangeType` – specifies the type of change detected

- ❑ `Name` – the name of the file or directory involved in the change

- ❑ `OldName` – the old name of the file or directory if the change was a `Renamed` event

- ❑ `TimedOut` – indicates if the operation timed out

For example, the following code monitors the `C:\Access` directory for all types of changes:

```
using System.IO;

public class MyWatcher
{
  public static void Main()
  {

    FileSystemWatcher watcher = new FileSystemWatcher("C:\\Access");
    WaitForChangedResult res = watcher.WaitForChanged( WatcherChangeTypes.All );

    Console.WriteLine( res.ChangeType );
  }
}
```

This code waits indefinitely for any change in the `C:\Access` path, and it prints the type of change on the console once detected.

Events of the FileSystemWatcher Class

Changed Event

This event is triggered when a file-system object is changed in the path being monitored.

```
public event FileSystemEventHandler Changed;
```

This event is not triggered when a directory is renamed, but it is triggered if a file is renamed.

Example: MyWatcher

The following code, from the file `MyWatcher.cs`, shows how you can set your own event handler to deal with changed events. It is a console application that creates an instance of the `FileSystemWatcher` class, sets its own event handler for the `Changed` event and waits for any changes to the `C:\Access` directory. Once detected, the name of the file involved is written to the console.

```
using System;
using System.IO;
```

```
public class MyWatcher
{
  public static void Main()
  {
    MyWatcher watcher = new MyWatcher();
    watcher.Go();
  }

  private void Go()
  {
    FileSystemWatcher watcher = new FileSystemWatcher("C:\\Access");

    watcher.Changed += new FileSystemEventHandler( this.MyWatcher_Changed );
    watcher.EnableRaisingEvents = true;
    Console.WriteLine("Waiting for any change in C:\\Access");
    Console.ReadLine();
  }

  private void MyWatcher_Changed( object s, FileSystemEventArgs e )
  {
    Console.WriteLine( e.Name );
  }
}
```

Created Event

A Created event is triggered when a file or directory is created in the path being monitored.

```
public event FileSystemEventHandler Created;
```

Created events are also triggered when you move or copy a file or directory, because in each case a new file or directory is created in the monitored path.

Deleted Event

This event is triggered when a file or directory is deleted from the path that is being watched.

```
public event FileSystemEventHandler Deleted;
```

Error Event

An Error event is triggered when there is an overflow of the internal buffer.

```
public event ErrorEventHandler Error;
```

All changes to the file system are notified through the internal buffer. By default this buffer is 8 kilobytes long, and it is quite possible for file system objects to change faster than the events thrown can be handled, resulting in a buffer overrun. This condition triggers an Error event. An ErrorEventArgs object containing information releated to the error is passed to the event handler.

Renamed Event

A Renamed event is triggered when a directory or file in the monitored path is renamed.

```
public event RenamedEventHandler Renamed;
```

If you change the directory name that is itself the path being monitored, no event will be triggered. This event only fires on the renaming of file-system objects in the path being monitored.

A `RenamedEventArgs` object is passed to the event handler, which contains information about the old name and new name of the object.

The StreamReader Class

Typically the `Stream` object provides you with access to byte-level data. That is, if you have a stream of data, normally you only have methods to read one byte of an array of bytes from the stream. But if the file is a Unicode file where each character is composed of two bytes, it becomes difficult to read from such a stream. Similarly, the file could also be in UTF7 or UTF8 encoding. This makes it even harder to read the data from the stream. In such cases, you have to perform two operations to read the data. First read the data from the stream and then decode it based on the encoding of the file. To solve this problem you can use a `StreamReader` object, which automatically detects the encoding of the file and does the decoding of the data automatically when you read data from the stream. The `StreamReader` provides a layer on top of `Stream` and allows you to read different types of string using different encodings.

The `StreamReader` class is derived from the `TextReader` class and is not thread-safe.

Constructor

The constructor creates an instance of the `StreamReader` object.

```
public StreamReader( string path );
public StreamReader( Stream stream );
public StreamReader( Stream stream, Encoding encoding );
public StreamReader( string path, Encoding encoding );
public StreamReader( string path, Encoding encoding, int bufferSize );
public StreamReader( Stream stream, Encoding encoding, int bufferSize );
```

The following table lists the different arguments used in the overloaded constructor:

Argument	Description
stream	The raw stream object that is to be wrapped
path	Filename along with the path that has to be opened
encoding	The `Encoding` object that will be used to decode the data to populate a string
bufferSize	The size of the `Stream` buffer in bytes

Properties of the StreamReader Class

BaseStream Property

This returns the reference to the underlying `Stream` object.

```
public virtual Stream BaseStream {get;}
```

This lets you access the underlying `Stream` object, and if you have to use some of the methods of this class on the stream, you can do it using this property. The following code shows the use of this property:

```
FileStream fs = new FileStream("C:\\VS.NET\\abc.txt", FileMode.OpenOrCreate );
StreamReader sr = new StreamReader(fs);
Response.Write( sr.BaseStream.GetType() );
sr.Close();
```

CurrentEncoding Property

Returns the current `Encoding` object that is used to decode the read data.

```
public virtual Encoding CurrentEncoding {get;}
```

All of the decoding of the stream is done by this object. Keep in mind that by default the `StreamReader` has the UTF8 Encoder as the current encoder. This means that the `StreamReader` assumes that the data in the file was encoded through the UTF8 encoding scheme. UTF8 Encoding is one of the available encoding scheme, in .NET Frameworks which maps the characters to byte using a specific algorithm. We will talk more about encoding and decosing in the `System.Text` namespace section. When the first call to the file is made, it automatically detects the encoding mechanism of the file and sets the appropriate `Encoding` object to this property.

For example, let's suppose we have a file `abcuni.txt` which uses Unicode encoding. The following code builds a `StreamReader` object, prints the default `Decoder/Encoder` object, then reads a line from the file, before again printing the `Encoder/Decoder` object:

```
FileStream fs = new FileStream("C:\\VS.NET\\abcuni.txt", FileMode.OpenOrCreate );
StreamReader sr = new StreamReader(fs);
Response.Write( sr.CurrentEncoding + "<BR>");
string line = sr.ReadLine();
Response.Write( sr.CurrentEncoding + "<BR>");
fs.Close();
```

We will see more about the `Encoding` object in our discussion of the `System.Text` namespace.

Methods of the StreamReader Class

Close Method

This method closes all resources associated with a `StreamReader` object.

```
public override void Close();
```

Internally, this method calls the `Dispose` method with a `true` argument and hence releases both managed and unmanaged resources.

DiscardBufferedData Method

This method discards data currently contained in the internal buffer of `StreamReader` object.

```
public void DiscardBufferedData();
```

Whenever a read operation is performed on a `StreamReader`, data is fetched from the stream source and placed in a buffer. To make the `StreamReader` efficient, data is cached in an internal buffer ready for subsequent read operations. The `DiscardBufferedData` method forces the `StreamReader` object to discard data currently held in the buffer.

Dispose Method

Releases managed and unmanaged resources held by the `StreamReader`.

```
protected override void Dispose( bool disposing );
```

A `true` value in the `Dispose` method's arguments tells it to release both managed and unmanaged resources. A `false` value only releases managed resources. The .NET framework provides a common run-time environment in which all .NET applications run. One of the purposes of this run-time environment is to manage resources such as RAM efficiently, and to prevent leaking of resources. All resources controlled by the .NET runtime are known as "**managed resources**", and those not under its control are referred to as "**unmanaged resources**". The latter includes resources used by Microsoft Word, ADO, and any custom applications built using native compilers. The following code releases both the managed and unmanaged resources of the `StreamReader` object.

```
sr.Dispose( true );
```

Peek Method

This method reads the next available character from the stream without changing the current position in the stream.

```
public override int Peek();
```

This method returns `-1` when called against a stream that does not support seeking, or if the stream has no more characters available to read.

Read Method

This method reads the next available byte or bytes from the stream.

```
public override int Read();
public override int Read( out char[] buffer, int index, int count );
```

The first overload allows you to read the next byte from the stream and returns it cast as an integer. It also moves the current position in the stream to the next character.

The second overload reads a certain number of characters from the stream and copies them to a character array at a given starting location. For example, the following line reads 100 characters from the stream and puts them into a buffer starting from the 35th character:

```
int res = sr.Read( myBuffer, 34, 100 );
```

This overloaded method returns the number of characters read from the stream.

ReadLine Method

This method reads a line from the stream using the `Encoding` object set in the `CurrentEncoding` property. This method returns a string.

```
public override string ReadLine();
```

A line in a stream is the sequence of characters up to the next line feed ('\n'), or line feed and carriage return pair ('\r\n'). Calling this method also moves the current position in the stream to the start of the next line. The following code reads the file line-by-line and writes it to a `Response` object.

```
FileStream fs = new FileStream("C:\\VS.NET\\abcuni.txt", FileMode.OpenOrCreate );
StreamReader sr = new StreamReader(fs);
```

```
while( (string line = sr.ReadLine()) != null )
Response.Write( line );
sr.Close();
```

The `ReadLine` method returns `null` when it reaches the end of the stream. The string returned does not include the carriage return or line feed characters.

ReadToEnd Method

This method reads the entire contents of the stream and returns it as a string. It moves the current position of the stream to the end.

```
public override string ReadToEnd();
```

The StreamWriter Class

As opposed to the `StreamReader` class, the `StreamWriter` allows you to write to a stream using a specific encoding. All .NET stream objects derived from the `Stream` object (`NetworkStream`, `FileStream`, `BufferedStream` etc.) provide byte access to the stream only. If you have to write a string, you first have to create a string, then convert it to an array of bytes, and then write this array of bytes to the stream. A problem arises when we have to convert the string to an array of bytes, due to the fact that there is more than one character set available. For example, you can convert the string to a Unicode string, or a UTF7 or UTF8 string. In all of these types of encoding scenarios, one-to-one encoding of character-to-byte is not possible. Only ANSI encoding has one-to-one correspondence between character and byte. In Unicode every character is composed of two bytes and in UTF7 the first three bytes of the string has special meaning. To cope with these encoding problems the Microsoft .NET platform comes with an `Encoding` object that can be used when we write to a stream. However, to make life even easier, it also comes with a wrapper class for the `Stream` object that hides the details of the encoding process from the developer. `StreamWriter` is wrapper class that encapsulates a `Stream` object and an `Encoding` object to provide you with a set of methods to write to streams without worrying about the encoding.

The `StreamWriter` is derived from the `TextWriter` object.

Constructors

The constructor for `StreamWriter` is overloaded:

```
public StreamWriter( stream stream );
public StreamWriter( string path );
public StreamWriter( stream stream, Encoding encoding );
public StreamWriter( string path, bool append );
public StreamWriter( stream stream, Encoding encoding, int bufferSize );
public StreamWriter( string path, bool append, Encoding encoding );
public StreamWriter(string path, bool append, Encoding encoding, int bufferSize);
```

Argument	Description
stream	The underlying raw Stream object that will be used by the StreamWriter object for writing data
path	This filename, along with its path, that is to be opened
encoding	The Encoding object that will be used to encode the string to bytes
append	True if the file has to be opened in append mode
bufferSize	The size of the stream buffer in bytes

For example, the following code opens a file with a specific encoding:

```
StreamWriter sw = new StreamWriter("abc.txt", true, Encoding.Unicode );
```

As we are using the Encoding class that is defined in the System.Text name space, you must add a using statement in the file to include a reference to the System.Text namespace.

Properties of the StreamWriter Class

AutoFlush Property

Returns a Boolean value indicating whether the StreamWriter commits all data to the underlying Stream on every call to the Write method.

```
public virtual bool AutoFlush {get; set;}
```

When data is written to a stream using a StreamWriter, the data is placed in a buffer. Once you are done writing data to the Stream, you can use the Flush method or close the StreamWriter to dump the data in the buffer to the underlying Stream. Using an intermediate buffer in this way makes the StreamWriter much more efficient, but is not appropriate in all circumstances.If you set the AutoFlush property to true all data is instantly committed to the stream on every call of the Write method.

BaseStream Property

This property returns a reference to the underlying Stream object.

```
public virtual Stream BaseStream {get;}
```

Every character is written to this stream. The following code demonstrates the use of this property:

```
StreamWriter sw = new StreamWriter("C:\\abc.txt");
Stream s = sw.BaseStream;
```

Encoding Property

This returns the Encoding object that is used to convert the characters into bytes.

```
public override Encoding Encoding {get;}
```

This is a read-only property. However, you can set an `Encoding` object at the time of creation of the instance of the `StreamWriter` object using one of its overloaded constructors. Once you set an `Encoding` object for the `StreamWriter`, every character written to a stream is first encoded using the specified `Encoder` object.

Methods of the StreamWriter Class

Close Method

This method closes and releases all the managed and unmanaged resources associated with the `StreamWriter` object.

```
public override void Close();
```

It calls the `Dispose` method internally with `true` as its argument. You must issue a `Close` method when you are done with the `StreamWriter` otherwise the resources will be held for an indefinite period until the run-time garbage collector automatically frees up unused resources.

Dispose Method

This method releases managed and unmanaged resources held by the `StreamWriter` object. If the `disposing` argument is `true`, both managed and unmanaged resources are released. Setting it to `false` will release only managed resources.

```
protected override void Dispose( bool disposing );
```

Managed resources are the resources maintained by the .NET run-time environment, while resources allocated to any processes not running under the .NET framework are referred to as unmanaged resources.

Flush Method

This method forces all data contained in the buffer to be written (flushed) to the stream, thus emptying the buffer.

```
public override void Flush();
```

`StreamWriter` uses an intermediate buffer to write data to the underlying `Stream` object. All of the data is written to a buffer and after a certain time (if the `AutoFlush` property is set to `true`) it is committed to the stream. This method forces all data present in the buffer to be written to the stream.

Write Method

This method writes data to the underlying stream. You can write a character, an array of characters, a string, or a range of characters from a character array.

```
public override void Write( char value );
public override void Write( char[] buffer );
public override void Write( string value );
public override void Write( char[] buffer, int index, int count );
```

For example, the following code writes first the 100 characters of an array to the stream.

```
StreamWriter sr = new StreamWriter("abc.txt");
sr.Write( myByffer, 0, 100 );
sr.Close();
```

System.Text Namespace

The System.Text namespace contains classes to handle the encoding and decoding of bytes to characters and characters to bytes. This namespace contains classes that provide built-in functionality for some of the widely used encoding schemes such as Unicode, ANSI, UTF8 and UTF7 encoding. It also provides a base class that can be used to build your own custom encoding and decoding scheme.

The Decoder Class

This class decodes a sequence of bytes into a sequence of characters. You cannot explicitly create an instance of this class as it is an abstract class.

```
public abstract class Decoder
```

However, you can derive your own classes from the Decoder class, and implement all of its methods. You can also get a reference to an instance of a Decoder object by calling the GetDecoder method on any Encoding object.

The Decoder class decodes bytes to characters based on some given algorithm or scheme. In Unicode for example, each character consists of a pair of bytes that will be 'translated' into a single character.

Constructor

As this an abstract class, you cannot directly create an instance of this class, so its constructor is protected.

```
protected Decoder();
```

To get an instance of a Decoder object, you can call the GetDecoder method on an Encoding object instance. For example, the following line of code gets a decoder object from Unicode encoding:

```
Decoder myDecoder = Encoding.Unicode.GetDecoder();
```

Methods of the Decoder Class

GetCharCount

This method returns the number of characters needed to decode a series of bytes. You can pass a byte array containing the sequence to be decoded. The index parameter indicates the location in the array where the sequence starts, while count is the number of bytes from that point that are to be decoded.

```
public abstract int GetCharCount( byte[] bytes, int index, int count );
```

GetChars

This method returns the sequence of characters decoded from a sequence of bytes.

```
public abstract int GetChars( byte[] bytes, int byteIndex, int byteCount,
                              char[] chars, int charIndex );
```

The `bytes` argument is an array of bytes that are to be decoded. The `index` parameter indicates the location in the array where the sequence starts, while `count` is the number of bytes from that point that are to be decoded. The decoded characters are copied to the target array given by the `chars` parameter. `charIndex` specifies the starting location in the `chars` array from which the decoded characters are to be inserted. The returned `int` represents the number of characters written to the target array.

The following code decodes eight bytes from the `myBytes` array starting from the third location, inserting the results into the `myChars` array at the beginning (offset 0):

```
Decoder dec = Encoding.Unicode.GetDecoder();
int i = dec.GetChars( myBytes, 2, 8, myChars, 0 );
```

The Encoder Class

This class offers the inverse functionality of the `Decoder` class, to encode a sequence of characters into a sequence of bytes according to a specific algorithm.

```
public abstract class Encoder
```

This is an abstract class and so you cannot create an instance of it directly. However, you can of course create a class derived from the `Encoder` class. You can also get an instance of an `Encoder` object by calling the `GetEncoder` method of the `Encoding` class. For example the following code obtains an instance of a UTF8 `Encoder`:

```
Encoder myEncoder = Encoding.UTF8.GetEncoding();
```

State can be maintained between calls on the derived `Encoder` object.

Constructor

As the `Encoder` class is an abstract class, its constructor is protected meaning that you cannot explicitly create an `Encoder` instance. You must instead derive a class from it, and such deriving classes must implement all the abstract methods of the `Encoder` class.

```
protected Encoder();
```

Methods of the Encoder Class

GetByteCount Method

This method returns the number of bytes needed to encode a range of characters in `chars` array. If you pass the value `true` for the Boolean `flush` argument, it indicates the object is to maintain its state after this call.

```
public abstract int GetByteCount( char[] chars, int index, int count, bool flush );
```

Example: EncodingByteCount

The following code, `EncodingByteCount.aspx`, first gets a Unicode `Encoder` object by calling the `GetEncoder` method in the `Encoding.Unicode` namespace. Then it checks and displays the number of bytes needed to encode the string `"WROX"`.

```
<%@ Page Language="C#" %>

<html>
<script language="C#" runat=server>

void Page_Load(Object sender, EventArgs EvArgs) {
  string msg = "";
  char[] carray = { 'W', 'R', 'O', 'X' };

  Encoder enc = Encoding.Unicode.GetEncoder();
  msg += enc.GetByteCount( carray, 0, 4, false );

  Message.InnerHtml = msg;
}

</script>

<body>
<span id="Message" runat=server/>
</body>
</html>
```

The output of this code is simply 8, because Unicode encoding requires two bytes per character, making a total of eight bytes to encode "WROX".

GetBytes Method

This method gets the sequence of encoded bytes for the range of characters passed in the argument.

```
public abstract int GetBytes( char[] chars, int charIndex, int charCount,
                              byte[] bytes, int byteIndex, bool flush );
```

Here, chars is a character array containing the sequence of bytes to be encoded. The range of the chars array to be encoded is given by the starting location, charIndex, and the number of characters after that point, charCount, to be encoded. The encoded bytes are returned as the byte array of the bytes argument. The byteIndex argument provides the location from which the encoded results are to be inserted. The flush parameter indicates whether you want this method to maintain its state. The returned int indicates the total number of bytes written to the bytes array.

Example: WroxEncoding

In the following code, WroxEncoding.aspx, the class WroxEncoding is derived from the Encoder class. This class implements a custom encoding scheme, in which each character is encoded by four characters. The third byte of each encoded sequence holds the ASCII value of the character, while remaining three bytes each contain the value zero. This custom encoder object is then used to encode the string "Wrox". The encoded bytes are displayed on the browser.

```
<%@ Page Language="C#" %>

<html>
<script language="C#" runat=server>
public class WroxEncoder : Encoder
{
  public override int GetByteCount( char[] chars, int index, int count, bool flush
  )
  {
    return (count - index)* 4;
  }
```

```
    public override int GetBytes( char[] chars, int charIndex, int charCount,
            byte[] bytes, int byteIndex, bool flush )
    {
      int i = 0;
      foreach( char c in chars )
      {
        bytes[i++] = 0;
        bytes[i++] = 0;
        bytes[i++] = (byte) c;
        bytes[i++] = 0;
      }
      return (charCount - charIndex) * 4;
    }
  }

  void Page_Load(Object sender, EventArgs EvArgs) {
    string msg = "";
    char[] carray = { 'W', 'r', 'o', 'x' };
    byte[] ba;
    WroxEncoder myEncoder = new WroxEncoder();
    ba = new byte[myEncoder.GetByteCount( carray, 0, 4, false )];

    myEncoder.GetBytes( carray, 0, 4, ba, 0, false );
    foreach( byte b in ba )
      msg += "[" + Convert.ToString(b) + "]";

    Message.InnerHtml = msg;
  }
</script>

<body>
<span id="Message" runat=server/>
</body>
</html>
```

Here is the output from the code:

[0][0][87][0][0][0][114][0][0][0][111][0][0][0][120][0]

The Encoding Class

The Encoding class provides access to some of the built-in encoding classes through its static properties. It also provides a basis for building your own encoding/decoding mechanisms. Encoding is the process of mapping characters to a byte representation. In its most simple form, each character is mapped to a single byte, but this restricts us to a maximum 255 character codes. Many languages, such as those of Far East countries like Japan, have far more than 255 distinct characters. To handle this, each single character must be represented by multiple bytes. How these characters are mapped to a corresponding byte format is dealt with by the Encoding class. There are several standard encoding schemes widely used in various situations, including ASCII, Unicode, UTF7, and UTF8. Each of these encodings has its own purpose and its own benefits. The Encoding class has static properties that can be used for indicating such standard encodings.

Example: EncodingComparison

The following code sample, `EncodingComparison.aspx`, encodes the string `"Jibran"` to the corresponding byte representation using ASCII and Unicode encoding. The encoded versions are then written into two files, and the length of file in bytes is displayed on the web page.

```
<%@ Page Language="C#" %>
<%@ Import Namespace="System.IO" %>

<html>

<script language="C#" runat=server>

void Page_Load(Object sender, EventArgs EvArgs) {
  string msg = "";

  string s = "Jibran";

  // Get the bytes for the string using ASCII Encoding
  byte[] ascii_ba = Encoding.ASCII.GetBytes(s);

  // Get the bytes for the string using Unicode Encoding
  byte[] unicode_ba = Encoding.Unicode.GetBytes(s);

  // Open a file and write the bytes of ASCII Encoding.
  FileStream ascii_fs = new FileStream("ASCII.txt", FileMode.OpenOrCreate );
  ascii_fs.Write( ascii_ba, 0, ascii_ba.Length );
  msg += "ASCII File Length in Bytes : " + ascii_fs.Length + "<BR>";
  ascii_fs.Close();

  // Open a file and write the bytes of Unicode Encoding.
  FileStream unicode_fs = new FileStream("Unicode.txt", FileMode.OpenOrCreate );
  unicode_fs.Write( unicode_ba, 0, unicode_ba.Length );
  msg += "Unicode File Length in Bytes : " + unicode_fs.Length + "<BR>";
  unicode_fs.Close();

  // Display the size of the file.
  Message.InnerHtml = msg;
}

</script>

<body>
<span id="Message" runat=server/>
</body>
</html>
```

Here is the output produced:

ASCII File Length in Bytes : 6
Unicode File Length in Bytes : 12

As you can see, in ASCII encoding each character is encoded into one byte, but in Unicode, each character is represented by two bytes.

Constructors

As both of the constructors for this class are protected, you cannot create an instance of the class explicitly. However, you can use these methods from a deriving class.

```
protected Encoding();
protected Encoding( int CodePage );
```

You can also pass a `CodePage` in the protected constructor. `CodePage` is an identifier and tells the `Encoding` class the code page that should be used during string operations.

Properties of the Encoding Class

ASCII Property

This is a static property that returns an `Encoding` object. This object can be used for encoding or decoding the ASCII character set.

```
public static Encoding ASCII {get;}
```

The ASCII encoding scheme uses the first seven bits of a byte to encode a character, allowing a total of 128 characters in the set.

BodyName and HeaderName Properties

The `BodyName` property contains the name of the encoding to be used by a mail application – MS Outlook and the like – for the message body. The `HeaderName` property is the same, but for message headers.

```
public virtual string BodyName {get;}
public virtual string HeaderName {get;}
```

The following code displays the header and body name for `BigEndianUnicode` and `Unicode` types.

```
Response.Write( Encoding.BigEndianUnicode.BodyName + "<BR>" );
Response.Write( Encoding.BigEndianUnicode.HeaderName + "<BR>" );
Response.Write( Encoding.Unicode.BodyName + "<BR>" );
Response.Write( Encoding.Unicode.HeaderName + "<BR>" );
```

CodePage and WindowsCodePage Properties

These are virtual properties that must be implemented by any deriving class. The `CodePage` property contains the code page identifier for the encoding, while the `WindowsCodePage` property contains the closest Windows code page for this encoding type.

```
public virtual int CodePage {get;}
public virtual int WindowsCodePage {get;}
```

Default Property

This property gets the default `Encoding` object. It is also a static property.

```
public static Encoding Default {get;}
```

The default is `CodePageEncoding`.

EncodingName Property

This property returns the descriptive name of the encoding.

```
public virtual string EncodingName {get;}
```

For example, the `EncodingName` property for UTF7 encoding returns `"Unicode (UTF-7)"`.

Unicode and BigEndianUnicode Properties

The `Unicode` property is also a static property and returns an object that provides Unicode encoding and decoding in little-endian byte order. `BigEndianUnicode` is also a static property and returns an object that provides Unicode encoding and decoding in big-endian byte order.

```
public static Encoding Unicode {get;}
public static Encoding BigEndianUnicode {get;}
```

Unicode encoding uses 16 bits (2 bytes) to store a character, and may be one of two types: little-endian or big-endian. It is based on the order of bytes and how they are used in the encoding. In big-endian encoding, the most significant byte is stored in the lowest memory address, while in little-endian the least significant byte goes into lowest memory address. The following figure shows the difference between big-endian and little-endian. Here two characters, "A" and "R", each take two bytes in a hypothetical encoding. The memory structure shows the byte ordering of each character for both big- and little-endian schemes.

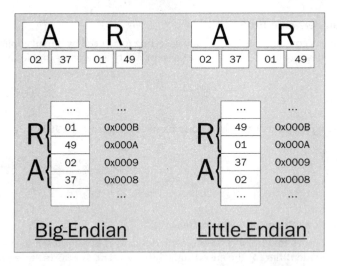

On Intel platforms, it is more efficient to store the bytes of a Unicode character in little-endian byte order. The Unicode little-endian and big-endian encoding is based on UCS-2.

UTF8 and UTF7 Properties

The UTF8 and UTF7 properties return the encoding objects that implement UTF8 and UTF7 encoding.

```
public static Encoding UTF8 {get;}
public static Encoding UTF7 {get;}
```

UTF8 and UTF7 are also Unicode encoding schemes. However, rather than two bytes they are based on just 8 bits and 7 bits, respectively. Each character is therefore mapped to an 8 bit or 7 bit item.

For example the following code encodes 'Adil' in UTF7 format:

```
byte[] ba = Encoding.UTF7.GetBytes("Adil");
foreach( byte b in ba )
{
  Response.Write( b );
  Response.Write( "<BR>" );
}
```

WebName Property

This property returns the list of IANA-registered names for the encoding, with the IANA-preferred name appearing first when there is more than one registered name.

```
public virtual string WebName {get;}
```

For example, ASCII has `"us-ascii"` as its IANA registered name.

Methods of the Encoding Class

Convert Method

This method converts an array of bytes from one encoding scheme to another, and returns a new array of bytes.

```
public static byte[] Convert( Encoding srcEncoding, Encoding dstEncoding,
                                               byte[] bytes );
```

This is a static method and can be used without creating an instance of the `Encoding` object.

Example: EncodingConversion

The following excerpt from `EncodingConversion.aspx` converts the string `"Adil Rehan"` from Unicode to ASCII encoding:

```
byte[] UnicodeBA = Encoding.Unicode.GetBytes("Adil Rehan");
Response.Write("Unicode Bytes:<BR>");
foreach( byte b in UnicodeBA )
{
  Response.Write(b);
  Response.Write("<BR>");
}
byte[] ASCIIBA = Encoding.Convert( Encoding.Unicode, Encoding.ASCII, UnicodeBA );
Response.Write("ASCII Bytes:<BR>");
foreach( byte b in ASCIIBA )
{
  Response.Write(b);
  Response.Write("<BR>");
}
```

GetBytes Method

This method returns an array of bytes after encoding is done on the provided string or character array. As this is a virtual method, the deriving class must override this method.

```
public virtual byte[] GetBytes( char[] chars );
public virtual byte[] GetBytes( string s );
```

Here "chars" represents an array of characters that has to be encoded. "s" is a string object that has to be encoded into bytes.

GetByteCount Method

This method returns an integer that indicates the number of bytes that will be required to encode the character array or string. It takes a character array or string as its argument, and you can also provide a starting offset and the number of characters to encode when using a character array for the source.

```
public virtual int GetByteCount( char[] chars );
public virtual int GetByteCount( string s );
public abstract int GetByteCount( char[] chars, int index, int count );
```

The following code snippet shows the use of this method:

```
Encoding unicode = Encoding.Unicode;
int count = unicode.GetByteCount( "Adil" );
Response.Write( "Count = " + count );
```

Here, the first line gets a reference to a Unicode Encoding static object, placing it into the variable called unicode. Next, we call the GetByteCount method to determine the bytes that will be needed to encode the "Adil" string.

GetCharCount Method

This method returns an integer indicating the number of decoded characters that will be produced by decoding a given byte array or subset of a byte array. The range is defined by specifying an initial offset with the index parameter, and the number of bytes after this point that are to be decoded with the count parameter.

```
public virtual int GetCharCount( byte[] bytes );
public abstract int GetCharCount( byte[] bytes, int index, int count );
```

The following C# code gets the number of characters that will be produced by a byte array that contains the Unicode equivalent of "ADIL".

```
byte[] ba = { 65, 0, 68, 0, 73, 0, 76, 0 };
Encoding unicode = Encoding.Unicode;
int count = unicode.GetCharCount( ba );
lblMessage.InnerHtml = "Count = " + count + "<BR>";
```

GetChars Method

This method returns the decoded characters as an array.

```
public virtual char[] GetChars( byte[] bytes );
public virtual char[] GetChars( byte[] bytes, int index, int count );
```

This method takes an array of bytes that have to be decoded using a certain encoding scheme. You can also specify the starting location and number of bytes in the array of bytes.

GetEncoder and GetDecoder Methods

These methods return an encoder and a decoder object respectively.

```
public virtual Decoder GetEncoder();
public virtual Encoder GetDecoder();
```

These objects can be used to encode or decode a text from one scheme to another. These are also virtual methods and must be overridden by the deriving class.

GetMaxByteCount Method

This is an abstract method that must be overridden by the deriving class. It returns the maximum number of bytes that will be needed to encode the specified number of characters.

```
public abstract int GetMaxByteCount( int charCount );
```

GetMaxCharCount Method

This method returns the maximum number of characters that will be decoded for a given number of bytes. It is another abstract method.

```
public abstract int GetMaxCharCount( int byteCount );
```

GetPreamble Method

This method returns an array of bytes that will be written to or read from the beginning of a stream. These bytes let the encoder or decoder figure out the encoding used in the stream.

```
public virtual byte[] GetPreamble();
```

For example, the following code lists the preamble bytes for UTF8 encoding:

```
byte[] ba = Encoding.UTF8.GetPreamble();
foreach( byte b in ba )
  lblMessage.InnerHtml += b + "<BR>";
```

GetString Method

This method returns the decoded string represented by an array of bytes, or a subset of elements from such an array. The range of the byte array is defined by its starting offset in the byte array, and the number of bytes after that location to be used.

```
public virtual string GetString( byte[] bytes );
public virtual string GetString( byte[] bytes, int index, int count );
```

The following code uses a `BigEndianUncode` encoding object to get a string from an array of bytes:

```
byte[] ba = { 0, 65, 0, 68, 0, 73, 0, 76 };
Encoding beu = Encoding.BigEndianUnicode;
lblMessage.InnerHtml = beu.GetString(ba);
```

System.Web.Services

Web Services are a new way of allowing communication and sharing of information between computers using HTTP. The ability to create and consume Web Services, quickly and simply, is one of the revolutionary features of the .NET framework. They can be made accessible from any point on an intranet or extranet, or over the Internet.

Not only are these services accessible over HTTP, but they also have the ability to describe themselves, what they offer, and how they can be accessed, using the emerging standards of UDDI and WSDL. Clients running on any system with support for HTTP communication can consume them, regardless of platform.

Web Services Overview

Understanding how Web Services work will be an important part of developing web applications in the near future. They bring a whole new group of programming tools to traditional ASP programmers, providing a mechanism for traditional enterprise programmers to expose their framework and business services in a brand new way.

The Web Services architecture will change the business model of many companies, as they will be able to easily connect to the internal systems of their suppliers, and offer direct connections for their customers to use. In this next phase of the Internet, a whole new group of client/server applications will be developed that will allow users to connect to business systems from a workstation on the Internet as seamlessly as if they were working on the local LAN.

What are Web Services?

The most basic definition of Web Services is that they are a new way of allowing communication, and the sharing of data, between software components. They are a method of invoking Remote Procedure Calls (RPC) over HTTP. The concept itself is nothing new, and has been implemented on network protocols many times over, using technologies like DCOM, RMI, CORBA, and EDI. What's different is that Web Services communicate using HTTP and XML.

Web Services overcome some of the limitations of previous technologies, including:

- ❑ **Platform interoperability** – clients of Web Services do not have to be based upon any particular platform to consume the services. Platforms such as operating systems, programming languages, component specifications, or language frameworks, are irrelevant.

❑   **Proprietary protocols** – Web Services use the standard HTTP protocol to communicate. As such, they can easily reach through firewalls and allow communication between servers anywhere on the Internet.

It is important to understand that Web Services are more than just a single specification. They are a whole set of specifications that have been adopted by major companies such as Microsoft and IBM. These specifications will be described briefly in the section on *Key Web-Service Standards*.

Discovery and Description

Web Services' standards include standards on their discovery and description. They allow application developers and integrators to easily find existing Web Services, discover their APIs, and build clients that can access them. The ASP.NET framework provides services that can be leveraged to provide discovery and description information for the Web Services that you build.

Why Use Web Services?

There are many reasons why you may want to consider exposing Web Services using ASP.NET. We list some of the most salient points below:

Widely Accepted Standards

Web Services are based upon a set of standards that have already been adopted by a number of large software companies, and the World Wide Web Consortium (W3C). To review the latest standards affecting Web Services, go to http://www.w3.org/. Microsoft is seriously backing all of the latest Web Service standards, and a mine of developer documentation can be found at http://msdn.microsoft.com/. A large number of tools for building Web Services have already been created, including Microsoft Visual Studio.NET, and more are being developed for other languages, such as Java and Perl.

Cross Platform

Because Web Services are built on standard protocols, such as XML and HTTP, they are accessible from any language that can communicate over HTTP. A component built in Visual Basic, C#, JavaScript, Perl, or Java can communicate with a component written in any other language and share data. This gives companies a new and exciting opportunity to begin integration with business partners, customers, and vendors, regardless of platform – the servers and programming backgrounds of the development teams you are trying to integrate with are no longer a barrier.

Scalable

Web Services built in ASP.NET scale similarly to the web sites we've been working on for years. A Web Service can be deployed to run on a single web server and then later scaled across multiple servers without any changes to the application code. This can be easily done using XCOPY deployment. Better still, application updates can be made at any time without taking down the Web Service, or interrupting its servicing of clients.

Loosely Coupled

Because Web Services communicate using a message-based protocol, the service and client can evolve separately. As long as the public APIs of the Web Service do not change, recompiling one side or the other and adding functionality will not break existing installed applications.

Software as a Service

This point will perhaps be the hardest one for business managers to wrap their minds around. Building software that can be exposed to the Web allows for a whole new vertical industry that software companies can get involved in. Companies that have a valuable repository of data or information can expose it to the world using Web Services. Company-to-Company systems integration will become much more commonplace and will reach down to the level of the small business.

One example of this would be a company that has a vast database of information. That company could expose this to the world via a Web Service. The information could then be accessed, for a fee, by media outlets such as web portals, newspapers, and other information providers. Prior to Web Services, information publishing to this broad a spectrum of customers was difficult to do.

Reasons You May Not Want to Use Web Services

In order to balance the discussion, we'll also mention some reasons why you might not want to use Web Services. They are, after all, not the answer to every application's needs.

Remoting May Better Suit your Needs

Remoting is a feature of .NET that allows objects written in .NET languages to be hosted on a server application and accessed remotely from .NET clients. It is a very similar technology to Distributed COM (DCOM). If all of the following bullet points are true, you may be better off using .NET Remoting, instead of Web Services:

❑   All of the clients of your server application will be running in the .NET platform

❑   You do not have a need for your server application to be accessible to the public on a variety of client platforms

❑   Performance is critical

> *This list is just a simple example; you should take the time to understand the Remoting and Web Services architectures if you are in the position of needing to make this kind of decision.*

Managing access to the Web Service

Once you have published a Web Service on the Internet, it will be accessible to anyone. If it is important that only authorized users or applications have access to your Web Service, so you'll have to create a way to manage access to it. This is quite easy to do, and is mentioned here merely to remind you that it is an issue.

Key Web-Service Standards

As mentioned previously, Web Services are built upon a number of standards. The base standards of HTTP and XML are well known, and will not be covered in detail. We will look, instead, at some of the newer standards, specific to Web Services, in this section.

SOAP

The core specification for Web Service communication is **SOAP**, which stands for Simple Object Access Protocol. SOAP is a protocol for messaging between applications using XML. The SOAP standard specifies three different aspects of the messaging process:

❑   **Messaging Envelope** – defines an XML schema for common information that is part of every SOAP message. This information is typically referred to as an envelope because it contains addressing information and routing rules. The envelope contains a message that is being sent to, or from, the Web Service.

❑   **Encoding Rules** – defines how specific base data types (strings, numbers, dates, etc.) are encoded in XML.

❑   **Procedural conventions** – defines how an actual component method can be represented in a SOAP message packet.

A sample SOAP message, complete with HTTP Headers is shown below:

```
POST /ProgrammersReference/AddingMachine.asmx HTTP/1.1
Host: localhost
Content-Type: text/xml; charset=utf-8
Content-Length: nnnn
SOAPAction: "http://wrox.com/programmersreference/AddTwoNumbers"

<?xml version="1.0" encoding="utf-8"?>
<soap:Envelope xmlns:xsi="http://www.w3.org/2001/XMLSchema-instance"
  xmlns:xsd="http://www.w3.org/2001/XMLSchema"
  xmlns:soap="http://schemas.xmlsoap.org/soap/envelope/">
  <soap:Body>
    <AddTwoNumbers xmlns="http://wrox.com/programmersreference">
      <FirstNumber>10</FirstNumber>
      <SecondNumber>5</SecondNumber>
    </AddTwoNumbers>
  </soap:Body>
</soap:Envelope>
```

In the example, you can see a `<soap:Envelope>` element. This is the root element of the XML document, and all other elements are nested inside it according to the rules of XML. Inside the root element we have a `<soap:Body>` element that acts as a container for the message sent to, or from, the Web Service. Within this container there is a nested group of elements defining the method call. If a Web Service returns an exception, the `Body` element will contain a `Fault` element describing the exception.

The ASP.NET framework automatically handles the creation and processing of SOAP packets. More information can be found by reading the SOAP specification (currently at revision 1.1). A copy can be found on the W3C's site at http://www.w3.org/TR/SOAP/

Data Types Supported in SOAP

In order to make cross-platform integration possible, SOAP defines a base set of data types that can be used in SOAP messaging. (It also allows for custom encoding and data type specifications, but using the base types will make for easier integration with other systems and platforms.)

Here is a list of the primitive data types that can be exposed as parameters and return values for web methods. They are likely to be supported on most programming platforms:

Types	Description
Simple types	Here is a list of the .NET types that are mapped to the simple types defined in the SOAP specification: `String`, `Int64`, `UInt64`, `Int32`, `UInt32`, `Int16`, `UInt16`, `Byte`, `Boolean`, `Decimal`, `Double`, `Single`, `DateTime`, and `XMLQualifiedName`
Enumerations	Enumerations can be built using any of the simple types defined above, except for the `Boolean` type
Arrays	Arrays of the above types

For Web Service applications that will be serving .NET clients exclusively, you have a lot more flexibility to use richer data types. Here is a list of some of the more common types that are specific to .NET that you can also expose as parameters from a Web Service:

Types	Description
XmlNode	A fragment of an XML document.
Classes and Structs	Any class or struct. Only the public properties and methods will be marshaled across the wire. It is also important to note that the effect is to pass the class or struct **by value**, not by reference. To use remote classes or structs by reference, you must use .NET Remoting.
DataSet	The ADO.NET DataSet.
Arrays	Arrays of the above types.

WSDL

WSDL stands for Web Services Description Language. It is closely tied to SOAP and is a specification for describing Web Services to developers. WSDL is a schema for an XML document that defines, in detail, the methods that are available from a specific Web Service. It also defines the SOAP messages that must be created to communicate with each web method. A WSDL document is commonly referred to as a **WSDL contract** because it is a documented description of a Web Service that a developer can rely upon to be accurate enough to build client access code against. ASP.NET can automatically generate WSDL for any Web Service that you create.

Here is an example piece of a WSDL contract that describes a web method that can add two numbers together to produce a result:

```
<?xml version="1.0" encoding="utf-8"?>
<definitions xmlns:s="http://www.w3.org/2001/XMLSchema">
  <service name="AddingService">
    <documentation>Adding Service web methods</documentation>
    <port name="AddingServiceHttpGet" binding="s0:AddingServiceHttpGet">
      <http:address location="http://localhost/WebService1/AddingMachine.asmx" />
    </port>
  </service>
</definitions>
```

This is just a small fragment of the entire contract that must be produced in order to fully document a Web Service. Because you are programming in ASP.NET, you may never have the need to fully understand the WSDL for your Web Service, because the .NET framework provides numerous tools to harness the power of WSDL for you. However, as with any technology, gaining an understating of the underlying ideas always makes you a more powerful programmer.

More information about WSDL, including the latest specifications and working drafts, can be found at the W3C web site at www.w3.org.

UDDI

UDDI (Universal Description, Discovery and Integration) is a specification to define a way of creating a registry of the Web Services available. This allows business to publish information about the Web Services that they are offering, and also search for providers of services that they need.

UDDI defines an XML schema for providing information about Web Services. It defines a SOAP API that the UDDI registry server must implement to allow for the publishing (and querying) of Web Services.

More information about UDDI, including current UDDI registries, can be found at http://www.uddi.org/. Microsoft is hosting one of the first UDDI registries available, at http://uddi.microsoft.com/.

> *UDDI is sometimes used to refer to the registry itself, rather than the specification.*

DISCO

DISCO (which is shortened from the word discovery) is a specification that allows an XML document to be created that can be queried for the locations of WSDL documents. The first part of the specification deals with how an application can go about finding and using documents describing Web Services. The second part defines an XML schema for documenting the locations of WSDL documents.

The ASP.NET framework ships with a handler to automatically search for ASP.NET Web Services located on a machine. It returns a DISCO document containing the locations of the WSDL files for those services. For more information about the discovery of Web Services, see Chapter 13.

The System.Web.Services Namespace

As you begin creating and using Web Services, you will need to start learning more about the classes that are available to you. `System.Web.Services` contains some of the most basic classes that are used to create a Web Service.

WebService Class

`WebService` is a class that you can inherit from when creating a Web Service in ASP.NET. When you do this you get immediate access, through your base class, to the ASP.NET intrinsic objects. You should be aware that these objects are the same ones used ASP.NET web form applications. In fact, the `Session` and `Application` objects are shared between Web Services and web forms if they are running within the same application scope in IIS.

Example: WebService Class

An example Web Service class with a single method is shown below:

> *Note that this Web Service uses the* `Context` *property, which is derived from* `WebService`.

C#

```
<%@ WebService Language="c#" Class="sample" %>
using System.Web.Services;
using System.Web;
public class sample : WebService
{
  [WebMethod]
  public string showRequestPath()
  {
    return Context.Request.ApplicationPath;
  }
}
```

VB.NET

```
<%@ WebService Language="vb" Class="sample" %>
Imports System.Web.Services
Imports System.Web
Public Class sample
```

```
      Inherits System.Web.Services.WebService
      <WebMethod()> _
      Public Function showRequestPath() As String
        showRequestPath = Context.Request.ApplicationPath
      End Function
    End Class
```

Because multiple inheritance is not supported in .NET, your Web Service class may need to inherit from other classes instead of `WebService`.

> It is not necessary to inherit from **WebService** to create a Web Service. Inheriting from **WebService** simply gives you intrinsic access to the **Application**, **Context**, **Server**, **Session**, and **User** objects.

If you expose a method as a Web Service in a class that does not inherit from `WebService`, you can still get the intrinsic ASP.NET objects from the current `HttpContext` object, by calling its static `Current()` method, as shown below:

C#

```
// Note that this class does not inherit from WebService
public class DataService
{
  [WebMethod]
  public string getData(string Query)
  {
    // Get a reference to the Context object
    HttpContext a_Context = HttpContext.Current();
    // Check the cache to see if we already have the data
    string a_ReturnValue = a_Context.Chache[Query].ToString();
    if(a_ReturnValue == null)
    {
      // Run the Query and then store the results in the cache
      // (the implementation of our fictional GetData() method is not shown)
      a_ReturnValue = GetData(Query);
      a_Context[Query] = a_ReturnValue;
    }
    return a_ReturnValue;
  }
}
```

VB.NET

```
' Note that this class does not inherit from WebService
Public Class DataService
  <WebMethod> _
  Public Fucntion getData(Query as String) as String
    ' Get a reference to the Context object
    Dim a_Context as HttpContext = HttpContext.Current()
    ' Check the cache to see if we already have the data
    Dim a_ReturnValue as String = a_Context.Chache(Query).ToString()
    If IsNull(a_ReturnValue) Then
      ' Run the Query and then store the results in the cache
      ' (the implementation of our fictional GetData() method is not shown)
      a_ReturnValue = GetData(Query)
      a_Context(Query) = a_ReturnValue
    End If
```

```
      return a_ReturnValue
   End Function
End Class
```

Application Property

The `Application` property returns an `HttpApplicationState` object. This object is similar to the `Application` object from the previous version of ASP.

Here is an example of using the `Application` property:

C#

```
[WebMethod]
public string getConnectionString()
{
    // This code will only work if we have previously stored
    // the connection string in the Application object
    return Application["ConnectStr"];
}
```

VB.NET

```
<WebMethod()> _
Public Function getConnectionString() As String
    ' This code will only work if we have previously stored
    ' the connection string in the Application object
    getConnectionString = Application("ConnectStr")
End Function
```

Context Property

The `Context` property returns the `HttpContext` object for the current request. The `HttpContext` class contains accessors for all of the normal objects you would use to retrieve the state of the current request, including the `Session`, `Request`, `Application`, `Server`, and `User` objects. Here is an example of getting the `Items` property of the `HttpContext` object:

C#

```
string aContextItem = Context.Items["ItemKey"].ToString();
```

VB.NET

```
Dim aContextItem As String = Context.Items("ItemKey")
```

Server Property

The `Server` property returns the current `HttpServerUtility` object. The `HttpServerUtility` object is similar to the `Server` object from previous versions of ASP. Here is an example of using the `Server` property of `WebService`.

C#

```
String aServerName = Server.MachineName;
```

VB.NET

```
Dim aServerName as String = Server.MachineName
```

Session Property

The `Session` property returns an `HttpSessionState` object. This object stores state for the current user between requests. The `Session` object is turned off by default in a Web Service. In order to enable it, you will need to set the `EnableSession` property on the `WebMethod` attribute to `True`. See the section on the `WebMethodAttribute` class, later in the chapter, for details.

Typically the `Session` object is not used in Web Services, as they are best designed to run in a stateless manner. In other words, each request will have all of the information the server needs to process the information and return a response. The server should not need to persist any information about the client in between requests. In some cases, however, session state within a Web Service may be a necessary and an important part of the design. An example of getting a piece of state information from the `Session` object is shown here:

C#

```
// Retrieve a string from the session object
string GetSessionItem = Session(SessionKey);
```

VB.NET

```
' Retrieve a string from the session object
Dim GetSessionItem as String = Session(SessionKey)
```

Note that the use of session state requires that the client application be able to process and return cookies for each subsequent request.

User Property

If user authentication has been enabled for the current Web Service, the `User` property will contain an object that implements the `IPrincipal` interface and represents the identity of the current user. See Chapter 9 for more details on user authentication. Here is an example of retrieving the current user's name.

C#

```
string aName = User.Identity.Name;
```

VB.NET

```
Dim aName as String = User.Identity.Name
```

WebServiceAttribute Class

The `WebServiceAttribute` contains three properties that you can attach to your class that contains web methods. These properties can partially change the SOAP and WSDL that is automatically generated for your code by ASP.NET at run time. It is good programming practice to set values for all three of these when you are ready to expose your Web Service to the world.

The properties are called `Description`, `Name`, and `Namespace`. Here's an example of them in use; we'll discuss them in a moment:

C#

```
[WebService(Name="Acme Calendar Service",
  Description="Use this Web Service to update your calendar",
  Namespace="Http://foo.bar/Calendars")]
```

```
public class Calendar
{
  [WebMethod]
  public DateTime GetTodaysDate()
  {
    return DateTime.Now;
  }
}
```

VB.NET

```
<WebService(Name:="Acme Calendar Service", _
    Description:="Use this Web Service to update your calendar", _
    Namespace:="Http://foo.bar/Calendars")> _
Public Class Calendar
  <WebMethod()> _
  Public Function getTodaysDate() As DateTime

    Return DateTime.Now
  End Function
End Class
```

All of these attributes are now available from the WSDL generated to describe your Web Service. The above class can now publish this information to anyone who might want to use your Web Service.

> Note that the name and description from our WebMethodAttribute were pulled in and used to help describe this Web Service.

Description Property

The Description property of the WebServiceAttribute can be set on your class to briefly describe your Web Service to consumers of your class. The WSDL that is generated will contain this description, as will the default ASP.NET Web Service description page for your Web Service. The description attribute is applied to your Web Service class as shown in the previous example.

Name Property

The Name property is where we store the name of the Web Service.

Namespace Property

The Namespace property is probably the most important attribute to use. It defines a unique URI that defines the XML namespace that will be applied to the specific XML elements in SOAP messages sent to, and from, your Web Service. Your namespace is what sets your Web Service apart from all other Web Services in the world. Other Web Services could have the same method names as yours, but if your namespace is unique, there is no ambiguity about which Web Service belongs to you. Typically, businesses that already have a unique domain name for their web site will use it for part of the namespace for their Web Services.

WebMethodAttribute Class

The WebMethodAttribute class is a required attribute for any method that you wish to expose to the world as a web method. When the ASP.NET runtime sees this attribute on your method, it does the necessary work of generating WSDL for it and mapping appropriate SOAP messages to it. All of the properties of this attribute class are optional.

BufferResponse Property

If this property is set to `true` (the default), the SOAP layer will create the complete response SOAP packet in a memory buffer before sending it back to the client. If it is set to `false`, the SOAP packet is sent back to the client in pieces, as it is built on the server. Normally you'll want to leave this with the default value.

C#

```
[WebMethod (BufferResponse=False)]
public string GetData()
{
  //We turned buffering off because we are going to return lots of data.
  return db.HugeDataSet();
}
```

VB.NET

```
<WebMethod(BufferResponse:=False)> _
Public Function GetData() As String
  'We turned buffering off because we are going to return lots of data.
  Return db.HugeDataSet()
End Function
```

You should only set `BufferResponse` to `false` if you anticipate that the web method will return very large amounts of data as its result. Note that if the `BufferResponse` property is set to `false`, SOAP extensions will be disabled for this method. See Chapter 13 for more information on SOAP extensions.

CacheDuration Property

Web Service output caching is a feature of ASP.NET that adds virtually automatic caching capability to methods exposed by your Web Service. If a web method is called more than once with the same parameters before the cached output expires, ASP.NET will return the cached output without calling your method again. The data that ASP.NET caches is the SOAP message packet that was generated as a response from the previous invocation of your Web Service.

> **Caching frequently used pieces of data for even short periods of time can dramatically increase the potential scalability of your web application.**

Here's an example of how to set up caching:

C#

```
[WebMethod (CacheDuration=60)]
public string GetTaskList(string UserID)
{
  return db.getTaskList(UserID);
}
```

VB.NET

```
<WebMethod(CacheDuration:=60)> _
Public Function GetTaskList(ByVal UserID As String) As String()
  Return db.getTaskList(UserID)
End Function
```

By default, the `CacheDuration` property is set to 0, which means that caching is disabled. If you set the `CacheDuration` property to a number greater than 0, then ASP.NET will cache the data for that many seconds.

A cached copy of the data will be maintained for each distinct set of parameters that are passed to the web method. If your web method will return large amounts of data and has a large number of different parameter combinations that it will be called with, caching the data may not be the right choice.

You should weight up the benefits against the amount of server resources you could be tying up to maintain the caches.

Description Property

The Description property is a string that describes the web method. This property is used to help generate user-friendly description documents for the web method.

C#

```
[WebMethod (Description="This method returns the current date") ]
public string GetDate()
{
  return DateTime.Now.ToString();
}
```

VB.NET

```
<WebMethod(Description:="This method returns the current date")> _
Public Function GetDate() as String
  Return DateTime.Now.ToString()
End Function
```

EnableSession Property

This property enables use of the Session object in a web method, if set to true. By default it is set to false. A Web Service can only maintain a Session object through the use of cookies.

> Web Service clients that do not properly handle cookies will not have any state maintained for them in their Session objects on the server between Web Service requests, regardless of whether this property is set to true or false.

MessageName Property

By default, the name SOAP uses to identify your web method is derived from the actual method name defined in the Web Service class. This behavior can be overridden by the use of the MessageName property.

This property is typically used to expose web methods that have several overloaded versions, as SOAP does not support overloading. If your Web Service class has overloaded versions of the same method, they must be distinguished from each other by having a unique SOAP message name.

Here is an example of an overloaded method. That is, the same name is used for two different methods, and the methods only vary by the data types of their parameters. In order for them to be exposed over SOAP as web methods, they must have a unique SOAP message name:

C#

```
[WebMethod]
public string GetCustomerName(Guid CustomerID)
{
  return db.GetCustomerName(CustomerID);
}
```

```
[WebMethod( MessageName="GetCustomerByID" )]
public string GetCustomerName(int CustomerID)
{
   return db.GetCustomerName(CustomerID);
}
```

VB.NET

```
<WebMethod()> _
Public Overloads Function GetCustomerName( _
    ByVal CustomerID As Guid) As String
   Return db.GetCustomerName(CustomerID)
End Function

<WebMethod(MessageName:="GetCustomerByID")> _
Public Overloads Function GetCustomerName( _
    ByVal CustomerID As Integer) As String
   Return db.GetCustomerName(CustomerID)
End Function
```

TransactionOption Property

This property sets the transactional behavior for the web method. Enabling transactional support in a web method means that it can participate as the root object in a COM+ (MTS) transaction.

Web methods in ASP.NET currently do not support sharing transactions with the application that is calling them. A Web Service is transactional only if it is the root object that started the transaction. In other words, if a web method begins a transaction and then calls another web method that requires a transaction, the two Web Services cannot mutually share the same transaction. Each web method participates solely in the context of its own transaction. This could change with future versions of ASP.NET as Web Service technology becomes more mature.

The `TransactionOption` property may be set with any of the values from the `TransactionOption` enumeration, which is shown below. By default, this property is set to `TransactionOption.Disabled`.

Note that this enumeration is from the `System.EnterpriseServices` namespace.

Enumeration Name	Description
Disabled	The web method will be run without any transaction in place.
NotSupported	Run this component outside of the context of a transaction. For a web method, this setting is effectively the same as `Disabled`.
Required	If a transaction is already in place, share in it. If not, create a new transaction. For a web method, this is always the same as `RequiresNew`.
RequiresNew	Always create a new transaction for this component.
Supported	If a transaction is already in place, share in it. Because web methods do not share in transactions, this setting effectively is the same as `Disabled`.

579

Here is an example usage of a web method with transaction support enabled:

C#

```
[WebMethod( TransactionOption = TransactionOption.RequiresNew)]
public void SaveCustomer()
{
    // run the save customer logic here within the scope of the transaction
}
```

VB.NET

```
<WebMethod(TransactionOption:=TransactionOption.RequiresNew)> _
Public Sub SaveCustomer()
    ' run the save customer logic here within the scope of the transaction
End Sub
```

WebServiceBindingAttribute Class

The `WebServiceBindingAttribute` is an attribute that can be applied to a Web Service class to declare that the class implements a binding, defined elsewhere, in a WSDL contract. Each Web Service has a default binding of which all of its operations are automatically made a part. The `WebServiceBindingAttribute` simply describes the details of one or more bindings that are described elsewhere in addition to these. For more information on bindings, see Chapter 12.

As Web Services evolve, the ability to be able to bind to a particular set of operations will become crucial to allow Web Services to seamlessly interact with one another. It is likely that standards bodies will define particular bindings for common types of Web Services that Web Service developers can then build to.

The behavior of this attribute is similar to declaring that a class implements an interface. Developing software based on interfaces is a familiar concept to those of you who have ever written a COM component in C++ or written an object-oriented application in VB. Interface based programming will continue to be extremely important in the Web-Services realm as well.

Here is an example binding that is applied to a Web Service class:

C#

```
[ WebServiceBinding(Name="ICalendarBinding",
      Namespace="http://www.foobar.org/Calendars",
      Location="http://www.foobar.org/Calendars/WSDL")]
public class Calendar
{
    // implementation goes here
}
```

VB.NET

```
<WebServiceBinding(Name:="ICalendarBinding", _
      Namespace:="http://www.foobar.org/Calendars", _
      Location:="http://www.foobar.org/Calendars/WSDL")> _
Public Class Calendar
    ' implementation goes here
End Class
```

Note that if you have applied a `WebServiceBindingAttribute` attribute to your Web Service, the individual methods that implement the binding interface must also be marked with a `SoapDocumentMethodAttribute` or a `SoapRpcMethodAttribute`. These attributes map the specific web methods to the associated binding that they are implementing.

Location Property

The `Location` property specifies the URL to the WSDL contract that this Web Service is bound to. The default value is the URL of the Web Service that this attribute is applied to.

Name Property

The `Name` property defines a unique name that identifies this binding from all other bindings. The default value is the name of the class with the word SOAP appended to it.

Namespace Property

The `Namespace` property sets the namespace that is associated with the particular binding.

System.Web.Services.Description

This chapter is divided into two sections. The first deals with conceptual ideas. It covers when you might find the System.Web.Services.Description namespace useful, how to read and write the WSDL files that it makes use of, and what the internal structure of a WSDL file looks like. It ends with an example of a complete WSDL file for a Web Service, and a brief discussion of WSDL extensibility.

In the second section of the chapter we deal with technical issues. we look in detail at the classes, properties, and methods that make up the System.Web.Services.Description namespace, and also at the different sections and elements that comprise a WSDL schema, using the previous WSDL example for illustration.

We will begin with a brief overview of what this namespace allows you to do, the WSDL files that it uses, and how this fits into the wider world of ASP.NET Web Services.

The Description namespace contains a hierarchy of object-oriented classes and collections that allow you to interrogate WSDL (Web Services Description Language) files. These XML files describe ASP.NET Web Services that are available for consumption by an ASP.NET client. They contain information on a Web Service's methods, arguments, and the location of the ASP.NET server.

WSDL files are not restricted to creation by an ASP.NET server; they are an industry-wide specification that all SOAP compliant servers adhere to. Therefore if you are consuming a Web Service from either an ASP.NET server or a SOAP server created by another organization then you will, in all cases, firstly need to locate the WSDL file that describes that service.

The information contained in a WSDL schema definition is used to construct a SOAP request message that can be sent to an ASP.NET Web Service. The Web Service then interprets the SOAP request and runs the specific methods identified. At the same time, it passes arguments into the methods that are contained within the SOAP message.

Displaying a WSDL File

To display the WSDL file for your ASP.NET Web Service you simply need to append the text "?wsdl" to the end of your ASMX address line:

```
http://localhost/webservice1/example1.asmx?wsdl
```

The WSDL file will now be displayed describing the location and structure of the Web Service.

Note that the above method displays a WSDL schema file for an ASP.NET Web Service; for Web Services that are not ASP.NET applications you will be supplied with a WSDL file Internet location.

How to Read a WSDL Schema

The ability to read and digest a WSDL schema at run-time is performed by using the following simple VB.NET code:

```
Dim oS As ServiceDescription
oS = ServiceDescription.Read("c:\calc.wsdl")
```

This code assumes that you have a valid WSDL schema file on your `c:` drive and then uses it to instantiate and populate the `ServiceDescription` base class. After this you can use the collections and objects contained within this class to interrogate any part of the WSDL schema definition.

The `ServicesDescription` class forms the basic building block for a WSDL schema, allowing you to read in, and subsequently interrogate, each of the schema's collections and associated objects.

How to Write a WSDL Schema

After you have read in a valid WSDL file you may want manipulate its values. For example, the following code shows you how to change the `TargetNamespace` property:

```
oS.TargetNamespace = "http://www.salcentral.com/wrox/tnspace.xml"
```

Once you have altered your schema, you can save it using one of the following methods:

❑   A `stream` object

❑   A `string` denoting a file name

❑   A `TextWriter` object

❑   An `XmlWriter` object

In the following example we alter our WSDL schema file and save it to a local file on our hard drive by using the following code:

```
Dim oS As ServiceDescription
oS = ServiceDescription.Read("c:\calc.wsdl")
oS.TargetNamespace = "http://www.salcentral.com/wrox/newnspace.xml"
oS.Write("C:\test.wsdl")
```

How Can I Use the WSDL Schema?

Reading in a schema definition is usually performed on a client, but in some cases where an ASP.NET server is using another ASP.NET server's Web Service to pass on processing, it may also be helpful to use this `Description` namespace on the server as well.

There is usually a little confusion about what the `Description` namespace can be used for, so an explanation using two scenarios will allow you to get a better grasp as to how this namespace can significantly help cure what are arguably two of the most common problems in any software development team today.

Scenario 1: Version Control

Say you wanted to implement versioning and as part of your versioning control management you set the `TargetNamespace` you wanted to use for the entire WSDL schema to include the name of the Web Service plus the version number as follows:

```
CalculatorWebService_v102
```

Setting the name for the Web Service on an ASP.NET server is done as follows:

```
Imports System.Web.Services
<WebService(TargetNamespace:="CalculatorWebService_v102")> Public _
                                          Class Service1
    Inherits System.Web.Services.WebService
    <WebMethod()> Public Function Add(ByVal X As Long, _
                           ByVal Y As Long) As Long
        Add = X + Y
    End Function
End Class
```

The client can now read the `targetNamespace` for the schema, by placing the following code wherever they require version checking:

```
Const sSupportedVersion As String = "CalculatorWebService_v101"
Dim oS As ServiceDescription
'Load up the remote Web Service into an XMLReader object
Dim oXmlReader As New Xml.XmlTextReader( _
                   "http://localhost/webservice1/service1.asmx?wsdl")
'Now populate the servicedescription class the root
'class for all WSDL schema definitions
oS = ServiceDescription.Read(oXmlReader)
If (oS.TargetNamespace <> sSupportedVersion) Then
    MsgBox("This version IS NOT supported")
Else
    MsgBox("This version IS supported")
End If
```

As can be seen, this value-added information for a WSDL definition enables you to programmatically determine business flow, and produce specialist SOAP interpretation and response routines.

Scenario 2: Naming Convention

In this scenario you have a strict naming convention within your organization for Web Services that states that all string variables must start with "`str`" and all other variables (independent of their type) must start with "`var`". Using the following code you can check through large quantities of Web Service schemas quickly looking for inconsistencies within your WSDL definitions.

In this case you could set the following code up in the manner outlined above:

```
Dim osd As New ServiceDescription()
Dim oMsg As Message
Dim oArg As MessagePart
Dim sPrefix As String
'You can read a local filename into
'the servicedescrption class using this method
```

```
osd = osd.Read("c:\calc.xml")
If osd.Messages.Count > 0 Then
    oMsg = osd.Messages.Item(0)
    For Each oArg In oMsg.Parts
        sPrefix = Microsoft.VisualBasic.Left(oArg.Name, 3)
        If oArg.Type.Name = "string" And sPrefix <> "str" Then
            'Raise an error or log an error
        ElseIf (sPrefix <> "var") Then
            'Raise an error or log an error
        End If
    Next
End If
```

WSDL Schema Definition

Before we attempt to describe the `Description` namespace we will discuss the hierarchy of WSDL/XML schema definitions.

Below we have outlined each of the classes within the `Description` namespace along with their related `<element>` names:

'*' denotes 0 or more entries allowed using a collection class
'?' denotes 0 or 1 entries allowed using a collection class

WSDL Section	Classes and Elements
Interface	**Types** (`<types>` element) *
	Message (`<message>` element) *
	InputMessage (`<input>` element) ?
	OutputMessage (`<output>` element) ?
	FaultMessage (`<fault>` element) *
	PortType (`<porttype>` element) *
	Operation (`<operation>` element) *
	OutputMessage (`<input>` element) ?
	OutputMessage (`<output>` element) ?
	FaultMessage (`<fault>` element) *
Binding	**Binding** (`<binding>` element) *
	OperationBinding (`<operation>` element) *
	InputBinding (`<input>` element) ?
	OutputBinding (`<output>` element) ?
	FaultBinding (`<fault>` element) *
Communication	**Service** (`<service>` element) *
	Port (`<port>` element) *

These classes will be covered in more detail later in the chapter. This table will serve as a reference as to which XML element they are associated with.

The WSDL schema structure adhered to by ASP.NET follows the standards defined by the W3C document at http://www.w3.org/TR/wsdl; the v1.1 WSDL draft specification.

WSDL Sections

The `ServiceDescription` class has many child collections and classes that map directly to WSDL elements. However, the bulk of the namespace's functionality lies within six classes. These classes represent the principal areas of a WSDL file, and each provides information relating to a particular aspect of a Web Service's functionality.

By instantiating the `ServiceDescription` class you are effectively mapping every element of a given WSDL schema to your class or property.

A WSDL file is split, not just by the XML tags within it, but also into definitive business sections. Each of these sections is self-describing, with regard to how one area of its internal structure can reference other internal areas. The three primary sections of a WSDL file are listed next.

The Interface Section

This section of a WSDL document defines the methods, arguments, and namespaces available for this Web Service on a remote SOAP server. It defines the format for SOAP Requests, Responses, Faults, and Data Types.

The main classes for handling the data contained in this section are:

❑ `Messages` (class correlates to the `<message>` element)

❑ `Types` (class correlates to the `<types>` element)

❑ `PortTypes` (class correlates to the `<porttype>` element)

The Communication Section

This section defines the supported communication methods for transferring a request to a server, such as HTTP GET, HTTP POST, and SOAP. This information is linked to an associated interface and protocol using a binding namespace.

The main classes that fall into this section are:

❑ `Services` (class correlates to the `<service>` element)

❑ `Ports` (class correlates to the `<port>` element)

The Binding Section

The binding section associates definitions given in the `Communication` section with definitions in the `Interface` section using the `<binding>` element.

The class in the `Description` namespace that deals with this section is:

❑ `Bindings` (class correlates to the `<binding>` element)

WSDL Example

To explain how the hierarchy of the `Description` namespace correlates to a WSDL schema, we have created some WSDL to describe a Web Service offering the functionality of a simple calculator. This WSDL is included in complete form here, and is also available in the download. Sections of this WSDL will also be shown throughout the rest of this chapter to highlight particular topics.

```xml
<?xml version="1.0" ?>
  <definitions name="SimpleCalculator.csimplecalc"
  targetNamespace="http://www.salcentral.com/wrox/calc.xml"
  xmlns:tns="http://www.salcentral.com/wrox/calc.xml"
  xmlns:xsd="http://www.w3.org/2001/XMLSchema"
  xmlns:soap="http://schemas.xmlsoap.org/wsdl/soap/"
  xmlns="http://schemas.xmlsoap.org/wsdl/">
  <import ref="http://www.salcentral.com/wrox/import.xml"/>
  <types>
    <schema targetNamespace="http://www.salcentral.com/xsd"
                           xmlns="http://www.w3.org/2001/XMLSchema">
      <element name="values">
        <complexType>
          <all>
            <element name="XI" type="long"/>
            <element name="YI" type="long"/>
          </all>
        </complexType>
      </element>
    </schema>
  </types>
  <message name="AddRequest">
    <part name="X" element="xsd:values" />
    <part name="Y" element="xsd:long" />
  </message>
  <message name="AddResponse">
    <part name="Return" element="xsd:long" />
  </message>
  <message name="AddFaultWarn">
    <part name="Source" element="xsd:string" />
    <part name="Description" element="xsd:string" />
  </message>
  <message name="AddFaultCritical">
    <part name="Source" element="xsd:string" />
    <part name="Description" element="xsd:string" />
    <part name="ErrorCode" element="xsd:long" />
  </message>

  <portType name="Calc.CalcType">
    <operation name="Add">
      <input name="AddReq" message="tns:AddRequest" />
      <output name="AddRes" message="tns:AddResponse" />
      <fault name="FaultWarning" message="tns:AddFaultWarn"/>
      <fault name="FaultCritical" message="tns:AddFaultCritical">
        <documentation>Message here</documentation>
      </fault>
    </operation>
  </portType>
  <binding name="Calc.CalcBind" type="tns:Calc.CalcType">
    <soap:binding style="rpc"
                     transport="http://schemas.xmlsoap.org/soap/http" />
      <operation name="Add">
      <soap:operation soapAction="www.salcentral.com#Add" />
      <input>
        <soap:body use="encoded" namespace="www.salcentral.com/1"
              encodingStyle="http://schemas.xmlsoap.org/soap/encoding/" />
      </input>
      <output>
        <soap:body use="encoded" namespace="www.salcentral.com/2"
              encodingStyle="http://schemas.xmlsoap.org/soap/encoding/" />
      </output>
      <fault>
```

```
            <soap:body use="encoded" namespace="www.salcentral.com/3"
                encodingStyle="http://schemas.xmlsoap.org/soap/encoding/" />
        </fault>
      </operation>

    </binding>
    <service name="Calc.Cadd" >
      <port name="Calc.CAddPort" binding="tns:Calc.CalcBind">
        <soap:address location="http://sal006.salnetwork.com/calc.cgi"/>
      </port>
    </service>
  </definitions>
```

Extensibility

This is a commonly used term within WSDL creation to denote the ability to enhance the basic function of WSDL's key elements, without changing the fundamental structure of the WSDL schema format.

Some situations where extensibility can be useful include:

❑   Extending style definitions (for example, RPC and Document)

❑   Specifying a location address for a port

❑   Providing MIME information for file attachments

❑   Providing message definitions

Extensions of these elements are defined using existing XML elements, such as `<soap:binding>`, which can be easily read and understood by a compliant WSDL reader, like ASP.NET.

Even though extensibility may seem, at first glance, like an issue for advanced users only, it does in fact include certain WSDL elements, which if not available would mean that the WSDL schema definition could not be read. Therefore you need to be aware that extensibility refers to mandatory XML elements of a WSDL file, as well as optional, and possibly more advanced, elements.

> *Extensibility elements must use a unique namespace within the WSDL schema in which they are defined.*

How Extensibility Classes Work

The following classes are all the extensibility classes that are supported within ASP.NET and can serve to extend functionality:

Extensibility Classes

❑   `HttpAddressBinding`

❑   `HttpBinding`

❑   `HttpOperationBinding`

❑   `HttpUrlEncodedBinding`

❑   `HttpReplacementBinding`

❑   `MimeMultipartRelatedBinding`

- ❏ MimePart
- ❏ MimeTextBinding
- ❏ MimeXmlBinding
- ❏ MimeContentBinding
- ❏ SoapAddressBinding
- ❏ SoapBinding
- ❏ SoapBodyBinding
- ❏ SoapFaultBinding
- ❏ SoapHeaderBinding
- ❏ SoapHeaderFaultBinding
- ❏ SoapOperationBinding

The way an extensibility class works is that certain classes within the `Description` namespace have an `Extensions` property; they are all listed below:

Classes with Extensions Property

- ❏ Binding
- ❏ FaultBinding
- ❏ InputBinding
- ❏ MimePart
- ❏ OperationBinding
- ❏ OutputBinding
- ❏ Port
- ❏ Service
- ❏ ServiceDescription
- ❏ Types

Extensibility can be simply described by stating if you add an extensibility class to a class with extensions capability (`Extensions` property) you extend the features of that class. Therefore if you add an `HttpBinding` class to a `Binding` class you are in the initial stages of indicating that you want this `Binding` class to support `HttpBinding`. This alteration is then reflected in the WSDL schema when written out to a file.

The following code outlines how you can add another operation to an existing class using extensibility classes:

```
Dim oS As ServiceDescription
Dim oOpBinding As New OperationBinding()
Dim oInputBinding As New InputBinding()
Dim oSoapOperation As New SoapOperationBinding()
Dim oOutputBinding As New OutputBinding()
Dim oSoapBodyBinding As New SoapBodyBinding()
Dim oXmlReader As New Xml.XmlTextReader( _
                "http://localhost/webservice1/service1.asmx?wsdl")
```

```
If oS.CanRead(oXmlReader) Then
    'Load WSDL schema
    oS = ServiceDescription.Read(oXmlReader)
    oSoapOperation.SoapAction = "CalculaterWebService"
    'Create encoded message format
    oSoapOperation.Style = SoapBindingStyle.Document
    oSoapBodyBinding.Use = SoapBindingUse.Encoded
    oInputBinding.Extensions.Add(oSoapBodyBinding)
    oOutputBinding.Extensions.Add(oSoapBodyBinding)
    'Add message formats, but now with encoding instead of literal
    oOpBinding.Input = oInputBinding
    oOpBinding.Output = oOutputBinding
    oOpBinding.Extensions.Add(oSoapOperation)
    'Use a distinct name
    oOpBinding.Name = "Add_Encoded"
    oS.Bindings(0).Operations.Add(oOpBinding)
    'Now lets write it to a local file
    oS.Write("C:\test.xml")
End If
```

After the above code was run, it automatically adds the following XML to the WSDL schema between the <binding> elements:

```
<operation name="Add_Encoded">
  <soap:operation soapAction="CalculatorWebService" style="document">
  <input>
  <soap:body use="encoded" />
    </input>
    <output>
      <soap:body use="encoded" />
    </output>
</operation>
```

The above code has now created a WSDL schema that states that the server can also handle encoded data within the SOAP message.

> Note that even though you have amended the schema this does not mean that your Web Service actually supports this functionality.

The ServiceDescription Class

The ServiceDescription class is the root class containing the Web Service definition in its entirety. Using ServiceDescription, you can import the WSDL schema definitions from an external WSDL schema file.

The Bindings Property

This property is the BindingCollection class containing the collection of binding elements extracted from the WSDL document. This binding class describes associations between the messages defined by the WSDL and the communication end-point.

```
BindingCollection = ServiceDescription.Bindings
```

This collection is read-only, meaning that you cannot assign a Bindings collection object directly to it, once it has be instantiated by reading in a WSDL schema; however, you are able to alter the underlying collection items.

The following is an extract from our example WSDL schema and identifies the `messages` element portion of the schema:

```
<binding name="Calc.CalcBind" type="tns:Calc.CalcType">
  ...
</binding>
```

As with any standard collection object within ASP.NET you can use the collection's built-in properties to better interrogate its values:

```
Dim iLoop As Integer
Dim osd As ServiceDescription
osd = osd.Read("calc.xml")
For iLoop = 0 To osd.Bindings.Count - 1
  Console.Write(osd.Bindings.Item(iLoop).Name)
Next
```

The Extensions Property

Extensibility refers to the enhancement of the WSDL schema with additions that are generally peculiar to a specific protocol or message format. The `Extensions` property of `ServiceDescription` provides the means for including such features.

```
ServiceDescriptionFormatExtensionCollection = ServiceDescription.Extension
```

It's worth noting that although extensibility properties can be found throughout a WSDL document, they represent unique features that are only related to the specific WSDL area to which they have been bound.

This collection is read-only, meaning that you cannot assign an `Extensions` collection object directly to it, once it has be instantiated by reading in a WSDL schema; however, you are able to alter the underlying collection items.

The Imports Property

WSDL allows for the definition of portions of its structure inside separate XML files external to the main WSDL document. Such external XML files are referenced by a WSDL document by means of an `<import>` element. The external XML is inserted into the WSDL document at the exact position of the import statement. The `Imports` property contains information about all `<import>` elements in a WSDL file as a `Collection`.

```
ImportCollection = ServiceDescription.Imports
```

The following is an extract from our example WSDL schema and identifies the `import` element portion of the schema:

```
<import ref="http://www.salcentral.com/wrox/import.xml"/>
```

You are unable to add a new collection to this property; however, you may alter the underlying collection items.

The Messages Property

The <message> elements in a WSDL file provide definitions of the arguments and method name for either the Request or the Response message, through sub-elements of the <part> elements in the WSDL schema. These are called "AddRequest" and "AddResponse". The Messages property contains collection information about all such <message> elements defined within the WSDL schema. See the section headed *The Message Class* later in the chapter for more complete details.

```
MessageCollection = ServiceDescription.Messages
```

It is again read-only, however, you may alter the underlying collection items.

The following is an extract from our example WSDL schema and identifies the message element portion of the schema:

```
<message name="AddRequest">
  . . .
</message>
<message name="AddResponse">
  . . .
</message>
<message name="AddFaultWarn">
  . . .
</message>
<message name="AddFaultCritical">
  . . .
</message>
```

Like any other collection within ASP.NET, this collection has a series of embedded properties that are available for the developer to interrogate, for example, count and item:

```
Dim osd As ServiceDescription
osd = osd.Read("c:\calc.xml")
if osd.Messages.Count > 0 Then
  msgbox "This WSDL file contains messages"
  msgbox "The name of the first message is " osd.Messages.Item(0).Name
End If
```

The Name Property

This property contains the WSDL schema name taken from the <definitions> element's name attribute in the header portion of the WSDL schema.

```
String = ServiceDescription.Name
```

This property has read/write access.

The PortTypes Property

This property represents an abstract collection of messages and operations. It is used to link the bindings section of the WSDL schema to the messages section of the WSDL schema.

```
PortTypeCollection = ServiceDescription.PortTypes
```

The following is an extract from our example WSDL schema and identifies the `porttype` element portion of the schema:

```
<portType name="Calc.CalcType">
  ...
</portType>
```

You are unable to add a new collection to this property, but you may alter the underlying collection items.

The ServiceDescriptions Property

The `ServiceDescriptions` property makes available the parent collection that contains this instance of `ServiceDescriptions` if the current `ServiceDescription` is attached to a collection. If this instance has no parent collection, then an exception will result.

```
ServiceDescriptionCollection = ServiceDescription.ServiceDescriptions
```

Exception Name	Description
NullReferenceException	Thrown when the ServiceDescription instance has not been assigned to a parent collection

This property allows for the collation of multiple schemas into a single business solution comprising a collection of various Web Services. For example the following code loads two WSDL schemas into a single `ServicesDescriptions` collection:

```
Dim iLoop As Integer
Dim oS As ServiceDescription
Dim oSCol As New ServiceDescriptionCollection()
Dim asWSDLSchema(2) As String
Dim oXmlReader As Xml.XmlTextReader

asWSDLSchema(0) = "http://localhost/webservice1/service1.asmx?wsdl"
asWSDLSchema(1) = "http://localhost/webservice2/service1.asmx?wsdl"

For iLoop = 0 To UBound(asWSDLSchema) - 1
    oXmlReader = New Xml.XmlTextReader(asWSDLSchema(iLoop))
    If oS.CanRead(oXmlReader) Then
        oS = oS.Read(oXmlReader)
        oSCol.Add(oS)
    End If
    oXmlReader = Nothing
    oS = Nothing
Next
```

Each schema added to the `ServiceDescriptions` collection must have its own unique `TargetNamespace`.

The Services Property

A Service groups together a set of related ports defined in the WSDL schema. A port is the destination and transport protocol to use when transferring messages to a SOAP-compliant server, for example below we have extracted the port element out of our previous WSDL example schema:

```
<soap:address location="http://sal006.salnetwork.com/calc.cgi"/>
```

This extract defines the transport protocol to be `soap`, which means send SOAP messages to the server and the destination address is: http://sal006.salnetwork.com/calc.cgi.

This collection allows you to interact with services and their associated ports for a specific Web Service.

```
ServiceCollection = ServiceDescription.Services
```

The following is an extract from our example WSDL schema and identifies the service element portion of the schema:

```
<service name="Calc.Cadd" >
  ...
</service>
```

Another read-only property that does not allow you to assign a new collection, it does however allow the underlying collection items to be altered.

The TargetNamespace Property

This specifies the namespace taken from the `<definitions>` element's `TargetNamespace` attribute in the WSDL header. This is the Internet or intranet location of the current WSDL file.

```
String = ServiceDescription.TargetNamespace
```

This property has read/write access.

The Types Property

It is possible to create your own data types tailored for specific messages and requirements. For example, when transmitting a customer's name and address, you could define a single complex data type to contain both name and address. The `Types` collection allows you to iterate through all user-defined types given in the current WSDL document.

```
Types = ServiceDescription.Types
```

Another read-only property that does not allow you to assign a new collection, it does, however, allow the underlying collection items to be altered.

The CanRead Method

You can determine whether a document conforms to the WSDL specification by loading it into an `XmlReader` object (a class for reading generic XML files) and subsequently using the `CanRead` method. The method returns `true` if the file is of the correct structure and is able to be read.

```
Boolean = ServiceDescription.CanRead(XmlReader)
```

Parameter	Type	Description
XmlReader	Object	Instantiates and populates an `XmlReader` file (see following example code)

Following is some example code for loading a WSDL Internet file from an Internet location, verifying that it can be read and is a valid WSDL schema file:

```
Dim oS As ServiceDescription
Dim oXmlReader As New Xml.XmlTextReader( _
                    http://localhost/webservice1/service1.asmx?wsdl")
If oS.CanRead(oXmlReader) Then
    oS = ServiceDescription.Read(oXmlReader)
    MsgBox("This is a valid WSDL schema")
End If
```

The Read Method

This method populates the `ServiceDescription` class. You can use any one of following four argument types to populate this class:

❑ A stream pointing to a WSDL file
    `ServiceDescription = ServiceDescription.Read(Stream)`

❑ A string denoting a WSDL file
    `ServiceDescription = ServiceDescription.Read(String)`

❑ A `TextReader` object associated with a WSDL file
    `ServiceDescription = ServiceDescription.Read(TextReader)`

❑ An `XmlReader` object associated with a WSDL file
    `ServiceDescription = ServiceDescription.Read(XmlReader)`

The following code shows how you could populate a `ServiceDescription` object by passing in the filename of a valid local WSDL document as a string argument:

```
Dim oS As New ServiceDescription()
oS = ServiceDescription.Read("c:\calc.wsdl")
```

Following is the corresponding syntax for this method:

```
ServiceDescription = ServiceDescription.Read(FileName)
```

Parameter	Type	Description
FileName	Object or String	One of:
		❑ Stream object
		❑ String filename
		❑ TextReader object
		❑ XmlReader object

The Namespace Constant

This constant identifies a unique namespace for the `ServiceDescription` class. The WSDL namespace used for this is http://schemas.xmlsoap.org/wsdl/. This description is similar to a constant that defines a data type, for example, the word `string` defines a `string` variable. In this instance the above namespace identifies that this WSDL schema construct adheres to the WSDL definition.

```
String = ServiceDescription.Namespace
```

Interface Section

This section contains definitions for the methods, arguments, and namespaces available on the SOAP server for the Web Service described by any WSDL schema. It defines SOAP Requests, Responses, Faults and Data Types.

Messages

A message refers to a single SOAP transaction; it requires particular arguments and data type definitions, and these are specified in corresponding `<message>` elements of a WSDL file. SOAP messages are either a request to a Web Service to perform a particular task, or a response from a Web Service to a previous request.

The `PortType` class can determine whether we are looking at a SOAP Request or a SOAP Response. This information is obtained from the associated WSDL file from the `name` attribute of each `<message>` element. Each `name` attribute value has a corresponding entry in the `<portType>` element of the WSDL file that declares that message to be either a Request, a Response, or a Fault.

> Note that the value of the name attribute is arbitrary, and need not contain the word **request** as in the extract below.

The following is a snippet from the WSDL example given at the start of the chapter, and shows the `<message>` elements, each with a `name` attribute that refers to a child of the `<portType>` element in the WSDL example file:

```
<message name="AddRequest">
  <part name="A" element="xsd:values" />
  <part name="Y" element="xsd:long" />
</message>
<message name="AddResponse">
  <part name="Return" element="xsd:long" />
</message>
<message name="AddFaultWarn">
  <part name="Source" element="xsd:string" />
  <part name="Description" element="xsd:string" />
</message>
<message name="AddFaultCrit">
  <part name="Source" element="xsd:string" />
  <part name="Description" element="xsd:string" />
  <part name="ErrorCode" element="xsd:long" />
</message>
```

The Message Class

The WSDL schema extract below shows a `<message>` element describing a SOAP Request. This element can be looked upon as describing the syntax for a remote method call:

```
<message name="AddRequest">
  <part name="A" element="tns:values" />
  <part name="Y" element="xsd:long" />
</message>
```

The `Message` class is contained within a `MessageCollection` and can be interrogated by the `Item` property and an appropriate index. The following code shows how an ASP.NET client could loop through all message types described by an imported WSDL file:

```
Dim iLoop As Integer
Dim osd As New ServiceDescription()
osd = osd.Read("c:\calc.xml")
For iLoop = 0 To osd.Messages.Count - 1
  Console.Write(osd.Messages.Item(iLoop).Name)
Next
```

Using our WSDL sample document, this code outputs the following:

AddRequest
AddResponse
AddFaultWarn
AddFaultCrit

The Message.Name Property

The `Name` property of the `Message` class corresponds exactly to the name attribute of a `<message>` element in the WSDL document. This naming convention is followed throughout the `System.Web.Services.Description` namespace and is very handy when correlating the property name of a class with its corresponding WSDL attribute or element.

In the following code example we extract the name of the first message in the WSDL schema:

```
Dim iLoop As Integer
Dim osd As New ServiceDescription()
Dim oMsg As Message
osd = osd.Read("calc.xml")
if osd.Messages.Count > 0 Then
  oMsg=osd.Messages.Item(0)
  msgbox(oMsg.Name)
End If
```

The name returned by this attribute is unique throughout the entire WSDL schema definition.

```
String = Message.Name
```

The above line assigns the value of the name attribute of the corresponding WSDL `<message>` element to the variable `String`.

The Message.Parts Property

Each `<message>` element in a WSDL file contains a set of child `<part>` elements describing each argument sent to, or received from, a SOAP server. This collection groups together all argument descriptions for a particular SOAP message.

Using our previously described WSDL schema definition we can iterate through all the arguments for the first method using the following code:

```
Dim osd As New ServiceDescription()
Dim oMsg As Message
Dim oArg As MessagePart
Dim sPrefix As String
osd = osd.Read("c:\test0.wsdl")
If osd.Messages.Count > 0 Then
  oMsg = osd.Messages.Item(0)
```

```
      For Each oArg In oMsg.Parts
        Console.Write(oArg.Name)
      Next
   End If
```

The above code will output the following text:

X
Y

```
   MessagePartCollection = Message.Parts
```

See the following section, *The MessagePart Class*, for more details.

The MessagePart Class

The `MessagePart` class defines the structure for the interface that the message requires, along with the data types, more commonly referred to as **method arguments**, that it accepts.

The following extract is taken from our example WSDL. It shows two of the elements that are consumed by the `MessagePart` class:

```
<part name="X" element="xsd:values" />
<part name="Y" element="xsd:long" />
```

The following code allows you to loop through all arguments for the message in the imported WSDL schema file:

```
Dim iLoop As Integer
Dim osd As New ServiceDescription()
Dim oPart As MessagePart
osd = osd.Read("calc.xml")
For iLoop = 0 To osd.Messages.Item(0).Parts.Count - 1
  oPart = osd.Messages.Item(0).Parts(iLoop)
  MsgBox(oPart.Name + " - " & oPart.Element.Name & " - " & _
                          oPart.Element.Namespace)
Next
```

Using the WSDL example schema the above code outputs:

X – values – http://www.salcentral.com/calc.xml
Y – long – http://www.w3.org/2001/XMLSchema

The MessagePart.Element Property

The `Element` property provides access to the data type information specified by the `element` attribute of a message's `<part>` elements (that is, the types of its method arguments). `MessagePart.Element` is used in place of `MessagePart.Type` for type definitions that conform to the XSD schema, as defined by the namespace specified in the `<schema>` element of the WSDL file.

This property returns an `XmlQualifiedName` object that can be interrogated to provide a namespace value, that when interrogated allows access to the defined type for this message part.

```
XmlQualifiedName = MessagePart.Element
```

This maps to the `element` attribute of the WSDL `<part>` element.

The MessagePart.Name Property

This property returns the name of this particular instance of the `MessagePart`. In our previous XML snippet it would return the value X. If no name is assigned, it returns an empty string.

```
String = MessagePart.Name
```

This maps to the `name` attribute of the WSDL `<part>` element.

The MessagePart.Type Property

The `Type` property refers to the WSDL **complex data type** definitions. The property is used instead of the `MessagePart.Element` property to obtain the data type for any specific message part; this is because the `messagepart.element` contains an XML namespace that has to be deconstructed. This property however just contains the data type information.

It returns an `XmlQualifiedName` object that can be interrogated to return a deconstructed namespace for the defined type.

```
XmlQualifiedName = MessagePart.Type
```

It maps to the `type` attribute of the WSDL `<part>` element.

You can extend the data types available by allocating a unique namespace, and then inserting a reference to the data type definition's location in the WSDL header. If an alternative data type definition is used, its namespace must be unique within this schema, see the next section, *Types*, for more details.

Types

Types are XML structures that define a custom data type for use within a particular context. They are helpful for defining data types that can be used within messages for transferring structured data sets or unique language-dependent data types.

The data definition can be anything from a high-level structure, such as a name and address record, to low-level redefinitions of a basic data type, such as `long`, `integer`, and `string`, to suit a particular requirement of a given message interface.

The Types Class

The `Types` class allows you to iterate through all types defined by the currently applicable WSDL definition.

These data types conform to standard XML notation. The following XML extract shows the `<types>` element of our example WSDL schema. This XML information is consumed by the `Types` class, and in turn the `Schemas` collection class instantiated inside it:

```
<types>
  <schema targetNamespace="http://www.salcentral.com/xsd" _
              xmlns="http://www.w3.org/2001/XMLSchema">
    <element name="values">
      <complexType>
```

```
          <all>
            <element name="XI" type="long"/>
            <element name="YI" type="long"/>
          </all>
        </complexType>
      </element>
    </schema>
  </types>
```

Our example defines a complex type that comprises the two `long` values `XI` and `YI` that may be passed as a single unit to our remote Web Service.

The `Types` class exposes such complex types through the `XMLSchema` object contained in the `Types` collection.

PortTypes

An abstract combination of operations and messages forms a single WSDL `<portType>` element for a particular function of a Web Service. This element dictates the message format and other conditions that apply when communicating with a SOAP end-point.

There are four primary interaction modes that can apply to a particular `PortType`, which are defined by using a combination of alternative messages:

❑ **One Way message**
  Transfer a message to a SOAP server, no reply expected
  `<input>` element only

❑ **Request/Response message**
  Transfer a message to a SOAP server and receive back a reply
  `<output>` and `<input>` elements

❑ **Solicit Response message**
  SOAP Server sends the client a message, a reply is expected in return
  `<output>` and `<input>` elements, but server initiates call

❑ **Notification message**
  SOAP Server notifies you, no reply expected
  `<output>` element only

As can be seen from the following WSDL schema extract, the `<fault>` message is also specified. This is simply for error reporting and does not indicate the direction of messages.

```
  <service ...>
    <portType name="Calc.CalcType">
      <operation name="Add">
        <input name="AddReq" message="tns:AddRequest" />
        <output name="AddRes" message="tns:AddResponse" />
        <fault name="FaultWarning" message="tns:AddFaultWarn" />
        <fault name="FaultCritical" message="tns:AddFaultCrit">
          <documentation>Message HERE</documentation>
        </fault>
      </operation>
    </portType>
  </service>
```

It is worth noting that the `<portType>` element does not specify transmission details. These are defined in the `<binding>` element where port types and communication end-points are linked together by the `<portType>`'s name attribute:

```
<binding name="Calc.CalcBind" type="tns:Calc.CalcType">
  <soap:binding style="rpc"
  transport="http://schemas.xmlsoap.org/soap/http" />
  <operation name="Add">
    <soap:operation soapAction="www.salcentral.com#Add" />
    <input>
      <soap:body use="encoded" namespace="www.salcentral.com"
        encodingStyle="http://schemas.xmlsoap.org/soap/encoding/" />
    </input>
    <output>
      <soap:body use="encoded" namespace="www.salcentral.com"
        encodingStyle="http://schemas.xmlsoap.org/soap/encoding/" />
    </output>
  </operation>
</binding>
```

The PortType Class

The `PortType` class groups together operations under a single port type name. With this in place, operations (an operation is a single entity that brings together the `<output>`, `<input>`, and `<fault>` messages into one coherent area) can define valid message groups associated with a specific operation.

> Note that the operation name does not have to be unique; however, the message name does therefore it can be a good idea to use the WSDL **name** attribute to ensure the uniqueness of a message when adding messages. See the later section headed *The Message Class* for more details.

The `<portType>` element's name attribute is used as the unique name to link to the binding section. See the section *The Binding Class* for details about how the `<portType>` element name is linked to the `<binding>` element.

The PortType.Name Property

This property holds the name assigned to the port type. It returns a blank string if its value has not been set. The name must be unique throughout the current WSDL schema.

```
String = PortType.Name
```

This maps to the name attribute of the WSDL `<portType>` element.

This property allows read and write access.

The PortType.Operations Property

This property provides access to the `<operation>` elements contained by the `<portType>` element of the WSDL schema.

```
OperationCollection = PortType.Operations
```

It maps to:

```
<portType name="Calc.CalcType">
   <operation name="Add">
      . . . . .
   </operation>
</portType>
```

This is a read-only property, however, you may alter the underlying collection items.

The PortType.ServiceDescription Property

This property returns the `ServiceDescription` class of which this `PortType` element is a member. It allows you to effectively interrogate the parent of the `PortType` class.

```
ServiceDescription = PortType.ServiceDescription
```

The Operation Class

The `Operation` class defines the structure of an action that can be performed by a communication endpoint such as an ASP.NET server.

The following extract shows the `<operation>` element within our example WSDL schema:

```
<portType ...>
   <operation name="Add">
     <input name="AddReq" message="tns:AddRequest" />
     <output name="AddRes" message="tns:AddResponse" />
     <fault name="FaultWarning" message="tns:AddFaultWarn"/>
     <fault name="FaultCritical" message="tns:AddFaultCrit">
       <documentation>Special fault message</documentation>
     </fault>
   </operation>
</portType>
```

Derived from the `DocumentableItem` class. This class cannot be inherited.

The Operation.Faults Property

This property allows access to the collection of fault messages assigned to an operation. Multiple fault messages can be defined to return information appropriate to the actual fault that occurred. For instance, our sample `<operation>` defines a critical fault error as well as a warning fault error.

```
OperationFaultCollection = Operation.Faults
```

Once again, this is read-only although you are able to alter the underlying collection items.

The Operation.Messages Property

This property allows access to the collection of messages for this instance of the `Operation` class. As any `<operation>` element may have no more than one `OperationInput` class and one `OperationOutput` class, there will only ever be a maximum of two items in this collection.

```
OperationMessageCollection = Operation.Messages
```

This property another read-only property, but you can alter the underlying collection items.

The Operation.Name Property

The Name property identifies this current instance of the Operation class, and need not be unique for all operations within the WSDL definition. If not set, this property returns an empty string.

```
String = Operation.Name
```

It maps to the name attribute of the WSDL <operation> element.

This property permits read and write access.

The Operation.ParameterOrder Property

This property allows access to an array of String values that have already been identified and extracted from the ParameterOrderString property. This property is only required if you are using an RPC binding style, as this style actually includes the requirement for a parameterOrder.

```
String Array() = Operation.ParameterOrder
```

The Operation.ParameterOrderString Property

Operations do not specify by default whether they use RPC-like bindings (RPC binding is a style/format for binding together the WSDL schema) This property therefore allows you to assign the original RPC function signature to the parameterOrder attribute within the operation element. The property contains a list of parameter names separated by a single space for SOAP Request-Response or Solicit-Response operations. When validating this property, you should note that it must adhere to the following rules:

- ❑ The part name order mirrors the order of the parameters in the RPC signature
- ❑ The **return** value part is not present in the list
- ❑ If a part name appears in both the input and output message, it is an **in/out** parameter
- ❑ If a part name appears in only the input message, it is an **in** parameter
- ❑ If a part name appears in only the output message, it is an **out** parameter

```
String = Operation.ParameterOrderString
```

This property may be ignored if you are not concerned with RPC signatures.

The Operation.PortType Property

This property returns a PortType object of which this Operation element is a member. In effect, this allows you to determine the parent <portType> element of the corresponding <operation> element in the WSDL schema.

```
PortType = Operation.PortType
```

The OperationFault Class

The OperationFault class defines the format and structure for error messages returned by a specific service identified within the WSDL schema.

The following snippet from the WSDL example shows the portion of the Interface section that describes the <fault> elements of an <operation> element:

```
<operation ...>
  <input ...>
  <output ...>
    <fault name="FaultWarning" message="tns:AddFaultWarn"/>
    <fault name="FaultCritical" message="tns:AddFaultCrit">
      <documentation>
        'Special fault message
      </documentation>
    </fault>
</operation>
```

Derived from the `OperationMessage` class. This class cannot be inherited.

The OperationFault.Message property

This property returns the value of the `message` attribute in the fault element of the operation. Includes data type information as well as a name binding to the associated message. The associated `fault` message describes the format that the expected error message will return.

```
XmlQualifiedName = OperationFault.Message
```

It maps to the `message` XML attribute of the `<fault>` element.

This is a modifier property (that is, it allows read/write access).

The OperationFault.Name property

This property allows access to the `Name` attribute of the operation fault message. If none is supplied, it returns an empty string.

```
String = OperationFault.Name
```

This maps to the `name` attribute of the `<fault>` element. This property allows read and write access.

The OperationFault.Operation

This property returns the `Operation` object of which this `OperationFault` is a member. The returned object represents the parent `<operation>` of the `<fault>` element mapped by the given `OperationFault`.

```
Operation = OperationFault.Operation
```

This property is read-only.

The OperationInput Class

The `OperationInput` class defines the format and structure for Request messages returned by a specific service described in a WSDL file.

The following snippet taken from our WSDL example shows the portion of the `Interface` section associated with the `OperationInput` class:

```
<operation ...>
  <input name="AddReq" message="tns:AddRequest"/>
  <output ...>
  <fault ...>
</operation>
```

Derived from the `OperationMessage` class. This class cannot be inherited.

The OperationInput.Message Property

This property returns the value of the `message` attribute of the `<operation>`'s child `<input>` element. This will include data type information as well as a name binding to the appropriate `<message>` element (which specifies the format for the Request message).

```
XmlQualifiedName = OperationInput.Message
```

It maps to the `message` attribute of the `<input>` element.

This is a modifier property (it allows read/write access).

The OperationInput.Name Property

This property returns the `name` attribute of the `<input>` element for an operation. The `name` attribute is an optional attribute: if not supplied, this property returns an empty string.

```
String = OperationInput.Name
```

It maps to the `name` attribute of the `<input>` element.

The OperationInput.Operation Property

The property returns the parent property. In the case of the `OperationInput` class, this is the `Operation` class.

```
Operation = OperationInput.Operation
```

It maps to the `<operation>` XML element.

The OperationOutput Class

The `OperationOutput` class defines the format and structure for Response messages returned by a specific service identified by the WSDL document.

The following snippet taken from the WSDL example shows the portion of the `Interface` section associated with the `OperationOutput` class:

```
<operation ... >
  <input ... >
  <output name="AddRes" message="tns:AddResponse"/>
  <fault ... >
</operation>
```

Derived from the `OperationMessage` class. This class cannot be inherited.

The OperationOutput.Message Property

This property returns the value of the `message` attribute of the `<operation>`'s child `<output>` element. This will include data type information as well as a name binding to the appropriate `<message>` element (which specifies the format of the returned Response message).

```
XmlQualifiedName = OperationOutput.Message
```

It maps to the `message` attribute of the `<output>` element.

This is a read/write property.

The OperationOutput.Name Property

This property returns the `name` attribute of the `<output>` element for an operation. The `name` attribute is an optional attribute: if it is not supplied, this property returns an empty string.

```
String = OperationOutput.Name
```

This maps to the `name` attribute of the `<output>` element.

The OperationOutput.Operation Property

This property returns the `Operation` object of which this `OperationOutput` instance is a member. The returned object represents the parent `<operation>` of the `<output>` element mapped by the given `OperationOutput` instance.

```
Operation = OperationFault.Operation
```

Communication Section

The Communication section of a WSDL document defines the supported communication methods for transferring a SOAP Request to a SOAP server. The only three communication methods supported at present in ASP.NET are HTTP GET, HTTP POST, and SOAP. This information is associated with an interface and protocol using a binding namespace.

Services

Services group together sets of related ports. Ports provide alternative communication methods for a service, allowing the developer to choose which communication method to use to transfer messages to the SOAP server.

The Service Class

The `Service` class defines **multiple** communication end-points for handling remote methods calls within the current service. The class is described in WSDL documents using the `<service>` element.

The following snippet taken from our WSDL example shows the portion of the `Communication` section associated with the `Service` class:

```
<service name="Calc.CAdd">
  <port name="Calc.CAddPort" binding="tns:Calc.CalcBind">
    <soap:address location="http://sal006.salnetwork.com/calc.cgi"/>
  </port>
</service>
```

This class cannot be inherited.

The Service.Extensions Property

This property provides access to a collection of extension elements contained within the current port. These elements can extend a Web Service by adding support for additional messaging formats for SOAP messages.

```
ServiceDescriptionFormatExtensionCollection = Service.Extensions
```

The Service.Name Property

This property returns the name of the service taken from the name attribute of the <service> element. This unique name links the service to a port type defined in the <bindings> element of the Interface section, such as "Calc.CalcType" in the case of our example.

```
String = Service.Name
```

This maps to the name attribute of the <port> element.

The Service.Ports Property

This property represents a collection containing all the ports available for the current Web Service. Each port holds the address of one communication end-point.

```
PortCollection = Service.Ports
```

This is a read-only property, but you may change the underlying collection items.

The Port Class

The Port class defines a **single** communication end-point for calling remote methods within the current service:

```
<service ...>
  <port name="Calc.CAddPort" binding="tns:Calc.CalcBinding">
  <soap:address location="http://sal006.salnetwork.com/calc.cgi"/>
  </port>
</service>
```

This class cannot be inherited. A port will not specify more than one address and will not specify any binding information other than the address information.

The Port.Binding Property

In WSDL, <port> elements are associated with the operations that the end-point supports through the binding attribute of the <port>. This attribute links to a <binding> element with a name attribute of the same value. <binding> elements are the underlying mechanism that collates messages, communications, and protocols to form a coherent WSDL schema. The Port.Binding property returns the value of this binding attribute.

```
XmlQualifiedNamespace = Port.Binding
```

This maps to the binding attribute of the <port> element.

The Port.Extensions Property

This property represents the collection of extension elements within the current <port>. These elements can extend the capability of the Port by adding support for additional messaging formats for SOAP messages.

```
ServiceDescriptionFormatExtensionCollection = Port.Extensions
```

The Port.Name Property

This is the name given to the Port class, taken from the name of the <port> element in the WSDL file. This name must be unique.

```
String = Port.Name
```

It maps to the name attribute of the <port> element.

The following code shows how you can use the name property and the Services collection to iterate through all services and ports defined by a WSDL document:

```
Dim iLoop1 As Integer
Dim iLoop2 As Integer
Dim osd As New ServiceDescription()
osd = osd.Read("calc.xml")
For iLoop1 = 1 To osd.Services.Count
  MsgBox(osd.Services.Item(iLoop1 - 1).Name)
  For iLoop2 = 1 To osd.Services.Item(iLoop1 - 1).Ports.Count
    MsgBox(osd.Services.Item(iLoop1 - 1).Ports(iLoop2 - 1).Name)
  Next
Next
```

The above code when used with the WSDL example outputs:

```
Calc.Add
Calc.AddPort
```

The Port.Service Property

This property returns the Service object of which this Port instance is a member. The returned object represents the parent <service> element of the <port> mapped by the given instance of the Port class.

```
Service = Port.Service
```

Binding Section

The Binding section of WSDL documents attaches definitions in the Communications section to definitions in the Interface section, at the same time specifying the transport protocol and encoding to be used (for example, SOAP or HTTP). These are selected according to the methods it supports and the specifics of the Web Service itself. This section creates crucial associations between elements of the WSDL schema to form a coherent whole.

The following XML extract from the WSDL example picks out the XML elements that are used to instantiate the Binding, Operation, and other child classes within this section:

```
<definitions ...>
  <binding name="Calc.CalcBind" type="tns:Calc.CalcType">
    <soap:binding style="rpc" _
                  transport="http://schemas.xmlsoap.org/soap/http" />
    <operation name="Add">
      <soap:operation soapAction="www.salcentral.com#Add" />
      <input>
        <soap:body use="encoded" namespace="www.salcentral.com/1" _
            encodingStyle="http://schemas.xmlsoap.org/soap/encoding/" />
      </input>
      <output>
        <soap:body use="encoded" namespace="www.salcentral.com/2" _
            encodingStyle="http://schemas.xmlsoap.org/soap/encoding/" />
      </output>
      <fault>
        <soap:body use="encoded" namespace="www.salcentral.com/3" _
            encodingStyle="http://schemas.xmlsoap.org/soap/encoding/" />
      </fault>
    </operation>
  </binding>
</definitions>
```

The Binding Class

The `Binding` class forms the basis of the mechanism that binds together messages and communication end-points, at the same time assigning a transmission protocol. You cannot directly specify any address or transmission information within this class.

Derived from the `DocumentableItem` class, this class cannot be inherited.

The Binding.Extensions Property

The WSDL format was designed to allow additions peculiar to a specific protocol or message format by the use of **extensibility elements**. These allow enhancements to be made available without changing the underlying WSDL standard.

```
ServiceDescriptionFormatExtensionsCollection = Binding.Extensions
```

In the case of transmission of SOAP messages, the schema contains the following specialist extension classes; the following classes are children of the binding class:

❑ SoapAddressBinding

❑ SoapBinding

❑ SoapBodyBinding

❑ SoapFaultBinding

❑ SoapHeaderBinding

❑ SoapHeaderFaultBinding

❑ SoapOperationBinding

> Please note that the namespace (if used) for such extensibility elements must be unique within any particular WSDL document.

The Binding.Name Property

This returns the name extracted from the `<binding>` element's name attribute in the WSDL schema. This name will be unique within the `Bindings` section.

```
String = Binding.Name
```

It maps to the name attribute of the `<binding>` element.

The following code shows how you can use the `Name` property in conjunction with the `Bindings` collection to iterate through all the bindings and operations defined by a schema.

```
Dim iLoop1 As Integer
Dim iLoop2 As Integer
Dim osd As New ServiceDescription()
osd = osd.Read("calc.xml")
For iLoop1 = 1 To osd.Bindings.Count
  MsgBox(osd.Bindings.Item(iLoop1 - 1).Name)
  For iLoop2 = 1 To osd.Bindings.Item(iLoop1 - 1).Operations.Count
    MsgBox(osd.Bindings.Item(iLoop1 - 1).Operations(iLoop2 - 1).Name)
  Next
Next
```

When used with the WSDL example, the above code outputs:

```
Calc.CalcBinding
Add
```

The Binding.Operations Property

An operation defines the valid protocols for messages between client and server during execution of a remote Web Service.

It does this by allowing the creation of groups of abstract definitions that match various messages with a particular communication protocol, potentially creating a quite diverse WSDL schema. However, in its simplest form, a single `<operation>` element represents a basic Web Service.

It can define the protocols for any of the following message types:

❑ Input message protocol

❑ Output message protocol

❑ Fault message protocol

```
OperationBindingCollection = Binding.Operations
```

This maps to:

```
<binding . . . . . . >
  <operation name="Add">
    . . .
  </operation>
</binding>
```

This property exposes a collection that contains the information extracted from the `<operation>` elements of the current WSDL definition.

The Binding.Type Property

This property can be used to set or retrieve the value linking to the `<portType>` element for the Web Service. This name also refers to an instance of the `PortType` class.

```
XmlQualifiedName = Binding.Type
```

This maps to the `type` attribute of the `<binding>` element.

The OperationBinding Class

The `OperationBinding` class, a child of the `Binding` class, defines the protocol to use for a particular operation, for instance, SOAP using extensibility.

Input, Output, and Fault Binding

The `OperationBinding` class provides a means to define the encoding and protocol for each of the message types. This is then used as a template against the `PortType` class when creating SOAP messages.

System.Web.Services.Description Enumerations

OperationFlow

This defines the values that indicate the direction of communication between a client and a Web Service.

It is used by the following property of the `Description` namespace:

❑   `OperationMessageCollection.Flow`

Member Name	Description	Value
None	Indicates that the Web Service end-point receives and makes no communication	0
OneWay	Indicates that the Web Service receives messages but is not expected to respond	1
Notification	Indicates that an end-point sends messages without a Request being issued	2
RequestResponse	Indicates that the Web Service receives Request messages, and returns Response messages	3
SolicitResponse	(Default) Indicates that an endpoint sends a message, and expects a reply by the client	4

ServiceDescriptionImportStyle

This Defines the point at which the XML parser should import an XML file defined by the `<import>` element of the current WSDL definition.

If this is specified as `Server` then when the client attempts to read the WSDL schema, the import XML file will be imported and embedded directly into the schema file at the location where the import element is situated. Therefore the client will simply see a single and completed WSDL file. If, however, it is set to `client` the client must import the XML file itself.

It is used by the following property of the `System.Web Services.Description` namespace:

❑   `ServiceDescriptionImporter.Style`

Member Name	Description	Value
Client	(Default) Indicates that the XML file should be imported by a client-based XML parser	0
Server	Indicates that the XML file should be imported before it reaches the client by a server-based XML parser	1

ServiceDescriptionImportWarnings

This is the return warning indication produced when attempting to import an XML file into the current WSDL schema definition, by either a client- or server-based XML parser.

It is returned by the following `System.Web Services.Description` method:

❑   `ServiceDescriptionImporter.Import`

Member Name	Value
NoCodeGenerated	1
OptionalExtensionsIgnored	2
RequiredExtensionsIgnored	4
UnsupportedOperationsIgnored	8
UnsupportedBindingsIgnored	16
NoMethodsGenerated	32

SoapBindingStyle

This indicates an appropriate programming model that can potentially affect the structure of the SOAP message body. It should be noted that RPC and Document binding styles simply indicate that schema definitions use different methods of structuring elements, most noticeably in the case of comparing these two methods with the definition of the messages and its arguments.

It is used by the following property in the `System.Web Services.Description` namespace:

❑   `SoapBinding.Style`

Member Name	Description	Value
Default	(Default) The default for this enumeration is Document	0
Document	Indicates that the operation involves document-oriented messages (messages contain documents)	1
Rpc	Indicates that the operation involves RPC-oriented messages (messages contain parameters, and return values)	2

SoapBindingUse

The `SoapBindingUse` enumeration specifies the parameter encoding styles available to an ASP.NET Web Service.

It is used by the following properties in the `System.Web Services.Description` namespace:

- ❑ `SoapBodyBinding.Use`
- ❑ `SoapFaultBinding.Use`
- ❑ `SoapHeaderBinding.Use`
- ❑ `SoapHeaderFaultBinding.Use`

Member Name	Description	Value
Default	(Default.)	0
Encoded	Identifies that the values are encoded as specified by the `encodingStyle` attribute. (To encode text means to translate it from one character set to another.)	1
Literal	Identifies that the class's values are explicitly stated by an XML Schema definition associated by either the `element` or the `type` attribute. This also refers to the fact that the value is non-encoded, in other words it is held in its original form.	2

System.Web.Services.Description Overview

The following section serves as summary of all classes within the `System.Web.Services.Description` namespace and is meant as a common reference lookup.

Please note: The following classes have been omitted from this summary and from this chapter, because as of the date of publishing this book there was still not information available. Please also note however that they are all extensibility classes and as such are generally covered in the extensibility section at the start of this chapter:

- ❑ `MimeContentBinding`
- ❑ `SoapAddressBinding`
- ❑ `SoapBinding`

❑   SoapBodyBinding

❑   SoapFaultBinding

❑   SoapHeaderBinding

❑   SoapHeaderFaultBinding

❑   SoapOperationBinding

The Binding Class

This class contains concrete definitions binding the different sections of the schema into a single WSDL schema. This class joins the protocols section to the messages section, introducing information on the format of the structure of the WSDL schema, for example RPC or Document binding styles.

Properties of the Binding class	Return Type	Description
Documentation	String	Assigns or interrogates a single line of documentation given for a particular Binding class instance. This is user-readable documentation. Documenation can be identified in the WSDL schema by the <documentation> element.
Extensions	Collection	Allows for extension of the basic abilities of the Binding class.
Name	String	Name of the binding.
Operations	Collection	Collection of Operations contained within the Binding. Reflects the <operation> elements of the WSDL document.
ServiceDescription	Object	Returns and allows access to the parent ServiceDescription class. The ServiceDescription class is the main class that contains the WSDL schema.
Type	Object	Assigns or interrogates the data type used by the Web Service. XML Namespace qualified.

The DocumentableItem Base Class

DocumentableItem acts as an abstract base class for a number of other classes in the System.Web.Services.Description namespace. It cannot be instantiated directly. It has one property, Documentation (read/write), which is inherited by all classes that use it as their base class.

The following classes are based on DocumentableItem:

❑   Binding

❑   Import

❑   Message

❑   MessagePart

❑   Operation

- ❑   OperationBinding
- ❑   OperationMessage
- ❑   Port
- ❑   PortType
- ❑   Service
- ❑   Types

The FaultBinding Class

Specifies the format for any error messages that may be generated by the Web Service interaction. Definition maps to the `<fault>` element, within the `<binding>` element, in our example WSDL schema definition at the beginning of this chapter.

Properties of the FaultBinding class	Return Type	Description
Documentation	String	Assigns or interrogates a single line of documentation provided for the `FaultBinding` class.
Extensions	Collection	Allows for extension of the basic abilities of the `FaultBinding` class.
Name	String	Name of the Fault binding.
OperationBinding	Object	Returns and allows access to the parent `OperationBinding` class. Reflects the `<operation>` element in the WSDL schema.

The HttpAddressBinding Class

Usually used to extend or enhance the WSDL schema to deal with a specific protocol or message format, where the binding uses the HTTP protocol. The address binding of the `Location` property supplies an Internet address for the port. Definition maps to a `<http>` element within the `<binding>` element of a WSDL schema that supports this protocol.

Properties of the Http AddressBinding class	Return Type	Description
Handled	Boolean	Indicates whether the current `HttpAddressBinding` statement is understood and able to be handled by ASP.NET.
Location	String	A relative URL to the XML definition that applies to this address binding type.
Parent	Object	Returns and allows access to the parent `class`.
Required	Boolean	If `true`, indicates that this `HttpAddressBinding` class must be fully understood. If not understood then parsing of this WSDL schema should be discontinued.

The HttpBinding Class

Used to extend or enhance the WSDL schema for a specific protocol or message format. If this definition is available it defines that the binding uses the HTTP protocol format.

Properties of the HttpBinding class	Return Type	Description
Handled	Boolean	Indicates whether the current `HttpBinding` statement is understood and able to be handled by ASP.NET.
Parent	Object	Returns and allows access to the parent class .
Required	Boolean	If `true`, indicates that this `HttpBinding` class must be understood. If not understood then parsing of this WSDL schema should be discontinued.
Verb	String	You can indicate whether this `HttpBinding` is associated with a GET or POST request.
Namespace	String	Identifies a unique namespace for the `HttpBinding` class.

The HttpOperationBinding Class

Used to extend or enhance the WSDL schema for a specific protocol or message format. HTTP operation binding links data formats and messages supported by the Web Service.

Properties of the Http OperationBinding class	Return Type	Description
Handled	Boolean	Indicates whether the current `HttpOperationBinding` is understood and able to be handled by ASP.NET.
Location	String	A relative URL to the XML definition that applies to this binding type.
Parent	Object	Returns and allows access to the parent class .
Required	Boolean	If `true`, indicates that this class must be understood. If not understood then parsing of this WSDL schema should be discontinued.

The HttpUrlEncodedBinding Class

Indicates that the parameters may be transferred to the server using standard URL encoding techniques, for instance appending the values of the `MessageParts` (arguments) to a URL (as in: `www.somedomain.org?name1=value&name2=value`).

Properties of the HttpUrl EncodedBinding class	Return Type	Description
Handled	Boolean	Indicates whether the current HttpUrlEncodedBinding is understood and able to be handled by ASP.NET.
Location	String	A relative URL to the XML definition that applies to this binding type.
Parent	Object	Returns and allows access to the parent.
Required	Boolean	If true, indicates that this class must be understood. If not understood then parsing of this WSDL schema should be discontinued.

The HttpUrlReplacementBinding Class

Indicates that all the message parts (arguments) are encoded into the HTTP request using a replacement algorithm.

Properties of the HttpUrl ReplacementBinding class	Return Type	Description
Handled	Boolean	Indicates whether the current HttpUrlEncodedBinding is understood and able to be handled by ASP.NET.
Parent	Object	Returns and allows access to the parent class.
Required	Boolean	If true, indicates that this class must be understood. If not understood then parsing of this WSDL schema should be discontinued.

The Import Class

The Import class indicates the location of an importable WSDL sub-document, that is, an external XML file to insert into the main document.

Properties of the Import class	Return Type	Description
Location	String	Holds the Internet location URL for the file that requires to be imported into this document when the schema is being parsed.
Namespace	Object	Allows for the assignment of a unique namespace for each <import> element. If not set defaults to an empty string.
ServiceDescription	Object	Returns and allows access to the parent ServiceDescription class.

The InputBinding Class

Operation binding names are not required to be unique, and so the `InputBinding` class defines a unique name attribute to correctly identify request methods. This class resides within the `OperationBinding` class.

Properties of the InputBinding class	Return Type	Description
Documentation	String	Assigns or interrogates a single line of documentation given for a particular `InputBinding` class instance
Extensions	Collection	Allows for extension of the basic features of the `InputBinding` class
Name	String	The name of this instance of `InputBinding`
OperationBinding	Object	Returns and allows access to the parent `Binding` class derived from the `<binding>` element of the WSDL schema

The Message Class

This class represents a single input, output, or fault message.

Properties of the Message class	Return Type	Description
Documentation	String	Assigns or interrogates a single line of documentation given for a particular `Message` class instance.
Name	String	The name of this instance of `Message`. Must be unique within `<message>` elements for any WSDL file.
Parts	Collection	Each message can contain any number of arguments. Every item in this collection is an argument for a message. An argument can be extracted from this collection by using the `MessagePart` object and an object/collection `For...Each` loop.
ServiceDescription	Object	Returns and allows access to the parent `ServiceDescription` class.

The MessageBinding Base Class

`MessageBinding` is an abstract base class for a number of other classes within the `System.Web.Services.Description` namespace. It cannot be instantiated directly. Its properties are inherited by all classes that use it as their base class.

The classes that use `MessageBinding` as a base class are:

❏ `FaultBinding`

❏ `InputBinding`

❏ `OutputBinding`

The MessagePart Class

This class identifies the arguments to a single input, output or fault message.

Properties of the MessagePart class	Return Type	Description
Element	Object	Defines the data type for the message's argument using linked schema definitions. XML namespace qualified.
Message	Object	Returns and allows access to the parent `Message` class derived from the `<message>` element of the WSDL schema.
Name	String	The name of this instance of `MessagePart`, more commonly known as the method argument name. Must be unique within the parent `Message` class.
Type	Object	Defines the data type by linking to definitions for XML Schema complex types. Specifies the data type for the message's argument. XML namespace qualified.

The MimeContentBinding Class

To avoid having to define a new element for similar MIME formats, the optional element `mime:content` may be used to indicate there is no special feature of the format other than its MIME type string.

Properties of the Mime ContentBinding class	Return Type	Description
Namespace	String	Namespace for this MIME content binding
Part	String	MIME content binding message part name
Type	String	MIME type string, for example `text/xml` or `text/html`

Inherits other properties from `ServiceDescriptionFormatExtension`

The MimeMultipartRelatedBinding Class

This class groups together multiple MIME content binding classes into one abstract set of MIME parts.

Properties of the Mime MultipartRelated Binding class	Return Type	Description
Parts	Collection	Collection of `MimePart` objects
Inherits other properties from `ServiceDescriptionFormatExtension`		

The MimePart Class

This class contains one or more `MimeContentBinding` extensibility classes.

Properties of the MimePart class	Return Type	Description
Extensions	Collection	Allows extension of the basic functionality of the `MimePart` class by adding `MimeContentBinding` classes
Inherits other properties from `ServiceDescriptionFormatExtension`		

The MimeTextBinding Class

No information was available on this class at time of going to publication.

Properties of the Mime TextBinding class	Return Type	Description
Namespace	String	Namespace for this MIME text binding
Inherits other properties from `ServiceDescriptionFormatExtension`		

The MimeTextMatch Class

No information was available on this class at time of going to publication.

Properties of the MimeTextMatch class	Return Type	Description
Capture	Integer	-
Group	Integer	-
IgnoreCase	Boolean	-
Matches	Collection	-
Name	String	-
Pattern	String	-
Repeats	Integer	-
RepeatsString	String	-
Type	String	-

The MimeXmlBinding Class

This allows non-SOAP XML-structured data to be sent or received as attachments to standard messages.

Properties of the Mime XmlBinding class	Return Type	Description
Inherits all properties from `ServiceDescriptionFormatExtension`		

The Operation Class

The `Operation` class defines the structure of a function provided by a communication end-point such as an ASP.NET server.

Properties of the Operation class	Return Type	Description
Documentation	String	Assigns or interrogates a single line of documentation given for a particular `Operation` class instance.
Faults	Collection	Fault messages assigned to this operation. Reflects the `<fault>` element in the WSDL schema.
Messages	Collection	Messages (excluding Faults) assigned to this operation. Reflects the `<input>` or `<output>` element in the WSDL schema.
Name	String	The name of this instance of `Operation`.
ParameterOrder	Array	Array extracted from the `ParameterOrderString` property.
ParameterOrderStr ing	String	The original RPC function signature. Only used for RPC calls.
PortType	Object	Returns and allows access to the parent `PortType` class derived from the `<portType>` element of the WSDL schema.

The OperationBinding Class

The `OperationBinding` class controls the binding of the messages section of the WSDL schema to the protocols section of the WSDL schema along with identifying the message formats to be used, for example RPC or document.

Properties of the OperationBinding class	Return Type	Description
Binding	Object	Returns and allows access to the parent `Binding` class derived from the `<binding>` element of the WSDL schema.
Documentation	String	Assigns or interrogates a single line of documentation given for a particular `OperationBinding` class instance.

Properties of the OperationBinding class	Return Type	Description
Extensions	Collection	Allows for extension of the basic functionality of the OperationBinding class.
Faults	Collection	Fault messages assigned to this operation binding. Reflects a <fault> element inside the operation <binding> element of the WSDL schema.
Input	Object	Input message assigned to this operation binding. Mirrors the <input> element inside the operation <binding> element of the WSDL schema.
Name	String	The name of this instance of OperationBinding.
Output	Object	Output message assigned to this operation binding. Mirrors the <output> element inside the operation <binding> element of the WSDL schema.

The OperationFault Class

The OperationFault class defines the format and structure for Fault messages returned by a specific service identified in the WSDL schema.

Properties of the OperationFault class	Return Type	Description
Documentation	String	Assigns or interrogates a single line of documentation given for a particular OperationFault class instance.
Message	Object	Message instance in the OperationFault class. XML namespace qualified.
Name	String	The name of this instance of OperationFault.
Operation	Object	Returns and allows access to the parent Operation class derived from the <operation> element of the WSDL schema.

The OperationInput Class

The OperationInput class defines the format and structure for Request messages returned by a specific service identified in the WSDL schema.

Properties of the OperationInput class	Return Type	Description
Documentation	String	Assigns or interrogates a single line of documentation given for a particular OperationInput class instance.
Message	Object	Message instance in the OperationInput class. XML namespace qualified.

Table continued on following page

Properties of the OperationInput class	Return Type	Description
Name	String	The name of this instance of `OperationInput`.
Operation	Object	Returns and allows access to the parent `Operation` class derived from the `<operation>` element of the WSDL schema.

The OperationMessage Class

The `OperationMessage` class is an abstract base class for a number of other classes within the `System.Web.Services.Description` namespace. It cannot be instantiated directly.

The classes that use `OperationMessage` as a base class are:

❑ `OperationFault`

❑ `OperationInput`

❑ `OperationOutput`

The OperationMessageCollection Class

Properties of the Operation MessageCollection class	Return Type	Description
Flow	Object	Gets the `OperationFlow` of the `OperationMessage-Collection`
Input	Object	Gets the first occurrence of an `OperationInput` instance within the collection
Item	Object	Gets or sets the value of the `OperationMessage` determined to the specified index
Output	Object	Gets the first occurrence of an `OperationOutput` instance within the collection

Inherits other properties from the generic `Collection` class

The OperationOutput Class

The `OperationOutput` class defines the format and structure for Response messages returned by a specific service identified within the WSDL schema.

Properties of the OperationOutput class	Return Type	Description
Documentation	String	Assigns or interrogates a single line of documentation given for a particular OperationOutput instance.
Message	Object	Message object corresponding to the OperationOutput class. XML namespace qualified.
Name	String	The name of this instance of OperationOutput.
Operation	Object	Returns and allows access to the parent Operation class derived from the <operation> element of the WSDL schema.

The OutputBinding Class

Operation binding names are not required to be unique, and so the OutputBinding class defines a unique name attribute to correctly identify request methods. This class resides within the OperationBinding class.

Properties of the OutputBinding class	Return Type	Description
Documentation	String	Assigns or interrogates a single line of documentation given for a particular OutputBinding instance
Extensions	Collection	Allows extension of the basic functionality of the OutputBinding class
Name	String	The name of this instance of OutputBinding
OperationBinding	Object	Returns and allows access to the parent OperationBinding class derived from the <operation> element of the WSDL schema

The Port Class

The Port class defines a specific communication end-point (commonly known as an address) for calling remote methods of the current service.

Properties of the Port class	Return Type	Description
Binding	Object	Namespace for the Binding class. XML namespace qualified.
Documentation	String	Assigns or interrogates a single line of documentation given for a particular Port class instance.

Table continued on following page

625

Properties of the Port class	Return Type	Description
Extensions	Collection	Allows for extension of the basic functionality of the Port class.
Name	String	The name of this instance of the Port class.
Service	Object	Returns and allows access to the parent Service class derived from the <service> element of the WSDL schema.

The PortType Class

The PortType class connects binding information to the Interface section of the current WSDL definition. The name of the class, taken from the name attribute of the WSDL <portType> element, references an element in the Binding section.

Properties of the PortType class	Return Type	Description
Documentation	String	Assigns or interrogates a single line of documentation given for a particular Paste class instance.
Name	String	The name of this instance of the PortType class.
Operations	Collection	Operation instances contained within this PortType class. Reflects the <operation> element in the WSDL schema.
ServiceDescription	Object	Returns and allows access to the parent ServiceDescription class derived from the <service> element of the WSDL schema.

The Service Class

Groups together all the ports related to the current WSDL schema definition.

Properties of the Service class	Return Type	Description
Documentation	String	Assigns or interrogates a single line of documentation given for a particular Service class instance.
Extensions	Collection	Allows for extension of the Types class.
Name	String	The name of this instance of Service.
Ports	Collection	Allow access to the ports declared within this service. Reflects the <port> element in the WSDL schema.
ServiceDescription	Object	Returns and allows access to the ServiceDescription class derived from the <service> element of the WSDL schema.

The ServiceDescription Class

The ServiceDescription class is the root class for the entire WSDL file structure. If you use the Read method within this class you can read in any valid WSDL file.

Properties of the Service Description class	Return Type	Description
Namespace	String	Identifies a unique namespace for the ServiceDescription class.
Documentation	String	Assigns or interrogates a single line of documentation for the ServiceDescription class.
Bindings	Collection	The BindingCollection collection of binding elements from the WSDL schema. The Binding class defines the associations between a protocol and the messages defined within the schema.
Extensions	Collection	Allows for extension of the basic functionality of the ServiceDescription class.
Imports	Collection	The collection of external files to include in the WSDL schema.
Messages	Collection	Contains collection information about all messages defined in the WSDL schema.
Name	String	Name of this instance of ServiceDescription.
PortTypes	Collection	Links the Bindings section of the WSDL schema to the Messages section.
RetrievalUrl	String	—
ServiceDescriptions	Collection	Makes available the parent collection that this instance of ServiceDescriptions may be contained within.
Services	Collection	Groups together a set of related ports defined by the WSDL schema.
TargetNamespace	String	This contains the namespace extracted from the <definitions> element's targetNamespace attribute in the WSDL schema.
Types	Collection	Types allow you to create data type definitions for particular message or operation requirements. For example, you can define a type reflecting an internal structure of the Web Service application, such as a customer record.

Methods of the ServiceDescription class	Return Type	Description
CanRead	Boolean	This function tests an `XmlReader` object to see whether it points to a valid and parsable WSDL file. It returns `true` if the file is of the correct structure.
Read	–	This method allows you to populate the `ServiceDescription` class.
Write	–	Writes the currently loaded WSDL schema to one of the four output methods within a class. For example: ❑ Stream ❑ XMLWriter ❑ Textwriter ❑ String

The ServiceDescriptionCollection Class

This `ServiceDescription` collection allows you to add multiple WSDL schemas (`ServiceDescription` objects) into a single collection. You can then use the methods of the collection to retrieve, search or manipulate a `ServiceDescription` (single WSDL schema) object.

Properties of the Collection definition	Return Type	Description
Inherits all properties of the generic `Collection` class		

Methods of the Collection definition	Return Type	Description
GetBinding	Binding Object	Returns the `Binding` instance from the `ServiceDescriptionCollection` matching the `Binding` name passed in
GetMessage	Message Object	Returns the `Message` instance from the `ServiceDescriptionCollection` matching the name passed in
GetPortType	PortType Object	Returns the `PortType` instance from the `ServiceDescriptionCollection` matching the name passed in
GetService	Service Object	Returns the `Service` instance from the `ServiceDescriptionCollection` matching the name passed in
Inherits other properties from the generic `Collection` class		

The ServiceDescriptionFormatExtension Class

ServiceDescriptionFormatExtension acts as an abstract base class for a number of other classes within the System.Web.Services.Description namespace. It cannot be instantiated directly.

The following classes use ServiceDescriptionFormatExtension as a base class:

- ❑ HttpAddressBinding
- ❑ HttpBinding
- ❑ HttpOperationBinding
- ❑ HttpUrlEncodedBinding
- ❑ HttpReplacementBinding
- ❑ MimeMultipartRelatedBinding
- ❑ MimePart
- ❑ MimeTextBinding
- ❑ MimeXmlBinding
- ❑ MimeContentBinding
- ❑ SoapAddressBinding
- ❑ SoapBinding
- ❑ SoapBodyBinding
- ❑ SoapFaultBinding
- ❑ SoapHeaderBinding
- ❑ SoapHeaderFaultBinding
- ❑ SoapOperationBinding

Properties of the ServiceDescription FormatExtension class	Return Type	Description
Handled	Boolean	Indicates whether the current statement is understood and able to be handled by ASP.NET
Parent	Object	Returns and allows access to the parent Service class
Required	Boolean	If true, indicates that this class must be understood

The ServiceDescriptionImporter Class

This class allows the developer to create client proxy classes for WSDL schemas.

Properties of the ServiceDescriptionImporter class	Return Type	Description
ProtocolName	String	The name of the protocol to import.
Schemas	Collection	The XML Schemas collection of the Web Service to be imported. This property is read-only.
ServiceDescriptions	Collection	Allows new ServiceDescription classes to be added.
Style	Enum	ServiceDescriptionImportStyle enumeration. See Enumerations for details.

Methods of the ServiceDescriptionImporter class	Return Type	Description
AddServiceDescription	–	Adds a ServiceDescription to the ServiceDescriptions collection. This method also assigns AppSettingUrlKey and AppSettingBaseUrl.

The ServiceDescriptionReflector Class

Properties of the Service DescriptionReflector class	Return Type	Description
Schemas	Collection	The XML Schemas collection
ServiceDescriptions	Collection	The ServiceDescriptions collection

The SoapAddressBinding Class

This is the SOAP address binding used to give a port an address.

Properties of the Soap AddressBinding class	Return Type	Description
Location	String	-

Inherits other properties from ServiceDescriptionFormatExtension

The SoapBinding Class

The purpose of the SOAP binding element is to signify that the message is based on the SOAP format of Envelope, Header, and Body.

Properties of the SoapBindng class	Return Type	Description
Namespace	String	Identifies a unique namespace for the SoapBinding class. This namespace must be unique throughout the WSDL schema definition.
Address	String	–
Binding	Object	XML Namespace qualified.

Inherits other properties from `ServiceDescriptionFormatExtension`

The SoapBodyBinding Class

No information was available on this class at time of going to publication.

Properties of the SoapBodyBinding class	Return Type	Description
Encoding	String	The character encoding used. Encoding refers to the translation of text into another style which is either readable, or can be more easily transported, for example when UrlEncoding URL values.
Namespace	String	Identifies a unique namespace for the SoapBodyBinding class. This namespace must be unique throughout the WSDL schema definition.
Parts	String Array	–
PartsString	String	–
Use	SoapBindin gUse enum	Enumeration `SoapBindingUse`.

Inherits other properties from `ServiceDescriptionFormatExtension`.

The SoapFaultBinding Class

Defines the protocol and contents of SOAP Fault messages.

Properties of the SoapFaultBinding class	Return Type	Description
Encoding	String	The character encoding used. Encoding refers to the translation of text into another style which is either readable or can be more easily transported, for example when UrlEncoding URL values.

Table continued on following page

Properties of the SoapFaultBinding class	Return Type	Description
`Namespace`	`String`	Identifies a unique namespace for the `SoapFaultBinding` class. This namespace must be unique throughout the WSDL schema definition.
`Use`	`SoapBinding Use enum`	Enumeration `SoapBindingUse`.

Inherits other properties from `ServiceDescriptionFormatExtension`.

The SoapHeaderBinding Class

Properties of the SoapHeaderBinding class	Return Type	Description
`Encoding`	`String`	The character encoding used. Encoding refers to the translation of text into another style which is either readable or can be more easily transported, for example when UrlEncoding URL values.
`MapToProperty`	`Boolean`	–
`Message`	`Object`	`Message` property of the `SoapHeaderBinding` class. XML namespace qualified.
`Namespace`	`String`	Identifies a unique namespace for the `SoapHeaderBinding` class. This namespace must be unique throughout the WSDL schema definition.
`Part`	`String`	–
`Use`	`SoapBinding Use enum`	Enumeration `SoapBindingUse`.

Inherits other properties from `ServiceDescriptionFormatExtension`

The SoapHeaderFaultBinding Class

If the SOAP header itself produces an error, the SOAP standard states that such errors must be notified and returned in headers. This class allows such header error messages to be defined.

Properties of the Soap HeaderFaultBinding class	Return Type	Description
`Encoding`	`String`	The character encoding style used. Encoding refers to the translation of text into another style, which is either readable or can be more easily transported.
`Message`	`Object`	`Message` property of the `SoapHeaderFaultBinding` class. XML namespace qualified.

Properties of the Soap HeaderFaultBinding class	Return Type	Description
Namespace	String	Identifies a unique namespace for the SoapHeaderFault Binding class. This namespace must be unique throughout the WSDL schema definition.
Part	String	–
Use	SoapBinding Use enum	Enumeration SoapBindingUse.
Inherits other properties from ServiceDescriptionFormatExtension		

The SoapOperationBinding Class

This class specifies the Request protocols supported by the ASP.NET server or other SOAP-compliant end-point.

Properties of the Soap TransportImporter class	Return Type	Description
SoapAction	String	Gets or sets SOAP action value. The SOAP action is only used in a SOAP request and is placed in the HTML header to indicate to the recipient server who the message is intended for. For example, it could be processed by the next server that receives it, or passed on to another server.
Style	SoapBindin gStyle Enum	Indicates the binding style of the WSDL schema. For example RPC or document. These two styles use a different technique for defining and binding within a WSDL schema definition.
Inherits other properties from ServiceDescriptionFormatExtension		

The Types Class

Types allow you to create user-defined types for particular message or operation requirements.

Properties of the Types class	Return Type	Description
Extensions	Collection	Allows for extension of the basic functionality of the Types class.
Schemas	Collection	Returns a collection of XML Schema data type definitions for objects within the current WSDL schema.

Collections

For the sake of simplifying this documentation, all the collections listed below inherit the properties and methods detailed in the generic `Collection` definition, an abstract definition for the context of this chapter only:

❏   BindingCollection

❏   FaultBindingCollection

❏   ImportCollection

❏   MessageCollection

❏   MessagePartCollection

❏   MimePartCollection

❏   MimeTextMatchCollection

❏   OperationBindingCollection

❏   OperationCollection

❏   OperationFaultCollection

❏   OperationMessageCollection

❏   PortCollection

❏   PortTypeCollection

❏   ServiceCollection

❏   ServiceDescriptionCollection

❏   ServiceDescriptionFormatExtensionCollection

> **Note that all the above collections are read-only, but members can be added to the collection, removed, and modified, using the methods exposed by the collection.**

The Generic Collection Definition

Properties of the Collection definition	Return Type	Description
Count	Integer	Returns the number of items within this collection
Item	Object	Returns a specific object from the collection

Methods of the Collection definition	Return Type	Description
Add	Integer	Adds an instance of a class to the end of the collection
Clear	–	Empties the collection
Contains	Boolean	Returns true if the specified object is in this collection
CopyTo	–	Copies the entire collection to a one-dimensional array
GetEnumerator	Object	Allows iteration through the collection

Methods of the Collection definition	Return Type	Description
IndexOf	Integer	Returns the item number in the collection of the supplied object
Insert	–	Adds an object at a specific position in the collection
Remove	–	Removes the first occurrence of a supplied object
RemoveAt	–	Removes the item found at a specific position

13

System.Web.Services.Protocols

The `System.Web.Services.Protocols` namespace controls the main connectivity between the client and the server, in that it is used by the ASP.NET client and ASP.NET server to transport SOAP messages and in turn to allow the processing of Web Service functionality.

It has been designed to be versatile but concise by encapsulating different methods of transport in one single area of functionality. Though it currently only supports three transport methods (SOAP, HTTP-GET and HTTP-POST, see later for detailed description of these communication techniques) we can expect that this area of the .NET framework will be expanded over the forthcoming years to support other more intrinsic protocols.

The ASP.NET server and the ASP.NET client produce SOAP messages according to the current SOAP standard and as such this Protocols namespace can be used to transfer messages to non-.NET SOAP servers and receive requests from non-.NET SOAP clients. The only requirement is that the third party client or server understands how to transport messages using one of the three .NET-supported communication techniques.

In addition to the Protocols namespace dealing with communication it also controls the construction (also known as "serialization") and deconstruction (also known as "de-serialization") of the SOAP message according to the currently supported SOAP standard. This allows the Protocols namespace to use its attributes and classes to manipulate these SOAP messages to produce advanced customized SOAP messages, for example adding compression, encryption, or even a header section that contains logon details and/or transaction information.

The `System.Web.Services.Protocols` namespace groups together the classes that handle the communication of the basic types of SOAP messages required by all Web Service applications and SOAP-compliant servers:

- ❑ **SOAP Request** – transmitted by the .NET client to the ASP.NET server
- ❑ **SOAP Response** – returned by the ASP.NET server to any client that is SOAP-compliant
- ❑ **SOAP Fault messages** – returned by the SOAP-compliant server in the event of an error

The Simple Object Access Protocol (SOAP) is a platform-independent specification currently at W3C Working Draft status, detailed at http://www.w3.org/TR/2001/WD-soap12-20010709. It defines a standard XML format for the interchange of messages between client and server when implementing Web Services. SOAP messages must be parsed by the client or server to extract the message content from the SOAP wrapper.

The `System.Web.Services.Protocols` namespace is useful in a number of situations:

❑ **Interrogate** – to interrogate the current Web Service session to find information about the transfer protocol. This allows you to programmatically determine which communication technique (SOAP, HTTP-GET, or HTTP-POST) to use or even change the values to send to the ASP.NET server at runtime, encrypting or compressing your SOAP message, for example.

❑ **XML Element Control** – to change XML elements within the SOAP message. The namespace grants you fine-grained control over SOAP messages, such as adding headers, performing user validation, and assigning specialist XML namespaces.

❑ **Proxy Class Wrapper** – to create your own client communication proxy class wrapper that encapsulates available communication calls to the remote ASP.NET server, and allows you to control the sending of SOAP requests at a very low level.

❑ **Customize Proxy Class Wrapper** – to customize a client proxy class or Web Service method using attributes. This allows you to introduce specific extensions to fulfill your own particular requirements not catered for by the default Web Service settings. For example, by changing the default SOAP action for a Web Method you can effectively tell the SOAP server to redirect your message to another SOAP server instead of processing it.

Note that during this chapter we will deal with the common classes, methods, and properties that are defined as part of the `System.Web.Services.Protocols` namespace. However, because of the inheritance ability of the .NET framework, we will not cover classes, methods, and properties that fall outside of the Protocols namespace. These items will be covered elsewhere within this book. We will start this chapter with a general discussion of the various communication protocols that are used with Web Services, and we will then move on to discuss in depth some of the most important classes in the namespace. We will then give a round up of all the classes and enumerations in `System.Web.Services.Protocols`. Finally, we will examine Web Service Discovery.

Communication Protocols

The basic SOAP specification as defined by W3C does not require the use of any particular mode of communication, and you are free to transfer SOAP messages over HTTP, COM, COM+, CORBA, and SMTP. The definition of which communication techniques are available for any Web Service is specified by the `<service>` element within the corresponding WSDL (Web Service Definition Language) file. This WSDL file defines the structure of the Web Services available along with the supported communication techniques.

When ASP.NET transmits SOAP messages between a client and a server, it first interrogates the communication information contained by this `<service>` element to ensure that the technique you wish to use is supported. Secondly, once ASP.NET finds a communication technique it understands (SOAP, HTTP-GET, or HTTP-POST) the information contained within that element provides the end-point server information required to pinpoint the location of the SOAP-compliant server address and port. This may be an ASP.NET server or it may in fact be another organization's server that supports SOAP standards for running remote Web Services.

Although WSDL schemas have the ability to handle a wide variety of communication techniques, the technology's strength lies in the transmission of SOAP messages over TCP/IP by either HTTP POST, HTTP GET, or the SOAP protocol. The real benefit of these protocols compared to any other is that they are supported by almost all operating systems, allowing your Web Service to be available to devices ranging from WAP phones to PCs, from Notebooks to UNIX-based servers. These protocols are also the most appropriate to use when corporate firewalls need to be crossed, as they work over the standard HTTP port.

Supported Communication Techniques

The `System.Web.Services.Protocols` namespace supports three communication techniques for transferring the three varieties of SOAP message between client and the Web Service server:

- ❑ **SOAP** – transfer messages with HTTP and SOAP wrappers using form post. This is the typical and default SOAP communication method.

- ❑ **HTTP GET** – transfer messages using HTTP GET with URL defined parameters. In this instance, a complete SOAP message is not created.

- ❑ **HTTP POST** – transfer messages using HTTP form post. In this instance a complete SOAP message is not created.

Please note that these techniques are supported by ASP.NET, but may not necessarily be supported by other SOAP servers. To find the technique supported by a Web Service hosted on another type of server, look at the `<service>` element within the WSDL schema that is being advertised by that Web Service.

SOAP

The most common communication technique, SOAP, uses the TCP/IP transport to send a SOAP request inside standard HTTP formatted text. The example below shows its two distinct sections:

Member Name	Text Sent to Server
HTTP Header	PORT /FirstTest/Service1.asmx HTTP/1.1 Host: localhost Content-Type: text/xml; charset=utf-8 Content-Length: length SOAPAction: "http://tempuri.org/HelloWorld"

HTTP Body	`<?xml version="1.0" encoding="utf-8"?>`
	`<soap:Envelope`
	`xmlns:xsi="http://www.w3.org/2001/XMLSchema-instance"`
	`xmlns:xsd="http://www.w3.org/2001/XMLSchema"`
	`xmlns:soap="http://schemas.xmlsoap.org/soap/envelope/" >`
	`<soap:Body>`
	`  <HelloWorld xmlns="http://tempuri.org/">`
	`    <Argument1>Hello</Argument1>`
	`  </HelloWorld>`
	`</soap:Body>""`
	`</soap:Envelope>`

❑ **HTTP Header** – this section contains the standard HTTP header information that you would normally find in any HTTP request: for example, when you want to display a page on a web site. However, one important key is added: the SOAPAction key is added to SOAP requests and indicates the intended recipient for this SOAP message. This can allow us to pass a request to one server but indicate that we wish it to be redirected to another server for processing (this is covered in more detail later in this chapter). SOAPAction is ignored if used for sending a SOAP response back to a client.

❑ **HTTP Body** – contains a valid message that conforms to the supported SOAP specification. In the above example we show the SOAP from the HelloWorld example we create as our first Web Service within ASP.NET. When we actually run our HelloWorld Web Service for the first time from a client this is the actual message that is sent to the ASP.NET server.

The above template is followed for every SOAP communication transfer, although naturally the content will reflect the actual Web Service you are calling.

The SoapHttpClientProtocol class is the highest-level class that controls this SOAP communication technique. This is the default class employed by the proxy class created from the Web Service schema using the wsdl.exe command-line tool included with the .NET SDK.

HTTP GET

HTTP GET describes a technique for passing data to an ASP.NET server by appending information to the server's URL. Arguments are passed to the server by using name-value pairs, as shown in the following example:

```
http://www.webserviceserver.com/FirstTest/Service1.asmx/HelloWorld?Argument1=Hello
```

The URL also indicates the name of the Web Service (Service1.asmx) and the name method of the (HelloWorld) that you wish to run.

The above parameter is passed to a fictional server at webservicesserver.com. A "?" character denotes the end of the URL proper, and the start of the list of passed parameters, known as the **querystring**. The name of each parameter is followed by the value of that parameter, separated by the = sign. The ampersand character (&) marks the start of additional and/or optional name-value pairs.

The above address line can be typed into any Internet browser as if you were browsing to a specific page on the Internet. Instead of displaying an HTML page however, this process now runs a specific ASP.NET Web Service and returns and displays an XML formatted string.

The HttpGetClientProtocol class is the highest-level class that controls the HTTP-GET communication technique. The HttpGetClientProtocol class simulates a URL GET by constructing a valid HTTP-GET header and sending it down to the relevant ASP.NET server.

In the case of HTTPGET, unlike the SOAP communication technique, a SOAP message is **not** created. The values for the method name and argument are sent down to the SOAP server using URL parameter passing.

Member Name	Text Sent to Server
HTTP Header	PORT /FirstTest/Service1.asmx/Helloworld?Argument1=Hello HTTP/1.1 Host: localhost

❑ **HTTP Header** – the above HTTP header is sent to the ASP.NET server. The header has no special keys or tags and in its simplest form can be reproduced by simply typing the address and name-value pairs for arguments into any browser capable of displaying an HTML file on the Internet.

> **The HTTP-GET communication technique is simply used for running a Web Service, rather than an actual implementation of the SOAP messaging standard. Its primary significance would be for testing a response from an already created ASP.NET Web Service.**

Note that there is a 2048 character limit on sending characters on an Internet Explorer URL address line. This limit varies depending on your browser, but it must be noted that the limitation exists and that transfer errors may occur when sending large quantities of information to the Web Service.

HTTP POST

The HTTP-POST method of communication is similar to HTTP GET, except that parameter name-value pairs are transmitted as part of the actual body of the HTTP request, rather than appended to the URL request line.

Member Name	Text Sent to Server
HTTP Header	PORT /FirstTest/Service1.asmx HTTP/1.1 Host: localhost Content-Type: text/xml; charset=utf-8 Content-Length: length
HTTP Body	Argument1=Hello

❑ **HTTP Header** – the above HTTP header is sent to the ASP.NET server or any SOAP server that understands HTTP-POST requests. It uses standard form post techniques and in its simplest form can be created using a web page with a form and suitably named fields.

The ASP.NET server receives form post fields representing names-values for the parameters in question, which are then used as arguments for the requested Web Service. As with HTTP GET, this method is simply a technique for running a Web Service, rather than an actual implementation of the SOAP messaging standard.

The `HttpPostClientProtocol` class is the highest-level class that controls the HTTP-POST communication technique. The `HttpPostClientProtocol` class simulates a form post by constructing a valid HTTP-POST header and HTTP body and sending them down to the relevant ASP.NET server.

> **One potential benefit of the HTTP-POST communication technique is that you can create your own form within a web site, which, as long as it has the correct named arguments, can actually run a remote Web Service. Its flaw however, is that it must then be able to capture and respond to an XML-formatted response.**

This technique gives this method of transfer an unlimited size. However, in reality the inherent limitations of traffic information on the Internet restricts size.

Customization of the ASP.NET Server

In ASP.NET, you can fine-tune or generally customize the format of SOAP messages using an attribute-based mechanism that is built into .NET. It provides sophisticated techniques allowing you to control SOAP constructs at a low level of detail, enabling the implementation of advanced features such as specialist encoding, transaction processing, compression, and more.

> **A general rule of thumb, for both server and client customization, is that classes suffixed with `MethodAttribute` serve to customize a Web Service method, while classes suffixed with *`ServiceAttribute`* are used to customize a Web Service class.**

The `System.Web.Services.Protocols` namespace contains a number of classes for altering the defaults set by the WSDL schema for a Web Service by providing values to override specific attributes from the WSDL file on the server. These attributes can either be assigned directly to the definition of the Web Service at design time or on the proxy class at the client in the same manner.

An example of method customization on an ASP.NET server is shown below:

```
< SoapDocumentMethodAttribute( RequestNamespace:="http://www.contoso.com", _
  ResponseNamespace:="http://www.contoso.com")> Public Function HelloWorld() _
  As String
```

The above example would be used within the `.asmx` Web Service file, prefixing whichever Web Service method you wished to customize. The example used actually changes the `Request` namespace and `Response` namespace within the SOAP message. This recommended alteration is required to change the default temporary name space from `http://tempuri.org/` to a recognizable namespace that uniquely identifies your Web Service.

You would want to change the namespace to make sure that when a SOAP request (or multiple SOAP requests) arrives from a client you can match up the specific SOAP request with a specific Web Service method.

When attribute customization is performed on the ASP.NET server, the alterations actually change the WSDL definition file created during the Web Service build process. This alteration can then be read and acted upon by any SOAP-compliant client. Not all attribute customizations are fed into the WSDL schema however, for example headers.

The classes from the `System.Web.Services` namespace that can perform this attribute customization at Web Service method level are:

- ❑ `SoapDocumentMethodAttribute`
- ❑ `SoapRpcMethodAttribute`
- ❑ `HttpMethodAttribute`
- ❑ `SoapHeaderAttribute`
- ❑ `WebServiceBindingAttribute`

In addition, you can similarly fine-tune the WSDL schema at class level by means of the following:

- ❑ `SoapRpcServiceAttribute`
- ❑ `SoapDocumentServiceAttribute`

An example of class customization for an ASP.NET server is shown below:

```
< SoapDocumentServiceAttribute(Use := SoapBindingUse.Literal)> Public Class _
                                            SoapDocumentServiceSample
```

The above example changes the encoding style for a class. The encoding style defines the definition rules of how to describe data types within an XML document.

Customization of the ASP.NET Client

By generating a proxy class using the WSDL.exe utility provided with the .NET SDK, you are able to customize each method contained within the proxy class to introduce alternative features. This allows you to perform advanced client tasks such as data compression, transaction processing, and so on.

Below are the customization classes applicable to proxy classes at Web Service method level:

- ❏ SoapRpcMethodAttribute
- ❏ SoapDocumentMethodAttribute
- ❏ HttpMethodAttribute
- ❏ SoapHeaderAttribute
- ❏ WebServiceBindingAttribute (System.Web.Services namespace)

Each of the above classes can be used to customize a proxy class. An example of proxy Web Service customization would be:

```
Public Function <System.Web.Services.Protocols.HttpMethodAttribute ( _
  GetType(System.Web.Services.Protocols.XmlReturnReader), _
  GetType(System.Web.Services.Protocols.HtmlFormParameterWriter))> _
  GetUserName() As UserName
  Return CType(Me.Invoke("GetUserName", Me.Url + "/GetUserName", _
  New Object(0) {}), UserName)
End Function
```

The above customization defines the return message type (XmlReturnReader) and transport technique (HtmlFormParameterWriter) for transferring messages. For example, using the term XmlReturnReader sets the method to expect an XML formatted (SOAP) message in response to the invoke command, and the term HtmlFormParameterWriter identifies that the invoke command will use the HTTP-POST protocol to send the request to the SOAP server. We can further alter this attribute by invoking the SOAP server Web Service using HTTP GET. To do this we simply change the above parameter to UrlParameterWriter.

As well as customizing a method within a proxy class you can use the following attribute classes to customize all Web Services within the current proxy. Therefore, unless these values are overridden by another assignment to each specific Web Service, every Web Service adopts the attributes of the class. Customization for proxy classes at class level can be performed by the following:

- ❏ SoapRpcServiceAttribute
- ❏ SoapDocumentServiceAttribute

In most circumstances though, Web Service method and class customization within a client proxy class should not be necessary, and in any case it is preferable to do this by modifying the Web Service definition on the server. However in certain circumstances, such as creating headers for transaction control (as headers are not defined within the WSDL specification and so do not filter up to the client), it is preferable to create a client proxy class and use attribute classes to add header information. Adding header information to a SOAP request and SOAP response is covered later within this chapter.

SoapMessageStage Process Trapping

When the ASP.NET client and ASP.NET server create and send SOAP messages, they both go through a series of common stages/events that can be captured by creating a specific framework of methods. This framework traps each stage of the lifecycle of the SOAP message transfer and allows you to programmatically react and perform specialist and advanced features, including, but not limited to:

❑ Logging the SOAP request or SOAP response. By trapping the transfer of a SOAP message after it has been created and before it has been transferred to either the client or the server, you can simply read it and store the message in a database. That way you can store the exact SOAP message you send or receive for your own organization's analysis or security purposes.

❑ Adding authority information to a header for security checking.

❑ Adding encryption to your SOAP message. This allows you to trap the message and perform encryption on the entire SOAP request or SOAP response, to make sure that the SOAP message remains unreadable during transfer.

❑ Adding compression to your SOAP message. One concern about SOAP messages is the amount of text that needs to be transferred. This allows you to compress your SOAP message before it is sent to the Client or Server.

During this event trapping you are supplied with the `SoapClientMessage` or `SoapServerMessage` object that allows you to query or amend the current SOAP message.

By default event trapping is turned off, and to turn it on, you need to ensure the appropriate code is inserted into either your Web Service file, or your client proxy class. The example below shows the template for introducing trappable events within the `HelloWorld` function on an ASP.NET server:

Example: Trapping Events – Service1.asmx.vb

```
Imports System.Web.Services
Imports System
Imports System.Web.Services.Protocols
Imports System.IO

Public Class Service1
  Inherits System.Web.Services.WebService

#Region " Web Services Designer Generated Code "

  Public Sub New()
    MyBase.New()

    'This call is required by the Web Services Designer.
    InitializeComponent()

    'Add your own initialization code after the InitializeComponent() call

  End Sub

  'Required by the Web Services Designer
  Private components As System.ComponentModel.Container

  'NOTE: The following procedure is required by the Web Services Designer
  'It can be modified using the Web Services Designer.
  'Do not modify it using the code editor.
  <System.Diagnostics.DebuggerStepThrough()> Private Sub InitializeComponent()
```

```
         components = New System.ComponentModel.Container()
      End Sub

      Overloads Overrides Sub Dispose()
         'CODEGEN: This procedure is required by the Web Services Designer
         'Do not modify it using the code editor.
      End Sub

   #End Region

      <WebMethod(), TraceExtensionAttribute()> Public Function HelloWorld(ByVal _
                                                Argument1 As String) As String
         HelloWorld = "Hello World"
      End Function
   End Class

   ' This class is a required class for the trace extension to work
   ' it defines the binding between the actual class that reacts to the
   ' events and the HelloWorld web service
   <AttributeUsage(AttributeTargets.Method)> Public Class TraceExtensionAttribute
      Inherits SoapExtensionAttribute

      Private m_Priority As Integer

      Public Overrides ReadOnly Property ExtensionType() As Type
         Get
            ' The following line binds your named class
            ' to the trace extension event
            Return GetType(TraceExtension1)
         End Get
      End Property

      Public Overrides Property Priority() As Integer
         Get
            Return m_priority
         End Get
         Set(ByVal Value As Integer)
            m_priority = Value
         End Set
      End Property
   End Class

   ' The following class allows you to develop a method to handle
   ' the events being raised from the trace extension
   Public Class TraceExtension1
      Inherits System.Web.Services.Protocols.SoapExtension

      Dim sLogFile

      Public Overloads Overrides Function GetInitializer(ByVal methodInfo As _
            LogicalMethodInfo, ByVal attribute As SoapExtensionAttribute) As Object
         'Place any initialization data that can
         'be cached ready for initialization
      End Function

      Public Overrides Sub Initialize(ByVal initializer As Object)
         'Initialise any local variables
         sLogFile = "c:\wroxlog.txt"
      End Sub

      Public Overrides Sub ProcessMessage(ByVal message As _
```

```
                                       Web.Services.Protocols.SoapMessage)
      Dim swLog As StreamWriter
      swLog = New StreamWriter(sLogFile, True)
      Select Case message.Stage
        Case Web.Services.Protocols.SoapMessageStage.BeforeSerialize
          swLog.WriteLine(Now + "-BeforeSerialize stage")
        Case Web.Services.Protocols.SoapMessageStage.AfterSerialize
          swLog.WriteLine(Now + "-AfterSerialize stage")
        Case Web.Services.Protocols.SoapMessageStage.BeforeDeserialize
          swLog.WriteLine(Now + "-BeforeDeserialize stage")
        Case Web.Services.Protocols.SoapMessageStage.AfterDeserialize
          swLog.WriteLine(Now + "-AfterSerialize stage")
        Case Else
          swLog.WriteLine(Now + "-Invalid stage")
      End Select
        swLog.Close()
    End Sub

  End Class
```

The above example is created within the `.asmx` Web Service file and shows how you can trap events in the stages of a SOAP message; the above example writes a single line of code to a log file so that you can see the order that events are performed. Note, if you intend to use the above example code make sure that the log file does not overwrite an existing file on your `C:` drive.

The previous code is a template for handling trace extension events and is used as the container for your code to allow you to interrogate or manipulate a SOAP message at predetermined stages of its creation. As you can see, the single parameter that is passed in is of the type `SoapMessage` class within the `ProcessMessage` subroutine; this method in fact receives either a `SoapServerMessage` or a `SoapClientMessage` depending on whether you have placed your code on the server or on the client.

> For trace extension event trapping to work on the client you must first create a proxy class for a specific WSDL Web Service schema using the **WSDL.exe** command-line utility.

Asynchronous Communication

The default method of communicating with a remote server relies on the `Invoke` method of the `SoapHttpClientProtocol`, `HttpPostClientProtocol`, and `HttpGetClientProtocol` classes. When called, this method initiates a data exchange, and does not terminate until the response has been fully received. This is known as **synchronous** communication, meaning the client has to wait for the end of the transfer before it is able to start processing any other tasks.

However, in some cases, it will be appropriate to select **asynchronous** communication, which is achieved with the `BeginInvoke` and `EndInvoke` method calls.

Asynchronous communication allows the client to continue processing independently of the call to the Web Service while waiting for responses to SOAP messages to be received from the ASP.NET server. This communication technique is handled by the client by using the `BeginInvoke` and `EndInvoke` methods from within a proxy class. A proxy class can be created by using the `WSDL.exe` command and then attaching the outputted class to your project. To create a proxy class simply type the following at an MS-DOS command line.

```
Wsdl /l:vb http://sal006.salnetwork.com:83/xmlone/SimpleCalculator/SimpleCalc.xml
```

The first parameter (/l:vb) signifies the language you want to create in, other available options are C# (/l:cs, also the default) or JScript (/l:js). The other argument is the full URL location of the WSDL schema you want to create a proxy class for.

Once you have created a proxy class, attach it to a new client project.

> **The proxy class you generate using the WSDL.exe command-line utility must be written in the same language that you have created your project with.**

Within this proxy class you will now notice sets of corresponding methods that are named Begin????? and End?????. For example, in our SimpleCalc Web Service you would have a BeginAdd and an EndAdd method, which allow the Web Service to be called asynchronously.

When you use the BeginAdd method to invoke the Web Service asynchronously you also pass in a delegate or callback object. This object has been created within your client, and, once the Web Service has completed, your callback object is run by the proxy class, and you then use the EndAdd method to retrieve the values returned from the remote Web Service.

Below is some client code that calls our demonstration HelloWorld method using asynchronous calls. It is a **non-callback asynchronous** example; instead it uses a process that waits for the AsyncResult object to complete its task:

```
Dim oF As New Service1()
Dim asResult As IAsyncResult

asResult = oF.BeginHelloWorld(Nothing, Nothing)
'Insert your code for extra processing here
asResult.AsyncWaitHandle.WaitOne()
MsgBox(oF.EndHelloWorld(asResult))
```

For the above code to work you must have created a client project and attached your HelloWorld demonstration Web Service.

The above code, although it's practical and shows how you can go back and test an AsyncResult object to see if it has completed processing, is not a true asynchronous event as it does not complete unattended. Therefore we can also use a callback method, which is called once the asynchronous event has completed.

Below is an example of a **callback asynchronous** event:

```
Dim oF As New Service1()
Dim cb As AsyncCallback
Dim asResult As IAsyncResult

public Sub RunAsynchronousEvent()
  cb = New AsyncCallback(AddressOf CallB)
  asResult = oF.BeginHelloWorld(cb, Nothing)
End Sub

Public Sub CallB(ByVal asResult As IAsyncResult)
  MsgBox(oF.EndHelloWorld(asResult))
End Sub
```

As can be seen it only differs from the previous example code by the inclusion of the passing in of an address pointer to a specific method. This method is then called once the asynchronous event has completed its task.

The Client Proxy Class

The .NET SDK comes complete with a command-line utility called `WSDL.exe`, which can automatically generate a proxy class wrapper for a remote Web Service from the WSDL schema file describing a Web Service. This utility simply reads the WSDL schema and creates a framework class that neatly controls all communication with the remote server and also supplies you with a ready-made interface containing methods that match those described in the WSDL schema document.

You can then access this class's functionality and subsequently call the Web Service by using one of two techniques:

❑   Adding this proxy class directly into your client project as a new class and then instantiating it

❑   Compiling the class within a new client project and adding its reference into your project

One interesting thing about this class is that it utilizes the `SoapHttpClientProtocol` class to communicate with the remote SOAP server, meaning you can now use it as a template to amend certain definitions such as adding headers, or changing the character encoding, all from the client's proxy class.

If you look at the proxy class in more detail, you will see that it inherits the `SoapHttpClientProtocol` class. See the command:

```
Inherits SoapHttpClientProtocol
```

This inherited class and the other communication classes, `HttpGetClientProtocol` and `HttpPostClientProtocol`, have the same template for the methods that are available in each class. Therefore if you wish your proxy to communicate with the ASP.NET server using HTTP GET instead of SOAP (a reason to do this would be for example reducing traffic in data-traffic-critical situations) you merely need to change the class declaration to inherit from `HttpGetClientProtocol` instead, then amend the `Invoke` method used within the proxy class to include the destination URL:

```
Inherits HttpGetClientProtocol
```

The Important Classes of the Protocols Namespace

SoapHeaderAttribute Class

This class can customize a client proxy class or a Web Service method by creating SOAP headers that can be transferred as part of the SOAP request or SOAP response. This class cannot be inherited.

A SOAP header is an XML structure that can be placed within a SOAP message to send additional information down to the server that is not included in the arguments to the Web Service. It usually defines environment variables that can be acted upon, for example advising the server that you want this SOAP request to be included within a transaction, or passing down a security username and password for authorization. A SOAP header within a SOAP message looks like this:

```
<?xml version="1.0" encoding="utf-8"?>
<soap:Envelope xmlns:xsi="http://www.w3.org/2001/XMLSchema-instance"
               xmlns:xsd="http://www.w3.org/2001/XMLSchema"
```

```
                    xmlns:soap="http://schemas.xmlsoap.org/soap/envelope/" >
    <soap:Header>
      <MyHeader xmlns="http://www.contoso.com">
        <Username>Admin</Username>
        <Password>MyPassword</Password>
      </MyHeader>
    </soap:Header>
    <soap:Body>
      <HelloWorld xmlns="http://tempuri.org/">
        <Argument1>Hello</Argument1>
      </HelloWorld>
    </soap:Body>
  </soap:Envelope>
```

The following example outlines a step-by-step approach for defining a client SOAP header and sending it to a SOAP server.

Client Code for Sending a SOAP Header

The following code reflects example code required for the `HelloWorld` proxy class created using the `WSDL.exe` command:

Example: Soap Header Client – Service1.vb

```
Imports System
Imports System.Diagnostics
Imports System.Web.Services
Imports System.Web.Services.Protocols
Imports System.Xml.Serialization

<System.Web.Services.WebServiceBindingAttribute(Name:="Service1Soap",
[Namespace]:="http://tempuri.org/")> Public Class Service1
   Inherits System.Web.Services.Protocols.SoapHttpClientProtocol

    'This defines the structure of a simple SOAP header
    'this SOAP header allows you to pass down two values to the server.
    Public Class MyHeader
      Inherits SoapHeader
      Public MyValue As String
      Public MyNumber As Integer
    End Class

    'This defines a specific instance of the header
    'it also defines the variable name to use within
    'the SOAP header attribute.
    Public hName As New MyHeader

    <System.Diagnostics.DebuggerStepThroughAttribute()> Public Sub New()
      MyBase.New()
      Me.Url = "http://localhost/helloworld/service1.asmx"
    End Sub

    ' Now by simply attaching the local SOAP header variable to the call
    ' that is being made to the remote ASP.NET server process, the system
    ' builds and sends the header.
<System.Diagnostics.DebuggerStepThroughAttribute(), SoapHeader("hName", _
   direction:=SoapHeaderDirection.InOut)> Public Function HelloWorld() As String
    'You can also now assign values to the header to send to the server.
    HName.MyValue="Hello to you"
      hName.MyNumber=42
```

```
    Dim results() As Object = Me.Invoke("HelloWorld", New Object(-1) {})
    Return CType(results(0), String)
End Function

    <System.Diagnostics.DebuggerStepThroughAttribute()> _
        Public Function BeginHelloWorld(ByVal callback As System.AsyncCallback, _
        ByVal asyncState As Object) As System.IAsyncResult
        Return Me.BeginInvoke("HelloWorld", New Object(-1) {}, callback, asyncState)
    End Function

    <System.Diagnostics.DebuggerStepThroughAttribute()> _
        Public Function EndHelloWorld(ByVal asyncResult As System.IAsyncResult) _
                                                                   As String

    Dim results() As Object = Me.EndInvoke(asyncResult)
    Return CType(results(0), String)
    End Function
End Class
```

❏   Define the class structure for the header, inserting the values that you wish to send to the SOAP
    server. The following code should be placed in your proxy class. As can be seen, the MyValue
    and MyNumber entries are the actual values that will be sent to the SOAP server:

```
Public Class MyHeader
    Inherits SoapHeader
    Public MyValue As String
    Public MyNumber As Integer
End Class
```

It's worth noting that to declare this header you can also create another project with a public
class and then simply reference that instead of declaring it locally. This gives the added
advantage of having the ability to share the same class within the ASP.NET server, guaranteeing
that you conform to the same Header structure.

The above definition is not restricted to simple variable definitions; you may also use get and
set definitions within your code.

❏   You must then declare a local MyHeader variable within your proxy to contain the header values:

```
Public hName As New MyHeader
```

❏   Now to complete the client end, you must make sure that the SoapHeaderAttribute class is
    used to add the SOAP header to the outbound SOAP request.

```
<System.Diagnostics.DebuggerStepThroughAttribute(), SoapHeader("hName", _
        direction:= SoapHeaderDirection.InOut ), > _
        Public Function HelloWorld() As String
    HName.MyValue="Hello to you"
    hName.MyNumber=42
        Dim results() As Object = Me.Invoke("HelloWorld", New Object(-1) {})
    Return CType(results(0), String)
End Function
```

Please note that you can assign values to the SOAP header internally within this proxy class.
However, you can also assign values to the SOAP header outside the proxy class, from the client
code. The following example shows code that can be used anywhere within your client application as
long as the proxy class you created with the WSDL.exe command has been attached to your project:

```
Dim oWS as new Service1
oWS.hName.Myvalue="Hello to you"
oWS.hName.MyNumber=42
msgbox(oWS.HelloWorld())
```

Server Code for Receiving a SOAP Header

Now that you have prepared the client to send a SOAP header to the server, you must also prepare the ASP.NET Web Service to receive the SOAP header and automatically assign it to a local variable which can then be interrogated or changed.

If the SOAP header was created as an `InOut`, you can also use this local variable to return values to the client. Reasons you would want to return values to the client include (but are not limited to) for returning the successful outcome of any transaction processing or returning the last date logged on for the username and password you passed to the server.

Example: SOAP Header Server – Service1.asmx.vb

```
Imports System.Web.Services
Imports System.Web.Services.Protocols

Public Class Service1
  Inherits System.Web.Services.WebService

  Public Class MyHeader
    Inherits SoapHeader
    Public MyValue As String
    Public MyNumber As Integer
  End Class

  Public hName As MyHeader

  'This method now receives a SOAP header from the client which can be
  'interrogated
  <WebMethod(), SoapHeader("hName", direction:=SoapHeaderDirection.InOut)> _
                                      Public Function HelloWorld() As String
    HelloWorld = "This is what you sent me - MyValue=" + _
                     + hName.MyValue + " and MyNumber=" & hName.MyNumber
  End Function
End Class
```

❑ Declare the local header variable, this time omitting the `new` keyword, as this variable will be instantiated when receiving the SOAP request:

```
Public hName As MyHeader
```

❑ Then within the web method attribute area, assign the SOAP header to the method. Because this is assigned to a web method this now means that the web method is ready to accept a SOAP header from the client and assign it to a local variable.

```
SoapHeader("hName", direction:=SoapHeaderDirection.InOut)
```

That's it. You can now run your project and pass values into the Web Service using this SOAP header. From inside the Web Service code, simply use the following to retrieve or set any values that are to be returned to the client.

```
hName.MyValue
'or
hName.MyNumber
```

651

Direction Property

This property indicates the intended recipient of a particular `SoapHeader`:

- ❑ `In` – the header is sent **to** the Web Service method only

- ❑ `Out` – the header is sent **from** the Web Service method only

- ❑ `InOut` – the header is sent **to and from** the Web Service

In the previous example we displayed some code that indicated the direction of the SOAP header:

```
SoapHeader("hName", direction:=SoapHeaderDirection.InOut)
```

The assignment of the enumeration `SoapHeaderDirection.InOut` indicates that the Web Service accepts a SOAP header and can populate it and send it back. Please note that this attribute setting should always be the same as the proxy class.

The other values for this property are that the Web Service only accepts a SOAP header but it does not return one to the client:

```
SoapHeader("hName", direction:=SoapHeaderDirection.In)
```

or the Web Service only sends a SOAP header but it does not accept one from the client:

```
SoapHeader("hName", direction:=SoapHeaderDirection.Out)
```

MemberName Property

The SOAP header will be held within an XML element name, and this property allows you to assign exactly what that element name will be. Note that this value must be the same as the locally declared variable that contains the SOAP header, and also correspond to the SOAP header name given to the ASP.NET Web Service method.

Required Property

This determines that the ASP.NET Web Service must either understand (`true`) the SOAP header before continuing or does not need to understand (`false`) the SOAP header. This property makes sure that ASP.NET does not ignore a Web Service header if it does not understand it. A typical example would be a client request that insists the server encrypts all returned SOAP messages.

SoapDocumentMethodAttribute Class

This method alters the structure of the generated WSDL schema created during the build process for an ASP.NET Web Service project. It consequently affects the SOAP message structure and format used, as this structure adheres to the rules set out by the WSDL schema.

The following code is taken from an ASP.NET Web Service project, detailing how you can define your own `Request` and `Response` namespaces that will override the default definitions during building the WSDL file:

```
<System.Web.Services.Protocols.SoapDocumentMethodAttribute( _
                RequestNamespace:="http://namespacelocalhost", _
                ResponseNamespace:="http://localhost"), WebMethod()> _
                Public Function HelloWorld() As String
```

Namespaces are used to assign a string value to uniquely identify a Web Service. The `SoapDocumentMethodAttribute` is used in the ASP.NET Web Service or in a Web Service proxy class.

Action Property

The `Action` request header field can be used to get or set the SOAP `Action` for the message. The SOAP `Action` specifies a URI that indicates the intended business processing end-point for the SOAP request. It can be used to indicate to the SOAP server that this message must be passed to another server or it can simply indicate that the next server receiving this SOAP message should process it.

SOAP places no restrictions on the format or specificity of the URI, and doesn't even require that it be resolvable. This property is used during SOAP, HTTP GET, and HTTP POST transfers, and is placed inside the HTML wrapper's header, not within the SOAP message.

```
Boolean := SoapDocumentMethodAttribute.Action
```

The SOAP `Action` is used by SOAP-compliant servers to redirect SOAP messages to the appropriate server where the Web Service requested is located. This may in fact not be the server communicating with the client.

Binding Property

This property identifies the binding a Web Service method implements during an operation. The `Binding`, as its name suggests, forms the namespace or interface that brings together different items within the WSDL schema to form a complete set of operations.

```
String := SoapDocumentMethodAttribute.Binding
```

A `Binding` is an XML definition for attaching Web Services to a known end-point or communication technique. This property can be used to create a new `Binding` for a Web Service that was not included within the original WSDL schema definition.

When assigning a `Binding` name you must first of all create a new binding XML construct using the `WebServiceBinding` statement at class level. This will create the XML within the WSDL schema; you can then use this binding construct by simply assigning its name to the Web Service with the `Binding` property (see Chapter 11 for more details on binding).

OneWay Property

This property can only be used for SUB methods as they do not return a result to the client, as opposed to FUNCTION methods, where the property is not valid. This property is useful for instructing the server to initiate a task where the result is not required or there is no result:

```
Boolean := SoapDocumentMethodAttribute.OneWay
```

One potential use of this property is to create an asynchronous message queuing system, where you create methods that do not return SOAP messages, but simply process requests. After you have asked for a Web Service to run, you can send another SOAP message to the server to find out the status of the previous Web Service. All state however will be controlled within the server using database activity.

ParameterStyle Property

The propert indicates the position within the message where the SOAP parameters are to be placed during transfer. Using this property, you can fine-tune exactly where the parameters are stored within the SOAP request and response.

```
SoapParameterStyle := SoapDocumentMethodAttribute.ParameterStyle
```

If you select a `SoapParameterStyle` of `Bare`, the method parameters are not wrapped by any container element, instead appearing directly beneath the body element of the SOAP request. The default for this property is `Wrapped`, meaning that parameters are wrapped within a container element, which is in turn held inside the SOAP body element.

See the section on the `SoapParameteStyle` enumeration near the end of this chapter for a full list of enumeration values.

RequestElementName Property

When `ParameterStyle` is `Wrapped`, this property can be used to define the element name to use for the element wrapper around the parameters of the **SOAP Request**. The default value is the name of the Web Service method being called.

```
String := SoapDocumentMethodAttribute.RequestElementName
```

ResponseElementName Property

As you may have guessed, this property serves the same purpose as `RequestElementName`, except that it defines parameter names for the **SOAP Response**. So, for a `ParameterStyle` of `Wrapped`, this property defines the element wrapper to use for the parameters of the SOAP Response. Again, the default value is the name of the Web Service method used.

```
String := SoapDocumentMethodAttribute.ResponseElementName
```

RequestNamespace Property

Each SOAP request has an XML namespace associated with it. The default namespace for all .NET Web Services is http://tempuri.org/. This property allows you to declare an alternative namespace for the Request.

```
String := SoapDocumentMethodAttribute.RequestNamespace
```

ResponseNamespace Property

This property mirrors the `RequestNamespace` property for the SOAP Response. Again, the default namespace for the response is http://tempuri.org/. This property lets you specify a different namespace for the Response.

```
String := SoapDocumentMethodAttribute.ResponseNamespace
```

It should be noted that the `ResponseNamespace` does not have to be different from the `RequestNamespace`. Namespaces are simply used to identify a particular SOAP message to a Web Service (if on the server) or match a request with a response message (if on the client).

Use Property

This property gets or sets the parameter encoding that applies to a Web Service method within the XML portion of a SOAP message.

Encoding describes the rules for defining an XML string data type. Therefore, if the encoding style states that when defining a numeric field data type you must indicate minimum and maximum values, then you must adhere to this rule.

SoapExtension Class

SOAP extensions give you the ability to extend the facilities of the basic ASP.NET framework by providing a means of accessing the underlying engine processing events.

The class does this by allowing you to trap any of the four stages/events in the lifecycle of a SOAP message so that you may process through your own handler whenever one of these events is caught. These stages are:

- ❑ BeforeSerialize

- ❑ AfterSerialize

- ❑ BeforeDeserialize

- ❑ AfterDeserialize

ChainStream Method

This method allows you to capture a Stream object containing either the SOAP Request or SOAP Response. This Stream object can then be used within SoapMessageStage to manipulate the SOAP message, for example to apply compression or encryption:

```
Stream := SoapExtension.ChainStream( Stream )
```

Note that the Stream object attached to the message during SoapMessageStage is read-only, so if you wish to amend the SOAP message, you must use the Stream object passed by the ChainStream method.

GetInitializer Method

This method can provide perfomance enhancement by specifying how data is to be cached during processing of a SoapExtension.

Initialize Method

Use this method to initialize a SoapExtension using the data cached during a previous GetInitializer method call.

ProcessMessage Method

This method forms the heart of the entire SoapExtension, allowing you to assign code to react to the various events that are triggered during the processing of a SOAP message.

SoapHttpClientProtocol Class

This class defines the means for sending SOAP requests to the server using the SOAP communication technique. It sits at the top of a hierarchy of inherited classes, each of which is responsible for a specific process within the transport mechanism.

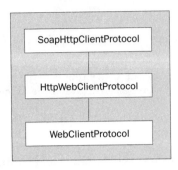

AllowAutoRedirect Property

The SOAP standard allows for the transfer of SOAP messages from a client to a SOAP server, but because it also allows for the redirection or "daisy-chaining" of SOAP servers, messages may be processed by a different server from the one you originally opened up communication with. This property allows you to prevent any such redirection from occurring, and is particularly useful when you are sending sensitive information with the SOAP message, such as name and password information:

```
Boolean = SoapHttpClientProtocol.AllowAutoRedirect
```

ClientCertificates Property

Certificates are digital documents that allocate unique public keys to identify an individual or other entity. They allow verification by ensuring that a public key does in fact belong to a given individual.

This property allows you to extract the certificate information from the `HttpGetClientProtocol` class during a SOAP request, which can be used to verify the identity of the client.

```
X509CertificateCollection = SoapHttpClientProtocol.ClientCertificates
```

ConnectionGroupName Property

This property enables you to associate a request with a specific and unique group name within your application session. This can be useful when your application makes requests to a server regarding different users, such as a web site that retrieves customer information from a database server.

Under normal circumstances, when a connection is opened to a .NET server, the connection pooling mechanisms built into .NET kick in. This is designed to save network latency by reusing already established connections rather than creating new ones. Problems can however occur if the connection requires a secure connection, and a user-specific authentication occurred between the client and the server. This creates a gray area when you then try to reuse a pooled secure connection for a non-secure user. By using `ConnectionGroupName` when establishing the connection, you create a new connection that is unique to that user, and will not be pooled for reuse by any other user.

```
String = SoapHttpClientProtocol.ConnectionGroupName
```

Note that each connection group creates an additional connection with the associated server. This may not be the same server for all connection groups. If many connection groups are used then this may result in exceeding the `ServicePoint.ConnectionPoint` for that server.

CookieContainer Property

Gets or sets cookies associated with the SOAP request.

```
CookieContainer = SoapHttpClientProtocol.CookieContainer
```

Cookies in Web Services can be used in a similar fashion to how cookies are used within web sites: to allow for the automatic retrieval of relevant data that can be stored on the client computer instead of the server. Note that this method of storing stateful data relies on many things, such as the client having cookies turned on, the client being able to understand cookies (non-cookie systems include PDA and WAP), also it invokes an additional round trip to retrieve cookie information that may significantly lengthen the time to run that Web Service.

Credentials Property

This property contains authentication information to identify the client for a SOAP request. When using the Credentials property, a Web Service client must instantiate the NetworkCredential class, and then set the client credentials according to the authentication mechanism employed. This information will then be used to authenticate your connection to an ASP.NET server or any server supporting basic, digest, NTLM, and Kerberos authentication mechanisms.

```
Credentials = SoapHttpClientProtocol.Credentials
```

Credential authentication is possibly the most important authentication technique available. It allows us to use the existing methods of username and password authority, which have over past years been tried and tested. Though some are not encrypted, such as basic authentication, with the addition of SSL connections this becomes a significant security benefit for transferring SOAP messages between client and server.

PreAuthenticate Property

When using the Credentials property and connecting to the ASP.NET server, the default behavior (PreAuthenticate=False) is to send authentication information to the server only if that server challenges the user for it. However, by setting the PreAuthenticate property to true, you can send authentication information in a WWW-authenticate HTTP header with every SOAP request. This will save any latency arising from the server having to request authentication information additionally.

```
Boolean = SoapHttpClientProtocol.PreAuthenticate
```

Proxy Property

If your local network setup requires that you process SOAP requests through a firewall, then you need to use this property to configure firewall authentication information. This can be used to bypass the default proxy settings for your machine.

```
WebProxy = SoapHttpClientProtocol.Proxy
```

This property can be used within the Web Service's proxy class. Below we have some example code that shows how the proxy class (which we built previously) can be altered to allow proxy connections:

```
Public Function HelloWorld() As String
  'Create a proxy object with your details
    Dim proxyObject As New WebProxy("yourproxyservername", 80)
```

```
      'Assign the object to the proxy class
       Me.Proxy = proxyObject
       Dim results() As Object = Me.Invoke("HelloWorld", New Object(-1) {})
    Return CType(results(0), String)
  End Function
```

As well as using it from within the proxy class you can also use it within the client code, for example:

```
Imports System.Net

Public Class Form1
  Inherits System.Windows.Forms.Form

  Private Sub Form1_Load(ByVal sender As System.Object, ByVal e As _
                                        System.EventArgs) Handles MyBase.Load

    Dim oHelloWorld As New Service1()
    Dim proxyObject As New WebProxy("yourproxyservername", 80)

    oHelloWorld.Proxy = proxyObject

    MsgBox(oHelloWorld.HelloWorld)

  End Sub
End Class
```

To pass in authentication information you must create credentials and assign that to the proxy class, before assigning the proxy class to your instantiated class.

RequestEncoding Property

This property allows you to get and set the character encoding method for all SOAP requests. You must use and populate the `Encoding` class appropriately, and pass it into this property. The response returned by the ASP.NET server will then reflect the encoding method given by `RequestEncoding`. The default encoding is Unicode. Valid encoding types are:

❑ `ASCIIEncoding`

❑ `UnicodeEncoding`

❑ `UTF7Encoding`

❑ `UTF8Encoding`

```
Encoding = SoapHttpClientProtocol.RequestEncoding
```

Timeout Property

Use this property to get or set the number of milliseconds to wait before SOAP requests time out.

```
Integer = SoapHttpClientProtocol.Timeout
```

Setting this value to -1 means wait for ever.

Url Property

This contains the base or listener URL of the Web Service the client is requesting. You can use this property to specify an alternative Web Service listener, for example to redirect the request to an alternative mirrored server in the event of failure on the main server.

```
String = SoapHttpClientProtocol.Url
```

This value includes a definitive URL address location, as well as a port number when relevant.

UserAgent Property

The user agent is a value in the HTTP header that identifies the client. By default, this is undefined and not sent to the server, but you can change it to uniquely identify your client either by type or even by location, for example "dotNET client in New York".

```
String = SoapHttpClientProtocol.UserAgent
```

Abort Method

The `Abort` method stops any currently executing asynchronous SOAP request from the client. This method is helpful when you start a long-running Web Service asynchronously on the server such as creating a report for a monthly meeting. If it seems to be taking too long you can stop it from running by executing this `Abort` command by simply attaching the abort to a button on your client form.

BeginInvoke Method

Use this method to initiate an asynchronous transfer of a SOAP request to a remote SOAP server.

```
AsyncResult = SoapHttpClientProtocol.BeginInvoke ( MethodName, _
                                   Parameters, Callback, AsyncState )
```

This method is called from within a client proxy class.

Parameter	Type	Description
MethodName	String	Name of the Web Service method that you wish to run asynchronously.
Parameters	Array of Objects	An array of objects containing the parameters to pass to the Web Service method. The order of values in the array must correspond exactly to the order of the parameters that the Web Service is expecting.
CallBack	Object	This argument defines the method/delegate to call on the client once the event for completion of the asynchronous SOAP message is performed. If `Callback` is nothing then no process is called on completion of the Web Service.
AsyncState	Object	A parameter type container object for holding useful information about the client responsible for using this asynchronous SOAP request. Once the asynchronous event completes, the `AsyncState` object is passed back to the `EndInvoke` method. This object can be used to retain any state values you wish to retrieve at the end of the asynchronous communication process.

An `AsyncResult` object is returned that can be used within your code while the asynchronous communication continues. Once the Web Service completes its processing the `AsyncResult` object is passed back into the `EndInvoke` method to obtain the return values. Typically, you would not call the `BeginInvoke` method directly, unless you were building your own proxy class for a Web Service.

Exception Name	Description
Exception	The request reached the server machine, but failed to process successfully

EndInvoke Method

This method is called to complete the asynchronous invocation of a Web Service method. Such methods must use either HTTP GET or HTTP POST. This method will be called on completion of the Web Service call to the SOAP server by the method identified as the callback delegate in the `BeginInvoke` method or simply from the client code.

```
Object Array = SoapHttpClientProtocol.EndInvoke ( asyncResult )
```

Parameter	Type	Description
AsyncResult	Object	The `AsyncResult` object instantiated by the `BeginInvoke` method that initiated this Web Service request.

An array of objects is returned that matches the return values produced by the Web Service in question; also includes "by reference" or "out only" return arguments. Normally within ASP.NET we deal with a function that returns an argument, this is classified as an "out only" argument, however SOAP allows for the return of multiple "out only" calls, similar to returning multiple function return values but from the same method.

Exception Name	Description
ArgumentException	The `AsyncResult` parameter does not match the one created by `BeginInvoke`

GetWebRequest Method

Similar to the `GetWebResponse` method, which we'll see next, this method overrides the default `WebRequest` specified by `HttpClientProtocol`. The new instance of the `WebRequest` class can then be used to further customize HTTP GET communication, such as by adding additional values to the HTTP header.

```
WebRequest = SoapHttpClientProtocol.GetWebRequest ( uri )
```

Parameter	Type	Description
Uri	String	Specific valid and existing Internet location

The method returns a `WebRequest` instance, which can be then be used to add new headers to the current HTTP communication.

Exception Name	Description
Uri	The parameter passed in was `null` or of zero length

GetWebResponse Synchronous Method

This method overrides the default `WebResponse`, as specified by `HttpClientProtocol`. It returns a `WebResponse` instance for a specified URL using synchronous communication.

```
WebResponse = SoapHttpClientProtocol.GetWebResponse ( WebRequest )
```

Parameter	Type	Description
WebRequest	Object	The `WebRequest` object associated with this connection to the SOAP server

The `WebResponse` object returned can be interrogated to determine the values returned by the SOAP server. Note that this method is only valid for **synchronous** HTTP GET-type communication.

GetWebResponse Asynchronous Method

As with the synchronous method, this overrides the default `WebResponse` specified by `HttpClientProtocol`, and it returns the `WebResponse` instance for a specified URL using asynchronous communication.

```
webResponse = SoapHttpClientProtocol.GetWebResponse ( webRequest, asyncResult )
```

Parameter	Type	Description
WebRequest	Object	The web request instance associated with the current connection to the SOAP server
AsyncResult	Object	The `AsyncResult` object that was instantiated by `BeginInvoke`

Again, a `WebResponse` object is returned, which can be interrogated to find out the return values for the Web Service call. Note that this method is valid for **asynchronous** HTTP GET communication only.

Invoke Method

This method initiates synchronous communication with a SOAP server via the HTTP GET transport.

```
Object = SoapHttpClientProtocol.Invoke ( methodName, parameters )
```

Parameter	Type	Description
MethodName	String	Name of the method you are attempting to run synchronously on the Web Service server.
Parameters	Array	An array of objects containing the parameters to pass to the Web Service. The order of values in the array must correspond to the exact order of the parameters expected by the Web Service.

The `WebRequest` object returned can then be used to add new headers to the current communication technique.

Exception Name	Description
Exception	The request reached the server machine, but was not processed successfully

HttpMethodAttribute Class

This class defines the method for serializing and de-serializing SOAP messages for the client and/or the ASP.NET server.

Serialization refers to the process of converting the current state of a class or object to a stream that can be processed or stored independently of the original object as a string variable. Once this object needs to be restored, the stream can be deserialized to re-create the original state of the object.

Serialization and deserialization is performed by different classes, resulting in different formats, such as a single text line, an XML string, or comma separated values. In the context of the Protocols namespace, the `HttpMethodAttribute` class handles serialization and deserialization from an object to an XML string to be sent within a SOAP message. Even though the serialization method can be changed, it is worth remembering that in practice, because SOAP messages and ASP.NET only understand certain `ParameterFormat` and `ReturnFormatter` values for SOAP interactions, you are constrained by these requirements for SOAP Requests and Responses.

ParameterFormatter Property

When a proxy client invokes a Web Service method using HTTP GET, this property must be set to `UrlParameterWriter`. When a proxy client invokes a Web Service method using HTTP POST or SOAP communication techniques, this property must be set to `HtmlFormParameterWriter` (the default).

```
Object = ParameterFormatter
```

This value is set by default within the proxy client but can be changed to alter the characteristics of the SOAP request. In the above example usage, setting the value to `UrlParameter` means that the SOAP message will be sent as part of a URL address line. Setting the value to `HtmlFormParameterWriter` means the SOAP message will be sent in the main body of the HTML request using a form POST.

ReturnFormatter Property

If a client invokes a Web Service using HTTP-GET, HTTP-POST, or SOAP, then this property must be set to `XmlReturnReader`.

```
<System.Diagnostics.DebuggerStepThroughAttribute(), _
            System.Web.Services.Protocols.HttpMethodAttribute_
            GetType(System.Web.Services.Protocols.XmlReturnReader),_
            GetType(System.Web.Services.Protocols.UrlParameterWriter))> _
            Public Function HelloWorld() As String
    Dim results() As Object = Me.Invoke("HelloWorld", New Object(-1) {})
    Return CType(results(0), String)
End Function
```

The above example shows how you set both the `ParameterFormatter` and the `ReturnFormatter` within a proxy client class using the `HttpMethodAttribute`.

```
Object = ReturnFormatter
```

This property simply states that the results will be returned as XML formatted text for all communication techniques.

HttpGetClientProtocol Class

This defines the mechanisms for sending SOAP requests to the server using HTTP GET. It is at the top of a hierarchy of inherited classes, each of which is responsible for a specific process within the transport:

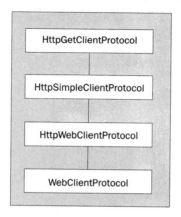

This class has the same methods and descriptions as the previously described SoapHttpClientProtocol with the exception of the following differences:

❑ The ParameterFormatter property must be set to UrlParameterWriter

❑ The invoke command must now be passed a URL in addition to its other arguments

BeginInvoke Method

This method commences the **asynchronous** transfer of a SOAP Request to a remote SOAP server.

```
asyncResult = HttpGetClientProtocol.BeginInvoke ( methodName, _
                            requestUrl, parameters, callback, asyncState )
```

Parameter	Type	Description
MethodName	String	Name of the method you are attempting to run asynchronously on the Web Service server.
RequestUrl	String	Internet location of the destination Web Service listener.
Parameters	Array of Objects	An array of objects containing the parameters to pass to the Web Service method. The order of the values in the array must correspond to the exact order of the parameters that the Web Service is expecting.
CallBack	Object	This argument defines the method/delegate on the client to fire on completion of this asynchronous SOAP message request.

Table continued on following page

Parameter	Type	Description
AsyncState	Object	A container object holding useful information about the client responsible for this SOAP request. Once the asynchronous event completes, this `AsyncState` object is returned to the `EndInvoke` method. This object can be used to retain any stateful values you wish to retrieve at the end of the asynchronous communication process.

The `AsyncResult` object returned can be used within your code while communication continues asynchronously.

Exception Name	Description
Exception	The request reached the server but failed to be processed successfully

Invoke Method

This method initiates a Web Service on a SOAP server using **synchronous** communication over HTTP GET transport. You would not normally call this method directly instead leaving it to the proxy class to call it instead:

```
Object() = HttpGetClientProtocol.Invoke ( methodName, requestUrl, parameters )
```

Parameter	Type	Description
MethodName	String	Name of the method you are attempting to run synchronously on the Web Service server.
RequestUrl	String	Internet location of the destination Web Service listener.
Parameters	Array	An array of objects containing the parameters for the Web Service method. The order of the values in the array must correspond to the exact order of the parameters expected by the Web Service.

The array of objects returned holds the arguments resulting from calling the remote Web Service method.

Exception Name	Description
Exception	The request reached the server machine, but was not processed successfully.

HttpPostClientProtocol Class

This class is used to define the mechanisms for sending SOAP requests to the server using HTTP POST. It is at the top of a hierarchy of inherited classes, each of which is responsible for a specific process of the communication.

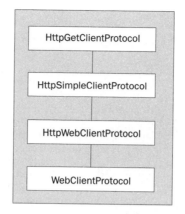

BeginInvoke Method

This method starts an **asynchronous** SOAP Request session with a remote SOAP server.

```
asyncResult = HttpGetClientProtocol.BeginInvoke ( methodName, _
                          requestUrl, parameters, callback, asyncState )
```

Parameter	Type	Description
MethodName	String	Name of the Web Service method you wish to run asynchronously on the server.
RequestUrl	String	Internet location of the destination Web Service listener.
Parameters	Array of Objects	An array of objects containing the parameters to pass to the Web Service method. The order of the values in the array must correspond to the exact order of the parameters expected by the Web Service.
CallBack	Object	This argument defines the method/delegate on the client to call once the SOAP Request is complete.
AsyncState	Object	A container object for holding useful information about the client responsible for using this SOAP Request. Once the asynchronous event completes, this AsyncState object is returned to the EndInvoke method. This object can be used to retain any values you wish to retrieve after the SOAP Request.

An AsyncResult object is returned that can be used within your code while communication continues asynchronously in the background.

Exception Name	Description
Exception	The request reached the server but was not processed successfully

Invoke Method

This method communicates with a SOAP server using **synchronous** communication and HTTP POST transport.

```
Object = HttpPostClientProtocol.Invoke ( methodName, requestUrl, parameters )
```

Parameter	Type	Description
MethodName	String	Name of the Web Service method you wish to run synchronously on the server.
RequestUrl	String	Internet URL of the destination Web Service listener.
Parameters	Array	An array of objects containing the parameters to pass to the Web Service method. The order of the values in the array must correspond to the exact order of the parameters expected by the Web Service.

The WebRequest object returned can be used to add new headers to the current HTTP communication.

Exception Name	Description
Exception	The request reached the server, but was not processed successfully

System.Web.Services.Protocols Classes

HtmlFormParameterReader Class

During the definition of a Web Service, this class can be used to indicate that parameter information will be received using HTML form post. This class is the default class for all SOAP and HTTP-POST communication techniques.

Methods of the HtmlForm ParameterReader Class	Return Type	Description
Read	–	Takes an object of the System.Web.HttpRequest class as an argument. This object contains all information pertaining to the HTTP Request, including header text and URL request values as well as the SOAP message.

HtmlFormParameterWriter Class

During the definition of the Web Service, this class can indicate that responses should be returned using HTML form post. This class contains the WriteRequest method called at the processing point where the transmission is performed. It is used as the main transport class for transmitting values back to the client using SOAP and HTTP-POST communication techniques.

Used by the HttpMethodAttribute class to customize the Web Service method.

Properties of the HtmlForm ParameterWriter Class	Return Type	Description
UsesWriteRequest	Boolean	

Methods of the HtmlForm ParameterWriter Class	Return Type	Description
WriteRequest	–	

HttpGetClientProtocol Class

As we saw in our previous discussion of the important classes of this namespace, this class can customize a Web Service method by using attributes assigned to either the Web Service method or to a client proxy class. It can control HTTP GET communication within a Web Service proxy created using the .NET SDK command WSDL.exe. An HTTP GET communication allows the transfer of name-value pairs as arguments within the Internet URL and simulates a typical GET-HTTP page request.

Properties of the HttpGet ClientProtocol Class	Return Type	Description
AllowAutoRedirect	Boolean	true indicates that the Web Service should allow server redirects. Set to false when sending sensitive data to the server to prevent the request being redirected. The default for this property is false.
ClientCertificates	Collection	Access to the client's collection of valid certificates for the current session.
ConnectionGroupName	String	Associates a communication request with a specific unique name during your application session. Allows you to have multiple sessions with different user authentications within a single application.
CookieContainer	Collection	A list of the cookies associated with this communication.
Credentials	Collection	Authentication information for the remote server.
PreAuthenticate	Boolean	If true, the Credentials authentication information is sent with each request. Otherwise the server must request the credentials separately. The default is false.
Proxy	Object	Allows you to assign and interrogate the proxy settings for the current communication session. This property allows you to pass proxy server authentication details.

Table continued on following page

Properties of the HttpGet ClientProtocol Class	Return Type	Description
RequestEncoding	Object	The character encoding to use for all SOAP messages in this communication.
Timeout	Integer	Sets the timeout that the communication session will wait (in milliseconds) without a response from the server. If −1 the process will wait indefinitely.
Url	String	The specific ASP.NET server end-point that will process the SOAP request.
UserAgent	String	Name of the calling process or application allowing the server to identify the client and act accordingly. Default is null.

Methods of the HttpGet ClientProtocol Class	Return Type	Description
Abort	–	Halts an asynchronous communication in progress.
BeginInvoke	Object	Starts a communication link to a remote Web Service using asynchronous invocation so the client can continue processing other tasks. Returns an AsyncResult object that is passed to the EndInvoke method.
EndInvoke	Object	Called when asynchronous communication with a remote Web Service is complete. Returns an AsyncResult object.
GetWebRequest	Object	Returns a WebRequest object: the base class for handling SOAP requests. You can use instances of this class to perform customization such as adding headers.
GetWebResponse	Object	Returns a WebResponse object: the base class for handling SOAP responses. You can use instances of this class to perform customization such as adding headers.
Invoke	Array Objects	Communicates with a remote Web Service synchronously, meaning the client must wait for a SOAP response before continuing. Returns an array of objects which are the "by reference" return values of the Web Service.

HttpMethodAttribute Class

As we saw in our discussion in the previous section, this class allows you to customize the classes that receive and send SOAP requests when defining the Web Service method.

Properties of the HttpMethodAttribute Class	Return Type	Description
`ParameterFormatter`	`Object`	Indicates the class to use for receiving SOAP requests. For SOAP and HTTP POST, the class should be `HtmlFormParameterWriter`. For HTTP GET, the class should be `UrlParameterWriter`.
`ReturnFormatter`	`Object`	Indicates the class to use for sending SOAP responses. For SOAP, HTTP POST, and HTTP GET, the class should be `XmlReturnReader`.

HttpPostClientProtocol Class

As detailed in the previous section, this class allows you to customize a Web Service method, and control HTTP-POST communication within a Web Service proxy created using the VS.NET `wsdl.exe` utility. An HTTP-POST communication allows the transfer of name-value pairs for arguments and simulates a typical form post.

Properties of the HttpPost ClientProtocol Class	Return Type	Description
`AllowAutoRedirect`	`Boolean`	`true` indicates to the Web Service to allow server redirects. Use `false` when sending sensitive data to the server that you want to ensure is not redirected. The default for this property is `false`.
`ClientCertificates`	`Collection`	Access to the client's collection of valid certificates for the current communication session.
`ConnectionGroupName`	`String`	Associates a communication request with a specific and unique name within your application session. Allows you to have multiple sessions for different user authentications within the same application.
`CookieContainer`	`Collection`	Contains a list of cookies associated with this communication.
`Credentials`	`Collection`	Authentication information for the remote server.

Table continued on following page

669

Properties of the HttpPost ClientProtocol Class	Return Type	Description
PreAuthenticate	Boolean	If true, the `Credentials` authentication information is sent with each request. Otherwise the server must request the credentials separately. The default is `false`.
Proxy	Object	Allows you to assign and interrogate the proxy settings for the current communication session. This property allows you to pass proxy authentication details.
RequestEncoding	Object	Character encoding used for all SOAP messages in this communication.
Timeout	Integer	Sets the timeout that the communication session will wait (in milliseconds) without a response from the server. If −1, the process will wait indefinitely.
Url	String	The SOAP server end-point. The specific server URL location that will process the SOAP request.
UserAgent	String	Name of the calling process or application allowing the server to identify the client and act accordingly. Default is `null`.

Methods of the HttpPost ClientProtocol Class	Return Type	Description
Abort	–	Attempt to stop an asynchronous communication.
BeginInvoke	Object	Starts a communication link to a remote Web Service using asynchronous invocation so the client can continue processing other tasks. Returns an `AsyncResult` object that is passed to the `EndInvoke` method.
EndInvoke	Object	Completes an asynchronous communication link with a remote Web Service. Returns an `AsyncResult` object.
GetWebRequest	Object	Returns a `WebRequest` object: the base class for handling SOAP requests. You can use instances of this class to perform customization such as adding headers.

Properties of the HttpPost ClientProtocol Class	Return Type	Description
GetWebResponse	Object	Returns a WebResponse object: the base class for handling SOAP responses. You can use instances of this class to perform customization such as adding headers.
Invoke	Array Objects	Communicates with a remote Web Service synchronously, meaning the client must wait for a SOAP response before continuing. Returns an array of objects, which are "by reference" and return values from the remote Web Service.

HttpSimpleClientProtocol Class

The HttpSimpleClientProtocol class acts as an abstract base class for other classes within the System.Web.Services.Protocols namespace. It cannot be instantiated directly.

The classes that use the HttpSimpleClientProtocol class as a base class are as follows:

- ❑ HttpGetClientProtocol class
- ❑ HttpPostClientProtocol class
- ❑ SoapHttpClientProtocol class

HttpWebClientProtocol Class

The HttpWebClientProtocol class acts as an abstract base class for other classes within the System.Web.Services.Protocols namespace. It cannot be instantiated directly.

The classes that use the HttpWebClientProtocol class as a base class are:

- ❑ HttpGetClientProtocol class
- ❑ HttpPostClientProtocol class
- ❑ SoapHttpClientProtocol class

MatchAttribute Class

Indicates the attributes or properties of a match. This class cannot be inherited.

Properties of the MatchAttribute Class	Return Type	Description
Capture	Integer	Allows you to interrogate or change the value representing the index of a match within a grouping.
Group	Object	Allows you to interrogate or change the value that represents a grouping of related matches.

Table continued on following page

Properties of the MatchAttribute Class	Return Type	Description
IgnoreCase	Boolean	Allows you to interrogate or change the value that indicates whether the pattern to match is case-insensitive.
MaxRepeats	Integer	Allows you to interrogate or change the value representing the maximum number of repeats.
Pattern	Object	Allows you to interrogate or change the Regular Expression describing the pattern to match.

SoapClientMessage Class

The SoapClientMessage class contains the SOAP Request and may be interrogated either by the client application or by the Web Service on the server. You can interrogate this class during the SoapMessageStage event. The class contains information pertaining to the SOAP message and HTTP header sent down from the client to the ASP.NET server.

Properties of the SoapClientMessage Class	Return Type	Description
Action	String	URI value giving the intent (that is, the destination for the current SOAP message). Embedded into the HTTP header for SOAP, HTTP GET, and HTTP POST. Can be used to redirect SOAP requests to the appropriate server.
Client	Object	Interrogates an instance of the proxy client class SoapHttpClientProtocol.
Exception	Object	If a SOAP exception is raised, this object contains information describing the error, otherwise it is null.
Headers	Collection	A list of all SOAP headers attached to the current SOAP message.
MethodInfo	Object	Provides access to the LogicalMethodInfo class, which holds detailed information on the current Web Service.
OneWay	Boolean	Indicates whether a Web Service client needs to wait for the server to process a given Web Service. Only valid for services that do not return any values.
Stage	SoapMessage Stage	Returns the current stage in the processing of this Web Service. Can be captured for a user-defined event handler. See the enumeration SoapMessageStage.

Properties of the SoapClientMessage Class	Return Type	Description
`Stream`		Obtains a `Stream` object that can be used to examine the SOAP Request during a `SoapMessageStage` event.
`Url`		Base location URL for the current Web Service.

Methods of the SoapClientMessage Class	Return Type	Description
`GetInParameterValue`	`Object`	Retrieves the SOAP Request parameters of the current Web Service. Use `index` to identify a particular one.
`GetOutParameterValue`	`Object`	Retrieves the SOAP Response parameters of the current Web Service. Use `index` to identify a particular one.
`GetReturnValue`	`Object`	Retrieves the SOAP return values of the current Web Service. Use `index` to identify a particular one.

SoapDocumentMethodAttribute Class

As detailed in our previous discussion, this class is used in conjunction with a Web Service to customize the nature of SOAP Requests and SOAP Responses that it deals with. Any changes made using this class will be reflected in the WSDL schema definition file produced by `wsdl.exe`.

Properties of the SoapDocument MethodAttribute Class	Return Type	Description
`Action`	`String`	URI value giving the intent (that is, the destination for the current SOAP message). Embedded into the HTTP header for SOAP, HTTP GET, and HTTP POST. Can be used to redirect SOAP requests to the appropriate server.
`Binding`	`String`	Name of the binding that is assigned to the current Web Service. You may change this name by assigning a new value using Web Service method attribute customization. This will allow you to alter the binding and introduce advanced features such as describing a new communication end-point that is not described in the WSDL schema.

Table continued on following page

Properties of the SoapDocument MethodAttribute Class	Return Type	Description
OneWay	Boolean	Indicates whether a Web Service client needs to wait for the server to process a given Web Service. Only valid for services that do not return any values.
ParameterStyle	Enum	wrapped indicates the SOAP parameters are placed within a wrapped element during transfer. bare means they are to be placed immediately beneath the body element of the SOAP message. See the ParameterStyle enumeration.
RequestElementName	String	XML element name for the Request message of the current Web Service.
RequestNamespace	String	Namespace that applies to SOAP Requests for the current Web Service.
ResponseElementName	String	XML element name for the Response message of the current Web Service.
ResponseNamespace	String	Namespace that applies to SOAP Responses for the current Web Service.
Use	Enum	Specifies the encoding for the Web Service using the SoapBindingUse enumeration in the Descriptions namespace.

SoapDocumentServiceAttribute Class

This class is used to customize SOAP Requests or SOAP Responses for a particular Web Service. Any changes made using this class will be reflected in the WSDL schema definition file produced by the WSDL.exe. Unlike the SoapDocumentMethodAttribute class, these values are set at service level using a service-level attribute. This class cannot be used at method level.

Properties of the SoapDocument ServiceAttribute Class	Return Type	Description
ParameterStyle	Enum	wrapped indicates the SOAP parameters are placed within a wrapped element during transfer. bare means they are to be placed immediately beneath the body element of the SOAP message. See the ParameterStyle enumeration.
RoutingStyle	Enum	Assign routing style as one of two values given by the enumeration SoapServiceRoutingStyle.

Properties of the SoapDocument ServiceAttribute Class	Return Type	Description
Use	Enum	Specifies the encoding for the Web Service using the `SoapBindingUse` enumeration in the `Descriptions` namespace.

SoapException Class

When an error occurs during the execution of a Web Service over SOAP, the `SoapException` class can provide the associated error information. This class is populated by the server when returning a SOAP Fault.

Properties of the SoapExceptionClass	Return Type	Description
Actor	String	The ASP.NET client code that caused the exception. The value is that assigned to the `Actor` of the `SoapMessage` during the initial WSDL processing.
Code	Object	Fault code element from the returned fault message. See the *Valid Fault Codes for SoapException.Code Property* table below for the currently supported values. `XmlNamespace` object.
Detail	String	Fault `Detail` element of the SOAP Fault.
OtherElements	Array	Returns an array of XML nodes that were passed back in the Soap Fault error message. Enables the Web Service or client to pass additional information about the error that occurred.
ClientFaultCode	Object	Specifies a SOAP fault code for a badly formatted or incomplete client call.
DetailElementName	Object	An XML Qualified Name representing the `Detail` element of a SOAP Fault
MustUnderstandFaultCode	Object	A SOAP Fault code indicating a SOAP element marked with the `MustUnderstand` attribute was not processed.
ServerFaultCode	Object	A SOAP Fault code for an error that occurred during the processing of a client call by the server, where the problem was not due to the message contents.
VersionMismatchFaultCode	Object	A SOAP fault code indicating that an invalid namespace for a SOAP Envelope was found during the processing of a SOAP message.

Valid Fault Codes for SoapException.Code Property	Return Type	Description
VersionMismatchFaultCode	Object	The SOAP envelope contains an invalid namespace. XmlNamespace object.
MustUnderstandFaultCode	Object	You can assign a MustUnderstand attribute to SOAP elements such as headers. This fault code is produced if a MustUnderstand attribute was set to 1, and the server or client recipient did not know how to process that particular element. XmlNamespace object.
ClientFaultCode	String	An error occurred during processing the SOAP message while at the client. XmlNamespace object.
ServerFaultCode	String	An error occurred during processing the SOAP message while at the server. XmlNamespace object.

SoapExtension Class

As we saw in more detail in our previous section, this class allows you to extend the processing power of your Web Service or client by trapping one of four events in the lifecycle of the SOAP message.

- ❑ BeforeSerialize
- ❑ AfterSerialize
- ❑ BeforeDeserialize
- ❑ AfterDeserialize

Your code can then react to each event by firing a user-defined handler to change the SOAP message or environment to suit your particular needs.

Methods of the SoapExtension Class	Return Type	Description
ChainStream	Object	Returns a copy of a Stream object containing the SOAP message– either a SOAP Request or SOAP Response
GetInitializer	Object	Caches any data required for this SoapExtension
Initialize	Object	Initializes this SoapExtension
ProcessMessage	Object	Processed when each of the four events is triggered

SoapExtensionAttribute Class

This class lets you assign a `SoapExtensionAttribute` to a specific Web Service. This enables the `SoapMessageStage` events to work.

Properties of the SoapExtensionAttribute Class	Return Type	Description
ExtensionType	Object	Type of the extension class
Priority	Integer	Priority of this `SoapExtension` over other `SoapExtensions` assigned to a given Web Service

SoapHeader Class

The `SoapHeader` class allows you to pass extra information to the Web Service not directly related to the SOAP message parameters. This allows for performing specialist tasks such as user authorization, or defining particular transaction requirements.

Properties of the SoapHeader Class	Return Type	Description
Actor	String	The name of the recipient of the header. If the recipient is the current Web Service but the message needs to be passed on to the next server then the header specific to the current Web Service should be stripped out. Also if the intended recipient is not the current Web Service server then the header should be ignored.
DidUnderstand	Boolean	If true then the intended recipient has already processed and understood this SOAP header.
EncodeMustUnderstand	String	The intended recipient must understand the encoding used by this header.
MustUnderstand	Boolean	The intended recipient must understand this header. If it does not understand, it **must** raise a `SoapException`.

SoapHeaderAttribute Class

As we saw in our more detailed examination previously, this class allows the customization of a Web Service by adding SOAP header information. The attribute is applied to the Web Service at design time, and is reflected in the actual WSDL schema file created. This class cannot be inherited.

Properties of the SoapHeaderAttribute Class	Return Type	Description
Direction	Enum	Using the SoapHeaderDirection enumeration, you can define who the header is intended for; namely the client, server, or both.
MemberName	String	Name of the SOAP Header contents. The default is an empty string.
Required	Boolean	Sets the MustUnderstand attribute on the Soap Header at design time for the Web Service.

SoapHeaderException Class

This class is used for exceptions thrown when a Web Service method is called over SOAP, and an error occurs during processing the SOAP header.

Properties of the SoapHeaderException Class	Return Type	Description
Actor	Enum	The name of the recipient of the header.
Code	Object	Error code created during the SOAP error handling. XmlNamespace object.
Detail	Object	Detailed text describing the SOAP error. XmlNode object.
OtherElements	Collection	Any additional information pertaining to the error. Array of XmlNode objects.

SoapHttpClientProtocol Class

As discussed previously, this class allows you to customize a Web Service method, and control HTTP communication within a Web Service proxy created using the .NET SDK `wsdl.exe` utility.

Properties of the SoapHttpClientProtocol Class	Return Type	Description
AllowAutoRedirect	Boolean	`true` indicates to the Web Service to allow server redirects. Use `false` when sending sensitive data to the server that you want to ensure is not redirected. The default for this property is `false`.
ClientCertificates	Collection	Access to the ASP.NET client's collection of valid certificates for the current communication session.
ConnectionGroupName	String	Associate a communication request with a specific and unique name within your application session. Allows you to have multiple sessions for different user authentications within the same application.
CookieContainer	Collection	Contains a list of cookies associated with this communication.
Credentials	Collection	Authentication information for the remote server.
PreAuthenticate	Boolean	If `true`, the `Credentials` authentication information is sent with each request. Otherwise the server must request the credentials separately. The default is `false`.
Proxy	Object	Allows you to assign and interrogate the proxy settings for the current communication session. This property allows you to pass proxy authentication details.
RequestEncoding	Object	The character encoding to use for all SOAP messages in this communication.
Timeout	Integer	Sets the timeout that the communication session will wait (in milliseconds) without a response from the server. If −1 the process will wait indefinitely.

Table continued on following page

679

Properties of the SoapHttpClientProtocol Class	Return Type	Description
Url	String	The SOAP server end-point that will process the SOAP request.
UserAgent	String	Name of the calling process or application allowing the server to identify the client and act accordingly. Default is null.

Methods of the SoapHttpClientProtocol Class	Return Type	Description
Abort	-	Attempts to stop an asynchronous communication.
BeginInvoke	Object	Starts a communication link to a remote Web Service using asynchronous invocation so the client can continue processing other tasks. Returns an AsyncResult object which is passed to the EndInvoke method.

Methods of the SoapHttpClientProtocol Class	Return Type	Description
EndInvoke	Object	Completes an asynchronous communication operation with a remote Web Service. Returns an AsyncResult object.
GetWebRequest	Object	Returns a WebRequest object: the base class for handling SOAP Requests. You can use instances of this class to perform customization such as adding headers.
GetWebResponse	Object	Returns a WebResponse object: the base class for handling SOAP Responses. You can use instances of this class to perform customization such as adding headers.
Invoke	Array Objects	Communicates with a remote Web Service synchronously, meaning the client must wait for a SOAP response before continuing. Returns an array of objects, which are the "by reference" return values of the Web Service.

SoapMessage Class

`SoapMessage` is as an abstract base class for a number of other classes within the `System.Web.Services.Protocols` namespace, and may not be instantiated directly.

The classes that use the `SoapMessage` class as a base class are:

❑ `SoapServerMessage`

❑ `SoapClientMessage`

SoapRpcMethodAttribute Class

This class allows you to alter the style by which a SOAP Request or Response encodes and formats parameters. This class defines the requirement to use RPC methods to encode a message. RPC style refers to encoding the Web Service method according to the SOAP specification for using SOAP for RPC; otherwise known as Section 7 of the SOAP specification.

Properties of the SoapRpcMethodAttribute Class	Return Type	Description
Action	String	URI value giving the intent (that is, the destination for the current SOAP message). Embedded into the HTTP header for SOAP, HTTP GET, and HTTP POST. Can be used to redirect SOAP requests to the appropriate server.
Binding	String	Name of the binding assigned to the current Web Service. You may change this name by assigning a new value using Web Service method definition customization.
OneWay	Boolean	Indicates whether a Web Service client needs to wait for the server to process a given Web Service. Only valid for services that do not return any values.
RequestElementName	String	Element name for the Request message for the current Web Service.
RequestNamespace	String	Namespace for the Request message for the current Web Service.
ResponseElementName	String	Element name for the Response message for the current Web Service.
ResponseNamespace	String	Namespace for the Response message for the current Web Service.

SoapRpcServiceAttribute Class

This class allows you to set encoding method to RPC for all Web Service methods within a specific class.

Properties of the SoapRpcServiceAttribute Class	Return Type	Description
RoutingStyle	Enum	Assign routing style as one of two values given by the enumeration SoapServiceRoutingStyle.

SoapServerMessage Class

This class is used during a SoapMessageStage event to interrogate the Web Service call during each of its processing stages.

- ❑ BeforeSerialize
- ❑ AfterSerialize
- ❑ BeforeDeserialize
- ❑ AfterDeserialize

This allows for manipulation, logging, or even amendment of any part of the process according to the needs of a particular situation.

Properties of the SoapServerMessage Class	Return Type	Description
Action	String	URI value giving the intent (that is, the destination for the current SOAP message). Embedded into the HTTP header for SOAP, HTTP GET, and HTTP POST. Can be used to redirect SOAP requests to the appropriate server.
ContentType	String	Describes the MIME category and sub-type of the current SOAP message, text/xml by default.
Exception	Object	If a SOAP exception is raised, this contains information describing that error, otherwise this property returns null.
Headers	Collection	A list of all SOAP headers attached to the current SOAP message.
MethodInfo	Object	Access to the LogicalMethodInfo class, which carries detailed information about the Web Service.

Properties of the SoapServerMessage Class	Return Type	Description
OneWay	Boolean	Indicates whether a Web Service client needs to wait for the server to process a given Web Service. Only valid for services that do not return any values.
Server	Object	Instance of the class implementing this Web Service.
Stage	SoapMessageStage Enum	Returns the current stage in the processing of this Web Service. Can be captured for a user-defined event handler. See the enumeration SoapMessageStage.
Stream	Object	Obtains a Stream object that can be used to examine the SOAP Request during a SoapMessageStage event.
Url	String	Base location URL for the current Web Service.

Methods of the SoapServerMessage Class	Return Type	Description
GetInParameterValue	Object	Retrieves the value of parameters in the SOAP Request for the current Web Service. Use index to specify a particular one.
GetOutParameterValue	Object	Retrieves the value of parameters in the SOAP Response for the current Web Service. Use index to specify a particular one.
GetReturnValue	Object	Retrieves the SOAP return value of the current Web Service. Use index to specify a particular one.

SoapUnknownHeader Class

This class allows you to interrogate headers that were transferred as part of the SOAP message, but whose structure was not known by the client or Web Service.

Properties of the SoapUnknownHeader Class	Return Type	Description
Actor	String	Sets the intended recipient of this header. This is not necessarily the server receiving the message; it may be another SOAP server that contains the Web Service in question.
DidUnderstand	Boolean	Set to `true` when the current ASP.NET process understood and was able to process the SOAP header. If set to `false`, a `SoapHeaderException` is thrown.
Element	Object	Allows interrogation and amendment of a SOAP header using an XML definition class.
EncodedMustUnderstand	Boolean	Specifies that the encoding attribute of this header must be understood.
MustUnderstand	Boolean	Specifies that this header must be understood by the intended recipient.

UrlParameterWriter Class

The `HttpMethodAttribute` makes use of this class to indicate the transmission method for SOAP messages when HTTP is used for communication. It is typically used when sending SOAP messages via HTTP GET.

The class that uses the `UrlParameterWriter` class is:

❑   `HttpMethodAttribute.ReturnFormatter`

Methods of the UrlParameterWriter Class	Return Type	Description
GetRequestUrl		

WebClientAsyncResult Class

Properties of the WebClientAsyncResult Class	Return Type	Description
AsyncState	Object	Holds useful information about the client responsible for the asynchronous SOAP Request.
AsyncWaitHandle	Object	Has a couple of wait methods, which are handy if you want to wait for Web Service calls to return. You can use it right after making a BeginXXX call.
Completed Synchronously	Boolean	Returns true if the BeginInvoke method has completed. Note that in Beta 1 and Beta 2, this property always returns false.
IsCompleted	Boolean	Returns true if processing has completed; also indicates that the client can now destroy any associated instantiated objects.

Methods of the WebClientAsyncResult Class	Return Type	Description
Abort	–	Stops the currently executing SOAP request.

WebClientProtocol Class

This class acts as an abstract base class for all ASP.NET Web Services using SOAP, HTTP POST, or HTTP GET. It contains the fundamental properties required for all currently supported transports.

The classes that use WebClientProtocol as a base class are:

❑ HttpGetClientProtocol

❑ HttpPostClientProtocol

Properties of the WebClientProtocol Class	Return Type	Description
ConnectionGroupName	String	Associates a communication request with a specific and unique name within an application session.
Credentials	Object	Contains authentication information to identify the client for a SOAP request.
PreAuthenticate	Boolean	If true, the Credentials authentication information is sent with each request. Otherwise the server must request the credentials separately. The default is false.
RequestEncoding	Object	The character encoding to use for all SOAP Requests in this communication.
Timeout	Integer	Synchronous timeout value. Note that the default is -1, which means wait indefinitely.
Url	String	Location of the end-point listener server.

Methods of the WebClientProtocol Class	Return Type	Description
Abort	–	Halts the currently executing SOAP request

XmlReturnReader Class

This class is employed by HttpMethodAttribute to provide methods to serialize messages being sent from the client to the Web Service. Used when sending SOAP messages via HTTP POST or HTTP GET.

The class that uses XmlReturnReader is:

❑   HttpMethodAttribute.ParameterFormatter

Methods of the XmlReturnReader Class	Return Type	Description
Read		

A typical SOAP Header will look something like this:

```
<?xml version="1.0" encoding="utf-8"?>
<soap:Envelope xmlns:xsi="http://www.w3.org/2001/XMLSchema-instance"
               xmlns:xsd="http://www.w3.org/2001/XMLSchema"
               xmlns:soap="http://schemas.xmlsoap.org/soap/envelope/" >
  <soap:Header>
    <MyHeader xmlns="http://www.contoso.com">
      <Username>Admin</Username>
      <Password>MyPassword</Password>
    </MyHeader>
  </soap:Header>
</soap:Header>
```

To learn more about SOAP you might want to some of these links:

http://www.w3.org/TR/SOAP
http://www.xml.apache.org/soap
http://msdn.microsoft.com/soap/default.asp
http://discuss.develop.com/soap.html
http://www.develop.com/soap/soapfaq.htm
http://www.w3.org/2000/xp

So up until this point in the chapter we have looked at the various methods and properties that are available in the System.Web.Services.Protocols namespace. To finish off this section we will look at the various enumerations that the namespace also exposes.

System.Web.Services.Protocols Enumerations

LogicalMethodTypes

This enumeration specifies the method by which the current Web Service was invoked.

Applies to the following member of the `System.Web.Services.Protocols` namespace:

❑ `LogicalMethodInfo`

Member Name	Description	Value
Sync	The current Web Service was invoked synchronously	1
Async	The current Web Service was invoked asynchronously	2

SoapHeaderDirection

This enumeration specifies the intended recipient of the attached `SoapHeader`.

Applies to the following member of the `System.Web.Services.Protocols` namespace:

❑ `SoapHeaderAttribute`

Member Name	Description	Value
In	The intended recipient for this header is the Web Service. The client should therefore ignore this header.	1
Out	The intended recipient for this header is the client. The Web Service should therefore ignore this header.	2
InOut	The current header contains information that is required by both Web Service and client.	3

SoapMessageStage

On trapping an event during the processing of a SOAP message, this enumeration determines the stage that the current SOAP message has reached.

The meaning of the enumeration depends on whether the event was trapped on the server or client, and therefore the table below contains two descriptions for each value.

Applies to the following members of the `System.Web.Services.Protocols` namespace:

❑ `SoapClientMessage`
❑ `SoapServerMessage`
❑ `SoapMessage`

Member Name	Description	Value
BeforeSerialize	CLIENT: Occurs after a client calls a Web Service, but before the SOAP request has been serialized. SERVER: Occurs after the Web Service returns results, but before the SOAP response has been serialized.	1
AfterSerialize	CLIENT: Occurs after a client call to a Web Service is serialized, but before sending the SOAP request to the server. SERVER: Occurs after the results from a Web Service are serialized, but before sending the SOAP response to the client.	2
BeforeDeserialize	CLIENT: Occurs after the network response for a Web Service has been received, but before the SOAP response has been de-serialized. SERVER: Occurs after a network request for a Web Service is received, but before the SOAP request has been de-serialized.	4
AfterDeserialize	CLIENT: Occurs after the network response for a Web Service has been de-serialized, but before the client receives the results. SERVER: Occurs after a network request for a Web Service has been de-serialized, but before the Web Service has been called.	8

SoapParameterStyle

Indicates the position of SOAP parameters during transfer. Using this enumeration, you can fine-tune exactly where the parameters for SOAP Requests and Responses are to be contained.

Applies to the following members of the System.Web.Services.Protocols namespace:

- ❑ SoapDocumentServiceAttribute
- ❑ SoapDocumentMethodAttribute
- ❑ SoapRpcServiceAttribute
- ❑ SoapRpcMethodAttribute

Member Name	Description	Value
Default	Indicates the default value for the Web Service. The default will either be `Wrapped`, or the value declared by `SoapDocumentServiceAttribute` if any.	0
Bare	The Web Service method parameters are not wrapped by a container element, and instead appear unadorned directly after the Body element of SOAP Requests and Responses.	1
Wrapped	The Web Service parameters will be wrapped within container elements, which are in turn held inside the SOAP Body element.	2

SoapServiceRoutingStyle

Applies to the following members of the `System.Web.Services.Protocols` namespace:

❑ `SoapRpcServiceAttribute`

❑ `SoapDocumentServiceAttribute`

Member Name	Value
RequestElement	1
SoapAction	0

Web Service Discovery

Web Service Discovery is a term given to the promotion and location of Web Services that are available on SOAP-compliant servers. The term is not restricted to ASP.NET and the Discovery standard has been publicized on the Internet to allow others to adopt it.

There are currently, however, only two industry adoptions of this standard, the first is UDDI; the industry-recognized directory service, the second is **www.salcentral.com**, a widely used Web Services search engine that creates DISCO files dynamically. As the Web Services industry starts to mature we would expect to see more appearing.

Web Service Discovery is the process of locating and interrogating Web Service definitions, which is a preliminary step for accessing a Web Service. It is through this discovery process that Web Service clients learn that a Web Service exists, what its capabilities are, and how to properly interact with it.

Discovery is performed by the creation of an XML file with a `.disco` extension (in the case of ASP.NET) at the time the Web Service project is built. It is not compulsory to create a discovery file for each Web Service, as you may simply want your Web Service to be for your organization's own internal use. In that particular case you can simply supply the location of the WSDL schema to people in your organization who will use it.

The term "Web Service Discovery" is often referred to as simply **DISCO**.

The DISCO standard is based around a strictly defined, XML-structured file that is available for Web Service clients to read to ascertain what Web Services are available. In the case of ASP.NET this file is created at run time by the `.asmx` file for a specific Web Service project. However, this is not a requirement and in fact you can create your own `.disco` file independently of the `.asmx` file that can be placed on IIS or another Internet server.

This XML `.disco` file uses its own internal attributes and elements to supply a Web Service client with information as to the location of Web Services that may be available on your server.

An example of an XML structured `.disco` file is shown below:

```
<?xml version="1.0" encoding="utf-8"?>
<discovery xmlns="http://schemas.xmlsoap.org/disco/">
  <contractRef ref="http://localhost/webservice1/service1.asmx?wsdl"
               docRef="http://localhost/webservice1/service1.asmx"
               xmlns="http://schemas.xmlsoap.org/disco/scl/" />
  <soap address="http://localhost/webservice1/service1.asmx"
               xmlns:q1="http://tempuri.org/" binding="q1:Service1Soap"
               xmlns="http://schemas.xmlsoap.org/disco/soap/" />
</discovery>
```

This simple XML file can be viewed and interrogated to identify the location of the WSDL schema files. These WSDL files describe the methods and arguments that a specific Web Service has available for a remote Web Service client to consume.

There is one `.disco` file for every ASP.NET Web Service `.asmx` file. However, `.disco` files can in fact point to other `.disco` files (more about this later) to allow for multiple Web Service promotion.

The location of this `.disco` file can be publicly advertised to a dynamic search engine (UDDI), or specialist environment (**www.salcentral.com**) that can openly use it to advertise the location of your Web Service. It can also be used within the '**Add Web Reference**' menu option in Visual Studio.NET to allow others to add your Web Services directly into their project (more about this later).

Whenever you build a Web Service, ASP.NET automatically generates a discovery file. The creation of a Web Service does not require the creation of a `.disco` file, so when consuming other organization's Web Services that have not been written in ASP.NET, it will most likely not be available. This does not mean that the creation of `.disco` files is peculiar to ASP.NET. It does however mean that ASP.NET is currently the only large-scale product that supports `.disco` files.

Displaying a Disco File

The discovery of Web Services is accomplished by making available to interested parties an XML file that adheres to the DISCO standard (more about the details of this standard later). To display the `.disco` file for your ASP.NET Web Service you simply need to append the words `?disco` to the end of your `.asmx` address line.

For example, create a basic VS.NET Web Service project and uncomment the `HelloWorld` example that is included within the `.asmx` file code. Then run the project. Once the HTML browser displays the `.asmx` file, on the address line simply change it from:

```
http://localhost/SoapHeaderServer/service1.asmx
```

to:

```
http://localhost/SoapHeaderServer/service1.asmx?disco
```

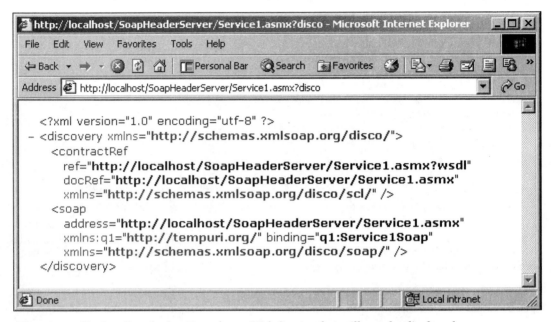

The disco file describes the location of your Web Service that will now be displayed.

The .disco file does not need to reside on the server where the Web Service is located; you can in fact create your own .disco file and place it on any Internet server. ASP.NET however generates the .disco file dynamically when you run the .asmx file, therefore by default it is always situated in the same location as the .asmx file.

Disco File Structure

A .disco file format can be split into five main constituent parts:

- ❑ Header (discovery element)
- ❑ Contract (contractRef element)
- ❑ Discovery (discoveryRef element)
- ❑ Schema (schemaRef element)
- ❑ SOAP message (soap element)

In the following sections we'll describe the attributes and structure for each of these.

```
<?xml version="1.0" encoding="utf-8"?>
<discovery xmlns="http://schemas.xmlsoap.org/disco/">
  <contractRef ... />
  <discoveryRef ... />
  <schemaRef ... />
  <soap ... />
</discovery>
```

Please note that all file locations referenced from within the `.disco` file can be either fully specified or relative; if relative then paths are always relative to the location of where the `.disco` file is described.

Header

This section is mandatory and defines the XML header along with all relevant namespaces. You will always see the `discovery` namespace in this file, which is the same for every `.disco` file and simply states that this file adheres to the DISCO XML structure:

```
<?xml version="1.0" encoding="utf-8"?>
<discovery xmlns="http://schemas.xmlsoap.org/disco/">
```

You may also add the `scl` namespace to the header. This allows you to state it only once within the `.disco` file instead of having to declare it on every `<contractref>` line. This namespace states that this file contains WSDL contract information that complies with the Service Contract Language structure. The SCL structure indicates that this file contains `<contractref>` elements that can be used to locate a WSDL schema definition. The following is an example of a header that includes the `scl` namespace:

```
<?xml version="1.0" encoding="utf-8"?>
<discovery xmlns:disco="http://schemas.xmlsoap.org/disco/"
           xmlns:sclns="http://schemas.xmlsoap.org/disco/scl">
```

If the `scl` namespace is used in the header, then the namespace, defined above as `sclns` (any name can be used), must prefix the `contract` elements within the `.disco` file. For example using the above header would mean that the `contractRef` elements would be prefixed as follows:

```
<sclns:contractRef ref="http://localhost/webservice1/service1.asmx?wsdl"
                   docRef="http://localhost/webservice1/service1.asmx" />
```

In addition to the `scl` namespace the following namespaces are also valid:

```
xmlns:soap="http://schemas.xmlsoap.org/wsdl/soap/"
xmlns:schema="http://www.w3.org/2000/10/XMLSchema"
```

If a Web Service client reads and does not understand the namespaces provided within the DISCO XML header then it means that there is some content within the `.disco` file that it also will not understand, and therefore it should discontinue reading and interpreting the rest of the `.disco` file. This would cause an exception to be raised on the client.

Please note that in the example below for the `contract` section the `scl` reference is placed within the `contractRef` element, which is also acceptable. If used, however, then the above header need not include a reference to that namespace.

Contract

A contract defines the location of a WSDL schema, but in addition a contract can optionally also include references to help or to any description document. The help document link generated for ASP.NET points to the `.asmx` file.

The `contract` section is located on the `contractRef` element line. An example of the `contractRef` line is shown overleaf:

```
<contractRef ref="http://localhost/webservice1/service1.asmx?wsdl"
             docRef="http://localhost/webservice1/service1.asmx"
             xmlns="http://schemas.xmlsoap.org/disco/scl/" />
```

This element contains the location information for the WSDL schema file within the `ref` XML attribute. The WSDL schema file describes the Web Service methods, arguments and the Web Service's server location. Please note that appending the `?wsdl` parameter to the end of the `.asmx` file location will always display the WSDL schema file:

```
ref="http://localhost/webservice1/service1.asmx?wsdl"
```

The `<contractRef>` element also contains the `docRef` attribute, which identifies the location of an associated page, which can contain any HTML browser-readable text:

```
docRef="http://localhost/webservice1/service1.asmx"
```

This text can constitute (but is not limited to) any of the following subjects:

- ❑ Help
- ❑ Testing tools (for example `.asmx` file)
- ❑ Service-level agreement
- ❑ Company information

In the case of a Web Service project for ASP.NET this attribute contains the location of the `.asmx` browsing page which allows you to test a Web Service using a web browser front end.

You can specify multiple `contractRef` elements within one `.disco` file.

It's worth noting that it is not just WSDL schema files that can be identified within this element. The WSDL file type is **the only** currently supported use of the `contractRef` element that the `http://schemas.xmlsoap.org/disco/scl/` namespace identifies. However, you can also refer to other file types defined by other standards which, if implemented, would simply mean changing the namespace to suit the definition being used.

Discovery

The `discovery` section allows you to put the icing on the cake. You can use this mechanism to point to other `.disco` files either on other servers or within your own organization. Its worth noting that the main (but not the only) use for this linking of `.disco` files is that it allows a search engine to browse through Web Services using a tree-like structure, discovering Web Services as it goes, and using this information to populate its search database.

The repercussions of this service are astounding, as it becomes apparent that it reproduces peer-to-peer technology. It provides the ability to connect together vast numbers of Web Services, in a similar manner to how you link web pages together. This simple addition to the DISCO standard definition in fact substantially increases the power of `.disco` file discovery.

An example of a discovery element is shown below:

```
<discoveryRef ref="http://localhost/anotherwebservice/service1.asmx?disco" />
```

You can specify multiple `discoveryRef` elements within one `.disco` file. The file linked to **must** be another DISCO XML file. The location of the file specified can be specific or relative.

Schema

The `<schemaRef>` element allows you to attach an XML schema to the `.disco` file. This allows extra information to be encapsulated within the `.disco` file to describe the Web Service:

```
<schema:schemaRef ref="http://localhost/webservice1/xmlschema.xml" />
```

An example of the use for this link would be an XML file that contained elements that described the service, named the service, supplied keywords for the service, and supplied examples for the service. This would, for instance, give a Web Service search engine extra information it could display to its users.

SOAP

The `<soapRef>` element reproduces a portion of the binding information found within a WSDL schema. It does this to allow a Web Service client to locate a service using lightweight information. Therefore, rather than having to load the WSDL schema file every time it needs to find the relevant information, it uses this summary information to identify the contents of a specific WSDL file.

An example of a `<soapRef>` element is shown below:

```
<soap:soapRef binding="s0:Service1Soap"
               address="http://localhost/webservice1/service1.asmx" />
```

Binding information is used to locate a specific Web Service.

Multiple Web Services

As mentioned in the above description of the `<contractRef>` element in the `.disco` file, this element can be placed in a `.disco` file multiple times. However, in contradiction to this fact, you may have noticed that you actually produce a `.disco` file by running the associated `.asmx` file, and that an `.asmx` file is directly correlated to a single Web Service schema.

This is where the `.vsdisco` file comes in. This VS.NET-specific file is either automatically produced by the ASP.NET Web Service application within your project, or can be created manually and placed on any server. When you browse to it, it lists **all** Web Services within the current project. The following is an example of a valid URL for a `.vsdisco` file.

```
http://localhost/webservice1/webservice1.vsdisco
```

To test this out, simply create two Web Service classes within the same ASP.NET Web Services project, (they do not have to contain any code), then run the project. Browse to the above URL and you will now see two `contractRef` elements, each one defining one of the classes:

```
<?xml version="1.0" encoding="utf-8"?>
<discovery xmlns="http://schemas.xmlsoap.org/disco/">
  <contractRef ref="http://localhost/Discovery/Service1.asmx?wsdl"
             docRef="http://localhost/Discovery/Service1.asmx"
             xmlns="http://schemas.xmlsoap.org/disco/scl/" />
  <contractRef ref="http://localhost/Discovery/Service2.asmx?wsdl"
```

```
               docRef="http://localhost/Discovery/Service2.asmx"
               xmlns="http://schemas.xmlsoap.org/disco/scl/" />
</discovery>
```

This `.vsdisco` file is important for two reasons. First it allows you to attach multiple Web Services to the same project and have them promoted either individually or with the aid of the `.vsdisco` file as a group of classes. Second it enables you to package together groups of functionality into a common project and release them all together for clients to consume.

Add Web Reference

Now for one of the great reasons why we should know what our `.disco` file is doing. Within ASP.NET we can consume someone else's Web Service by adding it directly into our ASP.NET project. This is done using the 'Add Web Reference' menu option from within VS.NET. You can access this option by doing the following steps:

1. Create a new client project

2. Click on the 'References' icon in your project

3. Right-click your mouse

4. Select 'Add Web Reference'

Using the Web Service project that you created earlier, browse to your Web Service by typing in the URL of your `.asmx` file, for example:

```
http://localhost/WebService1/Service1.asmx
```

Once the page is loaded you'll notice that the 'Add Reference' button has now become enabled. You can now click it and add your Web Service directly into your client project. The key question here is how does the 'Add Reference' button know that you have identified a Web Service?

It can all be revealed by looking at the source for your .asmx file. To view the source for your .asmx file click on the page within the above screen, then right-click your mouse, and choose 'View Source'. You will then be able to see the following link in the HTML header:

```
<link rel="alternate" type="text/xml" href="Service1.asmx?disco"/>
```

This identifies to the 'Add Web Reference' browser that there is an associated .disco file for this page, so when it loads your .asmx file it also looks for the location of the above HTML tag, and if it is found, the 'Add Web Reference' browser also reads and interprets the associated .disco file. Then, if a <contractRef> link exists (or even multiple <contractRef> elements), it enables the 'Add Reference' button.

This inbuilt facility is actually a designated use for the .disco file. However, at the moment only ASP.NET and www.salcentral.com support this function. In addition the .disco file is not the only way to add a web reference. You can also browse to the .wsdl file, which gives you the same effect of enabling the 'Add Reference' button. This gives you the ability to use WSDL schemas from other platforms and other SOAP servers.

It should be noted that in some cases, because the above project contains two Web Services, you may require that a customer consuming your Web Service adds both Web Services to their project to allow the application to work. Instead of browsing to the .asmx file for each Web Service, browse to the associated .vsdisco file using the 'Add Web Reference' menu option described above. This now displays the following screen:

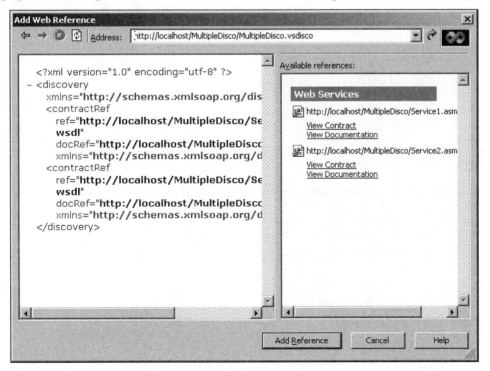

As you can see, there are now two `<contractRef>` element entries on the left of the screen, and when you press the 'Add Reference' button both are added to your project.

Customizing Disco

It seems that even though the `.disco` file is created by ASP.NET automatically, there is considerable flexibility for creating your own `.disco` file. This could be designed to group together related Web Services instead of simply one or two.

For example, say if you created three Web Services all separate from each other, offering your customers independent functionality. You want, however, to promote all of these Web Services together as a group. To do this simply create a `.disco` file with multiple `<contractRef>` elements and give this `.disco` file to your customer, who can subsequently browse to it from within their ASP.NET application. This `.disco` file can actually be placed anywhere so long as it is accessible remotely by the customer. For example, you could set up multiple `.disco` files, each one for a specific software package, each package containing links to multiple WSDL schemas.

One other benefit that this type of distribution gives you is reuse. It's now very simple to develop a component and reuse it within another application if it is a Web Service. There's now very little trying to get it to fit, you simply include the WSDL schema within your `.disco` file and your generic component always gets included with that application.

Customize 'Add Web Reference'

When you run the 'Add Web Reference' menu item (mentioned previously), the search engines you see listed are actually links to the UDDI registry using nothing more than a simple HTML browser. In fact, if you view the properties for the left browsing page (click your mouse on the left browser window and then right click and choose Properties) you will see that the home page is actually a standard HTML-formatted file called `HelpWatermark.htm` sitting on your local hard drive.

You can change `HelpWatermark.htm` yourself as easy as you change any other HTML page. This can allow you to either add additional search engines that support `.disco` (www.salcentral.com) files or add additional services that are peculiar to your own company's requirement, such as contact information or a list of in-house Web Services.

By making this customized `HelpWatermark.htm` file available to the rest of your company you can effectively roll out lists of your own in-house Web Services so that you can more easily share development between departments.

To share Web Services between departments would mean simply linking from your `HelpWatermark.htm` to a simple HTML file that contains a list of descriptions and links to each WSDL schema. If a developer wanted to use a Web Service they would simply decide by reading the text and then browse to a WSDL schema, which immediately activates the 'Add Reference' button at the bottom of the browser window.

UDDI

The Universal Description, Discovery and Integration project (UDDI) serves as a platform-independent database that contains information on the location and category of businesses and Web Services. This allows you to more easily find business partners or suppliers and also locate and consume Web Services.

The interface to UDDI is itself a Web Service. As with any Web Service it has a SOAP interface, which can be used to send messages to a SOAP server to search or edit the UDDI registry. It also has a WSDL schema definition, which defines its Web Service.

The UDDI WSDL Schema is split into two distinct functionality definition files:

❑ **Searching** – locating businesses and Web Services (http://www.uddi.org/wsdl/inquire_v1.wsdl).

❑ **Publishing** – adding, updating, and removing businesses and Web Services (http://www.uddi.org/wsdl/publish_v1.wsdl).

It should be noted that, as of the time of going to press, the above WSDL schema specifications are not supported from within ASP.NET by browsing to the schemas using the above mentioned 'Add Web Reference' menu option. This, however, may well be rectified in a future (non-beta) version of ASP.NET.

Both of these files contain a link to the following XML data type definition file:

http://www.uddi.org/schema/2001/uddi_v1.xsd

The UDDI registry is not run by Microsoft alone. IBM and Ariba are also controlling repositories for UDDI. This means that if you post information with one, it is replicated on all. The following are the server end-points for each of these organizations (the end-points described are purely for UDDI enquiries). The publishing end-points will be alternative server locations and are usually HTTPS secure transmissions.

❑ Microsoft enquiry server – http://uddi.microsoft.com/inquire

❑ Ariba enquiry server – http://uddi.ariba.com/UDDIProcessor.aw/ad/process

❑ IBM enquiry server – http://www-3.ibm.com/services/uddi/inquiryapi

There are currently two methods of searching or updating the UDDI registry, as outlined below:

❑ **Construct your own SOAP message** and send it using a TCP/IP communication to the correct server. This is certainly the most complex and means that you require a significant understanding both about the SOAP message and also of how the UDDI registry is structured.

❑ **Use the Microsoft UDDI SDK**. This SDK hides the creation of SOAP messages from the developer by wrapping them in a COM interface. A COM and VS.NET version is available at the following location: http://uddi.microsoft.com/developer/default.aspx.

Why have UDDI? Well one argument for UDDI is that if you have a central repository that all organizations can collaborate in populating, it has similar functionality to a phone book, in that you can find and locate organizations either in your area or in a specific category that you are interested in. At the moment we can trawl through vast quantities of Internet pages looking for that specific supplier. It certainly seems more sensible to simply search for a specific supplier (a supplier of tape backups for example) in your area (Washington for example). The UDDI registry helps you accomplish this.

Construct Your Own SOAP

On first inspecting the XML structure defined in the WSDL schema, it looks vague and difficult to understand. Learning a few simple concepts will allow you to greatly improve your understanding of the technical side of how UDDI works.

First of all, both of the above functionality files, "Searching" and "Publishing", contain definitions for the methods that are available for you to call using a SOAP message. They also outline the expected response. The following XML extract from the "Searching" WSDL schema outlines the methods used if you wish to find a business within UDDI:

```
<operation name="find_business">
  <soap:operation soapAction="" style="document" />
  <input message="tns:find_business">
    <soap:body use="literal" parts="body" namespace="urn:uddi-org:api" />
  </input>
  <output message="tns:businessDetail">
    <soap:body use="literal" parts="body" namespace="urn:uddi-org:api" />
  </output>
  <fault name="error" message="tns:dispositionReport">
    <soap:fault name="error" use="literal" />
  </fault>
</operation>
```

The above XML sits inside the `<binding>` element within the "Searching" schema.

This XML extract refers to the `find_business` and the `businessDetail` message. If you perform a text search within that same WSDL schema you will see the following two sections (they will not necessarily be situated together):

`find_business` message:

```
<message name="find_business">
  <part name="body" element="uddi:find_business" />
</message>
```

`businessDetail` message:

```
<message name="businessDetail">
  <part name="body" element="uddi:businessDetail" />
</message>
```

Both of these message definitions refer to the `uddi` namespace and athey refer to data types of `find_business` and `businessDetail` respectivley. Note that the data type names do not have to be the same as the message name, it's simply the naming convention that UDDI has used.

So far the above definitions have already described how the SOAP message will search, and below is an example of the expected SOAP envelope:

```
<?xml version='1.0' encoding='UTF-8'?>
<Envelope xmlns='http://schemas.xmlsoap.org/soap/envelope/'>
<Body>...</Body>
</Envelope>
```

Glancing through the WSDL schema you should also be able to see that every message conforms to the same format as our two for "Searching". Therefore, up to this point, we will also expect the SOAP envelope to be identical for all requests to UDDI for "Searching" **and** "Publishing".

Now for how UDDI actually works: the XSD file, which is linked by the `<import>` tag to each file, contains the structure for a packet of XML that actually defines what action you wish to perform on UDDI.

http://www.uddi.org/schema/2001/uddi_v1.xsd

Our above "Searching" messages referenced a data type of `find_business` and `businessDetail`. On searching the imported XSD file you will find the following two definitions:

`find_business` XML data type:

```
<xsd:element name="find_business" type="uddi:FindBusiness" />
  <xsd:complexType name="FindBusiness">
<xsd:sequence>
  <xsd:element minOccurs="0"
               maxOccurs="1"
               name="findQualifiers"
               type="uddi:FindQualifiers" />
  <xsd:element minOccurs="0"
               maxOccurs="1"
               name="name"
               type="xsd:string" />
  <xsd:element minOccurs="0"
               maxOccurs="1"
               name="identifierBag"
               type="uddi:IdentifierBag" />
  <xsd:element minOccurs="0"
               maxOccurs="1"
               name="categoryBag"
               type="uddi:CategoryBag" />
  <xsd:element minOccurs="0"
               maxOccurs="1"
               name="tModelBag"
               type="uddi:TModelBag" />
  <xsd:element minOccurs="0"
               maxOccurs="1"
               name="discoveryURLs"
               type="uddi:DiscoveryURLs" />
</xsd:sequence>
<xsd:attribute name="generic" type="xsd:string" use="required" />
<xsd:attribute name="maxRows" type="xsd:int" use="optional" />
</xsd:complexType>
```

`businessDetail` XML data type:

```
<xsd:element name="businessDetail" type="uddi:BusinessDetail" />
<xsd:complexType name="BusinessDetail">
  <xsd:sequence>
    <xsd:element minOccurs="0"
                 maxOccurs="unbounded"
                 name="businessEntity"
                 type="uddi:BusinessEntity" />
  </xsd:sequence>
  <xsd:attribute name="generic" type="xsd:string" use="required" />
  <xsd:attribute name="operator" type="xsd:string" use="required" />
  <xsd:attribute name="truncated" type="uddi:Truncated" use="optional" />
</xsd:complexType>
<xsd:element name="businessDetailExt" type="uddi:BusinessDetailExt" />
```

All you do now to find a business on UDDI is take the above request message (`find_business`) and send that within the `<body>` element of our template SOAP request, for example:

```
<?xml version='1.0' encoding='UTF-8'?>
<Envelope xmlns='http://schemas.xmlsoap.org/soap/envelope/'>
<Body>
  <find_business generic="1.0" maxrows=30 xmlns="urn:uddi-org:api">
    <name>Microsoft</name>
  </find_business>
</Body>
</Envelope>
```

That's it, just send this SOAP message to the Enquiry UDDI server
(`http://uddi.microsoft.com/inquire`), the returned result will be the `businessDetail`
XML structure.

The important thing to remember is that the above method can be used with all requests made to UDDI
for both searching and publishing, so you simply need to concentrate on understanding the definitions
outlined in the `<import>` file:

http://www.uddi.org/schema/2001/uddi_v1.xsd

Using the Microsoft UDDI SDK

There seems to be an SDK for everything these days and indeed UDDI is no exception. To access this
component you must first of all download and install the UDDI SDK for VS.NET, which is available at:

http://uddi.microsoft.com/developer/default.aspx

Once installed you need to add a reference to the DLL. The easiest way to accomplish this is to use the
'Add Reference' menu option to browse to the file `Microsoft.UDDI.SDK.dll` situated in the
directory where you installed the SDK.

Once this is done, use the following code to access UDDI:

```
Imports Microsoft.Uddi
Imports Microsoft.Uddi.Business
Imports Microsoft.Uddi.Service
Imports Microsoft.Uddi.Binding
Imports Microsoft.Uddi.ServiceType
Imports Microsoft.Uddi.Api

Public Class Form1
  Inherits System.Windows.Forms.Form

  Private Sub Form1_Load(ByVal sender As System.Object, ByVal e As _
                                  System.EventArgs) Handles MyBase.Load

    Dim oUDDI As New Microsoft.Uddi.FindBusiness()
    Dim oInquire As New Microsoft.Uddi.Inquire()
    Dim oBusinessList As Microsoft.Uddi.BusinessList

    oInquire.Url = "http://test.uddi.microsoft.com/inquire"
    oUDDI.Name = "Microsoft"
    oBusinessList = oUDDI.Send
    MsgBox(oBusinessList.BusinessInfos.Count)

  End Sub
End Class
```

The above code actually does exactly the same as our SOAP construct we created earlier, but this time the SOAP messages have been shielded away from us, and are all created and sent by the SDK.

Note that to send a "publish" message you need to replace the code:

```
oInquire.Url = "http://test.uddi.microsoft.com/inquire"
```

with the following code, which also sets up your login details:

```
Publish.Url = "https://test.uddi.microsoft.com/publish"
Publish.User = "PassportSignInName"
Publish.Password = "PassportPassword"
```

disco.exe

Included with VS.NET is the `disco.exe` tool. This tool scans a `.disco` file or a web site and creates files locally on your computer that correspond to all the information on Web Services it finds. It can create any combination of the following files while it scans the source location:

- ❑ WSDL Schema
- ❑ XSD Schema definition
- ❑ DISCO file
- ❑ DISCO.map file

The `disco.exe` tool is used through a command-line DOS command. Instead of having every developer in your organization referencing schemas and `.disco` files via the Internet, to keep data traffic at a minimum (SOAP messages only) you could locate all available Web Services on a series of servers and place their files on a local network drive. The network drive would then be referenced by everyone instead of the slower link to the Internet.

Below is an example use of this command, when you wish to inspect a single `.disco` file:

```
disco.exe http://www.proseware.com/prosewareWebservice.disco
```

In addition you can also interrogate a web server, saving the output to a specified output directory:

```
disco.exe /out:myDir http://www.proseware.com
```

Disco map file

A disco map file is published by a Web Service and is an XML document that typically contains links to any resources that describe the Web Service.

The disco map file is created in the VS.NET client project at the same time that the Web Service is added, is usually named `reference.map`, and is located within the reference section of your project. Below is an example of the disco map file:

```xml
<?xml version="1.0" encoding="utf-8"?>
<DiscoveryClientResultsFile xmlns:xsi="http://www.w3.org/2001/XMLSchema-instance"
                            xmlns:xsd="http://www.w3.org/2001/XMLSchema">
  <Results>
```

```
    <DiscoveryClientResult
        referenceType="System.Web.Services.Discovery.DiscoveryDocumentReference"
        url="http://localhost/WebService1/Service1.asmx?disco"
        filename="Service1.disco" />
    <DiscoveryClientResult
        referenceType="System.Web.Services.Discovery.ContractReference"
        url="http://localhost/WebService1/Service1.asmx?wsdl"
        filename="Service1.wsdl" />
  </Results>
</DiscoveryClientResultsFile>
```

The default entries for the disco map file (as shown above) are the location of the .disco file and the WSDL schema file. The disco map file is primarily used to notify the developer that additional information exists.

DiscoveryClientResult Element

The <discoveryclientresult> element within the disco map file can be repeated as many times as there are links related to the referenced Web Service. This element is broken down into three attributes. The first reference attribute must refer to a string value that is a recognized and a valid class name in the System.Web.Services.Discovery namespace. The only three valid entries are currently:

❑   System.Web.Services.Discovery.DiscoveryDocumentReference – points to a disco file

❑   System.Web.Services.Discovery.ContractReference – points to a WSDL schema file

❑   System.Web.Services.Discovery.SchemaReference – points to an XML schema file

The second url attribute points to the Internet URL location of the specified file

The third filename attribute points to the name of the file that was created **locally** when the Web Service was added to the current project.

The <discoveryclientresult> element is populated by the information contained in the .disco file it finds (if any) when adding a remote WSDL schema into the current ASP.NET client project. If no .disco file is found then only the ContractReference is created inside the disco map file.

Data in ASP.NET

In web development, it has long been the case that dynamic web sites have relied on a database to provide content. This has not changed in ASP.NET, except that now there are new tools available to developers to enable them to rapidly access and consume data from a variety of sources, including databases, text and XML files, and more.

This chapter will provide high-level coverage of the data access mechanisms in .NET. These mechanisms are referred to as ADO.NET. It is intended to not just provide an understanding of the way that data interacts with the ASP.NET framework and controls, but also an insight into the data access framework and the theory behind it. For a full reference to this topic, you may want to look at the *ADO.NET Programmer's Reference*, ISBN 1-861005-58-X.

Data in the .NET Framework

In recent years, Microsoft has been working on what is called Universal Data Access. The goal is to have a single API for accessing data from a variety of sources, including Exchange, databases, Active Directory, text, and many others. During the time that this strategy has been evolving, XML (Extensible Markup Language) has come to the forefront of the technology field as a platform-neutral mechanism for representing data and meta data. In ADO.NET, Microsoft has combined the two to create a very powerful and flexible system for accessing data.

A Brief History

One of the first big milestones in universal data access was ODBC or Open DataBase Connectivity. ODBC was an attempt to provide a cross-platform Application Programming Interface (API) to access data in relational databases. There are currently a large number of ODBC drivers on the market for accessing a wide variety of databases, from different vendors, on just about every platform, including Windows, Unix, and Macintosh. However, ODBC is a low-level interface, and not very easy to program.

Data Access Objects (DAO) was a technology introduced by Microsoft that provided an object model as an interface for accessing data. While this technology used ODBC, it provided an interface that was much easier to use, and was accessible from languages such as Visual Basic, which made it extremely popular in some circles. However, DAO was optimized for Microsoft's Access databases and therefore was not as widely accepted as ODBC.

Following DAO, Microsoft introduced OLEDB or Object Linking and Embedding for Databases. OLEDB is the technology used by Microsoft to allow operations such as embedding a spreadsheet in a Word document. This same concept of merging data is apparent in OLEDB in the concepts of providers and consumers. All providers expose a defined interface through which data can be accessed. This is the key element that allowed universal data access. Any source can be exposed through OLEDB simply by implementing the interface. A data consumer similarly implements an interface that allows the object to consume data from the provider. By doing this, Microsoft provided a framework in which almost any data source could be accessed using the same API.

One of the problems with OLEDB, however, is that it is a low-level API and does not provide support for languages such as Visual Basic, script languages, or traditional ASP. The answer to this was to create ActiveX Data Objects (ADO). ADO provides an easy-to-use interface that is accessible from languages as low-level as C++ and as high-level as the scripting languages used in ASP. ADO sits on top of OLEDB using the data providers to access data. A clear yet simple object model made ADO a popular choice for many developers. In addition, because there are so many data sources now accessible via OLEDB, and therefore ADO, the ability to work with a new data source requires only a small amount of learning on the part of the developer.

While there have been other milestones along the way, including varied attempts to provide access remotely over HTTP, they have all been only mildly successful. ADO.NET is touted as an evolution in data access. Taking the best features of ADO, including an easy to use object model and a framework that provides the ability to plug in a provider for any data source, ADO.NET extends the model and provides a more pertinent model that is architected for today's internet-based applications.

Like OLEDB and ADO, ADO.NET uses the concept of providers, referred to as managed providers. A managed provider talks directly to the data source and exposes a defined interface. The .NET framework currently includes three providers; a native provider for SQL Server, an ODBC provider, and an OLE DB provider. The SQL Server provider is the only one that currently works directly with the database. Both the OLEDB and ODBC providers are provided for interacting with large number of non-SQL Server data sources through their "legacy" interfaces using the existing OLEDB and ODBC drivers. Early benchmarks show large performance gains in using the SQL Server managed provider over using ODBC or OLEDB so it is recommended practice to use this provider instead of either of the others when working with SQL Server. As time progresses, managed providers will surface for a variety of data sources and will provide a performance boost wherever they are used.

When accessing data, regardless of the source, opening and maintaining a connection to the data source is a very costly operation in terms of time and resources. In traditional ADO programming, there were options when programming as to whether you wanted to work with the data on the server, or on the client. Often, when working with data for any period of time, it made sense to disconnect a `RecordSet` from the database by pulling the data to the client and closing the connection to the database. This performance-enhancing practice is at the core of ADO.NET. When working with data, it is retrieved and the connection closed, thus freeing up valuable resources. When updates or inserts are necessary, the connection is opened and the updates made. This disconnected method lends itself to distributed architectures where data is often read from the database and manipulated before updates are returned, or simply browsed.

In this chapter, we will cover the objects used to perform data access using ADO.NET and specifically how ADO.NET is used in ASP.NET. We'll cover the various mechanisms for accessing data, how and when to use each, and how to bind data to ASP.NET Web Controls.

A note about the examples in this chapter. While the intention of the examples is to provide a clear understanding of connecting to and working with a variety of data sources, there is also a need for some consistency in the examples. To that end, there are several examples of connecting to different databases, but many of the examples will use a simple example database on SQL Server, which holds information about movies and actors. Attempts will be made throughout the chapter to point out the differences in working with different data sources as they pertain to .NET. In order to use the examples, either set up the database manually, or use the script file included in the source code download to create the database on SQL Server or the Microsoft Data Engine (MSDE).

The structure of the database used for the examples is shown below and is extremely simple. The database consists of four tables: Movie, Actor, Genre, and MovieActor. Movies have a genre ID which relates them to a genre while the MovieActor table acts a go-between to connect Actors to Movies:

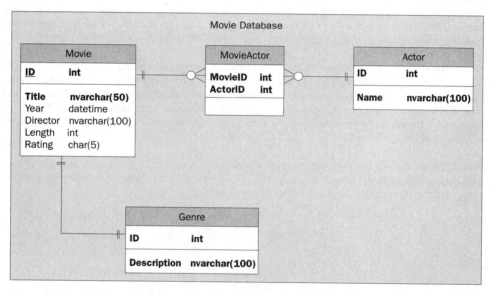

The System.Data Namespace

The `Sytem.Data` namespace contains the classes related to data access in .NET. These classes can be divided into three logical partitions. The first is the `DataSet` and its related classes, the second are .NET **Managed Providers**, and the third are common base classes.

The namespace itself is further divided to partition the included classes and interfaces. The namespace breaks down as follows:

- ❑ `System.Data` – this is the root of the namespace and holds the definition for the majority of the interfaces and classes used when accessing data, including the `DataSet` and `IDataReader`.

- ❑ `System.Data.Common` – contains classes that provide base functionality to .NET managed provider implementations such as Data Adapters and Table Mappings.

- ❑ `System.Data.Odbc` – contains the classes necessary to work with data using ODBC drivers. This namespace constitutes the managed provider for ODBC.

- ❑ `System.Data.OleDb` – contains the classes necessary to work with data from OLEDB-compliant data sources. This namespace constitutes the managed provider for OLEDB.

- ❑ `System.Data.SqlClient` – contains the classes necessary to work with data from SQL Server. This namespace constitutes the managed provider for SQL Server.

- ❑ `System.Data.SqlTypes` – provides classes that map directly to native data types in SQL Server to enhance performance when working with data from SQL Server.

> **The ODBC managed provider is currently available as a separate download from Microsoft. Upon final release to the public, this provider may be included in the framework installation.**

As you can see, each managed provider has its own namespace within the `System.Data` hierarchy. As future providers are written, they too will have their own namespace. For example, an Oracle Managed Provider would likely live in the `System.Data.Oracle` namespace. As the chapter progresses we will be using classes from all of the namespaces contained within the `System.Data` namespace.

Because managed providers will need to support a base level of functionality and expose standard interfaces, switching from one provider to another will not be difficult. In fact, using interfaces and configuration information, applications should theoretically be able to have the data source switched with no code changes. Of course, things never go this smoothly and every data source will have its intricacies and differences, but this makes for a very easy to use framework, with a gentle learning curve for new data sources, none the less.

Below is a diagram that shows the core components of the `System.Data` namespace and it is followed by a brief description of each class. A more detailed description of the classes, including their roles and how to use them, makes up the next section of this chapter.

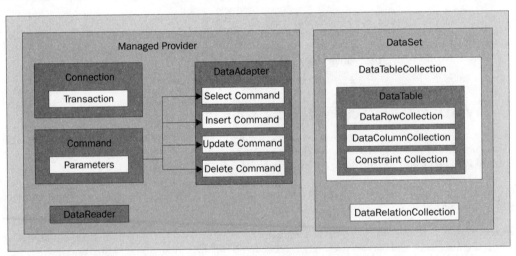

A managed provider represents a set of classes whose purpose is to communicate with a data source. This involves connecting to the source, executing commands against it, and extracting data from it. A managed provider includes the following classes to accomplish this:

❑ Command – the command class represents a command to be executed against the data source such as an INSERT, UPDATE, DELETE, or SELECT. A command uses the connection to execute against the data source.

❑ Connection – the connection class is responsible for opening and managing the physical connection to the data source.

❑ DataReader – the DataReader class is responsible for providing a fast, forward-only, stream of data from the data source. Its sole responsibility is to read the data out as fast as it can.

❑ DataAdapter – the DataAdapter class is responsible for the communication between a DataSet and the data source. The DataAdapter uses command objects to execute commands against the data source on behalf of a DataSet, and the DataAdapter is used to fill a DataSet with data.

❑ Parameter – the parameter class represents a parameter for a command. An example would be a parameter to be passed to a stored procedure in a database. Not all commands have parameters.

❑ Transaction – the Transaction class represents an executing transaction against the data source. Because the connection class is responsible for communication with the data source the Transaction class is tied to the connection.

In addition to those classes provided by each of the managed providers, the ADO.NET framework provides a base set of classes for working with data, which includes the following:

❑ Constraint – the Constraint class represents constraints placed on the data in a DataTable or DataSet that force the data to meet certain requirements. A typical example would be a constraint that indicates that a DataColumn must have unique values in each of its rows.

❑ DataColumn – the DataColumn class represents a specific column of data in a DataTable and provides the type information for all items in that column, such as whether they are an integer or a string.

❑ DataRelation – the DataRelation class represents a relation, or connection, between two DataTables. This relation can then be used to extract data from one table that is related to the data in another.

❑ DataRow – the DataRow class represents a single row of data in a DataTable.

❑ DataSet – The DataSet class is responsible for managing data outside of a data source. In fact, this object has no knowledge of the source of its data and can be used to manage data independent of any physical data source.

❑ DataTable – the DataTable represents a collection of rows and columns of data. Its structure is similar to that of a table in a relational database. The DataTable is often housed in a DataSet but can be used on its own as a collection of data.

As you can see, there is a rich set of objects that provide a great deal of power in working with data. In the sections that follow, we will go into more detail on how each of these classes plays a role in working with data, and how they can be used in ASP.NET.

Connections and Transactions

Connections provide the mechanism for opening and maintaining communication with the data source, so we'll mention them first. In addition, the Connection class is responsible for starting transactions and, optionally, creating Command objects. There is no concrete base class for a Connection, rather an interface, IDbConnection, is defined in the System.Data namespace. This interface is implemented by managed providers on their connection classes. Using interface inheritance in this way ensures that all managed providers support a base set of features.

Since, first and foremost, connections allow us to open communication with a data source, we will take a look at how to open a connection to a variety of data sources. In the examples below, we open connections to a variety of data sources using the various managed providers. Full namespace qualifications are given for the items to help make it clear which provider is being used. These samples can be run in almost any function, but can be found in the `ConnectionsAndCommands.aspx.cs` and `ConnectionsAndCommands.aspx.vb` files in the source code for the book.

Example: Opening Connections

C#: OdbcConnection.Open

```
System.Data.Odbc.OdbcConnection ExcelConnection = new
System.Data.Odbc.OdbcConnection("Driver={Microsoft Excel Driver
(*.xls)};DBQ=c:\\sales.xls");
ExcelConnection.Open();
```

VB.NET: OdbcConnection.Open

```
dim ExcelConnection as new
System.Data.Odbc.OdbcConnection("Driver={Microsoft_Excel Driver
(*.xls)};DBQ=c:\\sales.xls")
ExcelConnection.Open()
```

C#: OleDbConnection.Open

```
System.Data.OleDb.OleDbConnection AccessConnection = new
System.Data.OleDb.OleDbConnection("Provider=Microsoft.Jet.OleDb.4.0;Data
source=c:\\grocertogo.mdb;");

AccessConnection.Open();
```

VB.NET: OleDbConnection.Open

```
Dim AccessConnection as new
System.Data.OleDb.OleDbConnection(("Provider=Microsoft.Jet.OleDb.4.0;Data_source=c
:\\grocertogo.mdb;")

AccessConnection.Open()
```

As you can see, the only real difference that comes into play when opening connections is the connection string we pass to the constructor of our `Connection` class. This information points the provider to the database using the appropriate driver where necessary.

Connecting to a SQL Server database using the SQL Server Managed Provider is slightly different from the ODBC and OLEDB connection methods:

C#: SqlClientConnection Open

```
System.Data.SqlClient.SqlConnection SqlServer = new
System.Data.SqlClient.SqlConnection("server=(local);database=pubs;uid=sa;pwd=;");
SqlServer.Open();
```

VB.NET: SqlClientConnection Open

```
Dim SqlServer as new
System.Data.SqlClient.SqlConnection("server=(local);database=pubs;uid=sa;pwd=;")
SqlServer.Open()
```

Once we have a connection open to the data source, the other actions we take are very similar regardless of the provider. For that reason, the rest of the examples in this chapter will use the various providers at different points rather than showing all three providers for each example.

Now that we have a connection open, we can create a transaction in which our actions can be ensured to all complete or all fail. We do this by calling the `BeginTransaction` method of the connection object which returns an object implementing the `IDbTransaction` interface. We then use this object to either commit or roll back our transaction.

Example: Carrying Out Transactions

C#:

```csharp
//open connection to a SQL Server database using the SQL provider
SqlConnection SqlServer = new
SqlConnection("server=(local);database=pubs;uid=sa;pwd=;");
IDbTransaction PubsTransaction;    //SQL Transaction

//implement our logic in a try, catch, finally block to properly
//catch exceptions in our code
try
{
//open the connection
  SqlServer.Open();

  //get a connection object back as we begin the transaction
  PubsTransaction = SqlServer.BeginTransaction(IsolationLevel.ReadUncommitted);

  //DO WORK HERE IN TRANSACTION//

  //if there were no errors, commit the transaction
  PubsTransaction.Commit();
  Response.Write(SqlServer.ServerVersion.ToString() + "<br>");
}
catch(SqlException SqlEX)
{
  //output an error message to the UI
  Response.Write("Error opening connection to local server. Check logon details");
  Response.Write(SqlEX.ToString());

  //rollback our transaction if there was an error.
  PubsTransaction.Rollback();
}
finally
{
  //close the connection whether we succeeded or failed
  SqlServer.Close();
}
```

VB.NET:

```vbnet
'open connection to a SQL Server database using the SQL provider
Dim SqlServer As New_
                SqlConnection("server=(local);database=pubs;uid=sa;pwd=;")
Dim PubsTransaction As IDbTransaction        'SQL Transaction

'implement our logic in a try, catch, finally block to properly
'catch exceptions in our code
Try

  'open the connection
  SqlServer.Open()

  'get a connection object back as we begin the transaction
  PubsTransaction = SqlServer.BeginTransaction(IsolationLevel.ReadUncommitted)

  '''DO WORK HERE IN TRANSACTION'''
```

```
            'if there were no errors, commit the transaction
            PubsTransaction.Commit()
            Response.Write(SqlServer.ServerVersion.ToString() + "<br>")

        Catch SqlEX As SqlException

            Response.Write("Error opening connection to local server." & _
                            " Be sure the username and password are correct.")
            Response.Write(SqlEX.ToString())

            'rollback our transaction if there was an error.
            PubsTransaction.Rollback()

        Finally

            'close the connection whether we succeeded or failed
            SqlServer.Close()

        End Try
```

In this example, we open a connection and begin a transaction. We would then execute the code we want to have transacted and commit the transaction. Notice that in our error handler we roll back the transaction to ensure that all of our actions are reversed because they did not all complete successfully if there was an error.

When working with transactions, it is important to begin the transaction as late as possible and commit or roll back as soon as possible. Because the items in a transaction need to be able to be put back to their original state, the resources involved are often locked to other users, which can cause performance problems in your application. Likewise, when working with database connections, it is best to open the connection as late as possible and close it as early as possible to allow your application to scale appropriately.

Commands and Parameters

A command allows us to actually define a function for the data source to perform. Using a connection, we execute a command against the data source which may, or may not, return results. Commands have a `CommandText` property that defines the command action, which might be a SQL statement. The `CommandText` is interpreted based on the `CommandType` set for the command. If the command type is `"StoredProcedure"`, then the command text is interpreted as the name of a stored procedure. If the type is `"Text"`, then it is interpreted as a direct command. The two examples below show these two properties; we've defined one command with text and one with a stored procedure.

> Note that in order for a command to be executed, it must be associated with a connection that is open at the time the command is executed.

We associate a command with a connection by passing the `Connection` object to the constructor of the command, or by setting the `Connection` property of the command.

In this VB.NET example we open a connection and execute a stored procedure with the `ExecuteReader` method of the command object:

VB.NET: Executing a stored procedure
```
        'dimension connection and command objects as well as a reader
        Dim PubsConnection As New_
                        SqlConnection("server=(local);database=pubs;uid=sa;pwd=;")
```

```
Dim PubsCommand As SqlCommand
Dim PubsReader As SqlDataReader

'create the command object from the connection which associates the command
'with the connection (i.e. this is equivalent to setting the connection
'property on the command
PubsCommand = PubsConnection.CreateCommand()

'identify the name of the stored procedure as our command text
PubsCommand.CommandText = "AuthorTitles"

'identify the type of the command as a stored procedure
PubsCommand.CommandType = CommandType.StoredProcedure

'open connection right before needing it
PubsConnection.Open()

'execute the command put the resulting data into a data reader
'we identify the command behavior to close the connection when the reader
'is closed so that we don't have to explicitly close it.
PubsReader = PubsCommand.ExecuteReader(CommandBehavior.CloseConnection)

'DO WORK WITH READER'

'close the reader when we are done with it
PubsReader.Close()

'clean up our variables.
PubsReader = Nothing
PubsCommand = Nothing
PubsConnection = Nothing
```

We first have to define our connection and command objects. Next, we set the properties on our command object for the command text and command type. Finally, we execute our procedure, returning the results into a `DataReader` object. Notice that we specify the `CommandBehavior.CloseConnection` parameter to the `ExecuteReader` method, which tells the provider to close the connection when the `DataReader` is closing rather than waiting for an explicit command to close the connection as well.

In this next example we use the ODBC provider to query an Excel spreadsheet using a `Text` command. The primary differences are in the connection string used to connect to the data source and the command text and type set on the command object.

VB.NET: Executing a text based command

```
'dimension command and connection objects along with reader
Dim ExcelConnection As New_
OdbcConnection("Driver=Microsoft Excel Driver (*.xls);DBQ=c:\\sales.xls")
Dim ExcelCommand As OdbcCommand
Dim ExcelReader As OdbcDataReader

'create connection from command and set its properties
ExcelCommand = ExcelConnection.CreateCommand()
ExcelCommand.CommandText = "SELECT * FROM SalesFigures"
ExcelCommand.CommandType = CommandType.Text

'open the connection
ExcelConnection.Open()
```

```
'execute the command and retrieve the data into a reader
ExcelReader = ExcelCommand.ExecuteReader(CommandBehavior.CloseConnection)

''''DO WORK WITH READER HERE'''

'close the reader and therefore the connection
ExcelReader.Close()

'clean up our variables
ExcelReader = Nothing
ExcelCommand = Nothing
ExcelConnection = Nothing
```

In both of the above examples, we used the `ExecuteReader` method of the `Command` object to return an object implementing the `IDataReader` interface. This is the method to use if you are returning rows of data from a data source. There are three different methods to execute commands, however, each with its own purpose: `ExecuteNonQuery`, `ExecuteReader`, and `ExecuteScalar`. The `ExecuteNonQuery` method is used when the command you are executing will not return rows of data. You can still have output parameters, which we will cover next, available to retrieve data and the method will return the number of rows affected. The `ExecuteScalar` method is used to return a single value, such as a sum or average. It returns the first item in the first column of the resulting records from the command. In addition, the SQL Server managed provider adds another version of this method, `ExecuteXmlReader`. This method is used when querying SQL Server for XML data and can be consumed by the `ReadXml` method of the `DataSet`.

In the example above, we used a stored procedure to return data. In many cases, a stored procedure will require input, and possibly output, parameters. These parameters can be used to pass information into the stored procedure to allow it to be more dynamic. In order to pass parameters along with a command, we first create and define the parameters, and then add them to the command object's parameters collection. In the C# example below we call a simple stored procedure to return all movies with an R rating:

C#: Executing a parameterized procedure

```
//create connection and command objects
OleDbConnection MovieConnection = new OleDbConnection("Provider=SQLOLEDB;data
source=(local);database=WROXmovieDB;uid=sa;pwd=;");
OleDbCommand MovieCommand;
OleDbDataReader MovieReader;

//set the properties for the command object
MovieCommand=MovieConnection.CreateCommand();
MovieCommand.CommandText ="GetMovieByRating";
MovieCommand.CommandType = CommandType.StoredProcedure;

//create an input parameter and add it to the collection
OleDbParameter MovieParam=new OleDbParameter("@rating",OleDbType.VarChar,5);
MovieParam.Direction = ParameterDirection.Input;
MovieParam.Value="R";
MovieCommand.Parameters.Add(MovieParam);

//create a return value parameter to capture the return value of the
//stored procedure and add it to the collection.
OleDbParameter MovieRetVal = new OleDbParameter("@RetVal",OleDbType.Integer,4);
MovieRetVal.Direction = ParameterDirection.ReturnValue;
MovieCommand.Parameters.Add(MovieRetVal);
```

```
//open the connection when we need it, and not before
MovieConnection.Open();

//fill the reader with the movie details.
MovieReader=MovieCommand.ExecuteReader(CommandBehavior.CloseConnection);

//do some work with the data reader here

//close the data reader, and thus the connection
//based on the command behavior specified when we executed
MovieReader.Close();

//clean up variables
MovieReader=null;
MovieCommand=null;
MovieConnection=null;
```

In this example we created an input parameter by using the `Direction` property of the parameter class. We then also created a return value parameter, which has its own direction enumerated value specifying it as a return value only. We then open the connection and run the stored procedure, placing the results in the `DataReader`. We could have used an output parameter to retrieve information from the database as well.

Another item to notice is the parameter we passed to the `ExecuteReader` method of the `Command` object. This command behavior parameter allows definition of specific behaviors about how the command will execute. In our example, we have specified `CommandBehavior.CloseConnection`, which closes the database connection as soon as the associated `DataReader` is closed. This helps prevent problems that may arise from forgetting to close a connection.

A stored procedure may only need to return a few values, and not rows of data. In these cases we can use parameters to get data out of a data source. An example of using an output parameter is shown next. In this example, we query our database for the genre of a given movie and its rating. Rather than return a reader, we simply return the data in two output parameters to our stored procedure:

C#: Using Output parameters

```
//create connection and command objects
SqlConnection MovieConnection = new
    SqlConnection("server=(local);database=wroxmoviedb;uid=sa;pwd=;");
SqlCommand MovieCommand = new SqlCommand("GetGenreRating",MovieConnection);

//set command type to stored procedure
MovieCommand.CommandType = CommandType.StoredProcedure;

//create and add all of the parameters for the stored procedure
MovieCommand.Parameters.Add(new SqlParameter("@title", SqlDbType.VarChar, 50));
MovieCommand.Parameters.Add(new SqlParameter("@genre", SqlDbType.VarChar, 100));
MovieCommand.Parameters.Add(new SqlParameter("@rating", SqlDbType.VarChar, 5));

//set the direction attribute for all of the parameter and the value for
//the input parameter
MovieCommand.Parameters["@title"].Direction = ParameterDirection.Input;
MovieCommand.Parameters["@genre"].Direction = ParameterDirection.Output;
MovieCommand.Parameters["@rating"].Direction = ParameterDirection.Output;
MovieCommand.Parameters["@title"].Value = "Matrix";
```

```
//open the connection
MovieConnection.Open();

//execute the query getting the number of rows affected
int RecordsAffected = MovieCommand.ExecuteNonQuery();

//write out the parameters, we could also put them in variables
Response.Write("Matrix<br>");
Response.Write("Rating: " + MovieCommand.Parameters["@rating"].Value + "<br>");
Response.Write("Genre: " + MovieCommand.Parameters["@genre"].Value + "<br>");

//close the database connection as soon as we are done with it
MovieConnection.Close();

//clean up our objects
MovieConnection = null;
MovieCommand = null;
```

In this example we were able to get data from the database without getting an entire rowset, and thus gained better performance. We created our connection and command objects as before and then created the individual parameter objects and added them to the parameters collection of the command object. Next, we had to set the direction for the parameters to indicate those items that are our output parameters. Finally, we executed the query and accessed the parameters through the parameters collection of the command to get the output.

> If the data coming back from a query is a single row, consider using output parameters and the **ExecuteNonQuery** method to achieve the best performance. Because a **DataReader** does not have to be created, this method provides better performance.

DataReader

The DataReader provides read-only, forward-only, access to a data stream coming from a data source. A DataReader is not created directly; instead it is created by using the ExecuteReader method of the Command object. We have seen this in the prior examples, showing how to use a command object. Once a DataReader has been retrieved by executing a command the Read method moves the reader to the next record in the ResultSet. Usually, when looping through the results syntax similar to the following will be used:

C#:
```
while(Reader.Read())
{
  //access the values in the row
  Response.Write(Reader["title"]);
}
```

VB.NET:
```
While Reader.Read()
  'access the values in the row
  Response.Write(Reader.Item("title"))

End While
```

The Read method returns a Boolean value indicating whether or not the cursor was moved to the next record. A value of false indicates that the reader has reached the end of the ResultSet.

Once the `DataReader` is positioned on a row, there are a variety of methods that allow retrieval of items from the row in their native data type such as `GetString()` and `GetDateTime()`. In addition, using the `Item` property we can get an item from the row using the name or index of the field. When performance is a consideration, the methods that allow access to the native type should be used as they do not require casting the value to the appropriate type.

In the case where multiple `Resultsets` are returned in one query, the `NextResult` method allows movement to the next `ResultSet`. The following example loops through the `ResultSets` and the records within them outputting the values to the ASP.NET response.

VB.NET: DataReader example

```
'dimension variables
Dim MovieConnection As New SqlConnection(SqlConnStr)
Dim MovieCommand As SqlCommand
Dim MovieReader As SqlDataReader
Dim Counter As Integer

'create command and set properties
MovieCommand = MovieConnection.CreateCommand
MovieCommand.CommandText = "SELECT * from actor;SELECT * from movie"
MovieCommand.CommandType = CommandType.Text

'open the connection to the data source
MovieConnection.Open()

'execute command create reader
MovieReader = MovieCommand.ExecuteReader(CommandBehavior.CloseConnection)

'output the results to table in HTML
Response.Write("<table>")

'loop through the resultsets, being sure to execute at least once
Do
   'create headers for the table using the schema table information
   'from the datareader object. We get the column names from the first
   'column of the table returned.
   Response.Write("<tr>")
   For Counter = 0 To MovieReader.FieldCount - 1
Response.Write("<th>" & MovieReader.GetSchemaTable().Rows(Counter)(0) & "</th>")
   Next
   Response.Write("</tr>")

   'loop through the fields and write out their value in a
   'table cell element as long as there are more values
   While MovieReader.Read()
Response.Write("<tr>")
For Counter = 0 To MovieReader.FieldCount - 1
   Response.Write("<td>" & MovieReader(Counter) & "</td>")
Next
Response.Write("</tr>")
   End While

   'loop as long as their are more resultsets
Loop While MovieReader.NextResult()

'close the reader which closes the connection because of the
'parameter we passed to the ExecuteReader method
MovieReader.Close()
```

```
'close the table and cleanup
Response.Write("</table>")

MovieReader = Nothing
MovieCommand = Nothing
MovieConnection = Nothing
```

In this example we executed a command that, because it had multiple SQL statements in it, returned multiple `ResultSets`. Because of this, we were able to use the `NextResult` method of the `DataReader` to move to the second `ResultSet` and get its values as well. We loop through the `ResultSets` and, within that loop, we also loop through the rows and then the fields to build an HTML table. There are much easier ways to do this using both the `DataReader` and the `DataSet` as we shall see later, but this provides us with a simple way to see the `DataReader` in action.

DataAdapter

The `DataAdapter` serves as the communication mechanism between a managed provider and the `DataSet`. As can be seen from the figure earlier in the chapter, the `DataAdapter` is essentially a set of command objects. It uses these command objects to execute commands against the data source on behalf of the `DataSet`. There is a separate command for each of the four actions that can typically be taken: `SELECT`, `INSERT`, `UPDATE`, and `DELETE`. Each of these commands can be manipulated and configured independently of the others.

When creating a `DataAdapter`, the constructor optionally allows passing in information about the `SELECT` command and the connection. This allows easy creation of a `DataAdapter` that can extract data from a data source, but with no ability to update the data source. In order to update the data source, we would have to create the other commands. This can be done in one of two ways: manually define and assign the various commands, or use a `CommandBuilder` to automatically build the other commands based on the `SELECT` command and the table schema. In the examples below, we show both the manual process of setting up the commands and the automatic process.

VB.NET: Building Commands manually

```
'create data variables
Dim MovieDataAdapter As New SqlDataAdapter("SELECT * from actor", SqlConnStr)
Dim MovieDataset As New DataSet()
Dim MovieDataRow As DataRow

'create an textbased update command with parameters
MovieDataAdapter.UpdateCommand = New SqlCommand()
MovieDataAdapter.UpdateCommand.CommandText =_
                    "UPDATE actor SET name=@name WHERE id=@id"
MovieDataAdapter.UpdateCommand.CommandType = CommandType.Text
MovieDataAdapter.UpdateCommand.Connection =_
        MovieDataAdapter.SelectCommand.Connection
MovieDataAdapter.UpdateCommand.Parameters.Add(New SqlParameter("@name", & _
                                SqlDbType.VarChar, 50, "Name"))
MovieDataAdapter.UpdateCommand.Parameters.Add & _
                (New SqlParameter("@id", SqlDbType.Int, 4, "ID"))

'create an insert command to add new records to the database when
'they are added to the data set.
MovieDataAdapter.InsertCommand = New SqlCommand()
MovieDataAdapter.InsertCommand.CommandText = "INSERT actor(Name) values(@name)"
MovieDataAdapter.InsertCommand.CommandType = CommandType.Text
MovieDataAdapter.InsertCommand.Connection =_
        MovieDataAdapter.SelectCommand.Connection
```

```
MovieDataAdapter.InsertCommand.Parameters.Add(New SqlParameter("@name", & _
                                      SqlDbType.VarChar, 50, "Name"))

'create the delete command and set its parameters
MovieDataAdapter.DeleteCommand = New SqlCommand()
MovieDataAdapter.DeleteCommand.CommandText = "delete actor where id=@id"
MovieDataAdapter.DeleteCommand.CommandType = CommandType.Text
MovieDataAdapter.DeleteCommand.Connection =_
        MovieDataAdapter.SelectCommand.Connection
MovieDataAdapter.DeleteCommand.Parameters.Add(New SqlParameter("@id",_
        SqlDbType.VarChar, 50, "ID"))

'fill the dataset creating a table named "Actor"
MovieDataAdapter.Fill(MovieDataset, "Actor")

'add a new row to the dataset
MovieDataRow = MovieDataset.Tables.Item("Actor").NewRow()
MovieDataRow.Item("name") = "Geena Davis"
MovieDataset.Tables.Item("Actor").Rows.Add(MovieDataRow)

'update the database with the new changes.
MovieDataAdapter.Update(MovieDataset, "Actor")
```

In this example we have created the command objects, on their own, by manually assigning command text, command type, and parameters to the UPDATE, INSERT, and DELETE commands. Remember that the SELECT command can be specified in the constructor as we have done here. We will touch on the Fill and Update methods in a bit, but first we will look at another way to build the commands using the CommandBuilder object. The CommandBuilder is a class that works with the DataAdapter to automatically build INSERT, UPDATE, and DELETE commands for the DataAdapter as long as the source data is coming from a single table, and the schema information is known. The example below does just what we saw in the last example, but with much less code:

VB.NET: Using the CommandBuilder object

```
'create data variables
Dim MovieDataAdapter As New SqlDataAdapter("SELECT * from actor", SqlConnStr)
Dim MovieDataset As New DataSet()
Dim MovieDataRow As DataRow

'create a new SqlCommandBuilder to build our commands for us
'and pass in the data adapter to provide the SELECT command and
'allow the function to create the other commands
Dim MovieCommandBulider As New SqlCommandBuilder(MovieDataAdapter)

'fill the dataset creating a table named "Actor"
MovieDataAdapter.Fill(MovieDataset, "Actor")

'add a new row to the dataset
MovieDataRow = MovieDataset.Tables.Item("Actor").NewRow()
MovieDataRow.Item("name") = "Jeff Goldblum"
MovieDataset.Tables.Item("Actor").Rows.Add(MovieDataRow)

'update the database with the new changes.
MovieDataAdapter.Update(MovieDataset, "Actor")
```

The highlighted text in the above example takes the place of all the code we had to write in the previous example. The `CommandBuilder` can greatly reduce the task of creating commands when dealing with a single table. However, it is confined to working with a single table and therefore limited. The `CommandBuilder` uses the `SelectCommand` to get schema information about the table and uses that information to build the other commands, and you must therefore have a primary key defined on your table, and your data source must support the retrieval of schema information. In order to update and delete properly, the command must be able to reference a key for the row, or you need to build the command yourself to ensure that the proper rows are updated. Because of the need to get schema information, a trip to the database is required, which can also impact performance. Keep these things in mind as you consider whether to use the `CommandBuilder`, or to write the code yourself. Additionally, the commands built by the `CommandBuilder` are SQL statements executed as text commands. With data sources such as SQL Server, a large performance gain can be achieved by using stored procedures. In order to use stored procedures for these commands, you must define the commands manually.

In the previous examples, we also used two other methods of the `DataAdapter`: `Fill` and `Update`. Both take, as a parameter, a `DataSet` object and an optional table name. There are several overloaded versions of these methods. The `Fill` method actually executes the `SelectCommand` and loads the resulting data into the specified table, or a table with the name "Table1" if no name is specified. Internally, what this translates to is that the `DataAdapter` executes the `SELECT` command and gets a `DataReader` object back, which it then uses to create the structure of the `DataSet`. When updating, the `DataSet` and an optional table name are provided. The `DataAdaper` then uses information in the `DataSet` about the current state of the rows to call the `UPDATE`, `INSERT`, and `DELETE` commands to make sure the data in the data source matches that in the `DataSet`. The `DataAdapter` will open the connection associated with the `SELECT` command if it is not already open it and close it after loading the `DataSet` only if it needed to open it.

If all we need in our `DataSet` or `DataTable` is the schema of the data source, then we can use the `FillSchema` method, which will simply create the schema for the `DataTable` to match that of the data source. This provides a quick way to build the `DataTable` structure without having to write all the code. However, this does require a trip to the server so there is a performance cost. For most applications, it is best to define the table schema directly if the code does not already require a trip to the data source.

Another concept related to the `DataAdapter` is mapping. The `DataAdapter` provides the ability to create **table mappings** and **column mappings**. As it is the job of the `DataAdapter` to keep the `DataSet` and the data source up to date, the `DataAdapter` needs to be able to relate, or map, the tables and columns in the `DataSet` to the "tables" and "columns" in the data source. Having a mapping between the tables and columns allows the developer to use names for the tables and columns in the `DataSet` which differ from the names of their source table in the data source. By using the mappings, the `DataAdapter` can successfully execute the commands against the database, mapping the table names and columns where appropriate.

In the example below, we query our movie database for the list of movies and map the table name and several columns to make them easier to reference in the code:

C#: Querying a Database

```
using System;
using System.Data;
using System.Data.SqlClient;
using System.Web;
using System.Web.UI;
using System.Web.UI.WebControls;
using System.Web.UI.HtmlControls;
```

```
namespace AspProgRefData_c
{
  public class mapping : System.Web.UI.Page
  {
    public mapping()
    {
      Page.Init += new System.EventHandler(Page_Init);
    }

    private void Page_Load(object sender, System.EventArgs e)
    {
      // Call our function to map
      Mappings();
    }

    private void Page_Init(object sender, EventArgs e)
    {
      InitializeComponent();
    }

    private void Mappings()
    {
      //create connection, adapter and dataset
      SqlConnection MappingConnection = new
      SqlConnection("server=(local);database=wroxmoviedb;uid=sa;pwd=;");
      SqlDataAdapter MappingAdapter = new SqlDataAdapter("SELECT * FROM _
        MOVIE",MappingConnection);
      DataSet MappingDataSet = new DataSet();

      //create a new table mapping and then add new column mappings
      MappingAdapter.TableMappings.Add("movie","Favorite_Movies");

MappingAdapter.TableMappings["movie"].ColumnMappings.Add("Length","Minutes");
MappingAdapter.TableMappings["movie"].ColumnMappings.Add("Year","Release Date");

      //fill the dataset passing in the name of the table mapping above
      //to indicate that we want to use this mapping for our schema
      MappingAdapter.Fill(MappingDataSet,"movie");

      //write out the table name and the columns to an html table by
      //looping through the columns for the headings and then through
      //the rows for the data.
      Response.Write("<Table border='1'><caption>" +
                              MappingDataSet.Tables[0].TableName +
                              "</caption><tr>");

      //column headings
      foreach(DataColumn c in MappingDataSet.Tables["Favorite_Movies"].Columns)
      {
        Response.Write("<th>" + c.ColumnName + "</th>");
      }
      Response.Write("</tr>");

      //table cells
      foreach(DataRow r in MappingDataSet.Tables["Favorite_Movies"].Rows)
      {
        Response.Write("<tr>");
        foreach(Object item in r.ItemArray)
        {
```

```
            Response.Write("<td>" + item.ToString() + "</td>");
        }
        Response.Write("</tr>");
      }
    }

    private void InitializeComponent()
    {
      this.Load += new System.EventHandler(this.Page_Load);
    }
  }
}
```

VB.NET: Querying a Database

```
Imports System
Imports System.Data
Imports System.Data.SqlClient
Imports System.Web
Imports System.Web.UI
Imports System.Web.UI.WebControls
Imports System.Web.UI.HtmlControls


Public Class Mapping
  Inherits System.Web.UI.Page

  <System.Diagnostics.DebuggerStepThrough()> Private Sub InitializeComponent()

  End Sub

  Private Sub Page_Init(ByVal sender As System.Object, ByVal e As_
                                        System.EventArgs) Handles
MyBase.Init
    InitializeComponent()
  End Sub

Private Sub Page_Load(ByVal sender As System.Object, ByVal e As System.EventArgs)
                                                              Handles
MyBase.Load
    'Call mapping function
    Mappings()
  End Sub


  Private Sub Mappings()

    'create connection, adapter and dataset
    Dim MappingConnection As New
SqlConnection("server=(local);database=wroxmoviedb;uid=sa;pwd=;")
    Dim MappingAdapter As New SqlDataAdapter("SELECT * FROM MOVIE",
MappingConnection)
    Dim MappingDataSet As New DataSet()

    'create a new table mapping and then add new column mappings
    MappingAdapter.TableMappings.Add("movie", "Favorite_Movies")
    MappingAdapter.TableMappings.item("movie").ColumnMappings.Add("Length",
"Minutes")
    MappingAdapter.TableMappings.item("movie").ColumnMappings.Add("Year", "Release
Date")
```

```
'fill the dataset passing in the name of the table mapping above
'to indicate that we want to use this mapping for our schema
MappingAdapter.Fill(MappingDataSet, "movie")

'write out the table name and the columns to an html table by
'looping through the columns for the headings and then through
'the rows for the data.
Response.Write("<Table border='1'><caption>" + _
               MappingDataSet.Tables.Item(0).TableName + "</caption><tr>")

'column headings
Dim c As DataColumn
For Each c In MappingDataSet.Tables.Item("Favorite_Movies").Columns

    Response.Write("<th>" + c.ColumnName + "</th>")
Next

Response.Write("</tr>")

'table cells
Dim r As DataRow
For Each r In MappingDataSet.Tables.Item("Favorite_Movies").Rows

    Response.Write("<tr>")
    Dim item As Object
    For Each item In r.ItemArray

      Response.Write("<td>" + item.ToString() + "</td>")
    Next

    Response.Write("</tr>")
  Next
End Sub

End Class
```

After defining the connection and query information, we create a table mapping to map the source table, "Movie", to the local table named "Favorite_Movies". Two Column Mappings are added as well, mapping "year" to "Release Date" and "Length" to "Minutes". After filling the DataSet, we write the data out to an HTML table to show that the names changed:

Favorite_Movies						
ID	Title	GenreID	Release Date	Director	Minutes	Rating

DataSet

The DataSet is the core of the ADO.NET framework. Acting as the local storage mechanism for data, the DataSet can either be kept in synch with a data source using a DataAdapter, or it can be used as a standalone data storage object. In today's Internet-dominated world, user interaction with systems is often stateless and disconnected, occurring one request at a time. In order to address this change, the DataSet has been developed to operate independently of any data source. The difference between working with a DataSet and the disconnected options when using an ADO RecordSet object is that a DataSet cannot, ever, be connected.

With XML making a significant impact on how we manage data today, one of the most important features about the `DataSet` is its ability to work with XML. The `DataSet`'s native serialization format is XML so loading, reading, saving, and writing XML are native operations requiring less memory and processor overhead than similar methods of the `RecordSet` object in traditional ADO. Using the `DataSet` to work with XML is covered in Chapter 15, *XML in ASP.NET*.

In order to best mimic the data source from which it is loaded, the `DataSet` provides a framework for structuring the data in a fashion that resembles a relational database. `DataTables` and `DataRelations`, are the two components that make this possible. `DataTables` hold the data itself, and the `DataRelations` allow for tying these tables together. Each of these classes is covered in the following sections and several examples of working with the `DataSet` are found throughout the rest of the chapter.

DataTable

The `DataTable` plays a central role in managing the in-memory representation of data. A `DataTable` represents a set of rows and columns that provide access to the data. This structure is similar to that found in a relational database system. While the `DataTable` uses the `DataColumn` and `DataRow` classes to help manage the data within, it acts as the central point for gaining access to data for the `DataView` and `DataSet`.

The `DataColumns` in a `DataTable` define the schema of the table and act as the central element in defining constraints and relations. In addition, the `DataColumn` provides other mechanisms for defining the limits of data in the `DataTable` such as prohibiting null values in a column, marking a column as read-only, or identifying a column, or columns, as the primary key for a `DataTable`.

> *A primary key indicates that a column or columns provides a value which uniquely identifies each row of data.*

Each `DataColumn` has a data type assigned to it and can optionally have constraints defined, which ensure that the data exists within certain limits. A `DataColumn` can either hold a specific value or can have an expression defined to set the value to a calculated or aggregate value.

The `DataRow` provides access to data elements in a table. Each row in the data table must meet the schema set forth by the `DataColumns` in the table. In order to add new data, the `NewRow` method of the `DataTable` is called to return a `DataRow` object. This `DataRow` can then be modified to ensure that no constraints will be violated and added to the `DataRowCollection` of the `DataTable` exposed by the `Rows` property.

The example below builds a `DataTable` manually by adding columns and rows. The web form for this example is simply a declaration of the code running behind the page:

Example: Building a DataTable

ASP.NET: `BuildTable.aspx`

```
<%@ Page language="c#" Codebehind="BuildTable.aspx.cs" AutoEventWireup="false"
Inherits="AspProgRefData_c.BuildTable" %>
```

C#: `BuildTable.aspx.cs`

```
using System;
using System.Collections;
using System.ComponentModel;
```

```
using System.Data;
using System.Drawing;
using System.Web;
using System.Web.SessionState;
using System.Web.UI;
using System.Web.UI.WebControls;
using System.Web.UI.HtmlControls;

namespace AspProgRefData_c
{
  public class BuildTable : System.Web.UI.Page
  {
    public BuildTable()
    {
      Page.Init += new System.EventHandler(Page_Init);
    }

    private void Page_Load(object sender, System.EventArgs e)
    {
      // Call our function to build a table
      BuildDataTable();
    }

    private void Page_Init(object sender, EventArgs e)
    {
      InitializeComponent();
    }

    private void BuildDataTable()
    {
      //create a new data table object
      DataTable GenreTable = new DataTable("Genre");

      //add two data columns to the datatable indicating name and type
      GenreTable.Columns.Add(new DataColumn("ID",Type.GetType("System.Int32")));
      GenreTable.Columns.Add(new
                DataColumn("Description",Type.GetType("System.String")));

      //create a DataRow object
      DataRow Row;

      //set the row object to a new row created by the table
      //this gives a new row with the schema of the table
      Row = GenreTable.NewRow();

      //set the values of the data
      Row["ID"] = 1;
      Row["Description"] = "Drama";

      //add the row to the table
      GenreTable.Rows.Add(Row);

      //generate a new row as before
      Row = GenreTable.NewRow();
      Row["ID"] = 2;
      Row["Description"] = "Action";

      GenreTable.Rows.Add(Row);

      //write out the table name and the columns to an html table by
      //looping through the columns for the headings and then through
      //the rows for the data.
```

```
            Response.Write("<Table border='1'><caption>" + GenreTable.TableName +
                                                        "</caption><tr>");

        //column headings
        foreach(DataColumn c in GenreTable.Columns)
        {
          Response.Write("<th>" + c.ColumnName + "</th>");
        }
        Response.Write("</tr>");

        //table cells
        foreach(DataRow r in GenreTable.Rows)
        {
          Response.Write("<tr>");
          foreach(Object item in r.ItemArray)
          {
            Response.Write("<td>" + item.ToString() + "</td>");
          }
          Response.Write("</tr>");
        }
    }
    private void InitializeComponent()
    {
       this.Load += new System.EventHandler(this.Page_Load);
    }
  }
}
```

VB.NET: `BuildTable.aspx.vb`

```
Public Class BuildTable
  Inherits System.Web.UI.Page

  <System.Diagnostics.DebuggerStepThrough()> Private Sub InitializeComponent()

  End Sub

  Private Sub Page_Init(ByVal sender As System.Object, ByVal e As_
                    System.EventArgs) Handles MyBase.Init
    InitializeComponent()
  End Sub

  Private Sub Page_Load(ByVal sender As System.Object, ByVal e As_
                    System.EventArgs) Handles MyBase.Load
    'call function to build table
    BuildDataTable()
  End Sub

  Private Sub BuildDataTable()

    'create a new data table object
    Dim GenreTable As New DataTable("Genre")

    'add two data columns to the datatable indicating name and type
    GenreTable.Columns.Add(New DataColumn("ID", Type.GetType("System.Int32")))
    GenreTable.Columns.Add(New DataColumn("Description",_
                                      Type.GetType("System.String")))

    'create a DataRow object
    Dim Row As DataRow
```

```
'set the row object to a new row created by the table
'this gives a new row with the schema of the table
Row = GenreTable.NewRow()

'set the values of the data
Row.Item("ID") = 1
Row.Item("Description") = "Drama"

'add the row to the table
GenreTable.Rows.Add(Row)

'generate a new row as before
Row = GenreTable.NewRow()
Row.Item("ID") = 2
Row.Item("Description") = "Action"

GenreTable.Rows.Add(Row)

'write out the table name and the columns to an html table by
'looping through the columns for the headings and then through
'the rows for the data.
Response.Write("<Table border='1'><caption>" + GenreTable.TableName +_
                                      "</caption><tr>")

'column headings
Dim c As DataColumn
For Each c In GenreTable.Columns
   Response.Write("<th>" + c.ColumnName + "</th>")
Next

Response.Write("</tr>")

'table cells
Dim r As DataRow
For Each r In GenreTable.Rows

   Response.Write("<tr>")
   Dim item As Object
   For Each item In r.ItemArray

     Response.Write("<td>" + item.ToString() + "</td>")

     Response.Write("</tr>")
   Next
Next

   End Sub
End Class
```

We create a `DataTable` object and then add two columns to it using the `Add` method of the `Columns` property. These columns provide the schema for our table by defining the data types of the columns. We then use the `NewRow` method of the `DataTable` to return a new row, which we edit and then add into the table using the `Add` method of the `Rows` property. Once we have added a couple of rows, we write the data out to the response stream, manually creating an HTML table:

DataView

The `DataView` class provides a means for presenting and working with different views of a `DataTable`. Several different `DataViews` can be pointing to a single `DataTable` and provide different views on the same data. For example, the first view could show a sorted view of all the rows still containing the original data while a second view could be an unsorted view of the rows that have been added.

The `DataView` is also used to bind data to user interface (UI) controls such as a `DataGrid` on a Windows Form or on a Web Form. The `DataView` implements a variety of interfaces allowing it to be easily enumerated and bound to other items. Because of this, if you want to bind part of a `DataSet` to a UI element, the `DataView` will be the class to use to bind to the control.

The `DataTable` object has a `DefaultView` property, which provides a starting view on the data. This view, or a customized view of the data, can be used not only to view data, but to edit it as well. The `AllowDelete`, `AllowEdit`, and `AllowNew` properties on the `DataView` indicate the actions that can be performed on the `DataView`. These changes are then reflected in the `DataTable` that serves as the data source for the `DataView`.

The example below exhibits how to use the `DefaultView` property of a `DataTable` to retrieve a view of the data. This view is then sorted and filtered to provide a distinct look at the data and several values are edited. In addition, we create a second view, which only shows the newly added items from the table:

Example: Using the DefaultView property of a Datatable

ASP.NET: `ViewSort.aspx`

```
<%@ Page Language="vb" AutoEventWireup="false" Codebehind="ViewSort.aspx.vb"
Inherits="AspProgRefData_vb.ViewSort"%>
<!DOCTYPE HTML PUBLIC "-//W3C//DTD HTML 4.0 Transitional//EN">
<html>
  <head>
  </head>
  <body ms_positioning="FlowLayot">
    <form id="ViewSort" method="post" runat="server">
      <asp:datagrid id="MovieGrid" runat="server"></asp:datagrid>
      <br>
      <asp:datagrid id="MovieGrid2" runat="server"></asp:datagrid>
    </form>
  </body>
</html>
```

The web form for this example is a simple page containing two `DataGrid` controls, which will display the two views. These items are marked to run at the server so that we can use them in the code behind page.

C#: `ViewSort.aspx.cs`

```
using System;
using System.ComponentModel;
using System.Data;
using System.Data.SqlClient;
using System.Web;

namespace AspProgRefData_c
{
  public class ViewSort : System.Web.UI.Page
  {
    protected System.Web.UI.WebControls.DataGrid MovieGrid2;
    protected System.Web.UI.WebControls.DataGrid MovieGrid;

    public ViewSort()
    {
      Page.Init += new System.EventHandler(Page_Init);
      this.Load += new System.EventHandler(this.Page_Load);
    }

    private void Page_Load(object sender, System.EventArgs e)
    {
```

```
        ExampleView();
    }

    private void Page_Init(object sender, EventArgs e)
    {}

    private void InitializeComponent()
    {}

    private void ExampleView()
    {
        //create connection dataAdapter and dataset
        SqlConnection ViewConnection = new_
            SqlConnection("server=(local);database=wroxmoviedb;uid=sa;pwd=");
        SqlDataAdapter ViewAdapter = new SqlDataAdapter("SELECT * FROM
                                            movie",ViewConnection);
        DataSet ViewDataSet = new DataSet();

        //fill dataset
        ViewAdapter.Fill(ViewDataSet, "movie");

        //create a dataview and set it equal to the default view
        //of the movie table we have filled
        DataView MovieView = ViewDataSet.Tables["movie"].DefaultView;

        //sort the view on the Title column
        MovieView.Sort="Title";

        //filter the rows to only show those movies with an R rating
        MovieView.RowFilter = "Rating='R'";

        //add a new row to the view, which adds it to
        //the underlying table as well.
        DataRowView NewRow = MovieView.AddNew();

        //begin editing the new row
        NewRow.BeginEdit();
        NewRow["ID"]=8;
        NewRow["Title"]="Traffic";
        NewRow["Director"]="Barry Sonnenfeld";
        NewRow["Year"] = "1/1/2000";
        NewRow["Rating"] = "R";
        NewRow["GenreID"] = 4;
        NewRow["Length"] = 180;

        //end edit of new row
        NewRow.EndEdit();

        //create a new view which shows only added items
        DataView NewView = new DataView(ViewDataSet.Tables["movie"]);
        NewView.RowStateFilter = DataViewRowState.Added;

        //display the movies on the page, the first grid will show all
        //R rated movies sorted by title while the second will show
        //only the added item
        MovieGrid.DataSource=MovieView;
        MovieGrid2.DataSource = NewView;
        DataBind();
    }
}
}
```

VB.NET: `ViewSort.aspx.vb`

```vb
Imports System.Data.SqlClient

Public Class ViewSort
  Inherits System.Web.UI.Page
  Protected WithEvents MovieGrid As System.Web.UI.WebControls.DataGrid
  Protected WithEvents MovieGrid2 As System.Web.UI.WebControls.DataGrid

  <System.Diagnostics.DebuggerStepThrough()> Private Sub InitializeComponent()

  End Sub

  Private Sub Page_Init(ByVal sender As System.Object, ByVal e As_
System.EventArgs) Handles

 MyBase.Init
    InitializeComponent()
  End Sub

  Private Sub Page_Load(ByVal sender As System.Object, ByVal e As_
System.EventArgs) Handles

MyBase.Load
    'call method to build views
    ExampleView()
  End Sub

  Private Sub ExampleView()

    'create connection dataAdapter and dataset
    Dim ViewConnection As New_
        SqlConnection("server=(local);database=wroxmoviedb;uid=sa;pwd=")
    Dim ViewAdapter As New SqlDataAdapter("SELECT * FROM movie", ViewConnection)
    Dim ViewDataSet As New DataSet()

    'fill dataset
    ViewAdapter.Fill(ViewDataSet, "movie")

    'create a dataview and set it equal to the default view
    'of the movie table we have filled
    Dim MovieView As DataView = ViewDataSet.Tables.Item("movie").DefaultView

    'sort the view on the Title column
    MovieView.Sort = "Title"

    'filter the rows to only show those movies with an R rating
    MovieView.RowFilter = "Rating='R'"

    'add a new row to the view, which adds it to
    'the underlying table as well.
    Dim NewRow As DataRowView = MovieView.AddNew()

    'begin editing the new row
    NewRow.BeginEdit()
    NewRow.Item("ID") = 8
    NewRow.Item("Title") = "Traffic"
    NewRow.Item("Director") = "Barry Sonnenfeld"
    NewRow.Item("Year") = "1/1/2000"
    NewRow.Item("Rating") = "R"
    NewRow.Item("GenreID") = 4
    NewRow.Item("Length") = 180
```

```
        'end edit of new row
        NewRow.EndEdit()

        'create a new view which shows only added items
        Dim NewView As DataView = New DataView(ViewDataSet.Tables.Item("movie"))
        NewView.RowStateFilter = DataViewRowState.Added

        'display the movies on the page, the first grid will show all
        'R rated movies sorted by title while the second will show
        'only the added item
        MovieGrid.DataSource = MovieView
        MovieGrid2.DataSource = NewView
        DataBind()
    End Sub
End Class
```

After filling a `DataSet` with data from the "Movie" table in our database, we use the default view as a starting point and define, sort, and filter clauses to arrange the view. We then add a new row to the view and edit it, adding it to the `DataTable` as well. Once this is complete, we create a new view based on the "Movie" table and set the `RowStateFilter` option to show only newly added rows. When displayed, the first grid contains only 'R' rated movies sorted by their title. The second grid contains only the new record added in the code.

Constraints and Relations

In most relational database systems, there are the concepts of constraints and relations. A constraint defines a rule by which the data must abide in order to be valid. For example, a `UniqueConstraint` can be created on a column of data to indicate that all rows must have a unique value in that column. This is often used for columns that need to uniquely identify a row and might be an Employee ID, a Social Security number, or a machine-generated identifier or number. Constraints provide a means for ensuring the integrity of the data by keeping a user or application from inserting, updating, or deleting data that would violate the constraint. If a new record would violate the `UniqueConstraint`, most databases will throw an error to be caught by the calling application.

Relations provide another means to ensure data integrity, as well as a mechanism for finding items that are connected to one another. Relations allow a data item in one table to be associated with data items in other tables. The idea of related data is at the heart of relational database systems. As an example, the sample movie database we have been using in this chapter contains a Movie table. In this table there is column named GenreID. The GenreID column is related to the ID column of the Genre table to allow looking up the specific genre of a given movie. This provides a reduction in data redundancy because we do not need to specify the full genre name in the movie table, but can give a simple numeric ID. It also allows easier management of data, as we can change the genre in one place and all of the movies specifying that genre, by its ID, will then reflect the change.

The `DataSet` is intended to provide a local, disconnected, copy of the data found in a data source. Having the data local provides many benefits, but the data source is not able to enforce constraints or relations on the local data and any problems will not be known until an attempt is made to update the data source. Fortunately, the `DataSet` object has a collection of `DataRelations` and the `DataTable` has a collection of `Constraints`. By mimicking the constraints and relations of the data source, we can ensure that the data, when updated, will be more likely to successfully integrate back into the data source. In addition, we can create constraints or relations that do not exist in the data source, but which ensure that data entered into the `DataSet` meets certain requirements.

As of this writing, the .NET framework provides two constraints: `ForeignKeyConstraint` and `UniqueConstraint`. The `UniqueConstraint` was described above and ensures that a data column contains unique values. The `ForeignKeyConstraint` is used to constrain values in two different `DataTable` objects. This constraint is used when a relation exists between the two tables, though this does not have to be a defined `DataRelation`. The `ForeignKeyConstraint` identifies what action should be taken in a related table when a value in one of the specified `DataColumns` is updated or deleted.

Developers can define their own constraints by simply inheriting from the `System.Data.Constraint` class and implementing the abstract methods defined in the base class. For example, a constraint could be created that ensures that values in a particular column are valid US phone numbers.

> In order for constraints to be enforced, the **`EnforceConstraints`** property of the **`DataSet`** must be set to **`true`** (this is the default value).

`DataRelations` allow a developer to define relationships between two `DataTables` in a `DataSet`. In this way, a parent-child relationship can be created. In our example using the Movie database, the Movie table would be the parent and the Genre table would be the child. The `DataRelation` allows access to related data in the parent table from a row in the child table, and vice versa. Given a specific row in the Movie table, we can access the related row in the genre table using the `DataRelation` defined between them.

In order for a `DataRelation` to be created, the data type of the data columns in the respective data tables must be the same. It is not possible, for example, to relate two tables if the column in the first table is a `String` type, and the column in the second table is an `Integer` type. Regardless of whether the values in the `String` column are always numbers, the relationship cannot exist unless the actual types are the same.

Example: Constrains and Relations

ASP.NET: `ConstrintAndRelation.aspx`

```
<%@ Page language="c#" Codebehind="ConstraintAndRelation.aspx.cs"
AutoEventWireup="false" Inherits="AspProgRefData_c.ConstraintAndRelation" %>
<!DOCTYPE HTML PUBLIC "-//W3C//DTD HTML 4.0 Transitional//EN" >
<html>
  <head></head>
  <body>
    <form id="ConstraintAndRelation" method="post" runat="server">
      <asp:DataGrid id="MovieGrid" runat="server"></asp:DataGrid>
    </form>
  </body>
</html>
```

C#: `ConstraintAndRelation.aspx.cs`

```
using System;
using System.Data;
using System.Data.SqlClient;
using System.Web;
using System.Web.UI;
using System.Web.UI.WebControls;
using System.Web.UI.HtmlControls;

namespace AspProgRefData_c
{
```

```
    public class ConstraintAndRelation : System.Web.UI.Page
    {
      protected System.Web.UI.WebControls.DataGrid MovieGrid;

      public ConstraintAndRelation()
      {
        Page.Init += new System.EventHandler(Page_Init);
        this.Load += new System.EventHandler(this.Page_Load);
      }

      private void Page_Load(object sender, System.EventArgs e)
      {
        // Call method to do the work
        ConstrainAndRelate();
      }

      private void Page_Init(object sender, EventArgs e)
      {}

      private void InitializeComponent()
      {}

      private void ConstrainAndRelate()
      {
        //create connection, adapter and dataset
        SqlConnection MovieConnection = new
            SqlConnection("server=(local);database=wroxmoviedb;uid=sa;pwd=;");
        SqlDataAdapter MovieAdapter = new SqlDataAdapter("SELECT * from movie
                                      SELECT * from genre",MovieConnection);
        DataSet MovieDataSet = new DataSet();

        //create two table mappings
        MovieAdapter.TableMappings.Add("movie","movie");
        MovieAdapter.TableMappings.Add("genre", "genre");

        //fill the dataset using the first mapping
        MovieAdapter.Fill(MovieDataSet, "movie");

        //name the second table to match our mapping
        MovieDataSet.Tables[1].TableName = "genre";

        //create unique constraint on the "ID" column of the movie table
        DataColumn[] ConstrainedColumn = new

DataColumn[]{MovieDataSet.Tables["movie"].Columns["id"]};
        UniqueConstraint UniqueActorID = new UniqueConstraint("UniqueActorID",
                                          ConstrainedColumn);

        //create a relation between the movie and genre tables on the
        //genre id
        DataRelation MovieRelation = new DataRelation("MovieGenre",
            new DataColumn[]{MovieDataSet.Tables["movie"].Columns["genreid"]},
            new DataColumn[]{MovieDataSet.Tables[1].Columns[0]},false);

        //add the constraints to the table and the relation to the dataset
        MovieDataSet.Tables["movie"].Constraints.Add(UniqueActorID);
        MovieDataSet.Relations.Add(MovieRelation);
```

```
        //display the data on the page
        MovieGrid.DataSource = MovieDataSet.Tables["movie"].DefaultView;
        DataBind();

    }
    }
}
```

VB.NET: `ConstraintAndRelation.aspx.vb`

```
Imports System
Imports System.Data
Imports System.Data.SqlClient
Imports System.Web
Imports System.Web.UI
Imports System.Web.UI.WebControls
Imports System.Web.UI.HtmlControls
Public Class ConstraintAndRelation
    Inherits System.Web.UI.Page
    Protected WithEvents MovieGrid As System.Web.UI.WebControls.DataGrid

    <System.Diagnostics.DebuggerStepThrough()> Private Sub InitializeComponent()

    End Sub

    Private Sub Page_Init(ByVal sender As System.Object, ByVal e As_
System.EventArgs) Handles

MyBase.Init
        InitializeComponent()
    End Sub

    Private Sub Page_Load(ByVal sender As System.Object, ByVal e As_
System.EventArgs) Handles

MyBase.Load
        'call function
        ConstrainAndRelate()

    End Sub

    Private Sub ConstrainAndRelate()

        'create connection, adapter and dataset
        Dim MovieConnection As New _
                    SqlConnection("server=(local);database=wroxmoviedb;uid=sa;pwd=;")
        Dim MovieAdapter As New SqlDataAdapter
                        ("SELECT * from movie;SELECT * from genre",_
                                                    MovieConnection)

        Dim MovieDataSet As New DataSet()

        'create two table mappings
        MovieAdapter.TableMappings.Add("movie", "movie")
        MovieAdapter.TableMappings.Add("genre", "genre")

        'fill the dataset using the first mapping
        MovieAdapter.Fill(MovieDataSet, "movie")

        'name the second table to match our mapping
        MovieDataSet.Tables.Item(1).TableName = "genre"
```

```
        'create a unique constraint on the "ID" column of the movie table
        Dim ConstrainedColumn() As DataColumn = New DataColumn()

{MovieDataSet.Tables.Item("movie").Columns.Item("id")}
        Dim UniqueActorID As New UniqueConstraint("UniqueActorID", ConstrainedColumn)

        'create a relation between the movie and genre tables on the genre id
        Dim MovieRelation As New DataRelation("MovieGenre", New DataColumn()
{MovieDataSet.Tables.Item("movie").Columns.Item("genreid")}, _
            New DataColumn() {MovieDataSet.Tables.Item(1).Columns.Item(0)}, False)

        'add the constraint to the table and the relation to the dataset
        MovieDataSet.Tables.Item("movie").Constraints.Add(UniqueActorID)
        MovieDataSet.Relations.Add(MovieRelation)

        'display the data on the page
        MovieGrid.DataSource = MovieDataSet.Tables.Item("movie").DefaultView
        DataBind()
    End Sub
End Class
```

In this example, we first load a `DataSet` with **genre** and movie information using table mappings to provide our internal tables with names. We then create a new `UniqueConstraint` object and indicate that the "ID" column of the movie table should be constrained. A `DataRelation` is defined between the movie and genre tables specifying **genreID** as the column that relates the two tables. Finally, we must add the newly-created constraint and relation to their respective collections on the `DataTable` and `DataSet`. Now, any attempt to add a row to the **Movie** table with an "ID" that already exists will result in a `ConstraintException` being thrown. We also have the ability to use the **genreID** to get related records in one table from the other.

Data Binding

With the advent of server controls in ASP.NET developers have a very powerful set of tools at their fingertips. To make these objects even more powerful, Microsoft has implemented a data binding infrastructure, which is used by many of the controls. In the old days, a classic ASP developer had to write a lot of code to extract data from a database and write it out in an HTML table similar to the examples in the section on the `DataTable` earlier in the chapter. With ASP.NET, we bind a data source to the control and call its `DataBind` method – and that's it! Of course we have options to format the controls using standard HTML attribute tags and even more flexibility on others. Chapters 4, 5, and 6 cover the various controls in detail.

`DataBinding` allows a user interface element to be provided with a data source and then instructed to bind to that data. It is up to the control itself to manage this binding and determine how and where to display the data. This behavior is similar to data-bound controls that became popular in the client-server world. An example of these controls is the `DataGrid`, which presents data in an HTML table. As an example, the following code sample shows creating this type of output. We use the `DataGrid` server-side control and use an `SqlDataReader` to extract data and bind it to the `DataGrid`.

Example: Reading Data from a DataGrid

ASP.NET: `ReadGrid.aspx`

```
<%@ Page Language="vb" AutoEventWireup="false" Codebehind="readgrid.aspx.vb"
Inherits="AspProgRefData_vb.readgrid"%>
<!DOCTYPE HTML PUBLIC "-//W3C//DTD HTML 4.0 Transitional//EN">
<html>
```

```
  <head></head>
  <body>
    <form id="Form1" method="post" runat="server">
      <asp:DataGrid id="dgReader" style="Z-INDEX: 101; LEFT: 14px;
          POSITION: absolute; TOP: 8px" runat="server"></asp:DataGrid>
    </form>
  </body>
</html>
```

As you can see, this is a standard ASP.NET web page with a single DataGrid server control element declared. This control is marked to run at server so that the data can be bound to it in the code behind page.

C#: readgrid.aspx.cs

```csharp
using System;
using System.Data;
using System.Data.SqlClient;
using System.Web;
using System.Web.UI;
using System.Web.UI.WebControls;
using System.Web.UI.HtmlControls;

namespace AspProgRefData_c
{
  public class readerlist : System.Web.UI.Page
  {
    protected System.Web.UI.WebControls.DataGrid dgReader;

    public readerlist()
    {
      Page.Init += new System.EventHandler(Page_Init);
    }

    private void Page_Load(object sender, System.EventArgs e)
    {
      //declare database variables
      SqlConnection MovieConnection = new
        SqlConnection("server=(local);database=wroxmoviedb;uid=sa;pwd=;");
      SqlCommand MovieCommand = new
      SqlCommand("SELECT * from movie",MovieConnection);

      SqlDataReader MovieReader;

      //open the connection to the database and get our reader
      MovieConnection.Open();
      MovieReader = MovieCommand.ExecuteReader(CommandBehavior.CloseConnection);

      //set the datasource of the grid to our reader and bind them
      dgReader.DataSource = MovieReader;
      dgReader.DataBind();

      //close the reader, and thus the connection based on the
      //parameter used to get the reader
      MovieReader.Close();

    }
```

```
   private void Page_Init(object sender, EventArgs e)
   {

     InitializeComponent();
   }

   private void InitializeComponent()
   {
     this.Load += new System.EventHandler(this.Page_Load);
   }
  }
}
```

VB.NET: readgrid.aspx.vb

```
Imports System.Data
Imports System.Data.SqlClient

Public Class readgrid
  Inherits System.Web.UI.Page
  Protected WithEvents dgReader As System.Web.UI.WebControls.DataGrid

  <System.Diagnostics.DebuggerStepThrough()> Private Sub InitializeComponent()

  End Sub

  Private Sub Page_Init(ByVal sender As System.Object, ByVal e As System.EventArgs)
                                                            Handles MyBase.Init
         InitializeComponent()
  End Sub


  Private Sub Page_Load(ByVal sender As System.Object, ByVal e As System.EventArgs)
                                                            Handles MyBase.Load

       'declare database variables
       Dim MovieConnection As New
       SqlConnection("server=(local);database=wroxmoviedb;uid=sa;pwd=")
       Dim MovieCommand As New SqlCommand("SELECT * from movie", MovieConnection)

       Dim MovieReader As SqlDataReader

       'open the connection to the database and get our reader
       MovieConnection.Open()
       MovieReader = MovieCommand.ExecuteReader(CommandBehavior.CloseConnection)

       'set the datasource of the grid to our reader and bind them
       dgReader.DataSource = MovieReader
       dgReader.DataBind()

       'close the reader, and thus the connection based on the
       'parameter used to get the reader

       MovieReader.Close()

    End Sub
End Class
```

739

In the `Page Load` event we connect to the data source and use a command object to get a `SqlDataReader`. We then pass this `DataReader` to the `DataGrid` as its `DataSource` property. Calling the `DataBind` method on the `DataGrid` causes it to go through the `DataSource` and create the HTML output. If we just call `DataBind` within the page scope, all controls on the page will have their `DataBind` method called. This can be used as a shortcut, rather than trying to remember to call `DataBind` on each control.

The `SqlDataReader` is not the only object that can be passed to the `DataSource` property of a bound control. Any object that properly exposes the `IEnumerable` interface can be bound to a control. The `IEnumerable` interface allows for the "For...Each" syntax in accessing items of a collection. Many of the base classes in the .NET framework implement this interface including `Array`, `ArrayList`, `DataView`, and `Hashtable`. In fact, a single `DataSet` could have several of its tables loaded from one call to the data source and then views of each of those tables could be bound to different controls on the page.

In the rest of this section, we'll walk through building an ASP.NET page containing several data controls. We will work with a variety of the functions of the `DataSet` in order to provide a hands-on look at working with the `DataSet` in ASP.NET. Many of the functions have been described earlier in the chapter, and this example brings them together. As this example is intended to provide insight on working with data in relation to the controls, attention is focused on the functionality of the page and not the layout.

The final web form is shown in the figure below. The page consists of several controls on the left-hand side for sorting and filtering. In the main portion of the page is a `DataGrid` containing the various genres of movies in our sample movie database. Below this grid is another grid showing movies. The page is set up such that when sort and filter criteria are selected, the genres grid reflects these criteria. Upon clicking on any one of the genre ID values, the movie grid is updated to show only those movies that are in the specified genre.

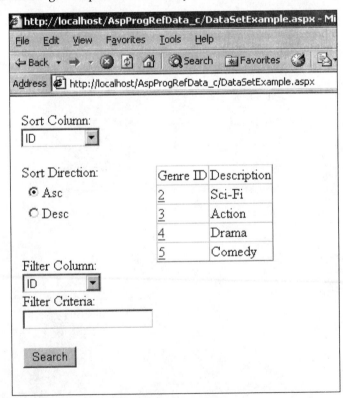

Example: Using the DataSet with Server Controls

ASPNET: **DataSetExample.aspx**

```
<%@ Page language="c#" Codebehind="DataSetExample.aspx.cs" AutoEventWireup="false"
Inherits="AspProgRefData_c.DataSetExample" %>
<!DOCTYPE HTML PUBLIC "-//W3C//DTD HTML 4.0 Transitional//EN" >
<html>
  <head></head>
  <body>
    <form id="frmExample" method="post" runat="server">
      <table>
        <tr>
        <!--Sort section -->
          <td rowspan="5" valign="top">
            Sort Column:
            <br>
            <asp:DropDownList ID="sortcol" Runat="server"></asp:DropDownList>
            <br>
            <br>
            Sort Direction:
            <br>
            <asp:RadioButtonList ID="sortdir" Runat="server">
              <asp:ListItem Text="Asc" Value="ASC" Selected="True"></asp:ListItem>
              <asp:ListItem Text="Desc" Value="DESC"></asp:ListItem>
            </asp:RadioButtonList>
            <br>
        <!--End Sort Section -->

        <!--Filter Section -->
            <br>
            Filter Column:
            <br>
            <asp:DropDownList ID="filtercol" Runat="server"></asp:DropDownList>
            <br>
            Filter Criteria:
            <br>
            <asp:TextBox ID="filtercriteria" Width="150"
                Runat="server"></asp:TextBox>
            <br>
        <!--End Filter Section -->
            <asp:Button id="postbackbutton" runat="server"
                text="Search"></asp:Button>
          </td>
          <td>
        <!--Genre grid definition -->
            <asp:DataGrid ID="genre" runat="server" AutoGenerateColumns="false">
              <Columns>
                <asp:HyperLinkColumn HeaderText="Genre ID" DataTextField="id"
                  DataNavigateUrlFormatString="datasetexample.aspx?genreid={0}"
                  DataNavigateUrlField="id"></asp:HyperLinkColumn>
                <asp:BoundColumn HeaderText="Description"
                                    DataField="description"></asp:BoundColumn>
              </Columns>
            </asp:DataGrid>
        <!--End Genre Grid-->
            <br>
            <br>
            <br>'
        <!--Movie Grid-->
```

741

```
          <asp:DataGrid ID="movies" Runat="server"></asp:DataGrid>
        </td>
      </tr>
    </table>
  </form>
</body>
</html>
```

We use an HTML table to lay out our page, providing a framework for organizing the various elements. The drop-down list and radio buttons for the sorting selection are defined and we indicate that these should run at the server so that we can get access to their values from the code behind our page. We do the same thing with the filter criteria and follow it with a button that we can use to post our form the server. We then define a `DataGrid` element to hold the genres, which we provide with some custom layout instructions for the columns to allow the ID to act as a link. For more information about working with the `DataGrid`, see Chapter 5, *System.Web.UI.WebControls*. Finally, we create a simple `DataGrid` to hold the movie information. Next, we take a look at the code behind this page in both C# and VB.NET.

C#: `DataSetExample.aspx.cs`

```csharp
using System;
using System.Data;
using System.Data.Common;
using System.Data.SqlClient;
using System.Web;
using System.Web.UI;
using System.Web.UI.WebControls;
using System.Web.UI.HtmlControls;

namespace AspProgRefData_c
{
  public class DataSetExample : System.Web.UI.Page
  {
    protected System.Web.UI.WebControls.DropDownList sortcol;
    protected System.Web.UI.WebControls.RadioButtonList sortdir;
    protected System.Web.UI.WebControls.DropDownList filtercol;
    protected System.Web.UI.WebControls.TextBox filtercriteria;
    protected System.Web.UI.WebControls.DataGrid genres;
    protected System.Web.UI.WebControls.DataGrid products;
    protected System.Web.UI.WebControls.DataGrid movies;
    protected System.Web.UI.WebControls.DataGrid genre;

    public DataSetExample()
    {
      Page.Init += new System.EventHandler(Page_Init);
    }

    private void Page_Load(object sender, System.EventArgs e)
    {
        SqlConnection MovieConnection = new
          SqlConnection("server=(local);database=wroxmoviedb;uid=sa;pwd=");
        SqlCommand MovieCommand = new  SqlCommand
          ("SELECT * from genre;SELECT * from movie", MovieConnection);
        SqlDataAdapter MovieAdapter = new  SqlDataAdapter();
        DataSet MovieDataSet = new  DataSet();


        //indicate that we want the primary key
        //da.MissingSchemaAction = MissingSchemaAction.AddWithKey;
```

```
        //set the select command and fill our dataset
        MovieAdapter.SelectCommand = MovieCommand;
        MovieAdapter.Fill(MovieDataSet, "genre");

    //name the second table from our query
    MovieDataSet.Tables[1].TableName ="movie";

        //set the datasource for our drop down lists to get the column names
        sortcol.DataSource = MovieDataSet.Tables["genre"].Columns;
        filtercol.DataSource = MovieDataSet.Tables["genre"].Columns;

        //if we are posting back to this page, then create a new view on our data
        //to bind to the grid
        if (IsPostBack)
    {

            //set the sort value in the format: column ASC|DESC
            MovieDataSet.Tables["genre"].DefaultView.Sort =
             sortcol.SelectedItem.ToString() + " " +
             sortdir.SelectedItem.ToString();

            //if we have filter criteria specified then filter the view
            if  (filtercriteria.Text != String.Empty)
        {
        MovieDataSet.Tables["genre"].DefaultView.RowFilter = _
                        filtercol.SelectedItem.ToString() +
                        filtercriteria.Text;
        }

            //set the categories grid to have the new view as the datasource
        genre.DataSource = MovieDataSet.Tables["genre"].DefaultView;
        }
        else
    {
            //no postback so we use the default view of the categories table
        genre.DataSource = MovieDataSet.Tables["genre"].DefaultView;
    }

        //if we get a request for a category, display the child rows of the

        //products table
    if(Request.QueryString["genreid"] != null)
    {
      movies.Visible=true;
      //create a new dataview and set its filter based on the
      //value selected
      DataView MovieView = new DataView(MovieDataSet.Tables["movie"]);
      MovieView.RowFilter = "genreid=" + Request.QueryString["genreid"];

      movies.DataSource = MovieView;
    }
    else
    {
      movies.Visible=false;
    }

        //bind all of our controls
        DataBind();
}
```

```csharp
    private void Page_Init(object sender, EventArgs e)
    {
      InitializeComponent();
    }


    private void InitializeComponent()
    {
      this.Load += new System.EventHandler(this.Page_Load);

    }
  }
}
```

VB.NET: `DataSetExample.aspx.vb`

```vbnet
Imports System
Imports System.Data
Imports System.Data.SqlClient
Imports System.Data.Common
Imports System.Web
Imports System.Web.UI
Imports System.Web.UI.HtmlControls
Imports System.Web.UI.WebControls

Public Class DataSetExample
    Inherits System.Web.UI.Page
    Protected WithEvents sortcol As System.Web.UI.WebControls.DropDownList
    Protected WithEvents sortdir As System.Web.UI.WebControls.RadioButtonList
    Protected WithEvents filtercol As System.Web.UI.WebControls.DropDownList
    Protected WithEvents filtercriteria As System.Web.UI.WebControls.TextBox
  Protected WithEvents movies As System.Web.UI.WebControls.DataGrid
  Protected WithEvents genre As System.Web.UI.WebControls.DataGrid

  <System.Diagnostics.DebuggerStepThrough()> Private Sub InitializeComponent()

  End Sub

 Private Sub Page_Init(ByVal sender As System.Object, ByVal e As System.EventArgs) _
                                                        Handles MyBase.Init

    InitializeComponent()
  End Sub

 Private Sub Page_Load(ByVal sender As System.Object, ByVal e As System.EventArgs) _
                                                        Handles MyBase.Load

    Dim MovieConnection As New _
                SqlConnection("server=(local);database=wroxmoviedb;uid=sa;pwd=")
    Dim MovieCommand As New SqlCommand & _
    ("SELECT * from genre;SELECT * from movie", MovieConnection)*
    Dim MovieAdapter As New SqlDataAdapter()
    Dim MovieDataSet As New DataSet()

    'set the select command and fill our dataset
    MovieAdapter.SelectCommand = MovieCommand
    MovieAdapter.Fill(MovieDataSet, "genre")

    MovieDataSet.Tables.Item(1).TableName = "movie"
```

```
'set the datasource for our drop down lists to get the column names
sortcol.DataSource = MovieDataSet.Tables.Item("genre").Columns
filtercol.DataSource = MovieDataSet.Tables.Item("genre").Columns

'if we are posting back to this page, then create a new view on our data to
' bind to the grid
If (IsPostBack) Then

    'set the sort value in the format: column ASC|DESC
    MovieDataSet.Tables.Item("genre").DefaultView.Sort =  & _
         sortcol.SelectedItem.ToString() & " " &_
         sortdir.SelectedItem.ToString()

    'if we have filter criteria specified then filter the view
    If Not filtercriteria.Text = String.Empty Then
      MovieDataSet.Tables.Item("genre").DefaultView.RowFilter = & _
                        filtercol.SelectedItem.ToString() &_
                        filtercriteria.Text
    End If

    'set the genre grid to have the new view as the datasource
    genre.DataSource = MovieDataSet.Tables.Item("genre").DefaultView
Else
    'no postback so we use the default view of the genre table
    genre.DataSource = MovieDataSet.Tables.Item("genre").DefaultView

End If

'if we get a request for a genre, display the child rows of the movie table
If Not Request.QueryString("genreid") = Nothing Then
    'create new view and set the filter based on the
    'item selected
    Dim MovieView As New DataView(MovieDataSet.Tables.Item("movie"))
    MovieView.RowFilter = "genreid=" & Request.QueryString("genreid")

    'set datasource of movie grid to the new view
    movies.DataSource = MovieView
End If

'bind all of our controls
DataBind()
End Sub

End Class
```

There is a lot happening in this example. We define our objects and then start by filling the `DataSet` with movie and genre information. We then set the data source for the drop-down controls to be the `Columns` property of the `Genre` table. Since the `DataColumns` collection is enumerable, these will be filled automatically when we call `databind`. We next check to see if the request for the page is a postback. If it is, then we create a new view of the data and set the sort and filter properties accordingly, using this view as the source for the main grid on the page. Next we check to see if a specific genre ID was sent with the request, and if one was, then we filter the movie table's default view to show only movies with that genre ID. If no ID was sent with the request, we hide the grid.

In a real application, we would not load the data on each request and would implement some form of caching. The repeated trips to the server in this scenario would not be acceptable for a high volume site, but serve to provde an example of using `DataSet` and `DataView` to view data.

Binding Templated Controls

In addition to those controls that allow binding simply by setting the data source, there are controls that can be bound, but require direction on layout as well as where to insert data items. These templated controls include the `DataList`, covered in Chapter 5. Here we'll show a simple example using the `DataList` and take a look at how we can bind data to the control using different databinding methods, which will be explained in more detail after the example. This example utilizes the `GrocerToGo` database, which comes as part of the Framework SDK for the .NET framework. Having the images associated with that sample provides for a much more impressive example when run in a browser.

Example: Databinding

ASP.NET: **`Databind_template.aspx`**

```
<%@ Page Language="vb" AutoEventWireup="false"
Codebehind="databind_template.aspx.vb"
Inherits="AspProgRefData_vb.databind_template"%>
<!DOCTYPE HTML PUBLIC "-//W3C//DTD HTML 4.0 Transitional//EN">
<html>
  <head></head>
  <body>
    <form id="Form1" method="post" runat="server">
      <asp:DataList id="dlProducts" runat="server" RepeatDirection="Horizontal"
                                                   RepeatColumns="3">

        <ItemTemplate>
          <table>
            <tr><td rowspan="5">
                <img src="<%# Container.DataItem("imagepath")%>">
              </td>
              <td>
                <b>
                  <%# Container.DataItem("productname")%>
                </b>
                <br>
                <font style="FONT-WEIGHT: bold; FONT-SIZE: smaller">from
                  <%# Container.DataItem("manufacturer")%>
                </font>
              </td>
            </tr>
            <tr>
              <td>
                <%# Container.DataItem("productdescription")%>
              </td>
            </tr>
            <tr>
              <td>
                Servings:
                <%# DataBinder.Eval(Container.DataItem,"servings")%>
              </td>
            </tr>
            <tr>
              <td>
                Serving Size:
                <%# DataBinder.Eval(Container.DataItem,"servingsize")%>
              </td>
            </tr>
            <tr>
              <td>
                Price:
                <%# DataBinder.Eval(Container.DataItem,"unitprice")%>
              </td>
            </tr>
```

```
                </table>
              </ItemTemplate>
          </asp:DataList>
        </form>
    </body>
</html>
```

VB.NET: databind_template.aspx.vb

```vb
Imports System
Imports System.Data
Imports System.Data.SqlClient
Imports System.Web
Imports System.Web.UI
Imports System.Web.UI.HtmlControls
Imports System.Web.UI.WebControls

Public Class databind_template
    Inherits System.Web.UI.Page
    Protected WithEvents dlProducts As System.Web.UI.WebControls.DataList

    <System.Diagnostics.DebuggerStepThrough()> Private Sub InitializeComponent()

    End Sub

    Private Sub Page_Init(ByVal sender As System.Object, ByVal e As_
System.EventArgs) Handles

MyBase.Init
        InitializeComponent()
    End Sub

    Private Sub Page_Load(ByVal sender As System.Object, ByVal e As_
System.EventArgs) Handles

MyBase.Load
    Dim GrocerConnection As New _
                SqlConnection("server=(local);database=grocertogo;uid=sa;pwd=;")
    Dim GrocerAdapter As New SqlDataAdapter( & _
    "SELECT productid,productname, productdescription,unitprice," & _
    "servingsize, servings, manufacturer,imagepath FROM products" & _
    , GrocerConnection)
    Dim GrocerDataSet As New DataSet("dsProducts")

    GrocerAdapter.Fill(GrocerDataSet, "Products")

    dlProducts.DataSource = GrocerDataSet.Tables.Item("Products").DefaultView
    dlProducts.DataBind()

    End Sub

End Class
```

The first thing we do is to add a DataList item to the page and set its attributes to have three columns of repeating templates. Then we define the ItemTemplate and in it we build a table to display our data. As we define the template we indicate where the data should go for the given item. We do this though ASP.NET's declarative data binding syntax.

> **The syntax of the declarative binding code is dependant on the language of the code defined for the page. In this case we used VB syntax because the language attribute of the page declaration is VB.**

Declarative data binding in ASP.NET uses the <%# ... %> tag syntax. Items within these tags are only evaluated when the DataBind method is called on the containing control, in this case the control serving as the container for the ItemTemplate. When the DataBind method is called on a control, including the page, all contained controls have their DataBind method called as well.

In our example, we have used two different methods of binding. The first, explicit binding, looks like the following:

C#:
```
<%# ((System.Data.DataRowView)Container.DataItem)["manufacturer"]%>
```

VB.NET:
```
<%# Container.DataItem("manufacturer") %>
```

This syntax explicitly casts the data item to a DataRowView object and then accesses the "manufacturer" item. Because this item is a string value, there is no need to cast it as well. If it were another type of object we could use the ToString method in order to be able to output it to the screen.

The other method for declarative binding involves the use of a static method on the DataBinder class. This method uses reflection to allow for using late-bound objects in the data-binding declarative output. For example we used this syntax on the price of the item in our page:

C#:
```
<%# DataBinder.Eval(Container.DataItem, "unitprice")%>
```

VB.NET:
```
<%# DataBinder.Eval(Container.DataItem, "servings")%>
```

While this method is easier to write, it comes with a performance penalty. Because the information is late bound and reflection is used, this method will cost you and should only be used in Rapid Application Development (RAD) environments where performance is not a major concern such as prototyping or small internal applications with few users.

Editing Data

Editing Data in ASP.NET, as in any web application, is a disconnected operation. As such, there are several ways to edit data. The templated controls, such as the datalist, make this much easier by providing a framework for submitting records and information to the page. This is accomplished by providing an edit template in which certain controls present their values in editable controls such as a textbox. See Chapter 5, *System.Web.UI.WebControls,* or more information on using these controls.

In order to update data in a data source, we must use a command object. However, this command can be freestanding or part of a DataAdapter connected to a DataSet. Using the Data Command objects, we simply create our SQL statement dynamically from the values passed in and execute our commands using the Command.ExecuteNonQuery method. In addition, a parameterized stored procedure can be used which, in most cases, will give the best performance.

When using the DataSet, we load it with the same data we displayed, or the specific row(s) we are going to update, and make the changes according to the information posted to the page. We then use the DataAdapter's update command to submit the changes to the database. It should be noted that this method involves overhead that the first method does not, especially if the data for the DataSet needs to be loaded from the data source in order to be edited. This method would only make sense in a limited number of cases and would most likely be accompanied by a caching framework that would remove the need to load the data from the data source before editing it.

In many enterprise-level applications, a middle tier of business objects will actually be providing data to our ASP.NET presentation layer and managing the updating of the database. In these cases, the mechanism for updating data will depend on the architecture and design of the application. However, as the Command objects are the mechanism for submitting commands to the data source, any .NET application directly updating the data source will be using the Command objects to do so.

Summary

In this chapter we saw how the DataReader and DataSet objects allow us to access data in a variety of datasources. We discussed how the Managed Providers take care of communicating with the data source and managing our connections for us. We also took a look at some of the data binding fundamentals.

The ADO.NET framework is extremely powerful and is geared towards a disconnected architecture like that found in web applications which makes it a perfect complement to ASP.NET. With the improved XML features that are an integral part of the ADO.NET framework, transmitting data between applications, and even platforms, is a simple operation.

In this chapter we have covered:

- ❑ **Connection and Transaction classes** – these classes provide the actual communication mechanism with the database and manage the context of that connection

- ❑ **Command and Parameter classes** – the command and parameter classes work in conjunction to allow the developer to execute commands against a data source to SELECT, INSERT, UPDATE, or DELETE data

- ❑ **DataAdapter** – the DataAdapter manages the interaction between the data source and the DataSet object to keep the two in synch

- ❑ **DataReader** – the DataReader provdes fast, forward-only, read-only access to data in a data source.

- ❑ **DataTable, DataColumn, and DataRow classes** – these classes work together to manage the schema and editing of data

- ❑ **DataSet** – the core of the disconnected architecture in ADO.NET, the DataSet serves as a local data storage mechanism

- ❑ **DataRelation and Constraint classes** – these classes allow constraint of the data in the DataSet in order to provide data integrity when keeping the local copy of the data in synch with the data source

- ❑ **ASP.NET DataBinding** – presenting data to the user through the ASP.NET framework utilizes the server controls and a binding framework that allows bindng many different collections to UI elements

XML in ASP.NET

The .NET Framework provides a range of useful classes for working with XML documents and resources. This includes support for the W3C XML DOM interface, and extensions to facilitate a wide variety of common tasks. There is also built-in support for translating data to and from the ADO.NET-style relational format.

All in all, there are an enormous number of classes in the System.Xml namespace and its subsidiary namespaces, and we can't cover them all in detail in a single chapter. However, we'll provide an overview of the complete namespace and then look at how we can use the objects it contains to accomplish the most common XML-related tasks.

This chapter will look at:

❑   The namespaces available for working with XML

❑   Details of the most useful classes in these namespaces

❑   How we can use these objects for everyday tasks

❑   The automatic synchronization of XML and relational data

We start, then, with an overview of the namespaces and the objects they provide

System.Xml Namespaces Overview

There are three namespaces that implement the main XML features of the .NET Framework. Note that the XML namespaces discussed in this chapter refer to the .NET class groupings, and should not be confused with namespaces in XML documents, that are used to distinguish elements of a particular XML dialect.

Namespace	Description
System.Xml	The primary namespace, containing the W3C-compliant XML document objects and the ancillary objects for working with XML documents. These include W3C-compliant objects that represent the nodes that make up any XML document, "reader" and "writer" objects for accessing XML disk files or streams, and a class for validating XML documents against a schema or DTD.
System.Xml.XPath	Provides a fast and compact document object for working with XML using XPath queries. It does not support the W3C XML DOM interfaces, so cannot be used where this type of access to the content is required. This namespace includes a pull-model "navigator" object that can be used to iterate XML documents, plus objects to represent XPath expressions and collections of elements selected by an XPath expression.
System.Xml.Xsl	Provides objects that can be used to perform XSL (or more precisely, XSLT) transformations on an XML document. This namespace includes a class for passing arguments to an XSLT stylesheet, allowing conditional transformations to be applied.

This chapter concentrates only on these three namespaces; however, there are two other namespaces available for more specialist XML tasks:

Namespace	Description
System.Xml. Schema	Contains a series of objects to represent the various parts of a W3C-compliant XML Schema, allowing them to be manipulated directly. This namespace also provides objects to represent collections of schemas and the event-handler objects required when validating XML documents against a schema or DTD.
System.Xml. Serialization	Contains a series of objects that can be used to serialize XML documents in a range of ways. It includes objects to represent SOAP messages, and also allows control over the encoding of the XML when serializing to a stream. Generally used only when building custom Web Services and when communicating XML-format in other non-standard ways.

A full reference to all of the System.Xml namespaces, classes, enumerations or other objects is provided in the SDK installed with the .NET Framework.

The System.Xml Namespace

The classes in the System.Xml namespace that are used most often are:

❑   XmlDocument

❑   XmlNode

❑   XmlNodeList

- ❏ XmlDataDocument
- ❏ XmlTextWriter
- ❏ XmlTextReader
- ❏ XmlNodeReader
- ❏ XmlValidatingReader

We'll look at each one in turn next.

The XmlDocument Class

This is the standard class for storing and manipulating XML documents. It provides objects such as XmlElement, XmlEntity, XmlAttribute, XmlComment, XmlNode, XmlNodeList, and so on that expose W3C-compliant interfaces for working with the document content. All of these objects have additional Microsoft-specific extensions that make common tasks such as persisting the data to disk or copying nodes from one document to another much easier. The XmlDocument class provides methods to create new nodes in an XmlDocument instance using either W3C standard approaches, or Microsoft's own proprietary extension mechanisms. This gives the developer much more choice over how they work with the objects.

This class provides the nearest equivalent to the MSXML parser supplied with Internet Explorer and the Microsoft Data Access Components (MDAC) for use with unmanaged code outside the .NET Framework.

Properties of the XmlDocument Class

The XmlDocument object has broadly the same set of properties as the XmlNode object, as covered in that section later in this chapter. However, it offers two properties of its own that are especially useful.

DocumentElement property

The DocumentElement property returns a reference to the root element for the document as an XmlElement object. Read-only.

```
XmlElement = objXmlDoc.DocumentElement
```

DocumentType property

This property returns the complete node containing the DOCTYPE declaration as an XmlDocumentType object. Read-only.

```
XmlDocumentType = objXmlDoc.DocumentType
```

Methods of the XmlDocument Class

Note that after creating a new node using any methods of this class, it must be inserted into an XML document using the InsertBefore, InsertAfter, PrependChild, or AppendChild method of another XmlNode object already in the document. These methods are covered in the later section on the XmlNode class.

CloneNode Method

The CloneNode method returns a copy of the root node of this document. When true, the Boolean parameter indicates that it should also clone all descendant nodes of this node:

```
'clone root node and all child nodes
objNewNode = objXmlDoc.CloneNode(True)
```

After cloning a node it must be inserted into an XML document using the `InsertBefore`, `InsertAfter`, `PrependChild`, or `AppendChild` method of another `XmlNode` object already in the document. These methods are covered in the later section on the `XmlNode` class.

CreateAttribute Method

To create an `XmlAttribute` object, use the `CreateAttribute` method. It accepts the name of the attribute, and optionally a namespace URI and a namespace prefix. The value of the attribute is set after it has been created:

```
Dim objAtr As XmlAttribute
'create an attribute named "Title"
objAttr = objXmlDoc.CreateAttribute("Title")
objAttr.Value = "Instant ASP.NET"
```

Or by specifying the namespace for the attribute:

```
'create the attribute  Title xmlns="http://wrox.com"
objAttr = objXmlDoc.CreateAttribute("Title", "http://wrox.com")
objAttr.Value = "Instant ASP.NET"
```

Or by specifying a namespace and namespace prefix:

```
'create the attribute  Wrox:Title xmlns="http://www.wrox.com"
objAttr = objXmlDoc.CreateAttribute("Wrox", "Title", "http://wrox.com")
objAttr.Value = "Instant ASP.NET"
```

CreateCDataSection Method

This method creates and returns an `XmlCDataSection` object, that can contain arbitrary character data including characters (like "<" and "&") that cannot legally be included in XML text elements except as escaped characters (such as `&lt;` and `&apos;`). For example:

```
Dim objCData As XmlCDataSection
objCData = objXmlDoc.CreateCDataSection("Check if X < 20 & Y = 50")
```

CreateComment Method

This method creates and returns an `XmlComment` object with the specified string as its text, for example:

```
Dim objComment As XmlComment
objComment = objXmlDoc.CreateComment("This is the comment text")
```

CreateDocumentFragment Method

This method creates and returns an empty `XmlDocumentFragment` object, for example:

```
Dim objDocFrag As XmlDocumentFragment
objDocFrag = objXmlDoc.CreateDocumentFragment()
```

CreateDocumentType Method

This method creates a new `XmlDocumentType` object that includes the specified name, system ID, public ID, and subset. The subset parameter is used to specify the entries for the document type, for example:

```
Dim objDocType As XmlDocumentType
Dim strDocName As String = "Book"
Dim strPublicID As String = "http://wrox.com"
Dim strSubset As String
strSubset = "<!ELEMENT MyElem ANY>" _
         & "<!ATTLIST MyElem MyAttr CDATA>"
objDocType = objXmlDoc.CreateDocumentType(strDocName, Nothing, _
                                          strPublicID, strSubset)
```

As we are not specifying a System ID in this example, we use a `null` value (`Nothing` in Visual Basic) for the second parameter to the method. The result is:

```
<!DOCTYPE PUBLIC http://wrox.com [
  <!ELEMENT MyElem ANY>
  <!ATTLIST MyElem MyAttr CDATA>
]>
```

CreateElement Method

This method creates an `XmlElement` object with the specified tag name, for example:

```
Dim objElem As XmlElement
objElem = objXmlDoc.CreateElement("Book")
```

As with the `CreateNode` method, the namespace URI and namespace prefix can be specified as well if required.

CreateEntityReference Method

This method creates and returns an `XmlEntityReference` object with the specified name, for example:

```
Dim objEntity As XmlEntityReference
objEntity = objXmlDoc.CreateEntityReference("MyEntity")
```

CreateNavigator Method

To create an an `XPathNavigator` object based on an `XmlDocument` object, use the `CreateNavigator` method. The `XPathNavigator` class is covered later in this chapter. If we call this method with no parameter provided, the navigator is automatically set to the start of the document:

```
Dim objNav As XPathNavigator
objNav = objXmlDoc.CreateNavigator()
```

We can create the navigator and locate it at a particular node by passing that node as an `XmlNode` object:

```
objNav = objXmlDoc.CreateNavigator(objXmlNode)
```

CreateNode Method

The non W3C-compliant (Microsoft-specific) method `CreateNode` is used to create a `XmlNode` object that can represent any type of node within the document by specifying the node type, the node name, and the namespace.

```
Dim objNode As XmlNode
'create an element node <Book xmlns="http://wrox.com">
objNode = objXmlDoc.CreateNode("element", "Book", "http://wrox.com")
```

We can alternatively specify the node type using the `NodeType` enumeration. In general, this is the preferred method:

```
'create an element node <Book xmlns="http://wrox.com">
objNode = objXmlDoc.CreateNode(NodeType.Element, "Book", "http://wrox.com")
```

Finally, we can also create the namespace and the namespace prefix:

```
'create an element node <Wrox:Book xmlns:Wrox="http://wrox.com">
objNode = objXmlDoc.CreateNode(NodeType.Element, "Wrox", _
                               "Book", "http://wrox.com")
```

CreateProcessingInstruction Method

This method creates and returns an `XmlProcessingInstruction` object with the specified name and data. For example this code creates a standard stylesheet reference:

```
Dim objPI As XmlProcessingInstruction
Dim strName As String = "xml-stylesheet"
Dim strData As String = "type='text/xsl' href='mystyle.xsl'"
objPI = objXmlDoc.CreateProcessingInstruction(strName, strData)
```

The result is:

```
<?xml-stylesheet type='text/xsl' href='mystyle.xsl'?>
```

CreateSignificantWhitespace and CreateWhitespace Methods

These methods create an `XmlWhitespace` or `XmlSignificantWhitespace` object using the text provided, which can only consist of the characters &#20 (space), &#10 (line feed), &#13 (carriage return) and &#9 (tab). For example:

```
Dim objWSpace As XmlWhitespace
objWSpace = objXmlDoc.CreateWhitespace(&#20&#20&#20&#13&#10)
```

Significant whitespace will normally be used to control the display of the document, whereas "ordinary" whitespace is generally removed by XML processors.

CreateTextNode Method

This method creates and returns an `XmlText` object with the specified text, for example:

```
Dim objText As XmlText
objText = objXmlDoc.CreateTextNode("This is the value of an element")
```

CreateXmlDeclaration Method

This method creates an `XmlDeclaration` object, for example:

```
Dim objDecl As XmlDeclaration
Dim strVersion As String = "1.0"
Dim strEncoding As String = "UTF-8"
objDecl = objXmlDoc.CreateXmlDeclaration(strVersion, strEncoding, "yes")
```

The first parameter is the version of the document, and the second is the encoding to be used. The common encoding type is "UTF-8". The third parameter defines the standalone attribute of the declaration, and must be "yes" or "no". The code above creates the declaration:

```
<?xml version="1.0" encoding="UTF-8" standalone="yes" ?>
```

GetElementById Method

To locate elements within an `XmlDocument` object we can use either the `GetElementById` or `GetElementsByTagName` method. The `GetElementById` method returns an `XmlElement` object. It requires the document to have an associated schema or DTD, and an attribute must be defined as of type ID. If the element is not located it returns `null` (`Nothing` in Visual Basic). For example, if we have the following excerpt from a DTD:

```
<!ELEMENT MyElem ANY>
<!ATTLIST MyElem MyAttr ID #REQUIRED>
```

then the first element in the document that has an attribute named `MyAttr` with the value 42 can be located using:

```
Dim objXmlElem As XmlElement
objXmlElem = objXmlDoc.GetElementById("42")
```

GetElementsByTagName Method

The `GetElementsByTagName` method takes a string that is the name of one or more elements to be located, and returns an `XmlNodeList` containing all elements that have this tag name:

```
Dim objNodeList As XmlNodeList
objNodeList = objXmlDoc.GetElementsByTagName("Book") 'return all book elements
```

If the elements in the document have a namespace defined in the top-level element, for example `<Wrox:Catalog xmlns:Wrox="http://wrox.com">`, the namespace URI is specified in the second optional parameter:

```
objNodeList = objXmlDoc.GetElementsByTagName("Book", "http://wrox.com")
```

ImportNode Method

Individual nodes can be read into an `XmlDocument` object using either the `ReadNode` or the `ImportNode` method. The `ImportNode` method takes an `XmlNode` object and an optional second Boolean parameter that indicates if it should also import all attributes, children, and descendant nodes of that node:

```
'import node and all child nodes
objNewNode = objXmlDoc.ImportNode(objExistingNode, True)
```

After importing a node it must be inserted into an XML document using the `InsertBefore`, `InsertAfter`, `PrependChild`, or `AppendChild` method of another `XmlNode` object already in the document.

Load Method

To load an XML document into an `XmlDocument` object, use the `Load` or the `LoadXml` method. The `Load` method can accept a stream object, an XML "reader" object, or a path and file name to provide an XML source for the `XmlDocument`. The following code:

```
Dim objXmlDoc As New XmlDocument()
Dim objXmlReader As New XmlTextReader("c:\docs\thisfile.xml")
objXmlDoc.Load(objXmlReader)
objXmlReader.Close()
```

has the same net effect as this:

```
Dim objXmlDoc As New XmlDocument()
objXmlDoc.Load("c:\docs\thisfile.xml")
```

Although the first example is clearly more verbose, by loading the XML file via an `XmlTextReader`, we can perform any required validation as it is loaded. We'll see how later when we look at the `XmlValidatingReader` object. It also means that the XML can come directly from another object via an `XmlTextReader` rather than a disk file.

LoadXml Method

If the source XML does not already exist in a form acceptable to the `Load` method, the `LoadXml` method can be used to populate the `XmlDocument` object with the data contained in its string argument. This string must itself constitute a well-formed XML document or an error will occur (it does not have to be valid, however, only well-formed):

```
Dim strXML As String
strXML = "<?xml version='1.0' standalone='yes' ?>" _
      & " <BookList>" _
      & "  <Book>" _
      & "   <ISBN>1861003323</ISBN>" _
      & "   <Title>Professional Visual Basic 6</Title>" _
      & "  </Book>" _
      & " </BookList>"
Dim objXmlDoc As New XmlDocument()
objXmlDoc.LoadXml(strXML)
```

ReadNode Method

Individual nodes can be read into an `XmlDocument` object using the `ReadNode` method. Unlike the `ImportNode` method, `ReadNode` accepts an `XmlTextReader` that is positioned at the required node and copies that node, plus all its attributes, children, and other descendants, into the document:

```
Dim objNewNode As XmlNode
Dim objXmlReader As New XmlTextReader("c:\docs\thisfile.xml")
```

```
objXmlReader.MoveToContent()
objXmlReader.Read()  'skip the root element
'read the first child of the root element
objNewNode = objXmlDoc.ReadNode(objXmlReader)
objXmlReader.Close()
```

After reading a node it must be inserted into an XML document using the `InsertBefore`, `InsertAfter`, `PrependChild`, or `AppendChild` method of another `XmlNode` object already in the document. These methods are covered in the later section on the `XmlNode` class.

Save Method

The content of an `XmlDocument` object can be saved via a `Stream`, via a "writer" object, or by specifying a path and filename for a disk file. For example:

```
objXmlDoc.Save("c:\docs\thisfile.xml")
```

Or (for example when you want to add output before or after the content) through an `XmlTextWriter` pointing to a disk file:

```
Dim objXmlWriter As New XmlTextWriter("c:\docs\thisfile.xml")
'... write other content here if required
objXmlDoc.Save(objXmlWriter)
'... write other content here if required
objXmlWriter.Close()
```

Or to a `Stream` object, as in the following – which dumps the contents to screen:

```
objXmlDoc.Save(Console.Out)
```

This might be useful if you want to dump the content direct into the output of an ASP.NET page:

```
objXmlDoc.Save(Response.OutputStream)
```

WriteContentTo and WriteTo Methods

The `WriteTo` and `WriteContentTo` methods work similarly in that they only accept an `XmlTextWriter` object. While they can be used at document level to write a document to disk, they are more usually used to output individual nodes. We'll see this when we look at the `XmlNode` object later. The sole difference between the `WriteTo` and `WriteContentTo` methods is that `WriteContentTo` writes out the child nodes of the document (or the node when called at `XmlNode` level) only:

```
Dim objXmlWriter As New XmlTextWriter("c:\docs\thisfile.xml")
Dim objXmlContentWriter As New XmlTextWriter("c:\docs\thatfile.xml")

objXmlDoc.WriteTo(objXmlWriter)
objXmlDoc.WriteContentTo(objXmlContentWriter)
objXmlWriter.Close()
objXmlContentWriter.Close()
```

Events of the XmlDocument Class

There are six events that are raised by modifications to an `XmlDocument`, and handlers can be created that receive these events. The events are:

❑ The `NodeChanging` and `NodeChanged` events occur when the value of a node in the document is being changed and after is has been changed. To cancel the change you must handle the `NodeChanging` event and raise an exception.

❑ The `NodeInserting` and `NodeInserted` events occur when a node in the document is being inserted and after it has been inserted into another node. To cancel the change you must handle the `NodeInserting` event and raise an exception.

❑ The `NodeRemoving` and `NodeRemoved` events occur when a node is being or has been removed from the document. To cancel the change you must handle the `NodeRemoving` event and raise an exception.

The XmlNode Class

The `XmlNode` object represents any node within an XML document. This allows nodes to be processed without having to know in advance what type of node they are. The following properties and methods are common to all types of node (elements, attributes, CDATA sections, comments, etc.).

Properties of the XmlNode Class

The `XmlNode` object has a series of properties that return information about the node itself. These properties are also available for the `XmlDocument` object itself. Each `XmlNode` object also exposes the `ChildNodes`, `FirstChild`, `LastChild`, `NextSibling`, `PreviousSibling`, and `ParentNode` properties that can be used to navigate through an XML document. Finally, there are the `OwnerDocument`, `DocumentElement`, and `DocumentType` properties that return information about the XML document that this node is contained within.

Attributes Property

This property returns an `XmlAttributeCollection` object containing all the attributes of this node. Read-only.

```
XmlAttributeCollection = objXmlNode.Attributes
```

ChildNodes Property

This property returns an `XmlNodeList` containing all the child nodes of the node. Read-only.

```
XmlNodeList = objXmlNode.ChildNodes
```

DocumentElement Property

This property returns an `XmlElement` object representing the root element of the document. Read-only.

```
XmlElement = objXmlNode.DocumentElement
```

DocumentType Property

This property returns an `XmlDeclaration` object representing the node in the document that contains the `DOCTYPE` declaration. Read-only.

```
XmlDeclaration = objXmlNode.DocumentType
```

FirstChild Property

This property returns an `XmlNode` object representing the first child of the node. Read-only.

```
XmlNode = objXmlNode.FirstChild
```

HasChildNodes Property

This property returns a Boolean value indicating if the node has any child nodes. Read-only.

```
Boolean = objXmlNode.HasChildNodes
```

InnerText Property

This is a Microsoft extension property that sets or returns the concatenated text values of the node and all its child nodes.

```
String = objXmlNode.InnerText
objXmlNode.InnerText = String
```

InnerXml Property

This is a Microsoft extension property that sets or returns the markup and text representing the children of the current node.

```
String = objXmlNode.InnerXml
objXmlNode.InnerXml = String
```

IsReadOnly Property

This property returns a Boolean value indicating if the node is read-only. Read-only.

```
Boolean = objXmlNode.IsReadOnly
```

LastChild Property

This property returns an `XmlNode` object representing the last child of the node. Read-only.

```
XmlNode = objXmlNode.LastChild
```

Name and LocalName Properties

The `Name` property returns the qualified name of the current node. The `LocalName` property is similar but ignores any namespace prefix. Read-only.

```
String = objXmlNode.Name
String = objXmlNode.LocalName
```

NamespaceURI Property

This property returns the namespace URI for the node. Read-only.

```
String = objXmlNode.NamespaceURI
```

NextSibling Property

This property returns an `XmlNode` object representing the node immediately following this node. Read-only.

```
XmlNode = objXmlNode.NextSibling
```

NodeType Property

This property returns the type of the current node (element, attribute, CDATA section, and so on). Read-only.

```
Integer = objXmlNode.NodeType
```

OuterXml Property

This is a Microsoft extension property that returns the markup and text content representing this node and all its child nodes.

```
String = objXmlNode.OuterXml
objXmlNode.OuterXml = String
```

OwnerDocument Property

This property returns a reference to the `XmlDocument` object that contains the document to which the node belongs. Read-only.

```
XmlDocument = objXmlNode.OwnerDocument
```

ParentNode Property

This property returns an `XmlNode` object representing the parent of this node (for nodes that can have parents). Read-only.

```
XmlNode = objXmlNode.ParentNode
```

Prefix Property

This property sets or returns the namespace prefix for the node. Read-only.

```
String = objXmlNode.Prefix
```

PreserveWhitespace Property

This property sets or returns a Boolean value indicating if whitespace is preserved.

```
Boolean = objXmlNode.PreserveWhitespace
objXmlNode.PreserveWhitespace = Boolean
```

PreviousSibling Property

This returns an `XmlNode` object representing the node immediately preceding this node. Read-only.

```
XmlNode = objXmlNode.PreviousSibling
```

Value Property

This property sets or returns the value of the node.

```
String = objXmlNode.Value
objXmlNode.Value = String
```

Methods of the XmlNode Class

The `XmlNode` object has a series of methods that we can use to work with the node itself. In addition to methods defined by the W3C for manipulating content of an XML document are a couple of Microsoft extensions, `SelectNodes` and `SelectSingleNode`, which locate nodes using a given XPath expression. The `XmlNode` object also exposes the Microsoft-specific method `CreateNavigator`, which returns an `XPathNavigator` based on the document.

AppendChild Method

This method adds a specified node to the end of the list of the children of this node. It takes an `XmlNode` object that represents the new node as its single parameter, and returns a reference to the new node after it has been inserted.

```
objNode = objThisNode.AppendChild(objNode)
```

CloneNode Method

This method creates a duplicate of the node. For details see the previous coverage of this method for the `XmlDocument` object.

CreateNavigator Method

This method creates an `XPathNavigator` object for the document, and locates it on this node. The `XPathNavigator` class is described later in the chapter.

```
Dim objNav As XPathNavigator
objNav = objNode.CreateNavigator()
```

GetNamespaceOfPrefix Method

Looks up the closest `xmlns` declaration for the given prefix that is in scope for the current node and returns the namespace URI from this declaration.

```
strNamespace = objNode.GetNamespaceOfPrefix("Wrox")
```

Nodes in an XML document can consist of a concatenated namespace prefix and a local name. Multiple namespaces can be declared, as in the following example that declares the namespace prefixes `Wrox`, and `Doc`.

```
<Wrox:Catalog xmlns:Wrox="http://wrox.com/catalog"
              xmlns:Doc="http://wrox.com/documentation">
```

Any descendant elements of this element can then qualify their tag name with either of these prefixes, as in `<Doc:updated date="02/06/2001" by="Joe Gillespie" position="Editor"/>`. Here, the local name of the element is `addedby`, and the namespace URI is `http://wrox.com/documentation`. The `xmlns` definition can also be located elsewhere in the document – in a parent node (where it applies to all descendant nodes), or in the document declaration node (depending on the type of document). This method, and the related `GetPrefixOfNamespace`, can be very useful for such documents, as they will search the document to find the corresponding namespace URI or prefix respectively.

GetPrefixOfNamespace Method

This method looks up the closest `xmlns` declaration for the given namespace URI that is in scope for the current node and returns the prefix defined in this declaration.

```
strPrefix = objNode.GetNamespaceOfPrefix("http://wrox.com/catalog")
```

InsertAfter Method

This method inserts a specified node immediately after another specified node. An `XmlNode` object is passed as the first parameter representing the new node, and an `XmlNode` object representing an existing node in the document is passed as the second parameter. The method returns a reference to the new node after it has been inserted:

```
objNode = objThisNode.InsertAfter(objNewNode, objExistingNode)
```

Note that if the "existing node" parameter is `null` (`Nothing` in Visual Basic), `InsertAfter` behaves just like the `PrependChild` method, in that the new node is placed at the beginning of the list of child nodes.

InsertBefore Method

Inserts a specified node immediately before another specified node. An `XmlNode` object is passed as the first parameter representing the new node, and an `XmlNode` object representing an existing node in the document is passed as the second parameter. The method returns a reference to the new node after it has been inserted:

```
objNode = objThisNode.InsertBefore(objNewNode, objExistingNode)
```

Note that if the "existing node" parameter is `null` (or `Nothing` in Visual Basic), `InsertBefore` behaves just as the `AppendChild` method, that is the new node is placed at the end of the list of child nodes.

Normalize Method

This method puts all descendant `XmlText` nodes of this node into "normal" form, where only markup (tags, comments, processing instructions, CDATA sections, entity references, etc.) separates `XmlText` nodes. In other words, there are no adjacent `XmlText` nodes.

```
objNode.Normalize()
```

For example, an element node named `<Extract>` might contain the following XML:

```
<Extract>A book about ASP.NET and Windows 2000</Extract>
```

However, if the text has been added in several operations, the actual structure of the document may mean that the <Extract> element has more than one XmlText child node containing the "value" of the element:

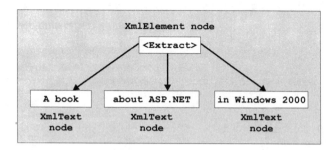

After normalizing it, all the text content is placed into one XmlText node:

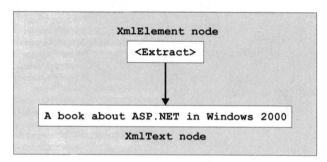

PrependChild Method

This method adds a specified node to the beginning of the list of the children of this node, such that the new node will then be returned by the FirstChild property. It accepts an XmlNode object that represents the new node as its only parameter, and returns a reference to the new node after it has been inserted:

```
objNode = objThisNode.PrependChild(objNode)
```

RemoveAll Method

This method removes all attributes and descendant elements of the current node. This method has no parameters, and does not return a value. It simply removes all child and descendant nodes and attributes of the current node:

```
objThisNode.RemoveAll()
```

RemoveChild Method

This method removes a specified child node. This method accepts an XmlNode object that represents the child node to be removed as the single parameter, and returns a reference to the removed node:

```
objNode = objThisNode.RemoveChild(objExistingNode)
```

ReplaceChild Method

This method replaces the specified child node with a new node. This method takes an `XmlNode` object that represents the new node as the first parameter, and an `XmlNode` object that represents an existing node in the document as the second parameter. It returns a reference to the new node once it has replaced the existing node:

```
objNode = objThisNode.ReplaceChild(objNewNode, objExistingNode)
```

If the existing node does not exist, the new node is simply inserted at that point in the document.

SelectNodes Method

This method selects all nodes matching the XPath expression and returns an `XmlNodeList` object representing these nodes.

To find all the `<Book>` nodes in a document we could use the `SelectNodes` method as below:

```
Dim strXPath As String = "descendant::Book"
Dim colNodeList As XmlNodeList
colNodeList = objThisNode.SelectNodes(strXPath)
Dim objNode As XmlNode
For Each objNode In colNodeList
  Response.Write(objNode.Name.ToString() & " = " _
                 & objNode.Value.ToString())
Next
```

SelectSingleNode Method

This method selects just the first node that matches the XPath expression and returns an `XmlNode` object that represents it.

The `SelectSingleNode` method is usually used when only one node in the document is expected to match the XPath expression (or when we are only interested in the first one that matches). For example here where we are specifying only the `<Book>` element that has an attribute named `ISBN` with the value `1861004885`:

```
Dim strXPath As String = "descendant::Book[@ISBN=1861004885]"
Dim objNode As XmlNode
objNode = objThisNode.SelectSingleNode(strXPath)
Response.Write(objNode.Name.ToString() & " = " _
               & objNode.Value.ToString())
```

WriteContentTo Method

This method saves all the children of the node to the specified `XmlWriter`. For details see the previous coverage of this method for the `XmlDocument` object.

WriteTo Method

Saves the current node to the specified `XmlWriter`. For details see the previous coverage of this method for the `XmlDocument` object.

Other XML "Node" Classes

While the `XmlNode` class can reference any type of node in a document, there are times when a more specific class of object is desired. These "more specific" classes inherit all the members of the `XmlNode` object, but provide extra properties and methods that carry out tasks specific to that type of node. They provide the W3C-compliant members, as well as several Microsoft-specific extensions. The specific node classes are described in this section.

The XmlDeclaration Class

This class represents the XML declaration element, such as:

```
<?xml version="1.0" encoding="UTF-8" standalone="yes" ?>
```

In addition to the properties and methods inherited from the `XmlNode` class, it has three properties reflecting the attributes specific to this type of node.

Encoding Property

This represents the encoding used within the document as a string. The default is "UTF-8".

```
String = objDeclaration.Encoding
objDeclaration.Encoding = String
```

Standalone Property

This is either "no" if the document has an associated DTD or schema, or "yes" if there is no external DTD or schema.

```
String = objDeclaration.Standalone
objDeclaration.Standalone = ["yes" | "no"]
```

Version Property

This is the XML version number of the document as a string. Read-only.

```
String = objDeclaration.Version
```

The XmlDocumentType Class

This class provides an interface to the `<!DOCTYPE [...]>` element of a document, and all its content. It has five properties in addition to the properties and methods inherited from the `XmlNode` class.

Entities Property

This property returns a collection of `XmlEntity` node objects that are defined within the DOCTYPE element as an `XmlNamedNodeMap` object. Read-only.

```
XmlNamedNodeMap = objDeclaration.Entities
```

InternalSubset Property

This property returns the complete content of the DOCTYPE element as a string. Read-only.

```
String = objDeclaration.InternalSubset
```

Notations Property

This property returns a collection of `XmlNotation` node objects that are defined within the `DOCTYPE` element as an `XmlNamedNodeMap` object. Read-only.

```
XmlNamedNodeMap = objDeclaration.Notations
```

PublicId Property

This property returns the public ID defined in the `DOCTYPE` element as a string. Read-only.

```
String = objDeclaration.PublicId
```

SystemId Property

This property returns the system ID defined in the `DOCTYPE` element as a string. Read-only.

```
String = objDeclaration.SystemId
```

The XmlElement Class

This class represents an XML element within the document. Bear in mind that elements never have an actual value of their own. They can have content such as other elements, markup, and text. The text value of an element is contained within an `XmlText` element that is a child of an `XmlElement` object. As well as the properties and methods inherited from the `XmlNode` class, one property and ten methods are introduced by this class.

IsEmpty Property

This is a boolean value indicating if an empty element is defined using the shortcut technique of a single tag with a closing backslash. For example `<MyElem />` returns `True`, while `<MyElem></MyElem>` returns `False`.

```
Boolean = objElement.IsEmpty
objElement.IsEmpty = Boolean
```

GetAttribute Method

This method returns the value of a specified attribute as a string using the attribute name or both the namespace URI and local name. If the attribute does not exist (and has no default value in any attached DTD or schema), an empty string is returned.

To get the value of an attribute named `ISBN` from an element referenced by `objThisNode`, use code like this:

```
Dim strISBN As String = objElement.GetAttribute("ISBN")
```

Or, if the attribute were defined within the namespace `"http://wrox.com"`, we would need:

```
Dim strISBN As String = objElement.GetAttribute("ISBN", "http://wrox.com")
```

GetAttributeNode Method

This method returns the specified attribute as an `XmlAttribute` object using the attribute name or both the namespace URI and local name. This is useful if we want to use the returned `XmlAttribute` object, perhaps to insert it elsewhere into the document rather than just getting the value as a string. So, to get the value of an attribute as an `XmlAttribute` object named `ISBN` from an element referenced by `objThisNode`, we can use this code snippet:

```
Dim objISBNAttr As XmlAttribute
objISBNAttr = objElement.GetAttributeNode("ISBN")
```

Or, if the attribute were defined within the namespace `"http://wrox.com"`, we would need:

```
Dim objISBNAttr As XmlAttribute
objISBNAttr = objElement.GetAttributeNode("ISBN", "http://wrox.com")
```

GetElementsByTagName Method

This method takes a string that is the name of one or more elements to be located, or both the namespace URI and local name, and returns an `XmlNodeList` containing all/any elements that have this tag name. See the previous section on the `XmlDocument` object for more details.

HasAttribute Method

This method returns a Boolean value indicating if the element contains the specified attribute. The attribute can be specified using the attribute name or both the namespace URI and local name.

```
If objElement.HasAttribute("ISBN") Then
  objElement.RemoveAttribute("ISBN")
End If
```

RemoveAllAttributes Method

This method removes all attributes from the element. Takes no parameters and does not return a value.

```
    objElement.RemoveAllAttributes()
```

RemoveAttribute Method

This method removes an attribute from the element. The attribute can be specified using the attribute name or both the namespace URI and local name. Does not return a value. The code below shows how it could be used:

```
If objElement.HasAttribute("ISBN") Then
  objElement.RemoveAttribute("ISBN")
End If
```

RemoveAttributeAt Method

This method removes an attribute from the element. The attribute is specified using its index within the `Attributes` collection (starting at zero for the first attribute). Returns the removed attribute as an `XmlNode` object.

```
Dim objAttrNode As XmlNode
objAttrNode = objElement.RemoveAttributeAt(1)
```

RemoveAttributeNode Method

This method removes an attribute from the element. The attribute is specified as an XmlAttribute object or both the namespace URI and local name. Returns the removed attribute as an XmlAttribute object.

```
Dim objISBNAttr As XmlAttribute
objISBNAttr = objElement.RemoveAttributeNode(objThisAttr)
```

```
Dim objISBNAttr As XmlAttribute
objISBNAttr = objElement.RemoveAttributeNode("ISBN", "http://wrox.com")
```

SetAttribute Method

This method sets the value of an attribute. The attribute can be specified using the attribute name or both the namespace URI and local name. This method provides the easiest way to set the value of an attribute (adding it if it doesn't already exist). The first parameter is the name of the attribute, and the second is the value to give that attribute:

```
objElement.SetAttribute("ISBN", "1861004885")
```

Or, if the attribute were defined within the namespace "http://wrox.com", the second parameter is the namespace URI, and the third the value for the attribute:

```
objElement.SetAttribute("ISBN", "http://wrox.com", "1861004885")
```

SetAttributeNode Method

This method adds an attribute to, or replaces one within the Attributes collection. The attribute can be specified as an XmlAttribute object, or by using both the namespace URI and local name. Returns the new or modified attribute as an XmlAttribute object. Useful if you already have a reference to an XmlAttribute object, or if you want to reference the attribute object after it has been added to the element:

```
objAttr = objElement.SetAttributeNode(objThisAttr)
```

The XmlAttribute Class

This class represents an attribute of an element node of an XML document. In addition to the properties and methods inherited from the XmlNode class, there is just one new property introduced by this class.

Specified Property

This is a Boolean read-only value indicating if an attribute with a specified default value (assigned in the DTD or schema) has actually been assigned a value (True), or if it has the default value (False). If the attribute has been assigned a value, you must delete the attribute to restore the default value – whereupon a new attribute with the default value is automatically created.

```
Boolean = objAttribute.Specified
```

The XmlText Class

This class represents the text within an element node, notionally the value of that element or the value of any other type of node that can have text content. For example, in the element:

```
<Title>Instant ASP.NET</Title>
```

the `XmlElement` node has the `Name` property of `"Title"` but the "value" of the element node is `null` (`Nothing` in Visual Basic). However, the child `XmlText` node has a `null` value for the `Name` property, but the `Value` property is `"Instant ASP.NET"`. There is one method specific to this type of node.

SplitText Method

This method divides an `XmlText` node into two separate `XmlText` nodes at the offset specified by the method's parameter. It is the opposite of the `Normalize` method, and is useful if you want to insert other nodes within the content of the node at a specific point.

```
objText.SplitText(24)
```

The XmlEntity Class

This object represents an XML Entity that is declared in the document using an `<!ENTITY ...>` element. There are two properties specific to this type of node.

PublicId Property

This property returns the public ID defined in the `ENTITY` element as a string. Read-only.

```
String = objEntity.PublicId
```

SystemId Property

This property returns the system ID defined in the `ENTITY` element as a string. Read-only.

```
String = objEntity.SystemId
```

The XmlNotation Class

This class represents an XML Notation that is declared in the document using a `<!NOTATION ...>` element. There are two properties specific to this type of node:

PublicId Property

This property returns the public ID defined in the `NOTATION` element as a string. Read-only.

```
String = objNotation.PublicId
```

SystemId Property

This property returns the system ID defined in the `NOTATION` element as a string. Read-only.

```
String = objNotation.SystemId
```

The XmlProcessingInstruction Class

This class represents a processing instruction in the document, for example:

```
<?xml-stylesheet type="text/xsl" href="mystyle.xsl" ?>
```

There is just one property specific to this type of node.

Data Property

This contains the complete content of the element except for the name of the instruction. For example, in the above, the `Data` property is the string: `type="text/xsl" href="mystyle.xsl"`. The instruction name (`xml-stylesheet`) is available through the `Name` property of this node.

```
String = objPI.Data
objPI.Data = String
```

The XmlCDataSection Class

This class represents a `<![CDATA...]>` section of a document, usually containing text that cannot legally be included in an XML document (such as un-escaped versions of the characters `"<"`, and `"&"`). It has no node-specific properties or methods.

The XmlComment Class

This class represents a comment in an XML document, such as `<!-- some comment -->`. It has no node-specific properties or methods. The comment text itself is available through the inherited `Value` property of the node.

The XmlDocumentFragment Class

This class represents a document fragment that can exist unattached within an XML document while nodes are added to it or removed from it. It has no node-specific properties or methods.

The XmlEntityReference Class

This class represents an entity reference in an XML document. It has no node-specific properties or methods.

The XmlSignificantWhitespace Class

This class represents a node consisting of just the characters `&#20` (space), `&#10` (line feed), `&#13` (carriage return), and `&#9` (tab), and which is not generally removed from the document by XML processors. It has no node-specific properties or methods.

The XmlWhitespace Class

This class represents a node consisting of just the characters `&#20` (space), `&#10` (line feed), `&#13` (carriage return) and `&#9` (tab). It has no node-specific properties or methods.

Note that we haven't listed all of the properties for the XmlNode and other node-type objects, as there are some that are rarely used. Full details can be found in the .NET Framework SDK, in the .NET Framework Class Library Reference section.

The XmlNodeList Class

This class represents a collection of `XmlNode` objects. It has a `Count` property that returns the number of items in the collection:

```
Dim intLoop As Integer
For intLoop = 0 To objNodeList.Count - 1
```

```
          Response.Write(objNodeList(intLoop).Name.ToString())
   Next
```

It can also be iterated using a `for each` (For Each...Next in Visual Basic) construct:

```
Dim objNode As XmlNode
For Each objNode In objNodeList
   Response.Write(objNode.Name.ToString())
Next
```

Or by calling the `GetEnumerator` method to return an `Enumerator` object:

```
Dim objEnum As objNodeList.GetEnumerator()
Dim objNode As XmlNode
While objEnum.MoveNext()
   'have to convert the members of the enumerator to XmlNode objects
   objNode = CType(objEnum.Current, XmlNode)
   Response.Write(objNode.Name.ToString())
End While
```

The XmlDataDocument Class

This is an extension of the `XmlDocument` object that provides three Microsoft-specific (non W3C-compliant) members that allow synchronization of relational and XML-formatted data. It allows you to access the same instance of the XML data using ADO.NET relational methods or XML techniques.

Properties of the XmlDataDocument Class

Fundamentally, this class works exactly the same as the `XmlDocument` class, and inherits all its properties, adding an extra property that makes it so useful.

DataSet Property

This property returns a reference to a normal ADO.NET-style `DataSet` object containing the data in the XML document that is currently loaded into the `XmlDataDocument` object. Changes made to the XML document within the `DataSet` are immediately reflected in the `XmlDataDocument` object itself, and vice versa. Read-only.

```
DataSet = objXmlDataDoc.DataSet
```

We've provided an example later in this chapter that demonstrates how these methods are used. For example, we can create an ADO.NET `DataView` object from the first table in a `DataSet` referenced by `objXmlDataDoc` using:

```
Dim objDataView As New DataView(objXmlDataDoc.DataSet.Tables(0))
```

Methods of the XmlDataDocument Class

There are two new methods provided by the `XmlDataDocument` class.

GetElementFromRow Method

This method takes as its single parameter a reference to a `DataRow` object, and returns a string containing an XML element that represents that row. This code (taken from the example at the end of this chapter) iterates through a table displaying the XML representation of each row:

```
Dim objDataTable As DataTable = objXMLDataDoc.DataSet.Tables(0)
Dim objRow As DataRow
Dim objXMLElement As XmlElement

For Each objRow In objDataTable.Rows
   objXMLElement = objXMLDataDoc.GetElementFromRow(objRow)
   Response.Write(Server.HtmlEncode(objXMLElement.OuterXML) & "<br />")
Next
```

GetRowFromElement Method

The inverse of the above, this method takes as its single parameter a reference to an element in the XML document and returns a `DataRow` object (as defined by the `System.Data` namespace) comprising the data contained by that XML element.

For example, given a reference to a node `objNode`, we can get an ADO.NET `DataRow` object that represents the data in that row using:

```
Dim objDataRow As DataRow = objXMLDataDoc.GetRowFromElement(objNode)
```

The XmlTextWriter Class

This class is used to create XML documents node by node, and send the output as it is created to a stream, another object, or a disk file. Each element and attribute, comment, text node or other node type can be created in the required order using code. It can also be used as the output for another object, whereupon that object calls the methods of the `XmlTextWriter` to create the output.

Properties of the XmlTextWriter Class

The properties of the `XmlTextWriter` determine how it formats the output, and the various special characters it uses in the new document.

Formatting Property

This sets or returns how the output is formatted. The only two possible values are `Formatting.Indented` or `Formatting.None`. A full reference to the enumerations available and their values is provided in the SDK installed with the .NET Framework.

```
Integer = objTextWriter.Formatting
objTextWriter.Formatting = [Formatting.Indented | Formatting.None]
```

Indentation Property

This sets or returns the number of `IndentChars` to write for each level in the hierarchy when `Formatting` is set to `Formatting.Indented`.

```
Integer = objTextWriter.Indentation
objTextWriter.Indentation = Integer
```

IndentChar Property

This sets or returns the character used for indenting when `Formatting` is set to `Formatting.Indented`. The default is a space (`&#20`).

```
Char = objTextWriter.IndentChar
objTextWriter.IndentChar = Char
```

Namespaces Property

This is a Boolean value that indicates whether the use of namespaces is supported.

```
Boolean = objTextWriter.Namespaces
objTextWriter.Namespaces = Boolean
```

QuoteChar Property

This sets or returns the character to use to quote attribute values. It can be either a single quote (`&#39`) or a double-quote (`&#34`). The default is a double-quote.

```
Char = objTextWriter.QuoteChar
objTextWriter.QuoteChar = Char
```

WriteState Property

This returns the state of the writer and indicates what type of node or output is currently being written. This is one of the values from the `WriteState` enumeration (`Attribute`, `Closed`, `Content`, `Element`, `Prolog`, `Start`). Read-only.

```
Integer = objTextWriter.WriteState
```

XmlLang Property

This returns the value of the current `xml:lang` that is in scope, as a string. Read-only.

```
String = objTextWriter.XmlLang
```

XmlSpace Property

This returns an `XmlSpace` object that represents the current `xml:space` setting that is in scope. Read-only.

```
XmlSpace = objTextWriter.XmlSpace
```

Methods of the XmlTextWriter Class

There are numerous methods available for the `XmlTextWriter` that can be classed as belonging to one of several specific groups.

Close Method

This method closes the stream or file.

```
objXmlTextWriter.Close()
```

Flush Method

This method flushes the write buffer to the underlying stream or file.

```
objXmlTextWriter.Flush()
```

Writexxxxx Method

This method writes a complete element or other type of node to the output with start and end tags where appropriate. Each of the variations takes parameters appropriate to the node type, for example the `WriteComment` method just takes one parameter, the text of the comment. The `WriteElementString` method takes two or three parameters to define the element name, optionally the namespace URI, and the value of the element. The full list is:

- ❑ `WriteAttributeString("prefix", "local-name", "namespace","value")`
- ❑ `WriteBase64("buffer-array", "start-index", "byte-count")`
- ❑ `WriteBinHex("buffer-array", "start-index", "byte-count")`
- ❑ `WriteCData("string")`
- ❑ `WriteCharEntity("char")`
- ❑ `WriteChars("char")`
- ❑ `WriteComment("string")`
- ❑ `WriteDocType("name", "public-id", "system-id","subset")`
- ❑ `WriteElementString("local-name", "namespace","value")`
- ❑ `WriteEntityRef("name")`
- ❑ `WriteName("name")`
- ❑ `WriteNmToken("name")`
- ❑ `WriteProcessingInstruction("name","text")`
- ❑ `WriteString("text")`
- ❑ `WriteWhitespace("text")`

WriteEndAttribute Method

This method writes out the closing quotes of the last attribute "started" with the `WriteStartAttribute` method.

```
objXmlTextWriter.WriteEndAttribute()
```

WriteEndDocument Method

This closes any open elements and attributes, and puts the writer back into the `Start` state.

```
objXmlTextWriter.WriteEndDocument()
```

WriteEndElement Method

This writes out the closing tag of the last element "opened" with the `WriteStartElement` method.

```
objXmlTextWriter.WriteEndElement()
```

WriteFullEndElement Method

This method writes out the closing tag of the last element that was "opened" with the `WriteStartElement` method and closes the corresponding namespace scope.

```
objXmlTextWriter.WriteFullEndElement()
```

WriteStartAttribute Method

This method writes out just the attribute name and subsequent = " characters so that the attribute's value can be appended using the `WriteString` method.

```
objXmlTextWriter.WriteStartAttribute("prefix", "local-name", "namespace")
```

WriteStartDocument Method

This method Writes an XML declaration element with the version `"1.0"`. The optional Boolean parameter indicates if the standalone attribute is included – when `True` the output includes `"standalone="yes"`, and when `False` the output includes `"standalone="no"`.

```
objXmlTextWriter.WriteStartDocument(True)
```

WriteStartElement Method

Writes out just the opening tag of an element so that content consisting of other nodes can be included in the element.

```
objXmlTextWriter.WriteStartElement("prefix", "local-name", "namespace")
```

Example: XmlTextWriterExample

As an example, consider the following code:

```
Dim objXMLWriter As XmlTextWriter

'default encoding (UTF-8) is used if second parameter is null
objXMLWriter = New XmlTextWriter("c:\temp\test.xml", Nothing)

With objXMLWriter
  .Formatting = Formatting.Indented
  .Indentation = 3
  .WriteStartDocument()
  .WriteComment("Created with XMLTextWriter - " & Now())
  .WriteStartElement("BookList")
  .WriteStartElement("Book")
  .WriteAttributeString("Category", "Technology")
  .WriteElementString("Title", "Professional VCR Programming")
  Dim intSales As Integer = 17492
  .WriteElementString("Sales", intSales.ToString("G"))
  .WriteEndElement()    'close <Book> element
  .WriteEndElement()    'close <BookList> element
  .WriteEndDocument()
  .Flush()
  .Close()
End With
```

which creates this XML document:

```
<?xml version="1.0">
<!-- Created with XMLTextWriter - 8/8/2001 -->
<BookList>
  <Book Category="Technology">
    <Title>Professional VCR Programming</Title>
    <Sales>17492</Sales>
  </Book>
</BookList>
```

The XmlTextReader Class

This class is used to connect a stream, a disk file, or output from another object to an XML document object, or simply to iterate through an XML document using code. It may also be used with an `XmlValidatingReader` to validate an XML document.

Properties of the XmlTextReader Class

The `XmlTextReader` object has a series of properties that return information about the current node that is being read. There are also properties that provide information about the XML document itself, and the state of the `XmlTextReader`, and allow some aspects of the reading process to be controlled.

AttributeCount Property

This property returns the number of attributes for this node. Read-only.

```
Integer = objTextReader.AttributeCount
```

Depth Property

This property returns an integer indicating the depth of this node within the hierarchy of the XML document. Read-only.

```
Integer = objTextReader.Depth
```

Encoding Property

This property returns the encoding of the document as a string, such as "UTF-8". Read-only.

```
String = objTextReader.Encoding
```

EOF Property

This property returns a Boolean value indicating whether the `XmlTextReader` is positioned at the end of the stream or file. Read-only.

```
Boolean = objTextReader.EOF
```

HasAttributes Property

This property returns a Boolean value indicating if this node has any attributes. Read-only.

```
Boolean = objTextReader.HasAttributes
```

HasValue Property

This property returns a Boolean value indicating if this node can have a value. Read-only.

```
Boolean = objTextReader.HasValue
```

IsDefault Property

This property returns a Boolean value indicating if this node is an attribute that was generated from the default value, as defined in the DTD or schema. Read-only.

```
Boolean = objTextReader.IsDefault
```

IsEmptyElement Property

This property returns a Boolean value indicating if this node is an empty element, `<MyElem/>` for example. Read-only.

```
Boolean = objTextReader.IsEmptyElement
```

LineNumber Property

This property returns the current line number. Read-only.

```
Integer = objTextReader.LineNumber
```

LinePosition Property

This property returns the current line position. Read-only.

```
Integer = objTextReader.LinePosition
```

Name Property

This property returns the qualified name of the current node. There is also a `LocalName` property, which ignores any namespace prefix. Read-only.

```
String = objTextReader.Name
```

Namespaces Property

This property sets or returns a Boolean value indicating if namespaces are supported.

```
Boolean = objTextReader.Namespaces
objTextReader.Namespaces = Boolean
```

NamespaceURI Property

This property returns any namespace URI that applies to this node. Read-only.

```
String = objTextReader.NamespaceURI
```

NodeType Property

This property returns the type of the current node. Read-only.

```
Integer = objTextReader.NodeType
```

Prefix Property

This property returns any namespace prefix for this node. Read-only.

```
String = objTextReader.Prefix
```

QuoteChar Property

This property returns the character used to quote attribute values. Can be either a single quote (') or a double-quote ("). Read-only.

```
Char = objTextReader.QuoteChar
```

ReadState Property

This property returns the state of the reader and indicates what type of node or output is currently being read. Read-only. It has one of the following values of the ReadState enumeration: Closed, EndOfFile, Error, Initial, or Interactive. Read-only.

```
Integer = objTextReader.ReadState
```

Value Property

This properyt returns the text value of this node if available. Read-only.

```
String = objTextReader.Value
```

WhitespaceHandling Property

This property sets or returns a value that specifies whether whitespace is returned when reading. One of the values from the WhitespaceHandling enumeration (All, None, Significant).

```
Integer = objTextReader.WhitespaceHandling
objTextReader.WhitespaceHandling = Integer
```

XmlLang Property

This property returns the value of the current xml:lang that is in scope, as a string. Read-only.

```
String = objTextReader.XmlLang
```

XmlSpace Property

This property returns an XmlSpace object that represents the current xml:space setting that is in scope. Read-only.

```
XmlSpace = objTextReader.XmlSpace
```

Methods of the XmlTextReader Class

The `XmlTextReader` provides a number of methods that can be used to read XML from a stream, another object or a disk file. The `XmlTextReader` can be used in code, where you read each node one at a time and process it yourself. If used as the source of another object (for example, in the `Load` method of an `XmlDocument` object), that object will call the methods of the reader automatically to read the document.

Close Method

This method changes the `ReadState` to `Closed`.

```
objXmlTextReader.Close()
```

GetAttribute Method

This method returns the value of an attribute from the current node given the integer index position, the attribute name, or both the name and the namespace URI.

```
strValue = objXmlTextReader.GetAttribute("local-name", "namespace")
```

GetRemainder Method

This method reads the remaining content of the XML document and returns it as a "reader" object.

```
Dim objNewReader As XmlTextReader
objNewReader = objXmlTextReader.GetRemainder()
```

IsStartElement Method

This method returns a Boolean value indicating wether the current node is a start tag.

```
blnStart = objXmlTextReader.IsStartElement()
```

LookupNamespace Method

This method looks up the closest `xmlns` declaration for the given prefix that is in scope for the current node and returns the namespace URI from this declaration.

```
strNamespace = objXmlTextReader.LookupNamespace("prefix")
```

MoveToContent Method

This method checks if the current node is a content node (non-whitespace text, `CDATA`, `Element`, `EndElement`, `EntityReference`, or `EndEntity`). If not it skips to the next content node, or to the end of document, ignoring all `ProcessingInstruction`, `Comment`, `DocumentType`, `Whitespace` and `SignificantWhitespace` nodes. Returns the node it moves to:

```
objNode = objXmlTextReader.MoveToContent()
```

MoveToxxxx Methods

These methods advance the current reading point to the next node of a specific type. They return `True` if the move succeeds, or `False` if not. The methods are:

❑ blnOK = MoveToElement()

❑ blnOK = MoveToAttribute("*local-name*", "*namespace*")

❑ blnOK = MoveToFirstAttribute()

❑ blnOK = MoveToNextAttribute()

Read Method

This method reads the next node (of any type) and returns True if it succeeds or False if there are no more nodes to read (the reader is positioned at the end of the document). The node itself is then accessed as an XmlNode object through the reader.

```
blnOK = objXmlTextReader.Read()
```

ReadAttributeValue Method

This method parses the attribute value into one or more Text and/or EntityReference node types.

```
blnOK = objXmlTextReader.ReadAttributeValue()
```

ReadEndElement Method

This method checks that the current node is an element, and if so advances the reader to the next node.

```
objXmlTextReader.ReadEndElement()
```

ReadInnerXml Method

This method reads and returns the complete content of the current node including text and markup, but excluding the current node tags themselves.

```
strXML = objXmlTextReader.ReadInnerXml()
```

ReadOuterXml Method

This method reads and returns the complete content of the current node including text and markup, and including the tags of the current node.

```
strXML = objXmlTextReader.ReadOuterXml()
```

ReadStartElement Method

This method checks that the current content node is an end tag, and if so advances the reader to the next node.

```
objXmlTextReader.ReadStartElement("local-name", "namespace")
```

Readxxxx Methods

These methods read the appropriate set of characters from the document and return them as a specific type. The methods are:

❑ *bytes-read* = ReadBase64(*buffer-array*, *start-index*, *byte-count*)

❑ *bytes-read* = ReadBinHex(*buffer-array*, *start-index*, *byte-count*)

- ❑ *bytes-read* = ReadChars(*buffer-array*, *start-index*, *byte-count*)
- ❑ *string* = ReadElementString(*"local-name"*, *"namespace"*)
- ❑ *string* = ReadString()

Skip Method

This method advances the read point to the next node without retrieving the current node.

```
objXmlTextReader.Skip()
```

Example: XmlTextReaderExample

The following extract from the examples at the end of the chapter shows how the properties and methods of the XmlTextReader can be used to read an XML disk file:

```
Dim objXMLReader As XmlTextReader
objXMLReader = New XmlTextReader("c:\temp\booklist.xml")
objXMLReader.WhitespaceHandling = WhitespaceHandling.None
While objXMLReader.Read()
  Response.Write("NodeType: " & objXMLReader.NodeType.ToString() & "   ")
  Response.Write("Name: " & objXMLReader.Name.ToString() & "   ")
  If objXMLReader.HasValue Then
    Response.Write("Value: " & objXMLReader.Value.ToString())
  End If
  Response.Write("<br />")
  If objXMLReader.AttributeCount > 0 Then
    While objXMLReader.MoveToNextAttribute()
      Response.Write("Attribute Name: " & objXMLReader.Name  & "   ")
      Response.Write("Value: " & objXMLReader.Value & "<br />")
    End While
  End If
  Response.Write("<p />")
End While
objXMLReader.Close()
```

For a simple XML document, this is a section of the output that the code above produces:

```
NodeType: XmlDeclaration   Name: xml   Value: version="1.0" standalone="yes"
Attribute Name: version   Value: 1.0
Attribute Name: standalone   Value: yes

NodeType: Element   Name: BookList

NodeType: Element   Name: Book
Attribute Name: Category   Value: XML
Attribute Name: Language   Value: VB

NodeType: Element   Name: ISBN

NodeType: Text   Name:   Value: 1861003323
```

The XmlNodeReader Class

This class is used to read fragments of XML from a stream, another object, or a disk file. It works in almost exactly the same way as the `XmlTextReader`, but is used to read single nodes or fragments of a document from the source, rather than reading a whole document. It has the same set of properties and methods as the `XmlTextReader`, with the following exceptions.

The properties listed below are **not** supported by the `XmlNodeReader` class:

- ❑ Encoding
- ❑ LineNumber
- ❑ LinePosition
- ❑ Namespaces
- ❑ Normalization
- ❑ WhitespaceHandling

The methods below are **not** supported by the `XmlNodeReader` class:

- ❑ GetRemainder
- ❑ ReadBase64
- ❑ ReadBinHex
- ❑ ReadChars

The XmlValidatingReader Class

This is a special reader class that allows the validation of an XML document, or a set of nodes taken from an XML document, against a schema or Document Type Definition (DTD). It is created from an existing `XmlTextReader` or `XmlNodeReader`, and raises events as the document is read to indicate any validation errors encountered.

The `XmlValidatingReader` class inherits the properties and methods defined by the `XmlTextReader` class, and adds the properties described below to manage the validation process.

Properties of the XmlValidatingReader Class

Reader Property

This property returns a reference to the `XmlTextReader` object from which this object was constructed. Read-only.

```
XmlTextReader = objValidatingReader.Reader
```

Schemas Property

This property returns a reference to an `XmlSchemaCollection` containing the schemas that will be used for validation. It allows the use of external schemas and DTDs.

```
XmlSchemaCollection = objValidatingReader.Schemas
objValidatingReader.Schemas = XmlSchemaCollection
```

SchemaType Property

This property indicates the type of element in the schema currently being used for the validation of the corresponding node in the document. When using an XSD schema, it returns either an `XmlSchemaType` or an `XmlSchemaDatatype`, which expose properties such as the name, content type, data type, and namespace URI for the element in the schema.

The `SchemaType` property always returns `null` (`Nothing` in Visual Basic) if validation is being carried out against a DTD. Read-only.

```
[XmlSchemaType | XmlSchemaDatatype] = objValidatingReader.Schemas
```

ValidationEventHandler Property

This property contains a reference to the event handler that is to be called when validation errors are encountered.

In Visual Basic:

```
AddHandler objValidator.ValidationEventHandler, AddressOf MyHandler
```

In C#:

```
objValidator.ValidationEventHandler += new ValidationEventHandler(MyHandler);
```

Example: XmlValidatingReaderExample

In this example, the XML document has an in-line schema or DTD, meaning that we don't need to set any of the properties for our `XmlValidatingReader` instance:

```
Dim objXTReader As XmlTextReader
objXTReader = New XmlTextReader("c:\temp\test.xml")
Dim objValidator As New XmlValidatingReader(objXTReader)
While objValidator.Read()
   'use or display the XML content here as required
End While
objXTReader.Close()
```

By default, none of the XML document objects (`XmlDocument`, `XmlDataDocument`, and `XPathDocument`) validate the XML they load – they only check that it is well-formed. An `XmlValidatingReader` can be used as the source for one of these objects, for example in the `Load` method of an `XmlDocument` object, so that the document is validated as it is loaded:

```
...
Dim objXMLDoc As New XmlDocument()
objXMLDoc.Load(objValidator)
```

If the DTD or schema is in a separate file (or if there is more than one schema to validate a document against), an `XmlSchemaCollection` must be created and assigned to the `XmlValidatingReader`:

```
Dim objXTReader As XmlTextReader
objXTReader = New XmlTextReader(strXMLPath)
Dim objValidator As New XmlValidatingReader(objXTReader)
Dim objSchemaCol As New XmlSchemaCollection()
```

785

```
objSchemaCol.Add("", "c:\temp\test.xsd")
objValidator.Schemas.Add(objSchemaCol)

Dim objXMLDoc As New XmlDocument()
objXMLDoc.Load(objValidator)
```

To trap validation errors, an event handler is created and assigned to the `ValidationEventHandler` property of the `XmlValidatingReader`. In Visual Basic, calling the `AddHandler` statement performs this. The name of the event handler must be specified in conjunction with the `AddressOf` operator:

```
AddHandler objValidator.ValidationEventHandler, AddressOf MyHandler
```

A simple event handler looks like this:

```
Public Sub MyHandler(objSender As Object, objArgs As ValidationEventArgs)
  Response.Write("Validation error: " & objArgs.Message & "<br />")

  Dim strSeverity As String
  If objArgs.Severity = 0 Then strSeverity = "Error"
  If objArgs.Severity = 1 Then strSeverity = "Warning"

  Response.Write("Severity level: " & strSeverity & "<br />)
End Sub
```

We use this code in the example at the end of the chapter, and it produces the following output from a simple invalid document:

Validation error: Element 'Books' has invalid content. Expected 'LastName'. An error occurred at file:///c:/inetpub/wwwroot/530X/bad-booklist.xml(22, 6).
Severity level: Error

Validation error: The 'MiddleInitial' element is not declared. An error occurred at file:///c:/inetpub/wwwroot/530X/bad-booklist.xml(22, 6).
Severity level: Error

The System.Xml.XPath Namespace

The classes in the `System.Xml.XPath` namespace that we use most often are:

❑   XPathDocument

❑   XPathNavigator

❑   XPathNodeIterator

We'll look at each of these classes next.

The XPathDocument Class

This class is used to store an XML document. Unlike the other two "document" classes in .NET, it does not support the W3C XML DOM interface. Instead, all access to the content of the document is made through an `XPathNavigator` that can be attached to it.

To create an `XPathDocument`, we must provide details of the XML document that will be loaded. There is no `Load` or `LoadXml` method that can be used afterward to load XML into it. The source of the XML can be a stream object, the path and name of a disk file, a `TextReader` object, or an `XmlReader` object such as an `XmlTextReader` or `XmlNodeReader`.

```
Dim objXPathDoc As New XPathDocument("c:\temp\test.xml")
```

Or using an `XmlTextReader`:

```
Dim objXMLReader As XmlTextReader
objXMLReader = New XmlTextReader("c:\temp\test.xml")
Dim objXPathDoc As New XPathDocument(objXMLReader)
```

When using a disk file or an `XmlReader` as the source a second optional parameter can be used to specify how whitespace should be handled. It must be one of the values from the `XmlSpace` enumeration (`Default`, `None`, or `Preserve`).

```
Dim objXPathDoc As New XPathDocument("c:\temp\test.xml", XmlSpace.Preserve)
```

The `XPathDocument` object has only one method that is commonly used.

CreateNavigator Method

This method creates an instance of an `XPathNavigator` object based on the `XPathDocument` object.

```
Dim objXPNav As XPathNavigator = objXPathDoc.CreateNavigator()
```

The XPathNavigator Class

This object provides "push-model" access to an XML document. It provides methods that can be used to iterate through a document, and select specific nodes using an XPath expression. It can be used to move to a specific element, attribute, or other node type, or to move to the sibling, child, or parent of the current element. Note that an `XPathNavigator` can be used with **any** of the three XML document objects. Although located in the `System.Xml.XPath` namespace, it is not specific to the `XPathDocument` object.

Properties of the XPathNavigator Class

As an `XPathNavigator` instance iterates through an XML document, it exposes details of the current node through its properties. Many of these are similar to the properties of the `XmlNode` object.

GetAttribute Property

This property returns the value of the attribute for the current node given a `LocalName` and a `NamespaceURI`. Read-only.

```
String = objNavigator.GetAttribute
```

GetNamespace Property

This property returns the value of the namespace node corresponding to the specified local name. Read-only.

```
String = objNavigator.GetNamespace
```

HasAttributes Property

This property returns a Boolean value indicating if the node has any attributes. Read-only.

```
Boolean = objNavigator.HasAttributes
```

HasChildren Property

This property returns a Boolean value indicating if the node has any child nodes. Read-only.

```
Boolean = objNavigator.HasChildren
```

IsEmptyElement Property

This property returns a Boolean value indicating whether the current node is an empty element, for example, `<MyElem/>`. Read-only.

```
Boolean = objNavigator.IsEmptyElement
```

Name and LocalName Properties

The `Name` property returns the qualified name of the current node. The `LocalName` property is similar but ignores any namespace prefix. Read-only.

```
String = objNavigator.Name
String = objNavigator.LocalName
```

NamespaceURI Property

This property returns the namespace URI for the node. Read-only.

```
String = objNavigator.NamespaceURI
```

NodeType Property

This property returns the type of the current node (element, attribute, CDATA section, etc). Read-only.

```
Integer = objNavigator.NodeType
```

Prefix Property

This property returns the namespace prefix for the node. Read-only.

```
String = objNavigator.Prefix
```

Value Property

This property returns the value of the node. Read-only.

```
String = objNavigator.Value
```

XmlLang Property

This property returns the value of the current `xml:lang` that is in scope, as a string. Read-only.

```
String = objNavigator.XmlLang
```

Methods of the XPathNavigator Class

The `XPathNavigator` provides methods that can be used to move the current position of the `XPathNavigator`. The class also exposes methods for creating another `XPathNavigator` for the same document object, and finding information relating to the relationship between the two `XPathNavigator` objects. Finally, there are methods to select nodes using XPath expressions, and to handle these expressions.

Clone Method

This method creates and returns a reference to a new `XPathNavigator` object positioned on the same node as this `XPathNavigator`.

```
objNewNavigator = objXPNavigator.Clone()
```

ComparePosition Method

This method compares the position of the current `XPathNavigator` with the position of the specified `XPathNavigator`.

```
intNodeOrder = objXPNavigator.ComparePosition(objOtherNavigator)
```

The return value is a member of the `XmlNodeOrder` enumeration, and can be one of: `After`, `Before`, `Same`, or `Unknown`.

Compile Method

This method compiles the specified XPath expression and returns it as an `XPathExpression` object.

```
objXPExpression = objXPNavigator.Compile("string")
```

Evaluate Method

This method evaluates the specified expression (as a string or `XPathExpression` object) and returns the typed result (as an `Integer`, `Boolean`, or `String`).

```
result = objXPNavigator.Evaluate("string")
result = objXPNavigator.Evaluate(objXPExpression)
```

It can also be used to evaluate an expression using a set of nodes contained in an `XPathNodeIterator` object:

```
result = objXPNavigator.Evaluate(objXPExpression, objXPNodeIterator)
```

IsDescendant Method

This method returns a Boolean value indicating if the specified `XPathNavigator` is a descendant of the current `XPathNavigator`.

```
blnResult = objXPNavigator.IsDescendant(objXPNavigator)
```

IsSamePosition Method

This method returns a Boolean value indicating if the current `XPathNavigator` is at the same position in the document as a specified `XPathNavigator`.

```
blnResult = objXPNavigator.IsSamePosition(objXPNavigator)
```

Matches Method

This method returns a Boolean value indicating if the current node matches a specified XPath expression (which can be a string or an XPathExpression object).

```
blnResult = objXPNavigator.Matches("string")
blnResult = objXPNavigator.Matches(objXPExpression)
```

MoveTo Method

moves this XPathNavigator to the same position as another specified XPathNavigator.

```
objOK = objXPNavigator.MoveTo(objXPNavigator)
```

MoveToAttribute Method

This method moves the XPathNavigator to the attribute of the current node that has the specified LocalName and NamespaceURI.

```
blnOK = objXPNavigator.MoveToAttribute("local-name", "namespace")
```

MoveToFirst, MoveToNext, and MoveToPrevious Methods

These three methods move the XPathNavigator between nodes that are siblings – are at the same level within the document. They take no parameters and return True if the move succeeds, or False if there is no node to move to.

```
blnOK = objXPNavigator.MoveToFirst()
blnOK = objXPNavigator.MoveToNext()
blnOK = objXPNavigator.MoveToPrevious()
```

MoveToId Method

This method moves the XPathNavigator to the element node that has an ID-type attribute containing the specified value.

```
blnOK = objXPNavigator.MoveToId("string")
```

MoveToNamespace Method

This method moves the XPathNavigator to the namespace node that has the specified name.

```
blnOK = objXPNavigator.MoveToNamespace("string")
```

MoveToxxxx Methods

This set of methods move the XPathNavigator to a specified node. Some of them return True if the move succeeds, or False if there is no node to move to. The various methods are:

- ❑ MoveToRoot()

- ❑ blnOK = MoveToParent()

- ❑ blnOK = MoveToFirstChild()

- ❑ blnOK = MoveToFirstAttribute()
- ❑ blnOK = MoveToNextAttribute()
- ❑ blnOK = MoveToFirstNamespace()
- ❑ blnOK = MoveToNextNamespace()

Select Method

This method takes a string containing an XPath expression or an `XPathExpression` object and returns an `XPathNodeIterator` containing the nodes that match the XPath expression.

```
objXPNodeIterator = objXPNavigator.Select("string")
objXPNodeIterator = objXPNavigator.Select(objXPExpression)
```

SelectAncestors Method

This method takes one of the values from the `XPathNodeType` enumeration (`All`, `Attribute`, `Element`, `Text`, `Namespace`, etc.), or a node name and namespace URI as strings, plus a Boolean value that indicates if the current node should be included. Returns an `XPathNodeIterator` containing all ancestor nodes of the current node that match these criteria.

```
objXPNodeIter = objXPNav.SelectAncestors(node-type, match-self)
objXPNodeIter = objXPNav.SelectAncestors("name", "namespace", match-self)
```

SelectChildren Method

This method takes the same parameters and has the same return type as the `SelectAncestors` method (but omitting the *match-self* parameter), and returns only child nodes that match the specified criteria.

```
objXPNodeIter = objXPNav.SelectChildren(node-type)
objXPNodeIter = objXPNav.SelectChildren("name", "namespace")
```

SelectDescendants Method

This method takes the same parameters and has the same return type as the `SelectAncestors` method, but returns only descendant nodes that match the specified criteria.

```
objXPNodeIter = objXPNav.SelectDescendants(node-type, match-self)
objXPNodeIter = objXPNav.SelectDescendants("name", "namespace", match-self)
```

Example: XPathNavigatorExample

To demonstrate moving around an XML document, this code moves to the root of the document, then the first child, which is an element named `<BookList>`, and then to the first child of this element, which is an element named `<Book>`. Then it displays details about this element, and checks if there are any attributes – if so it iterates through them. Finally it iterates through all the child nodes of this node displaying information about them:

```
Dim objXPathDoc As New XPathDocument("c:\temp\booklist.xml")
Dim objXPNav As XPathNavigator = objXPathDoc.CreateNavigator()

objXPNav.MoveToRoot()
```

```
objXPNav.MoveToFirstChild()
objXPNav.MoveToFirstChild()

Do
  Response.Write("Node type: " & objXPNav.NodeType.ToString() & "   ")
  Response.Write("Name: " & objXPNav.Name.ToString() & "   ")
  Response.Write("Value: " & objXPNav.Value.ToString() & "<br />")
  If objXPNav.HasAttributes Then   'see if there are any attributes
    objXPNav.MoveToFirstAttribute()
    Do
      Response.Write("Attribute Name: " & objXPNav.Name.ToString() _
                  & "   ")
      Response.Write("Value: " & objXPNav.Value.ToString() & "<br />")
    Loop While objXPNav.MoveToNextAttribute()
    objXPNav.MoveToParent()
  End If
  If objXPNav.HasChildren Then   'see if there are any child nodes
    objXPNav.MoveToFirstChild()
    Do
      Response.Write("Node type: " & objXPNav.NodeType.ToString() & "   ")
      Response.Write("Name: " & objXPNav.Name.ToString() & "   ")
      Response.Write("Value: " & objXPNav.Value.ToString() & "<br />")
    Loop While objXPNav.MoveToNext()
    objXPNav.MoveToParent()
  End If
Loop While objXPNav.MoveToNext()
```

The result is something like this:

Node type: Element   Name: Book   Value: 1861003323Professional Visual Basic 6 XML2000-03-01T00:00:00
Attribute Name: Category   Value: XML
Attribute Name: Language   Value: VB
Node type: Element   Name: ISBN   Value: 1861003323
Node type: Element   Name: Title   Value: Professional Visual Basic 6 XML
Node type: Element   Name: PublicationDate   Value: 2000-03-01T00:00:00
Node type: Element   Name: Book   Value: 1861003382Beginning Active Server Pages 3.01999-12-01T00:00:00
Attribute Name: Category   Value: ASP
Node type: Element   Name: ISBN   Value: 1861003382
Node type: Element   Name: Title   Value: Beginning Active Server Pages 3.0
Node type: Element   Name: PublicationDate   Value: 1999-12-01T00:00:00

Notice that the Value property of a node in an XPathNavigator is the concatenation of all the text nodes within that node, in other words it is the same as the InnerText property of an XmlNode object.

Example: XPathNavigatorExample2

To select all the <Book> nodes in a simple XML document, we could use the following code:

```
Dim objXPathDoc As New XPathDocument("c:\temp\test.xml")
Dim objXPNav As XPathNavigator = objXPathDoc.CreateNavigator()
Dim objXPIter As XPathNodeIterator
```

```
objXPIter = objXPNav.Select("descendant::Book")
While objXPIter.MoveNext()

  Response.Write("Name: " & objXPIter.Current.Name & "   ")
  Response.Write("Value: " & objXPIter.Current.Value & "<br />")

End While
```

The XPathNodeIterator Class

When selecting one or more nodes within an `XPathNavigator`, the result is an `XPathNodeIterator` object that represents a collection of XML nodes. Methods provided by this object can be used to iterate through the nodes to access their values. This object was demonstrated in the previous code listing.

Properties of the XPathNodeIterator Class

There are just three commonly used properties of this class.

Count Property

This property returns an integer indicating the number of nodes in the object. Read-only.

```
Integer = objXPIter.Count
```

Current Property

This property returns a reference to the current node in the object. Read-only.

```
XmlNode = objXPIter.Current
```

CurrentPosition Property

This property returns an integer index indicating the position of the current node within the object. Read-only.

```
Integer = objXPIter.CurrentPosition
```

Methods of the XPathNodeIterator Class

The two methods described here are the only two in this class that are commonly used.

Clone Method

This method creates a copy of the current `XPathNodeIterator`.

```
objNewIter = objXPIter.Clone()
```

MoveNext Method

This method moves the pointer to the next node in the `XPathNodeIterator`. It returns `True` if the move was successful, or `False` if there are no more nodes to move to.

```
blnOK = objXPIter.MoveNext()
```

The System.Xml.Xsl Namespace

There are two classes within this namespace that are commonly used for transforming XML documents:

❏ XslTransform

❏ XsltArgumentList

We'll look at these objects next.

The XslTransform Class

This class provides features for performing XSL or XSLT transformations. The input XML document can be a single XML node, an XPathNavigator, or the path and name of a disk file. The resulting transformed document can be specified as any of the XML "reader" or "writer" objects, a stream, or the path and name of a disk file.

Methods of the XslTransform Class

There are just two methods of the XslTransform class that are commonly used.

Load Method

This method accepts an XmlNode, an XPathDocument, an XmlTextReader, an XmlNodeReader, an XPathNavigator, or the path and name of a disk file and loads the stylesheet document it references into the XslTransform object. An optional second parameter is used to load an XmlUrlResolver object for importing external resources.

The simplest way to load a stylesheet from disk is by specifying the path and filename:

```
Dim objTransform As New XslTransform()
objTransform.Load("c:\temp\mystyle.xsl")
```

Alternatively, use an XPathDocument as the source:

```
Dim objXPathDoc As New XPathDocument("c:\temp\mystyle.xsl")
objTransform.Load(objXPathDoc)
```

Or use an XmlTextReader:

```
Dim objXMLReader As New XmlTextReader("c:\temp\mystyle.xsl")
objTransform.Load(objXMLReader)
```

Or you can use an XPathNavigator:

```
Dim objXPathDoc As New XPathDocument("c:\temp\mystyle.xsl")
Dim objXPNav As XPathNavigator = objXPathDoc.CreateNavigator()
objTransform.Load(objXPNav)
```

The choice of which method to use depends really on where you actually have the stylesheet; is it currently referenced by an XPathNavigator or an XmlTextReader, or in an XmlDocument? If not, and it's on disk as a file, the easiest way to access it is by specifying the path and filename.

An `XmlUrlResolver` object is used when a stylesheet or XML document includes any `xsl:import` or `xsl:include` elements. It accesses other systems, using the URL provided in the `xsl:import` or `xsl:include` elements, to fetch the resources that are required. It can also accept a username, password, and domain name where anonymous access to the target system is not available. For more details, see the SDK section .NET Framework Class Library.

Transform Method

Takes an XML document and transforms it using the loaded stylesheet. The output can be sent to an XML "reader" object (`XmlTextReader` or `XmlNodeReader`), a "writer" object (`XmlTextWriter` or any of the other `TextWriter` objects), a stream, or a specified disk file. It can also accept an `XsltArgumentList` containing the arguments to be passed to the stylesheet.

Once the `XslTransform` object is loaded with a stylesheet, the `Transform` method is used to perform the transformation and create the output. The simplest approach is to specify the source XML document and the target document using a path and filename. In this example, we are creating an HTML output file (but it could be any format, depending on the stylesheet used):

```
objTransform.Transform("c:\temp\xmldoc.xml", "c:\output\newfile.htm")
```

Or, if the XML source document is in an `XPathDocument` object, and the required output is to the console (a stream):

```
objTransform.Transform(objXPathDoc, Console.Out)
```

Example: Loading and Transforming an XML Document

To create a valid XML document as the output of a transformation, you may need to add the opening `<?xml version="1.0" ?>` declaration element, and possibly other content. An `XmlTextWriter` object is useful here:

```
'create XslTransform and load XSL style sheet
Dim objTransform As New XslTransform()
objTransform.Load("c:\temp\mystyle.xsl")

'load XML source, can be an XPathDocument or an XPathNavigator
Dim objXPathDoc As New XPathDocument("c:\temp\xmldoc.xml")

'create XmlTextWriter to write the output
Dim objWriter As New XmlTextWriter("c:\temp\result.xml", Nothing)

'create output document, no arguments for stylesheet
objWriter.WriteStartDocument()   'create XML declaration element
objWriter.WriteComment("New XML file created: " & Now())
objTransform.Transform(objXPathDoc, Nothing, objWriter)
objWriter.WriteEndDocument()
objWriter.Close()
```

There are also versions of the `Transform` method that return the result as a "reader" object such as an `XmlTextReader`, `XmlNodeReader`, or `XmlValidatingReader` rather than accepting it as a parameter. The source XML document must be specified as an `XmlNode`, an `XPathDocument`, or an `XPathNavigator`, and the second argument (the reference to an `XsltArgumentList` object) must be provided. If there are no arguments for the stylesheet, `null` (`Nothing` in Visual Basic) is used:

```
Dim objXPathDoc As New XPathDocument("c:\temp\xmldoc.xml")
Dim objXMLReader As New XmlTextReader("c:\temp\newfile.htm")
objXMLReader = objTransform.Transform(objXPathDoc, Nothing)
```

The XsltArgumentList Class

When performing XSLT transformations (XSL does not support stylesheet arguments), an
XsltArgumentList object is used to hold the parameters and values for the stylesheet.

Methods of the XsltArgumentList Class

The commonly used methods of this class are described below.

AddParam Method

This method takes a parameter name, namespace URI, and a value and adds them to the
XsltArgumentList object. The value of a parameter can be a String, a Boolean, a Double (for
numbers), an XPathNavigator, or an XPathNodeIterator.

```
objArgList.AddParam("name", "namespace", value)
```

Clear Method

This method removes all existing parameters from the XsltArgumentList object. It takes no
parameters and returns no result.

```
objArgList.Clear()
```

GetParam Method

This method takes a parameter name and a namespace URI, and returns the matching parameter from
the XsltArgumentList as an Object type, or null (Nothing in Visual Basic) if the parameter
is not found.

```
objParameter = objArgList.GetParam("name", "namespace")
```

RemoveParam Method

This method takes a parameter name and a namespace URI, and removes **and** returns the matching
parameter from the XsltArgumentList as an Object type, or null (Nothing in Visual Basic) if the
parameter
is not found.

```
objParameter = objArgList.RemoveParam("name", "namespace")
```

Example: XsltArgumentListExample

As an example, this code creates an XsltArgumentList and adds two parameters to it, then uses it in
a transformation:

```
Dim objArgList As New XsltArgumentList()
Dim strParam1 As String = "Wrox Press"
objArgList.AddParam("SearchText", "", strParam1)
Dim dblParam2 As Double = 42
objArgList.AddParam("SearchText", "", dblParam2)
```

```
Dim objTransform As New XslTransform()
objTransform.Load("c:\temp\mystyle.xsl")
Dim objXPathDoc As New XPathDocument("c:\temp\xmldoc.xml")
objTransform.Transform(objXPathDoc, objArgList, Console.Out)
```

Common XML Task Examples

To demonstrate some of the most common tasks we perform with XML documents, we've provided some examples of the different ways that we can accomplish the following everyday requirements:

- ❑ Writing XML Documents
- ❑ Reading XML Documents
- ❑ Validating XML Documents
- ❑ Creating, Searching, and Modifying Documents
- ❑ Transforming XML Documents

We provided this selection of sample files, taken from several sources, in order to demonstrate the basic techniques available. You can download or run them online. To download the files go to:

http://www.wrox.com/Books/Book_Details.asp?isbn=186100530X

and select the **"Download code"** link. To run the samples online, go to:

http://www.daveandal.com/aspnetprogref/

Each page of the online samples has a **[view source]** link at the bottom that you can use to view the source code.

Within the samples, the default.htm menu page contains links to the various files, with a selection from each of the categories listed above and some for the final section of this chapter.

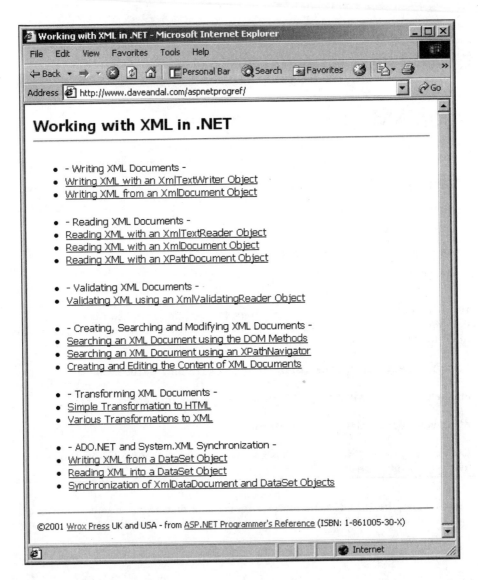

Writing XML Documents

There are two examples in this category, demonstrating how we can write XML using an `XmlTextWriter` object and save it from an `XmlDocument` object.

Example: Writing XML Using an XmlTextWriter – write-textwriter.aspx

The `XmlTextWriter` example creates a simple XML document and writes it to disk. It then opens the file and displays the contents. There is also a link you can use to view the disk file directly:

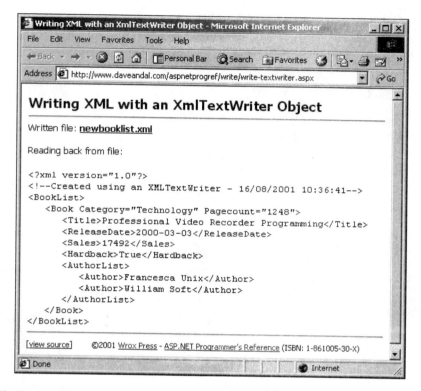

How It Works

The code used is similar to that we listed when we look at the XmlTextWriter object earlier in this chapter. Note that we're using a Try...Catch construct to catch any errors while creating and opening the disk file:

```
'create physical path for the new file (in same folder as ASPX page)
Dim strCurrentPath As String = Request.PhysicalPath
Dim strXMLPath As String = Left(strCurrentPath, _
                        InStrRev(strCurrentPath, "\")) & "newbooklist.xml"

'declare a variable to hold an XmlTextWriter object
Dim objXMLWriter As XmlTextWriter

Try

    'create a new objXMLWriter object for the XML file
    objXMLWriter = New XmlTextWriter(strXMLPath, Nothing)

Catch objError As Exception

    '... display error details here
    Exit Sub  ' and stop execution

End Try

'now ready to write (or "push") the nodes for the new XML document
```

```
'turn on indented formatting and set indent to 3 characters
objXMLWriter.Formatting = Formatting.Indented
objXMLWriter.Indentation = 3

'start the document with the XML declaration tag
objXMLWriter.WriteStartDocument()

'write a comment element including the current date/time
objXMLWriter.WriteComment("Created using an XMLTextWriter - " & Now())

'write the opening tag for the <BookList> root element
objXMLWriter.WriteStartElement("BookList")

  'write the opening tag for a <Book> element
  objXMLWriter.WriteStartElement("Book")

    'add two attributes to this element's opening tag
    objXMLWriter.WriteAttributeString("Category", "Technology")
    Dim intPageCount As Integer = 1248    'numeric value to convert
    objXMLWriter.WriteAttributeString("Pagecount", intPageCount.ToString("G"))

    'write four elements, using different source data types
    objXMLWriter.WriteElementString("Title", _
                              "Professional Video Recorder Programming")
    Dim datReleaseDate As DateTime = #03/03/2000#
    objXMLWriter.WriteElementString("ReleaseDate", _
                              datReleaseDate.ToString("yyyy-MM-dd"))
    Dim intSales As Integer = 17492
    objXMLWriter.WriteElementString("Sales", intSales.ToString("G"))
    Dim blnHardback As Boolean = True
    objXMLWriter.WriteElementString("Hardback", blnHardback.ToString())

    'write the opening tag for the <AuthorList> child element
    objXMLWriter.WriteStartElement("AuthorList")

      'add two <Author> elements
      objXMLWriter.WriteElementString("Author", "Francesca Unix")
      objXMLWriter.WriteElementString("Author", "William Soft")

    'close the <AuthorList> element
    objXMLWriter.WriteEndElement()

  'close the <Book> element
  objXMLWriter.WriteEndElement()

'close the root <BookList> element
objXMLWriter.WriteEndElement()

'flush the current content to the file and close it
objXMLWriter.Flush()
objXMLWriter.Close()
```

Example: Writing XML from an XmlDocument – write-xmldoc.aspx

The second example uses a mixture of W3C-compliant and Microsoft-specific code techniques to create a new XML document within an XmlDocument object, and then saves the new document to a disk file using the Save method. Again, there is a link where you can view the new document directly:

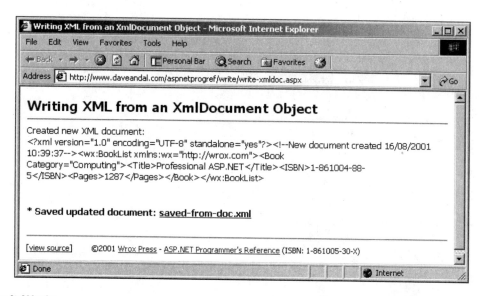

How It Works

The code starts by creating the path and filename for the new document, and then creates an empty `XmlDocument` object. Within this document is created a new `XmlDeclaration`, and this is inserted into the new document. Then a new `Comment` element is created and added after the declaration:

```
'create physical path to booklist sample files in same folder as ASPX page
Dim strCurrentPath As String = Request.PhysicalPath
Dim strXMLPath As String = Left(strCurrentPath, _
                      InStrRev(strCurrentPath, "\")) & "saved-from-doc.xml"

'create new empty XmlDocument object
Dim objXMLDoc As New XmlDocument()

'create a new XmlDeclaration object
Dim objDeclare As XmlDeclaration
objDeclare = objXMLDoc.CreateXmlDeclaration("1.0", "UTF-8", "yes")

'and add it as the first node in the new document
objDeclare = objXMLDoc.InsertBefore(objDeclare, objXMLDoc.DocumentElement)

'create a new XmlComment object
Dim objComment As XmlComment
objComment = objXMLDoc.CreateComment("New document created " & Now())

'and add it as the second node in the new document
objComment = objXMLDoc.InsertAfter(objComment, objDeclare)
```

Next, the code creates an `XmlElement` named `<BookList>` and makes it the root element of the document, and another `XmlElement` named `<Book>`, which it inserts within this element as a child element. It also creates a new `XmlAttribute` object named `Category`, assigns it the value `"Computing"`, and adds it to the `<Book>` element:

```
'create a new XmlElement object, including namespace and prefix
Dim objRootElem As XmlElement
objRootElem = objXMLDoc.CreateElement("wx", "BookList", "http://wrox.com")

'and add it as the root element in the new document
objRootElem = objXMLDoc.InsertAfter(objRootElem, objComment)

'create another new XmlElement object
Dim objBookElem As XmlElement
objBookElem = objXMLDoc.CreateElement("Book")

'and add it as a child of the root element
'don't need to save the returned reference
objRootElem.AppendChild(objBookElem)

'create a new XmlAttribute object
Dim objAttr As XmlAttribute
objAttr = objXMLDoc.CreateAttribute("Category")

'set the attribute value
objAttr.Value = "Computing"

'and add it to the <Book> element
'don't need to save the returned reference
objBookElem.SetAttributeNode(objAttr)
```

To create content for the <Book> element we use a Microsoft-specific shortcut technique. We can create a string that is an XML document fragment and then set the value of an element's InnerXml property to that string – effectively adding several elements and their values in one go. Then we can save the new document to disk ready to display it:

```
'create some content for the <Book> element
Dim strContent As String
strContent = "<Title>Professional ASP.NET</Title>" _
           & "<ISBN>1-861004-88-5</ISBN>" _
           & "<Pages>1287</Pages>"

'put it into the element using the InnerXml property
objBookElem.InnerXml = strContent

'write the new document to a disk file
objXMLDoc.Save(strXMLPath)
```

Other Options for Writing XML Documents

Among the other options for writing XML, to disk or to another object or stream, are:

- ❏ Using the Save method of an XmlDataDocument object.

- ❏ Using the WriteTo or WriteContentTo methods of an XmlDocument or XmlDataDocument, or any individual XmlNode within the document.

- ❏ Extracting XML from a document or node using the InnerXml or OuterXml methods of the XmlNode class and writing it to a disk file or stream. Remember that the ASP.NET Response object (from which many other specialized classes are also derived) can accept a Stream object to output XML to the client directly.

Reading XML Documents

Our examples show three techniques for reading XML, using an `XmlTextReader`, an `XmlDocument`, and an `XPathDocument` object.

Example: Reading XML with an XmlTextReader – read-textreader.aspx

This example reads a disk file using an `XmlTextReader`, and examines each node to see what kind (what `NodeType`) it is. Based on this, it displays the value by accessing the appropriate node. (Remember that an `XmlElement` node has its "value", or text content, held in a child `XmlText` node.)

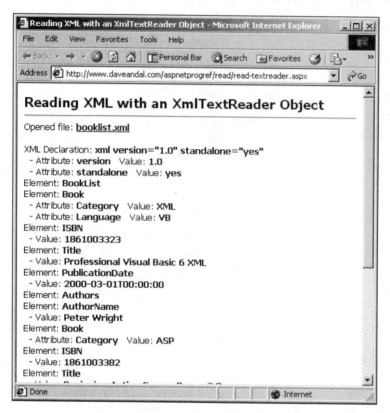

How It Works

The code creates a new `XmlTextReader` for the document within a `Try...Catch` construct, and (providing it could open the XML file) repeatedly calls the `Read` method of the `XmlTextReader` to fetch each node in turn:

```
'declare a variable to hold an XmlTextReader object
Dim objXMLReader As XmlTextReader

Try

    'create a new XmlTextReader object for the XML file
    objXMLReader = New XmlTextReader(strXMLPath)
```

```
Catch objError As Exception

   '... display error details here
   Exit Sub  ' and stop execution

End Try

'now ready to read (or "pull") the nodes of the XML document
Dim strNodeResult As String = ""
Dim objNodeType As XmlNodeType

'read each node in turn - returns False if no more nodes to read
Do While objXMLReader.Read()
```

As each node is read, the code examines the `NodeType` property to see what type of node it is. In this example, we're only handling three node types: `XmlDeclaration`, `Element`, and `Text`. For each type we display the appropriate property values:

```
'select on the type of the node (these are only some of the types)
objNodeType = objXMLReader.NodeType

Select Case objNodeType

   Case XmlNodeType.XmlDeclaration:
      'get the name and value
      strNodeResult += "XML Declaration: <b>" & objXMLReader.Name _
                       & " " & objXMLReader.Value & "</b><br />"

   Case XmlNodeType.Element:
      'just get the name, any value will be in next (#text) node
      strNodeResult += "Element: <b>" & objXMLReader.Name & "</b><br />"

   Case XmlNodeType.Text:
      'just display the value, node name is "#text" in this case
      strNodeResult += "  - Value: <b>" & objXMLReader.Value _
                       & "</b><br />"

End Select
```

The `XmlTextReader` fetches a complete element opening tag when it encounters an element node, and this contains any attributes that are declared on that element. Our code checks if there are any attributes, and if so iterates through them displaying the name and value of each one:

```
'see if this node has any attributes
If objXMLReader.AttributeCount > 0 Then

   'iterate through the attributes by moving to the next one
   'could use MoveToFirstAttribute but MoveToNextAttribute does
   'the same when the current node is an element-type node
   Do While objXMLReader.MoveToNextAttribute()

      'get the attribute name and value
      strNodeResult +=  "  - Attribute: <b>" & objXMLReader.Name _
                        & "</b>   Value: <b>" & objXMLReader.Value _
                        & "</b><br />"
```

```
      Loop

   End If
```

Then the code goes back to do the next node, and closes the reader when there are no more to read:

```
   Loop      'and read the next node

   'finished with the reader so close it
   objXMLReader.Close()
```

Example: Reading XML with an XmlDocument – read-xmldoc.aspx

The second example in this section produces roughly the same output, but this time by loading the XML into an `XmlDocument` object and parsing it into an XML DOM "tree" internally. Then it uses recursion to follow all the branches of the tree and display details about each node:

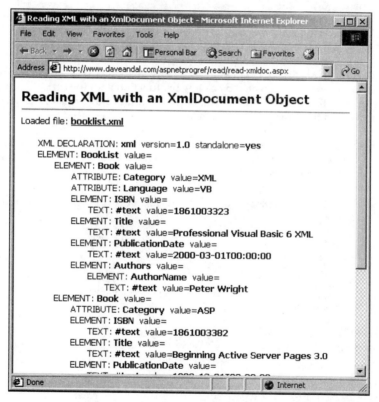

Recursion is an extremely useful approach for manipulating the contents of an XML parser (such as the `XmlDocument` and `XmlDataDocument` objects), as it can cope with any structure within the XML of the document.

How It Works

The code creates a new `XmlDocument` object and loads the XML file within a `Try...Catch` construct in case the file cannot be opened. Then it calls the recursive function that reads and displays the nodes within the document by stepping through each "branch" of the parsed XML "tree" in turn:

```
Dim objXMLDoc As New XMLDocument()

Try

    'load the XML file into the XMLDocument object
    objXMLDoc.Load(strXMLPath)

Catch objError As Exception

    '... display error details here
    Exit Sub  ' and stop execution

End Try

'now ready to parse the XML document. It must be well-formed to have
'loaded without error so call a recursive function to iterate through
'all the nodes in the document creating a string that is placed in
'a <div> element elsewhere in the page
Dim strNodes As String
outResults.innerHTML = strNodes & GetChildNodes(objXMLDoc.ChildNodes, 0)
```

The recursive function is listed next. It works in a similar way to the previous code, though now the source is an `XmlNodeList` object created by calling the function with the `ChildNodes` property of the `XmlDocument` object. This `XmlNodeList` contains all the nodes at the root of the document (basically the XML declaration and the root `<BookList>` element).

For each node in the `XmlNodeList`, the code examines the type of node and adds display details for the appropriate values to a string named `strNodes`. When it encounters an `XmlElement` node, it also iterates through the attributes collecting their values:

```
Function GetChildNodes(objNodeList As XMLNodeList, intLevel As Integer) _
        As String

    Dim strNodes As String = ""
    Dim objNode As XMLNode
    Dim objAttr As XMLAttribute

    'iterate through all the child nodes for the current node
    For Each objNode In objNodeList

        'display information about this node
        strNodes = strNodes & GetIndent(intLevel) _
                & GetNodeType(objNode.NodeType) & ": <b>" & objNode.Name

        'if it is an XML Declaration node, display the 'special' properties
        If objNode.NodeType = XMLNodeType.XmlDeclaration Then

            'cast the XMLNode object to an XmlDeclaration object
            Dim objXMLDec =CType(objNode, XmlDeclaration)
            strNodes = strNodes & "</b>  version=<b>" _
                    & objXMLDec.Version & "</b>  standalone=<b>" _
                    & objXMLDec.Standalone & "</b><br />"

        Else
```

```
            'just display the generic 'value' property
            strNodes = strNodes & "</b>  value=<b>" & objNode.Value _
                & "</b><br />"

        End If


        'if it is an Element node, iterate through the Attributes
        'collection displaying information about each attribute
        If objNode.NodeType = XMLNodeType.Element Then
            'display the attribute information for each attribute
            For Each objAttr In objNode.Attributes
                strNodes = strNodes & GetIndent(intLevel + 1) _
                    & GetNodeType(objAttr.NodeType) & ": <b>" _
                    & objAttr.Name & "</b>  value=<b>" _
                    & objAttr.Value & "</b><br />"
            Next
        End If
```

The magic comes at the end of this function, where it then recursively calls the same function again for each set of child nodes of this node. Afterwards, the cumulative result is passed back to the previous instance of the function:

```
        'if this node has child nodes, call the same function recursively
        'to display the information for it and each of its child node
        If objNode.HasChildNodes Then
            strNodes = strNodes & GetChildNodes(objNode.childNodes, intLevel + 1)
        End If

    Next   'go to next node

    Return strNodes   'pass the result back to the caller

End Function
```

There are a couple of other functions in the page that accomplish the peripheral tasks like getting a text representation of the element type and building up a string with the correct number of   characters to provide the indenting seen in the screenshot.

Example: Reading XML with an XPathDocument – read-xpathdoc.aspx

The third example in this section gives a similar result to the previous one, but does it by loading the XML into an XPathDocument and then accessing it through an XPathNavigator object. The "move" methods of the XPathNavigator are used to access each node recursively and output the information about the nodes:

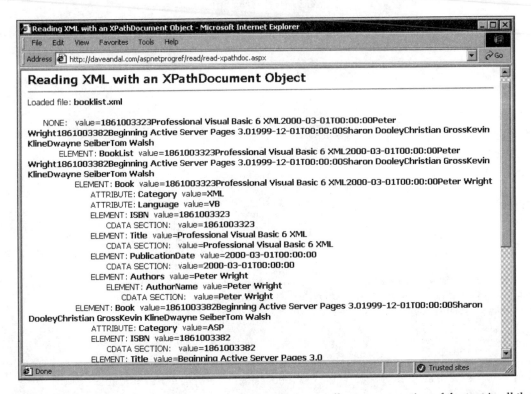

Note that the value of a node in an `XPathNavigator` is actually a concatenation of the text in all the child nodes. In an `XmlDocument`, when using the DOM methods, the value is just that of the node itself or the appropriate child TEXT (`XmlText`) node.

How It Works

The code is shown next. After creating an `XPathDocument` based on the XML source document, it creates an `XPathNavigator`, moves to the root of the document, and calls a recursive function named `GetXMLDocFragment` – passing in the `XPathNavigator` just created:

```
'declare a variable to hold an XMLDocument object
Dim objXPathDoc As XPathDocument

Try

   'create a new XPathDocument object and load the XML file
   objXPathDoc = New XPathDocument(strXMLPath)

Catch objError As Exception

   '... display error details here
   Exit Sub  ' and stop execution

End Try

'now ready to parse the XML document
'it must be well-formed to have loaded without error
```

```
'create a new XPathNavigator object using the XMLDocument object
Dim objXPNav As XPathNavigator = objXPathDoc.CreateNavigator()

'move the current position to the root #document node
objXPNav.MoveToRoot()

'call a recursive function to iterate through all the nodes in the
'XPathNavigator, creating a string that is placed in a <div> element
outResults.innerHTML = GetXMLDocFragment(objXPNav, 0)
```

The recursive function in this case is much the same in outline approach to the previous example, but now navigation through the document is carried out using the special methods of the XPathNavigator object. The technique is to display information about the current node, see if there are any attributes and – if so – iterate through these collecting the name and value of each one:

```
Function GetXMLDocFragment(objXPNav As XPathNavigator, intLevel As Integer) As
String

Dim strNodes As String = ""
Dim intLoop As Integer

'display information about this node
strNodes = strNodes & GetIndent(intLevel) _
        & GetNodeType(objXPNav.NodeType) & ": <b>" & objXPNav.Name _
        & "</b>  value=<b>" & objXPNav.Value & "</b><br />"

'see if this node has any Attributes
If objXPNav.HasAttributes Then

  'move to the first attribute
  objXPNav.MoveToFirstAttribute()

  Do

    'display the information about it
    strNodes = strNodes & GetIndent(intLevel + 1) _
            & GetNodeType(objXPNav.NodeType) & ": <b>" & objXPNav.Name _
            & "</b>  value=<b>" & objXPNav.Value & "</b><br />"

  Loop While objXPNav.MoveToNextAttribute()

  'then move back to the parent node (the element itself)
  objXPNav.MoveToParent()

End If
```

Then the function iterates through all the children of this node. For each node, it recursively calls the same function to get information about the child nodes and their children. Finally, it moves to the next sibling node of the start node and does the same again:

```
'see if this node has any child nodes
If objXPNav.HasChildren Then

  'move to the first child node of the current node
  objXPNav.MoveToFirstChild()
```

```
Do

   'recursively call this function to display the child node fragment
   strNodes = strNodes & GetXMLDocFragment(objXPNav, intLevel + 1)
Loop While objXPNav.MoveToNext()

'move back to the parent node - the node we started from when we
'moved to the first child node - could have used Push and Pop instead
objXPNav.MoveToParent()


End If

'must repeat the process for the remaining sibling nodes (nodes
'at the same 'level' as the current node within the XML document)
'so repeat while we can move to the next sibling node
Do While objXPNav.MoveToNext()

   'recursively call this function to display this sibling node
   'and its attributes and child nodes
   strNodes = strNodes & GetXMLDocFragment(objXPNav, intLevel)

Loop

Return strNodes   'pass the result back to the caller

End Function
```

Validating XML Documents

This example demonstrates the XmlValidatingReader object, which is created from an XmlTextReader object. Code in the page then creates an XmlSchemaColletion and loads an XSL stylesheet into it, then attaches this to the XmlValidatingReader. The XML is read one node at a time using the Read method of the XmlValidatingReader, and an event handler that is attached to the XmlValidatingReader object's ValidationEventHandler property outputs details of any validation errors:

Example: Validating XML Documents – validating-xml.aspx

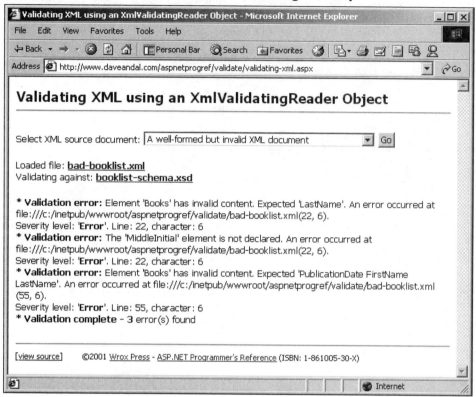

There are three appropriately named documents you can experiment with. One is not well-formed, and in this case the error handler set up for the `XmlValidatingReader` itself reports this error when the `Read` method is called.

How It Works

The code in the page creates two global variables, then (in the `Page_Load` event handler) it creates the paths to the appropriate documents. Next it loads the XML source document into a new instance of an `XmlTextReader` object, and from this creates an `XmlValidatingReader` object with the validation type set to `Schema`. Next a new `XmlSchemaCollection` is created, and the schema we're using is added to it. The `XmlSchemaCollection` object can then be assigned to the `XmlValidatingReader`:

```
'declare a variable to hold an XmlTextReader and one to hold the
'number of errors found.
Dim objXTReader As XmlTextReader
Dim intValidErrors As Integer = 0

...
...


'create physical path to booklist sample files (in same folder as ASPX page)
Dim strCurrentPath As String = Request.PhysicalPath
```

```
Dim strXMLPath As String = Left(strCurrentPath, _
    InStrRev(strCurrentPath, "\")) & selXMLFile.SelectedItem.Value
Dim strSchemaPath As String = Left(strCurrentPath, _
    InStrRev(strCurrentPath, "\")) & "booklist-schema.xsd"

'create the new XmlTextReader object and load the XML document
objXTReader = New XmlTextReader(strXMLPath)

'create an XMLValidatingReader for this XmlTextReader
Dim objValidator As New XmlValidatingReader(objXTReader)

'set the validation type to use an XSD schema
objValidator.ValidationType = ValidationType.Schema

'create a new XmlSchemaCollection
Dim objSchemaCol As New XmlSchemaCollection()

'add the booklist-schema.xsd schema to it
objSchemaCol.Add("", strSchemaPath)

'assign the schema collection to the XmlValidatingReader
objValidator.Schemas.Add(objSchemaCol)
```

Then the code specifies the event handler that will be used to detect validation errors, and finally it can read all the nodes of the document. We're not actually using the XML here, but it could be displayed or used in the same way as in the other examples in this section of the chapter. The reading is done within a `Try...Catch` construct, which means that any errors from a document that is not well-formed will be trapped here and displayed:

```
'add the event handler for any validation errors found
AddHandler objValidator.ValidationEventHandler, AddressOf ValidationError

Try

    'iterate through the document using the contents as required
    'we simply read each element here without using it for anything
    While objValidator.Read()
        'use or display the XML content here as required
    End While

    'display count of errors found in a <div> element in the page
    outXMLDoc.innerHTML += "<b>* Validation complete - " _
                    & intValidErrors & "</b> error(s) found"

Catch objError As Exception

    'will occur if there is a read error or the document cannot be parsed
    outXMLDoc.innerHTML += "<b>* Read/Parser error:</b> " _
                    & objError.Message & "<br />"

Finally

    'must remember to always close the XmlTextReader after use
```

```
        objXTReader.Close()

    End Try
```

The event handler specified for the `ValidationEventHandler` property of the `XmlValidatingReader` is shown next, and because this exists validation errors won't stop the document being read from disk (if we don't set up an event handler, the validation errors are picked up by the `Try...Catch` construct around the `Read` method instead, and so the first validation error would stop the document from being read any further.

```
Public Sub ValidationError(objSender As Object, objArgs As ValidationEventArgs)
    'event handler called when a validation error is found

    intValidErrors += 1    'increment count of errors

    'check the severity of the error
    Dim strSeverity As String
    If objArgs.Severity = 0 Then strSeverity = "Error"
    If objArgs.Severity = 1 Then strSeverity = "Warning"

    'display a message
    outXMLDoc.innerHTML += "<b>* Validation error:</b> " _
                        & objArgs.Message _
                        & "<br /> Severity level: '<b>" _
                        & strSeverity & "</b>'. "
    If objXTReader.LineNumber > 0 Then
      outXMLDoc.innerHTML += "Line: " & objXTReader.LineNumber _
                        & ", character: " & objXTReader.LinePosition _
                        & "<br />"
    End If

End Sub
```

Creating, Searching, and Modifying Documents

The three examples in this section demonstrate a range of techniques for manipulating XML documents. This includes using the W3C-compliant DOM methods with an `XmlDocument` object, an XPath search using an `XPathNavigator` and `XPathDocument` object, and a mixture of operations on XML documents to insert, remove, and copy nodes from one document to another.

Example: Searching XML Documents Using the DOM Methods – search-dom.aspx

The first example loads the XML document into an `XmlDocument` object, and then uses the `GetElementsByTagName` method to locate all the `<AuthorName>` elements:

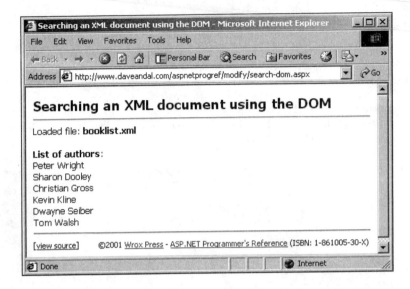

How It Works

The code in this example is quite simple. After creating the `XmlDocument` object and loading the XML from disk, it uses the `GetElementsByTagname` method to create an `XmlNodeList` containing the matching element nodes. Then it's just a matter of iterating through the list and displaying the values from the child `XmlText` node from each element:

```
'create physical path to booklist.xml sample file
Dim strCurrentPath As String = Request.PhysicalPath
Dim strXMLPath As String = Left(strCurrentPath, InStrRev(strCurrentPath, "\")) & _
                           "booklist.xml"

'create a new XMLDocument object
Dim objXMLDoc As New XmlDocument()

Try

   'load the XML file into the XMLDocument object
   objXMLDoc.Load(strXMLPath)

Catch objError As Exception

   '... display error details here
   Exit Sub  ' and stop execution

End Try

'now ready to parse the XML document
'it must be well-formed to have loaded without error

'create a string to hold the matching values found
Dim strResults As String = "<b>List of authors</b>:<br />"

'create a NodeList collection of all matching child nodes
Dim colElements As XmlNodeList
```

```
colElements = objXMLDoc.GetElementsByTagname("AuthorName")

'iterate through the collection getting the values of the
'child #text nodes for each one
Dim objNode As XmlNode
For Each objNode In colElements
  strResults += objNode.FirstChild().Value & "<br />"
Next

'then display the result in a <div> elsewhere in the page
outResults.innerHTML = strResults    'display the result
```

Example: Searching XML Documents using an XPathNavigator – search-navigator.aspx

The second example produces the same result, but this time using an `XPathDocument` and an `XPathNavigator`.

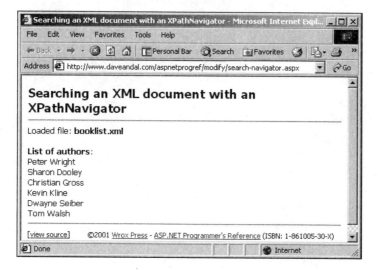

How It Works

The code executes the `Select` method of the `XPathNavigator` with the XPath expression "descendant::AuthorName", which returns an `XPathNodeIterator` object containing the matching elements. It's then just a matter of iterating through this list and displaying the values:

```
'declare a variable within current scope to hold an XPathDocument
Dim objXPathDoc As XPathDocument

Try

  'create XPathDocument object and load the XML file
  objXPathDoc = New XPathDocument(strXMLPath)

Catch objError As Exception

  '... display error details here
  Exit Sub  ' and stop execution
```

```
End Try

'now ready to parse the XML document
'it must be well-formed to have loaded without error

'create a new XPathNavigator object using the XPathDocument object
Dim objXPNav As XPathNavigator = objXPathDoc.CreateNavigator()

'create a string to hold the matching values found
Dim strResults As String = "<b>List of authors</b>:<br />"

'select all the AuthorName nodes into an XPathNodeIterator object
'using an XPath expression
Dim objXPIter As XPathNodeIterator
objXPIter = objXPNav.Select("descendant::AuthorName")

'iterate through the nodes. Each "node" in the XPathNodeIterator is
'itself an XPathNavigator, so Name and Value properties are available
Do While objXPIter.MoveNext()

  'get the value and add to the 'results' string
  strResults += objXPIter.Current.Value & "<br />"

Loop

outResults.innerHTML = strResults    'display the result
```

Example: Creating and Editing the Content of XML Documents – edit-xml.aspx

The third example in this section is somewhat more complex. It demonstrates four different techniques. The code for the page is fully commented, and broken down into the four steps shown:

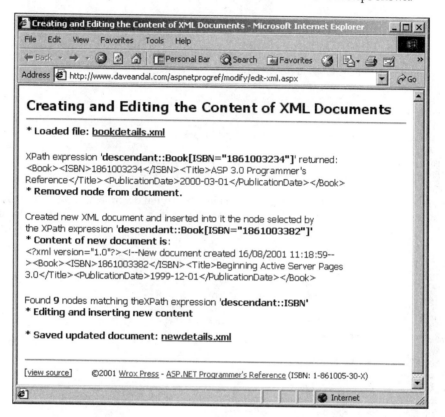

How It Works

First it loads an XML document into an `XmlDocument` object, selects a node using the `SelectSingleNode` method of the `XmlDocument`, and removes it using the `RemoveChild` method.

```
' 1: Select a Node, display content and then remove it

'specify XPath expression to select a book element
Dim strXPath As String = "descendant::Book[ISBN=" & Chr(34) _
                 & "1861003234" & Chr(34) & "]"

'get a reference to the matching <Book> node
Dim objNode As XmlNode
objNode = objXMLDoc.SelectSingleNode(strXPath)

'delete this node using RemoveChild method from document element
objXMLDoc.DocumentElement.RemoveChild(objNode)
```

Next, the code creates a new empty XML document and adds the XML declaration and a comment to it:

```
' 2: Create empty XML document, add declaration and comment

'create new empty XML Document object
Dim objNewDoc As New XmlDocument()

'create a new XmlDeclaration object
Dim objDeclare As XmlDeclaration
objDeclare = objNewDoc.CreateXmlDeclaration("1.0", Nothing, Nothing)

'and add it as the first node in the new document
objDeclare = objNewDoc.InsertBefore(objDeclare, objNewDoc.DocumentElement)

'create a new XmlComment object
Dim objComment As XmlComment
objComment = objNewDoc.CreateComment("New document created " & Now())

'and add it as the second node in the new document
objComment = objNewDoc.InsertAfter(objComment, objDeclare)
```

Then, in step three, it selects a single <Book> node in the original document, copies it into the new document using the ImportNode method, and inserts it as the root element of the new document. The contents of this document are then displayed in the page:

```
' 3: Select node in original document and import into new one

'change the XPath expression to select a different book
strXPath = "descendant::Book[ISBN=" & Chr(34) & "1861003382" & Chr(34) & "]"

'get a reference to the matching <Book> node
objNode = objXMLDoc.SelectSingleNode(strXPath)

'create a variable to hold the imported node object
Dim objImportedNode As XmlNode

'import the node and all children into new document (un-attached fragment)
objImportedNode = objNewDoc.ImportNode(objNode, True)

'insert the new un-attached node into document after the comment node
objNewDoc.InsertAfter(objImportedNode, objComment)
```

Finally, at step four, the code selects all the <ISBN> nodes using the SelectNodes method with the XPath expression "descendant::ISBN", and edits and inserts new content into these nodes. You can view the original and the edited documents using the links in the page:

```
' 4: Select and edit/insert new content into ISBN elements

'change the XPath expression to select all ISBN elements
strXPath = "descendant::ISBN"

'get a reference to the matching nodes as a collection
Dim colNodeList As XmlNodeList
colNodeList = objXMLDoc.SelectNodes(strXPath)

'display the number of matches found
outResult3.InnerHtml = "Found " & colNodeList.Count _
```

```
                        & " nodes matching the XPath expression '" _
                        & strXPath & "'</b><br />"
Dim strNodeValue, strNewValue, strShortCode As String

'create a variable to hold an XmlAttribute object
Dim objAttr As XmlAttribute

'iterate through all the nodes found
For Each objNode In colNodeList

    'create an XmlAttribute named 'formatting'
    objAttr = objXMLDoc.CreateAttribute("formatting")

    'set the value of the XmlAttribute to 'hyphens'
    objAttr.Value = "hyphens"

    'and add it to this ISBN element - have to cast the object
    'to an XmlElement as XmlNode doesn't have this method
    CType(objNode, XmlElement).SetAttributeNode(objAttr)

    'get text value of this ISBN element
    strNodeValue = objNode.InnerText

    'create short and long strings to replace content
    strShortCode = Right(strNodeValue, 4)
    strNewValue = Left(strNodeValue, 1) & "-" _
                & Mid(strNodeValue, 2, 6) & "-" _
                & Mid(strNodeValue, 8, 2) & "-" _
                & Right(strNodeValue, 1)

    'insert into element by setting the InnerXml property
    objNode.InnerXml = "<LongCode>" & strNewValue _
                & "</LongCode><ShortCode>" _
                & strShortCode & "</ShortCode>"

Next

'write the updated document to a disk file
objXMLDoc.Save(strNewPath)
```

Transforming XML Documents

We've provided two examples of transforming XML documents using the XslTransform object. The first transforms the XML into HTML using the simplest technique, and the second demonstrates several different ways of managing the transformation and the different objects that are available to handle the source and result documents.

Example: A Simple Transformation to HTML – simple-transform.aspx

This example takes an XML source file and an XSL stylesheet, and transforms the XML directly to a disk file in HTML format (the format is, of course, governed by the contents of the stylesheet):

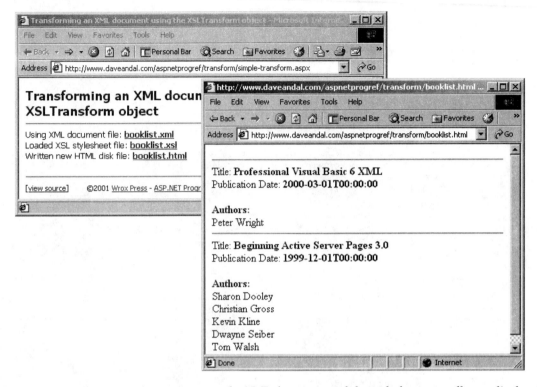

You can use the links in the page to open the XML document and the stylesheet, as well as to display the resulting HTML document.

How It Works

The code creates the three path and filename combinations it will need, creates the XslTransform object and loads the stylesheet. It then calls the Transform method to create the output file:

```
'create physical path to booklist sample files
Dim strCurrentPath As String = Request.PhysicalPath
Dim strXMLPath As String = Left(strCurrentPath, _
                        InStrRev(strCurrentPath, "\")) & "booklist.xml"
Dim strXSLPath As String = Left(strCurrentPath, _
                        InStrRev(strCurrentPath, "\")) & "booklist.xsl"
Dim strHTMLPath As String = Left(strCurrentPath, _
                        InStrRev(strCurrentPath, "\")) & "booklist.html"

Try

    'create a new XslTransform object
    Dim objTransform As New XslTransform()

    'load the XSL stylesheet into the XSLTransform object
    objTransform.Load(strXSLPath)

    'perform the transformation using the XSL file in the
    'XSLTransform and the XML file path in strXMLPath
```

```
        'the result is sent to the disk file in strHTMLPath
        objTransform.Transform(strXMLPath, strHTMLPath)

    Catch objError As Exception

        '... display error details here
        Exit Sub  ' and stop execution

    End Try
```

Example: Various Different Transformations to XML – multi-transform.aspx

In the second example, we use the `XslTransform` object to transform the source XML document into another XML document of a completely different format. We also use several different techniques to handle the process:

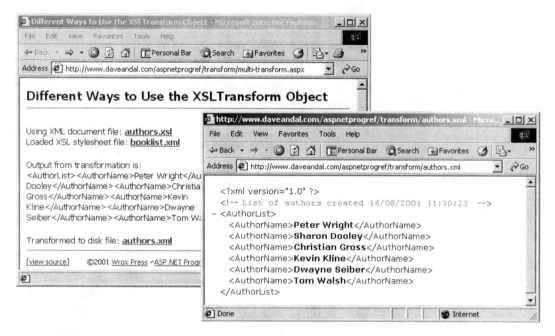

How It Works

After creating the paths and filenames required (as in the previous example) the code creates a new `XslTransform` object and loads the stylesheet. Next it demonstrates how an `XmlTextReader` and an `XPathDocument` can be used to load the source XML document. This would allow an `XmlValiatingReader` to be added if the document required validation aganst a schema along the way:

```
    'create a new XslTransform object to do the transformation
    Dim objTransform As New XslTransform()

    'load the XSL stylesheet into the XSLTransform object
    objTransform.Load(strXSLPath)

    'create a new XmlTextReader object to fetch XML document
```

```
Dim objXTReader As New XmlTextReader(strXMLPath)

'create a new XPathDocument object from the XmlTextReader
Dim objXPDoc As New XPathDocument(objXTReader)
```

The code next creates an `XPathNavigator` based on the `XPathDocument`. The `XPathNavigator` is used in the call to the `XslTransform` object's `Transform` method, which returns an `XmlReader` object. It then uses the `MoveToContent` and `ReadOuterXml` methods of the `XmlReader` to display the result of the transformation in the page:

```
'create a new XPathNavigator object from the XPathDocument
Dim objXPNav As XPathNavigator
objXPNav = objXPDoc.CreateNavigator()

'create a variable to hold the XmlReader object that is
'returned from the Transform method
Dim objReader As XmlReader

'perform the transformation using the XSL file in the
'XSLTransform and the XML document referenced by the
'XPathNavigator. The result is in the XmlReader object
objReader = objTransform.Transform(objXPNav, Nothing)

'display the contents of the XmlReader object in <div> on page
objReader.MoveToContent()
outResults.InnerText = objReader.ReadOuterXml()
```

Next, the code creates an `XmlTextWriter` object and uses it to write the opening `<?xml ... ?>` declaration and a comment element to a disk file. Then the `Transform` method of the `XslTransform` object is used to send the result of the transformation direct to the new disk file:

```
'create an XMLTextWriter object to write result to disk
Dim objWriter As New XmlTextWriter(strOutPath, Nothing)

'write the opening <?xml .. ?> declaration and a comment
objWriter.WriteStartDocument()
objWriter.WriteComment("List of authors created " & Now())

'transform the XML into the XMLTextWriter
objTransform.Transform(objXPNav, Nothing, objWriter)

'ensure that all open elements are closed to end the document
objWriter.WriteEndDocument()

'flush the buffer to disk and close the file
objWriter.Close()
```

XML and ADO.NET Synchronization

One of the biggest strengths of the new .NET data management classes is the inherent synchronization and interoperability between ADO.NET relational data access techniques and XML-based document management methods.

The ADO.NET `DataSet` object can be used to read and write XML documents in a pre-defined format. There is also a feature of the ADO.NET "command" objects that allow an XML "reader" object to be used to connect to the SQL Server XML output that is produced from a SQL "FOR XML" query statement (though we're not going to be exploring this aspect here).

However, the `System.Xml` namespace provides another useful way to integrate XML and relational data – the `XmlDataDocument` object. This can be loaded with an XML document in the same way as an `XmlDocument` object, but it exposes a "relational" view of the data through its `DataSet` property.

Some Synchronization Examples

We've provided three examples that allow you to explore the way that the ADO.NET `DataSet` object can provide support for working with XML data. They show:

❑ Writing XML from a `DataSet` object

❑ Reading XML into a `DataSet` object

❑ Synchronization of the `XmlDataDocument` and `DataSet` objects

Example: Writing XML from a DataSet Object – write-dataset.aspx

The first example uses ADO.NET relational data manipulation techniques to create a `DataSet`, add a new `DataTable` to it, and then add three rows to this table that contain information about some Wrox books. Afterwards, the contents of the `DataSet` object are written to disk, and links to the files are provided in the page:

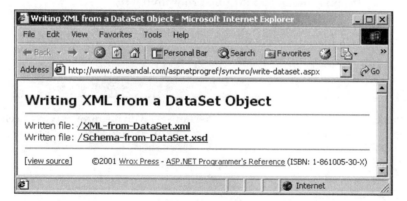

The standard (and only) persistence format for the ADO.NET objects is XML, and so they are well suited to transferring data from XML to relational format and vice versa. The page writes both the XML data itself, and the XSD schema for that data to the disk as two separate files. The XML representation of the data can be seen in the following screenshot:

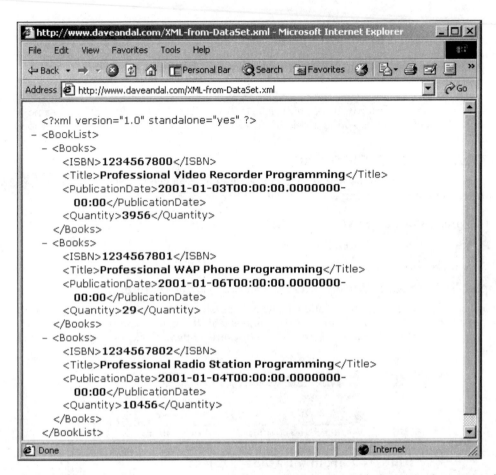

You can see that this is a very natural format, and relates well with the formats we've been using for XML documents throughout this chapter. The schema produced from the `DataSet` (and is therefore the schema for this XML document) is shown in the next screenshot:

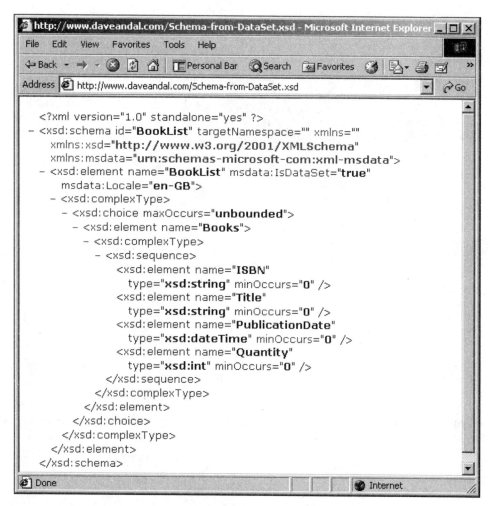

The two files, the data and the schema, are created using the `WriteXml` and `WriteXmlSchema` methods of the `DataSet` object.

How It Works

The first step is to create the ADO.NET `DataSet` object. ADO.NET is not the focus for this chapter, but the code used is listed next so that you can see what it does:

```
'create a new empty Table object
Dim objTable As New DataTable("Books")

'define four columns (fields) within the table
objTable.Columns.Add("ISBN", System.Type.GetType("System.String"))
objTable.Columns.Add("Title", System.Type.GetType("System.String"))
objTable.Columns.Add("PublicationDate", System.Type.GetType("System.DateTime"))
objTable.Columns.Add("Quantity", System.Type.GetType("System.Int32"))

'declare a variable to hold a DataRow object
```

```
Dim objDataRow As DataRow

'create a new DataRow object instance in this table
objDataRow = objTable.NewRow()

'and fill in the values
objDataRow("ISBN") = "1234567800"
objDataRow("Title") = "Professional Video Recorder Programming"
objDataRow("PublicationDate") = "2001-03-01"
objDataRow("Quantity") = 3956
objTable.Rows.Add(objDataRow)

'repeat to add two more rows
objDataRow = objTable.NewRow()
objDataRow("ISBN") = "1234567801"
objDataRow("Title") = "Professional WAP Phone Programming"
objDataRow("PublicationDate") = "2001-06-01"
objDataRow("Quantity") = 29
objTable.Rows.Add(objDataRow)

objDataRow = objTable.NewRow()
objDataRow("ISBN") = "1234567802"
objDataRow("Title") = "Professional Radio Station Programming"
objDataRow("PublicationDate") = "2001-04-01"
objDataRow("Quantity") = 10456
objTable.Rows.Add(objDataRow)

'create a new empty DataSet object and insert table
Dim objDataSet As New DataSet("BookList")
objDataSet.Tables.Add(objTable)
```

Now the code can save the DataSet contents to an XML disk file. It creates the path and filenames required, and calls the WriteXml and WriteXMLSchema methods of the DataSet object:

```
Try

    'use the path to the current virtual application
    Dim strVirtualPath As String = Request.ApplicationPath _
                                  & "XML-from-DataSet.xml"
    Dim strVSchemaPath As String = Request.ApplicationPath _
                                  & "Schema-from-DataSet.xsd"

    'write the data and schema from the DataSet to an XML document on disk
    'must use the Physical path to the file not the Virtual path
    objDataSet.WriteXML(Request.MapPath(strVirtualPath))
    objDataSet.WriteXMLSchema(Request.MapPath(strVSchemaPath))

Catch objError As Exception

    '... display error details here
    Exit Sub  ' and stop execution

End Try
```

Example: Reading XML into a DataSet Object – read-dataset.aspx

Once we've written the files from the previous example to disk, the next example can be used to read them again – back into a `DataSet` object. This demonstrates that, providing we have a valid XML document and (optionally) a matching XSD schema, we can load them into a `DataSet` and use ADO.NET relational data access techniques to work with the data – and, of course, export it or write it back to disk again if required.

The page loads the schema first using the `ReadXmlSchema` method, followed by the `ReadXml` method to load the XML data, and then it displays information about it. It shows the contents of the `DataSet` object's `Tables` collection (the table named `Books` that is created from the XML schema and data), and the content of this table:

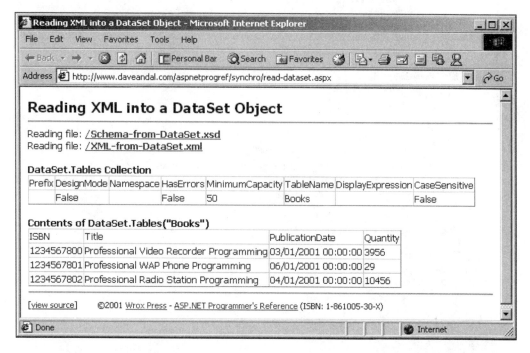

XML data can be loaded into a `DataSet` object without first loading a schema, and the `DataSet` will use its built-in heuristics to figure out the structure and build the appropriate tables. However, this may produce unpredictable results if the data is not uniform. If a schema is loaded first, the `DataSet` will allocate the values in the XML data to the appropriate pre-defined tables and columns, leaving `null` values in any that it can't fill.

How It Works

The code first creates a new `DataSet` object and then builds the paths and filenames for the schema and XML data files. The `ReadXmlSchema` and `ReadXml` methods are used to fill the `DataSet`, and then the results are displayed in an ASP.NET `DataGrid` server control:

```
'create a new DataSet object
Dim objDataSet As New DataSet()

Try

   'use the path to the current virtual application
   Dim strVirtualPath As String = Request.ApplicationPath _
                                 & "XML-from-DataSet.xml"
   Dim strVSchemaPath As String = Request.ApplicationPath _
                                 & "Schema-from-DataSet.xsd"

   'read the schema and data into the DataSet from an XML document on disk
   'must use the Physical path to the file not the Virtual path
   objDataSet.ReadXMLSchema(Request.MapPath(strVSchemaPath))
   objDataSet.ReadXML(Request.MapPath(strVirtualPath))

Catch objError As Exception

   '... display error details here
   Exit Sub  ' and stop execution

End Try

'now we can display the DataSet contents

'assign the DataView.Tables collection to the first DataGrid control
dgrTables.DataSource = objDataSet.Tables
dgrTables.DataBind()  'and bind (display) the data

'create a DataView object for the Books table in the DataSet
Dim objDataView As New DataView(objDataSet.Tables("Books"))

'assign the DataView object to the second DataGrid control
dgrValues.DataSource = objDataView
dgrValues.DataBind()  'and bind (display) the data
```

Example: Synchronization of XmlDataDocument and DataSet Objects – dataset-synchro.aspx

The final example demonstrates how an `XmlDataDocument` object's `DataSet` property, and the corresponding synchronized `DataSet` object that this property exposes, can be used. This is the result:

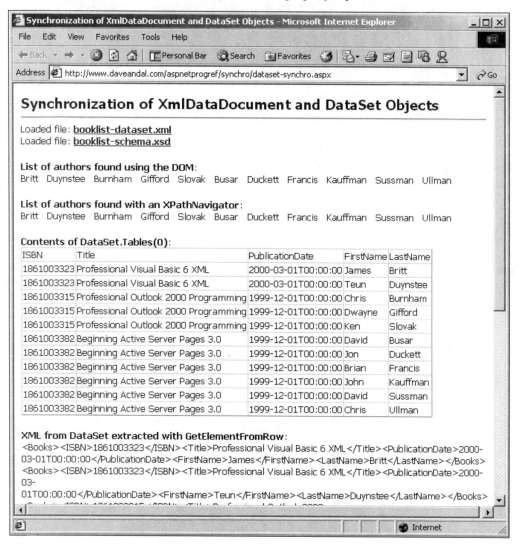

How It Works

The code in the page creates a new `XmlDataDocument` object and loads the schema using the path and filename created at the start of the code. As the `XmlDataDocument` object does not have a method for loading a schema, it does it by calling the `ReadXmlSchema` method of the synchronized `DataSet` object – via the `DataSet` property of the `XmlDataDocument` object. Then it loads the XML data itself using the `Load` method of the `XmlDataDocument` object:

```
'create physical path to booklist sample files
Dim strCurrentPath As String = Request.PhysicalPath
Dim strXMLPath As String = Left(strCurrentPath, _
            InStrRev(strCurrentPath, "\")) & "booklist-dataset.xml"
Dim strSchemaPath As String = Left(strCurrentPath, _
            InStrRev(strCurrentPath, "\")) & "booklist-schema.xsd"

'create a new XmlDataDocument object
Dim objXMLDataDoc As New XmlDataDocument()

Try

   'load the XML schema into the XmlDataDocument object
   objXMLDataDoc.DataSet.ReadXmlSchema(strSchemaPath)

   'load the XML file into the XMLDataDocument object
   objXMLDataDoc.Load(strXMLPath)

Catch objError As Exception

   '... display error details here
   Exit Sub   ' and stop execution

End Try
```

Once the XML schema and data are loaded, the page performs four separate operations to show how the data can be accessed in different ways. The first is to use the `GetElementsByTagName` method of the `XmlDataDocument`. As the `XmlDataDocument` is an extension of the normal `XmlDocument` object, these XML DOM techniques work just the same as in the earlier examples:

```
' 1: Extract the author names using the XML DOM methods

Dim objNode As XmlNode
Dim strResults As String = ""

'create a NodeList collection of all matching child nodes
Dim colElements As XmlNodeList
colElements = objXMLDataDoc.GetElementsByTagname("LastName")

'iterate through the collection getting the values of the
'child #text nodes for each one
For Each objNode In colElements
   strResults += objNode.FirstChild().Value & "   "
Next

'then display the result in a <div> on the page
outDOMResult.innerHTML = strResults
strResults = ""
```

Next, it creates an `XPathNavigator` for the `XmlDataDocument`, and uses this to search for the `<LastName>` nodes that contain the author names. This is accomplished through a recursive routine defined at the end of the code in the page. It is very similar to that used in earlier examples of reading an XML document, and so that routine code isn't repeated here:

```
' 2: extract the author names with an XPathNavigator object

'create a new XPathNavigator object using the XMLDataDocument object
Dim objXPNav As XPathNavigator
objXPNav = objXMLDataDoc.CreateNavigator()

'move to the root element of the document
objXPNav.MoveToRoot()

'and display the result of the recursive 'search' function
outXPNavResult.innerHTML = SearchForElement(objXPNav, "LastName")
```

To demonstrate that the `DataSet` property of the `XmlDataDocument` exposes a standard `DataSet` object, the third step is to bind the `DataSet` to an ASP.NET `DataGrid` server control. The code does this by creating an ADO.NET `DataView` object based on the table in the `DataSet`, and then assigning this to the `DataGrid` control's `DataSource` property. To display the contents of the `DataView` it can then simply call the control's `DataBind` method:

```
' 3: Display content of the XMLDataDocument object's DataSet property

'create a DataView object for the Books table in the DataSet
Dim objDataView As New DataView(objXMLDataDoc.DataSet.Tables(0))

'assign the DataView object to the DataGrid control
dgrResult.DataSource = objDataView
dgrResult.DataBind()   'and bind (display) the data
```

Finally, the code uses the `GetElementFromRow` method of each row in the `DataTable` object to retrieve an XML representation of the data for that row. This simply involves iterating through each member of the `Rows` collection of the table and calling `GetElementFromRow` to return that row as an XML element. It then displays the XML from that element by accessing its `OuterXml` property – using `Server.HtmlEncode` so that the individual elements within each `<Book>` element are visible:

```
' 4: Extract XML elements from the XMLDataDocument object's DataSet

'create a DataTable object for the Books table in the DataSet
Dim objDataTable As DataTable = objXMLDataDoc.DataSet.Tables(0)

Dim objRow As DataRow
Dim objXMLElement As XmlElement

'iterate through all the rows in this table
For Each objRow In objDataTable.Rows

   'get an XML element that represents this row
   objXMLElement = objXMLDataDoc.GetElementFromRow(objRow)

   'HTMLEncode it because it contains XML element tags
   strResults += Server.HtmlEncode(objXMLElement.OuterXML) & "<br />"

Next

'display the result
outFromRowResult.innerHTML = strResults
```

The format of the XML that is returned for each element looks like this:

```
<Books><ISBN>1861003323</ISBN><Title>Professional Visual Basic 6 XML</Title>
<PublicationDate>2000-03-01T00:00:00</PublicationDate>
<FirstName>James</FirstName><LastName>Britt</LastName></Books>
```

Summary

In this chapter, we've examined in some detail the three namespaces of the .NET Framework most often used when working directly with XML documents, XML Schemas, and related document formats. These namespaces are `System.Xml`, `System.Xml.XPath`, and `System.Xml.Xsl`.

We explored the namespaces in overview, seeing what classes are provided, before examining the most commonly used classes, their properties, methods, and (in some cases) the events that they expose. While the chapter doesn't exhaustively cover every member of each class in detail, we have seen those that are required for the vast majority of everyday tasks.

Towards the end of the chapter, we looked at some examples of the various objects that we described. These were broken down by task, covering techniques for writing and reading XML documents, validating XML documents against a schema, creating new XML documents, searching for information within XML documents, and modifying them using a range of methods. We also looked at how we can perform XSL or XSLT transformations on XML documents using stylesheets.

Finally, we briefly looked at how the ADO.NET and XML-based data manipulation techniques available within the .NET Framework can provide a boundary-free and synchronized approach to managing data.

The topics in summary were:

❑ An overview of the namespaces used for working with XML

❑ A summary of the common objects from these namespaces

❑ How we can use these objects for everyday tasks

❑ The automatic synchronization of XML and relational data

A full reference to all the XML classes, and other objects and classes within the Framework, can be found in the documentation that is installed with Visual Studio.NET and with the complete .NET Frameworks SDK. Open the topic .NET Framework Reference, and within it .NET Framework Class Library to see a summary of all the classes by namespace.

To find information about specific classes, enumerations or other objects, you can use the WinCV tool that is provided with the .NET Framework. WinCV is installed by default in the Program Files\Microsoft.NET\FrameworkSDK\Bin\ folder.

Examples

If a picture is worth a thousand words, then a code sample is worth ten thousand. While reading about programming and seeing small snippets of sample code can be helpful, it is often most helpful to see complete examples of what it is you are trying to do. In this chapter, you will get nothing but examples with brief explanations.

What follows is a series of code samples intended to provide a quick learning tool for the everyday tasks you will undertake when developing with ASP.NET. These samples should tie together nicely the items you have read about in the previous chapters to give you a more complete understanding of the ASP.NET framework.

The examples utilize the `Northwind` database from Microsoft's SQL Server 2000 to pull together a simple collection of pages that demonstrate the everyday programming tasks used in ASP.NET. For the sake of clarity, the samples are all presented in C#. However, the code for all the samples is available in C# and VB.NET online at http://www.wrox.com/.

Setup

In order to set up these samples on a server, follow the steps below:

- ❑ Make sure you have SQL Server or the Microsoft Database Engine (MSDE) installed on a server reachable over the network from the web server where you are setting up the samples. The application is currently configured to use the local machine as both the database server and the web server.

- ❑ Modify the connection string in the `Web.config` file, changing the server to a valid server name or IP address for the database server you will be using, and modifying the username and password to a valid SQL username and password with access to the `Northwind` database.

- ❑ Create a new virtual directory in Internet Information Server (IIS) and copy the contents of either the VB or C# application into the directory. To run both samples, create two virtual directories and place the code for each in a separate directory.

When running the sample, use "`wroxuser`" for both the login name and password. Note that you will have to login to the site before you can view any of the pages. If you do not login, and you attempt to read a page within the site, then you will be redirected to the home page to login. Once you login, you will be redirected to the originally requested page.

The sample site is a basic product-browsing site, which allows a user to examine the products in the Northwind database. The site consists of three pages: the home page, which describes the different categories, the products page, which displays the products and allows for their getting details, and the feedback page, which is a simple form to allow for submitting feedback about the site or company. In each of these pages we have an included header and a navigation bar. The specific files included in the site, their purpose, and the techniques they show are listed here to provide an overview of the site.

- ❑ **header.ascx** – a user control that serves as the header to our site and shows how to create a dynamic user control.

- ❑ **navigation.ascx** – a user control that provides the navigation for the site and shows how to implement page fragment caching and data caching.

- ❑ **login.ascx** – a user control that allows users to login to our site and shows some of the mechanisms involved in forms authentication.

- ❑ **home.aspx** – the home page to our site where we provide an overview of the categories and prompt the user to login. This page shows how to consume the user controls we have created as well as use the DataList control and data binding syntax.

- ❑ **products.aspx** – this detail page provide the means for presenting information about our products and their details and exhibits more advanced features of the DataGrid control and handling an event from the control on the server.

- ❑ **feedback.aspx** – this page is a simple form to allow a user to provide feedback. It shows how to use the validation controls and work with submitted form data as well as a sample of writing information to an XML document.

- ❑ **northwind.asmx** – this Web Service exposes two different methods, one to get all categories and another to get the products in a given category.

- ❑ **northwind.css** – the stylesheet for our site has class definitions for many of the items in the page, including the templates for our DataList on the home page.

- ❑ **web.config** – the configuration file for the application, which allows us to set parameters concerning how our application should run. This file demonstrates how to use custom errors and forms authentication.

The figure opposite shows a screenshot of the home page, which should provide a visual indicator as to how the site is organized.

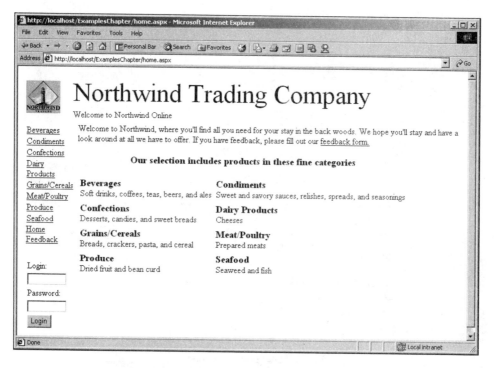

Example 1 – Web Controls Part 1

Web controls are one of the key pieces of the ASP.NET toolset. Being able to program using web page controls as full objects allows for a very powerful application. For a more complete discussion of Web Controls please see Chapters 4 to 6. This example shows a feedback form for the Northwind site that demonstrates some of the capabilities of just a few of the Web controls, including how to access forms and their values in the code files behind the web pages. We will build on this example later in the chapter to add form validation.

feedback.aspx

```
<%@ Page language="c#" Codebehind="feedback.aspx.cs" AutoEventWireup="false"
Inherits="ASPProgRefExamplesC.feedback_form" %>
<%@ Register TagPrefix="WROX" TagName="Header" Src="header.ascx"%>
<%@ Register TagPrefix="WROX" TagName="NavBar" Src="navigation.ascx"%>
<!DOCTYPE HTML PUBLIC "-//W3C//DTD HTML 4.0 Transitional//EN" >
<HTML>
  <HEAD>
    <LINK href="northwind.css" type="text/css" rel="stylesheet">
  </HEAD>
  <body>
    <form id="feedbackform" method="post" runat="server">
      <TABLE id="table_feedback" width="100%">
        <tr>
          <td colspan="2">
            <WROX:HEADER id="heading"
                         runat="server"
                         backcolor="white"
```

```
                      subheadingcolor="Blue"
                      subheadingsize="4 "
                      subheadingtext="Thank you for your input">
        </WROX:HEADER>
      </td>
    </tr>
    <tr>
    <td valign="top" rowspan="5">
      <WROX:NAVBAR id="nav" runat="server">
      </WROX:NAVBAR>
    </td>
    <td>
      <!--This is the message that will display when the form is submitted.
      -->
      <asp:label id="message" runat="server" visible="False"></asp:label>

      <!--This panel contains our controls in the form so we can hide them
      when the user posts the form. Panels are great for separating
      controls.-->

      <asp:panel id="formpanel" runat="server">
        <TABLE id="form_table">
          <TR>
            <TD>
              Name
              <BR>
              <asp:textbox id="person_name"
                           runat="server"
                           TextMode="SingleLine"
                           width="100">
              </asp:textbox>

            </TD>
          </TR>
          <TR>
            <TD>
              Email
              <BR>
              <asp:textbox id="email"
                           TextMode="SingleLine"
                           width="100"
                           Runat="server">
              </asp:textbox>
            </TD>
          </TR>
          <TR>
            <TD>
              Type of feedback
              <BR>
              <!--the RadioButtonList allows for defining a group of
              radio buttons that are mutually exclusive. The CheckBoxList
              does a similar thing with check boxes. -->
              <asp:RadioButtonList id="feedback_type"
                                   Runat="server"
                                   RepeatDirection="Horizontal">
```

```
            <asp:ListItem Text="Suggestion"
                        value="suggest"
                        Selected="True">
            </asp:ListItem>
            <asp:ListItem Text="Problem Report"
                        value="problem">
            </asp:ListItem>
            <asp:ListItem Text="Compliment"
                        value="compliment">
            </asp:ListItem>
            <asp:ListItem Text="Question"
                        Value="question">
            </asp:ListItem>
        </asp:RadioButtonList>
    </TD>
</TR>
<TR>
    <TD>
    Reason for visiting:
    <BR> <!--the dropdown list provides a select list that does
            not allow multiple items to be selected. -->
    <asp:DropDownList id="reason" Runat="server">
        <asp:ListItem Text="shopping"
            Value="shopping"></asp:ListItem>
        <asp:ListItem Text="research"
            Value="research"></asp:ListItem>
        <asp:ListItem Text="job search" Value="job"></asp:ListItem>
    </asp:DropDownList>
    </TD>
</TR>
<TR>
    <TD>
    Feedback
    <BR> <!--the generic textbox control has several textmodes
            which allow it to be a password, text box or text
            area in HTML terms. -->
    <asp:TextBox id="feedback"
                TextMode="MultiLine"
                Runat="server"
                Columns="40"
                rows="10">
    </asp:TextBox>
    </TD>
</TR>
<TR>
    <TD> <!--the button submits the server side form and we have
            indicated a function to run on the server when the
            button
            is clicked. This is where we will
        handle our form data-->
    <asp:button id="submit"
                onclick="ProcessForm"
                runat="server"
                text="Submit Feedback">
```

```
                    </asp:button>
                  </TD>
                </TR>
              </TABLE>
            </asp:panel>
          </td>
        </tr>
      </TABLE>
    </form>
  </body>
</HTML>
```

This example starts with a simple textbox that at first glance may not seem to offer much benefit over the regular HTML input tag. However with the `runat` attribute set to `server`, the control will be fully programmable from the code behind the page. Its value can be set or retrieved and all the other properties of the object can be accessed while the page is being processed on the server. The same is true for the drop-down lists and the radio buttons. However, there is more going on here than is apparent from this example. Several features are encapsulated in these new controls. Each of these controls generates standard HTML that targets the browser making the request, so the developer does not have to worry about browser compatibility when using these controls. In other words, if we use a radio-button list, it will get rendered correctly on both Internet Explorer and Netscape Navigator.

The screenshot below shows the page as it is rendered in a browser. While there is a lot more information in the code above than in a traditional HTML page, the output received by the browser is standard HTML that appears as we would expect a form to appear.

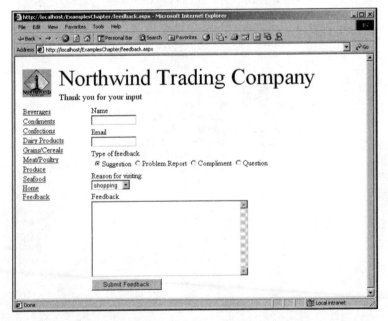

The page above is only half the story in this scenario. The file opposite represents the code behind the web page. It is in this file that we have the fullest capabilities to work with the C# and VB.NET languages to do the work of our page. In this code we handle the feedback form submission and write the contents of the form to an XML file. This portion of the example will also grow when we add validation to the form.

feedback.aspx.cs

```csharp
using System;
using System.Data;
using System.Web;
using System.Web.UI;
using System.Web.UI.WebControls;
using System.Web.UI.HtmlControls;
using System.Xml;

namespace ASPProgRefExamplesC
{
  public class feedback_form : System.Web.UI.Page
  {
    protected System.Web.UI.WebControls.TextBox person_name;
    protected System.Web.UI.WebControls.TextBox email;
    protected System.Web.UI.WebControls.RadioButtonList feedback_type;
    protected System.Web.UI.WebControls.DropDownList reason;
    protected System.Web.UI.WebControls.Table table_feedback;
    protected System.Web.UI.WebControls.Button submit;
    protected System.Web.UI.WebControls.TextBox feedback;
    protected System.Web.UI.WebControls.Label message;
    protected System.Web.UI.WebControls.Panel formpanel;
    protected System.Web.UI.HtmlControls.HtmlForm feedbackform;

    public feedback_form()
    {
      Page.Init += new System.EventHandler(Page_Init);
    }

    //This method handles the button event as defined
    //in the tag in the ASPX page. This will only get
    //processed when the button was clicked
    public void ProcessForm(object sender, EventArgs ea)
    {

      //get a path to a local file in the app path.
      string outpath = HttpRuntime.AppDomainAppPath + "formdata.xml";

      //create an XmlTextWriter to write out some XML
      XmlTextWriter xmlOut = new XmlTextWriter(outpath,
      System.Text.Encoding.UTF8);

      //indicate nested elements should be indented five spaces
      xmlOut.Indentation = 5;
      xmlOut.Formatting = Formatting.Indented;

      //write out the start and the root element: "feedback"
      xmlOut.WriteStartDocument();
      xmlOut.WriteStartElement("Feedback");

      //write out each of the elements from the form
      xmlOut.WriteElementString("Name", person_name.Text);
      xmlOut.WriteElementString("Email", email.Text);
      xmlOut.WriteElementString("Reason", reason.SelectedItem.Text);
      xmlOut.WriteElementString("Feedback_type",
```

```
                                      feedback_type.SelectedItem.Text);
      xmlOut.WriteElementString("Feedback", feedback.Text);

      //close the "feedback" tag and the document
      xmlOut.WriteEndElement();
      xmlOut.WriteEndDocument();

      //flush and close the writer
      xmlOut.Flush();
      xmlOut.Close();

      //clean up
      xmlOut = null;
   }
   private void Page_Load(object sender, System.EventArgs e)
   {
      //if we are posting back say thanks
      if(IsPostBack)
      {
         //if this is a postback, then the form has
         //been submitted. So, we hide all the form
         //controls and show the message saying, Thanks!
         //hiding the panel which makes it very easy to
         //work with a group of controls rather than to
         //have to deal with all of them.
         formpanel.Visible=false;

         this.message.Text = "Thank you for your feedback.";
         this.message.Visible=true;
      }
   }

   private void Page_Init(object sender, EventArgs e)
   {
      InitializeComponent();
   }

   private void InitializeComponent()
   {
      this.Load += new System.EventHandler(this.Page_Load);
   }
  }
}
```

In the code behind page, we have declared variables for all of the controls on our form. The Web Forms designer in Visual Studio.NET does this for you if you add items visually; otherwise, simply declare them in your class as they appear here. Keep in mind that the variable name must match the ID attribute of the control as it appears in the HTML. This allows us to access these items as full-blown controls rather than accessing form information from the Request object.

The processing for this form takes place in our `ProcessForm` method. This method simply creates an XML file in our application directory that contains the output of the submission. Notice that as each element is written out, we are accessing the variables declared above and using the methods and properties of these objects to get at the information in the form. This is made possible because we used the Web Controls and because we marked them as running on the server. This is not to say that we could not get the form variables out of the `Request` object. In fact, in many cases this would be more appropriate; however, it wouldn't make for a very good example of web controls!

We also make use of the `IsPostback` property of the page to determine if the page has been requested as a result of the form being submitted. If this property is `true`, then the page request is not an original request for the page. We use this property to determine what processing needs to take place to reduce the amount of code that is run when the page is processed. In our case, we hide the panel containing the form controls and display a "thank you" message.

Example 2 – Web Controls Part 2

One of the more powerful features of web controls is their ability to be **databound**. The following example demonstrates accessing data from a SQL Server database and binding several web controls to the data. The classes used in this example allow for connecting to SQL Server but there are other classes which allow for connecting to data sources using existing OLEDB and ODBC providers. For more information on data binding please refer to Chapter 14 and Chapters 4 to 6 to learn more about the controls. In addition to basic controls, **Templated** controls are also used in this example. Templated controls allow definition of the style and content of different portions of the control through the use of templates. In essence, the HTML element itself contains other elements that allow the developer to design the layout of the information in the control. This will become clearer as we take a look at this example.

Products.aspx

```
<%@ Page language="c#" Codebehind="Products.aspx.cs" AutoEventWireup="false"
Inherits="ASPProgRefExamplesC.Products" %>
<%@ Register TagPrefix="WROX" TagName="Header" Src="header.ascx" %>
<%@ Register TagPrefix="WROX" TagName="NavBar" Src="navigation.ascx" %>
<!--The Register directives as the top of the page indicate that the specified
    files provide source code for tags that are defined with a prefix and name.
    These
    tags are used below for our user controls. -->
<!DOCTYPE HTML PUBLIC "-//W3C//DTD HTML 4.0 Transitional//EN" >
<HTML>
  <HEAD>
    <link rel="stylesheet" href="northwind.css" type="text/css">
  </HEAD>
  <body>
    <form id="Products" method="post" runat="server">
      <table width="100%" border="0">
        <tr>
          <td colspan="2">
    <!--include the header user control setting properties for our page -->
            <WROX:Header subheadingtext="Product Listing"
                         subheadingcolor="Orange"
                         subheadingsize="4"
                         backcolor="white"
                         runat="server"
                         id="Header1"
```

```
                        name="Header1">
        </WROX:Header>
    </td>
</tr>
<tr>
<!--include the Navigation bar user control in our page -->
    <td rowspan="2" valign="top" width="15%">
        <WROX:NavBar runat="server">
        </WROX:NavBar>
    </td>
</tr>
<tr>
    <td width="85%">
        <div align="left">
        </div>
        <!--add a datagrid indicating not to auto-generate the columns
            and then specify the columns.-->
        <!--add a link button in the last column that will postback to
            the server firing the ItemCommand defined in the grid element-->
        <!--set the style for the items and headers to valid classes
            defined in the style sheet. -->
        <asp:DataGrid id="dg_products"
                    runat="server"
                    cssclass="CategoryTable"
                    AutoGenerateColumns="False"
                    OnItemCommand="productdetail">
        <Columns>
            <asp:BoundColumn
                Visible="False"
                DataField="productid">
            </asp:BoundColumn>
            <asp:BoundColumn
                DataField="productname"
                HeaderText="Name">
            </asp:BoundColumn>
            <asp:BoundColumn
                DataField="UnitPrice"
                HeaderText="Price">
            </asp:BoundColumn>
            <asp:BoundColumn
                DataField="QuantityPerUnit"
                HeaderText="Quantity">
            </asp:BoundColumn>
            <asp:BoundColumn
                DataField="UnitsInStock"
                HeaderText="In stock">
            </asp:BoundColumn>
            <asp:ButtonColumn
                ButtonType="LinkButton"
                Text="Details">
            </asp:ButtonColumn>
        </Columns>
        <ItemStyle
            CssClass="productlist">
        </ItemStyle>
        <HeaderStyle CssClass="productlistheader">
```

```
              </HeaderStyle>
            </asp:DataGrid>
          </td>
        </tr>
        <tr>
          <td colspan="2">
             
          </td>
        </tr>
        <tr>
          <td colspan="2">
             
          </td>
        </tr>
        <tr>
        <!--add the product list to the page to show the details.
            Auto-generating columns and providing the same style as above. -->
          <td colspan="2" align="center">
            <asp:DataGrid ID="dg_details"
                          Runat="server"
                          Visible="False"
                          AutoGenerateColumns="True">
              <ItemStyle CssClass="productlist"></ItemStyle>
                <HeaderStyle
                  CssClass="productlistheader">
                </HeaderStyle>
            </asp:DataGrid>
          </td>
        </tr>
      </table>
    </form>
  </body>
</HTML>
```

This example from our products page shows two different implementations of the DataGrid control. In the first, we list the high-level information about all of the products in the category but do not let the grid auto-generate its columns. Instead, we specify the types of the columns and the data fields associated with them. In order to do this, we add the Columns element in the DataGrid element and we set the AutoGenerateColumns attribute to false. In addition, we have included a hidden column holding the product ID to be used to access more detailed information. By specifying the OnItemCommand, we have identified a server-side function to be called when an item is selected using our ButtonColumn.

The screenshot overleaf shows the products page as it appears with a specific product selected, showing the details of the product in the lower grid.

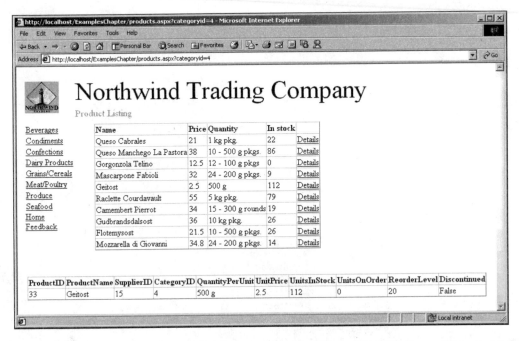

We have also used several of the style elements in this example to set the style for our `DataGrid`. In this case, we have set the style for the `Items` and the `Header` using the style classes defined in the `Northwind.css` file.

The second `DataGrid` holds detailed information on the selected product and is only marked visible when an item has been selected. The code that handles all of this is found in the code behind file, which we'll examine next.

Products.aspx.cs

```
using System;
using System.Configuration;
using System.Data;
using System.Data.SqlClient;
using System.Web;
using System.Web.UI;
using System.Web.UI.WebControls;
using System.Web.UI.HtmlControls;

//NOTE: this page queries the database multiple times.
//This is not an efficient use of db connection or
//an appropriate use of caching. This sample is to show
//how to handle the ItemCommand of the DataGrid.
//See the caching examples for details on how to cache data.

namespace ASPProgRefExamplesC
{
  public class Products : System.Web.UI.Page
  {
    //string variable and variables for our grids so we can
    //interact with them here. Notice the name is the same
```

```
    //as the id in the ASPX file.
    protected string cnn_String;
    protected System.Web.UI.WebControls.DataGrid dg_products;
    protected System.Web.UI.WebControls.DataGrid dg_details;

    public Products()
    {
        Page.Init += new System.EventHandler(Page_Init);
    }
```

After declaring our variables to allow access to the grid controls on the page, we create the page load event handler which is where we load the product summary information for the page. Keep in mind that some form of caching would be highly recommended for a page of this sort, but this sample is intended to show how to use the controls.

The first thing we do is extract our database connection string from the web.config file. We use the key name of the setting to retrieve the value using the static ("shared" in VB) AppSettings method. Next, we open a connection to the database and execute a command to get the product information. We load this data into a dataset and then set the source of the products grid to the default view of the products table in the dataset. A DataView is a class that allows provision of specific views on the data in a DataTable, and is used to bind controls to data. The DefaultView property returns a basic DataView object for the table. See Chapter 14 for more information on accessing and using data in ASP.NET. After calling DataBind on the grid to indicate that that control should bind to the data, the data will be displayed in the grid as we have defined it in the Products.aspx file above.

```
    private void Page_Load(object sender, System.EventArgs e)
    {

        //retrieve connection string from config file
        cnn_String =

            System.Configuration.ConfigurationSettings.AppSettings["cnnString"];

        //open connection and fill dataset with products from this category
        SqlConnection cnnProd = new SqlConnection(cnn_String);
        SqlDataAdapter daProd = new
                    SqlDataAdapter("SELECT * FROM products WHERE categoryid=" +
                    Request["categoryid"], cnnProd);
        DataSet dsProd = new DataSet("ds_products");

        //fill the dataset
        daProd.Fill(dsProd, "Products");

        //set the source for our data grid and call the data binding for this object
        dg_products.DataSource=dsProd.Tables["Products"].DefaultView;
        dg_products.DataBind();
    }
```

The product detail method was identified in the definition of our `DataGrid` in `Products.aspx` as handling the `ItemCommand` event of the products grid. This event is fired when the "Details" link button is clicked on the grid. The first thing we need to do is determine which link was clicked so that we can work with that row of data. We do this by getting the first, hidden, item in the row, and then extracting the text from this cell. We use the `DataGridCommandEventArgs` to get at this information. Next, we open a connection to the database and extract the detailed information about the product we picked. We then bind the `DefaultView` of the `DataTable` to the details grid.

```
public void productdetail(object sender, DataGridCommandEventArgs e)
{
    //get the table cell from which the ItemCommand was fired
    //and get the product id from that cell
    TableCell ProductCell = e.Item.Cells[0];
    string ProductID = ProductCell.Text;

    //open a connection to SQL Server and get the product details
    SqlConnection cnnDetails = new SqlConnection(cnn_String);
    SqlDataAdapter daDetails = new
            SqlDataAdapter("SELECT * FROM products WHERE productid=" +
            ProductID,cnnDetails);
    DataSet dsDetails = new DataSet();

    //fill the dataset and bind its default view to the grid
    daDetails.Fill(dsDetails, "details");
    dg_details.DataSource = dsDetails.Tables["details"].DefaultView;
    dg_details.DataBind();

    //show the details grid.
    dg_details.Visible = true;
}


private void Page_Init(object sender, EventArgs e)
{
    InitializeComponent();
}

private void InitializeComponent()
{
    this.Load += new System.EventHandler(this.Page_Load);

}
}
}
```

home.aspx

In the home page we have an example of the `DataList`. This control is a bit different from the `DataGrid` in that it has a more flexible layout. It also allows us to examine how templated controls work, and shows another mechanism for data binding. Templated controls allow explicit definition of the template to be used for such items as the header, footer, selected item, item, and so on, and the setting of styles for these templates. In this way, the page designer has much more control over the layout and presentation of the list, without having to do any coding.

```
<%@ Register TagPrefix="WROX" TagName="NavBar" Src="navigation.ascx" %>
<%@ Register TagPrefix="WROX" TagName="Header" Src="header.ascx" %>
<%@ Register TagPrefix="WROX" TagName="Login" Src="login.ascx" %>
<%@ Page language="c#" Codebehind="home.aspx.cs" AutoEventWireup="false"
Inherits="ASPProgRefExamplesC.home" %>
<!DOCTYPE HTML PUBLIC "-//W3C//DTD HTML 4.0 Transitional//EN" >
<HTML>
  <HEAD>
    <link rel="stylesheet" href="northwind.css" type="text/css">
  </HEAD>
  <body>
    <form id="home" method="post" runat="server">
      <table width="100%">
        <tr>
          <td colspan="2">
            <WROX:Header id="header"
                         backcolor="white"
                         subheadingtext="Welcome to Northwind Online"
                         subheadingcolor="blue"
                         subheadingsize="3"
                         runat="server">
            </WROX:Header>
          </td>
        </tr>
        <tr>
          <td rowspan="12">
            <P>
            <WROX:NavBar id="nav" runat="server">
            </WROX:NavBar>
            </P>
            <P>
              <WROX:Login id="login" runat="server">
              </WROX:Login>
            </P>
          </td>
          <td valign="top">
            <font color="navy">
              <P>
              Welcome to Northwind, where you'll find all you need for your stay
              in the back woods. We hope you'll stay and have a look around at
              all we have to offer. If you have feedback, please fill out our
              <a href="feedback.aspx">feedback form.</a>
              </P>
            </font>
            <asp:DataList ID="Categories"
                          Runat="server"
                          RepeatColumns="2"
                          RepeatDirection="Horizontal"
                          RepeatLayout="Table">
            <HeaderTemplate>
              <h3>
                Our selection includes products in these fine categories
              </h3>
            </HeaderTemplate>
            <HeaderStyle cssclass="CategoryHeader"></HeaderStyle>
```

```
        <ItemTemplate>
          <table id="category_item">
            <tr>
              <td>
                <span class="CategoryName">
                  <%#((System.Data.DataRowView)Container.DataItem)
                                            ["CategoryName"]%>
                </span>
                <br>
                <span class="CategoryDescription">
                  <%#((System.Data.DataRowView)Container.DataItem)
                                            ["Description"]%>
                </span>
              </td>
            </tr>
          </table>
        </ItemTemplate>
      </asp:DataList>
    </td>
  </tr>
</table>
</form>
</body>
</HTML>
```

The first thing to notice in using the `DataList` is the use of the `ItemTemplate` tag. Without this tag to guide it, the control would have no information as to how to render itself. There are many other templates that can be used with this control including the `HeaderTemplate` we have used above to create a heading for our list. Each of the templates defines a specific set of HTML code to be included in the output. For example, the `ItemTemplate` used here creates a table that contains two pieces of data from the data source. When the control is rendered, the `ItemTemplate` will get rendered once for every item in the data source.

When attempting to bind data to these templated controls, it often works best to use the shorthand data-binding syntax shown above. We first cast the `Container.DataItem` object to a `DataRowView`, and then index the view to get the column we want. By casting, rather than by using the alternative syntax shown below, we avoid the overhead of the reflection needed to do the data binding.

```
<%# DataBinder.Eval(Container.DataItem, "IntegerValue", "{0:C}") %>
```

This syntax uses reflection to get type information and should be avoided in any site where performance is a concern.

In the screenshot opposite we see the home page for our site. Comparing this with the code from `home.aspx` we see how the data binding of the `CategoryName` and `CategoryDescription` adds values into the list.

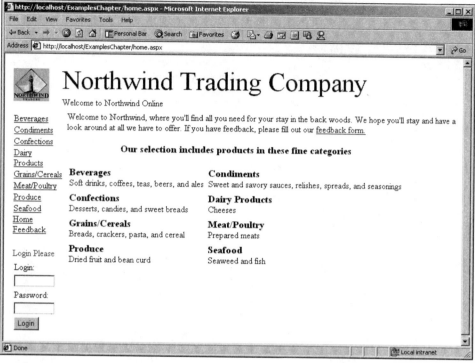

home.aspx.cs

In the code behind our page, we load the data for our `DataList` and bind it to the control.

```
using System;
using System.Configuration;
using System.Data;
using System.Data.SqlClient;
using System.Web;
using System.Web.Security;
using System.Web.UI;
using System.Web.UI.WebControls;
using System.Web.UI.HtmlControls;

namespace ASPProgRefExamplesC
{
  public class home : System.Web.UI.Page
  {
    protected System.Web.UI.WebControls.DataList Categories;
    private string cnnString;
    private DataView CategoryView;

    public home()
    {
      Page.Init += new System.EventHandler(Page_Init);
    }

    private void Page_Load(object sender, System.EventArgs e)
```

```
    {
        //retrieve connection string from the configuration file
        cnnString = ConfigurationSettings.AppSettings["cnnString"].ToString();

        //connect to sql database and fill our dataset
        SqlConnection cnnNW = new SqlConnection(cnnString);
        SqlDataAdapter daNW = new SqlDataAdapter("SELECT * FROM categories",cnnNW);
        DataSet dsNW = new DataSet("ds_categories");

        daNW.Fill(dsNW,"Categories");

        //set the DataView object equal to the DefaultView of the Categories table
        CategoryView = dsNW.Tables["Categories"].DefaultView;

        //set the datasource of our datalist to the dataview
        Categories.DataSource=CategoryView;
        Categories.DataBind();

    }

    private void Page_Init(object sender, EventArgs e)
    {
        InitializeComponent();
    }

    private void InitializeComponent()
    {
        this.Load += new System.EventHandler(this.Page_Load);
    }
    }
}
```

In order to load data into the control, we load data into a `DataSet` and bind the default view of the table in the dataset to the control. We could, alternatively, use a `DataReader` to bind to the control as well. Since a `DataSet` is loaded using a `DataReader`, by binding to the `DataReader` directly, we remove a step and improve the performance of our site. However, when using business objects or other mechanisms where data needs to be passed from one object to another, the `DataSet` is the preferred object. See Chapter 14 for more information on data access.

Example 3 – User Controls

User controls allow the creation of small sections of reusable code that can be included in ASP.NET pages. Similar to server-side includes, which allow for including files in an HTML page, the User control is much more powerful and extensible, allowing for parameters, caching, and compilation. This example demonstrates the use of a User control that acts as a header for the Northwind web site. The control allows the developer to pass in parameters for the subheading and the background color. This control will be updated in Example 5 to allow for caching.

The User Control (header.ascx)

```
<%@ Control Language="c#" AutoEventWireup="false" Codebehind="header.ascx.cs"

Inherits="ASPProgRefExamplesC.header"%>
```

```
<!--we use the BackColor variable to set the background color for the table-->
<table id="header_table" bgcolor="<%=BackColor%>" width="100%" border="0">
  <tr>
    <td rowspan="2">
      <img id="logo" src="./images/logo_sm.jpg"> </asp:Image>
    </td>
    <td>
      <font size="16" color="Navy">Northwind Trading Company</font>
    </td>
  </tr>
  <tr>
    <td>
      <!--use the SubHeadingColor, SubHeadingSize, and SubHeadingText to create
                                           the sub heading -->
<font id="SubHeading" color='<%=SubHeadingColor%>' size='<%=SubHeadingSize%>'>
        <%=SubHeadingText%>
      </font>
    </td>
  </tr>
</table>
```

The example starts out with the Control declaration at the top identifying this as a user control and indicating that the source for this control is found in the file named header.ascx.cs. Next, we create a simple table with an image and some text. Then we create some text that is dynamic:

```
<font id="SubHeading" color='<%=SubHeadingColor%>' size='<%=SubHeadingSize%>'>
  <%=SubHeadingText%>
</font>
```

This set of tags defines a font element with dynamic content for the color, size, and text that will be included. The values referenced between the <%= %> tags are variable names defined in the code behind our control. The control allows us to specify this information when we use it in another page as shown in the example host page. The syntax for dynamic content should be familiar to ASP developers.

header.ascx.cs

```
namespace ASPProgRefExamplesC
{
  using System;
  using System.Web;
  using System.Web.UI.WebControls;
  using System.Web.UI.HtmlControls;

  public abstract class header : System.Web.UI.UserControl
  {
    //having the public variables means that their values can be set in the
    //element declaration in an ASPX page. We could also have used public
    //properties rather than fields.
    public string SubHeadingText;
    public string SubHeadingColor;
    public int SubHeadingSize;
    public string BackColor="white";
```

```
   protected System.Web.UI.HtmlControls.HtmlGenericControl SubHeading;
   protected System.Web.UI.WebControls.Image logo;

   public header()
   {
     this.Init += new System.EventHandler(Page_Init);
   }

   private void Page_Load(object sender, System.EventArgs e)
   {}

   private void Page_Init(object sender, EventArgs e)
   {
     InitializeComponent();
   }

   private void InitializeComponent()
   {
     this.Load += new System.EventHandler(this.Page_Load);
   }
 }
}
```

In the code behind our control, we simply define public variables for the properties we want to expose. These items could also be exposed by using public properties as opposed to fields. As long as these items are publicly exposed, they can be manipulated from a web page using the attributes of the control. There is no logic or control manipulation in this file, only public fields, which are then used in the display for the control as seen in the header.ascx file.

The Host Page – home.aspx

To use the control in a web page, we register it and then add it like any other HTML element.

From **home.aspx**:

```
<@ Register TagPrefix="WROX" TagName="Header" Src="header.ascx" %>
...
<td>
  <WROX:Header id="head" SubHeadingText="Welcome to Northwind"
        SubHeadingColor="yellow"
        SubHeadingSize="3"
        BackColor="gray">
  </WROX:Header>
</td>
...
```

First, we must register our user control using the Register page directive to define the prefix and the tag name as well as the source, then we treat it as any other tag that we have in our toolbox. Notice that we have used the prefix and tag name declared in the Register directive to use the control. We use attributes of the tag to pass values to the user control. These parameter names match variable names in the code behind the user control and are then used to format the output. User controls can also contain logic and many of the same features as a full page. See the forms authentication example later in this chapter for a look at a user control that does some processing and logic.

Example 4 – Validating User Input

Form validation is a common task in web development. In ASP.NET, we have a set of controls that make form validation extremely simple. By creating a control and indicating another control it should validate, we ensure that our form is valid before working with data. The controls also have a mechanism built-in for prompting the user for further action to correct their input.

In many cases this validation helps take a load off the server by ensuring that the data that is sent to the server is already in a valid state and performing the validation at the client. This allows the server to focus its processing on submitting or working with the data rather than validating it. The validation controls will do client-side validation if the browser detected can support the rich level of scripting needed to do this. Internet Explorer 4 or higher, for example, will do the validation on the client before submitting the form, whereas Netscape will submit the form and return an error message if the page is not valid.

You can also indicate that you would like the controls to be validated at the client by setting the `EnableClientScript` attribute of the validation control and changing the `ClientTarget` property of the page class. See Chapter 5 for more information on the various validation controls and Chapter 3 for more information on the `Page` class. This example takes a look at how to validate data in a Web Form using the validation controls. Required fields and matching a particular pattern with regular expressions are both reviewed.

feedback.aspx (updated)

```
<%@ Page language="c#" Codebehind="feedback.aspx.cs" ClientTarget="uplevel"
          AutoEventWireup="false" Inherits="ASPProgRefExamplesC.feedback_form"
%>
<%@ Register TagPrefix="WROX" TagName="Header" Src="header.ascx"%>
<%@ Register TagPrefix="WROX" TagName="NavBar" Src="navigation.ascx"%>
<!DOCTYPE HTML PUBLIC "-//W3C//DTD HTML 4.0 Transitional//EN" >
<HTML>
  <HEAD>
    <LINK href="northwind.css" type="text/css" rel="stylesheet">
  </HEAD>
  <body>
    <form id="feedbackform" method="post" runat="server">
      <TABLE id="table_feedback" width="100%">
        <tr>
          <td colspan="2">
            <WROX:HEADER id="heading"
                  runat="server"
                  backcolor="white"
                  subheadingcolor="Blue"
                  subheadingsize="4 "
                  subheadingtext="Thank you for your input">
            </WROX:HEADER>
          </td>
        </tr>
        <tr>
          <td valign="top" rowspan="5">
            <WROX:NAVBAR id="nav"
                      runat="server">
            </WROX:NAVBAR>
          </td>
          <td>
```

```
<!--This is the message that will display when the form is submitted. -->
    <asp:label id="message" runat="server" visible="False"></asp:label>
    <!--This panel contains our controls in the form so we can hide them
    when a user posts the form. Panels are great for separating controls
    .-->
    <asp:panel id="formpanel" runat="server">

    <TABLE id="form_table">
      <TR>
        <TD> <!--The validation summary displays all of the error
        messages for any validation controls on the page. The display
        mode
        indicates how this list should be displayed. -->
        <asp:ValidationSummary id="validatorsummary"
                        runat="server"
                        displaymode="BulletList">
        </asp:ValidationSummary>
          Name
          <BR> <!--This text box is the name box on the form and we
          have
            attached a required field validator to it using the
            validator's ControlToValidate property. Setting Display
            equal to none allows for the validator message to only
            appear in the summary control defined above. We could
            use static which creates a placeholder for the error
            message or dynamic which does not create a placeholder
            but will display the message if necessary. -->
          <asp:textbox id="person_name"
                  runat="server"
                  TextMode="SingleLine"
                  width="100">
          </asp:textbox>
          <asp:RequiredFieldValidator id="valName"
                        display="None"
                        ControlToValidate="person_name"
                        ErrorMessage="Your name is required"
                              Runat="server">
          </asp:RequiredFieldValidator>
        </TD>
      </TR>
      <TR>
        <TD>
          Email
          <BR> <!--This is the email input with two validator
              controls.
              The second just makes sure the field has a value in
              it while the first makes sure the email is valid by
              testing it against a regular expressions pattern.
              -->
```

```
                        <asp:textbox id="email"
                                     TextMode="SingleLine"
                                     width="100"
                                     Runat="server">
                        </asp:textbox>
                        <asp:RegularExpressionValidator id="emailvalidator"
                                display="None"
                                ControlToValidate="email"
                                enableclientscript="True"
                                ErrorMessage="You must enter a valid email"
                                Runat="server"
                                ValidationExpression=
                                "\w+([-+.]\w+)*@\w+([-.]\w+)*\.\w+([-.]\w+)*">
                        </asp:RegularExpressionValidator>

                        <asp:RequiredFieldValidator id="emailreq"
                                display="None"
                                ControlToValidate="email"
                                ErrorMessage="You must enter your email"
                                Runat="server">
                        </asp:RequiredFieldValidator>
                    </TD>
                </TR>
                <TR>
                  <TD>
                    Type of feedback
                    <BR> <!--The RadioButtonList allows for defining a group of
                             radio buttons that are mutually exclusive. The
                             CheckBoxList does a similar thing with check boxes
                             . -->
                    <asp:RadioButtonList id="feedback_type"
                                         Runat="server"
                                         RepeatDirection="Horizontal">
                      <asp:ListItem Text="Suggestion"
                                    value="suggest"
                                    Selected="True">
                      </asp:ListItem>
                      <asp:ListItem Text="Problem Report"
                                    value="problem">
                      </asp:ListItem>
                      <asp:ListItem Text="Compliment"
                                    value="compliment">
                      </asp:ListItem>
                      <asp:ListItem Text="Question"
                                    Value="question">
                      </asp:ListItem>
                    </asp:RadioButtonList>
                  </TD>
                </TR>
                <TR>
```

857

```
<TD>
    Reason for visiting:
    <BR> <!--The dropdown list provides a select list that does
            not allow multiple items to be selected. -->
    <asp:DropDownList id="reason" Runat="server">
      <asp:ListItem Text="shopping"
                    Value="shopping">
      </asp:ListItem>
      <asp:ListItem Text="research"
                    Value="research">
      </asp:ListItem>
      <asp:ListItem Text="job search"
                    Value="job">
      </asp:ListItem>
    </asp:DropDownList>
  </TD>
</TR>
<TR>
  <TD>
    Feedback
    <BR> <!--The generic textbox control has several textmodes
         that allow it to be a password text box or text area in
             HTML terms. -->
    <asp:TextBox id="feedback"
                 TextMode="MultiLine"
                 Runat="server"
                 Columns="40"
                 rows="10">
    </asp:TextBox>
  </TD>
</TR>
<TR>
  <TD> <!--The button submits the server side form and we have
          indicated a function to run on the server when the
          button is clicked. This is where we will handle our
          form data-->
    <asp:button id="submit"
                onclick="ProcessForm"
                runat="server"
                text="Submit Feedback">
    </asp:button>
  </TD>
</TR>
</TABLE>
</asp:panel>
</td>
</tr>
</TABLE>
</form>
</body>
</HTML>
```

In the code above we have modified our feedback form to require certain information. For the first input box, we want to require that the user enter some value, but not put any restrictions on what that value is. Therefore, we use the `RequiredFieldValidator` tag. Using the `ControlToValidate` attribute, we specify the unique ID of the text box control we want to require. An error message is specified to present to the user when a value has not been entered.

For the e-mail field, not only do we require an input value, but we also want to make sure it is a valid e-mail address. To do so, we use a `RequiredFieldValidator` as we did for the name field, and we add a `RegularExpressionValidator` as well. The only difference between the two validator tags is that the `RegularExpressionValidator` includes a `ValidationExpression` attribute that specifies the required pattern to be matched. This allows the developer to specify a specific pattern of numerals, symbols, and characters that the input must match to be considered valid:

```
ValidationExpression="\w+([-+.]\w+)*@\w+([-.]\w+)*\.\w+([-.]\w+)*"
```

Let's dissect this expression. Below are the items in the expression in the order they appear and their meaning.

Element	Description
\w+	The beginning of our expression indicates any alphanumeric character "\w", which repeats one or more times "+"
([-+.]\w+)*	After the initial characters we will allow zero or more "*" hyphens or a period "[-+.]" followed by any number of alphanumeric characters "\w"
@	The "@" symbol must appear next
\w+	One or more alphanumeric values must follow the "@" symbol
([-.]\w+)*	Zero or more "*" instances of a hyphen or period "[-.]" followed by one or more alphanumeric characters
\.	A period, escaped to indicate that it is a literal character and must appear
\w+	One or more alphanumeric characters
([-.]\w+)*	Zero or more "*" instances of a hyphen or period "[-.]" followed by one or more alphanumeric characters

Either of the following examples would be a match for this expression:

my-name@mycompany.com
my.name@mycompany.region.com

In Visual Studio.NET the **Properties** pane of the `RegularExpressionValidator` control allows a choice of popular formats to match such as phone numbers, zip codes, and e-mail addresses. However, this property can easily be set manually. For further information on the `ValidationExpression` property refer to Chapter 5.

Note that the validators will work regardless of the browser, but may either work on the client using JavaScript, or by taking a trip back to the server if it is determined that the browser does not support the degree of scripting necessary for client-side validation.

Example 5 – Caching

In any high-performance or large-volume site, any efforts to reduce load on the web server or database server will strengthen the site. ASP.NET introduces several caching mechanisms to allow the developer to specify what content is cached and for how long. This example demonstrates caching an entire page, as well as a page fragment in the form of a User Control, and caching data from a database query. Note that caching a User Control is the only mechanism by which fragments of a page can be cached.

Page caching in its simplest form relies on adding a page directive to the `.aspx` file:

```
<%@ OutputCache Duration="120" VaryByParam="*" %>
```

This directive tells the ASP.NET framework to cache this page content for a duration of 120 seconds. It also indicates that the page content should be cached based on the parameters passed to it. This is a very powerful tool to have, as it allows the caching of dynamic content based on the parameters that are used to access the page. So, for example, if a page is passed different product ID values, the content produced will be cached for an ID of 1, 2, 3, etc. We also have the ability to cache based on particular parameters or no parameters, as well as all parameters as seen in this example. These parameters can be in the querystring or in POST data from a form. Caching can also be varied based on HTTP headers or by custom information. See Chapter 7 for more information on the specifics of caching.

> At the time this chapter was written, .NET was in Beta 2 and required the installation of "ASP.NET Premium Edition" for Output Caching to function. This product is available for free download from **msdn.microsoft.com**. However, this should no longer be necessary in future releases of ASP.NET as the availability of "premium" features will depend on the version of Windows installed and not on the runtime itself.

Caching fragments of a page involves creating User Controls for those portions of the page you wish to cache and actually caching the control. We will now do this for our `Header` control that we created in Example 3. We add the following code line to the top of our control:

```
<%@ OutputCache Duration="7200"
    VaryByControl="SubHeadingText;SubHeadingColor;SubHeadingSize" VaryByParam="*"
%>
```

We've introduced a new attribute of the `OutputCache` directive here, which is the `VaryByControl` attribute. This allows us to cache different versions of the control for the different values that are passed in to our variables. So if the site contains a version of the header with a green background, and one with a gray background, then both items will be cached.

With content like navigation bars, headers, and footers, the caching mechanism can really have an impact on performance by allowing the content to be cached and therefore lessening the processing load on the web server. In terms of performance, however, accessing data can be one of the most intensive activities that occurs on your site. So, wouldn't it be great if we could cache slowly changing data that was retrieved from a database rather than retrieve it each time the page is accessed?. We can! We'll use the categories that we displayed on our home page in the data list to demonstrate. By making some modifications to the `Page_Load` method, we'll transform our data intensive page to one that is simple to serve up and only accesses the database every two hours.

home.aspx.cs (updated)

```
using System;
using System.Configuration;
using System.Data;
using System.Data.SqlClient;
using System.Web;
using System.Web.Security;
using System.Web.UI;
using System.Web.UI.WebControls;
using System.Web.UI.HtmlControls;

namespace ASPProgRefExamplesC
{

  public class home : System.Web.UI.Page
  {
    protected System.Web.UI.WebControls.DataList Categories;
    private string cnnString;
    private DataView CategoryView;

    public home()
    {
      Page.Init += new System.EventHandler(Page_Init);
    }

    private void Page_Load(object sender, System.EventArgs e)
    {
    //try to load the data from the cache
      CategoryView = (DataView)Cache["CategoryData"];

      //if the value was not found in the cache,
      //then we need to load it from the database
      if (CategoryView == null)
      {
        //retrieve connection string from the configuration file
        cnnString = ConfigurationSettings.AppSettings["cnnString"].ToString();

        //connect to sql database and fill our dataset
        SqlConnection cnnNW = new SqlConnection(cnnString);
        SqlDataAdapter daNW = new SqlDataAdapter("SELECT * FROM
                                          categories",cnnNW);
        DataSet dsNW = new DataSet("ds_categories");

        daNW.Fill(dsNW,"Categories");

        //set the DataView object equal to the
        //default view of the Categories table
        CategoryView = dsNW.Tables["Categories"].DefaultView;

        //insert this data object into the cache so that we
        //can get it from the cache next time.
        Cache.Insert("CategoryData",CategoryView,null,DateTime.Now.AddHours(2),
                  TimeSpan.Zero);
```

```
        }

          //set the DataSource of our DataList to the view which may have come from
          // cache or been loaded from the database
          Categories.DataSource=CategoryView;
          Categories.DataBind();
        }

        private void Page_Init(object sender, EventArgs e)
        {
          InitializeComponent();
        }

        private void InitializeComponent()
        {
          this.Load += new System.EventHandler(this.Page_Load);
        }
      }
    }
```

The first thing we do in the Page_Load function is to check the **Cache** object for a DataView labeled CategoryData. Once we attempt to retrieve this object, we check to see if the object we got back is null. If so, then we know the cache is empty, so we retrieve the data from the database as we did before. However, instead of setting the DataGrid's DataSource property to the DefaultView of the table in the DataSet, we set our local DataView variable equal to that default view. In this way we have a local reference to a DataView object, which we then to insert into the Cache.

```
    Cache.Insert("CategoryData",CategoryView,null,DateTime.Now.AddHours(2),
                TimeSpan.Zero);
```

This function operates much like the old ASP Session and Application objects in that we insert items into the object and give it a key name. However, with the Cache object, we can also specify an expiration of the cached item that is explicit or relative to the last time it was accessed. In our example above, we have defined an explicit expiration of two hours for the data we are caching.

The next time our page is accessed, the Cache will contain our DataView and the data will be used for the DataSource of our DataList instead of making a trip to the database. This caching mechanism is specific to a server, and therefore, in a server farm each server will manage its own cache.

Caching also allows for setting up dependencies on files and other objects so that cached data or information can be updated as those items are updated. See Chapter 7 for more information.

Example 6 – Writing a Web Service

The .NET platform centers around Web Services, so no examples section would be complete without examining a simple Web Service. This example shows two methods of a Web Service, which allow a remote program to call in, via SOAP, to retrieve the categories of products in the Northwind database, or the products for a given category ID. This information is then returned to the calling program as XML.

northwind.asmx.cs

```
using System;
using System.Configuration;
using System.Data;
using System.Data.SqlClient;
using System.Diagnostics;
using System.Web;
using System.Web.Services;

namespace ASPProgRefExamplesC
{

  [WebService(Namespace="http://www.wrox.com/ASPNetProgRef/Northwind")]
  public class northwind : System.Web.Services.WebService
  {
    protected string cnn_String;
    public northwind()
    {
      InitializeComponent();
    }

    private void InitializeComponent()
    {}

    protected override void Dispose( bool disposing )
    {}

    //this method gets all products for a specified category
    [WebMethod(Description="This method gets the products for a given category")]
    public string GetProducts(int categoryid)
    {
      // Get Connection String from web.config file
      cnn_String =

System.Configuration.ConfigurationSettings.AppSettings["cnnString"];

      //open connection and load products data for the given category ID
      SqlConnection cnnProd = new SqlConnection(cnn_String);
      SqlDataAdapter daProd = new SqlDataAdapter("SELECT * FROM products WHERE
                                  categoryid="+categoryid.ToString(),
                                  cnnProd);
      DataSet dsProd = new DataSet("ds_products");

      //load dataset
      daProd.Fill(dsProd, "Products");

      //return the XML representation of the dataset.
      return dsProd.GetXml();
    }

    //this method gets all of the categories as XML
    [WebMethod(Description=
              "This method retrieves all of the categories of products")]
    public string GetCategories()
    {
```

```
        // Get the connection string from the web.config file
        cnn_String =

System.Configuration.ConfigurationSettings.AppSettings["cnnString"];

        //open a connection and get the category
        //information from the database
        SqlConnection cnnCat = new SqlConnection(cnn_String);
        SqlDataAdapter daCat = new SqlDataAdapter("SELECT categoryid, categoryname,
                                                  description FROM categories",
                                                  cnnCat);
        DataSet dsCat = new DataSet("ds_categories");

        //fill the dataset
        daCat.Fill(dsCat, "Categories");

        //return the XML representation of the data, including the schema
        return dsCat.GetXml();
      }
    }
  }
```

The first thing you might notice is that our Web Service is just another class. We define the class in a code-behind file, which exposes the methods using attributes, specifically the `WebMethod` attribute, and we call it through the simple, one-line `.asmx` file shown below:

northwind.asmx

```
<%@ WebService Language="c#" Codebehind="northwind.asmx.cs"
                                    Class="ASPProgRefExamplesC.northwind"
%>
```

The `.asmx` extension is handled differently by the ASP.NET runtime. For example, if we request the page directly, we get the output shown in the screenshot below:

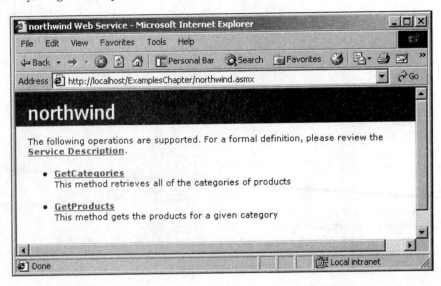

This web page interface allows us to get information on the different methods exposed by the service as well as invoke the methods in the service, passing parameters if appropriate. Notice the hyperlink in the first line of the page indicated as "Service Description". In order for clients to call into the Web Service, they need to know how to communicate with it. This information is provided in the service description, an XML file based on the Web Service Description Language (WSDL). This information is accessed by passing a parameter in the querystring of our request.

```
http://localhost/ExamplesChapter/northwind.asmx?WSDL
```

This information is used to create proxy classes to access the service. For more information on WSDL and Web Services, see Chapters 11 to 13.

In our class we first put a `WebService` attribute on the class itself to identify the XML namespace to be used in the SOAP messaging:

```
[WebService(Namespace="http://www.wrox.com/ASPNetProgRef/Northwind")]
```

This allows us to provide a unique namespace for the elements in our SOAP message and is applied to the class so that all methods from within the class will use this namespace.

Next, we define methods that access data from a database and use the `DataSet`'s `GetXML` method to return a string containing the XML representation of the data. Each of these methods is also marked by an attribute that identifies it as being available to be called via the Web Service:

```
[WebMethod]
```

This attribute, which can also take parameters to further specify how to handle the SOAP messaging, is all that is needed to mark your methods as part of the Web Service. In our example, we mark these methods with a `Description` attribute. This description appears when we examine the `.asmx` page in our web browser.

For the purposes of this example, we have removed security on this page to allow it to be accessed without logging in to the site. In order to do this, we added the following information to the `Web.config` file just before the closing `</configuration>` element:

```xml
<location path="northwind.asmx">
  <system.web>
    <authorization>
      <allow users="?" />
    </authorization>
  </system.web>
</location>
```

This instructs the runtime to allow access to anonymous users for this specific resource. We could have done just the opposite with this attribute, which is to restrict access to certain pages in a site such that anonymous users could browse certain sections of the page, but not others.

Now that we have a service, we need to be able to call it from a program. So, while it does not make a lot of sense that we would both define and call a Web Service from within the same assembly, we will do so here for simplicity's sake. In order to call a Web Service, we need to have its URL and we need to build the mechanisms for communicating with it. As was mentioned above, the WSDL file serves as a description of the service and a contract for interacting with it. We will use this file to build a proxy class that we can then use to contact the service.

We use the `WSDL.exe` utility that ships with the .NET Framework SDK to generate our proxy class. We simply run this application followed by the URL to the WSDL file and any options we want. For our purposes, we would call the application as follows from the command line:

```
wsdl http://localhost/aspprogrefexamplesc/northwind.asmx?WSDL
/namespace:AspProgRefExamplesC.localhost /language:CS
```

This instructs the tool to get the information from the WSDL file and create a C# file with the same name as the service name, and to use the namespace provided. We now have a class with methods on it corresponding to the web methods we defined in our service. The page below calls our Web Service to load some data and put it in a grid on the page.

ServiceConsumer.aspx.cs

```csharp
using System;
using System.Data;
using System.Web;
using System.Web.UI;
using System.Web.UI.WebControls;
using System.Web.UI.HtmlControls;
using System.Xml;

namespace ASPProgRefExamplesC
{
  public class ServiceConsumer : System.Web.UI.Page
  {
    protected System.Web.UI.WebControls.DataGrid ServiceDataGrid;

    public ServiceConsumer()
    {
      Page.Init += new System.EventHandler(Page_Init);
    }

    private void Page_Load(object sender, System.EventArgs e)
    {
      //create a dataset and an instance of our proxy class
      //for the Web Service
      DataSet ServiceDataSet = new DataSet();
      localhost.northwind NorthwindService = new localhost.northwind();

      //create an XmlTextReader to load up with the XML string from
      //our service
      XmlTextReader reader = new
          XmlTextReader(NorthwindService.GetCategories(),XmlNodeType.Document,
                        null);

      //load the dataset inferring the table schema from the XML
      ServiceDataSet.ReadXml(reader,XmlReadMode.InferSchema);

      //bind the data and grid
      ServiceDataGrid.DataSource=ServiceDataSet.Tables[0].DefaultView;
      DataBind();
    }

    private void Page_Init(object sender, EventArgs e)
    {
```

```
      InitializeComponent();
    }

    private void InitializeComponent()
    {
      this.Load += new System.EventHandler(this.Page_Load);
    }
  }
}
```

In our `Page_Load` event, we simply create a `DataSet`, an `XmlTextReader`, and an instance of our proxy class. We call the proxy class method to get categories and use this to construct the `XmlTextReader`. We then use the `ReadXml` method of the `DataSet` to load the data into the `DataSet` from the `XmlTextReader`. Finally, we bind this data to a `DataGrid`, the only control on our form.

The proxy class created by the WSDL tool is a simple wrapper around the inner workings of the communication happening between our client application and the service. This makes programming the client much easier than if we had to write all of this code ourselves. In the Visual Studio.NET environment we add a web reference, which uses the `WSDL.exe` tool to create a proxy class and adds it to the project. The proxy class generated is included below simply to show that it is a wrapper class and that it exposes methods with signatures just like our Web Service.

northwind.cs

```
//------------------------------------------------------------------------
// <autogenerated>
//    This code was generated by a tool.
//    Runtime Version: 1.0.2914.16
//
//    Changes to this file may cause incorrect behavior and will be lost if
//    the code is regenerated.
// </autogenerated>
//------------------------------------------------------------------------

namespace ASPProgRefExamplesC.localhost {
  using System.Diagnostics;
  using System.Xml.Serialization;
  using System;
  using System.Web.Services.Protocols;
  using System.Web.Services;


  [System.Web.Services.WebServiceBindingAttribute(Name="northwindSoap",
            Namespace="http://www.wrox.com/ASPNetProgRef/Northwind")]
  public class northwind : System.Web.Services.Protocols.SoapHttpClientProtocol {

    [System.Diagnostics.DebuggerStepThroughAttribute()]
    public northwind() {
      this.Url = "http://localhost/aspprogrefexamplesc/northwind.asmx";
    }


    [System.Diagnostics.DebuggerStepThroughAttribute()]
    [System.Web.Services.Protocols.SoapDocumentMethodAttribute
```

```
("http://www.wrox.com/ASPNetProgRef/Northwind/GetProducts",

RequestNamespace="http://www.wrox.com/ASPNetProgRef/Northwind",

ResponseNamespace="http://www.wrox.com/ASPNetProgRef/Northwind",

Use=System.Web.Services.Description.SoapBindingUse.Literal,

ParameterStyle=System.Web.Services.Protocols.SoapParameterStyle.Wrapped)]
    public string GetProducts(int categoryid) {
      object[] results = this.Invoke("GetProducts", new object[] {
        categoryid});
      return ((string)(results[0]));
    }

    [System.Diagnostics.DebuggerStepThroughAttribute()]
    public System.IAsyncResult BeginGetProducts(int categoryid,
                              System.AsyncCallback callback,
                              object asyncState) {
      return this.BeginInvoke("GetProducts", new object[] {
        categoryid}, callback, asyncState);
    }

    [System.Diagnostics.DebuggerStepThroughAttribute()]
    public string EndGetProducts(System.IAsyncResult asyncResult) {
      object[] results = this.EndInvoke(asyncResult);
      return ((string)(results[0]));
    }

    [System.Diagnostics.DebuggerStepThroughAttribute()]
    [System.Web.Services.Protocols.SoapDocumentMethodAttribute

("http://www.wrox.com/ASPNetProgRef/Northwind/GetCategories",

RequestNamespace="http://www.wrox.com/ASPNetProgRef/Northwind",

ResponseNamespace="http://www.wrox.com/ASPNetProgRef/Northwind",

Use=System.Web.Services.Description.SoapBindingUse.Literal,

ParameterStyle=System.Web.Services.Protocols.SoapParameterStyle.Wrapped)]
    public string GetCategories() {
      object[] results = this.Invoke("GetCategories", new object[0]);
      return ((string)(results[0]));
    }

    [System.Diagnostics.DebuggerStepThroughAttribute()]
    public System.IAsyncResult BeginGetCategories(System.AsyncCallback callback,
                                    object asyncState) {
      return this.BeginInvoke("GetCategories", new object[0], callback,
                        asyncState);
    }

    [System.Diagnostics.DebuggerStepThroughAttribute()]
```

```
      public string EndGetCategories(System.IAsyncResult asyncResult) {
        object[] results = this.EndInvoke(asyncResult);
        return ((string)(results[0]));
      }
    }
  }
```

While there is a great deal going on in this file, we have highlighted those items that map most easily to the service we have created. Most of the time you will not have to worry about the details of the proxy and the tools will do everything for you, but it is good to take a look at the inner workings a bit to get a better understanding in case things do not work as planned.

If you plan to use the client page to access the Web Service, be sure to update the URL in the constructor of this class to point to the Web Service as it is installed on your server.

Example 7 – Form-Based Authentication

In many web sites today it is common practice to either secure parts of the site, or keep track of users and their visits for the purposes of personalization and targeted campaigning. In ASP.NET there are a variety of methods to authenticate and secure a site. Form-based authentication provides the developer with a means to integrate the authentication of users into any portion of the site. This example shows how to use a User Control to provide a simple login framework.

Web.config

Before we can begin creating our User Control for logging in, we need to update our Web.config file to indicate that we wish to use form-based authentication. The following XML snippet should be placed inside the System.Web element:

```xml
<authentication mode="Forms">
  <forms loginUrl="home.aspx" protection="All">
    <credentials passwordFormat="SHA1">
      <user name="wroxuser" password="96FA6B10F13F47A8C50660DCF7CA87914E51F061" />
    </credentials>
  </forms>
</authentication>
<authorization>
  <deny users="?" />
</authorization>
```

The authentication element identifies the method of authentication as being form-based, which prepares the framework to search for an authentication cookie. The loginUrl indicates the page to redirect users to if they have not been authenticated. In this case, we have chosen to redirect users back to our home page, as that is where the login control will be displayed. The Protection attribute identifies the amount of security surrounding our cookie and involves encryption and other protective mechanisms. For our example we are asking for "All" protection which is the most secure. We could have used "None" which provides no encryption of the information and is the least secure. This is similar to having passwords sent in clear text and is not recommended unless the site is using SSL.

We have also specified a `credentials` element, which allows us to enter users' names and passwords. In this case, our passwords are hashed with the SHA1 algorithm, which is why the password for the site, "wroxuser" shows up as a long string of digits and characters. You can use the static ("shared" in VB) `HashPasswordForStoringInConfigFile` method of the `FormsAuthentication` class to create the hash of a password. Once we have identified the valid users and the authentication method, we then need to determine the authorization for the site. In our case we have simply indicated that anonymous users, denoted by the "?", are denied access to the site. This means that all users must authenticate in order to access any pages in our site. We have overridden this security for our Web Service page as described in the previous example.

Login.ascx

This is the HTML portion of our user control, which simply presents the textboxes and buttons for entering the login information. Notice that we have used a panel control to contain the input boxes so that we can show or hide these controls as a group.

```
<%@ Control Language="c#" AutoEventWireup="false" Codebehind="Login.ascx.cs"
Inherits="ASPProgRefExamplesC.Login" %>
<!--this control is a simple layout of nested tables and server controls to create
a
     login form the real work happens in the code file. -->
<TABLE>
  <tr>
    <td>
      <asp:label id="loginprompt" runat="server" style="COLOR: red">
        Login Please
      </asp:label>
    </td>
  </tr>
  <tr>
    <td>
      <asp:panel id="loginpanel" runat="server">
        <table>
          <TR>
            <TD>
              <asp:label id="login_label" runat="server" text="Login:">
              </asp:label>
            </TD>
          </TR>
          <TR>
            <TD>
              <asp:textbox id="login" runat="server" width="75">
              </asp:textbox>
            </TD>
          </TR>
          <TR>
            <TD>
              <asp:label id="pwd_label" runat="server" text="Password:">
              </asp:label>
            </TD>
          </TR>
          <TR>
            <TD>
              <asp:textbox id="pwd" runat="server" width="75" textmode="password">
              </asp:textbox>
            </TD>
```

```
            </TR>
            <TR>
              <TD colspan="2">
                <asp:button id="submit" onclick="LoginUser" runat="server"
text="Login">
                </asp:button>
              </TD>
            </TR>
          </table>
        </asp:panel>
        <asp:button id="logoff"
                    onclick="SignOut"
                    visible="false"
                    runat="server"
                    text="Sign out">
        </asp:button>
      </td>
    </tr>
  </TABLE>
```

Login.ascx.cs

This file represents the code behind our login user control where the processing of the control takes place. The first thing we do is to add the `System.Web.Security` and `System.Security.Principal` namespaces to the list of `using` statements. This allows easy access to the forms authentication objects and methods and the `GenericPrincipal` class. Next, we declare the variables for the UI objects that are going to be involved in the login control including the two textboxes, the labels, and the buttons.

```
using System;
using System.Data;
using System.Security.Principal;
using System.Web.Security;
using System.Web;
using System.Web.UI.WebControls;
using System.Web.UI.HtmlControls;

namespace ASPProgRefExamplesC
{
  public abstract class Login : System.Web.UI.UserControl
  {
    //fields for our controls in the ASCX file.
    protected System.Web.UI.WebControls.Label login_label;
    protected System.Web.UI.WebControls.Label pwd_label;
    protected System.Web.UI.WebControls.TextBox login;
    protected System.Web.UI.WebControls.TextBox pwd;
    protected System.Web.UI.WebControls.Button submit;
    protected System.Web.UI.WebControls.Label loginprompt;
    protected System.Web.UI.WebControls.Panel loginpanel;
    protected System.Web.UI.WebControls.Button logoff;

    public Login()
    {
      this.Init += new System.EventHandler(Page_Init);
    }
```

The `SignOut` method is called when the sign out or "logoff" button is clicked. This method uses the static method of the `FormsAuthentication` class to sign the user out. This removes the cookie information such that a new request by the user will force them to authenticate again. Once the user has signed out, we want to show the login controls in case they decide to log back in, and erase any text in the prompt.

```
//this method signs the user out of the site. They will have to
//reauthenticate to the site if they make another request.
public void SignOut(Object sender, EventArgs ea)
{
   //sign out using the FormsAuthentication class and show
   //the login controls so they can login again if they want to
   FormsAuthentication.SignOut();
   ShowLoginControls();
   loginprompt.Text="";
}
```

Two helper methods, `ShowLoginControls` and `HideLoginControls`, simply change the visibility of the controls involved to indicate whether the user is logged in. In the `Page_Load` method we simply check to see if the user has logged in, indicated by the `IsAuthenticated` property of the `HttpRequest` object. This property will tell us if the user has been authenticated to the site, no matter what authentication method is in place. If the page is not being posted back to, then `ShowLoginControls` is called if the user has not been authenticated, or `HideLoginControls` is called if the user has already authenticated. The result of this is that if the user has not yet logged in, they get the controls to do so, and if they have, then they get a nice welcome message. We use the `HttpContext` to get the user's name. This value is read/write so we can not only find out who is making the request, but force the request to run under another security context by assigning a user to it.

```
//this method displays the controls to allow for logging in
private void ShowLoginControls()
{
   //if no URL was given, then the user did not try to
   //access another page in the site. The ReturnURL is added
   //to the query string when a resource is requested and the
   //user has not been authenticated.
   //if(Request.QueryString["ReturnURL"]!=null)
   loginprompt.Visible=true;

   //show the controls on the panel
   //and hide the signout button
   loginpanel.Visible=true;
   logoff.Visible=false;

}

//this method hides all the controls to just allow for showing
//a message of some sort.
private void HideLoginControls()
{
   //hide the panel and add a welcome message
   //because we must be logged in.
   loginpanel.Visible=false;
   loginprompt.Text = "Welcome, " + Context.User.Identity.Name;
```

```
                 //make sure to display the sign out button
                 logoff.Visible=true;
             }
```

The `LoginUser` method is where the bulk of the work for this control takes place. We start by attempting to authenticate the user with the static ("shared" in VB) `Authenticate` method of the `FormsAuthentication` class passing in the values entered into the textboxes. If the user is valid, then this will return `true` so we continue on with the login process. Next we create an authentication ticket, which represents the information that will be stored in a cookie for this user. We check to see if the "ReturnURL" query parameter is present. If it is, then that means the user requested another page and was redirected by the runtime to the login page. If the user was redirected, then we use the `RedirectFromLoginPage` method to both set the authentication information and redirect the user to the page they originally requested.

If there is no "ReturnURL" parameter, we do not want to use the `RedirectFromLoginPage` method because it will try to redirect the user to "`default.aspx`", which does not exist on our site. So, we use the `SetAuthCookie` method to set the authorization cookie for the user passing in the username and indicating that we do not want this authentication to persist beyond this session. Next we set the `HttpContext` for the request to be running as the requesting user, which allows the appropriate name to display in the welcome message. We create a new `GenericPrincipal` based on the identity of our requesting user, which we get based on their ticket. We then assign this principal to the `User` property of the context. Without this, the name would not appear in the label until the next request was made because the request is not automatically running in the context of the user. Finally, if the user was authenticated, we hide the login controls.

```
        public void LoginUser(Object sender, EventArgs ea)
        {
           //use the FormsAuthentication class to try and authenticate the
           //user. If the login and password match in the credentials section
           //of the web.config file, then they will be given access and this will
           //return true.
           if(FormsAuthentication.Authenticate(Request.Form["login:login"],
                                               Request.Form["login:pwd"]))
           {
              //create an authentication ticket
              FormsAuthenticationTicket Ticket = new
                                    FormsAuthenticationTicket(login.Text,
                                    false,5000);

              //if a return URL was not specified, then set the AuthCookie and do
              //not redirect them
              if(Request.QueryString["ReturnURL"]==null ||
                        Request.QueryString["ReturnURL"]==String.Empty)
              {
                 FormsAuthentication.SetAuthCookie(login.Text, false);

                 //set the context of the current request to be the user
                 //making the request so our welcome message indicates the
                 //right name. Otherwise, this won't happen until the next
                 //request is made.
                 Context.User = new GenericPrincipal(new FormsIdentity(Ticket),null);
              }
```

```
                    //but if there was an original request, redirect them to
                    //that request.
                else
                    FormsAuthentication.RedirectFromLoginPage(login.Text, false);

                    //hide control because we were authenticated
                    HideLoginControls();
                }
                else
                {
                    //we did not validate so we need to let them know to try again
                    loginprompt.Text="Invalid credentials";
                }

            }

            private void Page_Load(object sender, System.EventArgs e)
            {
                //only set the control values if this is not a
                //postback, otherwise we are logging in or signing out
                if(!IsPostBack)
                {
                    // Check to make sure we are authenticated for this user
                    //and hide/show controls accordingly
                    if (Request.IsAuthenticated)
                    {
                        HideLoginControls();
                    }
                    else
                    {
                        ShowLoginControls();
                    }
                }
            }

            private void Page_Init(object sender, EventArgs e)
            {
                InitializeComponent();
            }

            private void InitializeComponent()
            {
                this.Load += new System.EventHandler(this.Page_Load);

            }
        }
    }
```

This control, along with the configuration information, provides a simple implementation of Forms authentication. It could certainly be extended to check the username and password against a data store and to store more information about the user and their habits. However, as a simple control, the only changes needed would be to change the loginUrl attribute in the configuration file to point to a page containing the user control.

There are many other ways to extend the authentication modules in ASP.NET to provide a custom security mechanism. See Chapter 9 for more details on authentication and authorization.

Example 8 – Custom Error Handling

The last sample in our chapter is a simple configuration example, which shows how to provide custom error handling for your site. In many cases, when an error occurs, the last thing we want is for the user to think it was unplanned and get an ugly error message generated by the system or error information that is not branded and customized. Using the configuration file for a site, we can specify a default error page as well as specific pages for the different status codes that a user might encounter when requesting resources.

In the `web.config` file, we make sure we have a `<customErrors>` element inside the main `<system.web>` element as shown below.

```
<configuration>
  <system.web>
...

    <customErrors mode="On" defaultRedirect="DefaultError.html">
      <error statusCode="404" redirect="404.html" />
    </customErrors>

...
  </system.web>
</configuration>
```

In this section, we specify that we want to enable custom errors by setting the mode to "On". The other options include "Off", which shows standard runtime error messages, and "RemoteOnly", which shows custom errors only to remote users and runtime-generated errors for a user on the local machine. We also specify a `defaultRedirect` attribute, which indicates the page to redirect the user to if they get an error that is not specifically directed to another page, such as a runtime error.

Within the custom errors element we can place any number of error elements indicating the status code to watch for and the page to which users should be redirected. Thus, in our site, if we request a page that is not part of the site, we would be presented with the contents of `404.html`. This is shown in the screenshot below.

Summary

In this chapter we have provided a number of samples for practices that are part of many web applications. These examples should give you a start and when you want more detail about these operations, refer to the chapters that cover the topic in more detail.

In this chapter we have covered:

- **Server controls** – how to declare them in an ASPX page and how to code against them in the code behind our pages

- **Data Binding** – getting data from a database and binding it to controls, providing style information and templates where appropriate

- **User Controls** – creating controls and allowing access to the properties or fields in a control to make it more dynamic

- **Caching** – page, fragment (User Control), and data caching were covered as well as parameterizing the cached item

- **Web Services** – creating a basic Web Service and reviewing it in a browser as well as creating a simple client to consume the Web Service

- **Forms Authentication** – securing a site with Forms authentication, defining users, and handling the authentication and sign out process

- **Input validation** – using the validation server controls to validate user input

- **Custom Errors** – how to initiate custom error handling and provide custom error pages

There is a great deal of rich functionality in the ASP.NET framework. Unfortunately examples cannot be given for everything. However, refer to the reference chapters in the book for more detailed information and other examples of specific tasks.

Language Syntax Comparison in .NET

As well as Visual Basic, the Microsoft .NET Platform currently offers built-in support for two other languages, **C#** (pronounced "C Sharp") and **JScript**. The main differences between the three languages are syntactical, but to give you a clearer idea of specific differences, here are the three languages side by side for you to compare. For more information regarding the syntax of the other languages, refer to the complete documentation for the .NET Framework SDK.

	VB	C#	JScript

Variable Declarations	`Dim x As Integer`
	`Dim s As String`
	`Dim s1, s2 As String`
	`Dim o 'Implicitly Object`
	`Dim obj As New Object()`
	`Public name As String`
		`int x;`
		`String s;`
		`String s1, s2;`
		`Object o;`
		`Object obj = new Object();`
		`public String name;`
			`var x : int;`
			`var s : String;`
			`var s1 : String, s2 : String;`
			`var o;`
			`var obj : Object = new Object();`
			`var name : String;`

Statements	`Response.Write("foo")`	`Response.Write("foo");`	`Response.Write("foo");`

Comments	`' This is a comment`
	
	`' This`
	`' is`
	`' a`
	`' multi-line`
	`' comment`
		`// This is a comment`
		
		`/*`
		`This`
		`is`
		`a`
		`multi-line`
		`comment`
		`*/`
			`// This is a comment`
			
			`/*`
			`This`
			`is`
			`a`
			`multi-line`
			`comment`
			`*/`

Accessing Indexed Properties	`Dim s, value As String`
	`s = Request.QueryString("Name")`
	`value = Request.Cookies("Key").Value`
		`String s = Request.QueryString["Name"];`
		`String value = Request.Cookies["key"];`
			`var s : String = Request.QueryString("Name");`
			`var value : String = Request.Cookies("key");`

Declaring Indexed Properties	`'Note that default non-indexed properties`
	`'must be explicitly named in VB`
	
	`' Default Indexed Property`
	`Public Default ReadOnly Property`
	`DefaultProperty(Name As String) As String`
	`  Get`
	`    Return CStr(lookuptable(name))`
	`  End Get`
	`End Property`
	
	`JScript does not support the creation of`
	`Indexed or Default Indexed properties.`
		`// Default Indexed Property`
		`public String this[String name] {`
		`  get {`
		`    return (String) lookuptable[name];`
		`  }`
		`}`
			To emulate these properties in JScript it is suggested that function declarations are used instead. Even though the functions can't be accessed using indexed property syntax in C#, it'll provide the illusion for VB.
			
			`public function Item(name:String) : String {`
			`  return String lookuptable(name));`
			`}`

Declaring Simple Properties	`Public Property Name As String`
	`  Get`
	`    ...`
	`    Return ...`
	`  End Get`
	
	`  Set`
	`    ... = Value`
	`  End Set`
	
	`End Property`
		`public String name {`
		`  get {`
		`    ...`
		`    return ...;`
		`  }`
		`  set {`
		`    ... = value;`
		`  }`
		`}`
			`function get name() : String {`
			`  ...`
			`  return ...;`
			`}`
			`function set name(value : String) {`
			`  ... = value;`
			`}`

	VB	C#	JScript

Declare and Use an Enumeration	`' Declare the Enumeration`
	`Public Enum MessageSize`
	`    Small = 0`
	`    Medium = 1,`
	`    Large = 2`
	`End Enum`
	`' Create a Field or Property`
	`Public MsgSize As MessageSize`
	`' Assign to the property using the`
	`Enumeration values`
	`MsgSize = small`
		`// Declare the Enumeration`
		`public enum MessageSize {`
		`    Small = 0,`
		`    Medium = 1,`
		`    Large = 2`
		`}`
		`// Create a Field or Property`
		`public MessageSize msgsize;`
		`// Assign to the property using the`
		`Enumeration values`
		`msgsize = Small;`
			`// Declare the Enumeration`
			`public enum MessageSize {`
			`    Small = 0,`
			`    Medium = 1,`
			`    Large = 2`
			`}`
			`// Create a Field or Property`
			`public var msgsize:MessageSize;`
			`// Assign to the property using the`
			`Enumeration values`
			`msgsize = Small;`

Enumerating a Collection	`Dim S As String`
	`For Each S In Coll`
	`    ...`
	`Next`
		`for each ( String s in coll ) {`
		`    ...`
		`}`
			`var s:String;`
			`for ( s in coll ) {`
			`    ...`
			`}`

Declare and Use Methods	`' Declare a void return function`
	`Sub VoidFunction()`
	`    ...`
	`End Sub`
	`' Declare a function that returns a value`
	`Function StringFunction() As String`
	`    ...`
	`    Return CStr(val)`
	`End Function`
	`' Declare a function that takes and`
	`returns values`
	`Function ParmFunction(a As String, b As`
	`String) As String`
	`    ...`
	`    Return CStr(A & B)`
	`End Function`
	`' Use the Functions`
	`VoidFunction()`
	`Dim s1 As String = StringFunction()`
	`Dim s2 As String = ParmFunction("Hello",`
	`"World!")`
		`// Declare a void return function`
		`void voidfunction() {`
		`    ...`
		`}`
		`// Declare a function that returns a value`
		`String stringfunction() {`
		`    ...`
		`    return (String) val;`
		`}`
		`// Declare a function that takes and`
		`returns values`
		`String parmfunction(String a, String b)`
		`{`
		`    ...`
		`    return (String) (a + b);`
		`}`
		`// Use the Functions`
		`voidfunction();`
		`String s1 = stringfunction();`
		`String s2 = parmfunction("Hello",`
		`"World!");`
			`// Declare a void return function`
			`function voidfunction() : void {`
			`    ...`
			`}`
			`// Declare a function that returns a value`
			`function stringfunction() : String {`
			`    ...`
			`    return String(val);`
			`}`
			`// Declare a function that takes and`
			`returns values`
			`function parmfunction(a:String, b:String) :`
			`String {`
			`    ...`
			`    return String(a + b);`
			`}`
			`// Use the Functions`
			`voidfunction();`
			`var s1:String = stringfunction();`
			`var s2:String = parmfunction("Hello",`
			`"World!");`

Custom Attributes	`' Stand-alone attribute`
	`<STAThread>`
	`' Attribute with parameters`
	`<DllImport("ADVAPI32.DLL")>`
	`' Attribute with named parameters`
	`<DllImport("KERNEL32.DLL",`
	`CharSet:=CharSet.Auto)>`
		`// Stand-alone attribute`
		`[STAThread]`
		`// Attribute with parameters`
		`[DllImport("ADVAPI32.DLL")]`
		`// Attribute with named parameters`
		`[DllImport("KERNEL32.DLL",`
		`CharSet=CharSet.Auto)]`
			`// Stand-alone attribute`
			`STAThreadAttribute`
			`// Attribute with parameters`
			`DllImportAttribute("ADVAPI32.DLL")`
			`// Attribute with named parameters`
			`DllImportAttribute("KERNEL32.DLL",`
			`CharSet=CharSet.Auto)`

Arrays	`Dim a(2) As String`
	`a(0) = "1"`
	`a(1) = "2"`
	`a(2) = "3"`
	`Dim a(2,2) As String`
	`a(0,0) = "1"`
	`a(1,0) = "2"`
	`a(2,0) = "3"`
		`String[] a = new String(3);`
		`a[0] = "1";`
		`a[1] = "2";`
		`a[2] = "3";`
		`String[][] a = new String(3)(3);`
		`a[0][0] = "1";`
		`a[1][0] = "2";`
		`a[2][0] = "3";`
			`var a : String[] = new String[3];`
			`a[0] = "1";`
			`a[1] = "2";`
			`a[2] = "3";`
			`var a : String[][] = new String[3][3];`
			`a[0][0] = "1";`
			`a[1][0] = "2";`
			`a[2][0] = "3";`

	VB	C#	JScript

Initialization	`Dim s As String = "Hello World"`
	`Dim i As Integer = 1`
	`Dim a() As Double = { 3.00, 4.00, 5.00 }`
		`String s = "Hello World";`
		`int i = 1;`
		`double[] a = { 3.00, 4.00, 5.00 };`
			`var s : String = "Hello World";`
			`var i : int = 1;`
			`var a : double[] = [ 3.00, 4.00, 5.00 ];`

If Statements	`If Not (Request.QueryString = Nothing)`
	`...`
	`End If`
		`if (Request.QueryString != null) {`
		`...`
		`}`
			`if (Request.QueryString != null) {`
			`...`
			`}`

Case Statements	`Select Case FirstName`
	`  Case "John"`
	`    ...`
	`  Case "Paul"`
	`    ...`
	`  Case "Ringo"`
	`    ...`
	`  Case Else`
	`    ...`
	`End Select`
		`switch (FirstName) {`
		`  case "John" :`
		`    ...`
		`    break;`
		`  case "Paul" :`
		`    ...`
		`    break;`
		`  case "Ringo" :`
		`    ...`
		`    break;`
		`  default:`
		`    ...`
		`    break;`
		`}`
			`switch (FirstName) {`
			`  case "John" :`
			`    ...`
			`    break;`
			`  case "Paul" :`
			`    ...`
			`    break;`
			`  case "Ringo" :`
			`    ...`
			`    break;`
			`  default:`
			`    ...`
			`    break;`
			`}`

For Loops	`Dim I As Integer`
	`For I = 0 To 2`
	`  a(I) = "test"`
	`Next`
		`for (int i=0; i<3; i++)`
		`  a(i) = "test";`
			`for (var i : int = 0; i < 3; i++)`
			`  a[i] = "test";`

While Loops	`Dim I As Integer`
	`I = 0`
	`Do While I < 3`
	`  Console.WriteLine(I.ToString())`
	`  I += 1`
	`Loop`
		`int i = 0;`
		`while (i<3) {`
		`  Console.WriteLine(i.ToString());`
		`  i += 1;`
		`}`
			`var i : int = 0;`
			`while (i < 3) {`
			`  Console.WriteLine(i);`
			`  i += 1;`
			`}`

Exception Handling	`Try`
	`  ' Code that throws exceptions`
	`Catch E As OverflowException`
	`  ' Catch a specific exception`
	`Catch E As Exception`
	`  ' Catch the generic exceptions`
	`Finally`
	`  ' Execute some cleanup code`
	`End Try`
		`try {`
		`  // Code that throws exceptions`
		`} catch(OverflowException e) {`
		`  // Catch a specific exception`
		`} catch(Exception e) {`
		`  // Catch the generic exceptions`
		`} finally {`
		`  // Execute some cleanup code`
		`}`
			`try {`
			`  // Code that throws exceptions`
			`} catch(e:OverflowException) {`
			`  // Catch a specific exception`
			`} catch(e:Exception) {`
			`  // Catch the generic exceptions`
			`} finally {`
			`  // Execute some cleanup code`
			`}`

	VB	C#	JScript
String Concatenation	```' Using Strings
Dim s1, s2 As String
s2 = "hello"
s2 &= " world"
s1 = s2 & " !!!"```	```// Using Strings
String s1;
String s2 = "hello";
s2 += " world";
s1 = s2 + " !!!";```	```// Using Strings
var s1 : String;
var s2 : String = "hello";
s2 += " world";
s1 = s2 + " !!!";```
	``' Using StringBuilder class for performance
Dim s3 As New StringBuilder()
s3.Append("hello")
s3.Append(" world")
s3.Append(" !!!")```	```// Using StringBuilder class for
performance
StringBuilder s3 = new StringBuilder();
s3.Append("hello");
s3.Append(" world");
s3.Append(" !!!");```	```// Using StringBuilder class for
performance
var s3:StringBuilder = new StringBuilder();
s3.Append("hello");
s3.Append(" world");
s3.Append(" !!!");```
Event Handlers Delegates	```Sub MyButton_Click(Sender As Object,
E As EventArgs)
...
End Sub```	```void MyButton_Click(Object sender,
EventArgs E) {
...
}```	```function MyButton_Click(sender : Object,
E : EventArgs) {
...
}```
Declare Events	```' Create a public event
Public Event MyEvent(Sender as Object, E as
EventArgs)

' Create a method for firing the event
Protected Sub OnMyEvent(E As EventArgs)
    RaiseEvent MyEvent(Me, E)
End Sub``` | ```// Create a public event
public event EventHandler MyEvent;

// Create a method for firing the event
protected void OnMyEvent(EventArgs e) {
    MyEvent(this, e);
}``` | JScript does not support the creation of events. JScript may only consume events by declaring Event Handler Delegates and adding those delegates to the Events of another control. |
| Add/Remove Event Handlers to Events | ```AddHandler Control.Change, AddressOf
Me.ChangeEventHandler
RemoveHandler Control.Change, AddressOf
Me.ChangeEventHandler``` | ```Control.Change += new
EventHandler(this.ChangeEventHandler);
Control.Change -= new
EventHandler(this.ChangeEventHandler);``` | ```Control.Change += this.ChangeEventHandler;
Control.Change -= this.ChangeEventHandler;``` |
| Casting | ```Dim obj As MyObject
Dim iObj As IMyObject
obj = Session("Some Value")
iObj = CType(obj, IMyObject)``` | ```MyObject obj = (MyObject)Session["Some
Value"];
IMyObject iObj = obj;``` | ```var obj : MyObject = MyObject(Session("Some
Value"));
var iObj : IMyObject = obj;``` |
| Conversion | ```Dim i As Integer
Dim s As String
Dim d As Double

i = 3
s = i.ToString()
d = CDbl(s)
' See also CDbl(...), CStr(...), ...``` | ```int i = 3;
String s = i.ToString();
double d = Double.Parse(s);``` | ```var i : int = 3;
var s : String = i.ToString();
var d : double = Number(s);``` |

	VB	C#	JScript
Class Definition w/ Inheritance	```Imports System``` ```Namespace MySpace``` ```Public Class Foo : Inherits Bar``` ```Dim x As Integer``` ```Public Sub New()``` ```MyBase.New()``` ```x = 4``` ```End Sub``` ```Public Sub Add(x As Integer)``` ```Me.x = Me.x + x``` ```End Sub``` ```Overrides Public Function GetNum() As Integer``` ```Return x``` ```End Function``` ```End Class``` ```End Namespace``` ```' vbc /out:libraryvb.dll /t:library``` ```' library.vb```	```using System;``` ```namespace MySpace {``` ```public class Foo : Bar {``` ```int x;``` ```public Foo() { x = 4; }``` ```public void Add(int x) { this.x += x;``` ```} override public int GetNum() { return``` ```x; }``` ```}``` ```}``` ```// csc /out:librarycs.dll /t:library``` ```// library.cs```	```import System;``` ```package MySpace {``` ```class Foo extends Bar {``` ```private var x : int;``` ```function Foo() { x = 4; }``` ```function Add(x : int) { this.x += x; }``` ```override function GetNum() : int {``` ```return x; }``` ```}``` ```}``` ```// jsc /out:libraryjs.dll library.js```
Implementing an Interface	```Public Class MyClass : Implements``` ```IEnumerable``` ```'... Function IEnumerable_GetEnumerator()``` ```As IEnumerable Implements``` ```IEnumerator.GetEnumerator``` ```...``` ```End Function``` ```End Class```	```public class MyClass : IEnumerable {``` ```...``` ```IEnumerator``` ```IEnumerable.GetEnumerator() {``` ```...``` ```}``` ```}```	```public class MyClass implements``` ```IEnumerable {``` ```...``` ```function IEnumerable.GetEnumerator() :``` ```IEnumerator {``` ```...``` ```}``` ```}```
Class Definition w/ A Main method	```Imports System``` ```Public Class ConsoleVB``` ```Public Sub New()``` ```MyBase.New()``` ```Console.WriteLine("Object Created")``` ```End Sub``` ```Public Shared Sub Main()``` ```Console.WriteLine("Hello World")``` ```Dim cvb As New ConsoleVB``` ```End Sub``` ```End Class``` ```' vbc /out:consolevb.exe /t:exe console.vb```	```using System;``` ```public class ConsoleCS {``` ```public ConsoleCS() {``` ```Console.WriteLine("Object Created");``` ```}``` ```public static void Main (String[] args)``` ```{``` ```Console.WriteLine("Hello World");``` ```ConsoleCS ccs = new ConsoleCS();``` ```}``` ```}``` ```// csc /out:consolecs.exe /t:exe``` ```console.cs```	```class ConsoleCS {``` ```function ConsoleCS() {``` ```print("Object Created");``` ```}``` ```static function Main (args : String[]) {``` ```print("Hello World");``` ```var ccs : ConsoleCS = new ConsoleCS();``` ```}``` ```}``` ```// jsc /out:consolejs.exe /exe console.js```
Standard Module	```Imports System``` ```Public Module ConsoleVB``` ```Public Sub Main()``` ```Console.WriteLine("Hello World")``` ```End Sub``` ```End Module``` ```' vbc /out:consolevb.exe /t:exe console.vb```	```using System;``` ```public class Module {``` ```public static void Main (String[] args) {``` ```Console.WriteLine("Hello World");``` ```}``` ```}``` ```// csc /out:consolecs.exe /t:exe``` ```console.cs```	```print("Hello World");``` ```// jsc /out:consolejs.exe /exe console.js```

Index

D

H

M

R

T

U

p2p.wrox.com
The programmer's resource centre

A unique free service from Wrox Press
with the aim of helping programmers to help each other

Wrox Press aims to provide timely and practical information to today's programmer. P2P is a list server offering a host of targeted mailing lists where you can share knowledge with your fellow programmers and find solutions to your problems. Whatever the level of your programming knowledge, and whatever technology you use, P2P can provide you with the information you need.

ASP — Support for beginners and professionals, including a resource page with hundreds of links, and a popular ASP+ mailing list.

DATABASES — For database programmers, offering support on SQL Server, mySQL, and Oracle.

MOBILE — Software development for the mobile market is growing rapidly. We provide lists for the several current standards, including WAP, WindowsCE, and Symbian.

JAVA — A complete set of Java lists, covering beginners, professionals,and server-side programmers (including JSP, servlets and EJBs)

.NET — Microsoft's new OS platform, covering topics such as ASP+, C#, and general .Net discussion.

VISUAL BASIC — Covers all aspects of VB programming, from programming Office macros to creating components for the .Net platform.

WEB DESIGN — As web page requirements become more complex, programmer sare taking a more important role in creating web sites. For these programmers, we offer lists covering technologies such as Flash, Coldfusion, and JavaScript.

XML — Covering all aspects of XML, including XSLT and schemas.

OPEN SOURCE — Many Open Source topics covered including PHP, Apache, Perl, Linux, Python and more.

FOREIGN LANGUAGE — Several lists dedicated to Spanish and German speaking programmers, categories include .Net, Java, XML, PHP and XML.

How To Subscribe

Simply visit the P2P site, at **http://p2p.wrox.com/**

Select the 'FAQ' option on the side menu bar for more information about the subscription process and our service.